SO-AIS-908

9950
.R635
2009

Third
Edition

JUSTICE BLIND?

Ideals and Realities
of American Criminal Justice

Matthew B. Robinson

Appalachian State University

PEARSON

Prentice
Hall

Upper Saddle River, New Jersey
Columbus, Ohio

KVCC KALAMAZOO VALLEY
COMMUNITY COLLEGE
LIBRARY

MAY 0 7 2008

Library of Congress Cataloging-in-Publication Data

Robinson, Matthew B.
   Justice blind? : ideals and realities of American criminal justice / Matthew B. Robinson. — 3rd ed.
      p.   cm.
   Includes bibliographical references and index.
      ISBN 0-13-514774-3
   1. Criminal justice, Administration of—United States.   2. Social justice—United States.
I. Title.
   HV9950.R635   2009
   364.973—dc22

                                                                                          2007031587

Vice President and Executive Publisher: Vernon Anthony
Senior Managing Editor: JoEllen Gohr
Associate Managing Editor: Alex Wolf
Acquisitions Editor: Tim Peyton
Editorial Assistant: Alicia Kelly
Project Manager: Alicia Ritchey
Design Coordinator: Diane Ernsberger
Cover Designer: Kristina Holmes
Cover Art: Bill Burrows, SIS.Images.com
Operations Specialist: Deidra Schwartz
Director of Marketing: David Gesell
Marketing Manager: Adam Kloza
Marketing Coordinator: Alicia Dysert

This book was set in Times Ten Roman 10/12 by TexTech. It was printed and bound by R. R. Donnelley & Sons Company. The cover was printed by R. R. Donnelley & Sons Company.

Copyright © 2009, 2005, 2002 by Pearson Education, Inc., Upper Saddle River, New Jersey 07458.
Pearson Prentice Hall. All rights reserved. Printed in the United States of America. This publication is protected by Copyright and permission should be obtained from the publisher prior to any prohibited reproduction, storage in a retrieval system, or transmission in any form or by any means, electronic, mechanical, photocopying, recording, or likewise. For information regarding permission(s), write to: Rights and Permissions Department.

Pearson Prentice Hall™ is a trademark of Pearson Education, Inc.
Pearson® is a registered trademark of Pearson plc.
Prentice Hall® is a registered trademark of Pearson Education, Inc.

Pearson Education Ltd.
Pearson Education Canada, Ltd.
Pearson Education Australia Pty. Limited
Pearson Educación de Mexico, S.A. de C.V.

Pearson Education Singapore Pte. Ltd.
Pearson Education—Japan
Pearson Education North Asia Ltd.
Pearson Education Malaysia Pte. Ltd.

10 9 8 7 6 5 4 3 2 1
ISBN-13: 978-0-13-514774-0
ISBN-10:   0-13-514774-3

This third edition is dedicated to Bella and Marley.
You are the future.

ABOUT THE AUTHOR

Matthew B. Robinson is Associate Professor in the Department of Political Science and Criminal Justice at Appalachian State University (ASU). He earned his Ph.D. in Criminology and Criminal Justice at Florida State University in 1997. Robinson teaches and does research in the areas of criminological theory, the war on drugs, capital punishment, and injustices of the criminal justice system. He has published more than 50 pieces of research, including six books: *Justice Blind? Ideals and Realities of American Criminal Justice* (Prentice Hall, 2002, 2005, 2008), *Why Crime? An Integrated Systems Theory of Antisocial Behavior* (Prentice-Hall, 2004), *Spatial Analysis of Crime: Theory and Practice* (with Derek Paulsen, Allyn & Bacon, 2004), *Lies, Damned Lies, and Drug War Statistics* (State University of New York Press, 2007), and *Death Nation: The Experts Explain American Capital Punishment* (Prentice Hall, 2008). He also has served as Board Member and President of the Southern Criminal Justice Association (SCJA). Robinson was awarded the William C. Strickland Outstanding Young Scholar Award from Appalachian State University in 2002 and the Donald W. Sink Outstanding Scholar Award from Appalachian State University in 2007.

BRIEF CONTENTS

Foreword   xix
Preface   xxi

PART I: THE "CRIMINAL JUSTICE SYSTEM": IDEALS AND
            REALITIES   1

            Chapter 1   What Is the Criminal Justice System? Ideals   3
            Chapter 2   The Role of Politics and Ideology in Criminal Justice:
                        Realities   30
            Chapter 3   The Law: Providing Equal Protection or
                        Creating Bias?   52

PART II: CRIME: IMAGES AND REALITIES   83

            Chapter 4   Crime: Which Is Worse, Crime on the Streets or Crime in
                        the Suites?   85
            Chapter 5   The Sky Is Falling! The Sky Is Falling! — Media Portrayals
                        of Crime and Criminal Justice   123

PART III: COMPONENTS OF CRIMINAL JUSTICE: POLICE,
            COURTS, AND CORRECTIONS   161

            Chapter 6   Law Enforcement: To Serve and
                        Protect?   163
            Chapter 7   Right to Trial? Injustice in Pretrial and Trial
                        Procedures   200
            Chapter 8   Punishment: Does It Work and Is It Fair?   236
            Chapter 9   Incarceration: Lock 'Em Up and Forget
                        About 'Em   270

PART IV: FAILING CRIMINAL JUSTICE POLICY AND HOPE
            FOR THE FUTURE   305

            Chapter 10 The Ultimate Sanction: Death as Justice?   307
            Chapter 11 The "War on Drugs": Focusing on the
                        Wrong Drugs?   361

Chapter 12 The War on Crime as a Threat to Equality:
            Innocent Bias Against the Poor, People of Color,
            and Women   411
Chapter 13 Summary, Conclusions, and Recommendations
            for the Future   444

References   **469**

Index   **501**

CONTENTS

Foreword   xix
Preface   xxi

PART I: **THE "CRIMINAL JUSTICE SYSTEM": IDEALS AND REALITIES   1**

CHAPTER 1   What Is the Criminal Justice System? Ideals   3

Introduction   3

What is a system?   4

     What is the "criminal justice system"?   *4*

     Why the "criminal justice system" is not a system   *5*

Ideal goals of criminal justice   13

     Reducing crime   *14*

     Doing justice   *14*

What is justice?   15

     Conflicting views of justice   *16*

     Due process versus crime control   *17*

     Justice today   *21*

Conclusion   25

Issue in Depth—Justitia—The Lady Justice   26

Key Terms   29

Discussion Questions   29

CHAPTER 2   The Role of Politics and Ideology in Criminal Justice: Realities   30

Introduction   30

Alternative goals of criminal justice   31

     Serving interests and controlling the population   *31*

Functions versus purposes of criminal justice   33

What is politics?   34

What is ideology?   35

How are politics, ideology, and criminal justice
related?   35

*How did criminal justice become so political and
ideological?   41*

Crime, politics, and ideology today   43

Conclusion   44

Issue in Depth—McDonaldization of America's Police, Courts,
and Corrections   45

Key Terms   50

Discussion Questions   50

**CHAPTER 3   The Law: Providing Equal Protection or
Creating Bias?   52**

Introduction   52

What is the law?   53

Where does the law come from?   55

Types of law   56

Natural law   56

Positive law   57

Common law   61

Criminal law and civil law   63

What is the purpose of the criminal law?   64

Who makes the law?   66

Demographics of lawmakers   66

Voting behavior   70

Special interests/lobbying   72

How the criminal law fails to protect Americans   74

Big tobacco   75

Big oil   76

Conclusion   77

Issue in Depth—New Antiterrorism Laws   77

Key Terms   81

Discussion Questions   81

PART II: CRIME: IMAGES AND REALITIES   83

CHAPTER 4   Crime: Which Is Worse, Crime on the Streets or Crime in the Suites?   85

Introduction   86

What is a crime?   86

Legal definition of crime   87

Types of crime in the United States   89

Serious/street crime   89

Other conceptions of crime: Elite deviance   94

What Is Victimization?   97

A comparison of harms associated with crimes and "noncrimes"   99

Sources of crime information: Do we really know how much crime is out there?   106

Uniform Crime Reports   106

National Crime Victimization Survey   108

American crime trends, according to the UCR and NCVS   110

Self-report studies   113

Sources of data on elite deviance   116

Conclusion   117

Issue in Depth—Enron, WorldCom, Tyco, and the Other Corporate Bandits   117

Key Terms   121

Discussion Questions   122

CHAPTER 5   The Sky Is Falling! The Sky Is Falling!—Media Portrayals of Crime and Criminal Justice   123

Introduction   123

An introduction to the media   124

What the media do and do not do   128

Does it matter? Are people exposed to the media?   129

Media coverage of crime and criminal justice   130

Focus of media reporting on crime: What the media cover and ignore   134

Crime trends   138

Lack of critical coverage: Where's the context?   139

Media and fear of crime: The Chicken Little phenomenon   *143*

Explanations of media inaccuracy   146

Organizational factors: Entertainment for profit   *147*

Peer culture   *148*

Lack of criminal justice education   *149*

The role of politics in the "framing" of crime   *149*

Conclusion   151

Issue in Depth—Media Coverage of September 11th and
the War on Terror   152

Key Terms   159

Discussion Questions   159

**PART III: COMPONENTS OF CRIMINAL JUSTICE: POLICE,
COURTS, AND CORRECTIONS   161**

CHAPTER 6   Law Enforcement: To Serve and Protect?   163

Introduction   163

The organization of policing in the United States   164

Basic roles and responsibilities of police officers: What police do
and how they do it   168

How police serve crime victims   *169*

The move to community policing   171

How police are supposed to behave   175

Innocent bias: Why even good policing produces bias   178

The particular focus of police on certain types of crime   *178*

The location of police on the streets of the United States   *179*

The use of police discretion   *180*

The use of police profiling   *181*

Policing the war on drugs   *184*

American stop rates and arrest rates   186

Use of force   189

Corruption in American policing   192

Conclusion   195

Issue in Depth—Corruption in the Criminal
Justice Network   195

Key Terms   198

Discussion Questions   199

CHAPTER 7   Right to Trial? Injustice in Pretrial and Trial Procedures   200

Introduction   201

What are the courts?   201

The organization of courts in the United States   201

What courts do   202

Types of crimes handled by courts   203

Characteristics of court clients   204

The courtroom workgroup   204

An imbalance of power in the court: From judge to prosecution   209

Pretrial procedures and justice   210

Bail as an injustice   210

Plea bargaining as an injustice   218

The unequal right to a defense in the United States: Public versus private attorneys   221

The "exceptional case" of trial   223

Stages of the criminal trial   224

Conclusion   227

Issue in Depth—Wrongful Convictions   228

Key Terms   234

Discussion Questions   235

CHAPTER 8   Punishment: Does It Work and Is It Fair?   236

Introduction   237

An introduction to sentencing   237

Types of sentences   237

Methods of punishment   241

Punishment facts   244

Why do we punish?   246

Retribution   247

Incapacitation   248

Deterrence   250

Rehabilitation   252

Toward restoration   253

Punishment: A summary   253

Is punishment effective?   255

    What we've learned from offenders   255

    *What we've learned from other criminal
      justice research   257*

Bias in the sentencing process   260

Conclusion   267

Issue in Depth—C. Ray Jeffery Explains the Failure of
    American Punishment   267

Key Terms   269

Discussion Questions   269

**CHAPTER 9   Incarceration: Lock 'Em Up and Forget
           About 'Em   270**

Introduction   271

The organization of corrections in the United States   271

America's incarceration rate   271

    What it costs   277

Who's in prison and jail?   277

What happens in prison? Pains of imprisonment   282

    Loss of liberty   283

    Loss of autonomy   289

    Loss of security   290

    Deprivation of heterosexual relationships   291

    Deprivation of goods and services   292

    Loss of voting rights   293

    Loss of dignity   293

    Stigmatization   293

    Summary of Pains of imprisonment   294

Forgiving the offender: Why harass parolees?   296

How and why corrections reflects criminal justice bias   297

Conclusion   300

Issue in Depth—The Convict School of Criminology   301

Key Terms   303

Discussion Questions   303

PART IV: FAILING CRIMINAL JUSTICE POLICY AND HOPE FOR THE FUTURE   305

CHAPTER 10   The Ultimate Sanction: Death As Justice?   307

Introduction   307

A brief history of capital punishment   308

Death penalty facts   315

Public support for capital punishment   326

Justifications for capital punishment:
   Logical or not?   332

   Vengeance   332

   Retribution   333

   Deterrence   338

   Incapacitation   341

What's wrong with the death penalty? Alleged problems
   with the administration of death   341

Conclusion   353

Issue in Depth—Expert Opinion on Capital
   Punishment   353

Key Terms   360

Discussion Questions   360

CHAPTER 11   The "War on Drugs": Focusing on the Wrong Drugs?   361

Introduction   362

The War on Drugs   362

   Goals of the drug war   363

   Elements of the drug war   364

   Drugs and crime   366

   A brief history of the drug war   367

What is a drug?   369

Types of drugs   371

Extent of drug use in the United States   373

Harms associated with drugs   378

Legal status of each drug: Why are the most harmful drugs
   legal while some relatively harmless drugs
   are illegal?   384

   The role of the media in drug scares   386

Harms caused by the drug war   390

Alternatives to the drug war: Legalization and
decriminalization   394

Conclusion   403

Issue in Depth—Drug War Lies?   404

Key Terms   410

Discussion Questions   410

**CHAPTER 12   The War on Crime as a Threat to Equality:
Innocent Bias Against the Poor, People of Color,
and Women   411**

Introduction   411

Is the war on crime a war on the poor?   412

The rich are getting richer and the poor are getting poorer   *417*

Is the criminal justice network biased against
people of color?   419

Race, ethnicity, and social class   *425*

Race, ethnicity, government policy, and criminal justice   *429*

Gender and criminal justice   433

Conclusion   438

Issue in Depth—The Greatest Threat to Civil Rights Is the
Criminal Justice Network   439

Key Terms   442

Discussion Questions   442

**CHAPTER 13   Summary, Conclusions, and Recommendations
for the Future   444**

Introduction   444

Summary: The criminal justice network fails to achieve
justice and reduce crime   445

Where to go from here: Alternatives to current criminal
justice practice   449

*General recommendations about government and informing
citizens*   *450*

Recommendations about reforming the law and crime   *452*

Recommendations about the media   *453*

Recommendations about the police   *454*

Recommendations about the courts and about sentencing   *456*

Recommendations about corrections   *458*

Likelihood of success   459

Conclusion   460

Issue in Depth—Toward Social Justice: Groups
        Doing the Work Now   460

Discussion Questions   467

References   469

Index   501

FOREWORD

This edition of *Justice Blind? Ideals and Realities of American Criminal Justice* is substantially different from the first edition. While the main ideas from the first edition remain—because so much about American criminal justice has remained the same—America's reaction to the attacks of September 11, 2001 has fundamentally changed our country.

Since that day, the people and government of the United States of America have been obsessed with *terrorism*. Terrorism generally refers to the use of violence to instill fear in order to achieve some political purpose. Merriam-Webster's Collegiate Dictionary provides this definition of terrorism: "the systematic use of terror (a state of intense fear) especially as a means of coercion . . . violence (as bombing) committed by groups in order to intimidate a population or government into granting their demands."

America's obsession with terrorism means that to some degree, *crime* has taken a back seat in terms of importance. Public opinion polls show that the things Americans used to worry about (for example, school shootings and child abductions) are less worrisome than terrorism. Interestingly, Americans are also greatly concerned about the direction of their country and the domestic and foreign policy decisions pursued by their leaders. A recent poll showed that two-thirds of Americans think their country is heading in the wrong direction.

In addition to making thousands of arrests and detaining hundreds of people for years, the "war on terror" has given us military action against Afghanistan and a disastrous war in Iraq. Congress quickly passed the USA PATRIOT Act of 2001 and later created the Department of Homeland Security. It then passed the Military Tribunals Act, a law that is so extreme it allows the use of hearsay evidence and evidence obtained by coercion in military trials, and it excuses any abuses committed by U.S. military officials in the war on terror.

Further, President Bush has also authorized the indefinite detention of American citizens as "enemy combatants" without criminal charges, created a top-secret domestic spying program under the auspices of the National Security Agency, and authorized government agencies to read the e-mail and open the postal mail of any American citizen. Some civil libertarians claim that the right to privacy implicit in the Fourth Amendment to the U.S. Constitution no longer exists.

Because of the significance of the war on terror for our country, as well as its clear implications for criminal justice practice, I give as much attention to issues related to terrorism as I can throughout the book. While the book is still not about terrorism, per se, you'll see that the problems that plague our wars on crime and drugs—thoroughly analyzed in the first and second editions of this text—also plague America's war on terror.

In this edition, I examine America's war mentality and discuss how it is relevant to the main thesis of this text. For example, I show that the anti-terrorism laws in the United States have swung the pendulum farther toward a *crime control model* of criminal justice by eroding the Constitutional protections that Americans enjoy in order to make it easier for police, courts, and corrections to investigate, arrest, detain, convict, and punish alleged terrorists. Additionally, I illustrate how media coverage of September 11 (and America's subsequent wars in Afghanistan and Iraq) maintained fear in Americans so they would be more likely to support tougher methods of fighting terrorism, even if it means giving up some of their own freedoms. Americans were also less likely to question their own government and its actions, which inevitably led to the types of abuses of official power (such as corruption and wrongful conviction) and erosions of Constitutional protections that I documented in the first and second editions of this book.

To end on a more positive note, there are real signs that Americans are rising to resist the policies that got us into the situation in which we now find ourselves. For example, American citizens elected enough Democrats into Congress to rustle away both the House and the Senate from Republican control. Now there is significant debate about the war in Iraq, and Congress has begun to question other American policies related to the war on terror. This is not to say that the problem is Republicans, but rather that with Democrats in control of Congress, it is once again possible that the checks and balances of America's democratic form of government will once again function properly. Further, public opinion has unquestionably turned against the war in Iraq. Americans are even willing to consider a complete withdrawal of U.S. forces from the country. Such developments suggest the possibility that Americans may be willing to question America's war approach itself, offering hope that our wars on crimes, drugs, and terrorism might soon be replaced by more efficacious methods of reducing the problems that face our nation.

PREFACE

Injustice anywhere is a threat to justice everywhere.
— MARTIN LUTHER KING, "Letter from Birmingham Jail"

Dr. Martin Luther King, Jr., wrote these words in his letter from a jail cell in Birmingham, Alabama, on April 16, 1963, after being jailed for "civil disobedience"—a peaceful, nonviolent form of resistance. The letter was his response to criticisms that, as an "outsider" from Atlanta, he had no business in Birmingham.

King countered that he could not "sit idly by in Atlanta" and be unconcerned about what was occurring in Birmingham, Alabama. He explained: "We are caught in an inescapable network of mutuality, tied in a single garment of destiny. Whatever affects one directly, affects all indirectly." King explained that the notion of an "outside agitator" was an outdated idea, saying: "Anyone who lives inside the United States can never be considered an outsider anywhere within its bounds."

So, injustice anywhere in America is a threat to all persons living in the United States. And injustice in America is every American's business. The injustices of American criminal justice are the motivation for this book.

When I began my college experience as a criminology and criminal justice major, I had some ideas in my head about what agencies of criminal justice were supposed to achieve. I thought that police, courts, and corrections were supposed to protect us from harmful acts committed intentionally by other people. In my first semester, however, I learned that these agencies of criminal justice in the United States are focused on only a small portion of all harmful acts. Many other behaviors that are committed intentionally—acts that kill and injure people and result in loss of property—nevertheless are not "crimes" or are not vigorously pursued by such agencies.

Later, in graduate school, I learned about the notion of "doing justice"—upholding due process, being fair, and so forth. Yet, massive criminal justice expansion of the several decades of the twentieth century driven by politics, fear, and the desire to be punitive severely threatened our commitment to justice.

To me, the incongruence between the ideals of American criminal justice and the realities of American criminal justice didn't seem right. How can the United States spend so much money and direct so much effort toward punishing a relatively small portion of harmful behaviors while virtually ignoring so many others? Why would we disinvest in the nation's future by overrelying on methods of crime control that we know are ineffective, while failing to try methods that seem more promising? None of this seemed "just" to me.

If justice really meant what I had always thought it meant, how could criminal justice in the United States, of all places, be so unjust? This is the question addressed in this book. *Justice Blind? Ideals and Realities of American Criminal Justice* attempts to demonstrate how and why American criminal justice agencies fail to live up to their ideals, and thus are unjust.

This book grew out of my experiences with teaching an introductory criminal justice course more than 30 times. Through my teaching, I realized that no introductory criminal justice text on the market exposed readers to many important realities of criminal justice in the United States. This book strives to do that.

THE MAIN ASSERTION OF *JUSTICE BLIND?*

The book proceeds from the following assertions:

- Myths and stereotypes about crime, criminals, and criminal justice are created when acts are defined as crimes by the criminal law
- These myths and stereotypes are reinforced as the mass media broadcast stories about crime, criminals, and criminal justice
- These myths and stereotypes are also reinforced as police, courts, and corrections enforce the criminal law
- Because the criminal law in the United States is inherently biased against certain groups (for example, the poor, people of color, and in some cases women), the activities of police, courts, and corrections are also biased against these groups.

This does not suggest that the U.S. media, police, courts, and corrections are intentionally biased. Rather, by focusing on those acts that come to be defined as "serious" in the criminal law, each of these institutions becomes biased in an "innocent" way. The figure below illustrates how this "innocent bias" is created in the United States. The arrows suggest that each step of the process affects all other stages—that is, that myths and stereotypes about crime, criminals, and criminal justice created by the criminal law are strengthened while agencies of criminal justice and the media operate. Throughout this book, I elaborate on this process and provide evidence for the main assertions listed here.

The Process of Innocent Bias

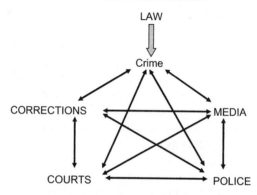

Source: Adapted from Robinson (2000: p.136)

CHAPTER BY CHAPTER

The book is divided into four main parts. Part I, The "Criminal Justice System": Ideals and Realities, discusses the most important issues necessary to gaining a complete understanding of the reality of criminal justice practice in the United States. In Chapter 1, I define the common term criminal justice system and show that there really is no such thing as a system of criminal justice in the United States. Nevertheless, I seek to identify the ideal goals of what I term the criminal justice network—that is, what criminal justice is supposed to be aimed at achieving in America. At the end of this chapter, in *Issue in Depth*, I take a close look at Lady Justitia, whose image adorns the cover of this book.

In Chapter 2, I explore alternative goals of criminal justice, including serving limited interests and controlling the population. In this chapter, I discuss the role of politics and ideology in American criminal justice to provide a more realistic assessment of what criminal justice is really all about. The *Issue in Depth* at the end of the chapter examines the issue of how "McDonaldization" has affected American criminal justice, showing that the overriding ideology of American criminal justice clearly parallels that of our fast-food industry.

In Chapter 3, I begin my analysis of actual criminal justice practice with an examination of the law-making process. In this chapter, I explore American law, including types of law, purposes of criminal law, and a detailed examination of who makes the law and votes for it. I also investigate the role that money plays in American politics. *Issue in Depth* examines laws that have been passed to fight terrorism in the United States. These laws erode basic freedoms and thus provide a good example of the struggle to balance crime prevention efforts with protections of our own rights.

Part II of the book, Crime: Images and Realities, addresses the most important issues necessary to gaining a complete understanding of crime in the United States. In Chapter 4, I define the term *crime* and lay out different types of crime in the United States. In this chapter, I also discuss different sources of crime data and examine long-term crime trends. Most importantly, I identify the most dangerous forms of crime in America—elite deviance. A detailed examination of recent large-scale financial scandals involving companies such as Enron, WorldCom, Tyco, and many others is discussed in the *Issue in Depth* at the end of the chapter.

In Chapter 5, I examine the role of the media in crime and criminal justice. Since no one can fully understand crime or criminal justice activity without understanding how these issues are framed in the mass media, this chapter is one of the most important of the book. *Issue in Depth* shows how the tragedy of September 11, 2001, has been used for political gain and ratings by mainstream media outlets. My goal in this chapter is to illustrate how media inaccuracy drives dangerous criminal justice policies.

Part III of the book, Components of Criminal Justice: Police, Courts, and Corrections, covers the basics of police, courts, and corrections (as in all introductory texts) and provides detailed, critical assessments of each component of criminal justice (unlike most introductory texts). In Chapter 6, I not only offer descriptions of who the police are, how policing is organized in the United States, and basic responsibilities of American police officers, I also carefully examine the realities of American policing. I introduce the concept of "innocent bias" to show the fundamental flaws of policing in the United States and examine differential stop rates and arrest rates and issues such as the use of force, opinion of the police, and corruption in American policing. *Issue in Depth* at the end of the chapter deals with corruption in criminal justice generally and law enforcement particularly.

In Chapter 7, I examine basic court issues such as the organization of courts in the United States, basic court functions, and responsibilities of the courtroom work group. I also discuss injustices in pretrial procedures such as bail and plea bargaining, as well as in trial procedures. The section on the imbalance of power in the court demonstrates how power has been shifted from judges to prosecutors over the past 30 years. *Issue in Depth* at the end of the chapter examines the causes of wrongful conviction.

In Chapter 8, I examine numerous aspects of punishment, including sentencing and justifications for punishment. In this chapter, I also examine the relative effectiveness of certain types of punishment and the issue of bias in the sentencing process. *Issue in Depth* claims by a well-known criminologist as to why criminal justice is so ineffective at reducing crime.

In Chapter 9, I deal with issues related to incarceration and compare America's incarceration rate with that of other countries. In this chapter, I illustrate who is in the nation's jails and prisons and what happens to inmates while in prison and after release. Finally, I explain how and why corrections reflect criminal justice bias. At the end of the chapter, *Issue in Depth* examines the emergence of "The Convict School of Criminology."

Part IV of the book, Failing Criminal Justice Policy and Hope for the Future examines criminal justice practices that many people in criminology and criminal justice have now come to see as massive failures. In Chapter 10, I discuss the most extreme form of punishment available, capital punishment. In this chapter, I specify key death penalty facts and critically assess justifications for capital punishment. I also carefully examine the issue of public support for capital punishment and provide a thorough summary of alleged problems with the administration of the death penalty. *Issue in Depth* presents findings from a national survey of capital punishment experts that explain why they do not think the death penalty is an effective policy.

In Chapter 11, I discuss the war on drugs, a significant part of America's war on crime. In this chapter, I examine the extent of drug use in the United States, harms associated with drugs, and provide a critical assessment of why some drugs are legal while others are not. Finally, using government data, I show precisely how the war on drugs causes more harm than it prevents. *Issue in Depth* at the end of the chapter details a study of drug war claims made by the federal agency responsible for the drug war—the Office of National Drug Control Policy (ONDCP).

In Chapter 12, I consider the implications of America's war on crime against relatively less powerful groups in the United States, including the poor, racial and ethnic minorities, and women. *Issue in Depth* examines the claim by a major civil rights group that American criminal justice practices pose a serious threat to civil rights.

Chapter 13, concludes the book with a summary and a series of 50 recommendations for overcoming the problems identified in the book. I discuss the likelihood of success and end with *Issue in Depth* that introduces the concept of social justice and documents various groups already working to overcome the problems outlined in the book and to achieve social justice.

FEATURES

Justice Blind? contains several useful features for students of criminology, criminal justice, sociology, social problems, political science, and related disciplines. Each chapter contains an *Issue in Depth* section that explores one issue raised in the chapter. Each chapter concludes with a series of discussion questions that deal with the important material discussed. Finally, the website for *Justice Blind?* (www.justiceblind.com) will continue to offer various forms of activities, links, and PowerPoint slides that students, instructors, and general readers will find useful. Throughout the book, highlighted key terms appear that are listed on the website and can be defined by students to promote active learning.

TO THE READER

Unlike many introductory criminal justice texts, *Justice Blind?* contains a careful analysis of the role that race, class, and gender play in crime and criminal justice. The critical approach of *Justice Blind?* is also unique. Most introductory criminal justice texts start with the perspective that the American criminal justice system meets its ideal goals. They introduce and discuss main concepts and terms without offering critical assessments. I want you, the reader, to learn not only about the ideals of criminal justice in America, but also about the realities. Whereas other texts emphasize the way things are supposed to operate, this book emphasizes on the way agencies of the American criminal justice system *really* operate.

This book focuses on injustice in criminal justice, an important topic for students and citizens alike to understand. Of course, people who study criminal justice and who work within agencies of American criminal justice need to gain an understanding of basic, introductory-level concepts and issues in order to become more knowledgeable and to become better employees. Many fine texts are on the market to meet this need. But this book takes a different approach: It begins with injustice as a problem.

In fact, I suggest that injustice is a social problem that plagues the United States. Lauer and Lauer (2000) in *Troubled Times* write that social problems begin "as a sense of something wrong in society—of suffering and deprivation growing out of a situation of injustice." I hope this book convinces you that something is very wrong with criminal justice in America. I hope that, because of this work, injustice within American criminal justice will be viewed as a significant social problem. This is why several of the topics addressed in this book (for example, the death penalty; drug use; the role of race, class, and gender in criminal justice) also may be appropriate for social problems classes.

As you read this book, I challenge you to keep an open mind. Do not allow your deeply entrenched beliefs about crime, criminal justice, or politics interfere with your understanding of the main argument of the book. If this reading has been assigned to you, remember that you do not have to agree with the arguments I put forth in this book, but you do need to understand them. In fact, I challenge you to read the book from a critical perspective, not automatically believing everything you read. Read the book from a perspective that will allow you to discover your own truth. Your own truth, after all, is the only truth that will matter to you.

ONLINE INSTRUCTOR'S RESOURCES

To access supplementary materials online, instructors need to request an instructor access code. Go to **www.prenhall.com**, click the **Instructor Resource Center** link, and then click **Register Today** for an instructor access code. Within 48 hours after registering you will receive a confirming e-mail including an instructor access code. Once you have received your code, go to the site and log on for full instructions on downloading the materials you wish to use.

Instructor
Resource
Center

Register today at www.prenhall.com
to access instructor resources digitally.

ACKNOWLEDGMENTS

This book is the product of many years of thought and study, both formal and informal. I would like to thank the faculty and staff of the Florida State University School of Criminology and Criminal Justice for the wonderful education I received. Much of what I learned there inspired this book. Also, I want to thank my colleagues at Appalachian State University for their support and friendship.

I also want to sincerely thank friends and colleagues around the country, especially within the Southern Criminal Justice Association (SCJA), many of whom have written and spoken about some of the same issues in their careers. I hope you know my work would not have been possible without yours.

I want to thank each of the reviewers for their hard work. I especially appreciate the feedback I got from David Friedrichs, Sarah Eschholz, and Ronald Iacovetta for the first edition; Chuck Brawner, Gwen Hunnicutt, Long Le, Ray Newman, Gary Perlstein, and Gary W. Potter for the second edition; and Lisa Anne Zilney, Demetra Pappas, Gray Perlstein, and Joan Crawley for this edition. These individuals went above and beyond the call of duty. Thanks also to Derek Paulsen for reviewing my original chapter on the media. I offer my sincere thanks to my research assistants, Anna Sheely and Dickie Lee Brown, who helped me compile the extensive bibliographies. I also want to thank Kim Davies, who was senior acquisitions editor with Prentice Hall when she saw promise in the project, and all the fine people behind the scenes who worked very hard making the final product come together. Thanks so much to my students, especially those who took my special topics class, Injustice in America, at Appalachian State University, which led directly to this book. Finally, I must thank my loving and supportive families—the Robinsons, Andersons, Chiodos, Kings, Murphys, Clements, and Johnsons: I appreciate all of you so much more than you know.

PART I

THE "CRIMINAL JUSTICE SYSTEM": IDEALS AND REALITIES

Chapter 1   What Is the Criminal Justice System? Ideals

Chapter 2   The Role of Politics and Ideology in Criminal Justice: Realities

Chapter 3   The Law: Providing Equal Protection or Creating Bias?

1

WHAT IS THE CRIMINAL JUSTICE SYSTEM? IDEALS

1. Introduction
2. What Is a System?
   a. What Is the "Criminal Justice System"?
   b. Why the "Criminal Justice System" Is Not a System
   • Box 1-1. The Typical Criminal Justice Process
3. Ideal Goals of Criminal Justice
   a. Reducing Crime
   b. Doing Justice
4. What Is Justice?
   a. Conflicting Views of Justice
   b. Due Process Versus Crime Control
   • Box 1-2. Upholding *Miranda*
   c. Justice Today
   • Box 1-3. Resources Devoted to Criminal Justice in the United States
5. Conclusion
6. Issue in Depth—Justitia—The Lady Justice
7. Key Terms
8. Discussion Questions

INTRODUCTION

What is the "criminal justice system"? Why do we have it? Does it achieve its goals? Are we winning the war on crime? If not, why not? This chapter introduces the ideal goals of what is called the "criminal justice system," including doing justice and reducing crime. Although justice is difficult to define, at least two conflicting conceptions of justice emerge, consistent with two competing ideal models of justice known as the **crime control** and **due process** models. This chapter demonstrates how criminal justice policy in the United States has shifted toward a crime control model of criminal justice over the past three decades, at the expense of individual constitutional protections and due process. I suggest that failures of American criminal justice are explained by this shift.

3

Finally, I examine the meaning of the lady justice, "Justitia," whose image adorns this book. I suggest that she should serve as a reminder of what justice is supposed to mean in terms of American criminal justice policy.

WHAT IS A SYSTEM?

According to *Merriam-Webster's Collegiate Dictionary,* 11th ed. (2003), a **system** is a:

> regularly interacting or interdependent group of items forming a unified whole . . . a group of interacting bodies under the influence of related forces; an assemblage of substances that is in or tends to equilibrium; a group of body organs that together perform one or more vital functions; the body considered as a functional unit; a group of related natural objects or forces; a group of devices or artificial objects or an organization forming a network especially for distributing something or serving a common purpose; a form of social, economic, or political organization or practice; an organized set of doctrines, ideas, or principles usually intended to explain the arrangement or working of a systemic whole; a harmonious arrangement or pattern.

In this definition, the key words and phrases include *interdependent, unified whole, equilibrium, functional, common purpose, organized,* and *harmonious.* Thus, a system can be thought of as a group of parts that make up a unified whole, in balance, that depend on one another and that serve a common purpose in an organized and harmonious manner.

What Is the "Criminal Justice System"?

When people talk about the *criminal justice system,* they are talking about its interdependent components—the police, courts, and correctional facilities within the federal government, as well as the agencies of criminal justice of each of the 50 states. Walker (2005) thus claims that the United States actually has 51 criminal justice systems. Additionally, each state has scores of municipalities, each with its own law enforcement agencies and, in some cases, its own forms of courts and correctional facilities, as does the District of Colombia.

You can think of the criminal justice system as a whole, made up of these three interdependent components, something like a pie with three pieces. Although each of these components has its own functions and personnel, they are expected to work together as a unified whole, in balance, to serve some common purposes in an organized and harmonious manner (Cole and Smith, 2006). This is why scholars refer to the process of arresting, convicting, and punishing criminals as the processes of the criminal justice system.

The primary responsibilities of each component of criminal justice include the following:

- *Police:* Investigating alleged criminal offenses, apprehending suspected criminal offenders, assisting the prosecution with obtaining criminal convictions at trial, keeping the peace in the community, preventing crime, providing social services, upholding constitutional protections.
- *Courts:* Determining guilt or innocence of suspected offenders at trial (adjudication), sentencing the legally guilty to some form(s) of punishment,

interpreting laws made by legislative bodies, setting legal precedents, upholding constitutional protections.

- *Corrections:* Carrying out the sentences of the courts by administering punishment, providing care and custody for accused and convicted criminals, upholding constitutional protections.)

Although each of these agencies of criminal justice has its own goals, ideally they will also share some larger goals. This means personnel of police, courts, and corrections should refrain from behaving in ways that may threaten these ideal goals. One goal I will discuss later in this chapter is doing justice, which means holding the guilty accountable for their criminal acts while ensuring that the criminal justice process is fair and impartial.

When police investigate criminal offenses and make arrests, their desire to reduce crime should not interfere with ensuring that the right person is caught. Additionally, their own personal prejudices and animosities should not affect their behaviors when interacting with citizens. Furthermore, members of the courtroom workgroup, including the prosecutor and defense attorney, should always remember that they are, first and foremost, officers of the court and therefore not entitled to allow their desire to win cases to interfere with their commitment to the ethics of their profession. Judges also should be fair in administering sentences so that justice is achieved and should ensure that prosecutors and defense attorneys follow the law. Finally, correctional facilities must not permit offenders to be assaulted or unduly humiliated for the sake of the enjoyment or empowerment of their employees. Punishment should be administered humanely and fairly. As you will see throughout this book, this logic has been lost on U.S. politicians, who have made criminal justice more and more punitive over the past 35 years.

Why the "Criminal Justice System" Is Not a System

It's easy to see why some are reluctant to refer to criminal justice in the United States as a "system." With three main components, each acting at three levels of government, the fight against crime is not an efficient, smoothly running process. Some view the three criminal justice components as a system, but many do not. As you will learn in this book, what is referred to as the criminal justice system is not organized, harmonious, uniform, or in equilibrium. And police, courts, and corrections have developed separately from the others. Each has "developed within different governmental structures, each has different sources of support and different budgets, and each has different objectives. Each has developed its own requirements for staffing, drawing on different resource pools for personnel and requiring different programs of training and education" (Gottfredson, 1999, p. 8).

As explained by the National Criminal Justice Commission, "the decisions made at each level of the system can severely impact other elements. Yet there is no systematic process used in making decisions. Rather, each component is left to its own, often fighting for resources against other parts of the system" (Donziger, 1996, p. 181). Indeed, every dollar invested in one component of criminal justice is a dollar not invested in another component.

These are some of the reasons that many criminal justice scholars do not view criminal justice agencies as a system and why some instead call it a "network" (e.g., Cox and Wade,

2001). In this book, I follow this lead and refer to the collection of agencies of police, courts, and corrections as the **criminal justice network** (except when I am quoting directly from another source). A network is a group of parts, agencies, or organizations that are interconnected and interrelated, but not necessarily organized and harmonious.

All of the agencies of criminal justice are expected to work together to achieve the goals of criminal justice as a whole, and each component of criminal justice is affected by the actions of the others. No one component can operate without the others. Police must solve crime by making arrests of suspects; otherwise, courts have no need to hold trials. Similarly, if courts do not convict people, correctional facilities such as prisons have no one to punish. Finally, if correctional facilities do not effectively administer punishment in communities, police will surely be overrun by crime. If we are to achieve our overall criminal justice goals, the three components must work together efficiently. The fact that they do not currently work this way in reality does not mean they should not ideally work this way.

The three parts of the criminal justice network are not equal in size, as law enforcement has historically employed the most personnel and has had the largest operating budget (see Figure 1-1). The rationale for this will be discussed in more depth later in this chapter. For now, keep in mind that all criminal justice cases must come into the criminal justice network through police contact, so to some degree it is logical for police to be the largest part; that is, police are the source of input for the criminal justice process. Box 1-1 illustrates how crime is typically processed through the entire criminal justice network.

From this brief introduction, you can conclude that one thing the U.S. criminal justice network is aimed at doing is reacting to crime—catching, convicting, and punishing criminals. But is that all? Is this the only reason we have police, courts, and corrections—to deal with the nation's crime problem? Or is there something else that the criminal justice network is supposed to do?

FIGURE 1-1   Relative Size of American Police, Courts, and Corrections (Percentage of All Criminal Justice Employees, 2000)

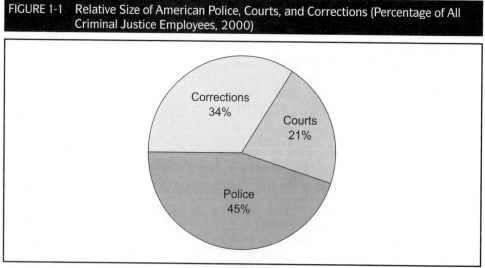

Data refer to percentage of total criminal justice employees.
Source: Bureau of Justice Statistics (www.ojp.usdoj.gov/bjs).

BOX 1-1

THE TYPICAL CRIMINAL JUSTICE PROCESS

The criminal justice network operates through numerous steps in a specified sequential order, although this does not necessarily mean that the criminal justice network operates like an efficient assembly line. There may be long delays between one stage and the next. For example, a crime may go unreported to the police for a long period of time, as happens when a victim does not discover his or her victimization immediately or when a murder goes unsolved for some period of time. Because murder cases have no statute of limitations, they can go to trial at any time in the future as long as a suspect has been identified and arrested. Additionally, accused offenders may sit in jail in preventive detention, awaiting trial, for more than a year.

When cases move quickly through the criminal justice process, the process can be accurately described as an assembly line. The criminal justice network moves more expeditiously for some types of cases and for some types of defendants than for others. Whether this is fair and therefore just will be discussed in Chapter 7. Typically, poor people are processed through criminal justice agencies quickly while wealthy citizens (who rarely are processed by the system at all) can afford to tie the process up if it is to their benefit to do so.

At each stage of the criminal justice process, many cases do not pass on to the next stage because of a process called *filtering,* which allows some cases to be screened out of the criminal justice network. Cases are filtered out for dozens of reasons. Examples are provided in this section as we move through each stage of the process.

CRIME

Obviously, the criminal justice process begins with the commission of a *crime.* The issue of what is crime will be discussed in Chapter 4. A short definition of a crime is "an act in violation of the criminal law." For example, theft occurs when a person takes property from its owner with the intent to deprive the owner of the property permanently. Normally, when a crime is committed, it is not immediately detected by the police (Wrobleski, 2006). Rather, it is typically reported to the police either by the victim or by another citizen who discovers the crime. Therefore, any law or criminal justice policy that discourages citizens from getting involved in the process will be detrimental to the operations of the criminal justice network.

Criminal offenses reported to the police by citizens are not automatically assumed to be crimes. That may sound strange, but citizens may think they have been victimized by crimes when, in fact, the act that was committed against them did not violate the criminal law. Whether reported acts violate the criminal law is determined by police when they conduct an investigation. Even when crimes have actually been committed, police do not necessarily conduct a thorough investigation; they use their **discretion** in deciding whether to act. Discretion is the ability of an agent to act according to his or her own professional judgment rather than some preset rules of procedures (Fuller, 2005). Using their discretion, police may determine that the crime committed is so minor that it does not warrant the expenditure of police resources, or that

(continued)

BOX 1-1   (*Continued*)

the likelihood of solving the crime or recovering stolen property is too remote.

Think about the disadvantage the police already face when a crime has been committed. The suspect is typically long gone before the police arrive. It is estimated that 75% of all crimes are **cold crimes**, crimes in which a suspect is not caught at the scene of the crime (Wrobleski, 2006). Given that policing in the United States is largely reactive and dependent on citizen reports, it is very difficult to do a good job of clearing cases by making arrests. Thus, the majority of crimes that are committed do not lead to an arrest.

Of course, the likelihood of **clearing a case by arrest** is a function of the type of crime committed. Murders are the most likely type of street crime to lead to an arrest, for several reasons. First, murder victims are almost always discovered by police. Second, the crime is heinous in nature, so police take this offense very seriously. Third, in about half of murders committed in the United States, the victim is killed by an acquaintance or relative. This makes it easier to locate the offender. Other crimes, such as theft, are less likely to be cleared by arrest. Thefts are not always discovered by the victims. Even when they are, they may be considered minor or not worthy of calling the police for some other reason. Also, thefts are more likely to be committed by strangers than by people known to the victim, so that locating suspects is much more difficult for the police.

The bottom line is that police do not even know about most crimes, even those committed on the street. Estimates suggest that police discover somewhere between 30% and 50% of all street crimes in any given year (Walker, 2005). The remaining 50% to 70% of street crimes never enter the criminal justice network because they are not discovered. The main reason this **dark figure of crime** remains hidden to the police and thus to the criminal justice network is that many crimes are simply not reported to the police by victims or witnesses. For reasons that are not the fault of police, law enforcement is highly ineffective at apprehending suspects and therefore at reducing crime and doing justice.

Furthermore, with about 800,000 sworn police officers in the United States for a population of 300 million Americans, there are only about 3 police officers on the street for every 1,000 people. If only 5% of these 1,000 persons are serious, repetitive criminals (as suggested by criminal careers research), this would mean that, on average, there are only 3 police officers on the street for every 50 career criminals (e.g., see Wolfgang, Figlio, and Sellin, 1972). And this figure includes only street criminals; it does not include those who commit white-collar and corporate crimes (see Chapter 4). Imagine 2.7 police officers in your community trying to keep up with the criminal acts of 50 career criminals, plus the occasional acts of other citizens who violate the law.

INVESTIGATION

Police investigation, the second stage in the criminal justice process, begins when the patrol officer responds to the scene of the alleged crime. If police determine that the act was not illegal, the case gets filtered out of the criminal justice network and does not lead to the next stage, arrest. If the responding officers determine that a crime was in fact committed, their primary job is to "solve the crime," which in law enforcement terms equates to making an arrest. Ideally, a criminal investigation leads the police to answer the question, "Who done it?" Patrol officers conduct a **preliminary investigation** at the crime scene; later, when the scene has been secured, trained detectives conduct a **secondary investigation**. The primary goal of the preliminary investigation is to secure the crime scene to protect the integrity of the evidence and to identify, locate, and question potential witnesses and/or victims. The secondary or follow-up investigation will lead to a more thorough collection, preservation, and presentation of evidence (Wrobleski, 2006).

ARREST

Once police identify a suspect by collecting enough high-quality evidence, their goal is to remove the alleged offender from the street. This is usually accomplished through an **arrest**. An arrest occurs when the police take a suspect into custody so that prosecution of the suspect may begin. Generally, arrests must be based on **probable cause**—a reasonable belief that a particular person has committed a crime. For serious crimes such as felonies, police officers "must have knowledge of sufficient facts and circumstances that would allow a person of reasonable caution to believe that a crime has been committed" (Gottfredson, 1999, p. 31).

At this point in the process, some cases are filtered out before the next stage, booking. For example, juveniles may be sent directly to the "juvenile justice system." If police discover they arrested the wrong person, the suspect may be immediately released.

At the point of arrest, police are required to read a suspect his or her *Miranda* rights, so named because of the 1966 Supreme Court case, *Miranda v. Arizona*. Since this ruling, police have been required to read suspects their constitutional protections when an arrest occurs or is imminent. The *Miranda* warning reads:

> You have the right to remain silent. If you choose to give up this right, anything you do say can and will be used against you in a court of law. You have the right to an attorney. If you cannot afford one, one will be appointed to you.

Suspects are then asked if they understand these rights and, if so, whether they want to give up their rights and make statements or answer questions. Many claim that this requirement places an undue burden on the police and makes it harder for the criminal justice network to obtain convictions because it encourages criminals to withhold vital information from the police. As a result of such concerns, numerous exceptions to this rule have been established through case law (see Chapter 6).

BOOKING

After arrest, **booking** occurs. At this point, an administrative record is made of the suspect. Typically, his or her photograph and fingerprints are taken, and he or she may be questioned further by the police and/or placed in a lineup for witness or victim identification.

After booking, the suspect may be charged with specific criminal offenses if the prosecutor thinks there is a sufficient quality and quantity of evidence indicating that the suspect is indeed guilty of the offenses charged. A person can always be released and later rearrested if further evidence of the suspect's guilt is discovered. Release is another form of filtering.

INITIAL APPEARANCE

After being formally charged with a crime or crimes by the prosecution, the

(*continued*)

BOX 1-1   (*Continued*)

suspect makes an **initial appearance** before a judge. At this stage, the suspect is notified of the charges against him or her and is advised of his or her rights. The judge determines whether **bail** is necessary; if not, the suspect is released on his or her promise to reappear for trial (called **release on own recognizance**). When a flight risk exists because the judge fears the suspect may flea the jurisdiction to avoid trial, suspects may be required to post bail or may even be held in **preventive detention** in cases where the judge determines there is a flight risk and some danger to the community (see Chapter 7). If the judge determines there is not enough evidence to warrant the charges, the case may be dismissed by the judge and hence filtered out of the criminal justice network.

PRELIMINARY HEARING/ GRAND JURY

Assuming a case is not dismissed, the next stage in the criminal justice process is either a *preliminary hearing* or a *grand jury,* depending on the jurisdiction in which the case is being heard. Both of these mechanisms are ideally intended to ensure that innocent persons are not hastily, maliciously, or arbitrarily prosecuted. In reality, these processes are typically one-sided and almost always result in a finding that there is probable cause to warrant a person being detained until trial (Walker, 2005). This can be a major impediment to fairness in the criminal justice process, because findings of preliminary hearings and grand juries are routinely published in local media, perhaps creating assumptions among the public that named defendants are already guilty of crimes, even though in fact they have not yet been convicted of anything.

In about half of the states, a preliminary hearing is held to determine if there is enough evidence to hold the case over for trial. If the judge does not find probable cause that the named person(s) committed the named offense(s), the case may be dismissed and filtered out of the criminal justice network. In cases where the judge finds probable cause, the accused is held for trial on the basis of an **information**, which is a formal charging document against the accused.

In federal cases and in other states, a grand jury is impaneled to determine if there is enough evidence to file an **indictment** charging the suspect with the named crime(s). If the grand jury, made up of a panel of civilians, finds that there is sufficient evidence to warrant a trial, it issues a true bill (which charges the defendant with a crime); if not, it issues a no bill (which means the defendant is not charged with a crime) and he or she is filtered out of the criminal justice network. Again, the vast majority of cases heard by a grand jury lead to an indictment. This has led some to call the grand jury process a "rubber stamp" for the prosecution (Walker, 2005).

ARRAIGNMENT

At **arraignment**, the next step in the process, the accused is read the information or indictment by the judge. The suspect then has the right to enter a plea of guilty, not guilty, or *nolo contendere* (no contest). Upon a plea of guilty or no contest, sentencing may take place immediately because a trial is not necessary to determine guilt. Pleas of guilty are not to be accepted by the judge unless several assurances from the accused are received. The reality is that **plea bargaining** occurs in more than 90% of all cases before U.S. courts, and the suspect is presumed guilty by virtually all involved, including the suspect's own attorney (see Chapter 7).

TRIAL

Although the right to **trial** is mentioned in the Declaration of Independence, three amendments to the U.S. Constitution, and numerous Supreme Court decisions, very few U.S. citizens have a reasonable expectation of a criminal trial when charged with a crime. As noted, more than 90% of defendants plead guilty to the charge(s) and thus do not need a trial. When a trial does occur, it becomes a contest between the government (prosecution) and the accused (defense) to win and secure their own interests. Ideally, our agencies of criminal justice are **adversarial** in nature because they are supposed to feature two adversaries fighting it out for the truth. But the ideal is very different from the reality. Gaines, Kaune, and Miller (2000, p. 286) state it this way: "Television dramas often depict the courtroom as a battlefield, with prosecutors and defense attorneys spitting fire at each other over the loud and insistent protestations of a frustrated judge. Consequently, many people are somewhat disappointed when they witness a real courtroom at work." Even when trials do occur, they commonly produce cooperation rather than battle.

The typical trial process is discussed in Chapter 7. Ideally, the truth of a suspect's guilt will emerge at trial, where guilt must be established **beyond a reasonable doubt** by the prosecution. In plea bargaining, by contrast, guilt or innocence is not determined. Instead, guilt is assumed and sentencing is the only issue to be resolved.

Trials are most likely to occur in cases where suspects are charged with serious offenses, particularly violent offenses such as murder (Schmalleger, 2006). Criminal trials are very expensive; for minor offenses, plea bargains are less time-consuming and therefore a much more cost-effective use of government resources to carry out justice. Criminal trials are rare precisely because, in most cases, all parties involved assume the guilt of the suspect simply because some evidence suggests the suspect is guilty. Many ask, "If they weren't guilty, why would we be arresting them in the first place?" The answer is that the standard of evidence needed to make an arrest (probable cause) is much lower than that needed to sustain a criminal conviction (beyond a reasonable doubt). Yet even the typical defense attorney in the United States (a public defender assigned to a poor client) has little financial incentive and limited resources to determine whether due process was followed or whether his or her client is actually innocent of the charges (see Chapter 7). Although the ideal of American justice is the trial, in reality, trials are the exception to the rule of plea bargaining.

According to Langbein (2000, p. 25):

> We are accustomed to viewing the Bill of Rights as a success story. With it, the American constitution-makers opened a new epoch in the centuries-old struggle to place effective limits on the abuse of state power. Not all of the Bill of Rights is a success story, however . . . we would do well to take note of that chapter of the Bill of Rights that has been a spectacular failure: The Framers' effort to embed jury trial as the exclusive mode of proceeding in cases of serious crime.

Think of the Sixth Amendment to the U.S. Constitution, which states: "In all criminal prosecutions, the accused shall enjoy the right to a speedy and public trial, by an impartial jury of the State and district wherein the crime shall have been committed. . . ." Langbein (2000) writes: "'All' is not a word that constitution-makers use

(continued)

BOX 1-1 *(Continued)*

lightly. The drafters of the Sixth Amendment used it and meant it." Article III of the Constitution says the same thing: "The Trial of all Crimes, except in Cases of Impeachment, shall be by Jury. . . ." Today in the United States, "[i]n place of 'all,' a more accurate term to describe the use of jury trial in the discharge of our criminal caseload would be 'virtually none.'" Thus, "our guarantee of routine criminal trial is a fraud" (p. 26).

SENTENCING

When defendants are found guilty by a jury of their peers or by a bench trial (where a judge determines guilt or innocence), the next step in the process is **sentencing**. When suspects are found not guilty or acquitted, they are filtered out of the criminal justice network and cannot be retried for the same offense because of the Fifth Amendment protection of freedom from double jeopardy. Sentencing addresses the questions: "What do we do with the legally guilty? What punishment should be administered?" Judges typically bear the responsibility for passing sentences, which are recommended by juries. Judges have discretion within certain guidelines in indeterminate sentences (which specify a range of possible sanctions), but have less discretion in determinate sentences (which are specific to the type of crime committed) and no discretion in mandatory sentences (see Chapter 8).

APPEAL

Those convicted of criminal offenses, particularly serious crimes, have the right to **appeal** their convictions to appellate courts, or courts of appeal. Those convicted through plea bargains give up this right, along with many others. Convicted offenders can appeal on the basis of any matter of law—for example, that the trial court somehow failed to follow proper procedures or that constitutional rights were violated at some point in the process. Perhaps unlawfully obtained evidence was admitted into trial, or maybe a defendant's evidence was wrongfully excluded from trial. In these cases, appeals may be allowed, yet in the vast majority of cases, appeals are denied (Meeker, 1984; Williams, 1991). Because appeals are made on matters of law rather than fact, a convicted criminal cannot simply argue that he or she is "really innocent!" Calls to review jury decisions often fall on deaf ears.

Some claim that such appeals are based on "legal technicalities" and should be limited so criminal justice processes can operate more efficiently and effectively. Others point out that procedural errors may lead to mistakes in adjudication, meaning that innocent persons may be wrongfully convicted; therefore, constitutional protections should not be equated with legal technicalities.

CORRECTIONS

Once a sentence is passed, correctional services such as probation, jails, prisons, and numerous other agencies administer the sanctions imposed by the court. **Probation**, a form of punishment that allows the offender to live in the community under certain rules, is the most widely used form of the criminal justice sanction in the United States (see Chapter 8). Probation, the cheapest sanction available, is intended for less serious offenders. Jails and prisons are forms of incarceration, where offenders are deprived of their freedom and locked away from the rest of society. The destructive nature of incarceration is discussed in Chapter 9. **Jails** are intended for persons sentenced to less than 1 year of incarceration, **prisons** for those sentenced to more than 1 year of incarceration (Clear, Cole, and Reisig, 2005).

RELEASE

Once a sentence has been fully served, a person is released from the criminal justice network in what is supposed to be the final stage of the process. Offenders are also commonly released early from incarceration through the process of **parole**, which allows the offender to be released back into the community prior to serving his or her full sentence, as long as he or she agrees to live under certain rules. In the current "get tough" environment in the United States, parole has been abolished at the federal level and in many states (see Chapter 9).

Although release is supposed to be the final stage of the criminal justice process, the reality of release is that offenders are routinely harassed by police and/or their parole officers after being released from the criminal justice network (Evans, 1997). When crimes are committed nearby, especially when they fit the modus operandi (M.O.) of a known offender out on parole, he or she is automatically considered a likely suspect. So much for "paying your debt to society"! Police and parole officers also may seek cooperation in developing leads for crimes committed by known associates of the offender.

IDEAL GOALS OF CRIMINAL JUSTICE

Believe it or not, there is no "official" source one can consult to find out what the U.S. criminal justice network is intended to do. You might find this curious: How can we possibly know how well we are really doing if we do not know what we are intended to do? The closest we can come to a government statement of intended criminal justice outcomes is the 1967 President's Commission on Law Enforcement and Administration of Justice report, *The Challenge of Crime in a Free Society*. The authors wrote that criminal justice agencies were intended to "enforce the standards of conduct necessary to protect individuals and the community."

This seems straightforward enough, but exactly whose standards of conduct should be enforced? And what is meant by "to protect individuals and the community"? Does this mean only that the criminal justice network should protect individuals and communities from criminals? If so, how? Does it also mean that suspected criminals should be protected from the government? Does protecting the community from crime mean eroding constitutional protections of all Americans? Answers to these questions are not clear.

This is partly because the last national report on crime was published decades ago by the Eisenhower Commission. In fact, the last time *specific* recommendations for criminal justice reform were *formally* reported was by the 1967 President's Commission. Since that time, no president of the United States has appointed a group to analyze crime or criminal justice policy.

In the 1990s, a group called the National Criminal Justice Commission initiated an investigation of the U.S. criminal justice network (Donziger, 1996). The findings of their scathing indictment, published under the title *The Real War on Crime*, will be discussed at various points in this book. Their overall argument is that American criminal justice agencies mostly fail to meet their goals. Although it has been more than 10 years since their book was published, the conclusions of the National Criminal Justice Commission hold true today.

One thing we can cull from this source, and most basic introductory criminal justice texts, is that the criminal justice network has at least two goals:

- Reducing crime
- Doing justice

Reducing Crime

Police, courts, and corrections are obviously aimed at **reducing crime**, or "crime-fighting" as some like to call it. This can be achieved through reactive means (after the crime occurs) or proactive means (before the crime occurs). The former type of crime fighting is generally called *crime control,* whereas the latter is often referred to as **crime prevention** (Lab, 2004). Amazingly, the U.S. Constitution does not list "crime control" as a responsibility of the U.S. government. Therefore, the U.S. Congress was not explicitly empowered with this authority. The Constitution does state, however, that our government must "establish Justice, [and] insure domestic tranquility," and this makes crime control an implied power of government (Marion, 1995, p. 6). Because crime control activities are not specifically granted to the federal government, and because they are not specifically denied to the states, crime control has historically been the responsibility of state governments. Since the 1960s, however, crime control has become increasingly a national issue as a consequence of the politicization of crime in elections (see Chapter 2) and media coverage of crime (see Chapter 5).

In the United States, crime reduction is mostly reactive in nature. For example, American policing has historically been aimed at reacting to calls for service from crime victims (after the crimes occur). Our agencies of criminal justice try to apprehend, prosecute, convict, and punish offenders after a crime is discovered by or reported to the police. It is important to point out here that reactive criminal justice operations are not likely to reduce crime because they do not eliminate the root causes of crime. This is why the National Criminal Justice Commission claims: "We cannot expect the criminal justice system to create strong families, deliver jobs, or provide hope to young people" because it is not charged with doing so (Donziger, 1996, p. 61). In fact, because the criminal justice network does little to address the major sources of criminal behavior, crime prevention through criminal justice is not likely (Sherman et al., 1997).

Crime prevention includes any means to eliminate the causes of crime so that crime does not occur and does not need to be dealt with by criminal justice agencies (Robinson, 1999). Although some American criminal justice activity is aimed at crime prevention, the great bulk of it can be described as crime control. There is some evidence that crime prevention can be effective, if appropriately designed, implemented, and supported (Sherman et al., 1997).

Reducing crime is obviously a desirable goal. But the most important point to remember while reading this book is that there is another, more important goal of our criminal justice network—doing justice. Although reducing crime is an important goal, it is of secondary importance to doing justice (Cole and Smith, 2006).

Doing Justice

First and foremost, the basis of the criminal justice system is **doing justice**. There are two somewhat conflicting conceptions of justice, one concerned with holding the guilty accountable for their crimes and the other with ensuring that the criminal justice process is fair and impartial. Doing justice implies both that guilty people will be punished for their wrongful acts and that innocent persons will not wrongly be subjected to the criminal justice process. Which is the more important conception of justice? If you had to choose to emphasize one conception of justice over the other, which would you choose?

WHAT IS JUSTICE?

The meaning of justice depends on who is being asked. To crime victims, justice may simply mean getting even with the offenders who harmed them. For example, a rape victim may define justice for the attacker as imprisonment, or even castration or death, and might perceive anything less as unjust. When people are intentionally victimized and the guilty are not held accountable for their actions, justice clearly has not been obtained. This is because the offender has unfairly gained an advantage over the victim; the mythical scales of justice shown in Figure 1-2 have wrongfully been tilted in favor of the offender. The scales of justice depicted in the figure are in balance only when the harms inflicted on crime victims are righted by administering punishment to their offenders.

Retribution, a main reason for administering criminal sanctions to offenders (see Chapter 8), implies that the harm inflicted by the criminal upon the victim will in some way be returned by the government to the offender. In the United States, when a criminal hurts someone, he or she is viewed as deserving of punishment: "An eye for an eye, a tooth for a tooth," so to speak. Victims now regularly view punishment of their offenders as one of their rights (Beckett and Sasson, 2003). This is one conception of justice.

Justice has an alternative meaning, as well. In some ways, this definition is related to the one above, for it is concerned with assuring that the scales of justice are not imbalanced. This conception of justice is based on fairness and impartiality. It assumes

FIGURE 1-2   The Scales of Justice

that all persons will be treated equally in the eyes of the law—that justice will be blind. Justice thus would not be present when any group is somehow left out or singled out for differential treatment by the law.

This conception of justice is represented by the figure of "a blindfolded woman with a scale in one hand and a sword in the other" (see Issue in Depth at the end of this chapter for a discussion of Lady Justitia, whose image adorns this book). It is also what is meant by "With liberty and justice for all" in the pledge of allegiance—that the government will treat its citizens with "fairness, equity" and in a manner that is right (Kappeler and Potter, 2004).

From the title of this book—*Justice Blind?*—you may guess that I am not sure whether our criminal justice network achieves this measure of justice. In fact, I will provide evidence that our criminal justice practices are unjust in many ways. Justice must be blind or it is not just at all. I will demonstrate in this book that the American criminal justice network is in some ways biased against the poor and people of color, and that, in some situations, it discriminates on the basis of gender (see Chapter 12).

The depiction of justice on the cover of this book is also reflected in the American Declaration of Independence. American settlers criticized their "British brethren" for being "deaf to the voice of justice" (Gottfredson, 1999, p. 50). Ideally, this was one reason that people came to found this country in the interests of justice apart from the interests of the British monarchy. Of course, history testifies to a different reality. Early Americans wiped out numerous indigenous peoples and enslaved other groups in the name of "Manifest Destiny," a nineteenth-century doctrine based on the premise that the Americans had the God-given right—indeed, the duty—to expand their territory and cultural influence throughout North America (e.g., see Koning, 1993). Howard Zinn, in *A People's History of the United States* (2003), tells history from the people that are least recognized in accounts of U.S. history—the poor, working people, women, Native Americans, slaves, and other minority groups—and shows that much of what we believe about American history is simply not true. Further, James Loewen, in his book, *Lies My Teacher Told Me* (1995), explains how and why Americans are raised to believe their country was founded based on the ideals of freedom for all when in fact freedoms were structured by social class, ethnicity, and so forth. Still, early Americans envisioned a country where all "men" could live, thrive, and further their own interests without the burdens imposed by the British monarchy.

Conflicting Views of Justice

Each conception of justice is important when it comes to studying and understanding the criminal justice network. Americans will not support criminal justice practices that fail to punish those who deserve it. Ideally, they will not support them when they wrongfully convict the innocent or are biased against any group. Pound (1912) wrote long ago that justice requires that serious offenders be convicted and punished and that the innocent and unfortunate not be wrongly oppressed. Similarly, Harrigan (2000, p. 315) notes that "Justice is served neither if a guilty person is let go nor if an innocent person is punished."

These two conceptions of justice—punishing the guilty but ensuring fairness and impartiality—often conflict. The law places restrictions on the actions of criminal justice actors so that constitutional rights of individuals are not violated. With unlimited powers, law enforcement agencies probably could do a much better job at fighting crime, but numerous liberties that we currently enjoy (such as the right to privacy) would have to be sacrificed. Imagine how much more effectively police could detect crimes if they could enter your home, peek into your windows, tap your phones, and monitor your e-mail without first having to establish probable cause!

This fictional example has great relevance for America today when considering our current "war on terror." For example, it has been reported that President Bush authorized—by executive order—a domestic spying program under the direction of the National Security Agency that tapped the phones and monitored the computer usage (e-mail) of American citizens for the purpose of disrupting terrorist plots. Critics of the program claimed it violates American citizens' rights to privacy, as well as federal law. Are such programs acceptable to you if they actually disrupt terrorist plots? Are they unacceptable to you no matter what benefit they provide? What if they lead to significant abuses?

Given the limits within which the criminal justice network must operate, it is difficult to catch, convict, and punish criminal offenders. For example, the "exclusionary rule" states that illegally seized evidence cannot be used to establish legal guilt against a defendant. The Supreme Court held, in *Mapp v. Ohio* (1961), that the rule had to be applied universally to all criminal proceedings, including those by state governments against individual citizens. This requirement may make it less likely that a factually guilty criminal will be found legally guilty in a court of law. Alternatively, our current efforts to fight crime at almost any cost have led to the establishment of measures intended to protect "victims' rights . . . [that] have lowered evidentiary requirements, eliminated the insanity defense, and weakened exclusionary rules designed to block the introduction of illegally obtained evidence" (Beckett and Sasson, 2000, p. 163).

Walker (1998, p. 176) argues that many so-called victims' rights initiatives are really efforts to get "tough on crime." He writes that the President's Task Force on Victims of Crime, for example, "recommended legislation 'to abolish the exclusionary rule,' 'to abolish parole,' to permit hearsay evidence at preliminary hearings, and to authorize preventive detention." Part of the frustration that victims feel when they suffer harm at the hands of criminals stems from the fact that, technically, the only "victim" of crime is the government. This means that victims are not entitled to get justice for themselves; rather, the state is authorized to conduct crime control efforts in the interest of community safety.

Yet the U.S. justice network must strive to achieve a balance between fighting crime (to do justice for its victims) and being fair and impartial (to do justice for the accused). Justice for the community requires both. Thus, throughout our history, the priorities of American justice have shifted back and forth, much like a pendulum or a set of scales being continually rebalanced. During some periods, emphasis has been placed on apprehending and punishing criminals over ensuring fairness in the criminal justice process. At other times, crime fighting has taken a back seat to ensuring that the criminal justice network operates impartially.

Due Process Versus Crime Control

There has always been tension between those who believe in **due process** and those who believe in **crime control.** These terms represent two models of justice put forth by Herbert Packer (1968) in his book, *The Limits of the Criminal Sanction.* Although neither of the two models actually exists or ever can in reality, Packer attempted to describe two polar extremes—one model most concerned with preserving individual liberties and the other with maintaining order in the community and fighting crime.

Figure 1-3 depicts these models at opposite ends of a continuum. The **due process model** is aimed at ensuring that individual liberties are protected at all costs, even if guilty people sometimes go free. In other words, the due process model values individual freedom, and the way to protect individual freedom is to uphold constitutional protections. It places a high value on the adversarial nature of justice, whereby a prosecutor and defense attorney battle it out in court to find the truth and make sure that justice is achieved. Reliability is the most important value of the due process model, for it is imperative that the right person be convicted of the crime of which he or she is accused. Packer's metaphor for this model was an "obstacle course" because, to ensure that no innocent persons were wrongfully convicted, the prosecution would have to overcome numerous obstacles to convict anyone.

The **crime control model** is aimed at protecting the community by lowering crime rates, even if, on occasion, innocent persons are mistakenly convicted. The crime control model also values individual freedom but suggests that the way to protect individual freedom is to protect people from criminals. It places a high value on informal processes such as plea bargaining (when a prosecutor and defense attorney agree out of court to an appropriate sentence for an accused criminal) to expedite criminal justice operations. In this model, very few criminal trials are held because they are expensive and unnecessary for establishing legal guilt. Efficiency is the most important value of the crime control model, for it is imperative that the criminal justice network operate as quickly as possible to keep up with the large numbers of criminal cases that enter it each day. Packer's metaphor for this model was an "assembly line" because individual defendants would be quickly processed through the criminal justice network outside the courtroom through plea bargaining (see Chapter 7).

Note that justice is an important value in both models. Yet proponents of each model view justice differently. Figure 1-4 illustrates how justice can be viewed either as an outcome or as a process. People who view **justice as an outcome**, usually supporters of the crime control model, think that justice means giving people what they deserve: Guilty people deserve punishment. I call this version of justice **corrective justice**. Others, typically proponents of the due process model, see **justice as a process**. People who value what I call **procedural justice** are more concerned with ensuring that everyone is treated fairly and equally while being processed through the criminal justice network. This means protecting people's constitutional rights and not allowing discrimination on the basis of factors such as race, class, or gender.

FIGURE 1-3   Due Process and Crime Control Models of Justice

	Crime Control	**Due Process**
Most Important Goal	Reduce crime	Protect rights
Cherished Value	Efficiency	Reliability
In Practice	Increase powers of police, prosecutors	Limit discretion of police, prosecutors

FIGURE 1-4	Justice as an Outcome and Justice as a Process		
Justice as . . .	**would mean . . .**	**Example**	**Term**
an outcome	giving one what he or she is due	Convicting the guilty	Corrective
a process	treating everyone fairly, equally	Not discriminating based on race, class, gender	Procedural

Each of these conceptions of justice is important to many Americans, but criminal justice activity over the past few decades reflects an emphasis on corrective justice at the expense of procedural justice. In other words, U.S. policy makers are more concerned with holding the guilty accountable for their crimes than with ensuring fairness and equity in criminal justice practice, even in the face of overwhelming evidence that innocent people have been convicted of crimes they did not commit (for evidence of wrongful convictions, see Issue in Depth at the end of Chapter 7). Apparently, the same can be said with regard to America's "war on terror." Generally, lawmakers seem far more concerned with catching and punishing terrorists than the freedoms the terrorists supposedly want to destroy. This is unfortunate, because of the inherent infallibility associated with all human activity.

In case you were wondering, Democrats historically tended to support due process protections, whereas Republicans tended to support crime control efforts. Traditionally, Democrats have been more "liberal" and have placed greater value on individual rights than on community protection, whereas Republicans have been more "conservative" and thus more supportive of government efforts to fight crime (Baker and Meyer, 1980; Biskupic, 1991; Van Horn, Baumer, and Gormley, 1992). Because the crime control and due process models are ideals, and because of the competing values of reducing crime and doing justice, the history of criminal justice in the United States can be characterized as a pendulum swinging back and forth between the two ideals, much as the political affiliation of voters shifts over time. For example, the Warren Supreme Court (1953–1969) can be considered a "due process" court because its rulings were more consistent with upholding individual rights. The Burger Supreme Court (1969–1986) is more accurately characterized as a "crime control" court because it was less protective of individual rights and made decisions that limited *Miranda* protections (for more, see Marion, 1995; O'Brien, 1993; Steel and Steger, 1988). Beckett and Sasson (2000, p. 59) go as far as to characterize Burger Court activity as an "assault on defendants' rights." The Rehnquist Supreme Court (1986–2005) was also generally a crime control court, as it made it easier to convict the "factually guilty" and to avoid losing cases as a result of legal technicalities that previously made it easier for the guilty to go free. The Rehnquist Court gave "greater flexibility to the police and corrections personnel, making changes in the death penalty, unreasonable searches and seizures, and the exclusionary rule" (Marion, 1995, p. 51). Some of its rulings, however, such as *U.S. v. Dickerson* (2000), which upheld the requirement that police read suspects the *Miranda* warning prior to interrogation, were more consistent with the due process model. This is discussed in Box 1-2.

BOX 1-2

UPHOLDING *MIRANDA*

In the case of *U.S. v. Dickerson* (2000), the U.S. Supreme Court upheld the *Miranda* requirements by a vote of 7–2. At issue was a 1968 federal law that allowed voluntary confessions by suspects to be admitted into court even if the defendant had not been read his or her rights. This law conflicted with the Supreme Court's decision in *Miranda v. Arizona* (1966). Chief Justice William Rehnquist wrote the majority opinion of the Court, in which he stated: "We hold that *Miranda*, being a constitutional decision of this Court, may not be . . . overruled by an Act of Congress, and we decline to overrule *Miranda* ourselves. We therefore hold that *Miranda* and its progeny in this Court govern the admissibility of statements made during custodial interrogation in both state and federal courts."

Rehnquist added that because the "advent of modern custodial police interrogation brought with it an increased concern about confessions obtained by coercion," *Miranda* requirements were considered more important than ever by the Court. Rehnquist wrote, for example, that being questioned by the police places a "heavy toll on individual liberty and trades on the weakness of individuals."

Ironically, the appeal of the original 1966 *Miranda* decision did not come from a law enforcement agency. In fact, most police administrators have always believed that *Miranda* provides an important protection for all Americans. They recognize that reading *Miranda* warnings to suspects is part of their professional responsibility of upholding the constitutional right of

suspects not to incriminate themselves. Because police have always been able to use strategies to convince suspects to waive their right not to incriminate themselves, *Miranda* is not and never has been a major impediment to effective policing.

Edward Lazarus (2000), author of "How *Miranda* Really Works and Why It Really Matters," wrote (about 3 weeks before the decision came down):

> As matters currently stand, when police officers fail to observe *Miranda*, judges almost always limit themselves . . . to finding "technical" violations of *Miranda*, thereby allowing prosecutors to use evidence derived from challenged confessions and to keep defendants from testifying in their own defense. Judges almost never take the extra step of finding a confession to be actually involuntary — which would deprive the prosecution of any evidence obtained as a result of the tainted confession.

Indeed, in practice, and wholly apart from the much-debated issue of whether *Miranda* inhibits police from obtaining confessions, the ruling has become largely symbolic. It allows judges to scold police for misbehavior and pay lip service to the right against self-incrimination, while minimizing the actual effect on police and prosecutors.

In 2000, the Court ruled that *Miranda* warnings have become intertwined with the fabric of American society. That is, *Miranda* protects a right that is crucial to being free from unwarranted government interference into our lives, a right that is so cherished by Americans that it cannot be eliminated by Court order.

It is too early to tell whether the Roberts Court (2005–) will rule more in favor of the crime control or due process model of criminal justice. Some speculate that since Chief Justice John Roberts is very conservative, was nominated by a Republican President, and was approved by a Republican Senate that the Court will shift further to the right and further toward the crime control model; yet past justices have ruled in ways often opposite of what one might expect.

Which model of criminal justice—crime control or due process—do you most support? Whether you would support a crime control model or due process model may depend on which you feel is more important, protecting the community from crime or protecting your individual constitutional rights. This may not be an easy choice, because both are worthy pursuits. Before you decide, remember that your rights as an American are the major difference between living in a democracy such as the United States or an authoritarian police state such as China, Afghanistan under the rule of the Taliban, or Iraq under Saddam Hussein.

Sometimes, ensuring that all individuals' rights are protected means that guilty people will go free. Alternatively, getting all the "bad guys" means that some "good guys" may get caught up in criminal justice processes, too. Ask yourself, which would be worse—being confronted by a criminal who was wrongly freed, or being wrongfully accused of a crime by your own government? In which situation would you be more likely to win?

How you answer such questions may determine whether you are a proponent of a due process model of justice or a crime control model of justice. Whatever the case, you must remember that the U.S. criminal justice network will never be 100% representative of either the due process or the crime control models. Rather, our criminal justice network attempts to stay in balance by upholding individual constitutional protections while effectively fighting crime. Gottfredson (1999, p. 27) writes: "Because we value freedom, we react strongly to violations or threats of violation of our persons or property. We resist any threat to our liberty by agencies of our government. [But] [b]ecause we value safety, we expect the criminal justice system to protect us. We want both protection for ourselves and for our own liberty."

The most important lesson to be learned from Packer's discussion is that there is an inherent conflict between protecting individuals' constitutional rights and fighting crime. It is difficult to do one well without being somewhat of a failure at the other.

Justice Today

Where are we today? And what are the implications for justice in America? Box 1-3 illustrates that most criminal justice resources go to police and corrections, with courts receiving the fewest resources. What does this suggest about whether we are following a crime control or due process model of justice?

From the discussion in the box on resources devoted to criminal justice, it appears that we as a nation have embraced crime control values. The past several presidents of the United States—Presidents Reagan, Bush (the first), Clinton, and Bush (the second)—have made this clear. Each sanctioned significant expansions of the wars on crime, drugs and now, terrorism.

Other chapters of this book will provide evidence that U.S. policy makers have chosen a crime control model at the expense of individual constitutional protections. The result is that many of our civil liberties are being or have been eroded. Remember that

BOX 1-3

RESOURCES DEVOTED TO CRIMINAL JUSTICE IN THE UNITED STATES

A criminal justice network that places a higher value on crime fighting than on due process might allocate a larger percentage of its resources to police because they are responsible for making arrests of suspected offenders, and/or to corrections because its agencies have sole authority over punishing offenders. A criminal justice network that places a greater value on due process might allocate a larger share of resources to courts because the judicial process determines the guilt or innocence of criminal justice clients. The primary protection innocent persons have from government overzealousness is high-quality defense attorneys and neutral, objective judges. If we value due process, these actors ought to be well equipped to do their jobs.

The following discussion is organized around these issues:

- Which component of criminal justice has the most employees?
- Which component of criminal justice is allocated the most financial resources?

EMPLOYEES OF CRIMINAL JUSTICE

As of March 2003, the U.S. criminal justice network employed more than 2.4 million people, including over 1 million working in law enforcement, about 500,000 working in courts, and more than 700,000 working in corrections (Bureau of Justice Statistics, 2007). So, of the three components of justice, the fewest people work in U.S. courts (about 20% of total employees work for courts). This is more consistent

with a crime control model of criminal justice than a due process model.

There are about 18,000 law enforcement agencies in the United States, employing a total of approximately 800,000 sworn officers. There are about 13,000 city police departments, employing nearly 450,000 sworn officers. The next largest type of agency is the county sheriff's office, with about 3,000 departments and more than 160,000 sworn deputies. Special police departments total about 1,400 agencies and more than 40,000 officers, and there are approximately 625 Texas constable agencies employing 2,600 officers. Compare these numbers with the 49 primary state police agencies that employ just over 56,000 officers, and the very small number of federal agencies (with more than 100 agents) that employ fewer than 90,000 officers (Bureau of Justice Statistics, 2007). Clearly, law enforcement in the United States is a local phenomenon, as most police officers work for local (city and county) agencies.

Courts employ far fewer employees than police departments. Given that prosecution is a state-level phenomenon (because most crimes are acts against the state government), I'll limit my discussion to state courts. There are 2,344 state court prosecutors' offices employing more than 78,000 attorneys, investigators, and support staff. In 2005, these employees were responsible for closing more than 2.4 million felony cases and about 7.5 million misdemeanor cases. Were the millions of people in these cases convicted "beyond a reasonable doubt" by a "jury of their peers"? Given the imbalance in criminal justice employees, it would be hard to imagine having trials for all of these defendants. In fact, almost all convictions by state courts were achieved through the process of plea bargaining. Half the prosecutors' offices in the United States employed 9 or fewer people and had a budget of $355,000 or less (Bureau of Justice Statistics, 2007).

Given that the largest share of defendants charged with felonies in state courts are indigent clients who cannot afford their own attorneys, an examination of defense systems for these indigent clients will help us learn about the state of defense attorneys generally in the United States. Of all felony case terminations, court-appointed counsel represent more than 80% of state defendants in the 75 largest counties. The poor traditionally receive legal representation from assigned counsel systems and public defenders' offices (see Chapter 7).

At the end of 2001, in the nation's 100 most populous counties, 90 had public defender programs, 89 had assigned counsel programs, and 42 had contract programs. Although the numbers are a bit dated—a possible sign of disinterest in the issue by the federal government—public defender offices in the nation's largest 100 counties employed 12,700 people in 1999. Defense attorneys for indigent clients handled 4.2 million cases in that year, 80% of which were criminal cases. Public defenders handled 82% of these cases, followed by 15% by appointed attorneys and 3% contract attorneys (Bureau of Justice Statistics, 2007). Whether publicly provided counsel provides defense of a lower quality than private attorneys is a matter of interesting debate (see Chapter 7), but the facts may speak for themselves. For example, the majority of inmates in state prisons and federal prisons were represented by publicly provided attorneys.

Private attorneys may not be any more likely than public defenders to gain acquittals for their clients or to achieve less severe sentences for them, but recall that justice is a process as much as it is an outcome. Clearly, publicly assigned defense attorneys have less financial incentive than private attorneys to assure fair and constitutional proceedings for their clients. The average public defender has more than 5 cases per day, 7 days per week, 52 weeks per year (assuming they work weekends, holidays, and vacation time); it is hard to fathom holding trials for all of these clients (Cole and Smith, 2006).

It should not be hard to imagine that, with more than 2 million felony criminal convictions in any given year, correctional facilities must employ a large number of people: In 2005, the number was greater than 700,000. At the end of 2005, more than 7 million people were under some form of criminal justice supervision, including probation, parole, and incarceration in jail or prison. State and federal prisons housed nearly 1.5 million inmates; jails housed another 750,000 (Bureau of Justice Statistics, 2007). How much does all of this cost? You must be wondering, especially since criminal justice is funded by taxpayer dollars. That's your money, after all. This is the next issue addressed.

FINANCIAL RESOURCES FOR CRIMINAL JUSTICE

In 2004, federal, state, and local governments spent over $193 billion for civil and criminal justice. For every resident, the three levels of government together spent $660 (this means you paid more than $600 for civil and criminal justice in 2004). State and local governments combined
(continued)

BOX 1-3 *(Continued)*

spent 82% of all direct justice dollars, and the federal government spent the rest. The federal government spent more than $34 billion on criminal and civil justice in 2005, compared to $61 billion spent by state governments and $97 billion by local governments (Bureau of Justice Statistics, 2007).

This is more than three times the amount spent in 1985, when justice spending was approximately $65 billion. In Chapter 4, I will review what happened with crime rates during this same time period. One might expect to have seen huge decreases in crime rates during this time period, but that is not what happened.

The vast majority of justice spending is incurred by state and local governments. The largest share of justice spending goes to law enforcement ($89 billon), followed by spending on corrections (including jails, prisons, probation, and parole) ($62 billion). The smallest share of resources is spent on prosecution and other legal services ($43 billion). These figures are more consistent with a crime control model than a due process model of criminal justice.

In American criminal justice, government agencies allocate much more funding for police to apprehend suspected criminals and for correctional facilities to punish convicted criminals. Overburdened courts receive relatively little funding, despite the fact that it is the role of the courts to ensure that justice is served—that is, that the innocent are not wrongfully convicted and that the guilty do not go free. Implications for justice in the United States are hard to understand fully, but the bottom line appears to be that we are less concerned with spending resources to determine that we get the "right" people than we are at just getting any people and punishing them. This may be an alarming realization for Americans who believe in justice.

much of the law was set up to protect individuals from their own government. Historical accounts of the purpose of the U.S. criminal justice network suggest that it was originally created to protect innocent citizens from an arbitrary and overzealous government. The founders of the U.S. government carefully crafted government practices, including criminal justice practices, to be limited by law. In Chapter 3, you will see how your constitutional rights allow you to enjoy certain protections from unwarranted government interference in your life.

In the past three decades, the United States has witnessed a rapid expansion of American criminal justice, an expansion driven not by facts about crime or increasing crime rates but, instead, by politics, fear, and an increasingly punitive attitude about crime and criminals (Beckett and Sasson, 2003; Donziger, 1996). During this time, spending increased dramatically for correctional budgets but fell for non-Medicare welfare, highway construction and repair, and higher education (Gold, 1990). This led Jerome Miller (1994, p. 479), affiliated with the National Center on Institutions and Alternatives, to write:

> During the 1980s and 1990s, in the midst of two decades of social neglect, America's white majority presented its inner cities with an expensive gift—a new and improved

criminal justice system. This new and improved system would, the government promised, bring domestic tranquility—with particular relevance to African Americans. No expense was spared in crafting and delivering it inside city gates. It was, in fact, a Trojan Horse . . . [because] . . . [a]s governmental investment in social and employment programs in the inner city held stable or decreased, the criminal justice system was ratcheted up to fill the void. With it came a divisive philosophy, destructive strategies, and particularly vicious tactics that would exacerbate violence and social disorganization.

Miller utilized investments in criminal justice activity over the past several decades, coupled with simultaneous disinvestments in social programs, to argue that the United States has shifted its efforts to solve social problems from a "social safety net" approach to a "dragnet" approach. This means U.S. policy makers seem more willing to spend tax-payer money catching criminals (after they commit crime) than preventing crime by helping people deal with the life-shattering effects of poverty.

In fact, corrections spending at the national level increased three times as fast as military spending in the 1980s and 1990s (Donziger, 1996, p. 48). So, during this time, when you were talking about the nation's "enemy," you were much more likely to be talking about an American than at any previous time in our history. Clearly, things changed a bit with the "war on terror" because the United States stepped up its fight against enemies abroad.

Was the increasingly punitive approach for dealing with crime attributable to citizen demand? Public opinion polls did show support for many current criminal justice approaches (Roberts and Stalans, 2000), but many claim that public support for "get tough" criminal justice approaches comes from public misconceptions about who is subject to these policies. That is, when citizens answer questions about their degree of support for a particular type of punishment, they are typically thinking about violent criminals. In fact, most offenders are nonviolent and actually produce little harm to society, even those in prison (see Chapter 9). When given more information about less punitive sentencing alternatives, Americans are far less punitive than politicians seem to believe (Donziger, 1996, pp. 60–61).

So, is the criminal justice network intended to do what criminal justice scholars claim it is intended to do? Some question the stated goals of the criminal justice network and posit that they are really intended to do something else entirely. In Chapter 2, I will examine these claims and address the role of politics and ideology in criminal justice to provide a more realistic impression of what our criminal justice network achieves.

CONCLUSION

The U.S. criminal justice network is made up of police, courts, and corrections. The main responsibilities of police include investigating alleged crimes and apprehending alleged offenders, whereas the main responsibilities of courts include determining legal guilt or innocence of accused offenders and upholding the presumption of innocence supposedly enjoyed by all Americans. The main responsibility of corrections is to carry out the punishment imposed by the courts under the laws that stipulate how punishment must be imposed on convicted offenders. The U.S. criminal justice network ideally aims to do justice and reduce crime. There are at least two conflicting meanings of justice, one concerned mostly with holding the guilty accountable for their crimes and the other with ensuring fairness in the criminal justice process. American criminal justice has, over the past few decades, prioritized its crime control concerns over its due process concerns. The result has been an erosion of U.S. constitutional protections, with little benefit in terms of crime reduction.

Issue in Depth—Justitia—The Lady Justice

The lady justice who appears on the cover of this book has a name. This figure, named Justitia after the Roman goddess of justice, may have its origins in the Greek mythological goddess Themis, who is considered the goddess of divine justice (Hansen, 1999). Justitia has also appeared in Christian imagery "as a personification of the ancient virtue" of justice (Curtis and Resnick, 1987, p. 1729).

Justitia has outlasted symbols of every other virtue of humankind. As Curtis and Resnick (1987, p. 1733) write, "show us a hulking woman with scales, blindfold, and sword, and the association is immediate: Justice."

What is the significance of the symbol of lady justice? The most common understanding of this symbol today is that the figure of "a blindfolded woman with a scale in one hand and a sword in the other" demonstrates that we are dedicated to treating all Americans with "fairness, equity" and in a manner that is right (Kappeler et al., 2000, p. 215). Such a figure implies that the imposition of justice will not be affected by demographic characteristics such as race, social class, or gender.

In essence, according to the myth of Justitia, everyone deserves equal justice: "Justitia is blindfolded so that she may be impartial" (Curtis and Resnick, 1987, p. 1727). Hansen (1999, p. 1) explains that she is a symbol of "the fair and equal administration of the law, without corruption, avarice, prejudice, or favor."

What follows is a summary of six main points about the lady justice made by Dennis Curtis and Judith Resnick (1987), published in the *Yale Law Journal*. I've also added my own commentary. Consider these points when deciding for yourself what "justice blind" is supposed to mean.

- *Justitia is not always depicted as blind.* At many times in history, Justitia wears no blindfold but simply stares forward. In other depictions, her eyes can be seen beneath or through wide spaces in a blindfold, or she is depicted peeking out. It is claimed that the appearance of Justitia's blindfold "coincided with the establishment of professional, independent judges, who stood apart from the sovereign and were not simply acting at its behest" (p. 1757). Thus, the blindfold signified that justice was to be carried out neither in the interests of the powerful nor in fear of the powerful. Generally, the blindfold represents fairness — individuals will be treated fairly by criminal justice agencies regardless of their status in society. An alternative conception of the blindfold is discussed later.
- *Justitia typically carries scales.* The meaning of her scales may be traced back to the Egyptian Book of the Dead (c. 1400 B.C.), the Old Testament (Job 31:6), and to weighing as a symbol of judgment in the Koran. Clearly, scales imply some type of weighing, although there is disagreement about what is to be weighed.

The most commonly accepted meaning of the scales is that "each man receives that which is due him, no more and no less" (p. 1749). Generally, the scales represent the issue of balance. In criminal justice, the scales signify the use of punishment for the guilty as well as an adequate defense for those accused of crimes (to protect the innocent).

- ***Justitia also is commonly depicted holding a sword.***   The significance of the sword, like that of the blindfold, is not clear. Most agree, however, that the sword is a symbol of the power of Justitia to condemn or punish those who "fail in their public duties" (p. 1744). It "represents the rigor of justice, which does not hesitate to punish" (p. 1749). Generally, the sword represents "just desserts" and shows that there ought to be punishment for those who commit crimes. The sword is thus a symbol of the power of the state.
- ***Justitia has been depicted with other ambiguous items, including a cornucopia, a fasces (bundle of rods), a scepter, books, a human skull, an ostrich or a crane, and a dog and snake.***   The meaning of these symbols is not clear. Some claim that they have positive meanings while others suggest negative meanings. For example, is the ostrich a symbol of gluttony (an ostrich will eat anything before it) or of valor and endurance (its diet might even include metal)? An ostrich puts its head in the sand. Is this an indication of fear, forgetfulness, or stupidity? Or is the ostrich another symbol of impartiality, because its feathers are so evenly distributed across its body (p. 1742)? Most illustrations of Justitia do not contain such items, but when they are included, no one can be certain of their significance.
- ***Justitia may create a false impression of what justice is.***   The more negative images of Justitia have been relegated to archives, while the more common images—Justitia in white robes, with the blindfold, scales, and sword—adorn courthouses and other government buildings in the United States. Many of us have never become aware of some of the more grotesque images of Justitia, or they have disappeared from our consciousness. For example, Justitia has been depicted without hands, which may suggest that she will avoid accepting bribes or punishing the guilty too brutally (p. 1754). Other images of Justitia surrounded by severed human heads are also generally unrecognizable. It is possible that our current conception of justice is thus sanitized so that only positive images come to mind in the presence of Justitia.

An alternative view of Justitia is possible: "Sword and scales need not only remind us that Justice can be powerful and correct; they can also be interpreted as indications of Justice as harsh, unsympathetic, and unyielding." The blindfold may be interpreted as an indication that justice is blind—to abuses that occur right under her nose. It may thus suggest "a failure to see the truth" (p. 1756). Perhaps the blindfold symbolizes Justitia's limitations or is a censure for past faults. Or is she blindfolded "not to see the many injuries imposed in her name" (p. 1757)?

For these reasons, Gottfredson (1999, p. 21) argues that the blindfold should be removed from figures showing Justitia. He writes: "Much of the criticism of the criminal justice system concerns a perceived lack of fairness and evenhandedness in decisions about accused and convicted offenders. The blindfold makes a good point, but it should be removed." Gottfredson suggests that, with "eyes open," Justitia will be able to ensure that American justice will be fair, ethically sound, and more effective.

- ***Justitia is a symbol used by the powerful to justify their actions in the name of "justice."***   For example, when a person is convicted of a crime by a jury of his or her peers, the government is granted the right to punish the person: "The imposition of judgment, with its requisite violence, is an essential, inevitable aspect of governance. How convenient, how distancing from human subjectivity and fallibility, if such decisions go forth in the name of Justice" (Curtis and Resnick, 1987, p. 1748).

No other cardinal or theological virtue is essential to the acts of lawmakers and law enforcers in exacting justice: "All sovereigns claim (notwithstanding evidence to the contrary) that their violence goes forth in the name of Justice." Clearly, humankind is fallible — we make mistakes. In the name of justice and its implied impartiality, governments have used and will continue to use force against their citizens, to restrict their citizens' liberty, and even to execute their citizens (p. 1734). The "conscious use of justice imagery by governments" may be an effort by them to "legitimate their exercises of power by associating themselves with the concept of justice" (p. 1743). In some ways, Justitia is "propaganda" to reassure Americans that actions of the government are in line with a "higher right" (p. 1746).

Images of justice may "teach, inspire, pacify, or otherwise influence viewers" (p. 1743). In the United States, Justitia suggests to young people that this is a fair country. It inspires us as a symbol of dedication against vices and injustices. It can pacify us as well, for in the presence of Justitia we may assume that our government is just, even in the face of evidence suggesting that it is not. We may tend to ignore conspicuous injustices, perhaps because we are forced to accept the judgments of powerful people in the name of justice (p. 1767).

Whatever Justitia is really intended to mean, I concur with Dennis Curtis and Judith Resnick (1987, p. 1764) when they write, "our hopes that justice . . . simultaneously be attuned to individual nuances and be evenhanded; that objectivity and subjectivity both be present; that justice know all that is needed but not know that which might corrupt or unfairly influence; that justice be rigorous in its equality yet 'now and then' relax in compassion."

In this book, I assume that American criminal justice should be blind to factors such as race, social class, and gender; thus, the cover of the book is adorned by a blind-folded lady justice. In this book, I suggest that perhaps American justice is not blind. Throughout the book, I examine how well the U.S. criminal justice network achieves its goals of doing justice and reducing crime. The main concern is, "How just is American criminal justice?" That is, "Is justice really blind?"

KEY TERMS

adversarial
appeal
arraignment
arrest
bail
beyond a reasonable doubt
booking
clearing a case by arrest
cold crimes
corrective justice
crime control
crime control model
crime prevention

criminal justice network
dark figure of crime
discretion
doing justice
due process
due process model
indictment
information
initial appearance
jails
justice as a process
justice as an outcome
parole

plea bargaining
preliminary investigation
preventive detention
prisons
probation
probable cause
procedural justice
reducing crime
release on own recognizance
secondary investigation
sentencing
system
trial

DISCUSSION QUESTIONS

1. What is a system?
2. What is the criminal justice network?
3. List some of the reasons that some claim that *system* is not an accurate term for the operations of the criminal justice network.
4. What are the three main components or parts of the criminal justice network?
5. Outline the main stages of the criminal justice network; that is, explain how a case proceeds from commission of a crime all the way to release from corrections.
6. What are the ideal goals of the American criminal justice network?
7. What is justice?
8. Compare corrective justice (justice as an outcome) and procedural justice (justice as a process).
9. Compare the ideal models of justice described by Herbert Packer: the due process and crime control models.
10. Which ideal model of criminal justice does American criminal justice more closely resemble? Why?
11. What are the differences between crime control and crime prevention?
12. What types of activities of police, courts, and corrections are aimed at preventing crime?
13. Which component of the criminal justice network has the most resources? Why?
14. Which component of the criminal justice network employs the most people? Why?
15. What is the significance of the fact that most criminal justice resources are devoted to police and corrections and the least to the courts?
16. What does the symbol of Lady Justitia, the Lady Justice, mean?

CHAPTER

2

THE ROLE OF POLITICS AND IDEOLOGY IN CRIMINAL JUSTICE: REALITIES

1. Introduction
2. Alternative Goals of Criminal Justice
   a. Serving Interests and Controlling the Population
   • Box 2-1. How Does Population Control Serve Interests?
3. Functions Versus Purposes of Criminal Justice
4. What Is Politics?
5. What Is Ideology?
6. How Are Politics, Ideology, and Criminal Justice Related?
   • Box 2-2. Politically Oriented Comments About Terrorism
   • Box 2-3. Planned Change Versus Unplanned Change
   a. How Did Criminal Justice Become So Political and Ideological?
   b. Crime, Politics, and Ideology Today
7. Conclusion
8. Issue in Depth—McDonaldization of America's Police, Courts, and Corrections
9. Key Terms
10. Discussion Questions

INTRODUCTION

Is our nation's criminal justice network really intended to reduce crime and do justice, or could there be some alternative goals? Is it a coincidence that the people who are most likely to have run-ins with police, courts, and corrections are disproportionately poor and minorities? This chapter introduces two alternative goals of criminal justice, including serving limited interests and population control. Although I do not think there is a criminal justice conspiracy in the United States, I do show how criminal justice activity performs functions such as serving interests of the powerful through population control. This chapter introduces two important concepts for understanding the reality of criminal justice activity in America—power and ideology. In this chapter, I show how politics, ideology, and criminal justice are related. Finally, I examine the political nature of defining and reacting to terrorism to demonstrate its relevance for American criminal justice policy.

ALTERNATIVE GOALS OF CRIMINAL JUSTICE

As noted in Chapter 1, some question the stated goals of the criminal justice network and posit that it is intended to do something else entirely besides reducing crime and doing justice. For example, Jeffrey Reiman (2006), as might be guessed from the title of his book, *The Rich Get Richer and the Poor Get Prison*, suggests that the criminal justice network is really intended to fail at reducing crime and doing justice. Although this may seem silly at first, Reiman's argument is that some failures amount to success, depending on what is really sought.

Serving Interests and Controlling the Population

Reiman posits the **pyrrhic defeat theory**, which suggests that "the failure of the criminal justice system yields such benefits to those in positions of power that it amounts to a success" (p. 5). Reiman suggests criminal justice processes are aimed at **population control and serving limited interests**. His main argument is that interests of those in power are served when we focus almost exclusively on street crimes rather than other types of harmful behaviors. At the same time, those people whom we fear most (e.g., young, minority males) are routinely rounded up by the police and sent off to some form of government-controlled institution or community alternative. This amounts to a form of population control, so that the enemies in the war on crime can never win, can never achieve the types of success enjoyed by those with the power to achieve. Box 2-1 discusses examples of how control of criminals serves limited interests.

Among other things, Reiman (2006) argues that the label of "crime" (particularly "serious crime") is not used for the most harmful and frequently occurring acts that threaten us. He claims that the criminal law distorts the image of crime so that the most dangerous threats are seen as coming from below us (i.e., from the lower class) when they really come from above us (i.e., from the upper class). In later chapters, I provide evidence that this is true by discussing how the law is biased against certain segments of the population (Chapter 3), by showing which types of crime are actually the most dangerous (Chapter 4), and how the media portray crime (Chapter 5). Additionally, the war on crime may, in effect, be a war against particular segments of the U.S. population (Chapter 12), and our efforts to curb drug use in the United States may be aimed primarily at what are perceived to be poor people's drugs (Chapter 11).

The segments of the population being controlled by America's crime control efforts are poor people and minorities. Several criminologists have noted that the criminal justice network is, in effect, the primary mechanism in the United States responsible for controlling the "poor masses" (Rusche and Kirchheimer, 1939), the "dangerous classes" (Shelden, 2001), the "problem populations" (Spitzer, 1975), and the nation's "surplus population" (Quinney, 2000). Such hypotheses have been supported by evidence showing that poor, unemployed members of racial minority groups are likely to receive

BOX 2-1

HOW DOES POPULATION CONTROL SERVE INTERESTS?

Think about all of the people in American prisons and jails. Currently, more than 2 million people are incarcerated in the United States. Guess what? The incarceration rate in the United States is now the highest in the world—we are number one! If there was an "Imprisonment Olympics," we would win the gold medal!

I guess this explains why some politicians celebrate our first-place standing in imprisonment as a success! For example, President Bill Clinton bragged, to a standing ovation of Congress, that the United States had incarcerated more than 1 million criminals. Why do we treat incarceration as a sign of success rather than a sign of failure? Perhaps if all Americans were safer as a result of our incarceration boom—both now and in the future—we would have reason to celebrate. Yet rates of violent crime in America, especially murders committed by handguns, are astonishingly high (see Chapter 4).

In fact, having so many people in prison is a success in so many ways. For example, even though inmates are not free people working outside in the labor force, they are not counted as part of the unemployment rate. If we assume, as many scholars do, that a very large percentage of these inmates are not employable (because they have a low educational level, criminal record, and many other disadvantages), what would happen to the unemployment rate if these people were free? Logic suggests the unemployment rate would be much higher if all the people in prison and jail were free and seeking work. Yet when politicians stand up in front of the American people and speak about unemployment, they do not have to count

incarcerated people as part of the unemployment problem, even though they really are. This serves their own political interests, as well as those of their parties.

Additionally, some criminologists have equated crime control, especially the nation's prisons and jails, with industry. Without any doubt, crime pays tremendous dividends for business interests. Businesses now compete for contracts to provide products and services to American jails and prisons. In fact, companies such as the Corrections Corporation of America and Wackenhut now run their own correctional facilities for profit. Once businesses have vested interests in making profits on crime control, it is logical that business-friendly government will do whatever it takes to ensure a steady supply of offenders, so that the criminal justice network will continue to pay off (Christie, 2000). Perhaps this is why correctional officer hiring and training became one of the "fastest-growing functions" of government in the 1990s (Lilly and Knepper, 1993, p. 155).

It is ironic, if you stop and think about it, how many people benefit from our "wars" against crime and drugs. Enormous sums of money and millions of jobs are created by criminal justice, including tens of billions of dollars spent on private security alone (Kappeler and Potter, 2004). Can you make a list of all the people who benefit from our crime problem? Be sure to include not only individuals working for police, courts, and corrections, but also all the private businesses who service these agencies. Additionally, be sure to think about all the students and professors who now have something to study and write about. If politicians in the 1970s, 1980s, and 1990s had not chosen to pursue crime with such vigor, leading to staggering increases in criminal justice spending and tremendous growth in criminal justice, what would all these people be doing right now?

harsher sentences than employed minority group members and Caucasians (e.g., see Chiricos and Bales, 1991; Chiricos and DeLone, 1992; Nobling, Spohn, and DeLone, 1998).

Consistent with this evidence, Morris (1988, p. 113) writes that "the whole law and order movement that we have heard so much about is, in operation though not in intent, anti-black and anti-underclass—not in plan, not in desire, not in intent, but in operation." It is hard to imagine criminal justice processes in the United States aimed at serving limited interests and controlling certain segments of the population. Before you dismiss this possibility, however, consider that our criminal justice network may achieve certain functions without actually intending to achieve them.

FUNCTIONS VERSUS PURPOSES OF CRIMINAL JUSTICE

Criminal justice in the United States may achieve certain functions without actually intending to achieve them. This is an important distinction to understand. As Reiman (2006) points out, political processes can achieve certain outcomes without being purposeful. Reiman argues that criminal justice network failure was not set in place by some vast conspiracy of old, rich, white men who wanted to protect their limited interests. Instead, Reiman argues, criminal justice evolved over time into processes that are unjust and that protect limited interests. Those who benefit from this obviously have no reason to change the status quo, and those harmed by the inherent biases of the criminal justice network do not have the intellectual or financial means to change it.

Herbert Gans (1995) makes a similar argument in his book, *The War Against the Poor*. I will return to the thrust of this argument in Chapter 12, but essentially Gans argues that American government has always been engaged in a war against poor people (including criminals), particularly the "undeserving underclass." Gans writes that "labeling the poor as undeserving . . . has some uses, or positive functions, or beneficial consequences, for more fortunate Americans . . . resulting in material and immaterial benefits, even though they are not immediately apparent, particularly to the people who benefit from them" (p. 91). Gans goes on to explain that functions are not the same as purposes:

> They are not what people intend to do, but are the consequences of what they actually do, whatever their initial purposes. Consequently, functions are usually neither intended nor recognized when they first emerge, and some are unintended but unavoidable because they follow from the demands of politically important groups. Whatever their origin, however, once these functions exist and produce benefits, their beneficiaries may develop an interest in them and even establish interest groups to defend them.

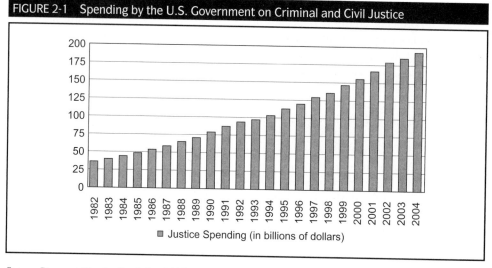

FIGURE 2-1 Spending by the U.S. Government on Criminal and Civil Justice

Justice Spending (in billions of dollars)

Source: Bureau of Justice Statistics (2006). Direct expenditures by level of government. http://ojp.usdoj.gov/bjs/glance/tables/expgovtab.htm.

Figure 2-1 shows spending by the U.S. government on criminal justice. Notice that spending on criminal justice has increased tremendously over the years. At the same time, government funding has decreased for assisting poor people, who are disproportionately likely to be minorities (Beckett and Sasson, 2003). Welfare reform laws and welfare-to-work programs are also aimed primarily at minorities, even though most people on welfare are not minority group members (Tonry, 1995). Tonry claims that such welfare reform laws are not likely to be effective in communities where African American males are absent (p. 6). And criminal justice efforts disproportionately affect minority males and their communities (see Chapter 12). Tonry writes: "Poor minority communities cannot prosper when so many of their young men are prevented from settling into long-term personal relationships, getting or keeping jobs, and living conventional lives" (p. vii). Ironically, criminal justice policy has created these outcomes. And government policies of the 1980s "openly and successfully fought to reduce federal funding for social, educational, and housing programs and for aid to cities . . . promoted a strategy of federal disinvestment in the inner cities, which accelerated their deterioration and diminished the scope and quality of urban public services" (p. 40).

Is it possible that the criminal justice network serves functions vital to preserving the status quo in the United States, even though these functions are not intended? And if this is so, why don't those with relatively less power rise up and demand change? Reiman (2006) explains that they simply do not have the power or the will to do so. Another reason may be that the criminal justice network is highly affected by politics and ideology, two terms discussed below.

WHAT IS POLITICS?

Politics is about who gets what economic benefits in society, when they get them, and how they get them (Lasswell, 1936). It is concerned with deciding who gets to keep most of the income generated in the United States, and how that income will be used (Harrigan, 2000). Politics is also about allocating society's values (Easton, 1953), at least for those who have the ability to have their values enacted into law. Then, resources are allocated for purposes of legitimating these values through government authority. Finally, politics is about competing for power—the ability to control others and make them do what you want them to do. One mechanism to achieve this is criminal justice. To the degree that politics is involved in criminal justice operations, an understanding of politics is necessary to fully understand the realities of criminal justice in America.

WHAT IS IDEOLOGY?

The term **ideology** was first coined by the philosopher Destutt de Tracy, and referred to a "science of ideas" that he hoped would reveal people's unconscious habits of mind. Ideology today "now tends to refer to those very habits of mind—beliefs, assumptions, expectations, etc.—which are superimposed on the world in order to give it structure and meaning and which then serve to direct our political or social activities" (Cline, 2002, p. 1). In essence, ideology is the way a group of people think about life and everything in it.

There is a dominant ideology that underlies the criminal justice network in the United States. Durham (1992, p. 49) writes: "Crime and the state response to crime are highly visible processes that involve many fundamental issues regarding the application of values to law formation, the use of coercion to regulate behavior, the definition and protection of individual rights, the limits of state power, and the maintenance of social order." To the degree this is true, an understanding of ideology is necessary to understand the realities of criminal justice in America.

HOW ARE POLITICS, IDEOLOGY, AND CRIMINAL JUSTICE RELATED?

Politics, ideology, and criminal justice are intimately linked and inseparable. Because of the close ties between them, it may be easier to understand how some interests get served while others are ignored or even harmed. For example, those with political power, or "the ability of individuals or groups to influence government as it allocates a society's resources" (Harrigan, 2000, p. 25), are more likely to have their interests served at the expense of others.

Although criminal justice policy development is affected by groups other than lawmakers, including the media, voters, lobbying groups, and other special interests (see Chapter 3), politicians play the largest role in setting the crime control agenda. Politicians have the largest ideological influence on what we do in criminal justice; this is because of their **power**. Power comes in various forms (e.g., political, economic, moral), and is "the ability to have a say, or to have influence, in what the government's policies are going to be" (Marion, 1995, p. 4, citing Lowi and Ginsberg, 1990). Because politicians create policies of criminal justice, they have power to determine the path of our nation's efforts to control and prevent crime. The U.S. Congress, for example, has the power to define crimes, create criminal justice agencies, provide or withhold funding from criminal justice programs (Steel and Steger, 1988), and act as a forum for public debate (Marion and Oliver, 2005).

Politics and ideology are involved in criminal justice in numerous ways. The most significant way is in deciding which behaviors should and should not be considered "crime." Crime is defined through a political process by a very small group of people in the United States (lawmakers or legislators) who, ideally, are representatives of the people. Richard Quinney's (2000) concept of the **social reality of crime** demonstrates that crime is imaginary rather than real; that is, it is invented by human beings with the power to do so (see Chapter 3). Therefore, all criminal justice policies that emanate from the criminal law are "merely definitions developed by people (authorities) who possess the power to shape, enforce, and administer such policies" (Arrigo, 1999, p. 6). According to Quinney (2000) "powerful individuals and groups promote particular conceptions of crime in order to legitimize their authority and allow them to carry out policies in the name of the common good that really promote their own self-interests" (Vold, Bernard, and Snipes, 2002). Crime and criminal justice practices are thus efforts by the powerful to control others and maintain power.

Kappeler and Potter (2004), in *The Mythology of Crime and Criminal Justice*, argue that since crime is defined in a political process, crime issues and criminal justice policy decisions will be affected by the same factors that influence all political issues. These factors include partisanship (e.g., Democrats fighting Republicans) and symbolic crusading (e.g., by moral entrepreneurs, claims-makers, the media, and others with vested interests in bringing crime problems to the public's attention). What may get lost in the shuffle are key truths about crime and criminal justice.

One recent example of a criminal justice policy illustrates how politics affects criminal justice processes. In 2007, the House of Representatives in the state of Texas passed a bill that allowed the death penalty for sex crimes against children, even if the victim does not die. The House created a new category of crime—"continual sexual abuse of a young child or children"—that carries a minimum of 25 years to life in prison and possibly the death penalty for a second offense. Basically, a person who is convicted twice of molesting or sexually assaulting a child could be sentenced to death (death sentences require more than one sex act committed against a victim younger than 14 years of age over a period of 30 or more days).

The bill was named "Jessica's law" after the Florida case of Jessica Lunsford. Jessica was abducted and killed, meaning her killer was already eligible for the death penalty in the state of Florida (because he committed an "aggravated" or "death eligible" murder). Because the abduction and killing of a child in the state of Texas—which leads the country in the number of executions in the modern era of capital punishment—is already a capital crime, many question whether "Jessica's law" is even needed.

In fact, more than a dozen states have already passed similar laws. And at least six states allow some child sex offenders to be sentenced to death even though the U.S. Supreme Court has made clear that for crimes to be eligible for capital punishment, a victim must be killed as part of the crime (Robinson, 2008).

Such laws exemplify symbolic crusading because the bill's sponsors (as well as those who voted for it) saw it as a "no lose situation." The law is in response to a horrific tragedy involving a young child, it sounds good to voters, and it promotes an easy solution to a complex problem. Voters will likely react with thoughts such as "Well, at least my representative will protect my children from child predators." The legislators who voted for the bill likely did not want to be seen by the public or portrayed by their opponents as "soft on crime." Since the 1960s, being "tough on crime" has been a necessary criterion for being a politician (Rosch, 1985).

Representative Dan Gattis, a Republican and former prosecutor who wrote the bill, said: "This bill is supposed to go after the true pedophiles . . . the worst of the worst." Representative Debbie Riddle, who helped write the bill, said: "Nothing we do will be more important." This statement is hard to believe, given that the law will rarely be enforced and may very well be struck down as unconstitutional.

The authors of the National Criminal Justice Commission's report, *The Real War on Crime,* describe efforts by U.S. politicians to deal with crime as a "hoax": "Politicians at every level—federal, state, and local—have measured our obsession, capitalized on our fears, campaigned on 'get tough' platforms, and won" (Donziger, 1996, p. 2). The gist of the argument by the National Criminal Justice Commission is that the war on crime, though a victory for politicians and other limited interests, has mostly been a failure for Americans.

Since September 11, 2001, when the United States was attacked by terrorists, our focus has shifted significantly to controlling and preventing terrorism. Thus, politics and ideology are now at work in dealing with forms of crime related to terrorism while common crimes occupy less of our common awareness. One need look no further than any major media outlet to find statements regarding terrorism and the U.S. response that likely reflect political motivations rather than sincere beliefs about the issues. Box 2-2 contains some examples.

BOX 2-2

POLITICALLY ORIENTED COMMENTS ABOUT TERRORISM

- "If [Usama bin Laden] thinks he can hide and run from the United States and our allies, he will be sorely mistaken." "I want justice. And there's an old poster out West, I recall, that says, 'Wanted: Dead or Alive.'" "Our objective is more than bin Laden." "We're going to find him." "[bin Laden is] a person who's now been marginalized. . . . I just don't spend that much time on him. . . . I truly am not that concerned about him." "I am deeply concerned about Iraq."—President George W. Bush, September 25, 2001–April 6, 2002. (President Bush had immediately spoken of bin Laden and promised revenge but then stopped mentioning him. He did not mention bin Laden in the January 2002 State of the Union speech and began answering questions about bin Laden

by providing information about Iraq and Saddam Hussein.)

- "Saddam Hussein is harboring terrorists and the instruments of terror, the instruments of mass death and destruction. And he cannot be trusted. The risk is simply too great that he will use them or provide them to a terror network . . . America must not ignore the threat gathering against us. Facing clear evidence of our peril, we cannot wait for the final proof—the smoking gun—that could come in the form of a mushroom cloud."—President George W. Bush, October 7, 2002. (In fact, the evidence suggested that Saddam Hussein was not a threat to the United States. A National Intelligence Estimate (NIE) prepared by the Central Intelligence Agency (CIA) said that Saddam Hussein

(continued)

BOX 2-2   *(Continued)*

would not likely use weapons of mass destruction (WMDs) against U.S. interests unless he was first attacked. Additionally, there was no credible evidence that Saddam Hussein was close to developing nuclear weapons.)

- "Clearly, al-Qaeda is operating inside Iraq. In the shadowy world of terrorism, sometimes there is no precise way to have definitive information until it is too late." — White House Press Secretary Ari Fleischer, September 25, 2002. (Actually, a single group affiliated with al-Qaeda was operating in the northern no-fly zone of Iraq, which was not under control of Saddam Hussein. The group openly called for the overthrow of Saddam Hussein. The Saddam Hussein regime and al-Qaeda were bitter enemies.)

- "In both word and deed, Iraq has demonstrated that it is seeking the means to strike the United States and our friends and allies with weapons of mass destruction for a reason: so that it can acquire the territory and assert influence over its neighbors" — Secretary of Defense Donald Rumsfeld, January 20, 2003. (In reality, both Colin Powell and Condoleezza Rice stated publicly in 2001 that Saddam Hussein's regime was not a threat to the United States or its allies.)

- "The area in the south and the west and the north that coalition forces control is substantial. It happens not to be the area where weapons of mass destruction were dispersed. We know where they are. They're in the area around Tikrit and Baghdad and east, west, south and north some" — Secretary of Defense Donald Rumsfeld, March 20, 2003. (In fact, no weapons of mass destruction have been found in Iraq. The evidence suggests the vast majority of his weapons were destroyed in the first Gulf War and by subsequent weapons inspectors — inspectors who were forced out because of the war initiated by the United States.)

- "We found the weapons of mass destruction. We found biological laboratories. You remember when Colin Powell stood up in front of the world, and he said, Iraq has got laboratories, mobile labs to build biological weapons. They're illegal. They're against the United Nations resolutions, and we've so far discovered two. And we'll find more weapons as time goes on. But for those who say we haven't found the banned manufacturing devices or banned weapons, they're wrong. We found them." — President George W. Bush, May 29, 2003. (Actually, the supposed biological weapons labs were trucks used to inflate large balloons.)

- "If we're successful in Iraq . . . then we will have struck a major blow right at the heart of The Base, if you will, the geographic base of the terrorists who had us under assault now for many years, but most especially on 9/11." — Vice President Richard B. Cheney, September 17, 2003. (In reality, al-Qaeda was not operative in Iraq prior to the U.S. invasion. The geographic base was more accurately in Afghanistan. Since the United States did not defeat the Taliban or al-Qaeda there, the Taliban are resurgent and al-Qaeda still operates from Afghanistan's soil as well as in Pakistan.)

- Saddam Hussein "had long-established ties with al-Qaeda."—Vice President Richard B. Cheney, June 14, 2004. (In fact, Saddam Hussein and al-Qaeda were opposed to each other for religious and political reasons. Usama bin Laden called for the overthrow of

secular leaders such as Saddam Hussein.)

- "The reason I keep insisting that there was a relationship between Iraq and Saddam and al-Qaeda, is because there was a relationship between Iraq and al-Qaeda."—President George W. Bush, July 17, 2004. (Again, there was no meaningful relationship between the two.)

Whether you examine our nation's responses to street crime or terrorism, the dominant ideology underlying the policies and practices of police, courts, and corrections is conservative, characterized by unplanned policies that are tough on crime, individualistic in their focus, and nonrehabilitative (Welsh and Harris, 2004). Most of our reactions to crime problems involve **unplanned change**, meaning they are designed on a whim, without much thought or study, because they sound good or appeal to common sense. They are tough on crime in the sense that they are aimed at punishing offenders as much as possible based on the assumption that criminal behavior is freely chosen by rational people who should be held accountable for their actions regardless of the conditions that gave rise to their behaviors. And they increasingly reject any calls for treatment or a rehabilitative focus. Finally, they are explicitly nonpreventive in the sense that they are almost never aimed at ameliorating the conditions that produced the behaviors in the first place. Box 2-3 differentiates planned change and unplanned change.

BOX 2-3

PLANNED CHANGE VERSUS UNPLANNED CHANGE

Planned change is an alternative way to reduce crime. Crime, despite its many functions and the interests it serves, has always been viewed as a problem, and problems require solutions. To be effective, solutions require time, thought, and planning. Criminal justice policy driven by short-term thinking and unplanned change results in inefficiency, wasted resources, and failure.

Planned change is spearheaded by change agents who have specifically thought about a problem and investigated

it thoroughly. *Unplanned change*, by contrast, involves little explicit or proactive planning and "comes about as a reaction to a crisis, a dramatic incident publicized by the media, a political opportunity, a lawsuit against criminal justice officials or an untested set of assumptions about a specific problem" (Welsh and Harris, 1999, p. 3).

In today's heated political environment, where U.S. crime problems are typically created and/or used at election time

(continued)

BOX 2-3 *(Continued)*

as political issues, criminal justice policy is often shortsighted and poorly planned (and at times reactive and altogether unplanned). Not surprisingly, current criminal justice policy fails to produce significant declines in crime-related problems. Such failure stems from poorly planned criminal justice policy.

To overcome our current path of injustice and ineffectiveness, we must dedicate ourselves to planned change and must insist that our policymakers use strategies of planned change to reduce crime. Planned change can be achieved through policies, programs, and projects. Policies are a "set of rules or guidelines for how to make a decision" (p. 5); programs are a "set of services aimed at achieving specific goals and objectives within specified individuals, groups, organizations or communities"; and projects are essentially time-limited programs (p. 6). Policies are more general than programs and projects and often motivate the development of specific programs and projects aimed at reducing some problem.

To solve problems related to crime, a step-by-step approach to problem analysis and criminal justice planning must be employed. This includes analyzing the problem, setting goals and objectives, designing programs and policies, developing action plans, developing monitoring plans, designing evaluation plans, initiating the program or policy, and then fully evaluating the program or policy so that it can be altered and continued.

The first step in policy or program design is analyzing the problem, including the need for change, the history of the problem, and potential causes of the problem. A systems approach to addressing causal factors based on the belief that crime problems stem from factors at various levels of analysis—individual, group,

organizational, community, and social-structural—will likely lead to the most fruitful policy changes. Policy and program designers or "change agents" should look for all causes of a problem and carefully document such causes with scientific evidence. Previous interventions that have been used to change the problem should be examined, and opponents and supporters of change should be identified. Once it is determined what works, what is promising, and what does not work, and once vital supporters are brought on board and opponents are appeased or defeated, effective crime reduction policies can be successful.

The next stage in policy and program development is setting goals and objectives. Goals lay out the general aims of the policy or program, and objectives more specifically restate the goals in measurable form. Clear goals and objectives are vital to success, for one cannot know if a policy has succeeded or failed unless one clearly specifies what one wants to achieve and sets forth a means of measuring the degree of effectiveness.

Effective action plans, the "blueprint" of policies or programs, must specify "all the necessary materials, supplies and tools required" to achieve successful planned change (p. 135). Action planning involves specifying the entire sequence of activities and completion dates required to carry out the program or policy design.

Monitoring must assess how well a planned policy or program is being implemented (i.e., how well the ideal matches the reality). Evaluation of the policy or program—assessing how well the policy or program achieved its goals and objectives—is also important. Data must be collected to monitor the implementation of the policy or program, to evaluate its degree of success, and to decide how to manage potential problems and confounding factors. How much longer can we afford to continue with our massive and failing American criminal justice experiments?

Nothing less than a dramatic transformation in the formulation of criminal justice policy is necessary if criminal justice in the United States is to turn its direction from one of disastrous failure to one of success. Policy makers must shift their focus from unplanned change to planned change.

SOURCE: Adapted from W. Walsh and P. Harris, *Criminal Justice Policy and Planning* (Cincinnati, OH: Anderson, 1999, 2004).

How Did Criminal Justice Become So Political and Ideological?

How did we as a nation get to such a point where criminal justice policy is so highly affected by politics and ideology? Numerous scholars have illustrated how crime originally became a significant political issue in the United States, used to advance a given ideological agenda (e.g., see Cronin, Cronin, and Milakovich, 1981; Marion, 1995; Scheingold, 1984; Wilson, 1975). Most attribute the politicization of crime at the national level to charges made by Republican senator Barry Goldwater, who ran for president in 1964 against Democratic president Lyndon Johnson. Goldwater blamed Johnson for rising crime rates and characterized the president as "soft on crime" (Rosch, 1985). One statement by Goldwater illustrates his beliefs clearly:

> History shows us that nothing prepares the way for tyranny more than the failure of public officials to keep the streets safe from bullies and marauders. We Republicans seek a government that attends to its fiscal climate, encourages a free and a competitive economy and enforcing law and order. (Quoted in Beckett, 1997, p. 31)

Goldwater also attacked public assistance programs by linking them to crime:

> If it is entirely proper for the government to take away from some to give to others, then won't some be led to believe that they can rightfully take from anyone who has more than they? No wonder law and order has broken down, mob violence has engulfed great American cities, and our wives feel unsafe in the streets. (Quoted in Beckett, 1997, p. 35)

This type of "tough" stance on crime was typical in the 1964 campaign.

Other events of the 1960s helped to make crime and criminal justice national concerns. For example, Beckett (1997, p. 28) claims that "the discourse of law and order was initially mobilized by southern officials in their effort to discredit the civil rights movement." Clearly, southern agencies of criminal justice—in particular, law enforcement agencies—characterized and fought civil rights activities as acts of crime rather than as struggles for civil rights. Peaceful protests, sit-ins, marches, and similar methods of civil disobedience were characterized as evidence of a disrespect for law and order rather than as struggles for basic human rights. This characterization permitted and even mandated government intervention against civil rights leaders and led to the characterization by the Federal Bureau of Investigation (FBI) of Martin Luther King, Jr., as the most dangerous man in America.

A statement from former Republican vice president Richard Nixon claimed that "the deterioration of respect for the rule of law can be traced directly to the spread of the corrosive doctrine that every citizen possesses an inherent right to decide for himself which laws to obey and when to disobey them" (in Beckett and Sasson, 2000, p. 50). Some claim that, even today, crime is a code word for race, because it refers "indirectly to racial themes but do[es] not directly challenge popular democratic or egalitarian ideals" (Omi, 1987, p. 120; also see Edsall and Edsall, 1991).

Since the 1960s, crime has been a national issue that has been used for political gain (and loss) in each presidential election and also in hundreds of elections at other levels of government (Gest, 2001; Marion, 1995; Oliver, 2003). The National Criminal Justice Commission claims: "Since 1968, six major anti-crime bills have passed Congress and been signed into law by presidents. In one way or another, all of these bills have been used by elected officials to convince the public that Washington was getting 'tough' on crime by increasing sentences for certain types of offenses" (Donziger, 1996, p. 13).

In the 1980s, Republican presidents Ronald Reagan and George Bush (the first) wanted more efficient, tougher criminal justice agencies (in line with a crime control model) and helped shift the perception of the causes of crime from society to the individual. A Reagan statement illustrates his party's stance on crime control: "Government's function is to protect society from the criminal, not the other way around" (in Beckett, 1997, p. 48). Under Democratic president Bill Clinton in the 1990s, the focus was much the same, including more police on the streets and tougher sentences for convicted criminals. Clinton's 1994 crime bill allocated $8.8 billion for hiring more police, $7.9 billion in state prison grants, and no money for crime prevention and rehabilitation programs. In the 1980s and 1990s, significant increases occurred in incarceration rates, and now both parties sell being "tough" on crime to the masses (Merlo and Benekos, 2000).

America's agencies of police, courts, and corrections now operate much like a fast food chain, aimed not only at being tough on crime but also at being as efficient as possible. Issue in Depth at the end of the chapter discusses how America's criminal justice network has become "McDonaldized."

The most well-known use of a crime as a political issue was seen in the "Willie Horton" charges made against Democratic presidential hopeful Michael Dukakis by future Republican president George Bush (the first) in 1988. As governor of Massachusetts, Dukakis had supported early release programs from prison as a means to reduce prison overcrowding and as a low-risk way to reintegrate offenders into the community through meaningful employment. An inmate from Massachusetts named Willie Horton, on his ninth furlough from prison, committed a brutal rape and assault. This incident led Bush to attack Dukakis as "soft on crime"; Bush assured citizens that if he were elected president, he would continue to expand criminal justice powers to fight crime. Even though the "Horton case was atypical and exaggerated," it worked: Bush was successfully elected president of the United States (Merlo and Benekos, 2000, p. 14).

Merlo and Benekos claim that the Willie Horton incident taught all politicians some important lessons about winning and losing:

- Don't be portrayed as being "soft on crime";
- Portray your opponent as "soft on crime";
- Simplify the crime issue; and
- Reinforce messages with emotional context. (pp. 14–16)

In each election since then, it has been hard to tell Republicans apart from Democrats on crime control issues, because both have supported more police, more power for prosecutors, more prisons, more money for the war on drugs, more executions, limiting appeals for death row inmates, and so forth.

A good example comes from the 2000 presidential debates between George W. Bush (the second) and Al Gore. When asked if he supported capital punishment, Bush—who was governor of Texas and oversaw more than 150 executions—said yes, "I believe it saves lives . . . I'm proud that violent crime is down in the state of Texas." Similarly, Al Gore answered yes, "I think it is a deterrence (sic) . . . I know that's a controversial view but I do think it's a deterrence (sic)." In a follow-up about whether capital punishment is a deterrent, Bush replied: "I do, it's the only reason to be for it . . . I don't think you should support the death penalty to seek revenge. I don't think that's right." Gore agreed, saying: "Yes. If it was not, there would be no reason to support it."

Such answers indicate how similar the positions of both candidates (one Republican, the other Democrat) were on the issue of capital punishment. Voters had the choice of a tough on crime Republican who supported the death penalty because he thought it was a deterrent, or a tough on crime Democrat who supported the death penalty because he thought it was a deterrent.

Of course, the answers of Bush and Gore could have simply been political—aimed at satisfying the public—because the available scientific evidence at the time, as well as since, suggests that the death penalty is not a deterrent (Robinson, 2008). Nearly every study ever conducted has failed to find evidence of a deterrent effect of capital punishment (see Chapter 10).

Crime, Politics, and Ideology Today

Today, criminal justice is highly influenced by both politics and ideology. Americans seem easily swayed by fear of violence—willing to sacrifice more and more of their civil liberties and due process rights in the name of public safety. One reason is that leading politicians promote fear of crime through the mainstream media.

Kappeler, Blumberg, and Potter (1996) argue:

> Exaggerating and distorting the amount and shape of the crime threat is standard fare for politicians. Democrats and Republicans compete to see who can spend the most money and appear the most punitive in putting together crime control legislation . . . It is not scientific proof which persuades, it is appeal to fear about serial killers, stalkers, drive-by-shootings, car-jackings, and violent predators. Supporting such measures will no doubt curry favor with the voting public; telling the truth could lead to premature retirement. (p. 49)

While the above statement is still likely true, fear over drive-by-shootings and car-jackings has waned. Currently it is fear of terrorism that convinces Americans to support criminal justice and foreign policies (regardless of how destructive they may be to the very freedoms that we are supposedly defending).

The dominant ideological messages driving criminal justice practice today (and likely U.S. foreign policy in places like Afghanistan and Iraq) are still to be tough on crime (and terrorism), portray your opponent as soft on crime (and terrorism), simplify the crime issue, and reinforce these messages with emotional context. President Bush successfully used this approach after 9/11 during the heated presidential campaign against Democrat John Kerry.

The tough on crime approach is one reason the United States leads the world in its incarceration rate (the number of people locked up in prisons and jails per 100,000 citizens) (see Chapter 9); has an ever-expanding war on drugs that is responsible for arresting, convicting, and punishing millions of people for simple possession and use of some relatively minor drugs (see Chapter 11); and is one of the top five nations in the world in its use of capital punishment (see Chapter 10). Virtually no politician is willing or able to question the logic or validity of such practices, despite their numerous flaws and lack of efficacy.

With an understanding of the role of politics and ideology in criminal justice practice, you should be able to understand the following points (Williams and Robinson, 2004).

1. Our criminal justice agencies are institutions of government social control.
2. As institutions of government social control, our agencies of criminal justice are political enterprises.
3. As political enterprises, the key phenomenon that drives criminal justice activity—from lawmaking through police, courts, and corrections—is ideology.
4. The American bipartisan government structure is represented by conservative and liberal political ideologies.
5. The conservative political ideology is currently the dominant American political ideology, ergo the behavior of our criminal justice network is presently under the dominant influence of the conservative crime control model.
6. Since the conservative crime control model is the dominant influence on our network of criminal justice, the nature and amount of our criminal justice activities will have little to do with actual crime rates and will have more to do with perceptions of crime problems generated by politicians.
7. Criminal justice processes are therefore not truly aimed at reducing crime or necessarily doing justice, but rather at achieving certain political and ideological goals. If true, this means the criminal justice network may not be pursuing the ideal goals of criminal justice introduced in Chapter 1 (i.e., doing justice and reducing crime).

Simon (2007) in his book, *Governing Through Crime: How the War on Crime Transformed American Democracy and Created a Culture of Fear,* identifies how our country became so obsessed with crime and convinced that "getting tough" through a conservative crime control model was the right approach to reducing crime. His analysis suggests that not only have the values of the crime control model become the dominant ideology of American criminal justice, but they have also significantly weakened other institutions of America society such as the family and schools. One result, according to Simon, is a less free country, with Americans sacrificing both civil liberties as well as much of their peace of mind.

CONCLUSION

Instead of doing justice, the U.S. criminal justice network may serve other functions, including serving limited interests and controlling certain segments of the population.

It is clear that criminal justice does not exist nor occur in a vacuum. Our efforts to do justice and to reduce crime are driven by political and ideological factors even more than by actual crime rates, evidence of criminal justice failure, or concerns over eroding constitutional protections. This in itself may be perceived as unjust by U.S. citizens and taxpayers, who should be able to expect more from their leaders than playing politics about crime and criminal justice, especially when so much is at stake.

ISSUE IN DEPTH—McDonaldization of America's Police, Courts, and Corrections

McDonaldization is a term created by sociologist George Ritzer (2000, p. 1) to describe the "the process by which the principles of the fast-food restaurant are coming to dominate more and more sectors of American society as well as the rest of the world." It is a process that represents the culmination of numerous practices of 20th century America, including bureaucratization, scientific management, and assembly line production.

According to Ritzer (2000), McDonaldization is made up of four elements:

1. **Efficiency** is "the optimum method for getting from one point to another" or for achieving some goal" (p. 12). In the fast food industry, efficiency is imperative, as the term *fast* implies.
2. **Calculability** is "an emphasis on the quantitative aspects of products sold and services offered . . . In McDonaldized systems, quantity has become equivalent to quality; a lot of something, or the quick delivery of it, means it must be good" (p. 12). In the fast food industry, more for your money is better than less for your money.
3. **Predictability** refers to "the assurance that products and services will be the same over time and in all locales" (p. 13). In the fast food industry, the goal is to make one's entire dining experience completely consistent with all previous visits; no matter where you go, the product will be exactly the same.
4. **Control** means that many aspects of production and consumption are governed by strict rules and an emphasis on one way of doing things. In the fast food industry, control is often achieved through the use of nonhuman technology (p. 236).

Any institution, system or, in this case, network of agencies that stresses efficiency, calculability, predictability, and control can be thought of as McDonaldized. According to my own research, America's agencies of criminal justice (police, courts, and corrections) have been McDonaldized, which means they tend to be aimed at efficiency, calculability, predictability, and control, perhaps even more than justice (Robinson, 2006).

EFFICIENCY AND CRIMINAL JUSTICE

The importance of efficiency in American criminal justice has always been stressed, perhaps never so much in our nation's history as in the past three decades. When agencies of criminal justice are more focused on controlling crime than assuring fairness and impartiality, efficiency of criminal justice becomes the most important value; informal processes such as plea bargaining are used in place of trials to expedite criminal justice operations and hold a larger proportion of criminals accountable for their criminal acts.

To the degree that cases move through the criminal justice network like an "assembly line," criminal justice practice is much like a fast-food production line. Modern criminal justice practice aims to be efficient, even at the cost of due process rights of defendants. As you saw in Chapter 1, most criminal justice resources go to police and corrections, with courts receiving the fewest resources. The result is that almost all convictions by courts are achieved through the assembly line process of plea bargaining; about 5% are convicted in criminal trials.

Allegiance to efficiency can be seen within the police, courts, and corrections. With regard to policing, the increased use of directed and aggressive patrol techniques (including foot and bike patrol) as part of a **problem-oriented policing** strategy provides evidence that law enforcement values efficiency. The **zero tolerance policing** in our nation's largest cities, aimed at eliminating small problems of disorder before they grow into large crime problems, is further evidence of an allegiance to efficiency. The shift from two- to one-man police cars, based on the realization that one-man cars are just as effective as those occupied by two officers, provides further evidence for the importance of efficiency in policing. Finally, the growth of technology in policing, from crime analysis and crime mapping to fingerprinting and computers in squad cars, suggests that policing is much more focused on proactive strategies than its has been historically.

With regard to courts, the popularity of plea bargaining provides tremendous evidence for the significance of efficiency in American courts. The ideal of American justice is an adversarial process whereby prosecutors and defense attorneys fight for truth and justice in a contest at trial. Yet an administrative system is in effect, as evidenced by the large use of plea bargaining in courts; these cases are handled informally in hallways and offices rather than in courtrooms. Instead of criminal trials where prosecutors and defense attorneys clash in an effort to determine the truth and do justice for all concerned parties, prosecutors, defense attorneys, and sometimes judges "shop" for "supermarket" justice through plea bargaining. Criminal trials are now the exception to the rule of plea bargaining. Plea bargaining achieves only one thing—a more efficient court. Most criminologists and criminal justice scholars view plea bargaining as an unjust process driven by large numbers of caseloads, understaffed courts, and the renewed emphasis on using law enforcement to solve drug use and public order offenses (see Chapter 7).

With regard to corrections, a renewed emphasis on efficiency can be found in the increased use of incarceration to achieve incapacitation and deterrence of large numbers of inmates. Increased use of imprisonment is discussed in the next section. Here, it simply should be noted that a greater use of imprisonment implies to consumers that the criminal justice network will be more efficient in preventing crime because it will prevent criminality by those currently locked up and instill fear in those considering committing crimes.

Other evidence of increased efficiency in corrections includes legislative efforts to expedite executions by limiting appeals and the elimination of gain time and parole by states and the federal government. The elimination of gain time and parole is a major factor contributing to prison overcrowding.

CALCULABILITY AND CRIMINAL JUSTICE

A greater emphasis has been placed on calculability in criminal justice over the past three decades—policy makers seem much more satisfied with more criminal justice (quantity) rather than better criminal justice (quality). **Victimless crimes** have, at virtually all times in our nation's history, been criminalized and we have fought numerous wars on drugs, yet the most recent war on drugs under Presidents Reagan, Bush (the first), Clinton, and Bush (the second) has stressed much more criminal justice intervention than at any time in our nation's history. As a nation, we have spent more than $300 billion on the war on drugs since 1980. The largest portion of recent drug war budgets has been for the least effective measures used in the drug war—law enforcement, interdiction, and drug eradication. The most effective measures—treatment and prevention—have received far less money (see Chapter 11).

In policing, we see calculability in the promises by politicians to place more cops on the street and to build more prisons. We also see calculability in asset forfeitures in the nation's drug war. The reward for police is being allowed to confiscate and keep some drug-related assets, including cars, houses, cash, and other property. To some degree, law enforcement officials have come to rely on drug assets to purchase equipment and conduct training so that police can exterminate drug use. The majority of law enforcement agencies in the United States have asset forfeiture programs in place (see Chapter 6).

In courts, the value of calculability is seen in the passing of longer sentences for virtually all crimes. It is also evident in laws that require offenders to serve greater portions of their sentences—the so-called "truth in sentencing" laws (see Chapter 8).

In corrections, calculability means building more prisons, sending more people to prison, and a renewed use of capital punishment. The imprisonment rate in America has historically been relatively constant. It has fluctuated over the years, but never until the 1970s did it consistently and dramatically increase. Beginning in 1973, America began to engage in an imprisonment boom based on the logic that more prisoners meant a safer America (see Chapter 9).

The ironic fact remains, however, that while violent crime rates fell in the 1990s, this had little to do with increased imprisonment (see Chapter 9). Further, drug use trends have largely been unaffected since 1988 and drug abuse levels have always hovered at approximately the same level (see Chapter 11). An increased commitment to calculability—more criminal justice—has not resulted in substantial reductions in crime rates, nor in drug use and abuse.

PREDICTABILITY AND CRIMINAL JUSTICE

If one were to fairly assess the performance of our nation's criminal justice network in terms of crime control over the past century, one could conclude that the likelihood of being subjected to it was always very unlikely; that is, the most predictable thing about it has been that reactive criminal justice processes fail. Even today, the chance of being apprehended, convicted, and sentenced to imprisonment is highly unlikely for all crimes other than murder.

The most important factor in the effectiveness of deterrence is the certainty of punishment, that is, the likelihood of being punished. Research on deterrence has consistently found that the severity of a sentence has less of a deterrent effect than sentence certainty (see Chapter 8). American criminal justice performs poorly in providing certain, swift punishments that outweigh the potential benefits of committing crimes. Putting more cops on the street and increasing the use of prison sentences are efforts to make criminal justice outcomes more predictable.

In terms of policing, law enforcement officers now attempt to apprehend suspects by using offender profiling methods, which allows them to develop a picture of the offender based on elements of his or her crime. The scientific method has always been a part of policing, yet only in the past two decades has offender profiling been used by police.

Police also try to accurately predict who is likely to get into trouble with the law before they commit criminal acts. They focus on particular types of people because of their own personal experience or that of their institution and profession, which suggests that certain people are more likely to violate the law. This practice, known as **police profiling**, results in startling disparities in police behavior based on class and race. Police use race, ethnicity, gender, and so forth, as a proxy for risk (see Chapter 6). Using race to establish probable cause is even supported by courts as legitimate when race is used in conjunction with other factors. Courts have stated that as long as the totality of the circumstances warrants the conclusion of the officer that the subject was acting suspiciously, race can be part of the circumstances considered by the officer. These elements of predictability in policing lead to difficulties in police–minority interactions, disproportionate use of force against people of color, and disrespect for the law generally.

American courts are also highly predictable in all they do. The main actors in this process within the criminal courts—the prosecutor, the defense attorney, and the judge—enter the courtroom daily knowing essentially what will happen each day before events actually take place. Ideally, each member of the courtroom work group serves its own roles and has its own goals; in reality, each member's main job is not to rock the boat in the daily operations of America's courts.

Because of the strong working interpersonal relationships among courthouse workers, **going rates** are established in bail and sentencing. The process of plea bargaining serves as an excellent example. In studies of plea bargaining, cases are disposed of with great regularity and predictability—meaning that the resulting sentence is reliably predicted based on the nature of the charges and the defendant's prior record. A going rate is established for particular types of crimes committed by particular types of people, one that becomes established over time and is learned by each member of the courtroom work group. Plea bargains typically closely parallel this going rate, and defendants charged with particular crimes can easily learn what sentence they likely face if they plead guilty (see Chapter 7).

At the sentencing phase of court proceedings, criminal penalties are highly predictable. Generally, the most important factors include the seriousness of the offense and the offender's prior record, so that the more serious the offense and the longer the prior record, the more severe the sentence will be. **Mandatory sentences** now establish a minimum sanction that must be served upon a conviction for a criminal offense. Thus, everyone who is convicted for a crime that calls for a mandatory sentence will serve that amount of time. Indeterminate sentences, which allowed parole and determinate prison sentences that could be reduced by good-time or earned-time credits, have been replaced by mandatory sentences across the country. Furthermore, **sentencing guidelines** have been established to make sentences more predictable and scientific based on a set of criteria including prior record, offense seriousness, and previous interactions with agencies of criminal justice. Sentencing grids reduce the discretion of judges and thus shift power to government prosecutors (see Chapter 8).

The best example of mandatory sentences are the **"three strikes" laws** in effect in more than half of our states. The logic of three strikes laws is to increase penalties of second offenses and require life imprisonment without possibility of parole for third offenses (see Chapter 8). These laws usually do not allow sentencing courts to consider particular circumstances of a crime, the duration of time that has elapsed between crimes, and mitigating factors in the background of offenders. The offender's potential for rehabilitation, ties to community, employment status, and obligations to children are also not taken into account.

Risk classification in corrections entails a great degree of prediction, as well. Individuals convicted of crimes can be put on probation, incarcerated in jail or prison, or subjected to some intermediate sanction; largely, one's punishment is determined by offense seriousness, prior record, and behavior during previous criminal justice interventions. Yet each form of punishment entails more or less supervision and fewer or greater rules to follow (e.g., probation versus intensive supervision probation) and/or greater restrictions on movement and activities (e.g., minimum versus maximum security) (see Chapter 9). The most violent and/or unmanageable inmates are now placed in isolation or incarcerated for 23 hours of the day in supermax prisons. These issues are discussed in the section on control that follows.

CONTROL AND CRIMINAL JUSTICE

As you saw in Chapter 1, in the past three decades America has witnessed a rapid expansion of American criminal justice. This is evidence of increased control efforts by the criminal justice network and is criticized for being a disinvestment in the nation's future.

This expansion is literally unparalleled in history; yet corresponding decreases in crime have not been achieved. Indeed, street crime decreased throughout the 1990s but only about one-fourth of this decrease is attributable to imprisonment (see Chapter 4). The clearest control issue in criminal justice revolves around corrections. Correctional facilities are now state of the art in terms of their use of technology to manage inmates. Increased use of other technologies include electronic monitoring of offenders under house arrest. Supermax prisons are the epitome of control. Offenders in **super-maximum** prisons have restricted contact with other inmates and with correctional personnel. Many inmates are locked in their cells for most of the day, in stark cells with white walls and bright lights on at all hours of the day and night. Cells have completely closed front doors and no windows. In these prisons, prisoners are confined to their cells for 23 hours per day and can take showers only 2–3 times per week. When inmates are transferred, they are shackled in handcuffs and sometimes leg irons. Temperatures inside these facilities consistently register in the 80s and 90s.

The supermax facility gives us another interesting parallel between criminal justice and the fast food industry. Technically, nothing can be more maximum than "maximum" custody, yet now we have supermax custody. In fast food, french fries used to come in small, medium, and large. Now they come in medium, large, and extra large; the extra large sizes are "super sized," "biggie sized," and even "super super sized" and "great biggie sized." French fries provide the fast food industry with great profit margins. The McDonaldized fast food industry tricks consumers into paying very high prices for a very small portion of one potato using deceptive terms such as *super supersized* and *great biggie sized* to convince consumers they are getting a good deal; the McDonaldized criminal justice network creates the illusion through the term *supermax custody* that these institutions keep Americans safe. In fact, most supermax inmates will one day be released back into society, having to readjust to living with other people. And the costs to taxpayers just to build such facilities can be more than $130,000 per inmate.

From this analysis, it is clear that our criminal justice network has fallen victim to McDonaldization. Each part of the network aims to be as efficient and predictable as possible, each uses quantity as an evaluative criterion, and each is highly controlling. Given the frequency of exposure to the efficiency, calculability, predictability, and control of the fast food environment, people have probably come to expect these qualities from many institutions and services other than fast food restaurants. This would make it easier for politicians to tout and sell fast and easy solutions to the nation's crime problem. Unfortunately, as American police, courts, and corrections have become McDonaldized, irrational policies have resulted. Although there is more criminal justice today than 30 years ago, although much of criminal justice practice is now highly predictable, and although Americans may now believe they are safer because more control is exerted over criminals by the government, the truth is that Americans are less sure of receiving justice from their agencies of criminal justice.

KEY TERMS

calculability	police profiling	serving limited interests
control	politics	social reality of crime
efficiency	population control	super-maximum
going rates	power	"three strikes" laws
ideology	predictability	unplanned change
mandatory sentences	problem-oriented policing	victimless crimes
McDonaldization	pyrrhic defeat theory	zero tolerance policing
planned change	sentencing guidelines	

DISCUSSION QUESTIONS

1. Summarize Reiman's pyrrhic defeat theory.
2. Do you agree with Reiman? Explain.
3. Is criminal justice really aimed at reducing crime and doing justice?
4. What are two alternative goals of America's criminal justice network?
5. Whose interests are served by a large criminal justice network? Provide examples.
6. What is the difference between intended goals of criminal justice and functions served by criminal justice? Provide examples.
7. Compare and contrast spending on criminal justice and spending on social services over the past three decades.

8. What is *politics*?
9. What is *ideology*?
10. Identify some ways in which politics, ideology, and criminal justice are related.
11. When did American criminal justice become so political and ideological?
12. Why is it so hard to distinguish between Republicans and Democrats when it comes to criminal justice?
13. Find some examples of how recent events related to crime or criminal justice serve as evidence of their political and ideological nature.
14. What is meant by the term *McDonaldization*? In what ways has America's criminal justice network become McDonaldized?

3

THE LAW: PROVIDING EQUAL PROTECTION OR CREATING BIAS?

1. Introduction
2. What Is the Law?
   - Box 3-1. Examples of Loony Laws and Silly Statutes
3. Where Does the Law Come From?
4. Types of Law
   a. Natural Law
   b. Positive Law
   - Box 3-2. The U.S. Constitution
   c. Common Law
   - Box 3-3. Some Interesting North Carolina Laws
   d. Criminal Law and Civil Law
5. What Is the Purpose of the Criminal Law?
6. Who Makes the Law?
   a. Demographics of Lawmakers
   b. Voting Behavior
   c. Special Interests/Lobbying
7. How the Criminal Law Fails to Protect Americans
   a. Big Tobacco
   b. Big Oil
8. Conclusion
9. Issue in Depth—New Antiterrorism Laws
10. Key Terms
11. Discussion Questions

INTRODUCTION

This chapter begins with a definition of law and a discussion of where the law comes from. Distinctions are made between natural law, or law dictated by a higher source, and positive law, or law made by sovereign human beings. Different types of positive law are discussed, including constitutional law, statutory law, case law, and administrative law. I also demonstrate the primary differences between criminal law, which defines acts as crimes against the government, and civil law, which regulates torts or acts against individuals. This chapter also outlines the purposes of the criminal law. A vital part of this chapter is a detailed exploration of who makes the law. To illustrate that the criminal law may not represent all Americans, I examine demographic characteristics of lawmakers and voters and illustrate how rare voting is in the United States. I show how special interests shape the criminal law through lobbying and financial donations to campaigns and elections. From this investigation, it seems likely that the U.S. criminal justice network is biased in favor of the wealthy and powerful. Finally, I examine new antiterrorism laws, such as the USA PATRIOT Act, to demonstrate how the events of September 11, 2001, have affected American criminal justice operations.

WHAT IS THE LAW?

Have you ever wondered how certain acts became criminal? For example, how did killing another person become the crime of murder? Has killing always been illegal? The answer is no. Even today, there are several ways of killing someone that still would not be considered crimes. These include killing someone in self-defense, killing someone in the line of duty as a police officer, execution of someone by the state through the administration of the death penalty, and killing "enemy" military personnel in times of war. Each of these means of killing is legal.

Why is it that some forms of killing are legal while other forms of killing are called "crimes"? Apparently, some forms of killing do not warrant the status of "crime." A behavior becomes a crime only when it is labeled a crime through the passage of a **law**. It is as simple as that. Rush (2000, p. 193) defines the law as "A general rule for the conduct of members of the community, either emanating from the governing authority by positive demand or approved by it, and habitually enforced by some public authority by the imposition of sanctions of penalties for its violation." Gilmer (1986, p. 194) defines the law as "a method for the resolution of disputes; a rule or action to which people obligate themselves to conform, via their elected representatives and other officials." From these two definitions, you can see that if lawmakers do not view an act as wrong, immoral, unethical, or harmful, the behavior will not be called a crime.

Thus, crimes are created when elected representatives decide to **codify**, or write down, behaviors as wrong, immoral, unethical, or harmful (Samaha, 2007). As you will see in Chapter 4, a crime occurs when a person either acts, fails to act, attempts to act, or agrees to act in a way that is in violation of the criminal law, without defense or justification. Because the law is what makes an act a crime, three important deductions can be made with regard to crime:

- No behavior is automatically a crime unless it is defined by the government as a crime.
- Any behavior can be made a crime.
- People often disagree about what acts should be called crimes and which should be treated as the most serious crimes.

With regard to the first point, many criminal justice scholars claim a distinction between **mala in se** crimes, those acts that are inherently evil or bad, and **mala prohibita** crimes, those acts that are evil or bad only because the government has labeled them criminal (Schmalleger, 2006). This is really an artificial distinction, because no behavior is inherently wrong. It only becomes wrong when the government says that it is wrong. This is why there is no behavior that has been considered wrong in every society at all times in history. In numerous places, in fact, rape is still not illegal despite its atrocious nature. Some states in the United States still do not consider it rape when a man is forced into sex. Others still do not call it rape when a husband forces his wife into unwanted sexual activity.

Sheryl Lindsell-Roberts (1994) demonstrates the second point in her amusing book, *Loony Laws and Silly Statutes*. In my state, North Carolina, for example, it is a crime for a man to talk to a woman who is attending an all-women's college while she is on campus. It is also a crime in North Carolina to shoot a deer if it is in water above its knees! In Florida, where I was born, it is against the law to take a bath with your clothes off. It is also a crime in Florida to doze off under a hair dryer. These types of criminal laws can be found in every state. Lindsell-Roberts's book provides examples of laws in every state that are unbelievable. Box 3-1 contains some examples from her book.

You may be wondering how such acts can be crimes. It is likely that at some time in history, these acts were considered problematic, probably because some people actually engaged in these acts and some type of harm resulted. Recently, the state of North Carolina created a new crime. It is now against the law to curse in the presence of a dead body. Apparently, a group of morticians grew tired of listening to all the foul language and thought it was disrespectful to the dead, so they lobbied to have such behavior prohibited by law. Every state has such loony laws and silly statutes on the books, even though they are not likely being enforced widely (if at all). When these laws are not enforced, do they need to be removed from the books?

BOX 3-1

EXAMPLES OF LOONY LAWS AND SILLY STATUTES

- In Tennessee, it is against the law to drive while sleeping.

- In California, it is against the law for a woman to drive her car in a housecoat.

- In Alabama, it is against the law to drive while barefoot or in bedroom slippers.

- In Florida, it is it is against the law to transport livestock aboard school buses.

- In Vermont, it is against the law to jump from a plane unless it is a true emergency.

- In Canada, it is against the law to board a plane after it has already taken off.

- In Washington, it is against the law to pretend that your parents are rich.

- In Kentucky, it is against the law to use a reptile as part of a religious service.

- In Massachusetts, it is against the law to eat peanuts while in church.

- In New Jersey, it is against the law to slurp soup.

- In Indiana, it is against the law to shoot open a can of soup.

- In Rhode Island, it is against the law to throw pickle juice on a trolley.
- In Tennessee, it is against the law to throw a banana peel on the sidewalk.
- In Wyoming, it is against the law to obstruct the view of fellow spectators by wearing a hat in a public theater.
- In Kansas, it is against the law to eat rattlesnake meat in public.
- In Minnesota, it is against the law to dance in public places.
- In Kentucky, it is against the law to remarry the same man four times.
- In Colorado, it is against the law to throw shoes at a wedding.

- In Missouri, it is against the law to carry a bear down the highway unless it is caged.
- In Washington, it is against the law to punch a bull in the nose.
- In Texas, it is against the law to milk someone else's cow.
- In Ohio, it is against the law to fish with explosives.
- In Indiana, it is against the law to take a bath during the winter.
- In Connecticut, it is against the law to chew tobacco without a doctor's permission.
- In Louisiana, it is against the law to gargle while in public.
- In Oregon, it is against the law to force a dead person to serve on a jury.

SOURCE: Adapted from Sheryl Lindsell-Roberts, *Loony Laws and Silly Statutes* (New York: Sterling, 1994).

WHERE DOES THE LAW COME FROM?

Acts are defined as crimes by human beings. Specifically, crimes are created by the U.S. Congress at the federal level, by legislatures at the state level, and by courts at every level of government when they interpret the law and set precedents through case law (Schmalleger, 2006). Congress at the federal level and all state legislatures have the power to define behaviors as crimes. For example, at both levels of government, it is against the law to steal a car forcibly from another person; this is often called **carjacking**. Rush (2000, p. 44) defines carjacking as "The unauthorized seizure of a vehicle by the use of force, threats, or coercion." According to Rush, federal law mandates a 15-year sentence for carjacking and a life sentence if a person is killed during the offense. In Louisiana, it is currently legal for a person to use lethal force against another if the person believes he or she is being carjacked. This became law after a winning beauty pageant contestant made this the issue she addressed upon her victory.

Courts interpret the meaning of the written law and, in so doing, actually clarify what the written law means. For example, if a man forced a driver out of his or her car so that he could take his pregnant wife to the hospital during labor, would that be considered carjacking? A court would likely have to decide this issue and, in essence, would be making law by setting a precedent that all other courts in the same jurisdiction would be required to follow (see Chapter 7). If a court heard a case in which a man was charged with carjacking under these circumstances and decided that such an act did not meet the definition of the crime in the statute (because the man did not intend to steal the car and thus did not intend to commit a carjacking), it would not be considered carjacking for human beings to engage in this behavior.

So where do we human beings get our law? Where did we get the notion that laws needed to be written down? The criminal law sets forth boundaries for acceptable behavior to ensure that we know what behaviors are wrong and what can happen to us if we commit wrongful acts. But where did the notions of right and wrong come from? An examination of different types of American law might answer these questions.

TYPES OF LAW

There are many types of law in the United States. Figure 3-1 depicts the main types of law and illustrates the relationships between them.

Natural Law

One type of law, known as **natural law**, is law from a higher source. If you are religious, this might be God's law—for example, the Ten Commandments delivered to Moses as explained in the Holy Bible. Natural law could also be considered "laws of the gods" (in polytheistic cultures). But natural law also exists for nonreligious people. Natural law might be the laws of "the force," for example, or laws of human nature. Natural law, whatever your beliefs about religion, is a recognition that there are wrong behaviors that are simply bad in themselves—these are the *mala in se* offenses. Other acts are inherently right, good, or just. Natural law in essence is greater than humankind—it was here before we got here and will be here after we depart. Schmalleger (1999, p. 16) defines natural law as those laws that "are fundamental to human nature and discoverable by human reason, intuition, or inspiration, without the need for reference to man-made laws."

The main problem with natural law is that no one can possibly know what it is. If there are universal truths, behaviors that are inherently good and bad, how can we know what they are? For example, if God has his or her own idea about what is right

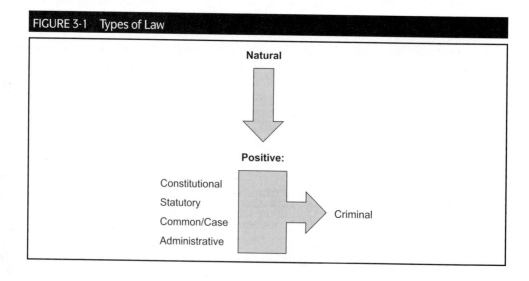

FIGURE 3-1   Types of Law

and wrong, how can we know unless he or she comes down from heaven and tells us? Since we cannot experience God directly with our empirical senses—that is, we cannot see, hear, or touch God—it is logically impossible to know God's laws.

Even if we rely on the Holy Bible to learn about natural law, which version do we use? How would we know which version is the correct one? Since religion is a matter of faith rather than evidence, you either believe it or you don't (Bohm, 2001). This makes natural law useless as a source of law for the purpose of informing us about right and wrong and for judging individuals' behaviors as right or wrong. So Americans end up disagreeing about rights and wrongs (even though we all do agree that there are rights and wrongs). Criminologists also disagree which behaviors are wrong and thus worthy of the status of crimes (see Chapter 4).

Positive Law

How do we decide whether some behavior should be considered right or wrong? How do we decide which behaviors are so wrong that they should be called crimes? We do this by electing people to make the law for us. Laws made by us—human beings—are referred to as positive law. **Positive law** consists of laws made by sovereign human beings. Those with the authority to make laws write them, and the rest of us have to abide by them in the face of potential sanctions for violating the law. The relationship between positive law and natural law is that natural law informs positive law. That is, positive law is based on or rooted in natural law. Legislators, on the basis of their conceptions of right and wrong and those of their constituents (natural law), define some acts as wrong by labeling them "crimes" or "torts." A crime is an act in violation of the criminal law. A tort is an act that is harmful against an individual; it is handled in a civil court rather than a criminal court. I'll return to the differences between criminal law and civil law later in this chapter. For now, think of this example: ex–football star O. J. Simpson was accused, but found not guilty at trial, of murdering his wife and her male friend. Murder is a behavior that leads to a trial in a criminal court. Later, O. J. Simpson was tried and found liable for the wrongful deaths of Nicole Brown and Ronald Goldman. He was not convicted for the murders of two people (a crime) in criminal court, but he was found responsible or liable for their wrongful deaths (a tort) in civil court.

The advantage of positive law is that it makes the law predictable. Because the law is written down by human beings, other human beings can consult the law and know what types of behaviors are permitted and which are prohibited. This is why "ignorance of the law is no excuse" for breaking it. We also can easily find out what the possible sanctions are for violating the law. If you want to know what is illegal in your state and what can happen to you if you break a particular law, just consult the criminal statute books in any law library in your state, or simply find the laws of your state online.

Positive law comes to us from many sources. Positive law includes constitutional law, statutory law, case law, and administrative law, all of which have been informed by common law (Cole and Smith, 2006). **Constitutional law** comes to us from the U.S. Constitution and from the Constitutions of each of the 50 states. Constitutional law establishes individual rights for people in the United States and thus sets forth limitations on government power. Box 3-2 discusses the U.S. Constitution.

Statutory law comes to us from legislatures of the federal government (the U.S. Congress) and each of the 50 states. Statutory law defines crimes and sets forth potential punishments for violations of the written law. **Case law** is made by courts at the

BOX 3-2

THE U.S. CONSTITUTION

The Constitution of the United States granted numerous rights to individual citizens. For example, the Bill of Rights guarantees individual citizens protection from acts of the federal government, including the following rights:

- Freedom from *unreasonable searches and seizures* (Fourth Amendment)
- Freedom from arrest or search without probable cause (Fourth Amendment)
- Freedom from *self-incrimination* (Fifth Amendment)
- Freedom from *double jeopardy* (Fifth Amendment)
- Freedom from being deprived of life, liberty, or property without due process of law (Fifth Amendment)
- Freedom from *cruel and unusual punishment* (Eighth Amendment)
- Freedom from *excessive bail or fines* (Eighth Amendment)
- Right to a *speedy, public, and fair trial by jury* (Sixth Amendment)
- Right to an *impartial jury* (Sixth Amendment)
- Right to *counsel* (Sixth Amendment)

The Equal Protection Clause and the Due Process Clause of the Fourteenth Amendment extended these rights to protect citizens from acts of their state government, as well. In essence, no level of American government can deprive its citizens of these rights.

These constitutional protections demonstrate that America's founders wanted to ensure, for all time, that its citizens would enjoy certain individual rights and would be free from such forms of government oppression. Some common sayings of criminal justice reinforce this ideal. Ever hear these?

- "All suspects are innocent until proven guilty."
- "It's better to let guilty men go free than to wrongfully punish innocent ones."

These sayings reflect an inherent belief that rules of criminal procedure are important to Americans. These rules of criminal procedure are referred to as due process, also defined as "ensuring that laws are reasonable and that they are applied in a fair and equal manner" (Rush, 2000, p. 120). No American is to be deprived of his or her life, freedom, or property without due process, because due process is required by the U.S. Constitution. Thus, when any American is subjected to some part of the criminal justice process (e.g., arrest, conviction, punishment) without due process, nothing less important than the U.S. Constitution is threatened.

The primary purpose of the U.S. Supreme Court is to interpret the meaning of individual cases for the Constitution. According to Walker, Spohn, and DeLone (2000, p. 289):

The Supreme Court consistently has affirmed the importance of protecting criminal suspects' rights. The Court has ruled, for example, that searches without warrants are generally unconstitutional, that confessions cannot be coerced, that suspects must be advised of their rights and provided with attorneys to assist them in their defense, that jurors must be chosen from a representative cross-section of the population, and that the death penalty cannot be administered in an arbitrary and capricious manner.

You might be surprised as you read this book that despite these ideal protections, many of them are not really enjoyed by many Americans.

WHAT WAS THE PURPOSE OF THE CONSTITUTION?

A more critical and perhaps even cynical interpretation of the Constitution suggests that the Constitution was and is biased against certain groups in society. Kappeler, Blumberg, and Potter (2000, p. 217) write: "The framers of the Constitution may have been engaged in unselfish efforts to construct an impartial rule of law, but women could not vote, and slavery was legal—constraints of the worldview at that time."

Charles Beard, in *An Economic Interpretation of the Constitution of the United States* (1913), discusses how the construction of the Constitution was a process biased against the poor. For example, of the five economic groups that existed in 1787 when the document was drafted in Philadelphia, "the four poorest groups had no representatives at the convention: women, slaves, indentured servants, and propertyless white men" (Harrigan, 2000, p. 45). Every delegate involved in drafting the Constitution was a white male who owned enough property to be allowed to vote. According to Beard, of the 55 delegates, 38 owned government bonds, 24 earned their living through banking or some other financial investment, 15 owned slaves, and 14 had investments in western lands. Feagin (2000, p. 9) suggests that of the 55 delegates, "at least 40 percent have been or are slave owners, and a significant proportion of the others profit

to some degree as merchants, shippers, lawyers, and bankers from the trade in slaves, commerce in slave-produced agricultural products, or supplying provisions to slaveholders and slave-traders." Given the makeup of the delegates, was the Constitution drafted at least partly to protect their limited interests?

Harrigan (2000, p. 47) suggests that three different types of provisions were written into the Constitution to protect the limited financial interests of wealthy, white male delegates:

- Those that protected their private property rights
- Those that insulated the national government from popular rule
- Those that minimized the influence of the lower-status population in the ratification process

The protections of private property rights included provisions that benefited businesses engaged in trade and economy, bankers and creditors, slave holders, and holders of securities under the Articles of Confederation.

Feagin (2000) explains that

at the heart of the Constitution was protection of the property and wealth of the affluent bourgeoisie in the new nation, including property of those enslaved. . . . For the founders, freedom meant the protection of unequal accumulation of property, particularly property that could produce a profit in the emerging capitalistic system. Certain political, economic, and racial interests were conjoined. This was not just a political gathering with the purpose of creating a new major bourgeois-democratic government; it was also a meeting to protect the racial and economic interests of men with substantial property and wealth in the colonies. (p. 10)

Popular rule was not set up in the Constitution because people did not directly

(continued)

BOX 3-2 *(Continued)*

vote for the president, the Court, or the Senate. Only House members were originally elected by the people, and people could vote only if their congressional districts had at least 30,000 people. This benefited the wealthy. Barriers to voting (such as property ownership requirements) were constructed to discourage a large percentage of people from voting. Because of this, Harrigan (2000) concludes:

> The lower-status population did indeed have nothing to say about the drafting of the Constitution and (whether by choice or coercion) had little to say about ratifying it. Important provisions in the Constitution protected economic interests that were more valuable to the upper-status population than to the lower-status population. (p. 53)

Similarly, Joe Feagin (2000), in his book, *Racist America; Roots, Current Realities and Future Reparations*, traces the roots of American racism to the U.S. Constitution and early colonial America. He suggests that many of our country's founders—including Thomas Jefferson, Benjamin Franklin, and James Madison—were greatly influenced by assumptions in Europe about the inherent inferiority of African Americans to Caucasians. Thus, African Americans would specifically be counted as only three-fifths of a man according to Article I, Section 2, of the U.S. Constitution.

Feagin (2000, p. 14) asserts that the U.S. Constitutional Convention was something other than what we have learned about in school. He suggests the structure of the nation, as laid out in the Constitution, "was created to maintain separation and oppression at the time and for the foreseeable future. The framers reinforced

and legitimated a system of racist oppression that they thought would ensure that whites, especially white men of means, would rule for centuries to come."

According to Feagin (2000, p. 15), the country's founders owned slaves and benefited from the unequal treatment of African Americans and Caucasians. "Men of politics like Thomas Jefferson, George Washington, Alexander Hamilton, Patrick Henry, Benjamin Franklin, John Hancock, and Sam Houston enslaved black Americans. Ten U.S. presidents (Washington, Jefferson, James Madison, James Monroe, Andrew Jackson, John Tyler, James Polk, Zachary Taylor, and Ulysses S. Grant) at some point in their lives enslaved African Americans." Many lawmakers (members of both houses of Congress) were also slave owners, as were those who would interpret the law (members of the U.S. Supreme Court). Not surprisingly, "few major decisions made by the federal legislative and judicial branches went against the interests of the nation's slaveholding oligarchy, and foreign and domestic policies generally did not conflict with the interests of those centrally involved with the slavery system" (p. 56).

Given such an apparent built-in bias in favor of the wealthy and white, it may not be hard to imagine that some biases would still be around today. Perhaps they would even have multiplied, expanded into areas such as tax codes and legal codes. If so, we would expect that a mechanism would need to be in place to support and maintain these biases in favor of the wealthy. Is it possible that the criminal justice network is this mechanism? If so, this would support Reiman's (2006) argument that the criminal justice network is really aimed at serving certain interests (see Chapter 2).

state and federal level when judges interpret statutes and make rulings on individual cases. Case law helps governments and citizens understand what statutes and constitutions mean. Rush (2000, p. 93) defines **administrative law** as "Statutes, regulations, and orders that govern public agencies ... rules governing the administrative operations of the government."

Common Law

Common law is a term used to describe the legal traditions of England before America was founded (Schmalleger, 2006). Common law consists of the traditions and customs of British judges that were passed down from judge to judge over time. Common law was not written down as strict legal rules but, rather, included "general principles to guide judges" (Gottfredson, 1999, p. 49). As noted, common law informs each of the types of positive law because American positive law grew out of the traditions and customs of England. Gottfredson explains that English common law informed American law by establishing these principles:

- The supremacy of the law
- The inviolability of person and property
- The local nature of criminal jurisdiction
- Due process of law
- The rule that no one should be compelled in any criminal prosecution to be a witness against himself or herself
- The right to a trial by jury

From these sources of positive law, we get the **criminal law**, which can be divided into two distinct types: substantive criminal law and procedural criminal law. **Substantive criminal law** is the "substance" of the law, as it defines which behaviors are illegal and what punishments can follow as a result of breaking the written law (Schmalleger, 1999). Box 3-3 provides examples of substantive criminal law in my state, North Carolina.

BOX 3-3

SOME INTERESTING NORTH CAROLINA LAWS

Each of the following is illegal in my state of North Carolina.

- *§ 14-72.3. Stealing a shopping cart:* It is unlawful to remove a shopping cart from the premises of a store without the consent, given at the time of the removal, of the store owner, manager, agent or employee, where "shopping cart" means the type of push cart commonly provided by grocery stores, drugstores, and other retail stores for customers to transport commodities within the store and from the store to their motor vehicles outside the store and "premises" includes the motor vehicle parking area set aside for customers of the store.

(continued)

BOX 3-3 *(Continued)*

- *§ 14-400. Tattooing; body piercing:* It is unlawful to tattoo the arm, limb, or any part of the body of any other person under 18 years of age.

- *§ 14-401.17. Unlawfully removing or destroying electronic dog collars:* It is unlawful to intentionally remove or destroy an electronic collar or other electronic device placed on a dog by its owner to maintain control of the dog.

- *§ 14-113. Obtaining money by false representation of physical defect:* It is unlawful to falsely represent yourself in any manner whatsoever as blind, deaf, dumb, or crippled or otherwise physically defective for the purpose of obtaining money or other thing of value or of making sales of any character of personal property. Any person so falsely representing himself or herself as blind, deaf, dumb, crippled or otherwise physically defective, and securing aid or assistance on account of such representation, shall be deemed guilty.

- *§ 14-444. Being intoxicated and disruptive in public:* It shall be unlawful for any person in a public place to be intoxicated and disruptive in any of the following ways: Blocking or otherwise interfering with traffic on a highway or public vehicular area, or Blocking or lying across or otherwise preventing or interfering with access to or passage across a sidewalk or entrance to a building, or Grabbing, shoving, pushing or fighting others or challenging others to fight, or Cursing or shouting at or otherwise rudely insulting others, or Begging for money or other property.

- *§ 14-197. Using profane or indecent language on public highways:* It shall be unlawful if any person uses, on any public road or highway and in the hearing of two or more persons, in a loud and boisterous manner, indecent or profane language.

- *§ 18B-1005.1. Sexually explicit conduct on licensed premises:* It shall be unlawful for a permittee or his agent or employee to knowingly allow or engage in any of the following kinds of conduct on his licensed premises: (1) Any conduct or entertainment by any person whose genitals are exposed or who is wearing transparent clothing that reveals the genitals; (2) Any conduct or entertainment that includes or simulates sexual intercourse, masturbation, sodomy, bestiality, oral copulation, flagellation, or any act that includes or simulates the penetration, however slight, by any object into the genital or anal opening of a person's body; or (3) Any conduct or entertainment that includes the fondling of the breasts, buttocks, anus, vulva, or genitals.

These acts must have been problematic in the state of North Carolina, or they would not likely be considered crimes. Your state has similar laws based on unique problems that its citizens experience. Remember, any behavior can be made criminal at any time.

Procedural criminal law puts forth the "procedures" that governments must follow when carrying out the law (Fuller, 2005). Procedural criminal law thus establishes limits on the government's power when attempting to apprehend and prosecute suspected criminals. An example of procedural criminal law is found in the Bill of Rights of the U.S. Constitution. Recall that the Bill of Rights lays out protections that all people ideally enjoy if and when they are subjected to criminal justice processes. Ideally, if these rights are somehow violated by police, the courts, or correctional facilities, consequences can include dismissal of charges, the overturning of criminal convictions, and even financial reimbursement to the victim (Peoples, 2000; Stuckey, Robertson, and Wallace, 2001).

Criminal Law and Civil Law

The criminal law and the **civil law** are very different. Table 3-1 illustrates these differences. For example, the criminal law is concerned with harmful acts committed against the government. All crimes are technically viewed as acts against the government rather than against individuals. Civil law, however, is concerned with harmful acts committed against individuals. The criminal law leads to trials involving the state or government against an individual—for example, the *State of California v. O. J. Simpson*. The civil law leads to trials where one individual faces another. When you think of the civil law, you may think of television shows like *Judge Judy* or *The People's Court*. Criminal trials can lead to either a **criminal conviction** or an *acquittal* (a finding of not guilty). When an offender is found guilty, he or she can be punished by any of a whole range of potential sanctions (see Chapter 8). For someone to be convicted, it must be demonstrated beyond reasonable doubt that the offender committed the named act(s) and did so intentionally (on purpose). Civil trials, however, lead to a finding of either liability or no liability. That is, the accused is either held responsible for the act or not. If found to be liable, the accused usually will be required to compensate the victim financially for the harm(s) inflicted. Intent is not required in civil court, and the standard of proof is much lower. In a civil court, the burden of proof is a **preponderance of evidence**, meaning that a simple majority of the evidence must suggest that the accused is responsible.

One final difference between the criminal law and the civil law is that the rules of evidence are much more stringent in the criminal law, meaning that is easier to get evidence admitted into a civil court than a criminal court. You might wonder how it is that a person can be tried twice for the same offense, given the constitutional right to freedom from double jeopardy. Because the criminal and civil courts have different jurisdictions and are intended for different purposes, being tried in each court does not constitute double jeopardy.

TABLE 3-1 Criminal Law and Civil Law		
	Criminal	*Civil*
Participants	State versus individual	Individual versus individual
Possible Outcome	Conviction, Punishment of offender	Liability, Financially compensate victim
Intent required?	Yes	No
Standard of Proof	Beyond reasonable doubt	Preponderance of evidence
Rules of Evidence	Very stringent	Less stringent

WHAT IS THE PURPOSE OF THE CRIMINAL LAW?

Early political theorists such as Hobbes, Locke, and Rousseau argued that when individuals form a society, they must enter into a **social contract** to surrender some of their individual rights in return for the protection of their personal safety and property. The social contract is codified by making law. In modern Western societies such as the United States, "crimes" are acts against the government rather than against individuals. This definition of crime gives the state the right to prosecute wrongdoers and to administer punishment in the name of the actual crime victims. At the same time, individual citizens are forbidden from engaging in vengeance or vigilantism.

For this type of system to work, the government must assure its citizens that their sacrifices are worth it. It does this primarily by providing protection, peace, and order. In other words, the government is responsible for enforcing laws, catching and punishing criminals, and protecting the community from harm (Marion, 1995). These efforts are aimed at crime control, a goal of the criminal justice network discussed in Chapter 1. But recall the inherent struggle between achieving our goal of crime control and our goal of ensuring due process. The law must be "both an engine of government and a brake which restrains government" (Gottfredson, 1999, p. 47). This means the government can use force to make sure the criminal law is not violated, but not so much force that it interferes with the rights of individual citizens. As I discuss each of the three components of the criminal justice network later in the book, you will see how each attempts to carry out the criminal law without violating individual constitutional protections.

For the purposes of this chapter, I will focus on the function of the criminal law that is concerned with defining behaviors that are illegal. There are at least two competing interpretations of whose interests are represented when behaviors are defined as illegal. Those who believe in the **consensus view of the law** believe that the law reflects societal interests and that "crimes" therefore are acts that a majority of the population view as immoral, wrong, and harmful. Crimes are thus deviations from the norm. This model is based on the belief that the "law reflects common consciousness and interests of society" (Marion, 1995, p. 21). According to its proponents, the criminal law "serves as a banner to announce the values of society. It tells us where the boundaries of acceptable behavior lie and links those who violate the boundaries—criminals—with evil, pain, incarceration, and disgrace" (Kappeler et al., 2000, p. 216).

Several studies have shown a remarkable level of agreement among citizens about which crimes should be considered most serious. These studies typically reveal a higher level of perceived seriousness for the violent street crimes included in the Uniform Crime Reports (e.g., see Carlson and Williams, 1993; Cohen, 1991; Cullen, Link, and Travis, 1985; Epperlein and Nienstedt, 1989; Gebotys and Dasgupta, 1987; Gebotys, Roberts, and Dasgupta, 1988; Meier and Short, 1985; Miethe, 1982; O'Connell and Whelan, 1996; Parton, Hansel, and Stratton, 1991; Rauma, 1991; Sebba, 1984; Warr, 1991). Some would claim that this is evidence that the criminal law clearly serves the interests of the public. But which came first—public support for the law or the law itself? Isn't it possible that people perceive harmful acts as more or less serious based on their status in the criminal law?

I advocate a different approach to determining crime seriousness, consistent with scholars such as Simon (2005) and Reiman (2006). This approach would pronounce acts as more or less serious on the basis of the degree of harm the acts cause. That is, more harmful acts would be considered more serious, and less harmful acts would be called less serious. The criminal law does reflect this approach in some ways—for example, murder is more serious than theft. Yet, in many ways, the criminal law does not define the most harmful acts as more serious, providing evidence for proponents of the conflict model of the law.

Proponents of the **conflict view of the law** believe that the law reflects the limited interests of powerful members of society. Thus, "crimes" are not necessarily the most harmful acts; instead, they are acts committed by relatively powerless people (e.g., the poor) (Vold, 1958). Those with political or economic power, and special-interest groups, are likely to have their beliefs reflected in the law, according to those who believe in the conflict model. As Goode and Ben-Yuhuda (1994b, p. 78) write: "Definitions of right and wrong do not drop from the skies, nor do they simply ineluctably percolate from society's mainstream opinion; they are the result of disagreement, negotiation, conflict, and struggle. The passage of laws raises the issue of who will criminalize whom." Similarly, Akers (1996, p. 142) writes: "The dominant groups can see to it that their particular definitions of normality or deviance will become enacted as law, ensconced in public policy, and protected by the operation of the criminal justice system."

In the United States, poor people are labeled as troublemakers more than any other group (Gans, 1995, pp. 18–21). Gans writes that the process begins with the "label-makers" (in the case of crime, they are legislators). Legislators define certain acts committed by the poor as crimes and then rely on "alarmists" to spread the word about the dangers of the acts (in the case of crime, they are the media) and on "counters" to supply numbers indicating that the problem is serious or widespread (in the case of crime, they are the police and politicians). So is the law biased against the poor? If you believe that the government should pass laws to protect us from harms, then you might feel that the law is biased if it only attempts to protect us from harms committed by poor people.

Hobbes argued that government's "sole purpose" was to give citizens the ability to "pursue their natural rights, including the rights to life, to liberty, and to enjoy personal property"—that is, to "provide safety for the citizens" (Marion, 1995, pp. 4–5). To the degree that the government does not do this, the government is failing to do its job. I will illustrate in Chapter 4 that our government ignores many harmful acts, such as white-collar and corporate crime. To the degree that they ignore these harms, our government is failing to provide us with justice and to protect us from things that kill us, injure us, and take our property. A violation of the law—a crime—is clearly a potential threat to the social order. Many crimes, because of the harms they cause to society, are considered serious and thus warrant criminal justice intervention. However, other crimes are not severe enough to warrant criminal justice intervention (see Chapter 11 for the example of drug crimes in the United States).

Failure to define intentional or other forms of culpable harms as "crimes" can also pose a threat to social order, because citizens may perceive that their government is failing to protect them. Reiman (1998, p. 59) states it this way: "The point of prohibiting an act by the criminal law is to protect society from an injurious act. . . . The label [of crime] is applied appropriately when it is used to identify all, or at least the worst of, the acts that are harmful to society. The label is applied inappropriately when it is attached to any harmless act or when it is not attached to seriously harmful acts." The label of "crime," especially "serious crime," is not reserved for the acts that actually threaten us the most. Instead, it is a label for harmful acts that we perceive to be crimes of the poor—that is, for street crime (see Chapter 4).

Before this information is discussed, there is a middle-ground between the consensus view and the conflict view called the **pluralist view of the law.** Proponents of this view suggest that there is intense competition between various parties with regard to any issue. The law reflects the interests of those who win this competition. Acts called crimes are those most lobbied for by interest groups. As it turns out, powerful groups and individuals are those most likely to win. To gain a clear understanding of why this is so, it is crucial to understand the legislative process in the United States, including who makes the law, who votes for the law, and how special interests shape the law.

WHO MAKES THE LAW?

The criminalization process, like all criminal justice activity, starts with the lawmaking stage. By defining crimes (substantive criminal law) and setting forth the rules that criminal justice actors must follow (procedural criminal law), the criminal law dictates what police, courts, and corrections do. That is, the criminal law sets forth what is considered a crime and what sanctions can follow from illegal behaviors. Therefore, the activities of police, courts, and corrections personnel all directly stem from the law. As introduced in Chapter 1, once the law is in place, police enforce the criminal law by responding to calls for service, investigating alleged crimes, and apprehending suspects. Courts determine the guilt of suspects and impose criminal sanctions on the legally guilty. Correctional facilities and programs carry out the sanctions of the courts and administer punishment to sentenced offenders. These institutions of criminal justice thereby reinforce the validity of the law and of all stereotypes created by that law.

This section examines who makes the law by illustrating key demographics of lawmakers. I then turn to voting behavior to illustrate who votes for the law and who does not. Then the effects of special interests and lobbying on the law are explored. Taken together, these analyses suggest that the criminal law may be biased in favor of the wealthy and powerful.

Demographics of Lawmakers

To the degree that lawmakers are representative of all of society, it is likely that laws will represent all people in society. Table 3-2 compares demographic characteristics of state and federal legislators with those of the general U.S. population.

At the federal level, in the 110th Congress, only 10% of U.S. House of Representatives members are African Americans and only 6% are Hispanics. The U.S. Senate contains 1 African American (1%) and 2 Hispanics (2%). Therefore, the majority of legislators at the federal level are Caucasians, including 84% of House members and 97% of Senators.

In terms of gender, 16% of the U.S. House is made up of women, and 14% of the U.S. Senate consists of women. Therefore, the majority of federal legislators are men, including 84% of House members and 86% of Senators. In fact, nearly 80% of members of Congress are white men.

In terms of age, less than 10% of the U.S. Congress is under the age of 40 years, in part because of constitutional requirements for age. The average age of federal legislators in

TABLE 3-2 Demographic Characteristics of Legislators				
	U.S. Population	*U.S. Senate*	*U.S. House*	*State Legislatures*
Median age	36.4 years	62 years	56 years	53 years
Percent women	51%	14%	16%	23%
Percent white	80.2%	97%	84%	89%
Percent black	12.7%	1%	10%	8%

Sources: U.S. Census (2006), Center for Voting and Democracy, and Congress Link.

the U.S. House is approximately 56 years and in the U.S. Senate it is 62 years. Thus, we can confidently say that the typical federal legislator is an older, white male.

At the state level, African Americans make up about 8% of state legislators and Hispanics comprise only 3%. Therefore, the majority of legislators at the state level are Caucasian (89%). In terms of gender, women make up just 23% of state representatives. Therefore, 77% of state legislators are men. The average age of state legislators is approximately 53 years. Thus, we can confidently say that the typical state legislator is an older, white male.

When we compare these numbers with the U.S. general population, we see that, demographically, lawmakers look very different from the average American. In 2005, according to the U.S. Census (2005), the average age of the population was 36 years. Legislators at both federal and state levels are older on average than the general population. Women make up 51% of the U.S. population. Women are thus underrepresented as federal and state lawmakers. Caucasians now make up about 80% of U.S. citizens, whereas African Americans make up 13% of the population and Hispanics make up 15% of the population. Caucasians are thus overrepresented as lawmakers at the federal and state level, while African Americans and Hispanics are underrepresented. It can be concluded that lawmakers are not representative of the general population in terms of demographic characteristics such as race, ethnicity, gender, and age.

Lawmakers are also much wealthier than the average person. For example, in 2006, the base pay of Senators and Representatives in Congress was $165,200. Congressional leaders receive $183,500 per year, whereas the Speaker of the House receives $212,100. This is more than four times the average pay of Congress' constituents. According to the U.S. Census (2006), the average income of all households in 2005 was $46,326, including $50,784 for Caucasian households, $35,967 for Hispanic households, and $30,858 for African American households.

Base salary is only what legislators get paid; it does not include their net worth nor the numerous benefits and perks they receive. About half of new lawmakers are millionaires, compared with only 1% of the American population. Many claim that these millionaire lawmakers have potential conflicts of interest given their financial interests in various corporations. This issue is discussed later in the chapter.

At the state level, legislator pay varied widely across the country. Table 3-3 shows data from the National Conference of State Legislatures (2005), illustrating the salaries of state legislators. In my state of North Carolina, pay varies based on the office held. According to the North Carolina General Assembly, pay of lawmakers in the state was nearly $14,000 per year, plus $104 in daily spending allowances. Keep in mind, however, that this is pay for a part-time job!

TABLE 3-3   Salaries of State Legislators

State	Salary	Per Diem (Allowance for Daily Expenses)
Alabama	$10/day	$2,280/month plus $50/day for three days during each week that the legislature actually meets during any session.
Alaska	$24,012/year	$200/day effective June 1, 2005, until october 1, 2005, then $156/day until May 1, 2006, then $200/day tied to federal rate. Legislators who reside in the Capitol area receive 75% of the federal rate.
Arizona	$24,000/year	$35/day for the 1st 120 days of regular session and for special session and $10/day thereafter. Members residing outside Maricopa County receive an additional $25/day for the 1st 120 days of regular session and for special session and an additional $10/day thereafter. Set by statute.
Arkansas	$14,067/year	$110.00/day plus mileage tied to federal rate.
California	$110,880/year	$138.00 per day for each day they are in session.
Colorado	$30,000/year	$45/day for members living in the Denver metro area. $99/day for members living outside Denver. Per diem is determined by the legislature.
Connecticut	$28,000/year	No per diem is paid.
Delaware	$39,785/year	No per diem is paid.
District of Columbia	$92,500/year	No per diem is paid.
Florida	$29,916/year	$117/day tied to federal rate. Earned based on the number of days in session. Travel vouchers are filed to substantiate.
Georgia	$16,524/year	$128/day set by the legislature.
Guam	N/R	N/R
Hawaii	$34,200/year ($35,000/year effective 2006)	$80/day for members living outside Oahu; $10/day for members living on Oahu set by the legislature. *NOTE: The per diem for legislators will be adjusted for the 2006 session. The specific amount is to be determined by the Speaker and the President.
Idaho	$15,646/year	$99/day for members establishing second residence in Boise; $38/day if no second residence is established and up to $25/day travel set by Compensation Commission.
Illinois	$57,619/year	$102/day tied to federal rate.
Indiana	$11,600/year	$134/day tied to federal rate.

Iowa	$21,380.54/year	$86/day. $65/day for Polk County legislators set by the legislature. State mileage rates apply.
Kansas	$82.12/day ($83.14 effective 12/4/05)	$91/day tied to federal rate.
Kentucky	$170.17/day	$100.10/day tied to federal rate (110% federal per diem rate).
Louisiana	$16,800/year	$113/day tied to federal rate. Additional $6,000/year expense allowance.
Maine	$11,384/year for first regular session; $8,655/year for second regular session. Annual COLAs apply. In addition, legislators receive a constituent service allowance ($2,000/year for Senators and $1,500/year for Representatives)	$38/day housing, or mileage and tolls in lieu of housing (at rate of 0.34/mile up to $38/day). $32/day for meals. Per diem limits set by statute.
Maryland	$40,500/year	Lodging $96/day; meals $32/day tied to federal rate and compensation commission. $225.00/day for out of state travel. Includes meals and lodging.
Massachusetts	$55,569.39/year	From $10/day to $100/day, depending on distance from State House set by the legislature.
Michigan	$79,650/year	$12,000 yearly expense allowance for session and interim set by compensation commission.
Minnesota	$31,140.90/year	Senators receive $66/day and Representatives receive $66/legislative day set by the legislature.
Mississippi	$10,000/year	$91/day tied to federal rate.
Missouri	$31,351/year	$76.80/day tied to federal rate. Verification of per diem is by roll call. $76.80/day tied to federal rate. Verification of per diem is by roll call.
Montana	$76.80/day (L)	$90.31/day.
Nebraska	$12,000/year	$91/day outside 50-mile radius from Capitol; $31/day if member resides within 50 miles of Capitol tied to federal rate.
Nevada	$130/day maximum of 60 days of session	Federal rate for Capitol area. Legislators who live more than 50 miles from the capitol, if require lodging, will be paid HUD single-room rate for Carson City area for each month of session.
New Hampshire	$200/two-year term	No per diem is paid.
New Jersey	$49,000/year	No per diem is paid.
New Mexico	None	$146/day tied to federal rate and the Constitution.
New York	$79,500/year	Varies; tied to federal rate.
North Carolina	$13,951/year	$104/day set by statute. $559.00/month expense allowance.

(*continued*)

TABLE 3-3 *(continued)*

State	Salary	Per Diem (Allowance for Daily Expenses)
North Dakota	$125/day during legislative sessions	Lodging reimbursement up to $900/month.
Ohio	$56,260.62/year	No per diem is paid.
Oklahoma	$38,400/year	$116/day tied to federal rate.
Oregon	$16,284/year	$91/day tied to federal rate.
Pennsylvania	$69,647/year	$128/day tied to federal rate. Can receive actual expenses or per diem.
Puerto Rico	$60,000/year	$122/day within 50 km. of Capitol; $132/day if outside the 50 km.
Rhode Island	$12,646/year	No per diem is paid.
South Carolina	$10,400/year	$95/day for meals and housing, for each statewide session day and committee meeting; tied to federal rate.
South Dakota	$12,000/two-year term	$110/legislative day set by the legislature.
Tennessee	$16,500/year	$141/legislative day tied to federal rate.
Texas	$7,200/year	$128/day set by Ethics Commission.
Utah	$120/day	$79/day lodging allotment for each calendar day, tied to federal rate, $39/day meals.
Vermont	$589/week during session; $118 per day for special sessions or interim committee meetings	Federal per diem rate for Montpelier $69/day for lodging and $35/day for meals for noncommuters; commuters receive $35/day for meals plus mileage.
Virgin Islands	$65,000	$30/day set by the legislature.
Virginia	$18,000/year Senate $17,640/year House	$130/day tied to federal rate.
Washington	$34,227/year	$90/day. Tied to federal rate (80% Olympia area).
West Virginia	$15,000/year	$115/day during session set by compensation commission.
Wisconsin	$45,569/year	$88/day maximum set by compensation commission (90% of federal rate).
Wyoming	$150/day	$85/day set by the legislature, includes travel days for those outside Cheyenne.

Source: National Conference of State Legislatures (2006). Pay of Legislators. [Online]. http://www.ncsl.org/programs/legismgt/about/05salary.htm.

Voting Behavior

These elected "representatives" may still represent the voter, but most people do not regularly vote. For example, according to the U.S. Census, in 2004 only 65.9% of people eligible to vote (18 years or older) were registered to vote, and only 58.3% reported voting in the 2004 elections. This is significant because the 2004 elections were among the most important and divisive elections in modern history. Harrigan (2000, pp. 178–179) explains that, in an indirect representative democracy such as the United States, "without meaningful elections, there is no meaningful democracy."

FIGURE 3-2   Extrasensory Political Participation (ESP): How Politicians Know What We Want When We Don't Vote

Before I move on to whether voters are representative of the population generally, think about this: If people do not vote, how do representatives know what normal citizens think? The law cannot represent the masses, and the **collective conscience** of society cannot be incorporated into the criminal law if people do not vote. Figure 3-2 shows what I call Extrasensory Political Participation (ESP), which is the only way that representatives can represent the people if the people do not speak for themselves.

Voters are not representative of the general population demographically, either. Voting behaviors are positively related to age. This means that as age increases, the like-lihood that one will be registered to vote and will bother to vote increases. The age group most likely to be registered to vote and to actually vote is people 65 to 74 years of age (76.9% and 70.8%, respectively), whereas the group least likely to be registered to vote and to actually vote is people 18 to 24 years old (51.5% and 41.9%, respectively).

As for race and ethnicity, 67.9% of Caucasians are registered to vote, and 60.3% reported voting in 2004, versus only 64.4% and 56.3% of African Americans and only 34.3% and 28% of Hispanics. Voter registration and voting is slightly higher for females than males (67.6% and 60.1% versus 64% and 56.3%, respectively).

Voting is highest among the most educated, as well as for government employees. Finally, in terms of income, there is a positive relationship between income and voting behaviors. For example, the highest level of voter registration and reported voting was for people who earn more than $150,000 per year (82.6% and 78.2%, respectively) ver-sus only 49.5% and 36.5% of people who earned less than $10,000 per year, respectively.

Voting is generally lowest in the South, where poverty and minority residence are very high. According to Harrigan (2000), lower rates of voting by the poor should be attributed to the fact that poor people have been systematically shut out of the electoral process, not that they are bad citizens. In essence, economic stress threatens good citizenship.

From these data, we see that voters are not demographically representative of the population either. Voters tend to be older, disproportionately Caucasian, and wealthier (just like the lawmakers).

Voters can have tremendous power to the degree that politicians fear voters will be antagonized. Yet Harrigan shows how very powerful interest **groups** have their will enacted into law, even when the interests of the voting public are not served.

Special Interests/Lobbying

Let there be no doubt about two key facts when it comes to American politics:

- There is a lot of money involved in the political system.
- Money determines the outcomes.

Figure 3-3 illustrates just how money is involved in the federal system. During the 2006 election cycle, Republicans and Democrats received $2.55 billion.

According to the Center for Responsive Politics in 2006 a total of $870.7 million was raised by 1,318 House candidates to run for office, and 167 Senate candidates raised a total of $637.2 million to run for office. This translates into an average of $660,638 for House candidates and $3,340,862 for Senate candidates. Incumbents, who already held seats and who generally win about 90% of federal elections, raised an average of $1,270,855 (versus $283,075 for challengers) in the House and an astounding $11,317,025 in the Senate (versus $1,814,844 for challengers). If candidates had to raise this money in 2 years in order to run, House incumbents would have to raise an average of $3,477.37 every single day, and Senate incumbents would have to raise $31,038.80 every single day! That gives you an idea of how much money is involved in federal politics.

Where does this money come from? Well, it does not come from average Americans. According to the Center for Responsive Politics, in 2006, far less than 1% of the U.S. adult population (0.35%) gave more than $200 to a political candidate, party, or lobbying group, and only 0.08% gave more than $2,000. Instead, the money comes from major corporations, wealthy individuals, and **political action committees** (PACs) in the form of campaign donations. PACs are groups organized to raise and spend money on political campaigns. According to the Center for Responsive Politics, PACs typically represent corporate, labor, and ideological interests, and are allowed to give $2,300 to

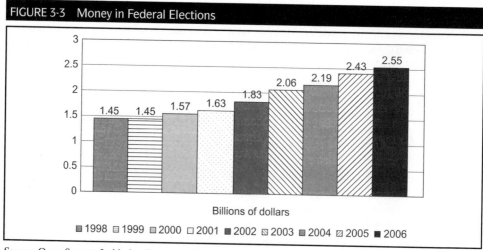

FIGURE 3-3   Money in Federal Elections

■ 1998 ▤ 1999 ▨ 2000 ☐ 2001 ■ 2002 ▨ 2003 ■ 2004 ▨ 2005 ■ 2006

Billions of dollars

Source: Open Secrets. Lobbying Database. [Online]. Available at http://opensecrets.org/lobbyists/index.asp.

any candidate per election, $5,000 to any other PAC, $10,000 to any state or local party committee, and $28,500 annually to any national party. Individuals can also donate the same amounts per election. Table 3-4 illustrates the top PACs between the years of 1998 and 2006 for federal elections. The data show that both major parties are well funded by PACs, and that Democrats are most represented by groups of workers and teachers, whereas Republicans are most represented by corporations. According to the Center for Responsive Politics, strongly Democratic industries include unions, lawyers, and entertainment (TV, movies, music), whereas strongly Republican industries include insurance, pharmaceuticals, and oil and gas. The top ten industries donating to American politics through lobbying include pharmaceuticals, insurance, computers, business associations, electric utilities, education, real estate, hospitals, oil and gas, and entertainment (TV, movies, music).

It is fair to say that American politics is essentially a fund-raising contest: Whoever raises the most money (and spends it) is almost guaranteed to win. While some may claim that the best candidates are the ones most likely to raise the most money—meaning that money does not really determine the winner but merely reflects citizen perceptions of quality candidates—the fact remains that in order to be heard by citizens through media coverage, candidates must raise enormous amounts of money to assure coverage by the mainstream media. For this reason, candidates for federal office must rely on wealthy individuals and PACs to be elected.

TABLE 3-4 Top Political Action Committees (PACs) in Federal Politics (1998–2006)	
Client	*Total*
US Chamber of Commerce	$317,164,680
American Medical Association	$156,375,500
General Electric	$137,770,000
American Hospital Association	$129,114,026
Edison Electric Institute	$105,642,628
AARP	$105,332,064
Pharmaceutical Research & Manufacturers of America	$104,302,000
National Association of Realtors	$97,530,000
Business Roundtable	$97,060,000
Northrop Grumman	$95,682,374
Blue Cross/Blue Shield	$84,156,418
Freddie Mac	$81,884,048
Lockheed Martin	$80,206,965
Boeing Co	$77,898,310
Verizon Communications	$75,836,522
Philip Morris	$75,500,000
General Motors	$71,158,483
Fannie Mae	$70,957,000
Ford Motor Co	$67,670,808
US Telecom Association	$65,280,000

Source: Open Secrets (2007). Lobbying database. [Online]. Available at http://opensecrets.org/lobbyists/index.asp?showyear=a&txtindextype=s.

The picture is the same at the state level. The Center for Public Integrity claims that private interests basically govern our states. According to the Institute on Money in State Politics (2005), candidates for legislative and statewide offices raised $1.8 billion during the 2004 election cycle. The institute reports that: "When combined, money and incumbency are nearly unstoppable. In legislative races, candidates who had the advantage of money, incumbency or both won 94 percent of the time. . . . Winning legislative candidates have more money to spend. Winning candidates raised about three times the amount, on average, that losing candidates raised: $91,360 compared with $33,980 for losing candidates." The average amount raised by a Senate candidate was $118,608 and the average for a House candidate was $52,625.

In 2004, the amount of money raised per voter ranged from $1.13 in North Dakota to $22.44 in New Jersey. This gives an idea of how much each vote costs a candidate to run for office. In my state of North Carolina, the cost per vote was $7.45. The average raised by a House candidate was $67,356 and the average raised by a Senate candidate was $134,181.

As with federal elections, Republicans were most supported by agriculture, construction, energy, finance, insurance, real estate, general business, health, and transportation. Democrats were most supported by labor, lawyers, lobbyists, retirees, and civil servants.

Even though PACs and wealthy individuals seem to have a stranglehold on lawmakers, groups other than powerful elites are involved in the codification of criminal law (Castellano and McGarrell, 1991). For example, the general public makes demands, and events such as media reporting and tens of thousands of lobbying actions among more than a dozen interest groups affect legislation (Brunk and Wilson, 1991; also see Hagan, 1989; McGarrell, 1993; Walker, Spohn, and DeLone, 1996; Wright, 1993). **Interest groups** are collectives of individuals with a common interest or goal who seek to influence public policy (Berry, 1984). Most of the lobbying groups in the United States represent corporations from the United States and abroad (Simon and Hagan, 1999, p.47) but some also represent average Americans. The latter are funded by their members and thus have greater difficulty raising funds.

Interest groups are the "core of democracy, because they represent channels through which people can band together to counteract the advantages that the economic elite have in a political system" (Harrigan, 2000, p. 165). But given that the poor are the least likely to belong to interest groups (Davis and Smith, 1996), and that the richest one-third of U.S. citizens are nearly twice as likely as the poorest one-third to belong to such a group, interest group activity is biased in favor of the wealthy. Simon and Hagan (1999, p. 13) thus claim that "the richest 1 to 5 percent of the population pays for political campaigns. The resultant system is something of a corrupt gravy train that only the rich and powerful may board." The voter is left with the realization that his or her vote, letter, phone call, fax, e-mail, or personal visit carries relatively little weight in a political process driven by money.

HOW THE CRIMINAL LAW FAILS TO PROTECT AMERICANS

Given that the law is made by people who are very different from the typical U.S. citizen, that most people do not inform the law through voting, and that lobbying and special interests influence the law so greatly, is it possible that the law does not really provide protection from the harms that most threaten us? Morgan-Sharp (1999, p. 383) explains that because the law is made "mainly by rich white men and persons who share their interests" but is sold as defining behaviors that are unacceptable to the majority of Americans, we may mistakenly believe that the law protects us. A couple of examples prove the point. First I examine the influence of money on tobacco legislation and then turn to its effects on legislation pertaining to energy policy (e.g., oil and gas).

Big Tobacco

According to the Center for Responsive Politics (2006), major tobacco companies gave $57.6 million in political contributions to national parties between 1990 and 2006, including $23.2 million in PAC money and $29 million in **soft money** (money paid to political parties rather than individual candidates, now banned by Congress). During this time, about 75% of tobacco money went to Republicans. The disparity in contributions to Republicans over Democrats grew from 51% in 1990 to 73% in 2006.

In June of 1998, Senate Republicans defeated legislation that would have raised more than $500 billion over 25 years through a $1.10 tax increase on a pack of cigarettes (Common Cause, 1999; Salant, 1999). The bill was aimed at reducing smoking among children, which has been shown to save lives. According to Common Cause, on June 17, 1998, senators who voted against the bill "received on average more than four times the tobacco industry . . . PAC contributions during the three most recent election cycles as those voting to move the bill forward."

Common Cause reports that between January 1993 through March 1998, the 43 senators who voted against the bill received an average of $20,761 from tobacco PACs, versus $4,970 received on average by the 57 senators voting for the bill. Given that more than 80% of tobacco money goes to Republicans, it is not surprising that 40 of the 42 senators voting against the bill were Republicans.

Is this bribery? No. Tobacco lobbyists are not buying votes, which is illegal. Tobacco companies and federal legislators alike insist that the money does not buy votes; instead it buys access for the companies. That is, large companies—like big tobacco— can afford greater access to lawmakers than everyday citizens and the groups that represent them. In the case of big tobacco, the result is that the most addictive drug on the planet continues to be abused by more than 20% of the American population.

Most significant is that both sides of the aisle regularly accept money from the same lobbying groups. This is one way to assure that the drug remains legal. Meanwhile, the public (more than 75% of whom are not smokers) suffers tremendous harms as a result of tobacco use. Given the harmfulness of this drug, its legal status does not make sense considering that some far less deadly drugs are illegal. Politicians routinely justify the illicit nature of many drugs on the grounds that they are dangerous or deadly. Yet, according to the federal government, deaths from all illicit drugs combined (including abuse of prescription drugs) is approximately 26,000 versus 430,000 for tobacco (see Chapter 11). That's right, according to our own government, tobacco kills more than 15 times more people than all illicit drugs including prescription drugs! Historically, it has been the leading cause of preventable death and illness in the United States every year!

Tobacco executives have avoided criminal convictions for their negligent and reckless behaviors in part because of the tobacco lobby's historical stranglehold on Congress (which has recently tightened even in the wake of increased realization of industry deception). At the same time, people continue to smoke and die because of big tobacco's seemingly bottomless advertising budget and willingness to target even children to ensure the sale of its products. In the 2006 election cycle, tobacco companies donated $19.1 million to federal candidates (82% to Republicans).

Big Oil

According to the Center for Responsive Politics (2006), major oil and gas companies gave $200.9 million in political contributions to national parties between 1990 and 2006, including $62 million in PAC money and $55 million in soft money (money paid to political parties rather than individual candidates, now banned by Congress). About 75% of this money went to Republicans, and the disparity in contributions to Republicans over Democrats grew from 62% in 1990 to 82% in 2006. Some might speculate that the growth in funding to Republicans reflects the fact that the President, Vice President, and Secretary of State in 2006 were all "big oil" people (President Bush ran an oil company, Vice President Cheney ran an oil company, and Secretary of State Condoleezza Rice served on the Board of Directors for an oil company). Logic would suggest that executives with major oil companies might feel a closer bond to such individuals and be more willing to donate money to them and their political party.

During the 1990s when Republicans controlled Congress, and also over the duration of the Bush Administration, big oil benefited greatly from its connections with members of Congress and the White House. In fact, documents show that representatives of major oil companies met privately with Vice President Dick Cheney and his energy task force to lay out strategies for the future of American energy policy (Milbank and Blum, 2005).

Evidence shows that officials from Exxon Mobil, Conoco, Shell, and BP America met with the energy task force when it was developing a national energy policy. Yet, in a joint hearing of the Senate Energy and Commerce committees, the CEOs of Exxon Mobil and Conoco (now ConcoPhillips) said their firms did not take part in any meetings with the White House, as did the CEO of Chevron. Shell's CEO said that the company did not participate to his knowledge, and the chief of BP America said he did not know. Chevron, not named in any document, still gave recommendations about energy policy to the Cheney task force.

This too is not bribery. As with big tobacco, the money (as well as the shared vision of the place of oil in the world) assured large oil companies greater access to policy makers, leaving average citizens without significant influence on issues related to the environment, foreign policy, and alternative energy sources.

Aside from the comfortable relationships between members of the White House and big oil magnates, and the numerous tax breaks and record profits large oil companies have enjoyed as a result, evidence obtained by Judicial Watch from the Commerce Department and reported by the Associated Press shows that the Cheney energy task force poured over "a detailed map of Iraq's oil fields, terminals and pipelines as well as a list entitled 'Foreign Suitors of Iraqi Oilfield Contracts'" (Eley, 2005). This raises the possibility that part of the reason for the invasion of Iraq was for energy concerns. Strangely, the original name for the war in Iraq was "Operation Iraqi Liberation" (its acronym: "OIL").

In Chapter 4, you will see how other corporations also commit harmful acts, many of them explicitly illegal. And you will learn how their acts cause far more damage than all street crimes combined, including more deaths than murder and more property loss than theft and bank robbery.

CONCLUSION

The law, which defines the behaviors that will be pursued by agencies of criminal justice and those that will be broadcast by the media, is created by human beings through a legislative process that is heavily skewed in favor of the wealthy and powerful. (Perhaps this is why some have said that there are two things you just do not want to see being made: sausage and the law.) Because legislators are predominantly Caucasian, male, and wealthy, because voters are also predominantly Caucasian, financially better off, and well educated, and because monied interests have greater access to legislators than other citizens do, the law is heavily biased against powerless groups in society. The first result is that the label of "crime" may not be used to identify the acts that are really the most dangerous to society.

ISSUE IN DEPTH—New Antiterrorism Laws

Although the terrorist attacks of September 11, 2001, against the World Trade Center in New York City and the Pentagon in Washington, D.C., may seem like the first time America was attacked by terrorists, this is not the case. There have been several notable attacks, even in recent history.

For example, on February 26, 1993, a rented van packed with explosives blew up in a basement parking garage within the World Trade Center, killing 6 people and injuring more than 1,000. The convicted bombers received life sentences for this crime, which was aimed at killing far more people using cyanide canisters that did not explode as planned. On April 19, 1995, a rented van packed with explosives blew up in front of the Murrah Federal Building in Oklahoma City, killing 168 people and injuring more than 400. The convicted murderer was executed by lethal injection in Terre Haute, Indiana.

As a result of such events, our federal government has passed various laws that have great importance for the activities of police, courts, and corrections at all levels of government. They also have great import for the main issues of this book, especially the balance between proponents of the crime control and due process models of criminal justice.

What follows is a brief summary of some of the most important antiterrorism laws and some commentary on their meaning for justice in the United States. First, *The Antiterrorism and Effective Death Penalty Act of 1996* was signed into law on April 24, 1996. According to the U.S. State Department, this law:

- prohibits U.S. foreign assistance to governments that provide assistance or lethal military equipment to terrorist-list governments;
- prohibits sales or licenses for export of defense articles or defense services to countries the president determines are not fully cooperating with U.S. antiterrorism efforts;
- authorizes exclusion of aliens who are members or representatives of foreign terrorist groups designated as such by the secretary of state;
- directs the Federal Aviation Administration to require foreign air carriers serving the United States to use the identical security measures utilized by U.S. carriers;

- criminalizes numerous forms of terrorism, such as possessing certain chemical and biological materials and conspiring to commit acts of terrorism; and
- makes dozens of types of killings involving terrorism eligible for the death penalty.

The aspects of the law that are most controversial deal with limiting *habeas corpus petitions,* which are judicial mandates to prison officials requiring that inmates be brought to the court to determine whether they are lawfully imprisoned based on the facts of their cases and the law. According to the federal judiciary, the law "creates one-year deadlines for filing habeas petitions, limits successive petitions, and generally restricts the review of state prisoner petitions if the claim was adjudicated on the merits in the state courts." The law also "establishes special habeas corpus procedures for capital cases in states with mechanisms for the appointment, compensation, and payment of reasonable litigation expenses of counsel in state post-conviction proceedings brought by indigent prisoners" and "establishes a 180-day time frame in which a petitioner must file a habeas petition, restricts the scope of federal review." When it comes to the death penalty, we know that expediting the process by limiting appeals increases the likelihood that errors (in this case, fatal errors) will be made (see Chapter 10). Any time an innocent person is punished for a crime, justice is not achieved. Finally, the law makes it easier to deport aliens by streamlining the deportation process after they serve their sentences.

The Aviation and Transportation Security Act was signed into law on November 19, 2001. According to the GOP, this law:

- establishes a new Transportation Security Administration (TSA) within the Department of Transportation (DOT) responsible for security for all modes of transportation and headed by a new Under Secretary;
- requires that the federal government assume responsibility for all passenger and baggage screening at commercial airports in the United States;
- requires that the TSA hire, train, and deploy federal screeners, federal security managers, federal security personnel, and federal law enforcement officers;
- requires the TSA to adopt new, stricter standards for airport baggage screeners;
- requires that 100% of checked baggage be screened;
- requires the deployment of Federal Air Marshals for certain flights; and
- directs the new Under Secretary, in consultation with the Federal Aviation Administration (FAA), to take action to strengthen cockpit doors and provides for pilots to carry firearms to defend their aircraft.

The aspects of the law that are most controversial deal with directing pilots to be armed. Many Americans feel uncomfortable with pilots being armed and/or pilots firing weapons while flying airplanes. Even pilots spoke out against being responsible for defending their planes, suggesting that the government and the airlines ought to take responsibility for preventing acts of violence in the air.

After 9/11 other new laws were passed by Congress and President Bush authorized by executive order other measures aimed at disrupting terrorist attacks. The net effect of these efforts has been a further expansion of crime control values and an erosion of due process values.

Perhaps the most controversial law to be passed in the wake of the attacks of September 11, 2001, is the *USA PATRIOT Act* (Uniting and Strengthening America by Providing Appropriate Tools Required to Intercept and Obstruct Terrorism), which was signed into law with almost no debate on October 24, 2001 (only 45 days after the attacks). The bill was 342 pages long, yet many members of Congress say they did not even read it before voting in favor of it.

The stated purpose of the law was "to deter and punish terrorist acts in the United States and around the world, to enhance law enforcement investigatory tools, and for other purposes." It is these "other purposes" that have legal experts and normal citizens very worried. This law is very complicated and modifies several existing laws, but essentially it allows the Federal Bureau of Investigation (FBI), Central Intelligence Agency (CIA), and agencies of the Office of Homeland Security to:

- access medical, financial, library, educational, and other personal records of any people as long as a "significant purpose" is for "the gathering of foreign intelligence";
- tap any and all phones of such people and monitor their Internet use, tracking every phone call made and received, and every Web site visited; and
- label people "domestic terrorists" if they criticize your government in any way that "influences the policy of a government by intimidation or coercion" or "intimidates or coerces a civilian population."

Legal experts have suggested that the law erodes elements of the First, Fourth, Fifth, Sixth, and Eighth Amendments to the U.S. Constitution, because it is possible that the U.S. government will use its unlimited authority to spy on American citizens without any evidence of criminal activity, to do so in secret, without judicial oversight, and without any accountability to the American people.

Perhaps this is why, at the time of this writing, more than 400 towns and counties have already passed resolutions against this law. Additionally, eight states have done the same. The cities that passed resolutions include New York City and Washington D.C., which witnessed the worst of the terrorist attacks on 9/11.

Together, these "civil liberties safe zones" represent more than 85 million Americans. Other bodies, such as the National League of Cities, representing 18,000 cities, towns, villages, and 225 million citizens, also passed resolutions.

While many sections of the USA PATRIOT Act were valid only to sunset at the end of 2005, Congress made 14 of the 16 provisions permanent law in March 2006 and renewed the remaining 2 for an additional four years. Thus, most of the USA PATRIOT Act—which was meant to be a temporary law designed to protect us from imminent attacks after 9/11—is now permanent law. Representative James Sensenbrenner, who had said that USA PATRIOT Act renewal would "be done over my dead body . . . I said at the time I did not think there were the votes to pass the [USA PATRIOT Act] in the House without the sunset and I still stand by that" (Gilbert, 2003), then said after the House renewed the law: "Why sunset legislation where there's been no actual record of abuse and vigorous oversight?"

In fact, reported abuses are widespread. In July of 2003, an Inspector General report documented 34 credible civil rights and civil liberties violations under the USA PATRIOT Act. This was out of the more than 1,000 complaints to the Justice Department about the law. The allegations included "unwarranted cell searches and illegal searches of personal residences and property" (Bohn, 2003). The report also contained "credible accusations . . . against employees of the F.B.I., the Drug Enforcement Administration, and the Immigration and Naturalization Service."

More recently, reports showed that the FBI has spied on thousands of Americans and simultaneously failed to report their investigations as required by law. The American Civil Liberties Union summarizes findings from a report of the Justice Department's Inspector General: "The FBI has issued significantly more National Security Letters than previously disclosed. The report found serious breaches of department regulations and numerous potential violations of the law. It also criticized the FBI for lax managerial controls that invited abuse, and found that agents had claimed 'exigent circumstances' where none existed, and that some recipients had provided more information than authorized by law."

National Security Letters can be used to acquire e-mail and telephone records, as well as financial information like credit and bank transactions. The USA PATRIOT Act ended the requirement that such records belong to someone under suspicion; today any innocent person's records can also be obtained as long as federal agents consider them relevant!

President Bush also authorized a top secret domestic wiretapping program under the auspices of the National Security Agency to spy on Americans, a program that top legal scholars referred to as illegal (Nolan et al., 2006). The program, leaked to the *New York Times,* allegedly allowed citizens' phones to be tapped, e-mails to be read, and mail to be opened. He also authorized the detention of American citizens as "enemy combatants."

Congress then passed the Military Commission Act of 2006, giving the president legal authority to utilize military tribunals in terrorism cases against "enemy combatants." According to the Bill of Rights Defense Committee, the law:

- allows military tribunals (which were rejected by the Supreme Court as unconstitutional in June 2006);
- makes legal any illegal acts committed by U.S. personnel during war (committed before December 30, 2005);
- disallows any person harmed by the U.S. from filing a claim in a U.S. court (in violation of the Geneva Conventions);
- strips legal U.S. residents of their right to challenge their detention in court if they're accused of being "enemy combatants";
- abolishes the right of Guantanamo detainees to challenge their detention;
- approves the CIA program that allows waterboarding and other forms of torture; and
- names any individual, including citizens, as an "unlawful enemy combatant" if they provide "material support" to those engaged in hostilities against the United States.

These laws and executive orders, as well as the reactions to them by Americans, serve as a good example of the struggle to maintain a balance between security (crime control or crime prevention) and individual liberty (due process). At this time, it is safe to conclude that efforts have been made by the U.S. government to restrict the liberties of all Americans in order to prevent or reduce the threat of terrorism on our soil.

We may be wise, then, to carefully consider the admonition of Benjamin Franklin, who wrote in 1755: "Those who would give up essential Liberty, to purchase a little temporary Safety, deserve neither Liberty nor Safety." A slightly altered version of this statement appears on a stairwell of the pedestal of the Statue of Liberty in New York Harbor, overlooking the very city that suffered the worst of the terrorist attacks on September 11, 2001.

KEY TERMS

administrative law
case law
carjacking
civil law
codify
collective conscience
common law
conflict view of the law
consensus view of the law

constitutional law
criminal conviction
criminal law
interest groups
law
mala in se
mala prohibita
natural law
pluralist view of the law

political action committees
positive law
preponderance of evidence
procedural criminal law
social contract
soft money
statutory law
substantive criminal law

DISCUSSION QUESTIONS

1. Define the law.
2. Explain the difference between so-called *mala in se* and *mala prohibita* crimes. Provide examples of each. Do you think this distinction is an important one? Why or why not?
3. Make a list of different types of law, and define each.
4. What is the difference between natural law and positive law?
5. Try to think of some behaviors that you think violate natural law but not positive law. Also, are there behaviors that violate positive law but not natural law? Give examples.
6. Where do the following types of law come from: constitutional law, statutory law, case law, and administrative law?
7. How did common law shape American criminal law?
8. Contrast substantive and procedural criminal law.
9. What are the main purposes of the law?
10. What do you think is the most important purpose of the criminal law?
11. Describe the typical lawmaker in the United States. How does he or she differ from the average American?
12 What are the implications for the law regarding legislators being so different from those whom they serve?
13. Describe the typical voter in the United States. How does he or she differ from the average American?
14. What is a PAC?
15. Provide an example of how money shapes the law.
16. Do you think the law represents the interests of Americans? Why or why not?
17. Which is more accurate in explaining the interests served by the law—the consensus model of lawmaking, the conflict model of lawmaking, or the pluralist model of lawmaking? Why?
18. What is the USA PATRIOT Act? In your opinion, is this law necessary to protect America from terrorism?
19. Which efforts by President Bush do you think are reasonable and which are unreasonable given the threat of terrorism faced by the United States?

PART

II

CRIME: IMAGES AND REALITIES

Chapter 4   Crime: Which Is Worse, Crime on the Streets or
             Crime in the Suites?
Chapter 5   "The Sky Is Falling! The Sky Is Falling!"—Media
             Protrayals of Crime and Criminal Justice

CHAPTER

4

CRIME: WHICH IS WORSE, CRIME ON THE STREETS OR CRIME IN THE SUITES?

1. Introduction
2. What Is a Crime?
    a. Legal Definition of Crime
    • Box 4-1.   Valid Defenses to Criminal Charges
3. Types of Crime in the United States
    a. Serious/Street Crime
    • Box 4-2.   Serious Crimes: Part I Offenses of the UCR
    • Box 4-3.   Less Serious Crimes: Part II Offenses of the UCR
    • Box 4-4.   NIBRS Offenses
    b. Other Conceptions of Crime: Elite Deviance
    • Box 4-5.   Iraq Study Group Criticizes Iraq War Spending
    c. What Is Victimization?
    d. A Comparison of Harms Associated with Crimes and "NonCrimes"
    • Box 4-6.   Section 2.07, Model Penal Code
4. Sources of Crime Information: Do We Really Know How Much Crime Is Out There?
    a. Uniform Crime Reports
    b. National Crime Victimization Survey
    c. American Crime Trends According to the UCR and NCVS
    • Box 4-7.   Abortion and Crime
    d. Self-Report Studies
    • Box 4-8.   Criminologists Are Criminals, Too!
    e. Sources of Data on Elite Deviance
5. Conclusion
6. Issue in Depth—Enron, WorldCom, Tyco, and the Other Corporate Bandits
7. Key Terms
8. Discussion Questions

INTRODUCTION

Close your eyes and picture a crime. What do you see? What does the offender look like? What about the victim? The image that you probably see is likely consistent with those vigorously pursued by American criminal justice agencies and portrayed in the American mass media. But what is a crime? Why are some crimes considered more serious than others? How do we know how much crime there is in the United States? Is the crime problem getting worse or is it getting better? This chapter answers these questions. I will argue that crime in the United States is probably not as bad as you think it is, unless you are thinking of some violent crimes such as murder and corporate crime. I also show that our criminal justice network is focused almost exclusively on street crimes committed by a small segment of our population. Implications for justice are discussed.

WHAT IS A CRIME?

When you think of the word **crime**, you probably have a good idea of what it means. Although there is a straightforward legal definition of crime, most of us think of crimes as any behaviors that are done intentionally and cause physical or financial harm to another person. For example, if you were standing on a street corner minding your own business, and someone came up and poked a pencil into your eye, causing a loss of vision, you would probably feel that you had been victimized by crime. Even if it was not against the law, you would probably think it should be. If a corporation manufactured a toaster that shot sparks into your eyes, you might also feel like a victim of crime, even if it was not specifically a violation of the criminal law to manufacture such a toaster. Whether or not any act violates the law, you may feel like a crime victim when you are harmed by another. The **natural definition of crime** is any act that is seen as "fundamentally wrong, strongly disapproved, and deserving of punishment," regardless of whether it is legal (Gottfredson, 1999, p. 47).

Recall the discussion of natural law in Chapter 3. Some argue that behaviors that violate natural law should be considered crimes. This natural view of crime, which appeals to our common sense, is very similar to the **legal definition of crime**, with one significant exception. Legally, a crime occurs only when an act violates the criminal law. As you saw in Chapter 3, there is no crime without law. Clearly, there are scores of behaviors that kill and injure us and take our property; many of them are committed intentionally but are not against the criminal law. Such acts are not legally considered crimes, even if we all think the act is wrong, immoral, deviant, or bad. What makes the act a crime is that it is written down as a crime by the government.

This means that crime is made up—invented—by people. Quinney (1970, p. 15) makes this point clear in his book, ***The Social Reality of Crime***, when he writes:

> Crime is a definition of behavior that is conferred on some persons by others. Agents of the law, representing segments of a politically organized society, are responsible for formulating and administering criminal laws. Persons and behaviors, therefore, become criminal because of the formulation and application of criminal definitions. Thus, crime is created.

Crime does not exist in nature. It is something that human beings have invented and continue to invent every day.

This is not to say that there is no harmful behavior in nature. Many behaviors in nature kill and produce harms. For example, on the plains of Africa, lions and hyenas fight for the right to kill zebras and other animals. This is part of Darwin's concept of "survival of the fittest." When lions and hyenas kill zebras or even one another in order to eat, defend their territory, or gain mating advantages, the zebra police are not called out to round up the killers in the interests of justice. Why not? I hope the answer is obvious—because zebras do not call such killings crimes. It is not illegal for lions or hyenas to kill zebras. Human beings are the only species to legislate killing as a crime (and only under certain circumstances, because there are plenty of ways to kill people, even intentionally, without committing a crime).

Since crime is invented, no behavior is inherently criminal and any behavior can be defined as a crime. These commonsense points are important to remember when thinking about crime. If you can remember these points, it will be much easier for you to understand this book. In Chapter 11, for example, I will explore decriminalization and legalization of drugs as alternatives to the war on drugs. In that chapter, you will see that many "drug crimes" are not really all that harmful. They are illegal only because human beings have made them illegal. Drugs that are illegal can also be made legal (whether they should be is also discussed in Chapter 11).

Because crime is a human invention, there is some disagreement about what behaviors should constitute crime among those who study crime for a living. Most criminologists and criminal justice scholars tend to limit their studies to behaviors that violate the criminal law, and a very large share of those study only **street crimes** (crimes committed on the streets of America). As you'll see in this chapter, this is problematic because street crimes are not the most harmful acts in America.

Legal Definition of Crime

Legally, a crime occurs when a person either acts, fails to act, attempts to act, or agrees to act in a way that is in violation of the criminal law, and without defense or justification. This legal definition of crime is made up of several elements. The first element, **acts**, includes any behaviors that are actually carried out, such as intentionally taking the life of another (murder) or taking someone's wallet from his or her back pocket (theft). **Attempts** are acts that are not successfully carried out, such as unsuccessfully trying to break into someone's home through a locked front door (attempted burglary). Agreeing to act is called a **conspiracy**. An example would be verbally agreeing with a friend to kill the president of the United States even if you did not ever attempt to do so. Examples of **failures to act** include not paying your taxes or not paying child support. The most important element of the definition of crime is the criminal law, which is made up of federal or state statutes that specify what behaviors are in violation of the criminal law. As noted, without the law, there is no crime.

The final element of this definition is **without defense or justification**. This is an important element, for a person may commit an act (**actus reus**) that is against the law, and even may do so with intent (**mens rea**), yet may not be a criminal if he or she has a valid reason for committing the act (Cole and Smith, 2006). Examples of valid defenses might include an alibi, a justification, an excuse, or a procedural defense (Schmalleger, 2001, p. 143). In addition to an **alibi**, which is a statement that suggests the defendant was somewhere else at the time of the crime and thus truly innocent, there are defenses that can be used that acknowledge the defendant did in fact commit the act. They are based on the premise that even though the defendant committed the act, he or she is still not responsible for the crime and thus not legally guilty.

Justifications assert that the crime was necessary in order to avoid some greater evil. **Excuses** assert that the crime can be accepted based on some special condition or emergency. **Procedural defenses** suggest either some form of discrimination by criminal justice officials or some form of misconduct, either intended or not. Examples of each are provided in the Box 4-1.

BOX 4-1

VALID DEFENSES TO CRIMINAL CHARGES

JUSTIFICATIONS

Self-defense: If you are afraid for your life and act to protect it (and sometimes to protect your property)—for example, if you attack someone who breaks into your house—you may plead not guilty because of self-defense.

Necessity: If you are personally at risk of dying or becoming ill unless you commit a crime—for example, if you find yourself in danger of freezing to death unless you break into someone's cabin in the middle of the woods—you may plead not guilty because of necessity.

EXCUSES

Duress: If you are coerced or forced to commit a crime by another—for example, if someone shoves a gun in your face and demands that you help him or her rob a bank—you may plead not guilty because of duress.

Immaturity: If you are too young to understand right from wrong—for example, if you are 5 years old and you playfully aim a gun at a playmate and pull the trigger—you may plead not guilty because of immaturity.

Insanity: If you are unable to understand the difference between right and wrong or are unable to adjust your behavior accordingly—for example, if

you have been diagnosed with a severe mental illness that impairs your thought processes—you may plead not guilty because of insanity.

Involuntary intoxication: If you become impaired by the action of another—for example, if someone slips a drug into your drink and you violently attack another person—you may plead not guilty because of involuntary intoxication.

PROCEDURAL DEFENSES

Entrapment: If a government agent such as a police officer approaches you and offers you the opportunity to commit a crime, and the offense did not originate in your own mind—for example, if you buy drugs from an undercover officer who has come to your door while you are at home enjoying a dinner with your family—you may plead not guilty because of entrapment.

Selective prosecution: If some people are singled out for a particular punishment based on extralegal factors such as race—for example, if you are pulled over for speeding and learn that blacks are more likely to be pulled over and ticketed, as well as prosecuted, because of "police profiling"—you may plead not guilty because of selective entrapment.

Additionally, for an act to be legally considered a crime, it must be committed with **culpability** (or responsibility). This includes acts that are committed under any of the following circumstances.

- **Intentionally:**   Committed with a guilty mind on purpose (e.g., sticking a gun in someone's face and pulling the trigger with the intent to kill)
- **Negligently:**   Committed as a result of a failure to meet normal or recognized expectations (e.g., failing to follow safety regulations meant to protect human life)
- **Recklessly:**   Committed without due caution for human life or property (e.g., driving while intoxicated)
- **Knowingly:**   Committed with knowledge that an outcome is likely (e.g., continuing to manufacture a product after product testing revealed a high likelihood of a deadly defect)

Generally, acts committed with intent are considered more serious than those committed negligently, recklessly, or knowingly. Considering that a person who is killed negligently, recklessly, or knowingly is just as dead as one killed intentionally, you may question the logic of such distinctions.

TYPES OF CRIME IN THE UNITED STATES

Serious/Street Crime

Remember what I asked you to do at the beginning of this chapter? Close your eyes and picture a crime. What do you see? What does the offender look like? What is he or she doing? What about the victim?

Chances are, if you do this, you will see a particular type of crime committed by a particular type of person against another particular type of person. In all likelihood, you saw a crime that is consistent with what our government perceives as **serious crime**, that which is visible to us as ordinary U.S. citizens. What does "serious" mean?

You may consider something serious that is important to you, perhaps something you fear or are worried about. You might consider crimes serious if they cause or threaten great danger and harm (either physical or financial).

The term *serious* also might be related to the frequency of a behavior. For example, a behavior may be very harmful but may occur so rarely that it does not create fear or worry in citizens. Would this type of act be considered serious?

The U.S. government has an answer to these questions. The Uniform Crime Reporting Program (UCR), to be discussed later in this chapter, is a source of crime information compiled by the Federal Bureau of Investigation (FBI) each year. This source of data was created because of a need to gather and disseminate national crime statistics. In the 1920s, the International Association of Chiefs of Police (IACP) formed a committee to create a uniform system for recording police statistics. Crimes were originally evaluated on the basis of the following criteria:

- Harmfulness
- Frequency of occurrence
- Pervasiveness in all geographic areas of the country
- Likelihood of being reported to the police

After a preliminary compilation in 1929 of a list of crimes that met these criteria, the committee completed its plan for developing the UCR. Statistics on these crimes were collected beginning in the 1930s.

As noted within each year's UCR publication, "Seven offenses were chosen to serve as an Index for gauging the overall volume and rate of crime." These offenses, known as **Part I Index Offenses**, included the violent crimes of murder and non-negligent manslaughter, forcible rape, robbery, and aggravated assault and the property crimes of burglary, theft, and motor vehicle theft. In 1979, arson was added to the UCR list, for a total of eight "serious" crimes. These terms are defined in Box 4-2.

BOX 4-2

SERIOUS CRIMES: PART I OFFENSES OF THE UCR

Criminal homicide: Includes murder and nonnegligent manslaughter, the willful (nonnegligent) killing of one human being by another. Deaths caused by negligence, attempts to kill, suicides, and accidental deaths are excluded. Justifiable homicides are classified separately, and traffic fatalities are excluded.

Forcible rape: The carnal knowledge of a female forcibly and against her will. Rapes by force and attempts or assaults with the intent to rape, regardless of the age of the victim, are included. Statutory offenses (where no force is used but the victim is under the legal age of consent) are excluded.

Robbery: Taking or attempting to take anything of value from the care, custody, or control of a person or persons by force, threat of force or violence, and/or by putting the victim in fear.

Aggravated assault: An unlawful attack by one person on another for the purpose of inflicting severe or aggravated bodily injury, which usually is accompanied by the use of a weapon or by means likely to produce death or great bodily harm. Simple assaults are excluded.

Burglary: The unlawful entering of a structure to commit a felony or a theft. Attempted forcible entry is included.

Larceny-theft: The unlawful taking, carrying, leading, or riding away of property from the possession or constructive possession of another. Examples are thefts of bicycles or automobile accessories, shoplifting, pocket-picking, or the stealing of any property or article that is not taken by force and violence or by fraud. Attempted thefts are included. Embezzlement, confidence games, forgery, worthless checks, and so on, are excluded.

Motor vehicle theft: The theft or attempted theft of a motor vehicle, defined as a vehicle that is self-propelled and runs on the surface and not on rails. Motorboats, construction equipment, airplanes, and farming equipment are specifically excluded from this category.

Arson: Any willful or malicious burning or attempt to burn, with or without intent to defraud, a dwelling house, public building, motor vehicle or aircraft, or personal property of another.

Given their own discussion of what constitutes a serious offense, you might expect that the street crimes listed in Box 4-2 would be the ones that cause the greatest harm (either physical or financial), occur with great frequency, are pervasive throughout the country, and are likely to be reported to the police. Since the majority of crimes overall are not reported to the police, you may wonder why some crimes that are highly unlikely to be reported to the police (e.g., theft) are included.

In discussing the eight types of serious crime in each annual UCR report, it is claimed that "these are serious crimes by nature and/or volume." That is, these crimes supposedly cause the most harm, occur with the greatest frequency, and are the most widespread.

Other types of crimes, known as **Part II Offenses** of the UCR, are literally considered "less serious." Presumably, it is because they either cause less harm, occur with less frequency, or are not as pervasive throughout the country. This list of Part II offenses is provided in Box 4-3. As a justification for their inclusion in this list, the FBI explains:

> Not all crimes, such as Embezzlement, are readily brought to the attention of the police. Also, some serious crimes, such as Kidnapping, occur infrequently. Therefore, for practical purposes, the reporting of offenses known is limited to the selected crime classifications because they are the crimes most likely to be reported and most likely to occur with sufficient frequency to provide an adequate basis for comparison.

No explanation is offered for their exclusion from the list of Part I or "serious" offenses based on the degree of relative harm they cause, how frequently they occur, and/or how pervasive they are throughout the country.

BOX 4-3

LESS SERIOUS CRIMES: PART II OFFENSES OF THE UCR

Simple assaults: Assaults and attempted assaults in which no weapon is used and which do not result in serious or aggravated injury to the victim.

Forgery and counterfeiting: Making, altering, uttering, or possessing, with intent to defraud, anything false in the semblance of that which is true. Attempts are included.

Fraud: Fraudulent conversion and obtaining money or property by false pretenses. Confidence games and bad checks, except forgeries and counterfeiting, are included.

Embezzlement: Misappropriation or misapplication of money or property entrusted to one's care, custody, or control.

Buying, receiving, or possessing stolen property: Buying, receiving, and possessing stolen property, including attempts.

Vandalism: Willful or malicious destruction, injury, disfigurement, or defacement of any public or private property, real or personal, without consent of the owner or persons having custody or control. Attempts are included.

(continued)

BOX 4-3 (*Continued*)

Prostitution and commercialized vice:
Sex offenses of a commercialized nature,
such as prostitution, keeping a bawdy
house, procuring or transporting women
for immoral purposes. Attempts are
included.

Sex offenses: Statutory rape and offenses
against chastity, common decency, morals,
and the like. Attempts are included.

Drug abuse violations: State and/or
local offenses relating to the unlawful
possession, sale, use, growing, and
manufacturing of narcotic drugs.

Gambling: Promoting, permitting, or
engaging in illegal gambling.

Offenses against the family and children:
Nonsupport, neglect, desertion, or abuse
of family and children. Attempts are
included.

Driving under the influence: Driving or
operating any vehicle or common carrier
while drunk or under the influence of
liquor or narcotics.

Liquor law violations: State and/or local
liquor law violations except drunkenness
and driving under the influence. Federal
violations are excluded.

Drunkenness: Offenses relating to
drunkenness or intoxication. Driving
under the influence is excluded.

Disorderly conduct: Breach of the
peace.

Vagrancy: Begging, loitering, and the
like. Includes prosecutions under the
charge of suspicious person.

Curfew violations and loitering:
Offenses relating to violations of local
curfew or loitering ordinances where
such laws exist.

Running away: Limited to juveniles
taken into protective custody under
provisions of local statutes.

Why are such acts considered less serious? We'll return to that issue later in this chapter when we compare harms caused by serious crimes with harms caused by other types of behaviors. I will illustrate that the acts we focus on least actually cause more harm, both physically and financially, and occur with greater frequency than the crimes we consider the most serious. You might correctly wonder, then, whether legal definitions of crime are appropriately limited. If not, why not? Recall the examination of who makes the law in Chapter 3. Why would legislators, who are predominantly older and wealthy Caucasian males, define acts committed by people like themselves as crimes and especially as serious crimes?

Apparently, even the federal government is aware of the contradiction in what they claim to be the most serious crimes and those that actually cause the most damage. The result is the creation of the **National Incident Based Reporting System** (NIBRS). This is a data set that includes information on individual criminal incidents, including arrests. NIBRS includes 22 categories of offenses and 46 specific crimes (called **Group A offenses**), as well as 11 categories of offenses for which only arrest data are collected (called **Group B offenses**). In NIBRS, typical street crimes such as theft have been combined with white-collar crimes such as embezzlement and fraud, which makes sense as each is a form of stealing someone else's property. However, NIBRS was not created to finally recognize the seriousness of white-collar crimes by treating them as "serious crimes." Instead, NIBRS is aimed at gathering more specific information about individual criminal incidents (such as time and place of occurrence, and characteristics of victims and offenders) to provide law enforcement with better information in their fight against crime.

The Bureau of Justice Statistics (2007) explains that, relative to the UCR, "NIBRS collects more details on more categories of crime, including concurrent offenses, weapons, injury, location, property loss and characteristics of the victims, offenders and arrestees." BJS explains that NIBRS increases what we know about crime because:

- It expands the number of offense categories included.
- It gives greater detail on individual crime incidents (offenses, offenders, victims, property, and arrests).
- It links arrests and clearances to specific incidents or offenses.
- It includes all offenses in an incident rather than only the most serious offense.
- It distinguishes between attempted and completed crimes.
- It links offense, offender, victim, property, and arrestee variables.

Box 4-4 lists NIBRS offenses. (Note: The offenses are not defined by the FBI except when listing specific types of offenses that fall into each category.)

BOX 4-4

NIBRS OFFENSES

Group A offenses

- *Arson*
- *Assault offenses*—aggravated assault, simple assault, intimidation
- *Bribery*
- *Burglary/breaking and entering*
- *Counterfeiting/forgery*
- *Destruction/damage/vandalism of property*
- *Drug/narcotic offenses*—drug/narcotic violations, drug equipment violations
- *Embezzlement*
- *Extortion/blackmail*
- *Fraud offenses*—false pretenses, swindle, confidence game, credit card/automatic teller machine fraud, impersonation, welfare fraud, wire fraud
- *Gambling offenses*—betting/wagering, operating/promoting/assisting gambling, gambling equipment violations, sports tampering
- *Homicide offenses*—murder and nonnegligent manslaughter, negligent manslaughter, justifiable homicide
- *Kidnapping/abduction*
- *Larceny/theft offenses*—pocket-picking, purse-snatching, shoplifting, theft from building, theft from coin-operated machine or device, theft from motor vehicle, theft of motor vehicle parts or accessories, all other larceny
- *Motor vehicle theft*
- *Pornography/obscene material*
- *Prostitution offenses*—prostitution, assisting or promoting prostitution
- *Robbery*
- *Sex offenses, forcible*—forcible rape, forcible sodomy, sexual assault with an object, forcible fondling

(continued)

BOX 4-4   (*Continued*)

- *Sex offenses, nonforcible*—incest, statutory rape
- *Stolen property offenses (receiving, etc.)*
- *Weapon law violations*

Group B offenses

- *Bad checks*
- *Curfew/loitering/vagrancy violations*

- *Disorderly conduct*
- *Driving under the influence*
- *Drunkenness*
- *Family offenses, nonviolent*
- *Liquor law violations*
- *Peeping Tom*
- *Runaway*
- *Trespass of real property*
- *All other offenses*

According to the FBI: "NIBRS has the capability of furnishing information on nearly every major criminal justice issue facing law enforcement today, including terrorism, white-collar crime, weapons offenses, missing children where criminality is involved, drug/narcotics offenses, drug involvement in all offenses, hate crimes, spouse abuse, abuse of the elderly, child abuse, domestic violence, juvenile crime/gangs, parental kidnapping, organized crime, pornography/child pornography, driving under the influence, and alcohol-related offenses." In fact, NIBRS still does not go far enough because it does not collect data on the behaviors that pose the greatest threats to Americans.

Other Conceptions of Crime: Elite Deviance

As noted at the onset of this chapter, you may feel like a "crime victim" when you are victimized by an act that is committed against you on purpose. But if this act was not legally defined as a "crime" at the time it was committed against you, then legally you were not a crime victim.

Does that mean you were not victimized? Of course not. You may be victimized by acts outside the scope of the criminal justice system. For example, **elite deviance** is a term put forth by Simon (2005) in his book of the same name. It includes not only criminal acts but also unethical acts, civil and regulatory violations, and other harmful acts committed intentionally, recklessly, negligently, or knowingly. Elite deviance is a term that encompasses **white-collar crime** (Sutherland, 1977a, 1977b), **corporate crime** (Clinard and Yeager, 2005), **corporate violence** (Frank and Lynch, 1992), **occupational crime** (Blount, 2002), **governmental deviance** (Erman and Lundman, 2001), **crimes of the state** (Michalowski and Kramer, 2006), **crimes of privilege** (Shover and Wright, 2000), **profit without honor** (Rosoff, Pontell, and Tillman, 2006), and those **crimes by any other name** (Reiman, 2006) committed by our **trusted criminals** (Friedrichs, 2006). These are acts that cause tremendous physical, financial, and moral harms to Americans.

Here's one example of elite deviance: Many Americans criticize "big government" for wasting tax money on social programs. Yet when money is wasted on national defense, Americans seem less concerned (this is not to say that national defense spending itself is a waste of money). Sherrill (1997) describes many defense-spending scandals. According to Sherrill, $13 billion paid to weapons contractors between 1985 and 1995 was simply "lost," and another $15 billion remains unaccounted for. Simon and

Hagan (1999, p. 33) claim that military waste and fraud cost taxpayers $172 billion per year.

President Bush's (the second) defense budget was $399 billion for 2003, but this did not include the costs of the war in Iraq and costs of the U.S. occupation of the country. By 2007, the defense budget was $439.3 billion per year (White House, 2007) and Congress had authorized nearly $400 billion for the wars in Iraq and Afghanistan, all of which was funded through emergency appropriations rather than the normal budget process. Box 4-5 contains a summary of spending for the Iraq war in the Iraq Study Group Report (2006).

BOX 4-5

IRAQ STUDY GROUP CRITICIZES IRAQ WAR SPENDING

Budget Preparation, Presentation, and Review

The public interest is not well served by the government's preparation, presentation, and review of the budget for the war in Iraq. First, most of the costs of the war show up not in the normal budget request but in requests for emergency supplemental appropriations. This means that funding requests are drawn up outside the normal budget process, are not offset by budgetary reductions elsewhere, and move quickly to the White House with minimal scrutiny. Bypassing the normal review erodes budget discipline and accountability.

Second, the executive branch presents budget requests in a confusing manner, making it difficult for both the general public and members of Congress to understand the request or to differentiate it from counterterrorism operations around the world or operations in Afghanistan. Detailed analyses by budget experts are needed to answer what should be a simple question: "How much money is the President requesting for the war in Iraq?"

Finally, circumvention of the budget process by the executive branch erodes oversight and review by Congress. The authorizing committees (including the House and Senate Armed Services committees) spend the better part of a year reviewing the President's annual budget request. When the President submits an emergency supplemental request, the authorizing committees are bypassed. The request goes directly to the appropriations committees, and they are pressured by the need to act quickly so that troops in the field do not run out of funds. The result is a spending bill that passes Congress with perfunctory review. Even worse, the must-pass appropriations bill becomes loaded with special spending projects that would not survive the normal review process.

RECOMMENDATION 72: Costs for the war in Iraq should be included in the President's annual budget request, starting in FY 2008: the war is in its fourth year, and the normal budget process should not be circumvented. Funding requests for the war in Iraq should be presented clearly to Congress and the American people. Congress must carry out its constitutional responsibility to review budget requests for the war in Iraq carefully and to conduct oversight.

SOURCE: The Iraq Study Group Report, http://www.usip.org/isg/iraq_study_group_report/report/1206/iraq_study_group_report.pdf (pp. 59–60).

As it turns out, tens of billions of dollars have simply been lost in Iraq! Is losing money intended for national defense a crime? No. Is spending money outside the normal budget process so that it is not accountable to the American people a crime? No.

Beyond such spending problems, evidence also clearly shows malfeasance involved in the Iraq war spending. Major contractors in all areas of business—from cell phone companies to security services—have earned in the tens of billions of dollars through no-bid contracts in Iraq. Companies such as Halliburton, Bechtel, and MCI (formerly WorldCom), along with dozens of others, have made billions there, often for shoddy work and work that was never completed (Campaign for America's Future, 2006; Center for Public Integrity, 2007). Some would argue that no-bid contracts ought to be illegal; yet many of them have been awarded to companies that made large financial contributions to Congress.

Another example of elite deviance is what Sennott (2000) calls "corporate welfare," which he claims costs Americans at least $150 billion per year. Essentially, businesses are subsidized by taxpayers in the form of trade missions, funding for support services, tax breaks, and state offices that guide corporations in their business affairs. Frivolous spending by the government also might be considered elite deviance. One prominent example is the "bridge to nowhere." The bridge was meant to connect the town of Ketchikan, Alaska (with a population of about 8,900), with an airport on the Island of Gravina (with a population of about 50) at a cost of about $320 million (Utt, 2005).

Congress regularly attaches such "pork" to its bills, often without much or any press coverage. One recent account claimed that **pork**—unnecessary and sometimes wasteful spending in a bill—costs taxpayers about $30 billion per year (Belzman, 2006). Citizens Against Government Waste (2007) characterize spending as pork if it:

- Is requested by only one chamber of Congress
- Is not subjected to congressional hearings
- Is not specifically authorized
- Is not competitively awarded
- Is not requested by the president
- Greatly exceeds the president's budget request or the previous year's funding
- Serves only local or special interests.

Some examples of pork projects identified by Citizens Against Wasteful Government include:

- $13,500,000 for the International Fund for Ireland, which helped finance the World Toilet Summit
- $6,435,000 for wood utilization research
- $1,000,000 for the Waterfree Urinal Conservation Initiative
- $500,000 for the Sparta Teapot Museum in Sparta, North Carolina
- $550,000 for the Museum of Glass in Tacoma, Washington
- $500,000 for the Arctic Winter Games in Alaska
- $250,000 for the National Cattle Congress in Waterloo, Iowa
- $234,000 for the National Wild Turkey Federation
- $100,000 for the Richard Steele Boxing Club in Henderson, Nevada.

Not all of the projects identified are so trivial. The group identified 2,658 projects at a cost of $13.2 billion in the Defense and Homeland Security Appropriations Acts for fiscal

2007. And of course, none of this is criminal—even though victimization is widespread—because the actors are members of Congress!

What Is Victimization?

Currently, the criminal justice network seldom views people as victims unless an individual person becomes a victim (suffers financial or physical harm) specifically as a result of a criminal act. Rush (2000, p. 353) defines **victimization** as "the harming of any single victim in a criminal incident." Champion (1997, p. 128) defines victimization as a "specific criminal act affecting a specific victim." The UCR definition of homicide also illustrates how crimes are typically perceived as being committed against one person by another. Murder is the "willful . . . killing of one human being by another."

Notice the common elements in these definitions:

- A single victim
- Suffering harm
- From a criminal act.

According to these definitions, victimization occurs when one person suffers some harm from a behavior that violates the criminal law. Yet people obviously are victimized by behaviors that do not meet these conditions. Table 4-1 sets forth a typology of victimization that illustrates four basic types of victimization:

- Harmful acts committed by an individual person against another individual person (Cell 1)
- Harmful acts committed by an individual person against an entity (e.g., a group of people or a corporation) (Cell 2)
- Harmful acts committed by an entity (e.g., a group of people or a corporation) against an individual person (Cell 3)
- Harmful acts committed by an entity (e.g., a group of people or a corporation) against another entity (e.g., a group of people or a corporation) (Cell 4).

Table 4-1 also provides examples of specific types of behaviors that would fall into each cell. I have provided one example of an act that causes financial harm to victims and one that causes physical harm. Examples in Table 4-1 of harmful acts committed by an individual against another individual include theft (e.g., taking property from another without consent and without the use of force or the threat of force) and battery

TABLE 4-1   A Typology of Victimization

	OFFENDER	
Victim	*Individual*	*Group/Corporation*
Individual	Cell 1 Theft Battery	Cell 3 Fraud Defective products
Group/Corporation	Cell 2 Forgery Terrorist acts	Cell 4 Price fixing Hazardous conditions

(e.g., physically striking or beating another person with force). Examples of harmful acts committed by an individual against a group of people or a corporation include forgery (e.g., signing another person's name to a check that is not yours in order to cash it) and terrorist acts (e.g., planting and detonating explosives at a building occupied by other people). Examples of harmful acts committed by a group of people or a corporation against an individual person include fraud (e.g., making false or deceptive claims about a product to trick the buyer into purchasing it) and manufacturing and selling defective products (e.g., making a car that explodes in a low-impact crash because of a faulty part). Finally, examples of harmful acts committed by a group of people or a corporation against another group of people or corporation include price fixing (e.g., when two corporations keep prices artificially high by agreeing to set a specific price on their products and simultaneously exclude smaller competitors that cannot lower prices to compete for buyers' business) and forcing or allowing employees to work in hazardous conditions (e.g., not complying with federally required safety regulations or ignoring warnings of potential problems).

Although these four types of victimizations are mutually exclusive, the examples provided in Table 4-1 are not. That is, some of the examples provided could also fit well into another category of victimization. For example, acts of fraud can also be committed by an individual against another individual (as when someone sells a fake fur coat to someone after claiming it is "a genuine mink coat") or by a group of people or a corporation against an individual person (as when a corporation sells a product guaranteed to "make you younger!"). Likewise, theft can be committed by individuals against other individuals or against groups and corporations. The examples simply serve to help illustrate the four different types of victimizations defined above.

The significant point is that victimization encompasses many more types of behaviors than can be adequately understood according to the most common definition in criminology. As noted by Karmen (1996, p. 2), the term **victim** most accurately "refers to all those people who experience injury, loss, or hardship due to any cause." In other words, a broader definition of victimization would be:

> people who experience any harmful behavior, such as "accident victims, cancer victims, flood victims, and victims of discrimination and similar injustices" and people who have been "physically injured, economically hurt, robbed of self-respect, emotionally traumatized, socially stigmatized, politically oppressed, collectively exploited, personally alienated, manipulated, co-opted, neglected, ignored, blamed, defamed, demeaned, or vilified." (Karmen, 1996, p. 2)

Although this definition is very broad, legal conceptions of crime and victimization are too restrictive to encompass the wide range of purposive behaviors that create victims, particularly given the fact that "crime" is a label applied by persons with power to have their will enacted into law while simultaneously creating a criminal law not focused on their own harmful and deviant acts (see Chapter 3). A compromise between the traditional definition of victim and the broader one proposed here would be a recognition of a specific set of harmful behaviors that more accurately captures the range of culpable behaviors that cause harm to their victims. As has been discussed, the key word pertaining to criminal justice is **culpability**, which indicates some degree of blameworthiness or responsibility for a resulting action. Because culpability encompasses more than intentionality, acts causing harm can lead to findings of responsibility even when they were not committed intentionally.

I have suggested that the concept of victimization be broadened to include any act that produces financial or physical harm and is committed intentionally, negligently, recklessly, or knowingly (Robinson, 2002). Following this logic, a new understanding of the term *victim* is in order, one that consists of individual persons, groups of people, or corporations that are victimized by acts committed intentionally, negligently, recklessly, or knowingly. Scholars such as Friedrichs (1983), Phipps (1986), and McShane and Williams (1992) have also been critical of the traditional conception of victims, for at least the following reasons.

- Current images of victims reinforce a focus on the state rather than the actual person(s) who suffered physical or financial harm. This "is a logical extension of a legal system which defines crimes as offenses against the state" (Zehr and Umbreit, 1982, p. 64).
- Current images of the state as victim reinforce a "conservative crime control agenda" or ideology "and have increased the power of the state in criminal proceedings" (McShane and Williams, 1992, p. 258).
- Criminal justice is focused on street crimes of the poor rather than on elite deviance, which allows white-collar and corporate offenders to escape relatively unscathed and unpunished despite their culpability (e.g., see Simon and Hagan, 1999).

Such criticisms have led scholars to call for a widening of the scope of criminal justice beyond street crimes committed by individuals against other individuals.

This is not to say that street crime is not tremendously harmful; it is just not as harmful as other acts that are either not against the law or not vigorously pursued by agencies of social control. Even violent crime, which Americans fear the most, is unlikely to result in actual harm to its victims. For example, fewer than 1 in 10 victims of violent crime will seek treatment for injuries at an emergency room (Donziger, 1996). In fact, the most common violent street crimes, simple assault and aggravated assault, do not even require any injury to be counted in the UCR. An attempt to injure is all that is required. As Kappeler et al. (2000, p. 122) explain: "all the violent crime, all the property crime, all the crime that we concentrate our energy and resources on combating is less of a threat to society than the crime committed by corporations."

A Comparison of Harms Associated with Crimes and "Noncrimes"

The label of "crime" is not a function of what is most harmful to society. If you believe that you are more likely to be victimized by street crime than by acts of elite deviance committed by wealthy individuals or corporations, you are wrong. The belief that elite deviance is less harmful than street crime is a myth (Kappeler and Potter, 2004).

There is considerable evidence that elite deviance causes more physical and property damage than all eight serious crimes combined. Kappeler and Potter (2004) estimate that economic losses from corporate crime alone cost somewhere between 17 and 31 times as much as street crime, although losses from corporate crime cost much more than this (see Issue in Depth at the end of this chapter for some stunning examples). And this says nothing about lives lost by corporate crime. One example proves this point: Tobacco use kills more people annually (approximately 430,000) than murder (approximately 17,000) and causes more financial loss (more than $75 billion in direct health care costs) than all street crime combined (about $20 billion). Whereas murder by definition is intentional, manufacturing and promoting the use of tobacco for the specific purpose of killing people is not intentional. Yet lawsuits against the tobacco industry have shown that the tobacco industry's recklessness and negligence have produced hundreds of thousands of deaths in the United States each year. Thus, some scholars claim that the law should criminalize any act that causes harm to others, as long as the act is done intentionally, negligently, recklessly, or knowingly, as discussed earlier.

Can a corporation be held responsible for a crime? According to Podgor and Israel (1997, p. 16):

> The initial common law view was that a corporation could not be held criminally liable, although the individual members of the corporation could. Lacking a mind, the corporation could not form the *mens rea* necessary for criminality. Not having physical attributes, there was no *actus reus*. Additionally, even if convicted of an offense, the corporation could not be imprisoned for the crime.

Currently, however, corporations can be held liable for their harmful acts. For example, Section 2.07 of the Model Penal Code suggests that corporate agents can be held responsible for harms inflicted in the course of their work, including harms resulting from a failure to act, and for actions authorized, performed, or recklessly tolerated by the board of directors. Box 4-6 shows this section of the Model Penal Code, which has been adopted in some form by many states.

BOX 4-6

SECTION 2.07, MODEL PENAL CODE

Liability of Corporations, Unincorporated Associations and Persons Acting, or Under a Duty to Act, in Their Behalf.

1. A corporation may be convicted of the commission of an offense if:

   a. the offense is a violation or the offense is defined by a statute other than the Code in which a legislative purpose to impose liability on corporations plainly appears and the conduct is performed by an agent of the corporation acting in behalf of the corporation within the scope of his office or employment, except that if the law defining the offense designates the agents for whose conduct the corporation is accountable or the circumstances under which it is accountable, such provisions shall apply; or

   b. the offense consists of an omission to discharge a specific duty of affirmative performance imposed on corporations by law; or

   c. the commission of the offense was authorized, requested, commanded, performed or recklessly tolerated by the board of directors or by a high managerial agent acting in behalf of the corporation within the scope of his office or employment.

2. When absolute liability is imposed for the commission of an offense, a legislative purpose to impose liability

on a corporation shall be assumed, unless the contrary plainly appears.

3. An unincorporated association may be convicted of the commission of an offense if:

a. The offense is defined by a statute other than the Code that expressly provides for the liability of such an association and the conduct is performed by an agent of the association acting in behalf of the association within the scope of his office or employment, except that if the law defining the offense designates the agents for whose conduct the association is accountable or the circumstances under which it is accountable, such provisions shall apply; or

b. The offense consists of an omission to discharge a specific duty of affirmative performance imposed on associations by law.

4. As used in this Section:

a. "corporation" does not include an entity organized as or by a governmental agency for the execution of a governmental program;

b. "agent" means any director, officer, servant, employee or other person authorized to act in behalf of the corporation or association and, in the case of an unincorporated association, a member of such association;

c. "high managerial agent" means an officer of a corporation or an unincorporated association, or, in the case of a partnership, a partner, or any other agent of a corporation or association having duties of such responsibility that his conduct may fairly be assumed to represent the policy of the corporation or association.

5. In any prosecution of a corporation or an unincorporated association for the commission of an offense included within the terms of Subsection (1)(a) or Subsection (3)(a) of this Section, other than an offense for which absolute liability has been imposed, it shall be a defense if the defendant proves by a preponderance of evidence that the high managerial agent having supervisory responsibility over the subject matter of the offense employed due diligence to prevent its commission. This paragraph shall not apply if it is plainly inconsistent with the legislative purpose in defining the particular offense.

6. a. A person is legally accountable for any conduct he performs or causes to be performed in the name of the corporation or an unincorporated association or on its behalf to the same extent as if it were performed in his own name or behalf.

b. Whenever a duty to act is imposed by law upon a corporation or an unincorporated association, any agent of the corporation or association having primary responsibility for the discharge of the duty is legally accountable for a reckless omission to perform the required act to the same extent as if the duty were imposed by law directly upon himself.

c. When a person is convicted of an offense by reason of his legal accountability for the conduct of a corporation or an unincorporated association, he is subject to the sentence authorized by law when a natural person is convicted of an offense of the grade and the degree involved.

The problem is that corporations are rarely held criminally responsible for the harms they inflict on Americans. Why not? Because the "most powerful organization in our society is the corporation. Corporations have become more powerful than governments, or religious institutions, or labor unions" (Mokhiber and Weissman, 1999, p. 96).

Other harms associated with legal acts and/or "crimes" that are not considered serious or worthy of criminal justice and media attention demonstrate that the label of "crime" is not reserved for the most harmful acts in society. For example, Frank and Lynch (1992) document the costs of physical damage to individuals and society by means of deadly pollutants, preventable work-related "accidents" (as they are called), occupational diseases and deaths, and faulty consumer products. Simon (2007) discusses individual cases of fraud by companies in the United States, illustrates the harms of the savings and loan (S&L) scandals, shows that tax breaks are given disproportionately to the rich, questions large corporate salaries (which have ballooned even as companies have lost money and workers have not gained greater wealth), business monopolies, public corruption, election fraud, human rights violations, and war crimes. Simon also demonstrates the harmful nature of price fixing and deceptive advertising and documents the dangers associated with unsafe working conditions and unsafe products, as well as of pollution. Friedrichs (1995) shows the harms associated with corporate violence against the public, consumers, and workers and illustrates harms resulting from fraud, tax evasion, price fixing, price gouging, false advertising, and so forth. He carefully examines environmental crimes, unfair labor practices, insider trading, computer crimes, and even various forms of state crimes. Weisburd and Schlegel (1992) document the nature and extent of antitrust violations, multiple types of fraud, bribery, tax violations, and embezzlement. Rosoff, Pontell, and Tillman (2002) discuss numerous examples of white-collar crimes, including medical crime and computer crime, which demonstrate the cold, calculated acts of individuals and corporations that result in mind-boggling financial and physical harms. They also examine consumer fraud, false advertising, price fixing, unsafe and defective products, crimes against the environment, securities fraud, banking and insurance fraud, as well as corruption.

Reiman (2006) estimates the costs of white-collar crimes to be at least $404 billion annually, far more than all street crimes combined, but even this number is an underestimate. Only one estimate of street crime costs has exceeded this estimate: A 1996 Justice Department report estimated that street crimes led to $450 billion per year in losses, but most of this was due to "quality of life costs" (Miller, Cohen, and Wiersman, 1997). The S&L scandals of the 1980s alone will cost Americans $500 billion over the next 40 years. Yet the "average prison term for savings and loan offenders sentenced between 1988 and 1992 was 36 months, compared to 56 months for burglars and 38 months for those convicted of motor vehicle theft," even though the average loss in an S&L case was $500,000 (Criminal Justice Newsletter, December 5, 1994, p. 5, reported in Reiman, 1998), while the loss in an average property crime during the time was $1,251 (Reiman, 1998, p. 128). Most recently, Enron, WorldCom, and other large corporations—with assistance from the accounting firm Arthur Anderson and numerous banks—engaged in numerous forms of elite deviance that caused thousands of Americans to lose their life savings and retirement resources. Their misdeeds are discussed in Issue in Depth at the end of the chapter.

Reiman, using both official and unofficial sources of data, shows that far more people are killed and injured by preventable occupational diseases and hazards than by crime every year. He convincingly argues that the majority of these—totaling 55,000 deaths and 3.1 million injuries—are as much beyond the control of the workers as being murdered is beyond the control of the murder victim. The fact that many of these deaths and injuries result from the negligence or recklessness of people who work for corporations demands our attention. McCaghy, Capron, and Jamieson (2000) suggest that as many as 100,000 workers each year die because of hazardous working conditions. Another 30,000 people die from unsafe and defective merchandise (Coleman, 1998). Additionally, studies in the 1990s showed that nearly 100,000 died every year from hospital errors (negligence and recklessness), although more recent studies show the number declined after several new regulations for safety were put into place. Another 300,000 die each year because of poor diet and inactivity.

The negligent and reckless acts that produce such harms are undeniably disproportionately committed by wealthier Caucasians. I illustrate this in Figure 4-1, which compares the typical offender and victim of street crime and elite deviance.

Whereas African Americans are rounded up for street crimes, particularly drug crimes (see Chapter 11), white-collar and corporate criminals typically walk away unscathed or with a slap on the wrist. Studies show that prosecution of white-collar and corporate criminals represents the "road not taken" (Shapiro, 1995) and that most white-collar criminals are repeat offenders who are nonetheless punished only with administrative sanctions or simple warnings (Weisburd, Chayet, and Waring, 1990). Reiman (1998, p. 110) writes that when we are talking about

> the kinds of crimes poor people almost never have the opportunity to commit, such as antitrust violations, industrial safety violations, embezzlement, and serious tax evasion, the criminal justice system shows an increasingly benign and merciful face. The more likely that a crime is the type committed by middle- and upper-class people, the less likely it will be treated as a criminal offense. When it comes to crime in the streets, where the perpetrator is apt to be poor, he or she is even more likely to be arrested and formally charged. When it comes to crime in the suites, where the offender is apt to be affluent, the system is most likely to deal with the crime noncriminally, that is, by civil litigation or informal settlement.

Reiman (2004, p. 119) even compares arrest data for street crimes that result in the loss of property with the crime of embezzlement (a property crime whereby property is

---

FIGURE 4-1   The Typical Offender and Victim of Street Crime and White-Collar Deviance

	Street		White-Collar	
	Offender	*Victim*	*Offender*	*Victim*
Gender	Male	Male	Male	All
Age Group	Young	Young	Older	All
Race/Ethnicity	Minority[*]	Minority[*]	Caucasian	All
Income Level	Low	Low	High	All

[*]Self-report studies and victimization surveys generally do not find the pronounced differences in offending by race and ethnicity that are evident in arrest and conviction statistics.

misappropriated—that is, stolen from its rightful owner after being left in the care or trust of another). He finds that the number of arrests for property crimes is 80 times greater than for embezzlement and that there is one arrest for every $14,000 stolen versus one arrest for every $898,000 "misappropriated." Arrests of white-collar offenders are made unlikely by deregulation efforts of politicians. **Deregulation** occurs when a government passes laws to limit its own control over an industry. In the 1980s, budgets of the Consumer Product Safety Commission, Occupational Safety and Health Administration, and Federal Trade Commission were slashed, and requirements relating to pharmaceutical and automotive safety were lifted or softened (Kappeler, Blumberg, and Potter, 2000, p. 135). Most of these changes in policy were attached as "riders" to large bills in Congress. The story is very similar today in the twenty-first century.

In fact, the history of government regulation has been one of businesses regulating themselves for their own benefit and gain. Many regulators are former corporate executives or go to work for corporations after their regulating days are over (Hagan, 1998). Thus, there is a double standard of justice in the United States. While we spend tens of billions of dollars each year fighting street crimes that produce relatively minor harms, we allow businesses to police themselves, and we give "little effort to enforce the law against [white-collar and corporate] criminals. When we do catch them at their nefarious deeds, we tap them on the wrist, make them say they are sorry, and send them about their criminal business" (Kappeler et al., 2000, p. 134). A recent example dealing with the Consumer Product Safety Commission (CPSC) illustrates the poor nature of regulation of business in the United States. The Cable News Network reported that in 2005, government scientists tested 60 soft, vinyl lunchboxes and found that one in five contained "amounts of lead that medical experts consider unsafe—and several had more than 10 times hazardous levels."

However, the CPSC did not tell the public! Instead, it released a statement saying they found "no instances of hazardous levels." Further, the CPSC "refused to release their actual test results, citing regulations that protect manufacturers from having their information released to the public." Only after the Associated Press issued a Freedom of Information Act request did the CPSC send along documents that led to the discovery of the test results. According to CNN, "The results of the first type of test, looking for the actual lead content of the vinyl, showed that 20 percent of the bags had more than 600 parts per million of lead—the federal safe level for paint and other products. The highest level was 9,600 ppm, more than 16 times the federal standard. But the CPSC did not use those results."

Amazingly, a CPSC spokesperson said: "When it comes to a lunchbox, it's carried. The food that you put in the lunch box may have an outer wrapping, a baggie, so there isn't direct exposure. The direct exposure would be if kids were putting their lunchboxes in their mouth, which isn't a common way for children to interact with their lunchbox."

Alexa Engelman, a researcher at the Oakland, California–based Center for Environmental Health, reacted: "They found levels that we consider very high. . . . They knew this all along and they didn't take action on it. It's upsetting to me. Why are we, as a country, protecting the companies? We should be protecting the kids. I don't think in this instance they did their job."

Since the Food and Drug Administration (FDA) reviewed the test results and sent a letter to lunchbox manufacturers telling them that the lunchboxes may be dangerous, it appears the action of the CPSC was negligent in nature. Even Wal-Mart stopped selling such lunchboxes due to safety concerns.

High levels of lead in blood can lead to learning problems, reduced intelligence, hyperactivity, and attention deficit disorder (Robinson, 2004). Further, no level of lead in the blood is considered safe. This led Dr. Bruce Lamphear, a lead poisoning specialist at the Children's Hospital Medical Center in Cincinnati, Ohio, to say: "I don't think the Consumer Product Safety Commission has lived up to its role to protect kids from lead. . . . As a public agency, their work should be transparent. And if one is to err on the side of protecting children rather than protecting lunch box makers, then certainly you would want to lower the levels."

When companies get bad press for engaging in dangerous acts, some just change their names. For example, Philip Morris tobacco became Altria and WorldCom became MCI. Imagine if after committing crimes, common street criminals were permitted to change their names and start over. Such is life for major corporations.

Why do white-collar and corporate offenders rarely receive "justice"? In their book *Corporate Predators,* Mokhiber and Weissman (1999, p. 9) claim it is because of their power to shape the definition of the law and to influence prosecutors not to bring criminal charges. To these, I would also add that they can afford the best defense that money can buy.

In Chapter 3, I showed how this owes itself to the criminal law, which does not usually label such acts as "crimes"; when it does, they are not considered "serious." In defining what is bad, evil, wrong, harmful, and criminal, the criminal law creates myths of crime that cause people to view certain acts as most serious and harmful even though they are not, and produces fear of certain actions and people instead of others that pose even greater threats.

The government basically views victims of elite deviance as deserving their own victimizations. The phrase "let the buyer beware" is a prime example: "American business has followed 'caveat emptor' (let the buyer beware) and 'laissez faire' economics (the doctrine of government noninterference in business)" (Simon and Hagan, 1999, p. 158). The former doctrine suggests that if you get ripped off by fraudulent salespeople, it is your own fault; you should have known better. The latter doctrine suggests that the government has no legitimate role in regulating business. Of course, if your house is burglarized because you left the windows unlocked, it is not your fault; you are seen as a victim of a "serious" crime, and the government has a legitimate role intervening in this type of activity.

Why does our own government fail to define the acts that are most dangerous to us as the most serious crimes? Kappeler et al. (2000) state:

> The government has a vested interest in maintaining the existing social definition of crime and extending this definition to groups and behaviors that are perceived to be a threat to the existing social order. . . . Similarly, the government has an interest in seeing that the existing criminal justice system's response to crime is not significantly altered in purpose or function.

According to these authors, the government's interests are served by promoting myths about crime and criminal justice. These myths are not only false but dangerous—dangerous because they allow harmful acts to be committed against innocent people by others with virtual impunity, even when done so intentionally. And they are promoted by the mass media, which are owned by powerful U.S. corporations (see Chapter 5). In essence, the definition of crime is a threat to justice in the United States, because people who intentionally, recklessly, negligently, and knowingly kill and injure Americans do so with virtual impunity.

SOURCES OF CRIME INFORMATION: DO WE REALLY KNOW HOW MUCH CRIME IS OUT THERE?

Now that you have a better understanding of what crime is (and perhaps what it should be), how much of it is out there? To answer this question, you first need to understand where we get our information about crime. Most people get their crime information from media outlets such as television and newspapers, as well as from popular forms of entertainment such as movies, books, and the Internet (see Chapter 5).

The government also collects information about crime. Government sources tend to be more representative of what street crime really is than media sources of crime information. I will use these government sources to illustrate the nature of crime in the United States.

We get our information about street crime from two main sources produced by the U.S. government. One may be better than the other, depending on what you want to learn. Major sources of crime data in the United States include the Uniform Crime Reports (UCR), the National Crime Victimization Survey (NCVS), and self-report studies. Each of these, as well as sources of data on other forms of harmful behaviors, are discussed next.

Uniform Crime Reports

The **Uniform Crime Reports** (UCR) is perhaps the most commonly cited source of crime data in the United States. The UCR is a city, county, and state law enforcement program that provides a national source of crime data based on the submission of crime statistics by law enforcement agencies across the country (UCR Handbook, 1999). More than 17,000 city, county, and state law enforcement agencies, employing more than 700,000 officers and representing roughly 260 million inhabitants of the United States (96% of the U.S. population), voluntarily send their crime statistics either directly to the Federal Bureau of Investigation or to their own state's bureau of investigation or department of law enforcement for inclusion in the UCR.

The UCR collects data primarily on a group of Index Offenses, including both **violent crimes** and **property crimes**. These crimes were listed as Part I and Part II offenses earlier in this chapter. The UCR has essentially been expanded to include the Group A and Group B offenses of the National Incidence Based Reporting System (NIBRS), also discussed earlier. Of the many limitations of the UCR (see Gove, Hughes, and Geerken, 1985), the most troubling in terms of both crime frequencies and crime trends is that the UCR measures only **crimes known to the police**. Most crimes are not known to the police, so the measure does not reflect actual crime frequencies accurately. Crimes not known to the police, commonly referred to as the **dark figure of crime**, are not addressed by the UCR. Statistics from the Bureau of Justice Statistics (BJS) suggest that victims report only about one out of every three property crimes and that victims are most likely to report their victimizations to the police when they are violent in nature, when an injury results, when lost items are valued at $250 or more, or when forcible entry has occurred (Bureau of Justice Statistics, 1997).

Additionally, because factors that affect the UCR figures fluctuate from one year to the next, it is not clear how valid the measure is of crime rates over time, known as **crime trends**. For example, rates of forcible rape may appear to be increasing according to the UCR when in fact they may be decreasing or remaining steady over time. If police across the United States get better at detecting rape or if citizens report more rapes to the police, the UCR will show an increase in rape rates even though the actual rate may not have changed at all.

One of the most striking limitations of the UCR as a source of valid crime data is that evidence is now available suggesting that police downgrade or upgrade serious crimes to less serious or more serious ones for political purposes (McCleary, Nienstedt, and Erven, 1982; Seidman and Couzens, 1974). Gaines, Kaune, and Miller (2000, p. 43) discuss evidence showing that police departments in Atlanta, New York, and Philadelphia seriously manipulated their crime data.

Despite these weaknesses, and keeping in mind that these figures represent only crimes known to the police, the UCR does teach some interesting facts about crime. First, the vast majority of crimes known to the police, including theft, burglary, and motor vehicle theft, are committed against property. If you include robbery, which is committed against individuals but is done for property gain, then property crimes make up more than 90% of all crimes known to the police. Given that property crimes are less likely to be reported than violent crimes, it is safe to assume that the true distribution of street crime in the United States would be more like 99% property crimes and 1% violent crimes. Second, the most common crime according to the UCR is theft, making up about 60% of all crimes known to the police. Third, the least common type of crime in the United States is murder, which makes up only 0.1% of all crimes known to the police. Table 4-2 depicts the numbers of crimes known to the police in 2006.

From these numbers, you might conclude that the United States is plagued by unusually high crime rates. In fact, this is not the case, with the exception of murder, which many attribute to our violent culture, economic and racial inequality, and the availability of guns in the United States (Beckett and Sasson, 2000, p. 8). This led some

TABLE 4-2 Number of Crimes Known to the Police (2005)		
Murder	16,692	(0.1%)
Rape	93,934	(0.8%)
Robbery	417,122	(3.6%)
Aggravated Assault	862,947	(7.5%)
MVT	1,235,226	(10.7%)
Burglary	2,154,126	(18.6%)
Theft	6,776,807	(58.7%)
TOTAL	**11,849,006**	**(100%)**

Source: Federal Bureau of Investigation (2006).

to claim that "crime is not the problem"—instead, the problem is lethal violence (Zimring and Hawkins, 1997).

National Crime Victimization Survey

In part to uncover some of the dark figure of crime—to assess some of the crimes not being reported to the police—the U.S. Department of Justice, Bureau of Justice Statistics designed the **National Crime Victimization Survey** (NCVS), originally known as the National Crime Survey (NCS). The survey was redesigned in the late 1980s, in part to improve survey techniques to increase people's ability to recall events, including previously undetected victimizations. The first annual results for the redesigned survey were published for the year 1993.

The NCVS is a survey of roughly 134,000 people age 12 years and older in approximately 77,000 households. The survey explores the experiences with criminal victimizations of a sample of respondents made up of a nationally representative group of individuals living in U.S. households. Demographic variables such as age, sex, race, and income are used to compare rates of victimizations for different subgroups within the population. The NCVS collects crime data on both personal crimes and household crimes, as noted in Table 4-3.

These crimes are very similar to those contained in the UCR, with the notable exception of homicide; the NCVS does not include statistics on homicide simply because it is impossible to ask a homicide victim how many times he or she has been murdered in the past 12 months! Neither the UCR nor the NCVS measures victimizations resulting from elite deviance.

Twice each year, citizens are asked about their experiences of victimization from the offenses in Table 4-3. Because the NCVS includes both crimes that citizens report to the police and those they do not report, it is a more valid measure of actual street crime rates than the UCR. This is why the NCVS always indicates higher rates of crime than the UCR. Table 4-4 shows how many actual offenses of each type were reported to NCVS researchers in 2005.

From these data, we can conclude that the vast majority of street crime is property crime, and the most common crime is theft. The most common violent crime is aggravated assault, but relatively little crime in the United States is violent (although, as noted, the United States is plagued by an alarmingly high murder rate).

TABLE 4-3 Crimes Measured by the Uniform Crime Reports (UCR) and National Crime Victimization Survey (NCVS)	
UCR	*NCVS*
Murder	—
Forcible Rape	Rape
Robbery	Robbery
Aggravated Assault	Aggravated Assault
Motor Vehicle Theft	Motor Vehicle Theft
Burglary	Burglary
Theft	Theft
Arson	—

TABLE 4-4 Criminal Victimization in the United States (2005)		
Type of Victimization	*Number*	*Percent*
Any NCVS crime	16,330,140	13.9%
Violent crime	3,271,760	2.8%
Rape	79,580	0.1%
Sexual assault	44,160	0.0%
Robbery	443,520	0.4%
Assault	2,796,900	2.4%
Aggravated	728,810	0.6%
Simple	2,183,110	1.9%
Personal theft	177,170	0.2%
Property crime	14,085,570	12.0%
Household burglary	2,970,000	2.5%
Motor vehicle theft	910,690	0.8%
Theft	11,109,290	9.5%

Source: Bureau of Justice Statistics. Crime and the Nation's Households 2005. http://ojp.usdoj.gov/bjs/pub/pdf/cnh05.pdf

Other than this, the U.S. crime rate is comparable to those of other industrialized countries. Findings from the **International Crime Victims Survey** (ICVS), first administered by the Dutch Ministry of Justice in 1988, suggested that crime rates are high in the United States but not much higher than in many other countries (Beckett and Sasson, 2000). More recent data from the ICVS suggest other countries have overtaken the United States as leaders in homicide rates. According to Barclay and Tavares (2002), the average rate of homicides in European Union countries from 1998 to 2000 was 1.7 homicides per 100,000 citizens, with the highest rates in Northern Ireland (3.1), Spain (2.8), Finland (2.6), Scotland (2.2), and Sweden (2.1). The highest rates for non-European nations include South Africa (54.3), Russia (20.5), Estonia (11.4), Lithuania (8.9), Latvia (6.5), and the United States (5.9).

Key findings from the 2000 ICVS, conducted in 17 industrialized countries (van Kesteren, Mayhew, and Nieuwbeerta, 2001), show the following:

- Countries where more than 24% of citizens were victims of any crime included Australia, England and Wales, the Netherlands, and Sweden.
- Countries where between 20 and 24% of citizens were victims of any crime included Canada, Scotland, Denmark, Poland, Belgium, France, and the United States.
- Countries where less than 20% of citizens were victims of any crime included Finland, Spain, Switzerland, Portugal, Japan, and Northern Ireland.

The most common crime in any country is a crime against property, and is typically theft of someone's property by another.

In terms of an individual's risk for criminal victimization from specific crimes, the 2000 ICVS finds the following:

- The highest risks for contact crime (robbery, assaults with force, and sexual assaults) were in Australia, England and Wales, Canada, Scotland, and Finland (all over 3%).

- The highest risks for theft were in Australia, Sweden, and Poland (between 5–6%).
- The highest risks for burglary were in Australia (7%), England and Wales (5%), and Canada, Denmark, and Belgium (all at 4%).
- The highest risks for car theft were in England and Wales (2.6%), Australia (2.1%), and France (1.9%).

Why, then, does the United States incarcerate more people than any other country? The answer—that we are tougher on crime than any other country—probably goes against all you have heard from "get tough" politicians attacking their "soft on crime" opponents. In fact, the notion that the U.S. criminal justice network is lenient is a myth, say Kappeler et al. (2000, p. 257), who write: "we lock up more people, for longer sentences, for more offenses than any nation on the face of the earth." Walker (1998, p. 146) writes that "the alleged 'loophole' of being soft on dangerous offenders does not exist." In fact, the opposite is true with regard to street crime. The United States is highly punitive against violent street criminals. It is only our response to white-collar and corporate crime that is "soft."

The NCVS is also considered a better measure of crime trends than the UCR because the factors that affect victim recall and reporting to researchers are more constant than the factors affecting UCR crime trends. "The victimization surveys are clearly superior to UCR data in that they measure both reported and unreported crime, and they are unaffected by technological changes in police record keeping, levels of reporting by victims and the police, and other factors which call into question the validity of UCR data" (Kappeler et al., 2000, p. 35). According to the NCVS, street crime rates are at their lowest rates since the inception of the survey and have almost consistently declined since 1973. The next section examines these street crime trends.

American Crime Trends According to the UCR and NCVS

In the 1990s, the bottom fell out of crime, meaning that street crime rates fell consistently in the last decade. Figure 4-2 illustrates crime trends according to the NCVS.

Several books have examined the causes of these declines. For example, *The Crime Drop in America* (Blumstein and Wallman, 2000) and *Why Crime Rates Fell* (Conklin, 2002) examine the effects of criminal justice (police, corrections) and noncriminal justice (economic, social) factors on crime. Blumstein and Wallman (2000) conclude that there is no single explanation for why crime fell in the United States. The factors analyzed in the book include economic improvement, an aging population, the stabilization of the illicit drug trade, reductions in gun crimes, and prison. The authors conclude that "no single factor can be invoked as *the* cause of the crime decline of the 1990s. Rather, the explanation appears to lie with a number of factors, perhaps none of which alone would have been sufficient and some of which might not have been of noticeable efficacy without reinforcement from others" (p. 11). The author who wrote the chapter on prisons (Spelman, 2000) concludes that prisons were only responsible for about one-fourth of the crime drop. He adds, ". . . Most of the responsibility for the crime drop rests with improvements in the economy, changes in the age structure, or other social factors" (p. 125). Additionally, Zimring's (2006) *The Great American Crime Decline* finds that numerous factors likely played a meaningful role in violent crime declines in the 1990s.

FIGURE 4-2   Trends in American Crime

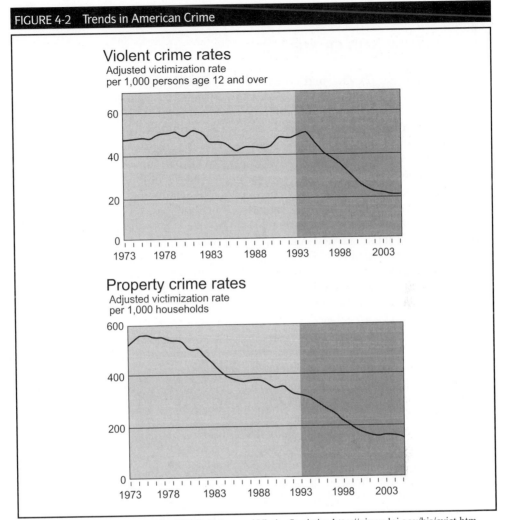

Source: Bureau of Justice Statistics (2006), Crime and Victim Statistics. http://ojp.usdoj.gov/bjs/cvict.htm.

One factor not considered by most authors but also demonstrated to have had a significant impact on crime rate declines is abortion, which was legalized by the U.S. Supreme Court in *Roe v. Wade* (1973). Box 4-7 reviews the claim that abortion reduced crime.

Unless you were born before 1973, you are safer today from street crime than at any time in recent U.S. history. Interestingly, Gallup polls taken every year show that public concern about crime is not a function of fluctuations in actual crime rates. For example, the percentage of people who indicated crime and violence as the nation's number one problem increased dramatically in the early 1990s and concern over crime peaked in 1994. Yet street crime was actually declining at this time. What explains this?

During the early to mid-1990s, concern rose about violent crime in response to several crimes that were given tremendous coverage. Some of these included the videotaped

BOX 4-7

ABORTION AND CRIME

Authors Steven Levitt and Stephen Dubner (2005), in their book, *Freakonomics*, claim that abortion is more common among the young, unmarried, and poor. Children born to these women are more likely to be raised in households characterized by poverty, single and teenage parents, stress, and "bad parenting." Therefore, with legalized abortion, there should be fewer children born to young, unmarried, and poor mothers, and less crime should be one result. In fact, violent crime began to decline roughly 21 years after abortion became legal, and murder began to decline 18 years after abortion was legalized.

Since the "crime peak" for street crime is 15–25 years—meaning people are at greatest risk for criminality during these ages — we would expect a surge in babies born in any year to result in higher crime rates some 15–25 years later. Conversely, a reduction in babies born (especially to mothers with lots of risk factors for crime) ought to be associated with a reduction in street crime. In the case of abortion, 18–21 years after it was legalized, violence started to decline.

The authors claim that several studies show it is true (in the United States, Canada, and Australia) and that state-specific analyses in the United States also support it. They conclude: "Legalized abortion led to less unwantedness; unwantedness leads to high crime; legalized abortion, therefore, led to less crime" (p. 139). However, other evidence finds that the relationship between abortion and crime rates is spurious, or false (e.g., Zimring, 2006).

Keep in mind that no one is advocating abortion as a crime control measure. In fact, Levitt and Dubner (2005) rightly conclude that "the trade-off between higher abortion and lower crime is, by an economist's reckoning, terribly inefficient" (p. 144). That is, one cost of reduced crime rates is roughly one million abortions per year.

One public figure—Bill Bennett (former Secretary of Education and former Drug Czar)—did say, "I do know that it's true that if you wanted to reduce crime, you could, if that were your sole purpose, you could abort every black baby in this country, and your crime rate would go down." He added this would be "an impossible, ridiculous and morally reprehensible thing to do, but your crime rate would go down." People responded with outrage, not so much over his assertion about abortion, but instead his reference to *black* babies specifically. His choice of black babies in particular clearly illustrates the widespread belief that blacks are more criminal than whites (see Chapter 12).

beating of Rodney King by police officers in 1991, as well as the subsequent acquittal of the officers in the case in 1992 and the rioting that occurred afterward, and the kidnapping and killing of young Polly Klaas from her parent's home by a stranger in 1993. Is it responsible of the mainstream media to devote enormous coverage to such crimes?

Even though street crime rates now are very low compared with other times in U.S. history, and relatively average compared to other countries, now Americans are afraid.

Americans report feeling less safe walking in their own neighborhoods after dark than citizens of other countries with higher crime rates (e.g., see Mayhew and Van Dijk, 1997). To some degree, the terrorist attacks of 9/11 changed this, as Americans became more afraid of terrorism than violent crime. Yet as concern over terrorism wanes, concern over violent crime will likely return.

Why are Americans so concerned about street crime even though it has decreased consistently since the 1970s? Is it that we see so much of it in the news and in television shows and movies? In Chapter 5, I attribute increases in fear to the politicization of crime and resulting media coverage.

Kappeler and Potter (2004) suggest that our own government must exaggerate the harms associated with street crime in order to justify intervening in it. Think about the massive criminal justice expansion detailed in Chapters 1 and 2. Does it make sense that we are spending more now than at any time in U.S. history to fight crime even though street crime rates are at their lowest rates in many years?

Kappeler and Potter (2004) argue that myths about crime and criminal justice are portrayed in ways that ensure that Americans will spend their tax dollars to expand the criminal justice network. They claim that this portrayal involves several steps:

- A distinct population is identified as "deviant" or "different" and then targeted.
- The harms associated with this population pose a threat to American norms, lifestyles, and traditions.
- Victims are portrayed as "innocent" or "helpless."
- Those who take on the dangerous class of offenders are portrayed as "virtuous" and "brave."

Is this how you see crime and criminal justice? While politicians and the media overemphasize street crime, more harmful acts of elite deviance are ignored. This is not consistent with either of the criminal justice network's goals of reducing crime and doing justice.

Self-Report Studies

Another way that criminologists have learned about crime is by studying actual offenders through **self-report studies**, including discussions with both incarcerated offenders and active offenders.

In general, these studies suggest that virtually all people have committed crimes during the course of their lives, including crimes for which they could have been incarcerated for at least 1 year. Even recent self-report studies measuring serious criminality and delinquency show that most people admit to committing harmful acts that are prohibited by law. Robinson and Zaitzow (1999a) even found that the nation's crime experts—members of the American Society of Criminology—admit to illegal, deviant, and unethical behaviors. Box 4-8 provides examples from the study.

The main problems associated with self-report studies revolve around reliability and validity issues. In self-report research, reliability refers to the likelihood that offenders will give the same answers to questions if the researcher asks the same question more than once over time. Validity means the likelihood that the offender is giving an honest, accurate answer. One thing we have learned about human behavior is that people misrepresent, exaggerate, and sometimes forget the truth. This makes self-report

BOX 4-8

CRIMINOLOGISTS ARE CRIMINALS, TOO!

Robinson and Zaitzow (1999) conducted a survey of criminologists affiliated with the American Society of Criminology. They examined 44 forms of crimes, deviance, and ethical violations. The authors focused on "serious" crimes of the Uniform Crime Reports (UCR), drug-related crimes, acts of sexual deviance, fraud-related crimes, computer crimes, occupational crimes and deviance, and other ethical violations.

Five hundred twenty-two out of 1,500 surveys were returned for a response rate of 35%. Most of the respondents (62%) had earned PhDs; another 29% had earned master's degrees, and 8% held bachelor's degrees. Many respondents were university professors, including 19% full professors, 13% associate professors, and 17% assistant professors. Another 25% were graduate students and 26% were criminal justice practitioners or "other" ASC-affiliated members.

Findings show that criminologists are criminals, too. Selected findings are reported below.

Percentage Who Engaged in Behaviors Ever and in Past 12 Months (Number of Respondents = 522)		
	Ever	Past 12 months
UCR Property Crimes		
Theft	55%	7%
Burglary	22%	4%
UCR Violent Crimes		
Assault	36%	15%
Battery	25%	2%
Rape	3%	2%
Robbery	2%	0%
Drug Crimes		
DUI/DWI	66%	35%
Bought Illicit Drugs	34%	17%
Illicit Drug Use	60%	27%
Sold Drugs	11%	3%
Permitted Use by Minor	42%	28%
Provided to Minor	26%	14%
Sexual Deviance		
Adultery	23%	16%
Obscene Phone Calls	9%	3%
Prostitution (buy sex)	7%	6%
Sex with Student in Class	7%	6%
Unwanted Sexual Advances	3%	0%
Fraud		
Tax Fraud	19%	7%
Written Bad Check	13%	5%

False Statement Under Oath	8%	2%
False Statement for Favor	4%	2%
Computer		
Free Computer Programs	66%	54%
Pornography	15%	11%
Hacking	1%	0%
Hate E-mail	5%	0%
Occupational/Property		
Use of Work Supplies	84%	43%
Sold Free Texts	48%	12%
Falsify Travel Receipts	20%	4%
Misrepresent Income	18%	2%
Violate Consulting Rules	12%	2%
Use Grant for Personal	11%	1%
Grant Inflation	8%	1%
Occupational/Ethical		
Workplace Violation	18%	10%
Avoid Responsibilities	9%	5%
Obtain Favor for Position	8%	4%
Give Grade for Favors	3%	2%
Embellish Résumé	9%	1%
Other		
Speeding	92%	88%
Not Report Crime	47%	24%

Robinson and Zaitzow (1999, p. 17) write: "These . . . data demonstrate that we criminologists are to a degree, what we study—i.e., we commit acts of crime and deviance. Depending on the type of behavior being referred to, many criminologists admit both to having committed them in the distant past and in the past twelve months, including many which are codified as 'serious' and 'harmful' in the criminal law . . . crime and deviance is normal, even among criminologists."

SOURCE: Robinson, Matthew B., and Barbara H. Zaitzow. 1999. Criminologists: Are We What We Study? A National Self-Report Study of Crime Experts. *The Criminologist* 24, 2:1, 4, 17–19. Available at http://www.asc41.com/March-April%201999.htm.

studies somewhat questionable. As stated by Nettler (1984), "Never bet on an animal that talks" (quoted in Jeffery, 1990).

What we have learned about offenders from self-report studies is still considered valuable by most criminologists. For example, we know that almost all offenders admit to having committed a crime for which they could have been incarcerated for at least 1 year. Self-report studies also indicate that much of what we do to fight crime in the

United States will not work. Offenders tell us that they are not highly concerned about getting caught or punished for their criminal acts. Instead, they are motivated by potential gains from their crimes, and they know from experience that the criminal justice network is highly ineffective at detecting crimes (e.g., see Cromwell, 1995).

Sources of Data on Elite Deviance

According to leading consumer advocate Ralph Nader, also the Green party presidential candidate in 2000 and 2004:

> Our country does not collect statistics on corporate crime the way that it does on street crime. For to do so would begin to highlight a little-attended agenda for law enforcement and other corporate reforms. Neither the Congress nor the White House and its Justice Department have made any moves over the years to assemble from around the country the abuses of corporations in quantifiable format so as to drive policy. (Mokhiber and Weissman, 1999, Introduction)

In fact, there are no national sources of data on elite deviance as there are on street crime: "No private or public institution—not the FBI, not the U.S. Department of Commerce—keeps up-to-date statistics on the cost of white collar crime. . . . The last public record was issued by the Department of Commerce in its 1974 *Handbook on White-Collar Crime*" (Kappeler et al., 2000, p. 123). This fact alone is proof that the U.S. government is less concerned with elite deviance than with street crime:

> Every year, the Federal Bureau of Investigation (FBI) issues its Crime in the United States report which documents murder, assault, burglary, and other street crimes. . . . The FBI does not issue a yearly Corporate Crime in the United States report, despite strong evidence indicating that corporate crime and violence inflicts far more damage on society than all street crime combined (Mokhiber and Weissman, 1999, pp. 8–9).

With the invention of the NIBRS program discussed earlier, at least there is a source of national white-collar crime data available that tells us something. Unfortunately, what we can learn from NIBRS data is very limited. This is because (1) the FBI's definition of white-collar crime is very limited, (2) NIBRS measures only a handful of white-collar offenses, and (3) UCR data on white-collar offenses is limited to arrests. The FBI defines white-collar crime as "those illegal acts which are characterized by deceit, concealment, or violation of trust and which are not dependent upon the application or threat of physical force or violence . . . [committed] . . . to obtain money, property, or services, to avoid the payment or loss of money or services, or to secure personal or business advantage" (Barnett, 2003, p. 1). This definition ignores most acts committed by corporations, as well as all acts of violence committed by corporations and wealthy individuals through their work, which I referred to earlier as elite deviance.

So how do we learn about harms associated with acts of elite deviance? Most of the evidence comes from studies of wealthy people, governments, corporations, and institutions, conducted by a handful of social scientists. These studies clearly demonstrate that the U.S. criminal justice network is failing to pursue the acts that most threaten us. There is also a National White Collar Crime center that provides "a nationwide support system for agencies involved in the prevention, investigation, and prosecution of economic and high-tech crimes and to support and partner with other appropriate entities in address-ing homeland security initiatives, as they relate to economic and high-tech crimes." Although the center is congressionally funded and has members in law enforcement, state regulatory bodies with criminal investigative authority, as well as state and local prosecution offices, it "has no investigative authority itself." Its last "public survey of white-collar crime" was completed in 1999. The survey found that Americans are aware of white-collar crime, think it is as serious or more serious than street crime, and that a large portion are even aware that they have been victimized by it.

CONCLUSION

Clearly, the label of "crime" is applied to only a small portion of acts that are harmful to Americans. The label of "serious crime" is reserved for those acts that the government perceives to be committed primarily by the poor. This explains the focus in the United States on street crime rather than on elite deviance, even though the latter is far more dangerous. The sources we rely on for understanding how much crime there is in the United States reflect this bias—we rely on the error-prone Uniform Crime Reports more than we do on more valid measures such as the National Crime Victimization Survey. Yet both sources show that street crime declined significantly in the 1990s and through the beginning of the twenty-first century, mostly in spite of criminal justice pol-icy. Meanwhile, sources of data on elite deviance in the government are almost nonexis-tent, forcing us to rely on individual studies of corporations and wealthy citizens to learn about the harms caused by elite deviance. If we know that elite deviance is far more dangerous and costly than street crime, why do we, as a nation, fear street crime more? This issue is explained in Chapter 5.

ISSUE IN DEPTH—Enron, WorldCom, Tyco, and the Other Corporate Bandits

Next to the terrorist attacks that shook our country on September 11, 2001, perhaps the largest crime story since 2001 was the massive frauds committed by dozens of major corporations—which I refer to here as the "corporate bandits."

The accused corporations included Arthur Andersen, Enron, WorldCom, Qwest, Tyco, ImClone, Global Crossing, Dynergy, CMS Energy, El Paso Corp., Halliburton, Williams Cos., AOL Time Warner, Goldman Sachs, Salomon Smith Barney, Citigroup, J.P. Morgan Chase, Schering Plough, Bristol-Myers Squibb, Kmart, Johnson & Johnson, Adelphia, Merrill Lynch, Rite Aid, and Coca-Cola.

Many of these corporations were accused of the same basic fraudulent activities—essentially "cooking the books" to inflate profits by hiding debts so investors would be more likely to invest money in the corporations. Many of the corporations allegedly treated debts as revenue to make them look more profitable. Think of it this way: Imag-ine you wanted to get a loan from your local bank and you treated every check that you wrote in the past month not as debts against your account but as payments made to you by the companies you sent the checks to. This is what many companies in the United States allegedly did.

Several of the corporations were accused of more, including Coca-Cola. Coca Cola was accused of knowingly allowing malfunctioning machines to leave metal residue in their products, rigging marketing tests to win business with Burger King, racial discrimination, antitrust violations, and accounting irregularities that boosted its net worth.

According to CNN/Money's "Fraud Inc.," this is what the following companies were accused or convicted of:

- *Adelphia Communications* — This major cable company filed for bankruptcy protection after it was discovered that the Rigas family used billions of dollars in loans to cover investment losses. Adelphia filed its own racketeering lawsuit against Rigas and other members of his family. The company faces civil charges by the Securities and Exchange Commission (SEC) and an ongoing Justice Department investigation.
- *AOL Time Warner* — This major corporation is under investigation by the SEC and the Justice Department for questionable accounting practices at the company's America Online unit in 2000 and 2001.
- *Arthur Andersen* — This major accounting firm was found guilty by a jury of obstructing justice for shredding Enron documents and received the maximum sentence of a $500,000 fine and 5 years' probation. This firm also served as the accounting agency for other numerous companies accused of crimes.
- *Bristol-Myers Squibb* — This drugmaker has restated sales by $2 billion, and federal regulators are investigating whether it purposely inflated sales by offering incentives to wholesalers.
- *Citigroup* — This financial services company agreed to pay $240 million to settle "predatory lending" charges in the largest consumer protection settlement in the history of the Federal Trade Commission (FTC). It has also been charged with helping Enron manipulate its finances to deceive investors.
- *Credit Suisse First Boston Corporation* — This company agreed to pay $100 million for taking millions of dollars from customers through inflated commissions in exchange for allocations of "hot" initial public offerings.
- *Enron* — This large energy company is accused of obscuring its finances with business partnerships (invented companies to hide debts) and questionable accounting practices that fooled debt-rating agencies, Wall Street analysts, and investors. Enron was forced to file for bankruptcy, causing billions of dollars in losses for investors and Enron employees, many of whose company retirement accounts became worthless. Many Enron rivals (including Dynergy, El Paso Corp., CMS Energy, Halliburton, and Williams Cos.) are also under investigation because of questionable accounting and trading activities. The Halliburton case concerns an accounting practice introduced at the company when it was headed by Vice President Dick Cheney.
- *Global Crossing* — This telecommunications company is being investigated for using "swap deals" with other telecom carriers to inflate sales. The company is suspected of selling capacity on its fiber-optic network to other carriers and then buying back a like amount, which is improper. Global Crossing filed for Chapter 11 bankruptcy protection and agreed to sell a majority stake in its fiber-optic network to two Asian investors for about $250 million in cash.

- ***Goldman Sachs*** — This investment bank has been asked to turn over documents to the House of Representatives, which is investigating potential conflicts of interest and the distribution of stock as companies went public.
- ***ImClone*** — This company's former CEO was convicted on charges of insider trading for allegedly trying to sell his stock and tipping off family members after learning the federal Food and Drug Administration (FDA) would refuse to review the company's application for the promising cancer drug Erbitux.
- ***Johnson & Johnson*** — This company is under investigation by the FDA for false record keeping at a plant that makes an anemia drug linked to serious side effects.
- ***J.P. Morgan Chase*** — This company is charged with helping Enron with $8 billion in financial dealings that made Enron look rich in cash rather than heavily indebted.
- ***Kmart*** — This major retailer filed for Chapter 11 bankruptcy protection. It is under investigation by the FBI and the SEC and has closed hundreds of stores and cut 22,000 jobs.
- ***Merrill Lynch*** — This Wall Street brokerage firm agreed to pay $100 million to settle charges from New York that its research analysts knowingly promoted stocks they privately ridiculed in order to win business for Merrill's investment banking unit.
- ***Qwest*** — This telecommunications company is being investigated by the SEC after admitting that it had improperly accounted for about $1.2 billion in revenue for part of 2000 and all of 2001, most of it from "swap deals" it made with other companies. It restated $950 million in revenue derived from making sales to other carriers and then buying back a similar amount.
- ***Rite Aid*** — Three former executives and one suspended executive of this drugstore company were indicted on charges that they cooked the books to make it appear more profitable. It restated results going back 3 years.
- ***Tyco*** — The former CEO and former CFO have been charged with looting $600 million from Tyco, but both men have pleaded not guilty. Tyco has sued its former CEO for at least $730 million.
- ***WorldCom*** — This company, now known as MCI, filed the largest bankruptcy in U.S. history. It has admitted that it overstated profits by hiding more than $7 billion in expenses over five quarters. Several former WorldCom executives have been charged and others have pleaded guilty.
- ***Xerox*** — This major company was forced to restate earnings to reflect $1.4 billion less in pretax profits over the past 5 years as part of a settlement with the SEC. It was forced to pay a $10 million penalty.

The total combined harms of the above corporate crimes are unknown, but estimates are in the hundreds of billions of dollars. Additionally, tens of thousands of people lost their jobs, hundreds of thousands have lost money from their retirement accounts, and millions lost money from the resulting stock market crash.

Whatever the actual harms, there is no doubt that the financial harms exceed those caused by street crime in any year by dozens of times (and numerous people have committed suicide as a result of losing all their money and/or killed their spouses and family members as a result of the stress of losing their jobs).

Keep in mind that these corporations are not nameless, faceless entities. Each is run by chief executive officers (CEOs), chief financial officers (CFOs), and a board of directors—in other words, real people who made real decisions and who can be held accountable for their actions. ImClone's CEO, Sam Waksal, was sentenced to 87 months in prison for his role in an insider trading scandal that has shed negative light on Martha Stewart. Waksal pleaded guilty to obstruction of justice, perjury, bank fraud, and sales tax evasion. He also was sentenced to pay a fine of $3 million and more than $1.2 million in restitution. Enron founder Kenneth Lay was convicted of fraud and conspiracy but then died in July 2006 and had his convictions overturned due to being unable to appeal them. Former Enron CEO Jeffrey Skilling was sentenced to more than 24 years in prison for nine counts of fraud, conspiracy, insider trading, and lying to auditors. He was also ordered to pay $50 million in restitution to victims. Former Enron CFO Andrew Fastow received a sentence of 6 years. Interestingly, Enron paid its senior executives more than $744 million in cash and stock in the year prior to its bankruptcy filing in December 2001!

In response to these crimes, Congress passed the Sarbanes–Oxley Act, which doubled the potential sentences that such corporate criminals can face. President George W. Bush (the second) signed the bill into law, appointed a corporate fraud task force (to be headed by the director of a credit card company that paid more than $400 million to settle fraud lawsuits), and allocated millions to the SEC to conduct investigations. Yet Jeffrey Reiman and Paul Leighton (2003) claim that there has mostly been "huff and puff and . . . do little" in responding to these actions. According to their analysis of the law, it will now be more difficult to prosecute alleged offenders in similar cases because the law raised the standard of proof from "recklessly" to "knowingly."

In fact, most of the companies have paid fines to get out of trouble. For example, WorldCom was fined $750 million to settle the case against it, an alarmingly high figure. Yet considering that investors lost $175 billion because of WorldCom, we learn that the company was charged about 0.4% of the amount of financial harm they caused. Imagine going to a bank and robbing it of $100,000 and being forced to pay back only 0.4% of it (which is $400)! As noted earlier, WorldCom also changed its name to MCI and continues to do business, including participation in the rebuilding effort in Iraq.

The banks that were involved with illegal loans to help these corporations hide their losses, and the accounting firms that oversaw them and turned a blind eye are each facing their own investigations. One notable example is that federal and state regulators settled with ten Wall Street investment firms (including Citigroup, Merrill Lynch, J.P. Morgan Chase, and Credit Suisse First Boston) because of knowingly pushing bad stocks, conducting and publishing flawed research, and for conflicts of interest. They agreed to pay $1.4 billion in fines and to separate their investment banking activities and research activities. Most of these firms did not admit guilt and some changed their names to distance themselves from these scandals.

Although these scandals have left the front pages of the paper, Caffrey (2003) reports that the FBI had launched about four new investigations of fraud per month, each of which has surpassed $100 million in damages. However, shortly thereafter the focus of federal law enforcement was shifted to counterterrorism, meaning there is less focus on elite deviance now than before (see Chapter 6).

KEY TERMS

acts
actus reus
aggravated assault
alibi
arson
attempts
burglary
"buying, receiving, or
    possessing stolen property"
conspiracy
corporate crime
corporate violence
crime
crime trends
crimes by any other name
crimes known to the police
crimes of privilege
crimes of the state
criminal homicide
culpability
curfew violations and
    loitering
dark figure of crime
deregulation
disorderly conduct
driving under the influence
drug abuse violations
drunkenness
duress
elite deviance
embezzlement

entrapment
excuses
failures to act
forcible rape
forgery and counterfeiting
fraud
gambling
governmental deviance
Group A offenses
Group B offenses
immaturity
insanity
intentionally
International Crime Victims
    Survey
involuntary intoxication
justifications
knowingly
larceny-theft
legal definition of crime
liquor law violations
mens rea
motor vehicle theft
National Crime Victimization
    Survey
National Incident Based
    Reporting System
natural definition of crime
necessity
negligently
occupational crime

offenses against the family and
    children
pork
Part I index offenses
Part II offenses
procedural defenses
profit without honor
property crimes
prostitution and
    commercialized vice
recklessly
robbery
running away
selective prosecution
self-defense
self-report studies
serious crime
sex offenses
simple assaults
street crimes
the social reality of crime
trusted criminals
Uniform Crime Reports
vagrancy
vandalism
victim
victimization
violent crimes
white-collar crime
without defense or
    justification

DISCUSSION QUESTIONS

1. Compare and contrast the terms *natural crime* and *legal crime*.
2. List and define the eight "serious" crimes of the Uniform Crime Reports (UCR).
3. What does the term *serious* mean?
4. List and define the main elements of a crime.
5. Is it possible to show that a person committed an act with intent? Why or why not?
6. Outline some defenses that can be used when someone is charged with a crime.
7. List and define the main types of culpability, including *intentionality, recklessness, negligence,* and *knowingly.*
8. In your opinion, are there any less-serious crimes (Part II offenses of the UCR) that should be considered serious crimes (Part I offenses of the UCR)? Why or why not?
9. What is victimization?

10. Discuss how the definition of criminal victimization is too limited.
11. Define elite deviance and provide a few examples.
12. Which is more harmful to Americans, street crime or elite deviance?
13. What interest does the U.S. government have in maintaining the current image of crime and criminals?
14. Identify and discuss the main sources of crime data in the United States, including the UCR, the NCVS, and self-report studies.
15. What is meant by the *dark figure of crime*?
16. Does the United States have more crime than other countries? Why or why not?
17. Why do you think that the American criminal justice system does not collect national statistics on elite deviance?
18. How do the harms caused by the corporations reviewed in Issue in Depth compare to street crimes? Were the harms caused by these corporations committed intentionally or with some other form of culpability? Explain.

CHAPTER 5

"THE SKY IS FALLING! THE SKY IS FALLING!"— MEDIA PORTRAYALS OF CRIME AND CRIMINAL JUSTICE

1. Introduction
2. An Introduction to the Media
    *   Box 5-1.   The Media and Business
    a. What the Media Do and Do Not Do
3. Does It Matter? Are People Exposed to the Media?
4. Media Coverage of Crime and Criminal Justice
    *   Box 5-2.   The D. C. Snipers
    a. Focus of Media Reporting on Crime: What the Media Cover and Ignore
    b. Crime Trends
    c. Lack of Critical Coverage: Where's the Context?
    *   Box 5-3.   The Homeland Security Advisory System
    d. Media and Fear of Crime: The Chicken Little Phenomenon
5. Explanations of Media Inaccuracy
    a. Organizational Factors: Entertainment for Profit
    b. Peer Culture
    c. Lack of Criminal Justice Education
    d. The Role of Politics in the "Framing" of Crime
6. Conclusion
7. Issue in Depth—Media Coverage of September 11th and the War on Terror
8. Key Terms
9. Discussion Questions

INTRODUCTION

This chapter introduces you to the media, a term that includes a wide range of sources of news-related information. I examine what the media do and do not do and then turn

123

to how much people are exposed to the media in the United States. In discussing how the U.S. media cover crime and criminal justice, I show what the media cover, what they ignore, and why the media are so inaccurate when portraying crime and criminal justice. I also examine media coverage of terrorism and the war on terror. Implications of media inaccuracy for justice are discussed.

AN INTRODUCTION TO THE MEDIA

Many of society's problems are blamed on the **media.** We hear, for example, that the prevalence of violence in the United States is "because of the media." When school shootings rocked communities across the country in the late 1990s, parents and community leaders called for tougher standards for showing violent content in "the media" because of their suspicion that the media are responsible for copycat crimes.

But what are the media? Surette (1992, p. 10) defines the mass media as: "media that are easily, inexpensively, and simultaneously accessible to large segments of a population." These sources include newspapers, magazines, books, television, radio, film, and recordings. Mass media broadcast and communicate with a large audience. They are "critical carriers and definers of popular culture" including print, billboards, and electronic media (Altheide, 2006, p. 48).

Media sources are organized within a hierarchy of controlling institutions. Hess (1981) describes the media as having an inner ring, a middle ring, and an outer ring. These sources of media information are depicted in Figure 5-1.

The **inner ring of the media** includes the major television networks such as ABC, NBC, CBS, CNN, and Fox News; major news magazines such as *Time, Newsweek,* and *U.S. News & World Report*; national newspapers such as *The New York Times,* the *Washington Post, USA Today,* and *The Wall Street Journal*; and the Associated Press wire service. The **middle ring of the media** and the **outer ring of the media** are more prevalent but have far less influence on the news than the institutions in the inner ring.

These inner-ring sources are the main sources of information for Americans about many issues (Lewis, 1981; Marion, 1995). Crime, as a major issue for society, is usually

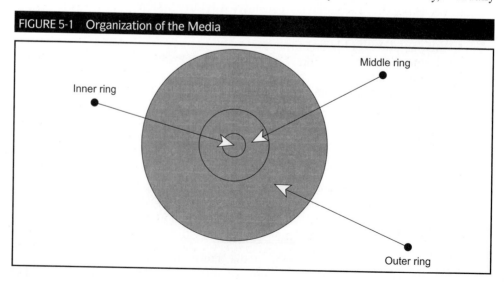

FIGURE 5-1   Organization of the Media

news (Merlo and Benekos, 2000). The Center for Media and Public Affairs, for example, found that almost 30% of local news is devoted to crime and criminal justice (Center for Media and Public Affairs, 2000). This number fluctuates based on national events; for example, after 9/11, a much larger portion of the news was devoted to coverage of terrorism and later to the war on Iraq.

The media are our main source for news about crime and criminal justice policy. As noted by Krajicek (1998, p. 139): "The press provides our window on public problems, on the government's strategies to solve them, and on how well those strategies succeed (or fail)." The media sources in the inner ring have greater influence than other sources. According to Harrigan (2000, p. 120), "The organization at the top of the media hierarchy decides what counts as news." This is true because most journalists consult these sources for their own news (Weaver and Wilhoit, 1986). Reporters of crime news commonly "copy" what other media reporters are doing. When reputable sources cover crime problems in the media, other reporters take their lead and follow with very similar stories.

As one example, virtually all of the 1,700 newspapers in the United States subscribe to the Associated Press (AP), the largest news organization in the world. The AP is a nonprofit cooperative that serves more than 5,000 television and U.S. radio stations and more than 8,500 media outlets throughout the world through AP online. The AP compiles thousands of stories each day, of which only a couple of dozen are sent to the local, regional, national, and international wires for inclusion in various media outlets (Krajicek, 1998). Historically, crime has been considered newsworthy by the media. Because newsworthy events are determined by media outlets that are owned by large corporations, the public's image of crime is at least partially defined by the wealthy and powerful. The issue of corporate ownership of the media is discussed in Box 5-1.

Figure 5-2 (see page 128) illustrates how the media can transform a minor problem into a major one. Try to imagine a recent crime story, for example, one related to a threat of terrorism against some place in your community. How does this threat become newsworthy in your community and ultimately to the whole nation? I suggest in the figure that crime problems (such as terror threats) are actually created and spread because of media coverage. For example, when a terror threat is received, local radio and television stations and newspapers will cover the story, leading to isolated local stories. As other, unrelated terror threats are received in other locations, the problem of terror threats becomes more newsworthy and leads to increased, diverse coverage in the media. To the consumer of news, with the increased coverage of terror threats, it appears that the problem is widespread or happening everywhere. With each new threat, all previous threats are rehashed, leaving the viewer with the perception that these threats are more common than they truly are and that they are probably connected. Now the public becomes concerned and legislative bodies begin to discuss what can be done about the problem, ultimately leading to some tough talk by politicians in the media and even some new laws. Anytime politicians talk tough or pass new laws, there is more coverage of the problem, some analysis, and justifications for the changes in law. Though the problem may not be much of a problem in reality, to the public it appears that the problem has grown immensely because there is much more evidence of the problem in all forms of media. So, in essence, the media are involved in constructing or creating crime problems.

BOX 5-1

THE MEDIA AND BUSINESS

The major news media are owned and thus controlled by major corporations: "By the late 1980s, eight corporations controlled eight of the inner-ring media and a host of middle- and outer-ring media, including 40 television stations, over 200 cable television systems, more than 60 radio stations, 59 magazines, and 41 book publishers" (Parenti, 1993, p. 26). Half of the nation's newspapers are controlled by just 10 large chains, and only about 2% of cities have competing newspapers (Graber, 1996). About 24 corporations control most of the U.S. culture industry (Herman and Chomsky, 1988).

Ben Bagdikian's book, *The New Media Monopoly* (2004), chronicles the ever-growing stranglehold that major corporations have on news in the United States. Since the 1980s, ownership of the media has narrowed. In 1983, 50 corporations owned the media. As of 2002, according to *The Nation,* just 10 corporations control all the mainstream news and entertainment media. Amazingly, only five corporations now own most of the mainstream news. For example:

- General Electric (GE), with revenues of $129.9 billion, owns NBC, CNBC, and part of MSNBC, at least 13 television stations, and numerous other channels, Internet companies, sports teams, and various other business such as aircraft engines and medical equipment.
- AOL/Time Warner, with revenues of $36.2 billion, owns CNN, Headline News, CNNfn, CNN/SI, at least 64 magazines, more than 40 music labels, several book companies,

Internet companies, and sports teams, and is the second largest provider of cable television.

- Walt Disney, with revenues of $25.4 billion, owns ABC, ESPN, ESPN2, at least 10 television stations, several magazines and book companies, as well as sports teams, movie companies, radio stations, and theme parks.
- Viacom, with revenues of $20 billion, owns CBS, MTV, MTV2, at least 39 television stations, major movie companies, several book companies, magazines, more than 100 radio stations, and Internet companies.
- News Corporation, with revenues of $11.6 billion, owns Fox, Fox News Channel, at least 26 television stations, major satellite and cable companies, books, newspapers, movies, and magazines, as well as sports teams.

In 2004, according to Bagdikian, "five huge corporations—Time Warner, Disney, Murdoch's News Corporation, Bertelsmann of Germany, and Viacom (formerly CBS)—own most of the newspapers, magazines, books, radio and TV stations, and movie studios of the United States." Bagdikian claims these media corporations "manufacture politics and social values," values that are consistent with conservative and "far right politics" according to Bagdikian . . . "It is not just national economics that is at stake. . . . Nor is it just the neglect of broadcast media giantism by the government agencies that by law are still required to operate 'in the public interest.' The public interest is to have the country's largest broadcasting system in the world provide diversity in news, opinion, and commentary that serves all Americans, right, left, and independent, as well as access to their local stations as well as true choices in national programs. What is at stake is American democracy itself. A country without all the significant news, points of view, and information its citizens need to be informed voters is risking the loss of democratic rights. Voters without genuine choices and without the information they need to choose what meets their own needs and wishes has produced something alarming: on Election Day our voters are forced to vote for what is the narrowest political choices among all industrial democracies of the world."

For the purposes of this book, what is most relevant is that many viewers are unaware that the crime and criminal justice news they see on TV and in the newspapers is the version that large corporations choose to air. Would it be logical to expect these corporations to focus on their own acts of deviance and harmful behaviors? As will be discussed later in this chapter, there is substantial evidence that the media tend to ignore corporate crimes.

Perhaps this is why street crime is more likely to be the focus of news than the more harmful behaviors of elite deviance discussed in Chapter 4. The disproportionate focus on street crime is a form of labeling whereby certain segments of the society are identified as bad, deviant, or immoral (Gans, 1995). In this process, evil is dramatized, and the notion of "us" versus "them" is reinforced, because we tend to think of criminals as being different from us. This "dualistic fallacy" is troubling because media coverage of crime is more reflective of crime myths than of realities (Kappeler and Potter, 2004). As images of crime tend to depict certain groups of society as bad, deviant, and immoral, they reinforce stereotypes created by U.S. criminal law.

U.S. corporations, through the inner ring of media outlets they own and control, define problems, identify crises, and thereby determine "what issues will be brought to the attention of political leaders" and U.S. citizens (Harrigan, 2000, p. 124). They also determine which issues and problems will be ignored.

The media are among the nation's group of elite individuals, corporations, and institutions because they have a direct impact on policies, including criminal justice activity, by limiting "the breadth of ideological views that enter the policy-making debate in the United States. The media also choose which stories to emphasize and which to ignore. . . . Finally, the media are merely a group of corporations that are owned by other corporations and financial institutions" (Simon and Hagan, 1999, p. 12).

If one of the fundamental purposes of government is to protect innocent human life, and if one of the fundamental duties of the media is to report on truths, where is the coverage of acts that are the most deadly to Americans—elite deviance? Why is there so much media focus on murder? Is it because corporations benefit from media ignorance that this occurs?

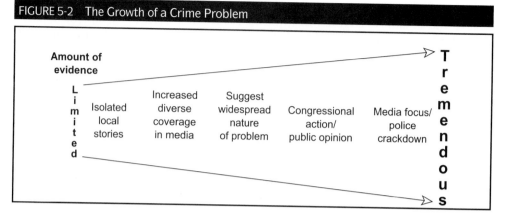

FIGURE 5-2   The Growth of a Crime Problem

What the Media Do and Do Not Do

Because people do not simply absorb ideological propaganda (Potter and Kappeler, 1998), the media do not tell the public what to think, but they may tell the public what to think about (Bennett, 1980; Iyengar and Kinder, 1987; McCombs and Shaw, 1972; Muraskin and Domash, 2006; Sacco, 2005). Whatever is covered in the media is perceived to be important and worthy of viewer attention. Whether the attention is actually warranted on the basis of the nature and severity of the issue being covered is debatable.

According to Altheide (2006, p. 61) the "news media contribute to public agendas, official and political rhetoric, and public perceptions of social problems as well as preferences for certain solutions. . . . For many people, the mass media in general and the new media in particular are a 'window' on the world." Further, the media "inform public opinion" and "contribute in no small way to setting social and political agendas" (p. 78).

Without question, the news media, in their broadcasts and editorials, alert and even alarm the public and lawmakers about important events and issues (Hollinger and Lanza-Kaduce, 1988; Muraskin and Domash, 2006; Sacco, 2005). Given that people are "passive consumers" of most forms of the media (such as television), it is not surprising that media coverage shapes a person's conception of reality: "People use knowledge they obtain from the media to construct a picture of the world, an image of reality on which they base their actions" (Surette, 1992, p. 2).

As explained by Potter and Kappeler (1998, p. 7), "Media coverage directs people's attention to specific crimes and helps to shape those crimes as social problems." The main problem with media coverage of crime, as you will see, is that it is dangerously inaccurate. The media alter the perceptions people have of criminal justice activity and distort the facts about crime (Marion, 1995; Van Horn, Baumer, and Gormley, 1992).

An alarming realization is that the media tend to cover the same crime repeatedly as it processes through the criminal justice network. With any recent development in a case, the details of the original crime are rehashed, fostering an impression that the crime occurred more than once. When the case goes to trial or is plea bargained, when a sentence is passed down, and so on, the viewer learns these details from the media once more. The effect is a general feeling that there is much more crime out there than there really is.

To the extent that media coverage of crime is repetitive and pervasive, it is more likely that it will affect people's attitudes about crime (Surette, 1992, pp. 86–87). This is true in terms of not only what the media cover, but also what they fail to cover: "By emphasizing or ignoring topics, [the media] may influence the list of issues that are important to the public" (p. 87). Corporate crimes are virtually ignored by the media; thus most people, even criminology and criminal justice students, do not perceive such acts as threatening to their own personal safety (Robinson, 1999).

Of course, the media are not the only sources of information from which a person constructs his or her own reality. According to Surette (1992, p. 4), four primary sources are used, including personal experiences, significant others (peers, family, friends), other social groups and institutions (schools, churches, government agencies), and the mass media (Altheide, 1984; Quinney, 1970; Tuchman, 1978): "Knowledge from all of these sources is mixed together, and from this mix, each individual constructs the 'world.'" Logically, the influence of the mass media likely increases as the influence of the other sources declines (Cohen and Young, 1981; Lichter, 1988).

Given that 90% of Americans will not be victimized by serious street crime (Barkan, 1997; Kappeler and Potter, 2004) and that most people do not know anyone who chooses to talk about personal experience of criminal victimization, the media are a prime source of information about crime (Potter and Kappeler, 1998). Other scholars make the same claim, that the U.S. media are basic sources about crime and criminal justice (Barak, 1994; Ericson, Baranek, and Chan, 1989; Graber, 1980).

In this chapter, I will examine how and why media coverage of crime is inaccurate and dangerous. This chapter will compare the realities of crime examined in the previous chapter with the way crime is portrayed on television, in the newspapers, and in popular entertainment. First, I examine the degree to which people actually are exposed to media sources.

DOES IT MATTER? ARE PEOPLE EXPOSED TO THE MEDIA?

Selective media coverage might be less problematic if viewers did not expose themselves to it. A study by the Pew Research Center for the People and the Press (2006) shows that 54% regularly watch local news, 34% watch cable TV news, 28% watch nightly network news, and 23% watch morning network news. About 40% read a newspaper and 36% listen to news on the radio. Finally, about 21% get news from the Internet regularly (three or more times per week). The average amount of time spent per day watching TV news was 53 minutes, followed by 43 minutes listening to radio news, 40 minutes reading the newspaper, and 32 minutes reading news online.

So most Americans do not follow the news closely. Yet the nature of crime news is that it does not have to be followed closely, particularly at the national level. As will be illustrated later, crime news is prevalent at all levels of news coverage, even the local level. It should not be surprising, then, that the media are the people's main source of information about crime (Beckett and Sasson, 2003). Tunnell (1992, p. 295) cites a National Crime Survey that found that 96% of Americans reported they relied on the media for information about crime. Fields and Jerin (1999, p. 94) cite research showing that most Gallup poll respondents report believing that the media are accurate in their depictions of crime.

Television is a more significant source of news than newspapers (Angolabahere, Behr, and Iyengar, 1993; Pew Research Center for the People and the Press, 2006). The average American spends more than three hours per day—about nine times as long as playing sports, exercising, and all other leisure-time physical activities combined—watching TV (Dong, Block, and Mandel, 2004). The average American child watches television between three and four hours per day (American Academy of Pediatrics, 2002; Center for Media Education, 2000). Further, 2- to 17-year olds spend more than four hours per day "in front of electronic screens (televisions, computers, and video games)" (Altheide, 2006, p. 53). People are less exposed to other sources of news information, such as newspapers, because television is more easily consumed; it can be taken in passively and does not require the ability to read in order to watch (Surette, 1992).

According to the Gallup Organization, which polls Americans on a variety of topics, "Americans are more likely now than at any point in the previous 15 years to say that news organizations' stories and reports are inaccurate. Additionally, about half of Americans perceive that there is a bias towards one political party or the other in the way news organizations report the news, and by a two-to-one margin, those who feel there is a bias say it favors the Democrats." Given that the mainstream media are owned by large corporations that tend to be conservative by definition, this is an interesting finding!

The Pew Research Center for the People and the Press (2006) adds, "Public displeasure with the national news media is clear, but this sentiment has not eroded the credibility of major news organizations. While public evaluations of most news organizations' credibility are lower than they were in the mid-1980s, the basic believability ratings have not changed since the center's last survey in 1996. The words people choose to describe the national media reflect their discontent. *Biased* and *sensational* were used nearly as often as *good* and *informative* when survey participants were asked to come up with one word to describe their impression of the national news media. On balance, negative words outnumbered positive ones 52% to 30%." Further, "Displeasure with the national news media in general does not translate, however, into lower believability ratings for specific news organizations. On average, majorities say they can believe most, but not all of what national news organizations say. A fair share of Americans are real doubters, however."

A Gallup poll in 2003 showed that a majority of Americans believe that crime has increased on a national scale over the past year. According to the Gallup Organization: "The poll was conducted as the news media were covering a series of sniper shootings in the Washington, D.C. area, which could affect the public's perceptions about the crime rate." Even though respondents were no more likely to report being worried about being a crime victim and were no more likely to report taking precautions to prevent their own victimization, this poll shows the power of the media when it comes to informing public opinion. As noted earlier, when the media cover crime more, it leads to the perception that crime is increasing, even when it is not. Coverage of the D.C. sniper shootings is discussed in Box 5-2.

MEDIA COVERAGE OF CRIME AND CRIMINAL JUSTICE

Fascinating research on the media and crime is found in *Scooped!*, written by former crime reporter David Krajicek (1998). The subtitle of this inside look at media coverage of crime reflects its author's informed opinion: *Media Miss Real Story on Crime*

BOX 5-2

THE D.C. SNIPERS

During a three-week period in October 2002, Americans along the mid-Atlantic United States suddenly became targets of a sadistic sniper who randomly shot 13 people while they shopped, pumped gas, and went about their normal lives. Since the attacks took place only 13 months after the terrorist attacks of September 11, 2001, mainstream media quickly asked whether the sniper attacks were being carried out by terrorists affiliated with al-Qaeda.

To some degree, this was a logical question, for our national leaders had pointed out the possibility of thousands of additional terrorists living in the United States even after 9/11. Additionally, several experts predicted al-Qaeda might very well attack "soft targets" next—people going about their daily business in places such as malls, shopping centers, apartment buildings, and so forth, who are hard to protect from such attacks.

As it turned out, the attackers were 41-year-old John Allen Williams, a former member of the U.S. military who later changed his name to John Allen Muhammad after joining the Nation of Islam, and 17-year-old Lee Boyd Malvo. Both men were also involved in robbery and murder in Alabama, Arizona, California, Georgia, Louisiana, and Texas. In total, the men allegedly killed 16 people, including 13 in the sniper attacks.

Since both men are African American, they do not fit the profile of the typical mass murderer, a middle-aged white male. In part because of intense media coverage of the "beltway sniper," "D.C. sniper," and "serial sniper," law enforcement officials were originally looking for a lone white male driving a white van or box truck. Officials involved in the investigation appeared on television frequently with large pictures of white vans and trucks asking for assistance in locating such vehicles which supposedly had been seen at the scene of several of the sniper attacks. As it turned out, the snipers were driving a dark blue Chevrolet Caprice automobile. The mistaken identification of the type of car being used by the killers was due to two factors: eyewitnesses who actually did see white vans and trucks near the scene of each attack, and intense media coverage of the type of vehicle—suggesting people should be on the lookout for this type of vehicle.

Given the nature of the sniper attacks, it is not surprising that media coverage was intense. After all, the attacks were violent, random, and bizarre. At several of the attacks, the killers left behind notes as well as tarot cards, leading some media outlets to call the killers the "tarot card killer." Consistent with the way the media tend to cover crime stories, media coverage of the sniper attacks focused on small details of the attacks, such as the type of vehicle being driven, the type of weapon being used, and the discovery of the notes and tarot cards at some of the crime scenes. Further, the media focused on the human elements of the crimes, telling the stories of the victims.

Mainstream media outlets developed their own special graphics and "theme songs" for the sniper story. They sent reporters to report live from the scenes (after the attacks were over and when nothing was happening at the scenes). Experts from law enforcement were

(continued)

BOX 5-2 *(Continued)*

disproportionately featured as guests, and numerous experts from psychology and forensic profiling were consulted to discuss possible motivations, as were those who specialize in terrorism. Coverage was redundant, making the same statements repeatedly over long hours of coverage and promoting fear in viewers. Because of a lack of context about how unlikely one was to become the victim of the snipers, given the massive population in Washington D.C. and the surrounding areas, people became afraid of being shot while shopping or pumping gas. Many people pumped their gas crouching beside their cars or lying beneath them!

Ultimately, Muhammad was convicted of murder and sentenced to death; Malvo was convicted of murder and sentenced to life in prison without the possibility of parole. Thereafter, the story subsided in the media, but not after much damage was done to the psyche of the American public.

While Chasing Sex, Sleaze, and Celebrities. Krajicek's main claim about the media is this: "Take a predisposition toward simplicity and anecdote, add unsophisticated reporting, a degenerating peer culture, an overworked news staff, the rapture of sex and celebrities, and—poof!—you've got today's crime journalism" (p. 180).

Disgusted with this type of crime reporting, Krajicek quit his job as a reporter. Why? In his words, he explains:

> While we [reporters] were sitting in vans counting arrests, we missed the most important story on the crime beat: the collapse of the U.S. criminal justice system as an effective means of fighting crime, maintaining order, ensuring public safety, and meting out equitable justice. . . . I came to conclude that the media had been scooped by myopia, sleazy story distractions, and an unhealthy devotion to the official police agenda. (p. 111)

Krajicek argues that the media misrepresent reality, much the same as what Reiman (2006) points out about the image of crime in U.S. society. As you may recall from Chapter 2, Reiman described the American conception of crime as a problem of the poor as distorted, much like a reflection in a carnival mirror. In Krajicek's words: "Today, reading a newspaper or watching a news telecast can be like looking at the country's reflection in a fun-house mirror. The society we see presented in the news is a warped place, often morbid and alarming" (p. 4). It should be no surprise to you that for a lot of people, "the term crime evokes an image of a young African American male who is armed with a handgun and commits a robbery, rape, or murder. In the minds of many Americans, crime is synonymous with black crime." Why? Because those "crimes that receive the most attention—from the media, from politicians, and from criminal justice policy makers—are 'street crimes' such as murder, robbery, and rape."

As explained by Krajicek (1998, pp. 5–6), the media provide crime-anxious Americans with excited accounts of horrible crimes; present tenuous evidence that the crimes, however anomalous, could happen to each of us; seek out the accountable individuals (judges and probation officers); devise snappy slogans to package the problem neatly; and serve up images of scowling politicians thumping their lecterns about the latest legislation that surely would stop such atrocities: "We're finally getting tough on crime. We're no longer coddling criminals. We're making America's streets safe again."

Whether crime news is based on fact and is representative of the truth is irrelevant — "the politicians wanted expedient answers, not information" — "efficacy means nothing; image is everything" (Krajicek, 1998, pp. 5, 17). I will return to the issue of how politics is involved in the "framing" of crime and criminal justice later in this chapter.

In terms of criminal justice, TV media coverage inaccurately portrays the U.S. criminal justice network. Marion (1995) explains that the "early steps in the [criminal justice] process (law enforcement, investigation and arrest) are emphasized, and the other steps are almost invisible, especially informal procedures such as plea bargaining. Lawyers are often shown as actively investigating crimes, which rarely occurs" (Potter and Kappeler, 1998, p. 108). This is especially true in the everyday cases of poor people represented by publicly assigned counsel (see Chapter 7).

In fact, most criminal justice cases receive no coverage from the media (Haltom, 1998, p. 157). Those rare cases that are covered tend to be atypical. As a result, false conceptions of what is "ordinary" are gained from these extraordinary cases. The O. J. Simpson trial wrongly showed Americans that the criminal justice network works too slowly and is more focused on defendants' rights than on victims' rights. For wealthy clients in highly publicized cases, the process of justice will be slow and deliberate. Yet most court clients are poor and do not receive a trial; instead, they are convicted through the informal process of plea bargaining (see Chapter 7).

Despite all the controversial issues regarding TV in the courts (e.g., see Surette, 1992), the most troubling aspect of the TV camera in the courtroom is the fact that what people see is not representative of the typical court case. While people see trials in their entirety on *Court TV* and in part on shows such as *Dateline NBC,* the reality is that more than 90% of cases do not lead to trial but are handled informally through plea bargaining (see Chapter 7). People think that trials are the rule when, in fact, they are the "exceptional case" (Cole and Smith, 2006). The media thus "emphasize the rare-in-reality adversarial criminal trial," which leads the viewer to believe that the typical court case in the United States is "a high-stakes, complicated, arcane contest practiced by expert professionals and beyond the understanding of everyday citizens" (Surette, 1992, p. 40), even though the reality is the assembly-line justice of plea bargaining. In other words, people think we are following a due process model of criminal justice when in fact we are using a crime control model. At the same time, corrections is the least shown aspect of criminal justice, so that the further one moves into the system, the worse the image becomes of American criminal justice (p. 41).

According to Haltom (1998, p. 157), media coverage of crimes in U.S. courts "tends to emphasize 'Crime Control' values" such as assuring "security from wrongdoers, just desserts, and punishment" while simultaneously devaluing due process concerns such as constitutional protections of the accused. Haltom maintains that only in celebrated cases do the media highlight due process values. From his analysis, it is clear that media coverage of criminal justice in the courts is partly responsible for the United States' shift to a crime control model of criminal justice.

Given that reporters rely on insiders for information, it is logical that media coverage of courts will support crime control values. The result is that reporters will be encouraged to "cover some aspects of the news more than others" (Haltom, 1998, p. 158). It is a symbiotic relationship in which the reporters get information and court personnel ensure the type of coverage that is favorable to their daily activities (Schlesinger and Tumber, 1994). Haltom suggests that "court sources 'feed' court reporters, and thus the news is largely what the reporters have 'eaten.'"

There are several reasons why crime control values will be emphasized over due process values. As noted earlier, the main reason is that members of the U.S. crime control bureaucracy are more likely to interact with the media than advocates of due process. Another reason that media slant their coverage of criminal justice in a manner more consistent with a crime control model is that it is simply

> easier to understand for reporters, their editors, and their audiences. Struggles between cops and robbers, good guys and bad guys, protectors and perpetrators are easy to write, to source, and to read or to view. Arcane rules and technicalities elude readers and viewers, many of whom have no idea what the rules are or what they mean (Haltom, 1998, p. 165).

One reason that it is easier is that reporters often rely on prosecutors' offices for their stories. Dreschel (1983) suggests that prosecutors are more helpful to reporters than defense attorneys in terms of clarifying facts and offering tips about stories. Because prosecutors are more concerned with crime control than with due process, logically their biases are reflected in any subsequent media coverage.

Finally, since the most common people seen in the news are criminals and suspected criminals, viewers will likely develop values consistent with the crime control model of criminal justice. After criminals and suspects, the next most likely group to be seen on the news is crime victims and their families (Project for Excellence in Journalism, 2001).

Media coverage of policing is plagued by numerous problems as well. Typically, police television shows such as *COPS* and *World's Wildest Police Videos* misrepresent crime, criminals, and typical police work. They tend to focus on the most violent, random, and bizarre stories while ignoring more routine calls for service. They also tend to characterize criminals as minorities who are typified as more threatening or suffering from some form of insanity (Chiricos and Eschholtz, 2002; Perlmutter, 2001).

Corrections is probably the least covered aspect of criminal justice by the media. Aside from documentaries and occasional stories of the nation's prisons, most Americans have no idea about the realities of American prisons, such as the enormous pains of imprisonment suffered each day by inmates (see Chapter 9).

Focus of Media Reporting on Crime: What the Media Cover and Ignore

As explained before, media portrayals of crime are "selectively determine[d]" by media outlets (Merlo and Benekos, 2000, p. 5). Generally, decisions are made to feature "the most sensational, emotional, significant, and universally appealing aspects" of crime for public viewing (Sacco, 1995). As Krajicek (1998, p. 95) said about his own work, crime reports focus on the miserable, the deviant, the strange, and the "particularly cruel." The common saying, "if it bleeds, it leads," accurately characterizes the philosophy of the media in the United States. Platt (1999) calls nightly news "Armageddon—Live at 6 (P.M.)!" Sabato (1993), in his book *Feeding Frenzy,* claims that American media coverage of politics is comparable to an attack of sharks on a helpless victim. Although his research focuses on politics generally, his arguments apply to media coverage of crime and criminal justice as well. Metaphorically speaking, if there is blood in the water, the media will likely cover a story about crime.

Research clearly demonstrates that crime news is focused on the most violent types of crime (Potter and Kappeler, 1998), at least those that occur at the street level (e.g., see Chiricos, 1995; Kooistra, Mahoney, and Westervelt, 1999). Of particular interest to the media are the rarest and "most egregious examples" of crime.

Television news generally shows violence at a rate much higher than its incidence in society would seem to justify (Newman, 1990). As noted by Krajicek (1998, p. 4): "Murder and sexual offenses are the marquee offenses . . . and certain cases, generally based upon nubility or celebrity, are anointed for extravagant coverage." A study cited in Surette (1992, p. 68) showed that 26% of news stories were focused on murder, even though murder regularly accounts for only 0.1% to 0.2% of all crimes known to the police (see Chapter 4). Although murder may be the most heinous of all crimes, this disproportionate focus does not seem justified by its prevalence in the United States. At the same time, even though about half of the crimes that are reported to the police are nonviolent, they made up only 4% of the stories in the same study. Additionally, it is the most heinous and bizarre of all murders that tend to be most widely discussed in the media (e.g., see Paulsen, 2000).

Altheide (2006, p. 63) discusses the significance of media focus on violent crime for the average citizen: "Serious personal criminal attacks happen rarely, but they are regarded as typical and quite common by American citizens because virtually all mass media reports about crime focus on the most spectacular, dramatic, and violent. With the images of blood, guns, psychopaths, and suffering in front of them and inside their heads, it is quite difficult to offer programmatic criticisms of our current approach to crime and accompanying issues such as prisons and other modes of dispute resolution, including restitution and negotiation. As long as crime and mayhem are presented in such familiar and fun formats, new information will not be forthcoming . . . only a recycling of affirmations tied to previous popular culture." Since violent crime is equated with crime in the media, viewers are more likely to support " 'tough crime legislation,' including mandatory sentencing, 'three strikes and you're out,' and capital punishment" (p. 75).

Terrorism is no different. As horrible as the events of September 11, 2001, were, the fact is that four planes were crashed that day by terrorists, out of thousands that were in the air that day. Consider this: If thousands of flights per day landed successfully before the terrorist attacks and roughly the same number per day since then, how was the intense media coverage of those flights justified? The rare nature of the event and the horrifying result is what is used to justify the coverage. The problem, however, is that such coverage may lead viewers to conclude wrongly that flying is unsafe and/or that such terrorism is likely to happen to them when they fly.

Marsh (1991) conducted a review of studies of media coverage and crime and found that for every two stories of property crimes, there were eight stories of violent crimes. Newspapers in the mid-1980s covered the violent crimes of murder, rape, robbery, and assault four times more than they did the property crimes of theft, burglary, and motor vehicle theft, even though property crimes make up at least 90% of street crimes in any given year (see Chapter 4).

By focusing on certain types of crimes over others, the media are thus involved in "constructing" the typical view of crime, even when they are only reporting "extreme, dramatic cases: the public is more likely to think they are representative because of the emphasis by the media" (Chermak, 1994, p. 580). Potter and Kappeler (1998, p. 7) explain: "Media coverage directs people's attention to specific crimes and helps to shape those crimes as social problems." This means Americans are much more concerned with violent crimes such as murder, even though they are much more likely to be victimized by property crimes such as theft and burglary and acts of elite deviance that receive virtually no coverage.

The media are also preoccupied with random crime (Merlo and Benekos, 2000), which partly explains the focus on terrorism (which is very rare in the United States). Not surprisingly, one type of crime that has received a tremendous amount of coverage in recent years is school violence. After the tragic mass murder of a dozen students and a teacher at Columbine High School in Littleton, Colorado, in 1999, the national news on each of the three major network news stations (ABC, NBC, CBS) devoted no less than half of each night's newscasts to this subject for approximately a month after the murders. But despite a commonsense impression to the contrary, in fact, school violence was not increasing during this time period, but rather was decreasing!

Figure 5-3 shows the number of homicides at schools in the United States in the 1990s. Lost in coverage about the mass murder at Columbine was the fact that school violence had declined in the 1990s. Further, homicides at school were the lowest in 1999 than any other year in the 1990s. That is, kids were safer that year than any other year in the 1990s.

How much news was devoted to the massacre at the campus of the Virginia Polytechnic Institute and University? While this was the worst mass murder ever committed by a single person with firearms in the United States, far more deadly things happened on that day. Yet since they were not "violent," "random," "rare" or "bizarre," they did not receive any coverage. For example, roughly 1,178 people died that day from tobacco use (and every day since), which kills 430,000 Americans every year. Another 821 died from poor diet and inactivity that day (and every day since), which kills 300,000 Americans every year. Another 110 died in car crashes (and every day

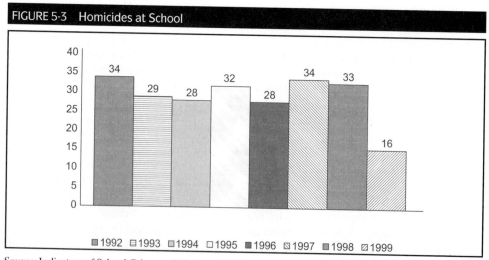

FIGURE 5-3   Homicides at School

Source: Indicators of School Crime and Violence 2004. http://nces.ed.gov/pubs2005/crime_safe04/figures.asp.

since), which kills 40,000 Americans every year. Another 82 died from defective products (and every day since), which kill 30,000 every year. And I could go on, but I think you get the point. While there clearly are differences between an intentional mass murder of 32 people committed by a troubled student, I already demonstrated in Chapter 4 that the other forms of killing just mentioned are also committed with **culpability**—responsibility or moral blameworthiness. When the media ignores these acts, it creates a false impression in the viewers of what is most likely to kill them.

Even though the media give much attention to crime, they typically ignore harmful acts committed by the wealthy, such as white-collar crime (Potter and Kappeler, 1998; Surette, 1992) and corporate crime (Evans and Lundman, 1987; Randell, 1995). This is troubling precisely because the harms associated with such acts clearly dwarf those resulting from all street crimes combined in any given year (see Chapter 4). Neglect of this topic stems from the risk of libel suits; interrelationships between the media and business; the pro-business orientation of the media; and difficulties associated with investigating white-collar crime (Potter and Kappeler, 1998, p. 15, citing Mintz, 1992). The media focus almost exclusively on street crimes, so that three classes of people are depicted—the upper class, the middle class, and the "criminal class" (Barak, 1994).

Recently, in the wake of the corporate scandals that sent our stock market crashing, led to hundreds of billions of dollars in losses to investors, and resulted in tens of thousands of Americans losing their jobs and retirement savings, the media finally began to tell the story of corporate crime in America. We learned of the fraud and embezzlement of Enron, Andersen, WorldCom, Tyco, and dozens of other corporations (recall the Issue in Depth at the end of Chapter 4). Unfortunately, once new laws were passed that supposedly "cracked down" on "bad apples," our attention was diverted away from such crimes toward a coming war with Iraq. And now, as if corporate crime is a thing of the past, the media rarely mention it.

At the time of this writing, some of the most closely followed stories deal with random violence committed by young people against the homeless. Some major networks hyped the story to make it appear that the United States is suffering from an epidemic of attacks by young people on the homeless. On the CNN website, for example, the news organization created figures showing an interactive map of the United States that depicted three attacks in Florida, two in California, and one attack each in the states of Colorado, Oregon, Michigan, Wisconsin, and Rhode Island. Each interactive "dot" (where an attack occurred) could be clicked on to learn the details of the attack. CNN thus created the illusion of a national epidemic based on nine recent attacks. Another figure by CNN showed the number of reported attacks on the rise from 1999 through 2006—from 52 to 141 attacks. Of course there is no official source of such data, meaning the number of attacks is a function of societal focus on the issue. Nor did CNN show a rate of attacks, controlling for population growth or the growth of the homeless. Either of these could create the appearance of an increase in attacks on the homeless.

All of this is problematic precisely because the media serve as the major source of information about crime for most people (Beckett and Sasson, 2003). As I have shown in Figure 5-4, crime stories funnel out to media viewers, but they are in no way accurate of what most crime really is—nor is public perception of crime.

The media also have historically not paid much attention to costly and misguided criminal justice policies. Krajicek writes: "Collectively, journalists were scooped on the biggest crime story of the last quarter of this century by neglecting to adequately

FIGURE 5-4   How the Media Shapes Public Opinion of Crime

inform a puzzled public that our system of law enforcement and punishment, cobbled together with razor wire and prison bars, has been an expensive folly" (1998, p. 5).

The media typically do not challenge the legal institution when it needs to be challenged. Although the media may question a particular enforcement (e.g., the vicious beating of Rodney King by Los Angeles police officers, captured on videotape, or of an unarmed, elderly man in New Orleans), they rarely challenge the legal institution as a whole (Reiman, 2006). What about police corruption and police brutality as a regular, everyday occurrence for some Americans? What about the way police discretion in the United States permits and perhaps even encourages such actions? The media rarely discuss such issues. As a result, media reporting reinforces the validity of law and the myths inherent in the law: "Crime news . . . tends to be ideological insofar as it represents a worldview of state managers" (Welch, Fenwick, and Roberts, 1998, p. 220).

Some specific events (e.g., Willie Horton's crimes, committed after he was released early on a prison furlough) have been used by politicians, through the media, to reinforce a need for new laws that crack down even harder on street crimes and poor minorities. In these cases, the media act as mouthpieces for sound-bite politicians.

Crime Trends

Even when crime is going down, stories about declines in crime are like "a dinghy bobbing in a rolling sea" of stories about individual, thoughtless, and salacious crime reports (Krajicek, 1998, p. 12). Individual stories erroneously suggest that crime is increasing even when it is not (Beckett and Sasson, 2003). This is one example of how media activity reinforces myths about crime: people believe that crime is increasing even when it is not (Kappeler and Potter, 2004). The media achieve this by providing "a steady diet of the growing and omnipotent danger of interpersonal crime" (Barak, 1995, p. 133).

For example, in the mid-1990s, when violent crime was decreasing to its lowest levels in 20 years, crime coverage on television and in the newspapers increased in one city by more than 400% (Chiricos, Eschholtz, and Gertz, 1997). In 1993, the three major news networks ran 1,632 crime stories on their evening newscasts, up from 785 in 1992 and 571 in 1991. This occurred even though victimization rates of the NCVS and crime rates of the UCR were down during this time (Potter and Kappeler, 1998, p. 3). Not surprisingly, 88% of Americans in 1994 thought crime was at an all-time high (Barkan, 1997; Jackson, 1994). Additionally, between 1992 and 1993, major network evening news coverage of homicide tripled even as homicide rates remained unchanged, and from 1993 to 1996, major network news increased coverage of homicide 721% (National Center on Institutions and Alternatives, 1999).

Studies of violent crime rates and drug use rates versus media coverage of violent crime and drug crimes on television and in the newspapers show clearly that amount of coverage is not directly related to actual trends of violence or drug use. Instead, coverage tends to increase for reasons unrelated to actual trends of crime. And public concern about crime peaks with media coverage, rather than actual crime or drug use trends (MacCoun and Reuter, 2001).

Approximately one-fifth of local television news relates to crime, as does more than one-tenth of national news and about one-quarter of newspaper space (Ericson et al., 1989; Surette, 1998). In many markets, stories about crime comprise about 25–35% of news in many news markets (Altheide, 2006, p. 75). Some studies find that crime stories make up as much as 61% of newscasts, and one found that "13% of all newscasts began with three crime stories in a row, back to back to back" (Project for Excellence in Journalism, 2005). In fact, you've probably seen a local newscast that follows the typical format of local news across the United States—crime, crime, bad story, crime, trivial story, crime, bad story, weather, sports, feel good story.

By trivial story, I am referring to so-called "soft" or "lifestyle" news pertaining to celebrity lifestyles, gossip, and similar stories. Between 1977 and 1997, coverage of "hard" news declined from 67.3% to 41.3%, whereas news about celebrities tripled from 2% to 7%! Additionally, "soft" news doubled from 13.5% to about 25%. "Network news times was increasingly devoted to celebrity news, and the 'morning news' shows emphasized more commercial and product advertising to promote the conglomerates that owned them" (Altheide, 2006, p. 167).

Crime is a popular news item for at least two reasons. First, it is connected to fear, which is "a staple of the entertainment format." Second, it is easy to cover and thus "fits well with scheduling and personnel constraints of local television" (Altheide, 2006, p. 74). News about crime is "institutionalized as a good way to 'hook' an audience and 'hold' them throughout the newscast" (p. 76). As I'll show later in the chapter, one main reason crime is given so much media coverage is because of organizational factors such as the fact that the media are for-profit entities.

The main problem with this overreporting is that news stories about crime are not rational and tempered. They are not in-depth, critical, informative accounts. Instead, they amount to numerous "raw dispatches about the crime of the moment, the frightening— and often false—trend of the week, the prurient murder of the month, the sensational trial of the year" (Krajicek, 1998, p. 4). The purpose of such coverage is to "hook and hold" viewers for purposes of achieving higher ratings.

Lack of Critical Coverage: Where's the Context?

Critical coverage about crime and criminal justice is typically lacking in American news. In terms of criminal justice policy, the media simply "cover" what politicians pledge and promise about getting tough on crime because the media are caught up in the same moral panic about crime, because they have become so caught up in the chase that they have forgotten to expose the public to intelligent crime reporting, and because crime news is inexpensive and attracts viewers (Krajicek, 1998, pp. 6–7).

A **moral panic** occurs when

> a condition, episode, person or group of persons emerges to become defined as a threat to societal values and interests; its nature is presented in a stylized and stereotypical fashion by the mass media; the moral barricades are manned by editors, bishops, politicians, and other right-thinking people; socially accredited experts pronounce their diagnoses and solutions. (Cohen, 1972, p. 9)

Eschholtz (1997, p. 48) adds that because moral panics "typically involve an exaggeration of a social phenomenon, the public response also is often exaggerated and can create its own long lasting repercussions for society in terms of drastic changes in laws and social policy."

One example of a recent moral panic is the threat of terrorism faced by the United States since September 11, 2001. The federal government developed an alert system whereby the color indicates the relative degree of risk faced by our country. Box 5-3 examines the color-coded threat system of the Department of Homeland Security.

Why do the media create moral panics about real problems such as terrorism and crime by blowing them out of proportion? As suggested by the term *terrorism*, acts of terrorism are aimed at creating terror (i.e., fear). Ironically, media coverage of terrorism is found to be related to increased fear in those exposed to it (Altheide, 2006, p. 128). This led one scholar to suggest that the media are operating in the same interests of the terrorists (Felling, 2004). Felling writes:

> Does terrorism exist without the media? Does coverage of terrorist acts empower or encourage the people behind them? If terrorism is directed more at the audience than at its victims, shouldn't television journalists stop giving terrorists the forum they covet? Can they? Now that attacks on American soil have begotten attacks on Americans abroad, these questions need to be answered in America's newsrooms.
>
> In [the] age of hype—where footage is run and rerun particularly in the absence of story developments—broadcasters need to start considering new internal guidelines in order to remove hype from terrorism coverage. Excerpts from the execution of

---

BOX 5-3

THE HOMELAND SECURITY ADVISORY SYSTEM

The Department of Homeland Security developed the Homeland Security Advisory System to alert Americans about the relative risks of terrorism. Five color-coded levels are provided: green, blue, yellow, orange, and red. At each level from green to red, the threat of terrorism increases. The threat level has been changed numerous times since it was developed, usually based on anonymous and false or dated information about alleged terrorist plots. On May 10, 2005, former Department of Homeland Security (DHS) head Tom Ridge said he wanted to "debunk the myth" that he had been responsible for repeatedly raising the threat level during his tenure at the DHS. Ridge reported that the Bush administration periodically put the United States on high alert for terrorist attacks even though he argued there was only flimsy evidence to justify raising the threat level. Ridge said he often disagreed with Bush officials who wanted to elevate the threat level to orange or a "high" risk of terrorist attack, but that he was over-ruled (Robinson, 2007).

Ridge commented: "Sometimes we disagreed with the intelligence assessment. Sometimes we thought even if the intelligence was good, you don't necessarily put the country on (alert).... There were times when some people were really aggressive about raising it, and we said, 'For that?'" An examination by MSNBC political commentator Keith Olbermann discovered 13 "coincidences" whereby a "political downturn" for the Bush administration was followed by a "terror event" that led to a change from yellow to orange in the national threat system. The implication is that the federal government was manipulating the terror threat level for political purposes—for example, to turn attention away from potentially embarrassing scandals (Robinson, 2007).

According to Robinson (2007), when pressed to explain what Americans should do when the threat is increased, we are told not to change our daily activities but rather to be "more vigilant" and "watchful for anything out of the ordinary." We are not told to look for anything or anyone specific or to avoid any given place at any given time, so many now question why the government should tell us anything unless it is very specific and may help us avoid becoming victims of terrorist crimes.

When the national terror alert level is at yellow, the website of the Department of Homeland Security says we should ensure our disaster supply kit is stocked and ready, check telephone numbers in our family emergency plan and update as necessary, develop alternate routes to and from work or school and practice them, and *continue to be alert for suspicious activity and report it to authorities*. At orange, we are told to exercise caution when traveling, pay attention to travel advisories, review our family emergency plan and make sure all family members know what to do, be patient, expect some delays as well as baggage searches and restrictions at public buildings, and check on neighbors or others that might need assistance in an emergency. A careful reading of this information shows that there is almost no differentiation between the advice for citizens when we are at yellow (the "elevated" level, when the risk of terrorism is "significant") or orange (the "high" level, when the risk of terrorism is "high").

What's more, a simple examination of the dictionary shows that the terms "elevated" and "significant" (at the yellow level) are virtually synonymous for the term "high" (at the orange level). Given this, one wonders whether the purpose of the terror threat system is simply to promote and maintain high levels of fear over and concern about terrorism (Altheide, 2006). Whatever the case, the color-coded threat level has been publicly acknowledged as a "joke" (Brigham, 2005).

Nick Berg, an American entrepreneur in Iraq, were aired repeatedly. When terrorists gave the U.S. 72 hours to comply with their demands before executing American contractor Paul Johnson, the cable networks breathlessly ticked down the time remaining. Network anchors lament global terrorism even as they become complicit partners. (p. 1)

It's not that Felling thinks the media should *not* cover terrorism when it occurs; it is just that the nature of the coverage may actually promote terrorism rather than help us understand it and better deal with it. He explains:

Certainly, television news covers terrorist attacks for the high-minded journalistic objective of informing viewers. But the zeal with which fear has been commoditized— from shark attacks to child kidnappings to the Washington sniper—is a product of TV executives realizing that frightened people put down the remote control and await news updates, ratcheting up ratings points. Unfortunately, this living-room fearmonger- ing plays right into the hands of terrorists who are attempting to rattle every American, turning television news reporters into de facto publicists for terrorists. (p. 2)

Harrigan (2000, p. 130) claims that the media are biased in favor of "visually dramatic or sensational events that will attract a wide viewing audience." Such media depictions of crime problems are inherently inaccurate—they have to be. The alterna- tive is to tell the truth, which is virtually guaranteed to be more mundane and therefore will not attract as many viewers. Imagine how many Americans have been caused sleepless nights and great worry over anonymous and very vague terrorist threats when the government has claimed it does not know how, where, when, or if America might be attacked, but that "intelligence" indicates that "recent chatter" among terrorist sus- pects "has increased."

Stories about crime and terrorism do not provide much real information about problems of crime and terrorism. Krajicek (1998) claims that media coverage of crime almost never attempts to answer the most important question of all: "So what?" Instead, the majority of crime coverage can be depicted as "drive-by journalism—a ton of anecdote and graphic detail about individual cases . . . but not an ounce of leavening context to help frame and explain crime" (Krajicek, 1998, p. 7). Zuckerman (1994, p. 64) writes: "Television, in particular, is so focused on pictures and so limited by time that in the normal run of reporting it cannot begin to provide the context that gives meaning and perspective."

Think of news reporters you have seen on the news, standing live at the scene of a crime that happened hours ago. The fact that there is nothing going on there now is apparently irrelevant. Because the reporter is there live, the illusion of importance is maintained. As noted by Grossman (1997, p. 21): "The crime scene, marked off in yel- low police tape, doesn't move; no matter when the reporter arrives there's always a pic- ture to shoot, preferably live. No need to spend off-camera time digging, researching, or even thinking. Just get to the crime scene, get the wind blowing through your hair, and the rest will take care of itself."

How many times have you seen reporters report from the scene of "ground zero" since September 11, 2001? What is added when news people report from the scene of an empty space? Reporting since the terrorist attacks against the United States suggests that the coverage has been mostly superficial and fails to provide any context for the attacks (see Issue in Depth at the end of this chapter). Why do some people hate us so much that they would sacrifice their own lives to spill blood on American soil? What are their goals? Where do they come from? Why didn't we see this coming? Why didn't we take action, given the clear warnings we had? What would be the best way to prevent such attacks in the future? Questions such as these have not been answered; in fact, they were rarely asked by members of the mainstream media.

Lack of context in the news does not serve Americans well because it misinforms them. It is beneficial for politicians who want to put forth brief and simplistic stances on crime and terrorism, most commonly depicted as the 10- or 15-second "sound bites" heard in any election year (Harrigan, 2000). The president's claim that terrorists are "evil" and we are "good" is one example of simplifying the problem of terrorism. As you'll see in Issue in Depth at the end of this chapter, the media generally portray terrorism very much in the same way that the media cover crime. Altheide (2006, p. 82) explains: "The 9/11 terror attacks were presented, essentially, as a 'crime story,' albeit a 'big crime,' and language that was developed over two decades of crime reporting was applied to terrorism." Basically, perfected narratives about crime were "transformed into the 'terror story'" (p. 111).

Media and Fear of Crime: The Chicken Little Phenomenon

One claim about media coverage of crime that has been confirmed recently is that it is related to the level of fear of crime (Livingston, 1996). In particular, so-called crime-time news leads to increased fear among its viewers (Cohen and Solomon, 1995).

Consider the prevalence of violence depicted on the nightly news. Kappeler, Blumberg, and Potter (2000, p. 42) provide an example of a study that illustrates the amount of violence in the television news: "The Center for Media and Public Affairs found that crime has been the most prominently featured topic on the evening news since 1993, with 7,448 stories, or about 1 in 7 evening news stories." And 1 in 20 stories since 1993 has been about murder (Center for Media and Public Affairs, 1997). A study of single crime stories featured on *ABC World News Tonight, CBS Evening News,* and *NBC Nightly News* by the Center for Media and Public Affairs (CMPA, 2000) found that murder led all stories by far, followed by gun control, the death penalty, and terrorism. Other studies by the CMPA show clearly that coverage of crime in the news is not related to crime trends—as crime goes down, coverage does not typically decrease but fluctuates in ways unrelated to crime rate changes.

Why do people who are exposed to media become afraid of crime? I suggest that it is because of what I call the **Chicken Little phenomenon**. News broadcasts merely cover violence without providing any context, leaving viewers with no real sense of their relative risks of violent crime victimization. All viewers, regardless of where they live or who they are, come to believe that their risk of victimization is significant and therefore become afraid. Media coverage of crime stories creates the sense that the sky is falling!

According to the CMPA (1999), "The American Psychological Association [APA] estimates that the average twelve-year-old has seen 8,000 murders and 100,000 acts of violence on network television." Also, the National Institutes of Mental Health (NIMH) illustrate the harmful effects of violent entertainment, including increased aggression among young viewers and "a callousness toward violence directed at others." The American Medical Association (AMA) thus passed a resolution declaring that TV violence "threatens the health and welfare of young Americans."

Krajicek (1998, p. 7) calls the result a "tattooing of the national psyche." The National Criminal Justice Commission demonstrates how the media have created the illusion that all Americans have a realistic chance of being murdered by strangers, even though murder is the rarest of all crimes and is most likely committed by people known to the victims (Donziger, 1996, p. 9). In the mid 1990s, *USA Today* published a headline that claimed: "Random Killings Hit a High." The subtitle claimed "All have 'realistic chance' of being victim, says FBI" (Davis and Meddis, 1994). This was absolutely false. According to Kappeler et al. (2000, p. 39), the chance that any U.S. resident over the age of 11 years will be murdered was only 1 in 14,286 in 1996. This risk has substantially declined since then, for not only has the U.S. population increased to just over 300 million people, the number of murders has declined significantly since the 1990s (see Chapter 4).

Generally, the more viewers are exposed to television, the more likely they are to see the world as a "mean and scary place" and the more likely they are to distrust others, feel insecure and vulnerable, and view crime as a serious problem (Gerbner et al., 1980; Morgan and Signorielli, 1990; Signorielli, 1990). Altheide (2006, p. 62) concurs, saying that television leaves people seeing the world as "'scary,' dangerous, and fearful."

Heavy TV exposure also leads to an increased fear of crime, an overestimation of the likelihood of becoming a victim of violence, beliefs that one's neighborhood is unsafe, assumptions that crime rates are increasing, and increased support for punitive anticrime measures (Gerbner, 1994). Another result of TV viewing is that it can "dull the critical-thinking ability" of Americans and lead to apathy (Harrigan, 2000, p. 131), thereby making simplistic solutions to complex problems more appealing and making Americans less interested in important issues.

An analysis of crime news and fear of crime by Chiricos et al. (1997) found that frequency of exposure to television news and radio news was related to fear of crime. Yet reading newspapers was not found to be related to fear of crime, even though most newspaper crime coverage is violent or sensational in nature (Marsh, 1991). Additional research supports this conclusion, that exposure to violence in the media is linked to fear of crime. For example, exposure to crime-related tabloid headlines and repeated exposure to violence-related stories are associated with higher levels of worry about becoming a victim of violence (Smolej and Kivivuori, 2006). Other outcomes of being confronted with numerous scenes of crime and violence include: (1) "having more favorable evaluations of people with similar religious and political beliefs and more unfavorable evaluations of those who differ on these dimensions, (2) being more punitive toward moral transgressors and more benevolent to heroic individuals, (3) being more physically aggressive toward others with dissimilar political orientations, and (4) striving more vigorously to meet cultural standards of value" (Altheide, 2006, p. 6).

According to some analyses, however, the effects of television viewing depend on who is doing the viewing (Heath and Gilbert, 1996). In some research, television viewing and fear of crime are related only in certain segments of the population (e.g., older Caucasian females). This finding can be attributed to the fact that the most likely depicted crime victims on television are middle-aged or older Caucasian women (Chiricos et al., 1997).

Thus, for some, "the media have the ability, indirectly at least, to manipulate the fear of crime" (Tunnell, 1992, p. 300). Eschholtz (1997, p. 50) summarizes the research by claiming that

> for newspaper consumption the character of the message is important: local, random, and sensational stories evoke the most fear, whereas distant, specific, and less sensational stories may have a calming effect on individuals. For television, the quantity of television viewed in general, violent programming in particular, and certain audience characteristics are generally associated with higher levels of fear.

After the attacks of 9/11 much research showed that increased coverage of terrorism leads to increased fear of terrorism. For example, analysis of the use of the words *fear, victim, terrorism* and *crime* 18 months before and after the 9/11 terrorist attacks found *terrorism* and *crime* were linked very closely with the expanding use of *fear.* The author found significant increases in linking *terrorism* to *fear* and to *victim* (Altheide, 2006). Victor (2006) calls the media coverage of terrorism after 9/11 a "moral panic," which he says led to dramatic increases in fear in spite of a very low threat for actual victimization. He says that most Americans didn't worry much about terrorism before the attacks of 9/11 "even though homegrown terrorists were blowing up fellow citizens in federal buildings and abortion clinics. There was no nationwide fear of terrorism. After 9/11, however, this changed. A majority of Americans came to believe that foreign terrorists could be lurking everywhere and might attack anywhere in the United States, even in small towns."

An interesting fact is that there are now at least 844 hate groups in the United States (Potok, 2007). Americans are more likely to be victimized by these groups than by foreign terrorists, yet mainstream media coverage of these groups is lacking.

Few go as far as to suggest that the media intentionally create fear in viewers. But the fear that is created reinforces mythology about crime and criminal justice (Kappeler and Potter, 2004), causing citizens to avoid, and police to apprehend, people who are perceived as posing the greatest threats to our well-being (e.g., see Culverson, 1998; Rome, 1998). As argued in Chapter 4, these people tend to be darker in skin color and lacking in wealth as compared to the average American. Michael Moore, in his Oscar-winning documentary film *Bowling for Columbine,* implies that media coverage of crime leads Americans to become afraid and spend more time at home watching television, where they are thus exposed to more commercial messages from the corporations that own the media and who pay to advertise their products.

Given all this coverage of crime in the United States, for many citizens "the United States must seem to be a hopelessly savage place that stands teetering on the lip of the Apocalypse" (Krajicek, 1998, p. 4). Gallup polls conducted throughout the 1980s and 1990s show that even as crime declined, people were more likely to call it the number one problem facing the nation. Additionally, the percentage of people who fear walking alone at night has been highly variable over the years despite relatively consistent declines in crime since the early 1970s. In March 1994, the Times Mirror Center for the People and the Press reported a poll showing that 50% of the respondents feared they would be victims of crime. Another 30% said that crime was the nation's number one problem. Compare this with the Gallup polls discussed in Chapter 4, which showed that a large number of citizens thought in 1994 that crime was the most important problem facing the country. Perhaps it is not surprising to learn that coverage of crime on the three major networks peaked a year earlier, in 1993.

Some research also links fear not only to media coverage but to the extent to which politicians highlight crime as a major concern (Lichter, Lichter, and Rothman, 1994). Perhaps this is why public concern about crime peaked at 52% in the same month in which President Clinton signed the 1994 federal crime bill into law, a law that promised more police and more prisons to make Americans feel safer.

In reality, there are acts that are likely to injure us, kill us, and take our property—those acts of elite deviance discussed in Chapter 4. Yet they are unlikely to be shown regularly in the mass media. Thus we do not fear them. Instead, as shown by Glassner (1999) in his book, *The Culture of Fear: Why Americans Are Afraid of the Wrong Things,* we are shown the most unusual and atypical threats—things like school violence—which promotes fear of crime. As explained by Victor (2006, p. 9): "One threat or another grabs attention on the evening news. There are child kidnappers and molesters, drug dealers who peddle to school children, teenage gang killers, teenage mass murderers in schools, and crack addicts. Moreover, an epidemic of single mothers and gay couples is said to threaten the fabric of society." Ironically, these things are the least likely to happen to us or to people we know.

With regard to terrorism, studies show that major politicians blew the threat of terrorism out of proportion by calling terrorists "evil," "fanatics," and similar terms. Then they exaggerate the threats of terrorism, calling it a threat to civilization itself. Coverage of terrorism thus fits the pattern of a moral panic (Victor, 2006).

EXPLANATIONS OF MEDIA INACCURACY

According to Cohen and Young (1981), there are two competing explanations for the news media's inaccuracy in covering crime. According to one explanation—the **market model**—crime is considered newsworthy because of the public interest in it, and thus it is covered. According to the other explanation—the **manipulative model**—crime is of interest to the owners of the media and is purposefully distorted to shape public interests in line with those of the owners of the media. Surette (1992, p. 57) describes both models as simplistic and inadequate and puts forth an alternative explanation—the **organizational model**—which posits that crime is inherently subjective and thus distorted, but also allows owners to generate profit from using crime.

Move On (2002) asserts that

the main problems with media are profoundly structural. The airwaves are supposed to belong to the public, but they've been hijacked by huge companies. With the government assisting the monopolization process, all the major forms of media—such as broadcasting, cable, newspapers, magazines, books, movies, the music industry, and, increasingly, the Web—are now dominated by the interests of capital, devoted to maximizing private profit. Some investors benefit; the public gets shafted.

This is a good starting point. In examining the literature in this area, however, there are other reasons that the media focus on crime and tend to be inaccurate in their coverage of it. Each of these reasons is discussed next. I begin with a discussion of organizational factors.

Organizational Factors: Entertainment for Profit

Reporters do not deserve all or even most of the blame for providing inaccurate coverage of crime and criminal justice. Most are simply following orders of their superiors. Instead, blame resides in "the moguls, stockholders, owners, and publishers" as well as the "editors, reporters, and photographers" (Krajicek, 1998, p. 5). Those who set the agenda for the media are the most to blame for inaccuracies about crime and criminal justice in the media.

Let's face it: Crime is almost always the top story. Studies of news by the CMPA show that crime is usually the top story in any given year, and at no time in the 1990s did it drop below the top 5 stories. Part of the reason that crime is so newsworthy is that violence is so prevalent in entertainment media, apparently because Americans like to watch it. Studies of American television shows, movies, and music illustrate that violence is a main theme. As noted earlier, stories about trivial matters have recently increased even in national media outlets, yet violence remains high in our entertainment media, particularly after the terrorist attacks on our country and the U.S. "wars" in Afghanistan and Iraq.

Given the finite resources of reporters and news space, the fact that crime is so prominent in the news means that other issues, such as international affairs, are not adequately addressed. Is this intentional? According to Krajicek (1998, p. 13), "The process of journalism—collecting, organizing, and disseminating information— happens in a series of priority-setting decisions about how to use . . . resources." Those who prioritize crime over other vexing social problems are the most accountable.

Who decides, then, what will be newsworthy? Beckett and Sasson (2000, p. 81) claim that news is simply defined as what is out of the ordinary (Ericson, Baranek, and Chan, 1989). Thus, television news comes to be seen as a form of entertainment, whereby the media are highly selective in what they broadcast. Violence is more "sellable" than the mundane aspects of theft and other forms of property crime. This explains what Surette (1992, p. 14) calls the recent blurring of news and entertainment in media outlets.

However, according to Surette (1992, pp. 22, 32), crime has been the "single most popular story element in the forty year history of U.S. commercial television, with crime-related shows regularly accounting for one-fourth to one-third of all the three major networks' prime time shows" from the 1960s to the 1990s. Why is this so? Since the media are businesses, economic factors are inherently involved in selecting content. The content of the media is shaped in line with the economic interests of the organization that owns the media outlet (Potter and Kappeler, 1998, p. 19).

According to Stevens and Garcia (1980), TV programming is aimed at attracting and keeping large audiences because the "larger the audience, the more that sponsors are willing to spend for advertising and the greater the profits" (Surette, 1992, p. 31). Given the organizational needs of the media, including profit-generating news (Beckett and Sasson, 2003; Marion, 1995), crime is valuable because it attracts viewers and because it is relatively easy to write about given the abundance of official sources of information in law enforcement personnel and politicians (Fishman, 1978; Sherizen, 1978). These officials are considered legitimate, authoritative, reliable, and consistently available (Beckett, 1997; Gans, 1979; Schlesinger and Tumber, 1994; Sigal, 1973).

Beckett and Sasson (2000, p. 118) conclude that crime entertainment narratives promote three related messages:

- Most offenders are professional criminals.
- Community safety is threatened by judges and defense attorneys who are too much concerned with offenders' rights.
- Criminal justice personnel are out there every day, fighting the war on crime.

These messages have the potential to be highly misleading to the general public. Therein lies the danger to doing justice, as well as to more honest crime control efforts. They also shift support toward a crime control model of criminal justice.

Research suggests that the media are focused on the interests of the state rather than the rights of the accused (Cavender, 2004; Ericson, 1995; Garland, 2001; Surette, 1998), sending the message that "the courts and legal protections like the Bill of Rights are hampering law enforcement and helping criminals, terrorists, and other merchants of fear" (Altheide, 2006, p. 212). Given this, when politicians are labeled as being "liberal" or "soft on crime," they are essentially being associated with "outsiders, deviants or the 'other,'" which is "a common propaganda technique that neutralizes the opposition" (p. 30).

Some claim that media are organized to promote fear. Altheide (2006, p. 61) refers to the combination of news and entertainment as a "fear-generating machine." The result is a **visual reality** that parallels actual reality; the visual reality is what affects people's perceptions of crime in the United States (p. 67).

And who benefits from this visual reality? According to Altheide (2006, pp. 34–35), "many businesses provide services and products to help solve or reduce the alleged sources of fear. . . . There is a massive home protection and security industry; the gun industry has fired up many neighborhoods to get involved in personal security and home protection by buying weapons and taking weapons training and has spawned numerous hobbies involving firearms. . . . Businesses also use security services that are very visible to customers in banks, offices, retail outlets, schools, and even places of worship."

Ironically, the academic field of criminal justice benefits enormously from fear and our fascination with crime and violence. Criminal justice is one of the more popular majors in the United States. Unfortunately, our academic discipline "tends to focus on police, court, and correctional operations and procedures . . . much of the curriculum concerns straightforward descriptions, evaluations, models, and recommendations for the organization of criminal justice agencies and the role that its workers . . . play in keeping crime under control and keeping us all safe" (Altheide, 2006, p. 36).

Peer Culture

Additionally, the "peer culture among journalists is as intense as that at any junior high school. Reporters and editors look to one another—both colleagues and competitors—to determine what is appropriate. If everyone else is doing it, that deserves an affirmation" (Krajicek, 1998, p. 35). Consistent with **social learning theories** of crime, the media imitate what others in the business are doing and will likely continue to cover it when the coverage is positively reinforced (Akers and Jensen, 2007).

As noted by Fishman (1978), simple **imitation** plays a role. Once a news agency picks up on a crime story or theme, other news organizations are likely to pick it up as well. When the theme runs throughout the media industry as a whole or through the mainstream media discussed earlier, it can lead to a "media crime wave" or "moral panic." As noted earlier, the inner circle media—who are owned by large corporations—are the ones who determine what is newsworthy. Yet more than imitation is involved. When media coverage of crime and terrorism is reinforced (e.g., with higher ratings and higher income), it is likely to be repeated, as predicted by differential reinforcement theory. Further, when reporters, editors, and other media personnel associate with others who are already promoting crime and terrorism through their media work, it is likely that this will impact other media outlets, as predicted by differential association theory (Robinson, 2004).

Lack of Criminal Justice Education

The problem with the peer culture of the media is that few reporters have expertise about crime and criminal justice. As Krajicek (1998) puts it, they do not know the difference between a VCR and the UCR. If media owners, reporters, and editors do not understand basic facts of crime and criminal justice, they will merely report what they are told by official sources. For example, you have likely seen headlines and stories about rising and falling crime rates that base their arguments on rising or falling arrest rates. Arrest rates are not valid measures of crime rates, but instead are a function of what police are doing. It is doubtful that many in the media understand the difference.

The journalist writes crime stories to get on the front page much as the academic criminologist or criminal justice professor writes articles to get published in the best journals. The goal of each is not necessarily to make an actual difference in criminal justice policy but, rather, to play the game successfully within the rules laid out by the discipline. Ultimately, personal and even financial reward may be gained by each, as well as by their respective employers.

While academics practice "real criminology" and have been highly critical of recent criminal justice policy, their findings do not seem to inform criminal justice policy. Politicians practice "kindergarten criminology" (Krajicek, 1998, p. 5), and reporters have not held politicians or criminal justice policy makers accountable for it.

The Role of Politics in the "Framing" of Crime

Ironically, the media, by reporting what such official sources report, create perceptions of the crime problem in viewers, thereby also creating support for particular crime control policies (Roberts and Edwards, 1992; Roberts and Doob, 1990). Because government sources are typically cited in crime reports, it is not surprising that Americans support "more police, more arrests, longer sentences, more prisons, and more executions" (Potter and Kappeler, 1998, p. 3). State managers cited in media reports about crime also tend to emphasize a crime control perspective over a due process model of criminal justice (Welch, Fenwick, and Roberts, 1998).

Logically, as news becomes routinized—as it follows similar formats to what has proved acceptable to owners of the media and news consumers and to what has evolved in line with needs of advertisers (Potter and Kappeler, 1998, p. 19)—sources that have been relied on in the past are relied on regularly. This makes getting the news relatively easy. Government sources can also be cited as "official" and thus reliable (Surette, 1992).

Given that the media are dominant institutions in society, they share similar characteristics with other dominant institutions, such as the state and corporations

(Potter and Kappeler, 1998, p. 17). They reproduce the status quo, which is beneficial to them (Alvarado and Boyd-Barrett, 1992; Gurevitch, 1982; Lapley and Westlake, 1988; McQuail, 1994; Stevenson, 1995; Strinati, 1995). An example can be characterized as a form of media inbreeding. Given that "media professionals are trained, educated, and socialized in a way as to internalize the values and norms of the dominant, mainstream culture . . . [they will] interpret or mediate news, information, and complex issues in a way that is usually consistent with the dominant culture and with the interests of powerful groups" (Potter and Kappeler, 1998, p. 18).

The media will also amplify viewpoints of the powerful, especially when these views are already shared by members of society because they appeal to our "common sense." Anything offensive to consumers, advertisers, or owners will be discouraged (Potter and Kappeler, 1998, p. 18). News stories about crime also often include "commentary from public officials" (Merlo and Benekos, 2000, p. 2) or "state managers" (Welch et al., 1998), which supposedly provide expert opinion about crime-related problems. Thus, politicians attempt to "capitalize on the news to further support their political agendas and to gain support of voters" (Merlo and Benekos, 2000, p. 2).

The best of these politicians—the most effective claims-makers about crime—have their views of crime turned into media coverage; thus, they determine the focus of crime coverage of the media (Edelman, 1988; Gusfield, 1967; Hilgartner and Bosk, 1988; Kitsuse and Spector, 1973). Strangely enough, politicians then see media coverage of crime problems as heightened public concern over crime (Beckett and Sasson, 2003). Yet most scholars posit that political action occurs before public concern and that public concern stems from actions of politicians, rather than the other way around.

In the media, the most common way in which crime is framed is as a failure of criminal justice agencies (Beckett and Sasson, 2003). For example, misleading and misinforming media coverage of crime highlights the failures of criminal justice agencies and characterizes the justice network as inefficient and soft on crime (Roberts, 1992; Roberts and Doob, 1990). This is one of the paradoxes of news coverage of criminal justice. Although the media depict the criminal justice network as ineffective, "the cumulative effect of these portraits appears to be increased support for more police, more prisons, and more money for the criminal justice system" (Surette, 1992, p. 14).

In other words, media coverage of criminal justice advances the status quo of big government when it comes to fighting crime by reinforcing the dominant ideology in American criminal justice (Fishman, 1978; Graber, 1980). That is, discourse on crime control is limited to present, get-tough policies (Potter and Kappeler, 1998, p. 7). Given that the media focus disproportionately on law enforcement crime-fighting activities, the end result is increased support for a crime control model rather than a due process model (Surette, 1992).

As if due process rights were the cause of crime in the United States, politicians have made us all less free in an effort to fight a crime problem that is actually less problematic today than it has been in a long, long time. This attack on due process is consistent with **social control theories** of crime, which hold that criminality is normal and should be expected in the absence of meaningful societal controls on individual behavior (Agnew, 2007).

Even as the United States has been cast by "get tough" politicians as "a victim of its own liberty"—that "U.S. society is too free for its own good and insufficiently fearful of authority" (Krajicek, 1998, p. 16)—the media have not alerted citizens to how their constitutional protections have been eroded in the move toward a crime control model of criminal justice. As explained by Krajicek (1998, p. 139), "the media have uncritically reproduced official, conservative, 'law-and-order' perspectives with little fundamental analysis of their success or failure."

The media tend to amplify the claims of politicians about crime (Beckett and Sasson, 2003). Sasson (1995, p. 13) states it this way: "People do crimes because they know they can get away with them. The police are handcuffed by liberal judges. The prisons, bursting at their seams, have revolving doors for serious offenders." Thus, the way to reduce crime is to reduce "loopholes and technicalities that impede the apprehension and imprisonment of offenders" and increase the "swiftness, certainty and severity of punishment"—in other words, to erode due process protections that interfere with the crime-fighting capacity of our criminal justice network (Surette, 1992, p. 14).

The term **politics of fear** refers to "decision makers' promotion and use of audience beliefs and assumptions about danger, risk, and fear in order to achieve certain goals" (Altheide, 2006, p. 15). It relies on "nationalism and perceived consensus against an enemy" (p. 39). Generally, the politics of fear correlates with the amount of social control in society, meaning the more prevalent the politics of fear, the more repressive is criminal justice. It results when "social control is perceived to have broken down and/or [when] a higher level of control is called for by a situation or events, such as a 'terrorist attack'" (p. 15).

The politics of fear begins with a definition of the situation and then a justification of it through propaganda "or the manipulation of information for a specific purpose" (Altheide, 2006, p. 17). Fear is "socially constructed and managed by political actors to promote their own goals," meaning it is ideological in nature (p. 18). It is most effective "when the messages and meanings are part of the broader culture and are recognized and taken for granted by a mass audience" (p. 47). In the case of crime, Americans generally agree that crime is bad; that is something that is taken for granted. So any policy that claims to be anti-crime is easily sellable as a good thing. The most effective messages are simple and often repeated.

CONCLUSION

Clearly, the media shape our world view about crime and criminal justice. Once the law has defined certain acts as crimes, the media tend to cover those acts that are the most unusual, bizarre, and violent. Coverage of criminal justice is front-loaded, focused on police but rarely on corrections or the reality of plea bargaining in courts. Because the inner ring of the American media is controlled by large corporations, which are concerned first and foremost with ensuring profits, the media sell crime to Americans—"if it bleeds, it leads." The media's coverage of criminal justice is biased in favor of "get tough" approaches to reducing crime. All of this threatens justice and due process in the United States. Using the media as their mouthpieces, politicians have become like Chicken Little, trying to incite the public about impending doom in the form of crime in this country. They claim we need a "war" to stop crime. When politicians and the media use terms like *war*, it suggests to the public that crime must be "fought" rather than "prevented." The costs to Americans include the failure to do justice or to reduce crime.

ISSUE IN DEPTH—Media Coverage of September 11th and the War on Terror

On September 11, 2001, the United States was attacked by terrorists like it had never been attacked before. Even the attacks of Pearl Harbor by the Japanese on December 7, 1941, were not as deadly.

And of course, clearly there were differences. Pearl Harbor was a military base and civilians were not the intended targets. Additionally, military planes and weapons were used in the attacks on Pearl Harbor. The attacks in New York City were intended to kill and injure civilians, and our own civilian airliners were used as weapons. Only the Pentagon was a targeted military facility, and one of the four doomed planes crashed into it. People have speculated that the fourth plane was intended for a government target in Washington, D.C., such as the White House or the U.S. Capitol building; that plane crashed into a field in rural Pennsylvania. But of course, you know all this.

What I have done in briefly describing the September 11, 2001, attacks—to set the stage for this discussion of media coverage of them and America's subsequent "war on terror"—is what mainstream media outlets did for months every time these issues were discussed. Think about it: How many times did you see the planes fly into the World Trade Center buildings? How many horrific images from that day—people running for cover, dead bodies and injured people, crushed police cars and fire engines, photos of missing persons posted on walls and fences—have you seen?

The media coverage of these attacks has been very similar to their typical coverage of crime and criminal justice discussed in this chapter: disproportionately focused on violence, creative of misperceptions of one's true risk of becoming a victim of such terrorism, ignorant of some key facts and issues about the causes and effects of terrorism, neglectful in failing to provide context for the attacks, and creative of much fear and anxiety.

Coverage of the U.S. response through its "war on terror" has been plagued by similar problems and distortions of its own. As you must know, the United States has responded to these attacks by launching two separate "wars"—one on the Taliban government in Afghanistan and one on the Saddam Hussein government in Iraq.

According to polls, most Americans cannot even identify these countries on a map, much less discuss the relationships that our government has had with these countries. Perhaps this is why some claim that the problem with the media coverage of the terrorist attacks began even before the attacks came. For example, Nisbet (2001) points out how American media essentially ignore world affairs, especially those that are complex and cannot be summarized in sound bites and short stories.

According to Altheide (2006, p. 166), the media "chose not to present important contextual and background information about the Middle East and especially Iraq because it was not consistent with other news themes, nor was it as entertaining. The dominant 'story' since the attacks of 9/11 was the 'war on terrorism.' This broad story included U.S. retaliation, the hunt for al Qaeda leaders . . . and plans to attack countries and 'outlaw regimes' that supported or harbored terrorists . . . invading Afghanistan and expanding the U.S. military presence throughout the world . . . adjustments were made in foreign policy, military budgets, domestic surveillance, and attacks on civil liberties. Threats to invade other countries (the 'axis of evil') that included Iraq were part of an effort to 'defend' the United States from future attacks."

More than this, media coverage of the terrorist attacks and the looming wars was prophetic. In essence, the media beat the drums of war with unique pro-war headlines and theme songs, making war seem inevitable, even before the United States launched any attacks. Americans just had to prepare for what was coming.

Early reports, beginning immediately after the attacks and continuing for months, focused almost exclusively on the human elements of the attacks. What was left out was any type of context for how rare these attacks were, where they came from, why they were initiated, the role the United States itself plays in the motivations, international reactions, appropriate or inappropriate responses from Congress and the president of the United States, or any information on what Americans should do in the wake of such events.

Lule (2002) focused on editorials in the *New York Times,* a member of the inner ring of the media, and found that their writers focused on four myths to portray the events of September 11, 2001: the end of innocence; the victims; the heroes; and the foreboding future. In essence, even editorials in top newspapers were simplifying the attacks and not providing any critical coverage of where the attacks emerged or why. Why did the attackers choose us? Why did they hate us so much that they were willing to give their own lives to kill innocent civilians? Since the *New York Times* is a member of the inner ring of the media, its coverage affects most other media outlets in America.

Questions like those above were not answered because they were not asked by inner-ring media. This is one reason why major media organization such as the *New York Times* ultimately apologized for its coverage—for not being critical enough, for not questioning evidence about Iraq presented to them from White House insiders. For those reporters and commentators who asked such questions, they received predictable answers given who was being asked—disproportionately those appearing on news broadcasts and talk shows were government and military spokespersons who simplified the motives for the attacks as jealousy of the United States and pure evil.

Altheide (2006, pp. 117–118) asserts that "government and military officials . . . dominated news reports about terrorism and fear. . . . Newspapers as well as television network news relied heavily on administration sources that directed the focus and language of news coverage." One study of a 6-month period found that 92% of the stories about Iraq broadcast on NBC, ABC, and CBS originated at the White House, Pentagon, and State Department (Tyndall, 2005). Another study of the time immediately following the speech to the United Nations by Secretary of State Colin Powell (which justified an invasion of Iraq) found that "two-thirds of the guests were from the United States, with 75 percent of these being current or former government or military officials, while only one . . . expressed skepticism or opposition to the impending war with Iraq" (Altheide, 2006, p. 118).

By relying almost exclusively on government insiders, the dominant ideology underlying the U.S. "war on terror" was served. According to Altheide (2006, p. 18), an important part of ideology "is the promotion of a mythology, a set of ideas or 'stories' that explains things, organizes our view of the world, and puts people, places, and events in convenient categories. . . . One of the most important myths that has been promoted by politicians is that of 'good' versus 'evil,' with 'your side' being good and the 'other side' being evil." In the case of 9/11 and terrorism, the United States is the good side, and thus the message by politicians was that terrorism "was cast as something that was done to the United States as barbaric, as unfair. A number of officials stated or implied that the United States . . . did not engage in terrorist activities—ever" (Altheide, 2006, p. 24). While the veracity of the statement that the United States has never engaged in terrorism is beyond the scope of this book, I hope you'll investigate alleged claims that our country has done this very thing (because the media do not).

Not surprisingly, one study found that pro-war voices in America dominated news coverage, outnumbering antiwar voices by a margin of about 25 to 1 (Rendell and Broughel, 2003). Zerbisias (2003) summarizes this study, conducted by Fairness and Accuracy in Reporting (FAIR):

> FAIR found a mere 3 per cent of U.S. sources represented or expressed opposition to the war, and that includes senators and members of Congress. With more than 1 in 4 U.S. citizens opposing the war and much higher rates of opposition in most countries where opinion was polled, none of the networks offered anything resembling proportionate coverage of anti-war voices. . . . The anti-war percentages ranged from 4 per cent at NBC, 3 per cent at CNN, ABC, PBS and FOX, and less than 1 per cent— 1 out of 205 U.S. sources—at CBS. . . . Anti-war voices were almost universally blown off in one-sentence sound bites while 42 per cent of them were never identified by name, labeled instead as 'protester" or 'anti-war activist.'"

Some outer-ring and middle-ring media agencies investigated the motivations for the war on Iraq and reported it for about a year before the war started; yet it was not until after the war began that any inner-ring media outlets even mentioned the *Project for a New American Century* (PNAC) or the *American Enterprise Institute* (AEI), two neo-conservative think tanks that had called for an invasion of Iraq. Shockingly, the founders and other key members of the PNAC ended up in the White House, and at least one key writer for the AEI was given significant access to President Bush on foreign policy matters. These groups planned the Iraqi war for more than 10 years!

Altheide (2006) shows that of 18 media reports regarding PNAC after the 9/11 attacks, five were on National Public Radio, seven were in major newspapers like the *New York Times* and *Los Angeles Times,* and only four were on major television networks such as NBC, ABC, or CBS. This matters because evidence suggests that the "general public derives most of its understanding of international affairs and foreign policy from news and particularly television news" (p. 165). Amazingly, members of PNAC regularly appeared in numerous mainstream media outlets, yet they were not identified as members of PNAC. Instead, they were identified by their position title within government. Of course, it is not surprising that such individuals were allowed to speak in favor of the "war on terror" and U.S. intervention in Iraq, given that so many members of PNAC were actually employed within the White House and/or other major government agencies.

Importantly, PNAC sources were used 85% more frequently after 9/11 than before it in the *New York Times*. This suggests they had an even greater ability to push their goals to invade Iraq through media coverage favorable to their claims, and one reason Altheide (2006, p. 174) concludes that "the media are indirectly responsible for encouraging the public's support of the war against Iraq through their acts of omission and/or compliance."

As the nation prepared for military action against Afghanistan and ultimately Iraq, mainstream media outlets provided little in the way of information about these countries, their cultures, and previous interactions between these countries and the

United States. For example, the U.S. government recently viewed the Taliban government as an ally in the war on drugs for destroying massive amounts of opium poppies. Since the Taliban government in Afghanistan had no air force and virtually no defenses, the U.S. military could easily move into and around Afghanistan, running nearly flawless air strikes against whatever military targets they located.

The Afghanistan "war" quickly was replaced by much bigger news, especially the large corporate crime stories of Enron, WorldCom, etc. (see Chapter 4). This was the focus of the news for an unprecedented few weeks, until President Bush signed a new law toughening sanctions for corporate crime and began openly discussing the possible invasion of Iraq, which then became the lead story. Coverage of the continuing "war" on Afghanistan—including the fact that Americans were still dying over there and that the Taliban was regrouping—was not widespread.

Almost nightly, the television news reported that the United States was already striking targets in Iraq, as they had been doing since the end of the first Gulf War with Iraq (for about 12 years). Yet rarely did we hear more than one sentence about the attacks, what their intended targets were, or how many civilians were killed in these bombings. As military actions against Iraq seemed imminent, despite overwhelming worldwide opinion against it, the media again began preparing the American people for the inevitable. Broadcasters on each of the major networks and writers for each of the major newspapers began predicting when the war would start and asked top officials in the U.S. government when they would launch the war. Much coverage was given to the U.S. plan to launch its "shock and awe" campaign against Iraq featuring military tactics never before seen in wartime.

Absent were questions pertaining to the just or unjust nature of the war (Cohen, 2003). Altheide (2006, p. 166) contends: "It is hard to believe that the American people would not have been interested in carefully presented reports about systematic efforts [by the Bush administration] to undermine international treaties, destroy the United Nations, expand the military, and engage in more military attacks, including preemptive first strikes." Yet these issues were not covered in the mainstream press.

Once it finally began, television news stations provided around-the-clock coverage initially, and major newspapers carried in-depth coverage and analysis of the war, including targets, weaponry, military personnel on both sides, and similar issues. Media coverage of Iraq fit certain themes, including victims, suffering, heroism, compensation, retaliation, the "war on terror," fear, homeland security, surveillance, and preparing for the wars (Altheide, 2004). Stories related to these themes were part of the "visual reality" of the war being created by the mainstream media.

With all the focus on U.S. weaponry, very few citizens probably had any reason to suspect that the United States would become entrenched in a long, drawn-out invasion. The mainstream media had some responsibility for this. For example, Cunningham (2003) found that there were 574 stories about Iraq on ABC, CBS, and NBC evening broadcasts between September 12, 2002, and March 7, 2003, and only 12 reports dealt with the potential aftermath of the U.S. invasion! While White House officials were publicly stating that U.S. forces would be greeted as liberators, Middle Eastern experts were predicting exactly what has happened in Iraq—a very prolonged and difficult occupation followed by a likely civil war. That the media did not give these experts voice and did not ask critical questions about postwar Iraq serves as evidence that media institutions are part of the problem.

Mainstream media developed special graphics with American flags—to be continuously broadcast on their television screens—that waved in the background or foreground as people were interviewed about the war. In a sense, the media were helping to create a sense that the war was not only inevitable but also necessary and right. Numerous scholars make the claim that the media have historically capitulated to the government during war (Altheide, 2006; Der Derian, 2002; Ellenius and European Science Foundation, 1998; Gerth, 1992; Herman and Chomsky, 2002; Jackall, 1999; Kellner, 2003; Shapiro, 1992).

Rutenberg and Carter (2001, p. C8) describe the media following the 9/11 attacks as "an arm of the government, as opposed to an independent, objective purveyor of information." Altheide (2006, p. 178) explains: "Major network television journalists, wearing American flag pins on their lapels, occasionally crying on camera, and offering constant moral support to an expanding network audience, offered very little perspective and understanding of the 9/11 events, seldom asking the most basic questions of administration officials who were pushing draconian legislation to limit civil rights through Congress while military appropriations were increasing drastically in pursuit of an emerging ambiguous war plan to attack Iraq. Clearly the pressure was on journalists to conform and not rock the boat, to not challenge those who were protecting us against evil and terror. . . . The coverage of the war was clearly influenced by such pressure, along with the availability of 'visuals' that permitted 'live' shots of advancing tanks, Marines, gunfire, and explosions. Other journalists covering the Iraq War reported censorship and intimidation." On top of this, the military only permitted members of the press to be "embedded" with certain military units. Only then could reporters convey what was happening at the time (e.g., live battles).

When President Bush declared an end to major combat operations only a few weeks into the military actions, the media began returning to normal, everyday stories, such as coverage of celebrity and random, violent crimes. Prior to the war, the leading story was the disappearance of a young woman who had some kind of relationship with a Congressman from California. Although no evidence ever surfaced to suggest the Congressman was involved in her disappearance or death (she was found dead in a public park long after she disappeared), intense media coverage followed the every move of the Congressman. The attacks of September 11, 2001, were supposedly a wake-up call to mainstream media: Many reporters even said this directly on the air, how they felt so badly for wasting so much time discussing the disappearance of one young woman and missed other, far more important stories. September 11th was going to teach us what was really important. Yet for the first several years after the attacks, the lead stories in the news dealt with things like the disappearance of a collegiate basketball player, the alleged sexual assault committed by a professional basketball player, acts of personal deviance committed by politicians, and a major corruption scandal in Congress centering around lobbyist Jack Abramoff.

Two years after that, even as Iraq disintegrated into full-fledged civil war—more than 3,000 U.S. service personnel had died and as many as 655,000 Iraqis were killed—the lead story in the press for weeks became the death of Anna Nicole Smith (an actress who was not particularly well-respected). Other stories covered widely in the media were the killing of a little girl in Florida, the sporadic beatings of homeless people across the country by teenagers, and celebrity gossip.

Even before the highest ranking officials of the Taliban government and the Hussein regime had been captured or killed, mainstream media began asking who the United

States would attack next in the war on terror. Top military officials appeared on television making their own predictions about countries like Iran, Syria, Lybia, and North Korea.

Before the "war" on Iraq, mainstream media institutions failed to provide coverage of the initial antiwar rallies in the United States, even though they were the largest-ever rallies against a war that were launched before the war started. When the media began covering these events as they grew still larger (the largest since the 1970s), in an effort to be fair, they gave equal time to the counterprotesters even though the counterprotesters were vastly outnumbered. Most media outlets did not investigate the claims of those against the war, such as the evidence against Iraq had been manipulated, misrepresented, exaggerated, and even fabricated, and that the war was actually against the law.

Claims such as these were finally investigated and more critical stories became more routine, questioning the intelligence that implicated the Hussein regime in attempting to obtain weapons of mass destruction. What was never asked, however, is whether it mattered that Hussein possessed or was attempting to possess these weapons. Could he reach us with them? Did he have good reason to? Would we be able to stop him without initiating a war? What would be the implications for the law, which explicitly forbids launching preemptive wars, and for our allies, who uniformly stood against the invasion? Such questions need answers.

Other efforts by the United States as part of its "war on terror" included new laws passed by Congress and executive orders of the president justifying major curtailments to civil liberties (see Issue in Depth at the end of Chapter 3). Yet media reports contained "little criticisms and dissent about administration incursions into civil liberties and violations of due process" (Altheide, 2006, p. 103) and "journalists referred to people concerned about civil liberties, especially government surveillance, as 'privacy advocates'" (p. 4). Once the media started to question whether the government had gone too far in its domestic efforts to prevent terrorism, reform of the law was unlikely due to the entrenchment of the new approaches.

As you saw in this chapter, media inaccuracies such as these stem, first and foremost, from the organizational nature of the media. Mainstream media are owned by corporations and will inevitably cover stories in a way that serves their own interests (including ignoring stories that call their interests into question). The media also attempt to give us what they think will help us sell the products that they advertise on their stations and in their newspapers. Since violence is so important and even celebrated in America, wars fit our preoccupation with violence nicely. Altheide (2006, pp. 18–19) says much "misinformation is quite intentional. This does not mean that everyone in the mass media lies. . . . Rather . . . it is the emphasis on entertainment and making profits that leads to the major distortions."

Additionally, the effects of the peer culture help explain the immense focus on the terrorist attacks and the war on terror. Once inner-ring media begin reporting on such stories, other media agencies follow so as not be left out. Furthermore, as the lack of criminal justice education partly explains the inaccurate media coverage of crime and criminal justice, so too does the lack of political science education partly explain the incomplete media coverage of the terrorist attacks on this country and the war on terror. Finally, as politics plays a role in "framing" crime, the war on terror has also been framed for a significant political reason: It reinforces patriotism and an unquestioning allegiance to government leaders who promote war rather than peace—even when the facts do not justify war (Nacos, 2002; Norris, Korn, and Just, 2003).

According to Jeff Cohen, founder of FAIR, the news media promote ignorance about important issues such as the war on Iraq. He writes:

> That half or more Americans [thought] Iraq was involved in the 9/11 attack—perhaps the most media-covered event in our history—stands as a horrific indictment of U.S. media today. Such levels of ignorance can't be found in other countries. . . . The run-up to the Iraq war offers a case study in news bias: how mainstream media, especially television, were incapable of getting the truth out in the face of administration lies and innuendo about Iraq's 9/11 role and weapons of mass destruction.

The "truth" includes the following facts: Iraq did not attack the United States on September 11, 2001; Iraq was not linked meaningfully with al-Qaeda; the majority of people in the world opposed the war (even among the countries that participated in it, aside from the United States); and the Saddam Hussein regime did not possess an ability to strike the United States with weapons of mass destruction.

A study by the Program on International Policy at the University of Maryland reports that a majority of Americans had significant misperceptions and these were highly related to support for the war with Iraq (Kull, Ramsay, Subias, Lewis, and Warf, 2003). The study found that 48% incorrectly believed that evidence of links between Iraq and al-Qaeda have been found, 22% that weapons of mass destruction have been found in Iraq, and 25% that world public opinion favored the United States going to war with Iraq. More than half (60%) had at least one of these three misperceptions.

The misperceptions were also found to be related to support for the war on Iraq. For example:

- Among those with none of the misperceptions, only 23% reported supporting the war.
- Among those with one of the misperceptions, 53% reported supporting the war.
- Among those with two of the misperceptions, 78% reported supporting the war.
- Among those with all three misperceptions, 86% reported supporting the war.

The frequency of Americans' misperceptions varied depending on their primary source of news. Viewers of Fox were most likely to have at least one misperception (80%), followed by CBS (71%), ABC (61%), and NBC and CNN (55%). Only about half (47%) of people who reported relying on print sources had at least one misperception, followed by only 23% of listeners of National Public Radio (NPR) and viewers of the Public Broadcasting System (PBS).

When Americans misperceive the facts after watching news coverage, it is clear that the media are failing to do their job. Because the free flow of information is at the heart of democracy, there is no greater threat to democracy than media that fail to do their job.

KEY TERMS

Chicken Little phenomenon
culpability
imitation
inner ring of the media
manipulative model

media
middle ring of the media
moral panic
organizational model
outer ring of the media

politics of fear
social control theories
social learning theories
visual reality

DISCUSSION QUESTIONS

1. What is meant by the term *media*?
2. Discuss how the inner ring of the media has more control over the stream of information than less well-known media outlets.
3. What are the main types of media that cover crime and criminal justice stories?
4. Explain how the media help shape our world view.
5. Why do you think the media are so heavily relied on for information about crime and criminal justice?
6. Why do the media tend to ignore elite deviance even though it causes so much harm?
7. What components of the criminal justice system do the media focus on most? Why?
8. Why do you think the media focus so much more on violent crimes than on property crimes?
9. Provide a few examples of how the media fail to provide the proper context when reporting about crime and criminal justice.
10. Do the media promote fear of crime? Why or why not?
11. Which reasons discussed in the chapter do you think best explain why the media are so inaccurate when reporting about crime and criminal justice?
12. On the basis of the research discussed in the chapter, do you the think the media are biased against any particular group in society? Why or why not?
13. What are some likely effects of media coverage of terrorism and American wars on our approach to criminal justice?

PART

III

COMPONENTS OF CRIMINAL JUSTICE: POLICE, COURTS, AND CORRECTIONS

Chapter 6   Law Enforcement: To Serve and Protect?

Chapter 7   Right to Trial? Injustice in Pretrial and Trial Procedures

Chapter 8   Punishment: Does It Work and Is It Fair?

Chapter 9   Incarceration: Lock 'Em Up and Forget About 'Em

CHAPTER

6

LAW ENFORCEMENT: TO SERVE AND PROTECT?

1. Introduction
2. The Organization of Policing in the United States
   - Box 6-1.   American Federal Law Enforcement Agencies
3. Basic Roles and Responsibilities of Police Officers: What Police Do and How They Do It
   a. How Police Serve Crime Victims
   - Box 6-2.   The Exclusionary Rule
4. The Move to Community Policing
   - Box 6-3.   Key Ideas of Sir Robert Peel
5. How Police Are Supposed to Behave
   - Box 6-4.   The Law Enforcement Code of Conduct
6. Innocent Bias: Why Even Good Policing Produces Bias
   a. The Particular Focus of Police on Certain Types of Crimes
   b. The Location of Police on the Streets of the United States
   c. The Use of Police Discretion
   d. The Use of Police Profiling
   e. Policing the War on Drugs
7. American Stop Rates and Arrest Rates
8. Use of Force
9. Corruption in American Policing
10. Conclusion
11. Issue in Depth—Corruption in the Criminal Justice Network
12. Key Terms
13. Discussion Questions

INTRODUCTION

What do images of police from television and movies suggest to you about American policing? What lessons does Hollywood teach you about what police do? This chapter will show you how police are mischaracterized in the United States. While police serve valuable functions to the American people, including crime victims, police spend very little time fighting crime. This is one significant reason that the criminal justice network is very ineffective at reducing crime. In this chapter, I discuss the basics of policing in the United States, including how policing is organized and the basic roles and responsibilities of American police. I also show that, because police are responsible for enforcing the criminal law, any biases in the criminal law will also be found in the activities of law enforcement. The term for unintended biases in law enforcement is *innocent bias*. In this chapter, I explain from where innocent bias against the poor and people of color arises.

THE ORGANIZATION OF POLICING IN THE UNITED STATES

The allocation of police officers to various government levels (i.e., city, county, state, and federal governments) in the United States will have major effects on what police do. Policing at different levels of government is focused on different forms of behaviors. An examination of the levels of government at which the police work in the United States provides a good picture of the types of harmful behaviors to which U.S. police generally dedicate their efforts.

As of 2000, there were 17,784 police agencies in the United States and 796,518 full-time sworn police officers. As shown in Table 6-1, a total of 12,666 (71%) of the police agencies were local police departments, and another 3,070 (17%) were county sheriff departments. Local police agencies have **jurisdiction** over cities and sheriff departments have jurisdiction over counties. Thus, 87% of police agencies are responsible for policing what can be thought of as local governments, or cities and counties.

As shown in Table 6-2, in 2000, city police departments employed 440,920 full-time officers (55% of the total), whereas sheriff departments employed 164,711 deputies (21% of the total). This means that 76% of police officers in the United States work for local cities and counties. Thus the typical police agency and the typical officer in the United States is at the local level of government. Meanwhile, only 56,348 officers work for state agencies (7% of the total) and 88,496 officers work for the federal government (11% of the total).

By 2005, the number of police officers employed by cities grew to 969,700, including 673,146 sworn employees and 295,924 civilians. These officers worked for 14,291 city-level police agencies (Federal Bureau of Investigations, 2006).

Most police departments are relatively small, as 5,894 departments (47%) employ fewer than 10 sworn officers. Almost 75% of local police departments serve communities

TABLE 6-1 American Police Agencies (2000)		
Total agencies	17,784	(100%)
City police	12,666	(71%)
County police (sheriff)	3,070	(17%)
State	49	(less than 1%)
Special jurisdiction	1,376	(8%)
Texas constable	623	(3.5%)

Source: Bureau of Justice Statistics (2002).

TABLE 6-2 American Police Employees (2000)		
Total officers	796,518	(100%)
City police	440,920	(55%)
County police (sheriff)	164,711	(21%)
State	56,348	(7%)
Special jurisdiction	43,413	(5%)
Texas constable	2,630	(less than 1%)
Federal	88,496	(11%)

Source: Bureau of Justice Statistics (2002).

with fewer than 10,000 people. Many sheriff's offices are also small, as 844 offices (27.5%) employed fewer than 10 personnel. Yet almost two-thirds of offices employed more than 100 officers.

From these data, we can conclude that police activities are very much a local phenomenon, and that most law enforcement officers work for small departments that serve small geographical areas. What types of harmful behaviors do local police agencies focus on? The answer is street crimes, such as the "serious" crimes listed in Chapter 4, as well as drug offenses and public order offenses. Later in this chapter, I will show you which of these types of offenses produces the most arrests (you may be surprised!). For now, keep in mind that most police agencies and officers are not focused on acts of elite deviance, the acts shown in Chapter 4 to cause the most harm to Americans.

Box 6-1 lists some of the main policing agencies at the federal level in the United States. The responsibilities of each are also discussed.

According to the Bureau of Justice Statistics (2006), the number of police officers working for the federal government in 2004 was 106,354. The majority of federal officers (63%) worked for the following agencies: U.S. Customs and Border Protection (28,200, or 27% of the total); Federal Bureau of Prisons (15,361, or 14% of the total), the Federal Bureau of Investigation (12,414, or 12% of the total); and U.S. Immigration and Customs Enforcement (10,691, or 10% of the total). FBI officers have broad investigative responsibilities for more than 250 federal crimes, including bank fraud, embezzlement, and kidnapping.

In 2004, the main functions of federal law enforcement officers included criminal investigation/enforcement (41%), police response and patrol (21%), inspections (16%), corrections/detention (16%), court operations (5%), and security/protection (4%). The numbers of agents assigned to each federal police agency has definitely changed since the terrorist attacks against the United States and the creation of the Department of Homeland Security, as have some of their basic responsibilities. The data now clearly show that attention of the FBI has shifted from white-collar crime to terrorism; thus there is even less of a focus on criminal acts of the powerful than probably at any time in our nation's history. In 2006, only 41% of FBI agents were assigned to criminal investigations, versus 55% who are assigned to counterterrorism or counterintelligence.

An examination by Shukovsky, Johnson, and Lathrop (2007) found: "Thousands of white-collar criminals across the country are no longer being prosecuted in federal court—and, in many cases, not at all—leaving a trail of frustrated victims and potentially

BOX 6-1

AMERICAN FEDERAL LAW ENFORCEMENT AGENCIES

U.S. DEPARTMENT OF JUSTICE

- *Drug Enforcement Administration*— Enforces the controlled substances laws and regulations of the United States and brings to the justice systems of the United States those organizations and principal members of organizations involved in the growing, manufacture, or distribution of controlled substances appearing in or destined for illicit traffic in the United States; recommends and supports nonenforcement programs aimed at reducing the availability of illicit controlled substances on the domestic and international markets (http://www.usdoj.gov/dea/agency/mission.htm).

- *Federal Bureau of Prisons*—Confines offenders in the controlled environments of prisons and community-based facilities that are safe, humane, cost-efficient, and appropriately secure (http://www.bop.gov/).

- *Federal Bureau of Investigation*— Protects and defends the United States against terrorist and foreign intelligence threats; enforces the criminal laws of the United States; provides leadership and criminal justice services to federal, state, municipal, and international agencies and partners; investigates terrorism, corruption, abuses of civil rights, white-collar crime, and significant violent crimes (http://www.fbi.gov/quickfacts.htm).

- *U.S. Bureau of Alcohol, Tobacco, Firearms, and Explosives*—Enforces federal criminal laws and regulates the firearms and explosives industries; investigates and reduces crime involving firearms and explosives, acts of arson, and illegal trafficking of alcohol and tobacco products (http://www.atf.gov/about/mission.htm).

- *U.S. Marshals Service*—Arrests more than half of all federal fugitives; protects the federal judiciary; operates the Witness Security Program; transports federal prisoners; seizes property acquired by criminals through illegal activities; provides judicial security; transports prisoners (http://www.usmarshals.gov/).

DEPARTMENT OF HOMELAND SECURITY

- *Bureau of Citizenship and Immigration Services*—Administers immigration and naturalization adjudication functions and establishes immigration services, policies, and priorities, including adjudication of immigrant visa petitions; adjudicates naturalization petitions; adjudicates asylum and refugee applications (http://www.uscis.gov/portal/site/uscis).

- *Bureau of Customs and Border Protection*—Manages, controls, and protects the nation's borders, at and between the official ports of entry (http://cbp.gov/xp/cgov/toolbox/about/mission/cbp.xml).

- *Immigration and Customs Enforcement*—Enforces immigration and customs laws and protects the United States against terrorist attacks. ICE does this by targeting illegal immigrants—the people, money, and materials that support terrorism and other criminal activities (http://www.ice.gov/about/index.htm).

DEPARTMENT OF TREASURY

- *U.S. Secret Service*—Established as a law enforcement agency to investigate the counterfeiting of U.S. currency; the primary investigative mission is to safeguard the payment and financial systems of the United States (http://www.secretservice.gov/investigations.shtml).

- *Internal Revenue Service* (IRS)—Assists with understanding and meeting tax responsibilities; enforces tax laws (http://www.irs.gov/irs/article/0,,id=98141,00.html).

---

billions of dollars in fraud and theft losses. . . . The White House and the Justice Department have failed to replace at least 2,400 agents transferred to counterterrorism squads, leaving far fewer agents on the trail of identity thieves, con artists, hatemongers and other criminals." Outcomes of the shift away from white-collar crime to counter-terrorism include:

- The number of criminal cases investigated by the FBI nationally has steadily declined. In 2005, the FBI brought more than 20,000 cases to federal prosecutors, compared with about 31,000 in 2000, a 34% decline.
- White-collar crime investigations by the FBI have plummeted in recent years. In 2005, the FBI sent prosecutors 3,500 cases, far less than the more than 10,000 cases assigned to agents in 2000.
- Civil rights investigations (e.g., hate crimes and police abuse) have steadily declined since the late 1990s. FBI agents pursued 65% fewer cases in 2005 than they did in 2000.

According to former FBI Executive Assistant Director Dale Watson (who oversaw counterterrorism operations): "The budget should be backfilled with additional agents. We've got to do this. But you could request 2,000 agents for white collar, and it would never see the light of day. . . . We realized we were going to have to pull out of some areas—bank fraud, investment fraud, ID theft—cases that protect the financial infra-structure of the country." In fact, the number of white-collar crime cases investigated and referred for prosecution declined 68% between 1997 and 2005, bank fraud cases declined 69%, and civil rights cases declined 71%. Virtually all of these declines occurred after 2001. During the same time period, the number of child pornography cases increased 213%, domestic terrorism cases increased 90%, and international ter-rorism cases increased 64%.

Given the federal cut-back in white-collar investigations, states would be left to pick up the slack; however, budget cuts have made this impossible. The net effect of this change is that white-collar offenders are less likely to be arrested and prosecuted, and they are also likely to spend less time in jail or prison than before. The main reason is that when convicted in state court, white-collar offenders generally receive much lighter sentences than when convicted and sentenced in federal **courts.** For example, for the crime of bank robbery the typical sentences in federal courts are 41–51 months versus 31–41 months in state courts. Similar differences are found for the crimes of extortion (27–33 months versus 6–12 months), racial harassment (6–12 months versus 3–9 months), identity theft (24 months versus 3–9 months), money laundering (15–21 months versus 0–12 months), fraud (6–12 months versus 0–3 months), embezzlement (6–12 months versus 0–3 months), and forgery (6–12 months versus 0–2 months).

Of all federal officers in 2004, women accounted for only 16% and minorities made up just 29.1% of all officers, including 17.7% Hispanics and 11.4% African Americans. At the local level in 2000, less than 11% of local officers were women and less than 23% were minorities, including less than 12% African Americans and just over 8% Hispanics. Less than 13% of sheriff's deputies were women and only about 17% were minorities, including less than 10% African Americans and just over 6% Hispanics. So, at all levels of government, women and minorities are underrepresented among police officers.

BASIC ROLES AND RESPONSIBILITIES OF POLICE OFFICERS: WHAT POLICE DO AND HOW THEY DO IT

Americans are exposed to a stereotypical view of policing from television entertainment shows and daily crime news. The typical view of police shows them encountering hardened criminals on a daily basis and fighting for their very survival each day (see Chapter 5). One surprising reality of policing in the United States is that police spend most of their time not dealing with crime. This fact runs counter to the image of high-speed car chases and "good guys versus bad guys" depicted in the media. In fact, most of what American police do on a daily basis is mundane and routine. According to Wrobleski (2006), police officers in the United States serve five basic roles:

- **Enforcing laws:**   This includes investigating reported crimes, collecting and protecting evidence from crime scenes, apprehending suspects, and assisting the prosecution in obtaining convictions.
- **Preserving the peace:**   This includes intervening in noncriminal conduct in public places that could escalate into criminal activity if left unchecked.
- **Preventing crime:**   This includes activities designed to stop crime before it occurs, such as education campaigns, preventive patrols, and community policing.
- **Providing services:**   This includes performing functions normally served by other social service agencies, such as counseling, referring citizens for social services, assisting people with various needs, and keeping traffic moving.
- **Upholding rights:**   This includes respecting all persons' rights regardless of race, ethnicity, class, gender, and other factors, and respecting individual constitutional protections.

Of these five roles, the **typical police officer** spends most of his or her time each day *not* fighting crime (Fyfe et al., 1997). So how do police spend their time? According to Wrobleski (2006), about 90% of a police officer's time is spent providing social services. Services provided by police include checking buildings for security violations, regulating traffic, investigating accidents, providing information to citizens, finding lost children, providing first aid, handling animal calls, mediating disputes, and negotiating settlements between citizens (Cox and Wade, 1998, pp. 99, 103). As noted by Manning (1997, p. 93), "Of the police functions or activities most central to accumulated police obligations, none is more salient than supplying the range of public services required in complex, pluralistic, urban societies." So, although "law enforcer" or "crime fighter" is the stereotypical image of the police officer, the typical city patrol officer or county sheriff in the United States spends the smallest amount of his or her day dealing with crime.

Others, such as Bayley (1994), claim that police spend about 75% of their time on routine patrol or administrative tasks. In fact, according to the Bureau of Justice Statistics, almost 70% of full-time local police officers were regularly assigned to responding to calls for service in 2000. Whatever the case, police spend only about 5% to 10% of their total time handling criminal matters (Cox and Wade, 1998, p. 99). An examination of activities of police officers at various levels of government illustrates this point equally well. According to the Bureau of Justice Statistics, approximately two-thirds of officers have primary responsibility for answering calls for service. Fewer than 1 in 5 have primary responsibility for investigative duties (15%), and fewer than 1 in 10 have primary responsibility for duties that are administrative or technical, or that involve training, jail-related duties, and court-related duties. When comparing city and county officers, the main difference is that city officers are more often on patrol, whereas county officers are more likely to have jail duties given that county sheriffs' departments often operate jails.

At the state and federal levels, the picture is very similar. State officers are most frequently assigned to responding to calls for service, followed by investigative duties; administrative, technical, and training duties; and court-related duties. At the federal level, most officers have primary responsibility for investigations and enforcement, followed by corrections-related duties, police services, court operations, and security and protection.

When politicians promise to put more police on the streets, they do not bother to tell us that it likely will make little difference in the fight against crime. This is because police officers spend so little time actually fighting crime. Given that fewer than one in two crimes is even known to the police (and this only counts street crimes), and only one in five of these leads to an arrest, it is not surprising that police have some free time on their hands (see Chapter 1). How could this time be better spent? I will discuss this issue in Chapter 13. Politicians offer more of the same—more police, even though the evidence suggests that what we need is not more—but better—policing (Sherman et al., 1997).

Efforts such as hiring more police, better arming police, and allowing increasingly tough and intrusive policing to crack down on relatively minor offenders interfere with one responsibility of police: to safeguard citizens' constitutional protections. A significant problem with "get tough," "law and order" approaches to reducing crime is that they interfere with citizens' constitutional rights. One example is the **exclusionary rule**, discussed in Box 6-2.

How Police Serve Crime Victims

Although police officers spend most of their time not dealing with crime, they do provide valuable services to victims of crime. Generally, as police "are the first representatives of

BOX 6-2

THE EXCLUSIONARY RULE

The *exclusionary rule* was applied to the states by the Supreme Court case, *Mapp v. Ohio* (1961). It requires that if evidence is obtained illegally it cannot be used against the accused in court. This rule grew out of the Fourth Amendment, which reads: "The right of the people to be secure in their persons, houses, papers, and effects, against unreasonable searches and seizures shall not be violated, and no Warrants shall issue, but upon probable cause, supported by Oath or Affirmation, and particularly describing the place to be searched, and the persons to be seized." Any evidence obtained without a valid warrant thus would not be admissible in court.

Yet, as we have become more and more entrenched in a crime control model of criminal justice, numerous exceptions have been created that allow police to get around the exclusionary rule. They include:

- ***Searches incident to lawful arrests:*** Police may search the area within the immediate control of the suspect upon arrest.

- ***Searches with consent:*** Police may search any area that is voluntarily consented to by citizens.

- ***The plain view doctrine:*** Evidence in plain view of the police may be seized without a warrant.

- ***The plain touch doctrine:*** Evidence that is felt by the police while they are legally searching a person or place may be seized without a warrant.

- ***The good faith exception:*** If it can be determined that the police officer was acting in good faith that a

warrant was valid even though it is not, then seized evidence can still be used against the accused.

- ***Inevitable discovery:*** Police can use illegally seized evidence against a suspect if they can demonstrate that the evidence would have ultimately been discovered by lawful means.

- ***Exigent circumstances:*** During emergencies, police may find evidence that can ultimately be used against a citizen.

These exceptions seem logical enough, but are they necessary? Fyfe (1983) has demonstrated that the exclusionary rule really does not make it harder for the police to gather and use meaningful evidence against guilty criminals. As explained by Walker (1998, p. 87), "[T]he police solve crimes when they immediately obtain a good lead about a suspect, from either the victim or a witness. Physical evidence, independent of some other kind of identification of the suspect, is rarely the primary factor in making an arrest and convicting the offender." This means that even fewer cases will be dismissed because of evidence that is thrown out as a result of the exclusionary rule. Fyfe described such a likelihood as "minuscule" and "infinitesimal." Does such a small likelihood that a guilty person will go free justify allowing ccourts to use illegally seized evidence against accused criminals?

Walker concludes that the exclusionary rule is valuable and in fact is supported by most police administrators. For example, former FBI Director William Sessions stated that "protections that are afforded by the exclusionary rule are extremely important to fair play and the proper carrying out of the law enforcement responsibility" (cited in Walker, 1998, p. 89). In essence, the exclusionary rule results in better police work and lowers the possibility that citizens will be wrongfully convicted by overzealous agents of government.

the criminal justice network that victims encounter after being victimized," they serve victims in the following ways.

- Responding quickly to calls for help
- Launching thorough investigations into alleged crimes
- Preserving and collecting evidence
- Solving crimes by capturing suspected offenders
- Assisting with criminal prosecutions of criminal suspects (Karmen, 2006)

Technically, all crime-related police work is in service to victims—recording crimes, investigating crimes, collecting and preserving evidence, apprehending and arresting suspects, interviewing witnesses and victims, interrogating and booking suspects, testifying in court, and so forth (Cox and Wade, 1998, p. 99). Such services are crucial to achieving justice as an outcome for victims of crime. The main problem with American policing is that it is structured to be reactive to crime, or **incident-driven**, rather than proactive, or **problem-oriented**.

Because street crime is "the product of social and economic disadvantage, much of it traceable to racial bias and discrimination" (Tonry, 1995, p. 3), police have little effect on crime rates. Such factors are beyond the reach of criminal justice agencies. Police themselves know this. For example, Klockars (1991, p. 250) writes:

> All of the major factors influencing how much crime there is or is not are factors over which police have no control whatsoever. Police can do nothing about the age, sex, racial, or ethnic distribution of the population. They cannot control economic conditions; poverty; inequality; occupational opportunity; moral, religious, family, or secular education; or dramatic social, cultural, or political change. These are the "big ticket" items in determining the amount and distribution of crime. Compared to them what police do or do not do matters very little.

This, in part, explains why American policing has shifted toward the community policing ideal. Wrobleski (2006) explains that community policing is more proactive and problem-oriented—a "customer service" approach to law enforcement.

THE MOVE TO COMMUNITY POLICING

A buzz word in policing is **community policing**, which refers to a crime prevention partnership between the police and the community (Wrobleski, 2006). Although the term has no clearly defined set of characteristics in practice, in philosophy it is aimed at solving problems before they become crimes rather than merely reacting to crimes after they occur. That is, it is an approach aimed at identifying problems with the community before they lead to crime (Goldstein, 1990).

Community policing is rooted in a problem-solving approach and is sometimes referred to as **problem-oriented policing**. Problem-oriented policing is based on the following principles, as described by the Bureau of Justice Assistance (1993, p. 5).

- A problem is something that concerns the community.
- A problem will likely indicate a pattern of related incidents that will require unique police interventions.
- Problem solving is a long-term strategy requiring increased police creativity and initiative.

Goldstein (2001) adds that problem-oriented policing is "an approach to policing in which discrete pieces of police business (each consisting of a cluster of similar incidents, whether crime or acts of disorder, that the police are expected to handle) are subject to microscopic examination (drawing on the especially honed skills of crime analysts and the accumulated experience of operating field personnel) in hopes that what is freshly learned about each problem will lead to discovering a new and more effective strategy for dealing with it." It places a high value on new responses that aim to prevent crime, that are not dependent on criminal justice, and that "engage other public agencies, the community and the private sector when their involvement has the potential for significantly contributing to the reduction of the problem." Finally, problem-oriented policing "carries a commitment to implementing the new strategy, rigorously evaluating its effectiveness, and, subsequently, reporting the results in ways that will benefit other police agencies and that will ultimately contribute to building a body of knowledge that supports the further professionalization of the police."

Community policing in its current forms began to take hold in the United States during the 1970s. It grew out of the recognition that professional policing was unsuccessful at reducing crime, as well as unpopular with certain segments of the public. From roughly 1920 to 1970, American policing was more professional in nature; that is, it placed a high value on efficiency and crime fighting while being separate and distinct from public influence. In the professional policing model, police intentionally keep themselves separate from the public in order to reduce corruption and special favors. Unfortunately, this leads to isolation from the community and hinders the ability of police to achieve cooperation from citizens. It also fosters hostilities in some neighborhoods where the police become seen as occupiers rather than service providers. Community policing places more emphasis on providing services to the community and developing police–community relations (Gaines, Kaune, and Miller, 2000, p. 178).

Research demonstrates that the success of formal social control depends, at least in part, on informal social controls in a community (Robinson, 2004). Police know that they need the help of communities to fight crime. Social control can be understood as "attempting to persuade persons or groups to conform to group expectations" (Cox and Wade, 1998, p. 94). **Formal social control** achieves that conformity through the use of official or governmental means, such as law enforcement, whereas **informal social control** is achieved through families, peers, teachers, and others. Coercing people to abide by the law (formal social control) depends to a great degree on a criminal justice network that can efficiently detect crime and apprehend criminals. Clearly, American criminal justice is highly inefficient. In part, this is because many Americans avoid getting involved in the process—for example, by not calling the police when they witness crimes. Given that there are fewer than 3 police officers per 1,000 citizens in the United States, it is highly unlikely that formal social control mechanisms will effectively deter would-be lawbreakers. This "should be enough to convince us that the likelihood of detection and apprehension for those who violate laws is quite low if we rely totally on the police for such detection and apprehension" (Cox and Wade, 1998, p. 94).

Community policing is also theoretically based on sound **crime analysis**, so that police resources and personnel are assigned to geographic areas where and when they are most needed. This goes back to a notion of Sir Robert Peel, who in 1829 founded the London Metropolitan Police Department in England. Box 6-3 illustrates the core ideas of Sir Robert Peel and discusses how and why they are still important for American policing. Compare this with the realities of policing discussed in this chapter.

BOX 6-3

KEY IDEAS OF SIR ROBERT PEEL

American policing evolved from English policing traditions. As the early colonists brought over their customs and traditions to this new country, they also brought over their law enforcement customs and traditions. In 1829, Home Secretary Sir Robert Peel established the London Metropolitan Police Department (LMPD) in England. The officers became known as "bobbies" after their founder. Peel put forth certain principles that he believed police should follow for law enforcement to be successful. As consistent as they are with today's version of community policing in the United States, keep in mind that he actually posited these ideas almost 200 years ago!

Peel insisted that the police be chosen from the people so that they would be familiar with and essentially the same as the people whom they policed. He insisted that police be uniformed and be unarmed except for a small truncheon beneath their coats. Peel clearly laid out his vision of the personality of the ideal police officer. Police, he said, should be highly trained, stable, quiet yet determined, and in control of their tempers.

Peel also thought officers should keep up a good appearance in order to gain respect.

Peel insisted that the police force be under government control and organized in military fashion to maximize accountability and ensure cohesiveness. He also held that officers should be required to keep records of all of their interactions with citizens, also for accountability purposes. Keeping records of all interactions would also allow the police to track incidents by time and place. Thus, Peel believed in what we now call crime analysis, which would allow police to be deployed to those areas and at those times when they were needed most. This would also permit the police department to distribute crime news for the benefit of the public (as is done in today's police newsletters).

Peel envisioned a police force whose officers would be hired on a probationary basis (much like today's probationary patrol officer, fresh out of the police academy). This would permit police officers to be adequately trained while on the street and would reduce the possibility of hiring

(continued)

BOX 6-3 *(Continued)*

negligent personnel. Unlike the current situation, in which law enforcement success has been measured in terms of more and more arrests, Peel believed that police efficiency could best be demonstrated by the absence of crime—that is, by crime prevention.

In the 1850s, Peel's law enforcement ideas spread across England, and England's police force became the largest and most organized in the world. Eventually, legislators from New York visited the LMPD to copy its ideas and to build a similar foundation for American police forces.

Has American policing become detached from its roots? Have we lost our way? Or is community policing a means to return to Robert Peel's core ideals?

According to the National Criminal Justice Commission, community policing is based on the notion that police "should serve residents in a neighborhood rather than simply police them" (Donziger, 1996). Yet one significant problem with community policing is that many minority communities "feel both **overpoliced and underprotected**—overpoliced because the drug trade flourishes with the same vitality as before, and because police are often slow to respond to 911 calls from minority neighborhoods" (p. 160; emphasis in original).

Legislators have voted to place more police in these neighborhoods on the basis of the belief that there is more crime there and that the presence of more police will reduce crime. The evidence from studies such as the now famous Kansas City Patrol Study (Kelling et al., 1974) and its replications (Police Foundation, 1981) suggests that more police will not reduce crime. These studies found no evidence that patrol activities of police, whether proactive, reactive, or even absent, had any effects on crime rates. This is why the National Criminal Justice Commission concludes that "we need to learn how to police *better* before we add new police" (Donziger, 1996, p. 160, emphasis added).

Walker (2005) explains why adding more police will have no effect on crime rates. He argues that patrol will always be spread thin in a geographic area, so that its crime-preventive benefits will be minimal. He also suggests that many crimes are not suppressible by patrol because they happen in private areas between people who know one another.

There is some research that suggests that adding more police to large cities will reduce street crime there, especially when patrols are directed at **hot spots of crime** (Sherman et al., 1997). The number of violent street crimes, as measured in the UCR, declined 34% between 1990 and 2000, and the number of UCR property crimes fell by 31%. During this time, the number of full-time officers increased 17% (Bureau of Justice Statistics, 2003). Policing likely had something to do with these declines but scholars generally agree that police were not responsible for most of the declines (see Chapter 4).

President Clinton boasted in the 1990s that crime rates fell in the nation's cities because he had put 100,000 new "community police officers" on the street. In fact, we still have not hired those additional 100,000 officers, and most of those whom we did hire are not engaged in community policing. The good news is that in 2000, of all city police departments, 66% had full-time sworn officers engaged in community policing activities, as did 62% of sheriffs' departments. Almost 70% of local police departments had a community policing plan of some type. The bad news is that only 18% of local police departments (who employed 52% of all officers) had a formally written community policing plan, and only 17% of departments offered training to citizens on community policing issues. As for sheriffs' offices, 55% had some community policing plan, and 62% used full-time community policing officers. Yet less than one-third (31%) of departments, employing 51% of deputies, trained all new recruits in community policing. And only 13% had formal policies on community policing. Only 9% of sheriffs' offices included problem-oriented projects in performance evaluations for officers and only 8% surveyed citizens regarding perceptions of crime problems in the community. Thus, it is safe to say that community policing is more of a buzz word than a widely used approach to crime prevention.

I suggest that even if we add more police, policing will probably be ineffective in reducing crime because police still will not spend a substantial amount of time fighting crime. Of crime calls, which make up only a small minority of calls for service, "almost all calls come when it is too late to catch the perpetrator" (Donziger, 1996, p. 162). These are known as **cold crimes**. The fact that about 75% of offenders are not caught at the scene of the offense is what makes arrest the weakest stage of the criminal justice process. Such facts have led even police chiefs to make statements such as, "Adding more police may be good politics, but it will do little to reduce crime and violence in America" (Moran, 1994; quoted in Krajicek, 1998).

Alternatively, better policing may reduce crime. A small portion of officers nationwide are assigned to crime prevention efforts. If we want to prioritize community policing, we must invest more resources in problem-solving approaches that are proactive rather than reactive. Such efforts offer great promise for preventing crime before it occurs.

HOW POLICE ARE SUPPOSED TO BEHAVE

Now that you have a better understanding of how policing is organized in the United States, what police do in a typical day, and what is happening with policing in the United States, you may be wondering how police actually behave. In fact, police are expected to behave in a very specific manner at all times. Box 6-4 contains *The Law Enforcement Code of Conduct* passed by the International Association of Chiefs of Police. Consider this the ideal of American policing.

Compare the ideal of police behavior with your own experiences with police. Are they generally consistent? I have personally had both good and bad experiences with police—sometimes I dealt with officers who behaved precisely the way the IACP expects they will and sometimes I dealt with officers who took job-related events personally and let it affect their behavior by acting unprofessionally.

The vast majority of police likely follow the IACP mandate. Yet, because of structural impediments, the reality of policing in the United States clearly runs counter to the ideals we expect. I would argue that for police to successfully carry out the IACP mandate, they would have to be highly educated. In 2000, almost all (98%) local police departments had some type of educational requirements for new officer recruits, but

BOX 6-4

THE LAW ENFORCEMENT CODE OF CONDUCT

All law enforcement officers must be fully aware of the ethical responsibilities of their position and must strive constantly to live up to the highest possible standards of professional policing.

The International Association of Chiefs of Police believes it is important that police officers have clear advice and counsel available to assist them in performing their duties consistent with these standards, and has adopted the following ethical mandates as guidelines to meet these ends.

Primary responsibilities of a police officer

A police officer acts as an official representative of government who is required and trusted to work within the law. The officer's powers and duties are conferred by statute. The fundamental duties of a police officer include serving the community, safeguarding lives and property, protecting the innocent, keeping the peace, and ensuring the rights of all to liberty, equality, and justice.

Performance of the duties of a police officer

A police officer shall perform all duties impartially, without favor or affection or ill will and without regard to status, sex, race, religion, political belief, or aspiration. All citizens will be treated equally with courtesy, consideration, and dignity.

Officers will never allow personal feelings, animosities, or friendships to influence official conduct. Laws will be enforced appropriately and courteously and, in carrying out their responsibilities, officers will strive to obtain maximum cooperation from the public. They will conduct themselves in appearance and deportment in such a manner as to inspire confidence and respect for the position of public trust they hold.

Discretion

A police officer will use responsibly the discretion vested in his position and exercise it within the law. The principle of reasonableness will guide the officer's determinations, and the officer will consider all surrounding circumstances in determining whether any legal action shall be taken.

Consistent and wise use of discretion, based on professional policing competence, will do much to preserve good relationships and retain the confidence of the public. There can be difficulty in choosing between conflicting courses of action. It is important to remember that a timely word of advice rather than arrest—which may be correct in appropriate circumstances—can be a more effective means of achieving a desired end.

Use of force

A police officer will never employ unnecessary force or violence and will use only such force in the discharge of duty as is reasonable in all circumstances.

The use of force should be used only with the greatest restraint and only after discussion, negotiation, and persuasion have been found to be inappropriate or ineffective. While the use of force is occasionally unavoidable, every police officer will refrain from unnecessary infliction of pain or suffering and will never engage in cruel, degrading, or inhuman treatment of any person.

Confidentiality

Whatever a police officer sees, hears, or learns that is of a confidential nature will be kept secret unless the performance of duty or legal provision requires otherwise.

Members of the public have a right to security and privacy, and information obtained about them must not be improperly divulged.

Integrity

A police officer will not engage in acts of corruption or bribery, nor will an officer condone such acts by other police officers. The public demands that the integrity of police officers be above reproach. Police officers must, therefore, avoid any conduct that might compromise integrity and thus undercut the public confidence in a law enforcement agency. Officers will refuse to accept any gifts, presents, subscriptions, favors, gratuities, or promises that could be interpreted as seeking to cause the officer to refrain from performing official responsibilities honestly and within the law. Police officers must not receive private or special advantage from their official status. Respect from the public cannot be bought; it can only be earned and cultivated.

Cooperation with other police officers and agencies

Police officers will cooperate with all legally authorized agencies and their representatives in the pursuit of justice.

An officer or agency may be one among many organizations that may provide law enforcement services to a jurisdiction. It is imperative that a police officer assist colleagues fully and completely with respect and consideration at all times.

Personal–professional capabilities

Police officers will be responsible for their own standard of professional performance and will take every reasonable opportunity to enhance and improve their level of knowledge and competence.

Through study and experience, a police officer can acquire the high level of knowledge and competence that is essential for the efficient and effective performance of duty. The acquisition of knowledge is a never-ending process of personal and professional development that should be pursued constantly.

Private life

Police officers will behave in a manner that does not bring discredit to their agencies or themselves.

A police officer's character and conduct while off duty must always be exemplary, thus maintaining a position of respect in the community in which he or she lives and serves. The officer's personal behavior must be beyond reproach.

most (83%) required only a high school diploma. Only 15% of city police departments and 11% of sheriffs' officers had college education requirements for new officers, including only 1% of local departments that required a 4-year degree. New police recruits were required to complete between 800 and 1,600 hours of academy and field training, depending on the city size. It is estimated that less than one-third of new officers work for departments that require college education (Law Enforcement Management and Administrative Statistics, 2003). The bottom line with police education requirements is that they are simply too low. Perhaps this is why the average starting salary of new officers in local police departments in 2000 was $25,500, whereas for sheriff's deputies it was only $23,700. Although these numbers have increased due to cost of living adjustments since 2000, starting police officers still make very little money given the amount of power and responsibility they hold.

What can we realistically expect from our police officers who are held to such high standards when we do not require a college education and when they are paid so poorly? I would argue that we should not expect the reality of policing to match the ideal. And you should be concerned about this. In 2000, local police departments spent nearly $37 billion, for an overall cost per resident of $179, whereas sheriffs' departments spent almost $18 billion for $65 per resident (Bureau of Justice Statistics, 2003). This is your money.

INNOCENT BIAS: WHY EVEN GOOD POLICING PRODUCES BIAS

If individual police officers are biased against certain groups of people, we may conclude that they are involved in unjust activity. Yet bias in policing does not require "bad cops." Biased law enforcement only requires bad law. In Chapter 3, it was shown that the criminal law is biased against poor people and people of color because it criminalizes their harmful behaviors as "serious crimes" even though their acts really aren't the most serious harms facing American citizens. Given this fact, enforcement of this law (through policing) will logically reinforce the bias within the law.

This means that even if every individual police officer was not biased, prejudiced, or bigoted, American law enforcement would still be biased because it simply reflects the biases of the law. This is what I call **innocent bias**.

Innocent bias can arise from the following factors.

- The particular focus of police on certain types of crimes
- The location of police on the streets of the United States
- The use of police discretion
- The use of police profiling
- Policing the war on drugs

The Particular Focus of Police on Certain Types of Crimes

Local policing in the United States focuses on street crime, the eight "most serious" Part I Index Offenses of the Uniform Crime Report (UCR): theft, burglary, motor vehicle theft, arson, homicide, aggravated assault, forcible rape, and robbery (see Chapter 4). These acts are generally perceived by society and government agencies alike to be the behaviors that cause the most physical and financial harm and occur with the greatest frequency. Usually police departments focus their law enforcement activities on crimes considered the most serious—those thought to pose the greatest threat to individuals and their property (Wrobleski, 2006). The main conclusion is that the general focus of law enforcement in the United States is on a very small number of criminal acts and an even smaller number of culpable harmful acts. The majority of types of victimizations, even those that stem from harmful, culpable behaviors, are virtually ignored by law enforcement in the United States.

Figure 6-1 illustrates the way in which law enforcement in the United States is most focused on criminal victimizations of individuals caused by acts of individual persons.

FIGURE 6-1   Focus of Law Enforcement on Victimization

The shaded region in Figure 6-1 indicates the main focus of police when it comes to victimizations. Law enforcement is much less concerned with victimizations against individuals that are committed by entities such as groups or corporations (these are usually under the jurisdiction of state or federal law enforcement). Victimizations against individuals or entities such as groups and corporations committed by other entities are generally not handled by the criminal justice network and hence do not fall within the primary domain of law enforcement. Instead, harms and victimizations resulting from such acts tend to be handled through civil law (as in the case of major lawsuits against large tobacco corporations) or regulatory agencies (as in the case of outbreaks of bacterial contamination in food products). Other harmful culpable behaviors, especially those that do not violate any law, are completely ignored.

These facts indicate that people can be victimized by acts that result in death, physical injury, and/or loss of property with virtual impunity from the U.S. criminal justice network. Given that doing justice implies that the guilty will be punished for their actions, the fact that our justice network ignores harmful acts committed with culpability means that the criminal justice network does not achieve justice as an outcome (or corrective justice). It also means that our network of justice is ineffective at reducing these types of crimes.

The Location of Police on the Streets of the United States

Police are disproportionately located in some areas of our country while being nearly absent from others. Specifically, more police are allocated to the nation's inner cities. Why? First, there is more demand for police services in these areas. Second, the nation's inner cities are characterized by very high poverty rates. This may explain why there are more police patrols directed at these areas. Residents in these areas have less power and are less able to resist police presence. Benjamin and Miller (1991, p. 21) provide an example with drug crimes. They claim that "the inner city is an expedient locale for police to rack up impressive arrest numbers, with little fear for consequences if mistakes are made."

The result of a differential location of police by city size and type is that police will make more arrests of the people who live in the areas where they patrol. Since poverty is higher in the nation's central cities, and since the poverty rate is highest among African Americans in these areas, we would expect police to disproportionately arrest poor people and African Americans, especially when they commit those street crimes on which officers are most focused.

The Use of Police Discretion

Discretion is the ability of an agent to act according to his or her own professional judgment rather than some preset rules or procedures. Even though all criminal justice decision making must occur within limits imposed by the U.S. Constitution, state constitutions, state laws, and precedents set forth by previous courts, many actors within the criminal justice network have wide discretion. The very nature of policing, whereby officers are entitled to use unchecked discretion to make decisions (e.g., see National Association of Criminal Defense Lawyers, 1996), allows racial stereotypes and myths of crime to infiltrate police work, resulting in racial disparities in stops, arrests, and police use of force (Cole, 1999).

Pratt (1992, pp. 99–100) argues that police officers are given discretion to act or not to act on the basis of their own judgment because we assume they are honest and trustworthy. In addition, extensive inservice training leaves police officers uniquely qualified to judge which behaviors pose significant threats to society. Finally, police must be allowed to use discretion for their own protection.

According to Bittner (1970, p. 107), police officers have "a greater degree of discretionary freedom in proceedings against offenders than any other public official." After all, if the police do not take people into custody, make arrests, and issue citations, the criminal justice network has no clients and thus cannot operate. This is why Gottfredson (1999, p. 30) writes about police: "To a great extent, they exercise discretion in deciding whether to invoke the criminal justice system."

When police are given discretion over criminal matters, the potential for abuse is clearly there. The National Criminal Justice Commission writes that American police have the power to decide how to apply the law and determine the crime-fighting agenda of a community:

> They have wide discretion to decide who will be stopped and searched, which homes will be entered into, and which businesses will be inspected. If misused, that power can cause everything from a minor inconvenience to the destruction of life and property. If used properly, it can save lives and help make neighborhoods safer (Donziger, 1996, p. 161).

Corruption in police departments and discrimination by the police were factors that led to the move by police away from the community and toward neutral, professional models of policing in the early twentieth century (Fyfe et al., 1997).

Discretion seems vital to the success of American policing; the problem is determining how to ensure that it will not be misused. It seems more likely that police will misuse their discretion when the political climate of their communities, states, and country is so focused on fighting street criminals that they lose sight of what should be the real goals of law enforcement: to serve citizens and reduce harmful behaviors while simultaneously upholding constitutional protections.

A prime example of misused discretion is seen in the enforcement of speeding laws. The police cannot possibly enforce laws regulating speeding on all roads at all times, so they selectively choose roads and times to patrol for speeding and even target individual cars. Cox and Wade (1998, p. 98) write, "While an officer is writing a citation to one speeder, several other speeders may escape his or her attention." The threat of a speeding ticket may deter some drivers from intentionally speeding at some times, but it is evident that most drivers exceed the speed limit at times, sometimes even intentionally. Robinson and Zaitzow (1999b) found that more than 90% of American criminologists admitted to speeding intentionally. There are times when one must speed to stay out of the way of other drivers or to keep up with the flow of traffic. This may explain why many speeders get upset with police officers for selecting them out of the dozens of surrounding vehicles on the roads.

The point is not that speeding should be allowed, that speed limits should be lifted, or that people should be free to drive as fast as they want. Rather, I want to demonstrate what can happen if police are looking for particular types of cars, or even types of people, to pull over for speeding. Because police have a wide range of discretion in deciding who to pull over, very little can stop them from abusing this discretion and applying the law differentially to different types of people.

Racial, cultural, or gender differences may lead officers to stop and arrest individuals from some groups of people more than others. African Americans may be more fearful and thus may run from or refuse to cooperate with the police. Hispanics may not make direct eye contact with officers, and this may be misinterpreted as a lack of respect. If police are not trained to recognize such group differences, their discretion may be biased against groups who are unlike the officers.

At the arrest stage, the police officer "possesses considerable discretionary power . . . [where] there is no one physically present to supervise the officer's actions, and he or she may respond to a variety of cues . . . [such as] the age, gender, race, dress, prior history, or location of a suspect" in deciding to arrest or not (Cox and Wade, 1998, p. 101). Granting police this awesome power is asking for trouble if police are dishonest, partial, bigoted, or unethical.

Cox and Wade (1998, p. 101) claim:

> It is the existence of discretion by individual police officers in thousands of police–citizen encounters everyday that helps shape public attitudes toward the police. . . . If an officer arrests one person for a particular offense but allows another who has committed the same offense to go free, the arrested party . . . can hardly be expected to feel that the criminal justice network is just.

Neither are everyday citizens who become aware of such discrepancies likely to think the criminal justice network is just. Decisions about who to stop, pull over, and suspect of criminal activity are informed by images of crime created by the criminal law and broadcast in the news media. Therefore, what is known as police profiling begins with the biases built into the law and the news media.

The Use of Police Profiling

American police focus on particular types of people because of their own personal experience or that of their institution and profession, which suggests that certain people are more likely than others to violate the law. For example, during police academy training, officer candidates may learn about crime rate differentials among different groups in society, using official rates of street crime from the Uniform Crime Reports. Also, during the time probationary officers spend with a **field training officer** (FTO), new police officers may pick up subtle hints of whom to be on the look out for, whom to stop and question, and so forth, from their senior officers. These experiences allow race and other extra-legal factors to affect police decision-making. This practice, known as **police profiling**, results in startling disparities in police behavior (Harris, 1999; Roberts, 1993; Son, Davis, and Rome, 1998).

One study found that although African Americans make up about 17% of drivers and only 17.5% of traffic violators, they made up nearly 73% of those pulled over and searched by the police (Gaines et al., 2000, pp. 645–646). Other research does not find evidence of racial profiling (e.g., see Alpert, Dunham, and Smith, 2007; Kowalski and Lundman, 2007; Lichtenberg, 2006; Ridgeway, 2006; Schafer et al., 2006; Skolnick, 2007; Stewart, 2007; Tomaskovic et al., 2006; Warren et al. 2006). One study, good news in my state, showed that state highway patrol officers did not appear to be engaging in racial profiling overall based simply on aggregate data on the number of people on the roads by race and their proportion of drivers stopped and ticketed (Smith et al., 2003). The authors note that "there is ambiguity as to whether any particular area is suspect as having unduly high levels of racial disparity. Such a finding of ambiguity may be disquieting to those who would want to know what might seem to be a straight answer to a simple question: Is a trooper racially biased or not? We interpret our evidence to mean that we can safely rule out widespread and large degrees of racial disparity in the behaviors of the [North Carolina State Highway Patrol] across districts. However, we cannot rule out with certainty the presence of small degrees of racial disparity" (p. 9). In fact, there is evidence of racial profiling in some places at some times.

Another way to look for racial profiling is to examine all face-to-face contacts with police. The Bureau of Justice Statistics (2007) reports that in 2005 about 19% of residents aged 16 years or older had some face-to-face contact with a police officer. This is down slightly from 21% in 2002. About 9 out of 10 people said the police acted properly, although blacks (82.2%) were less likely than whites (91.6%) to feel that police acted properly during a contact. At the same time, there were no differences found in the percentages of whites and blacks who felt that police behaved improperly when helping with a traffic accident or providing assistance.

Blacks tended to believe the police acted improperly during traffic stops and during criminal investigations. The percentage of drivers who felt their stop was legitimate varied by race. Nearly 9 in 10 white drivers felt the stop was legitimate (87.6%), versus 85.1% of Hispanic drivers and only 76.8% of black drivers. Pronounced differences by race were found in stops for vehicle checks, as 66.5% of blacks felt it was appropriate versus 72.2% of whites.

Those most likely to have face-to-face contacts with police include young people, males, and whites. In 2005, whites made up 71% of the U.S. population ages 16 years and older but 76% of persons with police contacts. Blacks ages 16 years and older made up about the same percentage of persons having police contact (10%) as their percentage of the population in 2005 (11%).

According to the data, the most common reason for contact with police in 2005 involved a traffic stop (41% of all contacts), and speeding was the most common reason for being pulled over in 2005. The vast majority of drivers (86%) said they were pulled over for a legitimate reason. Although white, black, and Hispanic drivers were stopped by police at similar rates, blacks and Hispanics were more likely than whites to be searched by the police. Only about 1 in 20 (5%) of all stopped drivers were searched by the police. This either suggests a higher rate of suspicious behavior on the part of people of color or racial profiling by the police.

Police found evidence of some form of wrongdoing (e.g., drugs, illegal weapons) in only 11.6% of searches, suggesting that the vast majority of people being searched were not involved in any criminal activity (at the time). Those drivers most likely to be arrested were males (three times more likely than female drivers to be arrested), and blacks (twice as likely as white drivers to be arrested). Black drivers were more likely than white drivers to be arrested (4.5% versus 2.1%, respectively). Hispanics were more likely than blacks or whites to receive a ticket (65% versus 56.2% and 55.8%, respectively). Whites were more likely to receive a warning than Hispanics (9.7% versus 5.9%) and also more likely than blacks to receive a verbal warning (18.6% versus 13.7%, respectively).

A higher arrest rate is suggestive of higher rates of wrongdoing by those stopped. The differential in warnings is consistent with possible differential favors by the police.

The same data show that males, as well as blacks and Hispanics, suffered from the highest rates of serious police actions following a stop. For example, male drivers were more likely than female drivers to be ticketed and/or arrested. Additionally, while less than 2% (1.6%) of the most recent contacts resulted in the use of force or a threat of force by the police, blacks and Hispanics were more likely than whites to have force used against them. Of those who had force used against them, a sizable majority (83%) said they thought the force was excessive. Whites (84.3%) involved in force incidents were only slightly more likely than blacks (81.5%) to feel the force was excessive (versus 85.6% for Hispanics), although the differences are likely due to random error.

Blacks (4.4%) and Hispanics (2.3%) were more likely than whites (1.2%) to have force used against them by police in 2005. Although blacks made up only 1 out of every 10 police, they made up roughly 1 out of every 4 contacts where force was used. This is suggestive of either differential suspect behavior by police or a greater willingness by police to use force against blacks.

Data from 2000 analyzed by the Bureau of Justice Statistics showed that among young males ages 16–24 years, neither African Americans nor Hispanics were more likely than Caucasians to be stopped by police. Yet African Americans (75.7%) and Hispanics (79.4%) were more likely than Caucasians (66.6%) to be ticketed for speeding. In this age group, African Americans (15.9%) and Hispanics (14.2%) were more likely than Caucasians (7.9%) to have their cars or persons searched.

Among males over the age of 24 years, African Americans (13.8%) were more likely than Caucasians (10.7%) to be stopped by police, and African Americans (3.2%) were more likely than Caucasians (2%) to be stopped by police more than one time. In this age group, African Americans (15.5%) and Hispanics (11.1%) were more likely than Caucasians (5.8%) to have their cars or persons searched. African American males over the age of 24 years faced searches of their persons during 11.4% of stops, versus only 5.8% of Hispanics and 4% of Caucasians.

Interestingly, African Americans (74%) and Hispanics (81.6%) were less likely than Caucasians (86%) to report that they felt the stop was legitimate. African American

(32%) and Hispanic (34.7%) males over age 24 years who were stopped more than once by police were far less likely than Caucasian (16.5%) males over 24 years to say the stop was illegitimate.

Given that the chance of arrest was not much greater for African Americans searched by police than for Caucasians (41.5% versus 37.3%), do these statistics suggest anything in particular? The Bureau of Justice Statistics suggests that among non-arrested motorists (those for which there was either no evidence or not enough evidence to warrant an arrest), African American males were more likely than Caucasian males to be searched (9.9% versus 5.1%). This seems like clear evidence of profiling, based on the assumption that people of color need to be searched more than Caucasians.

When police use race as a proxy for risk, being young, African American, and male equals probable cause (Gaynes, 1993), a phenomenon that is even supported by courts as legitimate when race is used in conjunction with other factors. Police profiling may explain why police target minority communities where drug dealing is committed out in the open and where it is more likely to lead to arrests (Walker, Spohn, and DeLone 2006).

Most of this perceived "social threat" to communities (Jackson, 1997) results from an honest, unintentional exaggeration of risk on the part of police, but it creates significant disparities nevertheless. "Race dependent policing erodes the difficult-to-maintain habit of individualizing persons and strengthens the reflex of lumping people together according to gross racial categories" (D. Kennedy, 1997, p. 157).

Other outcomes of police profiling of particular offenders include "a climate of alienation, hostility, social unrest, and violence in the nation's inner cities" and a basic distrust and resentment of the police. Not surprisingly, several studies reflect a lower view or approval of law enforcement and government among African Americans than among whites (e.g., see Donziger, 1996). In areas where it is the worst, such as Washington, D.C., courses are available to teach citizens how to handle themselves if stopped by the police (R. Miller, 1997, p. 26). Some studies show that police may overcharge arrestees with crimes they did not commit in order to make some charges stick (e.g., see Smith, 1990). Some of these arrests and overcharging practices have been found to be racially motivated (e.g., see Nazario, 1993). Therefore, jury nullification on the part of African Americans who refuse to convict other African Americans charged even with violent crimes may suggest that, for this targeted group, outrage against violent criminals may be dwarfed by apathy or hostility toward the justice network (J. Miller, 1997).

Profiling may be part of what Eddings (2000, p. 197) calls **stealth racism** in the United States. The term *stealth racism* suggests that racism is not gone but, rather, has become harder to see. It is more subtle because it is less likely to be admitted or is passed off as part of a legitimate function, such as maintaining order. Eddings suggests several examples of stealth racism—taxis that do not stop for minorities, shoppers who are identified as suspicious on the basis of their race, and customers who receive unequal service because of race. In Chapter 12, I explain how discrimination based on race persists in the United States, even today.

Policing the War on Drugs

One main focus of policing in the contemporary United States seems to be on drug offenses. Our nation's police spend a significant amount of time and resources fighting the war on drugs (see Chapter 11). In 2000, almost 90% of local police departments regularly engaged in drug enforcement activities, and 95% of sheriffs' offices engaged in drug operations. More than 20% of local police departments participated in a multidrug task force, and another 15% assigned officers full-time to a special drug unit. Nearly 30% of sheriffs' offices had special units for drug enforcement and 40% had deputies assigned full-time to drug task forces. Not surprisingly then, of the nearly 13.7 million total arrests from 2001, 1.6 million (11.4%) were for drug offenses. By 2005, the percentage of arrests for drug offenses grew to 13% as 1.4 million of the 10.4 million arrests were for drugs.

What is the result of these arrests? Our courts are now backlogged with too many cases (see Chapter 7) and our prisons and jails are filling up with drug offenders at unprecedented rates (see Chapter 9).

One outcome of the police focus on drug offenses is that police forces have become increasingly militarized, with more paramilitary units and better technology and weaponry (Kraska and Kappeler, 1997). In spite of this, the war on drugs is generally focused on low-level offenders engaged in illegal activity related to certain types of drugs. For example, 82% of all drug arrests in 2005 were for possession, 43% were for marijuana-related offenses, and 38% of the total were for marijuana possession. This means the largest share of drug arrests in any given year in the United States is for simple possession of marijuana. In Chapter 11, I show that marijuana is much less harmful than legal substances such as alcohol and tobacco. Is this a wise use of police resources?

One indicator of innocent bias in the war on drugs would be racial disparities in arrests, convictions, and sentences to prison for drug offenses. In 2005, African Americans made up just under 12% of the U.S. population, but 33.9% of arrests for drug abuse violations. Given that most drug arrests are for simple possession, are African Americans that much more likely to possess drugs? According to the Substance Abuse and Mental Health Services Administration's (SAMHSA) 2005 National Survey on Drug Use and Health, only 9.7% of African Americans reported using some illegal drug in the past month (current users), versus 8.1% of whites and 7.6% of Hispanics. In other words, African Americans were only slightly more likely than Caucasians to use an illegal drug. Differences in past-year use were also small (16% for blacks versus 14.5% for whites and 13.9% for Hispanics). In terms of lifetime use, whites were more likely than blacks and Hispanics to have tried an illegal drug at least once (48.9% versus 44.7% and 37.3%, respectively). So how can we explain the differential for race in drug arrests? One possible answer is that police are disproportionately located in the neighborhoods where poor African Americans live, thus making it more likely that they will be arrested.

The U.S. government has chosen to take a reactive approach to drug use rather than a proactive approach. This means American law enforcement spends more money attempting to reduce the supply of drugs coming into the United States than it spends on efforts to reduce the demand for drugs (see Chapter 11). According to an investigation into police corruption related to the war on drugs by the General Accounting Office (GAO) in 1998, police officers have become frustrated with their inability to stop drug use in their communities, despite their best efforts. This, along with general cynicism and dissatisfaction, leads to **police corruption**. Add to this the tremendous potential for profits to be had from stealing money and drugs from dealers, selling drugs, and so on, and it is easy to understand how some good cops turn bad (Gray, 2001; Merlo and Benekos, 2000). Issue in Depth at the end of this chapter discusses corruption in the criminal justice network.

Additionally, nearly half of local police departments and sheriffs' departments every year report drug asset forfeiture receipts totaling hundreds of millions of dollars in cash, goods, and property. The average seizure is typically $5,000 for police departments and $15,000 for sheriffs' departments. Guess what this money is used for? That's right, fighting the war on drugs!

With the U.S. war on drugs, police officers on our streets have been using more and more aggressive techniques. I believe our nation's law enforcement leaders are ignoring lessons from the past. In 1968, the National Advisory Commission on Civil Disorders, commonly referred to as the Kerner Commission, published a report that found a direct relationship between aggressive police patrols and tensions between police and minority communities. The type of intrusive law enforcement that is occurring in the United States' inner cities is aggravating racial tensions between citizens and the police in particular, and worsening racial relations in the United States generally. Ironically, some claim that law enforcement techniques used in the war on drugs run counter to the Law Enforcement Code of Conduct, discussed earlier. Police end up abusing their discretion, using excessive force, and occasionally even sullying their private lives.

AMERICAN STOP RATES AND ARREST RATES

Technically, anyone suspected of committing a criminal act can be arrested. An arrest occurs when a person is legally detained to answer to criminal charges (Rush, 2000, p. 20). Black's Law Dictionary (1991, p. 72) defines **arrest** as follows: "To deprive a person of his liberty by legal authority. Taking, under real or assumed authority, custody of another for the purpose of holding or detaining him to answer a criminal charge. . . ." Wrobleski and Hess (2000, p. 344) elaborate on this definition by demonstrating that arrest includes four main elements: (1) the officer must have intent to make an arrest, (2) the officer must have authority to make an arrest, (3) the person must be seized or restrained, and (4) the person must understand that he or she is being arrested. Typically, a **warrant** is required to make an arrest, but officers do not need warrants when crimes are committed in their presence or when they are responding to the scene of a crime and an offender is at the scene (Wrobleski, 2006).

The Supreme Court has explained that an arrest is not the same thing as a **stop**. A stop must only be justified by reasonable suspicion that some wrongdoing has occurred or is likely to occur (*Terry v. Ohio*, 1968). An arrest requires **probable cause**, meaning that all the facts and circumstances known to the officer would suggest to a person of reasonable caution that a crime has been committed or is likely to be committed (*Draper v. United States*, 1959).

Essentially, a stop will occur if police officers come upon a person they reasonably feel looks suspicious or is acting suspiciously. For their own protection, police officers are justified in conducting a frisk or pat-down search of the suspect if they feel the suspect is armed (Hess and Wrobleski, 1997, p. 122). This search is called a **Terry stop** after the Supreme Court case, *Terry v. Ohio* (1968). The Supreme Court ruled in *United States v. Cortez* (1981) that reasonable suspicion should be based on the **totality of**

circumstances, including the officer's inferences and deductions. A police officer who is carrying around a mental stereotype of the **typical criminal** may be more likely to stop some types of people than others.

If you can imagine that police might stop some people more than others, then consider the following scenario: A police officer sees a dark-skinned man (race unclear to the officer) lurking outside a store late at night and feels that the man looks suspicious. The man looks suspicious in part because the store is getting ready to close and because the neighborhood is mostly inhabited by Caucasians. The police officer approaches the man, stops him, and conducts a pat-down search of the man's outer clothing. In doing so, the officer feels something hard in the man's jacket pocket and then reaches inside to find a knife. If, by being in possession of the knife, the man has violated state law, the police officer would be justified in making an arrest of the man. This type of stop would likely be considered legal given that the officer is allowed to use his or her discretion to justify the stop and frisk, regardless of the man's intent. This man would likely have committed a crime against his state law. But what if the man was simply waiting for his girlfriend to get off work and was carrying the knife for his own protection? This probably would not matter to the police officer or to the court.

Now, what if the man outside the store was a Caucasian? Would the officer think that a Caucasian man hanging around a store at closing time in a Caucasian neighborhood was suspicious? Justifying a stop on the basis of the totality of circumstances allows officers to use their own discretion to determine who looks dangerous and who does not. This may allow police profiles of the typical criminal, created by the criminal law and reinforced by media coverage of crime and criminal justice, to come into play.

If every group in the United States committed equal amounts of crime and if police did not discriminate against any group, we would expect to see relatively equal stop rates and arrest rates for all groups. Any diversion from this expectation would suggest either that some groups commit more crime, that the police discriminate against some groups, or both.

Evidence suggests that Hispanics, African Americans, and other people of color are more likely to have run-ins with police (Bureau of Justice Statistics, 2007). Race is used as a cue for potential trouble-making activity on the part of citizens. In essence, police allow their personally held stereotypes to invade their professional work (Skolnick, 1994). The significance of being stopped by the police cannot be understated. Logically, being stopped would increase a person's risk of being arrested or of having force used against him or her, especially to the degree that the person does not cooperate with the police. Beyond this, being stopped can be bothersome and even intimidating if the police have bad attitudes or if a person is constantly harassed for no valid reason. Disproportionate arrest rates are accompanied by disproportionate harassment by the police (Chambliss, 2000).

The typical arrestee in the United States is a young, urban, poor, African American male: "This is the Typical Criminal feared by most law-abiding Americans. Poor, young, urban, [disproportionately] African American males make up the core of the enemy forces in the war against crime" (Reiman, 1998, p. 55). Kappeler, Blumberg, and Potter (2000, p. 221) concur: "The vast majority of people arrested and processed through the criminal justice system are poor, unemployed, and undereducated."

Given that police focus on crimes of the poor, and because the law defines their acts as criminal more often than those acts of the wealthy, the police target particular populations they perceive to be threatening, especially within inner cities. This calls into serious question official statistics suggesting that African Americans commit more than their "fair share" of criminal behavior. As noted by Kappeler et al. (2000, p. 222), "Research on the police clearly shows that suspects from lower socioeconomic groups and suspects who are members of minority groups are arrested more frequently, on weaker evidence, and for more crime than their white, affluent counterparts."

The fact that police typically arrest urban street criminals should not be surprising. Arrest rates from the UCR consistently are four to five times higher for African Americans over age 18 than for Caucasians over 18, and two to three times higher for African Americans under age 18 than for Caucasians under 18. It is alarming that African Americans make up roughly one-third of arrests in any given year, even though they account for only 12% of the U.S. population. The percentage of African American arrests is also higher in cities than in suburban communities and rural areas, as expected, given their relative residential concentration in inner cities. Walker et al. (2006) claim that the arrest rate for African Americans is two and one-half times higher than it would be if simply predicted by their proportion of the population.

American police officers in 2005 made 14.1 million arrests, the majority of which were not for "serious" street crimes. R. Miller (1997, p. 484) is thus correct when he asserts: "Most of the frenetic law enforcement in the black community has nothing to do with violent or serious crime." In fact, about 2.2 million arrests were for Index Offenses of the Uniform Crime Reports (15.7%), including 1.6 million arrests for property crimes and about 600,000 arrests for violent crimes. Of arrests in 2005, 27.8% were of African Americans who, as noted, account for 12% of the U.S. population. As shown in Table 6-3, African Americans are overrepresented in every category of arrests, for sencus crimes. They made up 38.8% of arrests for serious violent crimes and 28.6% of arrests for serious property crimes. Yet, African Americans are generally no more "criminal" than other groups of people.

Even when evidence does show that African Americans account for a disproportionate amount of some "serious" crimes (such as murder and robbery), *serious* is a term defined by lawmakers. As you learned in Chapter 3, legislators are less likely to be African American and not at all likely to be poor. Thus, if you learn that African Americans made up 56.3% of all arrests for robbery and 48.6% of all arrests for murder

TABLE 6-3   Arrests in the United States, by Race (2005)

	White	*Black*
Murder and manslaughter	49.1%	48.6%
Forcible rape	65.1%	32.7%
Robbery	42.2%	56.3%
Aggravated assault	63.3%	34.3%
Burglary	69.6%	28.5%
Theft	69.3%	28.0%
Motor vehicle theft	62.8%	34.8%
Drug abuse violations	64.7%	33.9%

Source: Sourcebook on Criminal Justice Statistics (2006).

in 2005, perhaps you should ask yourself: What is "robbery" and what is "murder"? No one would argue that these crimes are not serious or not harmful. But there are many ways to take someone's money by force or to kill a person that are not currently considered robbery or murder, respectively. The fact that these acts are not legislated as criminal or treated as serious is a function of who makes the law (see Chapter 3). The disproportionate focus of law enforcement on poor, minority communities, though rooted to a degree in the criminal law, is nevertheless extremely detrimental to minority communities. As Miller writes, "a major contributor to breakdown in the inner cities is the criminal justice system itself."

According to Walker et al. (2006), officers are more likely to arrest a suspect when there is strong evidence that he or she is guilty, when the crime is of a serious nature, when a victim requests that an arrest be made, when the alleged offender is a stranger rather than a person known to the victim, and when the suspect is disrespectful to the officer. The bulk of the evidence also suggests that race does matter when it comes to arrest because police are more likely to arrest alleged offenders when the victim is a Caucasian and the suspect is a member of a minority group.

USE OF FORCE

Limits have been placed on police use of force to protect citizens and police officers alike. Ideally, use of force by the police is determined by the behaviors of citizens with whom police come into contact. Police use of force can range from verbal commands to deadly force whereby a citizen is actually killed. Figure 6-2 shows a continuum of options for the use of force available to police based on the behavior of citizens. As the figure illustrates, the more resistant a citizen is to the police, the more force can be legally used against him or her.

A report by the U.S. Department of Justice entitled "National Data Collection on Police Use of Force" (1996) summarizes this issue very well:

> The feature distinguishing police from all other groups in society is their authority
> to apply coercive force when circumstances call for it. Police may be called on to use

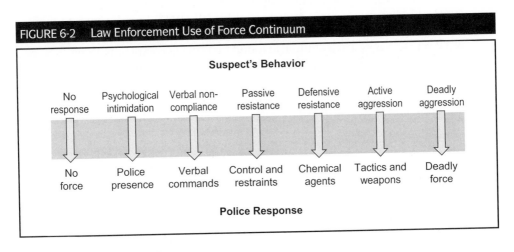

FIGURE 6-2   Law Enforcement Use of Force Continuum

Suspect's Behavior

| No response | Psychological intimidation | Verbal non-compliance | Passive resistance | Defensive resistance | Active aggression | Deadly aggression |

| No force | Police presence | Verbal commands | Control and restraints | Chemical agents | Tactics and weapons | Deadly force |

Police Response

force when making an arrest, breaking up an altercation, dispersing an unruly crowd, or performing a myriad of other official activities during their daily routines. The force may range from pushing a person to get his attention to using a firearm. Between those extremes are several other types of force, including firm grips on an arm, use of debilitating chemical agents, and blows with a baton. Whatever method is used, police are expected to apply only the force necessary to resolve a given situation.

The necessary degree of force to be used against a citizen is determined by the officer's own judgment (i.e., his or her discretion), based on the behaviors of the citizen. It is also constrained by the U.S. Constitution (Hall, 1992). McEwen and Leahy (1994) place force techniques along a continuum from no force to verbalization techniques to deadly force, with several nonlethal mechanisms somewhere in the middle, including the following:

- Impact weapons (e.g., batons and flashlights)
- Chemical weapons (e.g., pepper spray)
- Electrical weapons (e.g., electronic stun guns)
- Other less-than-lethal weapons (e.g., projectile launchers)

In 1999, the year when the latest data were available, nearly all (93%) of local police departments had a formal policy pertaining to the use of deadly force and 87% of local police departments had a formal policy pertaining to the use of non-deadly force. As for sheriffs' offices, nearly all (92%) had a formal policy pertaining to the use of deadly force and 85% had a formal policy pertaining to the use of non-deadly force.

Luckily for both citizens and the police, use of police force is relatively rare. Force is used in only about 1% of all citizen encounters (Bureau of Justice Statistics, 1996). In 2005, for example, only 1.6% of the 43.5 million persons who had contact with police had force used or threatened against them during their most recent contact. When considering all calls for police service, police use of force is even more rare. According to the International Chiefs of Police (2002), police used force at a rate of 3.61 times per 10,000 calls for service. Thus, the rate of use of force is only 0.0361%, meaning police did *not* use force 99.9639% of the time.

A large majority of instances of the uses of force are deemed justified. A national study of police use of force by Pate and Fridell (1994) found what one might expect about police use of force: Less serious types of force are used more frequently than more serious types. Their study also found that citizen complaints about excessive force were rarely filed. Nationally, the rate for city police departments was 11.3 complaints per 100,000 people.

We cannot know for certain the prevalence of excessive use of force by police. We do know, however, that it is minority men who are most likely to be subjected to it (Ross, 1999). Walker, Spohn, and DeLone (2000, p. 289) claim:

Pervasive evidence indicates that racial minorities suffer discrimination at the hands of the police. They are more likely than whites to be shot and killed, arrested, and victimized by excessive physical force. In addition, there is evidence of police misconduct directed at racial minorities, as well as evidence that police departments fail to discipline officers found guilty of misconduct.

Studies show that minorities in the United States are more likely to have force used against them by the police (Geller and Toch, 1995). According to the Bureau of Justice Statistics (2006), those most likely to experience force were young black males:

Among the persons who had police contact in 2005, females (1.0%) were less likely than males (2.2%) to have had contact with police that resulted in force . . . Males accounted for a larger percentage (72.4%) of contacts involving force compared to their percentage of all contacts (53.6%) . . . Blacks (4.4%) and Hispanics (2.3%) were more likely than whites (1.2%) to experience use of force during contact with police in 2005. Blacks accounted for 1 out of 10 contacts with police but 1 out of 4 contacts where force was used. Persons age 16 to 29 (2.8%) who had contact with police were more likely than those over age 29 (1.0%) to have had force used against them. Persons age 16 to 29 made up a smaller percentage of persons who had a police contact (34.5%) compared to the percentage of persons experiencing force during a contact (60.3%). The median age of those experiencing force was 26.

African Americans are also most likely to be shot and killed by the police, followed by Hispanics and then Caucasians (Geller and Scott, 1992). Disparities in police involvement in shootings have lessened since the Supreme Court abolished the fleeing felon rule in the 1985 case *Tennessee v. Garner.* Walker et al. (2006) suggest that since this case, police officers are less able to justify shooting a fleeing felon on the basis of his or her race alone as a sign of dangerousness. Thus, the law has made it more difficult for police to use their own stereotypes to inform split-second decisions about whether or not to kill a suspect.

The 1999 and 2000 shootings by New York City police of Amadou Diallo and Malcolm Ferguson, two unarmed African American men, show that questionable police shootings still persist. These two men were shot only two blocks away from each other by the New York City Police Department's Street Narcotics Enforcement Unit. Given that both men were unarmed, the police have been accused of using excessive force. Although the four officers in the first case, who shot a combined 41 rounds at the fleeing Diallo, were acquitted of criminal charges because they shot Diallo as he reached for his wallet (which the officers thought was a gun), many Americans are not satisfied with the verdicts, and marches on New York City and Washington, D.C., were organized in protest of these shootings.

I do not bring these cases up to question whether they were justified shootings. Technically, the officers followed their training and acted in an appropriate manner given their beliefs that the men were armed and their fear for their own personal safety. Yet I find the shootings unjustifiable, not because they did not follow proper procedure, but instead because the situation that precipitated the shooting should have never happened in the first place. It is never appropriate for police to approach a suspect (who is presumed innocent) in a militaristic manner, wearing all black with weapons drawn. The **war on crime** cannot actually be fought like a war, because the United States is not a war zone and its citizens will not tolerate this on their own soil.

The case of Abner Louima, a Haitain immigrant, shocked even those who already had a negative view of police. In the summer of 1997, Louima was attacked by four police officers. Two officers used the baton of one of the officers to sodomize Louima and then shoved the baton into his mouth, knocking out several of his teeth, as if they hated him personally. These officers were fired and convicted on criminal charges.

More recently, Robert Davis, a 64-year-old retired elementary school teacher, was beaten by three New Orleans police officers and two federal officers. He was charged with disorderly conduct, being intoxicated in public, and assaulting an officer. Although officers claimed he was drunk at the time of the arrest, Mr. Davis was in fact sober and had not consumed any alcohol for many years. Davis claimed he was going to the store to buy a pack of cigarettes when police began to harass him; subsequently, they beat him so badly he lay on the ground in a pool of his own blood. Film producer Rich Mathews, who was in New Orleans filming the aftermath of Hurricane Katrina and who happened to be on the scene of the Davis incident, was pushed into a police car by a police officer who shouted, "I've been here for six weeks trying to keep [expletive] . . . alive . . . [expletive] go home." Several of the officers in the case were fired and charged with crimes.

A report by the U.S. Department of Justice (1996) states, "When police go beyond reasonable force to use excessive force during an arrest or in precipitous response, as during the decades of protest demonstrations involving labor, civil rights, or other controversial issues, citizens become victims of police, and the public's confidence in a police force can plummet." In fact, statistics from the Sourcebook of Criminal Justice Statistics show that blacks are less likely than whites to view the police favorably. This is to be expected given their differential treatment by and experiences with the police.

CORRUPTION IN AMERICAN POLICING

Corruption, a perversion of policing stemming from a lack of integrity or honesty, is widespread and highly likely to affect poor people and people of color. Goldstein (1975, p. 3) defines corruption as a misuse of police authority "in a manner designed to produce personal gain." That is, corruption results in some benefit to the officer, even if the benefit is only emotional.

Criminologists do not know how extensive and prevalent police corruption in the United States is because problems such as citizen mistreatment and falsification of records and evidence have never been subjected to a national study (Donziger, 1996, p. 163). However, there are numerous well-known examples, particularly within larger American cities, of alarming corruption in American police departments (see Issue in Depth at the end of this chapter). For example, the Mollen Commission in New York found evidence of police involvement in theft, drug trafficking, drug use, falsification of police reports, lying in court, and police brutality (Mollen Commission, 1994). Shockingly, the most common form of corruption in New York was not police brutality (although the city has lost more than $100 million in lawsuits recently for brutality); rather, it was for falsifying police records and testimony at criminal trials, a practice known as **testilying**, whereby officers often made up testimony to ensure criminal convictions. They would invent stories to justify their illegal and unethical police techniques, which violated suspects' constitutional rights.

There can be no greater threat to justice—including the presumption of innocence and equality before the law—than such police misconduct. Imagine yourself, an innocent citizen, facing arrest, charges, and the threat of criminal prosecution for crimes you did not commit. Because you happened to be in the wrong place at the wrong time (e.g., in an inner-city neighborhood where police were patrolling) and because a police officer has lied in his reports and is willing to lie at trial, you know you are likely to be convicted. What would you do? Would you consider accepting a lesser sentence through a plea bargain? I'll return to the issue of how plea bargaining interferes with justice in Chapter 7.

Other large police departments have witnessed major corruption scandals, as well. In Washington, D.C., partly as a result of a massive hiring of unqualified officers, some of whom even had criminal records, more than 200 police officers since 1989 have been arrested and charged with crimes, including 79 officers in 1993 (Harriston and Flaherty, 1994). Departments that were faced with losing millions of dollars in federal funding if they did not hire more officers are the same ones that ended up hiring some very bad people.

In Philadelphia in 1995, officers confessed to planting evidence, personally profiting from the illegal drug trade, and making false arrests. This led to the reexamination of 2,000 criminal cases that may have led to wrongful conviction because of bad policing. Additionally, nearly 200 police officers in New Orleans were disciplined for their questionable activities, and 4 were charged with murder related to their involvement in drug offenses (Cromwell, 1995). The Christopher Commission in Los Angeles found "a significant number of LAPD officers who repeatedly misuse[d] force and persistently ignore[d] the written policies and guidelines of the Department regarding force" (Christopher, 1991).

Bernard Parks, former chief of police for Los Angeles, issued the report of the Rampart Area Corruption Incident. This involved police officers being involved in a bank robbery, false imprisonment and beating of a handcuffed arrestee at a police substation, and the theft of three kilograms of cocaine from a police evidence room (see Issue in Depth at the end of this chapter).

Other allegations of corruption pertained to the planting of cocaine in the automobiles of unsuspecting Mexican immigrant laborers in Dallas, Texas, and the framing of dozens of African Americans in Tulia, Texas, for drug crimes they did not commit. In Dallas, Police Chief Terrell Bolton admitted that "bricks of cocaine" seized as evidence actually turned out to be ground sheetrock. Two undercover police officers and a paid informant who received $200,000 for his tips reported that drugs had been sold or shown to them, which led to dozens of arrests. Prosecutors dismissed 86 drug cases and released dozens of defendants (all of them Mexican immigrants or legal Hispanic residents). In Tulia, 43 residents of the small town were arrested for alleged drug offenses (40 of them were African Americans, accounting for 10% of the entire town's African American population). The only evidence against them was the testimony of one undercover officer, Tom Coleman, who worked alone and had no audio tapes, video surveillance, or eyewitnesses. Essentially, these people were framed and have all subsequently been released.

Amazingly, the National Criminal Justice Commission reports that in several of the cases in Los Angeles, superiors were to some degree aware of the police corruption, yet decided not to intervene because of their fear of bad press (Donziger, 1996). Meanwhile, citizens were learning about corruption firsthand from the actions of the officers on the streets. Daily activities are far more important to the way police are perceived by citizens than public relations campaigns or bumper stickers aimed at promoting partnerships between citizens and the police (Wrobleski, 2006).

Unfortunately, several aspects of police corruption differentially affect the poor and citizens of color, which may explain the differential view of police by people of color and the poor. Police use of force is a significant problem in our inner cities where the poor and African Americans are more likely to reside. Not surprisingly then, in the 1990s, a majority of adults believed that the police were more likely to beat minorities than Caucasians (NAACP, 1993). This is why the authors of the NAACP report claimed that African Americans were more likely to be shot by police and bitten by police dogs, and thus concluded that the "risk of abuse, mistreatment or even death" accompanied any minority interaction with the police (p. vi).

Current law enforcement strategies revolving around zero-tolerance approaches exacerbate such problems. For example, the National Criminal Justice Commission discusses an antigang sweep of streets called Operation Sunrise in Los Angeles, which led to 63 arrests. Of those arrested, only 1% were charged with a violent felony. Such efforts were characterized as part of the "squeegee strategy," named after the street dwellers who, uninvited, wash the windows of cars that stop at red lights on city streets (Donziger, 1996, p. 169).

Zero-tolerance policing runs counter to community policing and logical crime prevention efforts. To whatever degree street sweeps are viewed by citizens as brutal, suspect, militaristic, or the biased efforts of "outsiders," citizens will be discouraged from taking active roles in community-building activities and crime prevention initiatives in conjunction with the police. Perhaps this is why the communities that most need neighborhood watch programs are least likely to be populated by residents who take active roles in them (Sherman et al., 1997). Zero-tolerance policing will fail because its practice destroys several important requisites for successful community policing, namely, police accountability, openness to the public, and community cooperation (Cox and Wade, 1998, p. 106).

Some link these types of police corruption to the unique nature of policing, particularly the **police subculture** that "exalts loyalty over integrity" and "a hostility and alienation between the police and the community in certain precincts which breeds an 'Us versus Them' mentality" (Mollen Commission, 1994). Walker (2005) argues that this allows police officers to treat suspects as if they did not have the same constitutional rights as the rest of us. This police subculture results in part from the nature of police work, but also from how citizens interact with police.

A subculture is a group of people in a larger society with its own way of life, norms, beliefs, attitudes, and values. The existence of a police subculture suggests that in some very real way, police are different from "civilians." These differences are attributable in part to the work environment of policing. According to Cole and Smith (2006), the main elements of the police subculture include the following:

- *Working personality of the officer:*   The personality of the officer changes over time as he or she is exposed to the threat of danger and is forced to exert his or her authority over citizens who do not automatically defer to the authority of the officer.
- *Social isolation:*   Police officers separate themselves from civilians professionally and personally because of the nature of their jobs. In part, this is because they are expected to live exemplary lives and are always on duty. Police officers use technical jargon to discuss their work and often literally speak in codes.

- *Stress:* Police officers face numerous sources of stress and thus suffer high rates of suicide, divorce, heart disease, alcoholism and other drug abuse.

Other research suggests that the police officer personality can be described as authoritarian and cynical in nature (Skolnick, 1966). Officers can also become suspicious, insecure, hostile, and prejudiced, in addition to several other characteristics (Schmalleger, 2006).

Cox and Wade (1998, p. 98) claim, "Many segments of the public are uncooperative with the police and some openly hostile a good deal of the time. Other segments criticize the police for being unable to do anything about the crime problem or appear largely apathetic regardless of police action or inaction." Thus, the police become "equally critical of and hostile toward some segments of the population." Others link police corruption to a lack of understanding on the part of the police of the people they are policing. Consistent with this are the findings that the largest police departments show more indications of police corruption and also tend to be the least diverse in terms of race and ethnicity (Donziger, 1996).

CONCLUSION

Police, the first component of the criminal justice network, are responsible for enforcing the criminal law. Despite the presence of the Law Enforcement Code of Conduct, which stipulates how police must behave, the practice of law enforcement in the United States results in innocent biases against the poor and people of color. This innocent bias owes itself to the use of police discretion, the particular focus of police on certain types of crimes, the location of police on the streets of the United States, the use of police profiling, and policing the war on drugs. Not only does policing create innocent bias, which in turn results in injustice, but it also is highly ineffective at reducing crime. Some police behavior, as well intentioned as it certainly is, is inconsistent with the goals of the U.S. criminal justice network.

Issue in Depth—Corruption in the Criminal Justice Network

Recall the discussion in Chapter 2 about the role of politics in criminal justice. The American criminal justice network was created by and is currently maintained by people with tremendous power. For example, legislators are the only people in the country who can define your behavior as a crime, even if it is relatively harmless or harms only you. Police officers are the only people in the country who can legally use force against you—in some cases, lethal force—if you violate the law. Criminal justice processes in the United States can thus be viewed as a system of oppressive power: "Criminal justice is, literally, state power. It is police, guns, prisons, the electric chair" (Friedman, 1993, p. 462). The problem with power is that it "corrupts; and power also has an itch to suppress."

With corruption comes wrongdoing and, potentially, criminal acts on the part of criminal justice officials. These crimes of the criminal justice network itself are virtually ignored, but according to Henderson and Simon (1994, p. xi), "there is clearly evidence that deviance, corruption, and immorality exist in the system." Crimes within the criminal justice network are "remarkably frequent" and "constant throughout the system" (Henderson and Simon, 1994, p. iii). They include corruption, abuse of authority, jury tampering, bribe taking and payoffs, brutality, sexual exploitation of prisoners, and formal approval of such acts by administrators. Such acts cause physical, financial, and moral harm.

Because power corrupts, "politicians probably represent the single most corrupt group involved with the criminal justice system" (Henderson and Simon, 1994, p. 61). Yet, because of the long history of corruption in American policing, it is the component of the criminal justice network most often identified with corruption (e.g., see Fyfe and Skolnick, 1993).

Research into police corruption has "consistently unearthed substantial and wide-ranging forms of police bribery" (e.g., see Coleman, 1990), including about a hundred drug-related cases that are heard by courts each year (Henderson and Simon, 1994). Drug law enforcement may present the most significant opportunity for police bribery (Gray, 2001; Kellner, 1988; Robinson and Scherlen, 2007).

According to the Drug Policy Alliance (2007):

> A 1998 report by the General Accounting Office notes that on-duty police officers involved in drug-related corruption engage in serious criminal activities such as (1) conducting unconstitutional searches and seizures; (2) stealing money and/or drugs from drug dealers; (3) selling stolen drugs; (4) protecting drug operations; (5) providing false testimony; and (6) submitting false crime reports. Approximately half of all police officers convicted as a result of FBI-led corruption cases between 1993 and 1997 were convicted for drug-related offenses and nationwide over 100 cases of drug-related corruption are prosecuted each year. Every one of the federal law enforcement agencies with significant drug enforcement responsibilities has seen an agent implicated.

In other words, the drug war produces a sizable amount of police corruption. However, police corruption also includes violation of search-and-seizure laws, evidence tampering (Douglas and Johnson, 1977), and perjured testimony (Kittel, 1986). Abuse of authority in corrections also has been described as a "nationwide problem" (Henderson and Simon, 1994, p. 47). Evidence exists that there is a "blue code of silence" among police (Juarez, 2004; Westmarland, 2005), meaning police, out of loyalty, often will not report their fellow officers for wrongdoing.

A recent example of a highly publicized corruption case in criminal justice is the Rampart Scandal in Los Angeles. According to the "Board of Inquiry into the Rampart Corruption Incident, Executive Summary":

a. In late 1997 and early 1998, three incidents occurred in which Los Angeles police officers were identified as suspects in serious criminal activity. The incidents began on November 6, 1997, when three suspects robbed a Los Angeles Bank of America. The investigation into that robbery led to the arrest of Officer David Mack, who was assigned to West Los Angeles Area at the time, and his girlfriend, an employee of the bank. The second incident occurred on February 26, 1998, and involved the false imprisonment and beating of a handcuffed arrestee at the Rampart Substation. The officer who beat the suspect was Rampart CRASH Officer Brian Hewitt. Two other CRASH officers, one of whom was Ethan

Cohan, were present and acquiesced to the beating. The third incident involved the March 2, 1998, theft of three kilograms of cocaine from the Department's Property Division. The investigation into that theft led to the arrest of Officer Rafael Perez, who was assigned to Rampart CRASH.

b. The investigations into these incidents disclosed that the suspect officers were closely associated, either as working partners or close friends, and all but one of them were assigned to Rampart Area. The only exception, David Mack, had previously been assigned to Rampart and was a close friend of Rafael Perez. Due to the seriousness of the criminal activity, commonality among the officers, and potential for involvement of more department employees, Chief of Police Bernard C. Parks formed a special criminal Task Force in May of 1998 to investigate these incidents.

c. Hewitt and Cohan were terminated following their Board of Rights hearings, but the third officer was found not guilty by his board. (In Los Angeles, a three-member Board of Rights, composed of two staff or command officers and one community member, hears allegations of major misconduct. Each accused officer may select a separate Board and the Chief of Police can impose no greater penalty than the Board recommends.) The case against Hewitt has been presented to the District Attorney on two occasions, but was rejected both times for a lack of sufficient evidence. The District Attorney's Office is now reconsidering the case. The case has also been presented to the State Attorney General's Office, which declined to take further action on the matter. David Mack was convicted in federal court of bank robbery and resigned from the Department in lieu of termination. He has been sentenced to 14 years and 3 months in prison. The $722,000 stolen in the robbery has not been recovered and his two accomplices have not been identified.

d. Rafael Perez's first trial resulted in a jury deadlock, eight-to-four in favor of a guilty verdict. The Department's investigative efforts during and after the first trial produced additional evidence that Perez was responsible for three additional cocaine thefts. He was also identified as being closely associated with known narcotics dealers, one of whom accompanied Perez, Mack, and a third officer on a trip to Las Vegas immediately after Mack committed the bank robbery.

e. As the evidence against Perez mounted, Perez offered to plead guilty to the charges and cooperate with the LAPD Task Force detectives in exchange for a reduced prison sentence. Perez indicated that he could provide information on other Rampart officers who were involved in serious criminal activity and misconduct. Just prior to the second trial in September 1999, an agreement was reached for a reduced prison sentence in return for Perez's guilty plea and cooperation in providing information on corruption activities within the Department. Subsequent interviews of Perez have indicated that much deeper corruption was occurring at Rampart than was originally suspected. The Task Force, in conjunction with the Los Angeles District Attorney's Office and Office of the United States Attorney General, pursued that investigation. On September 21, 1999, Chief Parks convened a Board of Inquiry (BOI) to assess the totality of the Rampart corruption incident without infringing on the work of the Task Force.

The final report was organized around more than 100 recommendations for positive change within the Los Angeles Police Department, in the following areas:

- Testing and screening of police officer candidates
- Personnel practices
- Personnel investigations and management of risk
- Corruption investigations
- Operational controls
- Anticorruption inspections and audits
- Ethics and integrity training
- Job-specific training

Despite the scores of breakdowns within the LAPD that led to this corruption scandal, the final report recommended that no outside investigation by the FBI take place.

According to news reports, LAPD Rampart officers routinely and unnecessarily punched, kicked, and choked suspects in an effort to intimidate them. The officers then fabricated stories in police reports to account for their victims' injuries. The corruption probe uncovered information about unjustified shootings, evidence planting, and even false arrests of innocent people. More than 50 convictions have been overturned, and more than 20 officers have been relieved of duty or fired, or have quit because of the scandal.

At a 1999 press conference, District Attorney Gil Garcetti expressed his concern about one very troubling aspect of the Rampart scandal—the fact that innocent people were coerced into confessing crimes that they did not commit. Garcetti said: "It raises the specter, obviously, that they pleaded guilty to something [even though] they were telling their lawyer, 'I'm not guilty, I'm innocent.' That raises a question for everyone in the criminal justice system."

Because crimes of the criminal justice network are not widely studied, we do not know precisely why they occur, but here are some likely reasons: There is only a small chance of such acts leading to punishment; criminal justice personnel become jaded over time in their fight against crime; and these crimes are supported to some degree by institutional factors (Henderson and Simon, 1994).

This book does not directly address the issue of criminality within the criminal justice network. Instead, I argue that even with completely "noncriminal" criminal justice personnel—that is, even in the absence of corruption—the criminal justice network fails to do justice or reduce crime effectively. At the same time, the criminal justice network tends to focus its attention on acts that, though harmful, are not the most harmful behaviors in the United States. All of this amounts to what I consider a "crime"—not in the legal sense, of course, but in the sense that it is not right or just.

KEY TERMS

arrest	discretion	formal social control
cold crimes	enforcing laws	hot spots of crime
community policing	exclusionary rule	incident-driven
corruption	exigent circumstances	inevitable discovery
crime analysis	field training officer	informal social control

innocent bias
jurisdiction
overpoliced and
  underprotected
police corruption
police profiling
police subculture
preserving the peace
preventing crime
probable cause

problem-oriented
problem-oriented policing
providing services
searches incident to lawful
  arrests
searches with consent
stealth racism
stop
typical police officer
Terry stop

testilying
the good faith exception
the plain touch doctrine
the plain view doctrine
totality of circumstances
typical criminal
upholding rights
war on crime
warrant
zero-tolerance policing

DISCUSSION QUESTIONS

1. Identify the main roles of police officers in the United States and provide a few examples of behaviors that fit into each role.
2. To which role do police officers devote most of their time? Why?
3. Compare the main functions of local police versus state and federal police.
4. Do you think more police on the streets will reduce crime in the United States? Why or why not?
5. What is the exclusionary rule? How does it protect you?
6. List some exceptions to the exclusionary rule. Do you think these exceptions are reasonable? Why or why not?
7. In what ways do police serve crime victims?
8. What is community policing?
9. Contrast the community police officer with the stereotypical view of the police officer.
10. Discuss the main tenets of Sir Robert Peel.
11. What does the term *innocent bias* mean?
12. What factors produce innocent bias in policing?
13. What do you think are the most important elements of the Law Enforcement Code of Conduct? Explain.
14. Why is it so important that police have discretion in deciding who to stop, detain, arrest, and so on?
15. On which types of crimes are American police most focused? Why?
16. Do you think there is a valid rationale for police profiling? Explain.
17. Why do more police officers work for local governments (e.g., cities, counties) than for states or the federal government?
18. Explain the difference between a stop and an arrest.
19. Explain why people of color are disproportionately more likely to be stopped by and arrested by the police.
20. In your opinion, when has excessive force been used by police against a citizen?
21. How does zero-tolerance policing run counter to the notion of community policing?
22. Identify and discuss the main elements of the police subculture.
23. What produces corruption in the criminal justice network?

CHAPTER

7

RIGHT TO TRIAL?
INJUSTICE IN PRETRIAL
AND TRIAL
PROCEDURES

1. Introduction
2. What Are the Courts?
   a. The Organization of Courts in the United States
   b. What Courts Do
   c. Types of Crimes Handled by Courts
   d. Characteristics of Court Clients
   e. The Courtroom Workgroup
3. An Imbalance of Power in the Court: From Judge to Prosecution
4. Pretrial Procedures and Justice
   a. Bail as an Injustice
   • Box 7-1. Types of Bail
   • Box 7-2. Bail Alternatives
   • Box 7-3. The U.S. Supreme Court and the War on Terror
   b. Plea Bargaining as an Injustice
5. The Unequal Right to a Defense in the United States: Public Versus Private Attorneys
6. The "Exceptional Case" of Trial
   a. Stages of the Criminal Trial
7. Conclusion
8. Issue in Depth—Wrongful Convictions
9. Key Terms
10. Discussion Questions

INTRODUCTION

This chapter continues the assessment of the criminal justice process by examining the operation of American courts. I begin with a brief examination of the U.S. court structure and then go on to discuss what courts actually do. Because of an imbalance in the courts in favor of the government, criminal proceedings are inherently biased against individual defendants. Additionally, because most defendants are indigent and therefore are appointed defense attorneys, biases against the poor and people of color continue in the courts. The institutions of bail, plea bargaining, and trials often do not promote the ideal goals of the criminal justice network. Trial processes also are fundamentally tilted in favor of the state and the wealthy. Finally, I examine the issue of wrongful conviction to identify why it occurs.

WHAT ARE THE COURTS?

The Organization of Courts in the United States

Because of the separation of powers clause of the U.S. Constitution, the United States has a **dual court system**; that is, federal and state governments each have their own distinct court systems, and the two systems operate independently of each other (Marion, 1995). There are more than 200 different court systems in the states, Washington D.C., and Puerto Rico, including more than 70 statewide trial courts systems with general jurisdiction and more than 130 courts of appeal.

State and federal courts can be differentiated by their **jurisdiction**—that is, where they have "the authority or power to hear a case" (Cox and Wade, 1998, p. 130). Where a case is heard depends on what type of law is violated. Crimes against states are typically handled in state courts, whereas crimes against the federal government are held in federal courts. And yes, cases can be heard in both courts without violating suspects' Fifth Amendment rights to freedom from double jeopardy. If both federal and state laws are violated, both courts can and often do hold trials.

Courts with **general jurisdiction** can hear most types of cases, whether they be criminal or civil matters, whereas courts of **specific or limited jurisdiction** can hear cases only within their specific expertise (e.g., juvenile courts hear only juvenile cases). Courts with original jurisdiction are typically trial courts, because their jurisdiction grants them the power to hear facts of cases initially. **Appellate courts**, or courts of appeals, do not decide matters of fact but, rather, decide matters of law. They hear cases that were first heard by courts with original jurisdiction and then appealed. The power of appeals courts lies in their ability to set precedents. Once a decision is made, a **precedent** is created that, under the principle of **stare decisis** (let the decision stand), must be followed by all other courts within the same jurisdiction.

There is no stereotypical court in the United States because the system is decentralized. Instead, there are a variety of types of courts, each with their own distinct names, purposes, and functions served (Cole and Smith, 2007; Schmalleger, 2006). Federal courts in the United States include 94 trial courts (called **district courts**) and 12 appeals courts (called **circuit courts**). Of course, the United States also has an appeals "court of last resort," the U.S. Supreme Court, made up of nine justices. State courts include trial courts of original jurisdiction, intermediate courts of appeals in about half of the states, and appellate courts of last resort (state supreme courts). As indicated earlier, not all states have intermediate courts of appeals, but states with larger populations tend to have them to relieve the burden on the state supreme courts (Chapper and Hanson, 1990). State courts are very diverse; Cox and Wade (1998, p. 132) write that the term that best describes state courts is variation because "there is no one state that adequately depicts the other fifty systems."

Most criminal justice scholars also differentiate between lower courts (e.g., courts that hear traffic cases or misdemeanors) and higher level courts (e.g., courts that hear felony cases). They are differentiated on the basis of how they ideally process defendants. Lower courts tend to emphasize speed and routinization of cases, so that large numbers of cases are disposed of quickly through fines, community service, and other such sanctions. Higher level courts are ideally less characterized by "assembly-line justice" and more accurately described as adversarial. The reality of even higher level trial courts for most defendants, as you will see later in this chapter, is that trials are the rare exception to the assembly-line nature of plea bargaining.

What Courts Do

When citizens are arrested by police, they become clients for the courts. What do courts do?

> Simply stated, a court is a place where arguments are settled. The argument may be between the federal government and a corporation accused of violating environmental regulations, between business partners, between a criminal and the state, or any other number of parties. The court provides an environment in which the basis of the argument can be settled through the application of the law. (Gaines, Kaune, and Miller, 2000, p. 270)

In deciding arguments, the primary function of American criminal courts is to determine the legal guilt of the accused—that is, to determine if a person is guilty beyond a reasonable doubt of committing a crime (Peoples, 2000; Stuckey, Robertson, and Wallace, 2001). The National Criminal Justice Commission writes of the courts: "Their responsibility is to be fair to all citizens charged with a crime and to impose a just punishment on those found guilty" (Donziger, 1996, p. 181). These are the key functions served by American courts.

But courts do much more than determine guilt or innocence. They also are "responsible for determining bail, conducting preliminary hearings (or grand juries), ruling on the admissibility of evidence, and determining the appropriate sentence when a finding of guilty has been reached" (Cox and Wade, 1998, p. 130).

Essentially, courts take over where the police leave off. As I will show later in this chapter, the U.S. courts are demonstrably biased against poor people and people of color. Pretrial procedures such as bail and plea bargaining, as well as trial procedures, are biased against relatively powerless groups. This bias begins with an imbalance in the power of the courtroom workgroup and occasionally results in wrongful convictions (see Issue in Depth at the end of this chapter).

Types of Crimes Handled by Courts

Types of crimes handled by federal and state courts are often very different. One example comes from those convicted of felonies in state and federal courts. State courts convicted about 1.1 million adults of felonies in 2002. Federal courts convicted approximately 78,000 people in 2002 (approximately the same number was convicted by federal courts in 2005 as well). Table 7-1 shows the types of felonies leading to convictions in each court in 2002 (Sourcebook of Criminal Justice Statistics, 2007).

Of all felony defendants in the state courts in 2002, the largest percentage was convicted of drug offenses (32%), followed by property offenses (31%) and violent offenses (19%). An additional 15% were convicted of "other offenses" (nonviolent offenses such as receiving stolen property and vandalism) and 3% were convicted of gun offenses. In federal district courts in 2002, 37% were convicted of drug offenses, 30% were convicted of public order offenses, 18% were convicted of property offenses, and 3% were convicted of violent offenses. Another 12% were misdemeanors (Sourcebook of Criminal Justice Statistics, 2007).

Thus, the majority of people convicted of felonies in each court were not convicted for violent crimes. Compare this with media coverage of crime in Chapter 5. Perhaps you are surprised that at this stage of the criminal justice process, most cases are not violent in nature. Further, given the harms caused by acts of elite deviance discussed in Chapter 4, you may be even more surprised to learn that at the state and federal level of courts, these types of crimes make up a small portion of all cases. Table 7-2 illustrates the percentage of cases dealing with various forms of elite deviance in state and federal courts, as well as the types of "elite deviance" cases handled there.

Almost all of these convictions come through plea bargains rather than jury trials. At the state level in 2002, 95% of convictions were achieved through plea bargains. Defendants charged with murder are most likely to go to trial (32%), followed by sexual assault and rape (10%). No other crime leads to a trial more than 10% of the time. At the federal level, about 96% of convictions are obtained by plea bargains.

TABLE 7-1 Convictions in American Courts (2002)		
	State Courts	*Federal Courts*
All offenses	1,051,000	77,339
Violent offenses	197,030	2,631
Murder/manslaughter	8,990	126
Sexual assault/rape	35,500	1,566
Robbery	38,430	1,327
Aggravated assault	95,600	661
Property offenses	325,200	13,197
Burglary	100,640	50
Theft	124,320	1,958
Motor vehicle theft	18,530	49
Fraud/forgery/embezzlement	100,240	9,464
Drug offenses	340,330	26,588

Source: Sourcebook on Criminal Justice Statistics (2006).

TABLE 7-2 Elite Deviance in the Courts		
	State Courts	*Federal Courts*
Fraud	47,610	9,464
Embezzlement	(included in above)	637
Forgery and counterfeiting	52,630	976

Source: Sourcebook on Criminal Justice Statistics (2006).

Not surprisingly, in light of our examination of American police, court defendants are disproportionately poor **indigents**. They make up more than 80% of people charged with felonies in the United States (Gaines et al., 2000). According to the Bureau of Justice Statistics, in any given year, roughly 80–85% of felony defendants in state courts and approximately 65–70% of federal defendants have publicly financed defense attorneys.

Characteristics of Court Clients

Characteristics of state and federal court defendants demonstrate who our criminal justice network pursues. At the state level, in the 75 largest counties in 2002, 82% of defendants were men, 43% of defendants were black (versus 31% white and 24% Hispanic), 33% of defendants were in their twenties, (versus 27% in their thirties, 21% over the age of 40, and 18% that were 20 years and under). State court statistics from the largest counties thus show that the typical defendant is a young, minority male. Of all those convicted of felonies in all state courts, 83% were male, 60% were white (versus 37% black and 3% other), and 41% were in their twenties (versus 29% in their thirties, 18% in their forties, 7% under 20, and 5% over 50) (Sourcebook of Criminal Justice Statistics, 2007).

In federal courts in 2003, most convicted for felonies were men (87%), white (71% versus 42% Hispanic and 25% blacks), and in their twenties or thirties (70% versus 25% over the age of 40, and 5% 20 years and younger). Further, 48% did not graduate from high school (versus 30% that were high school graduates, 17% with some college, and 6% who graduated from college) (Sourcebook of Criminal Justice Statistics, 2007). Thus, in federal courts, the typical conviction is of a young, uneducated white male, although blacks are overrepresented among felony convictions.

The Courtroom Workgroup

To ensure justice, the court is supposed to be impartial. Ideally, this means that neutral actors are involved in objectively determining the relevant facts of each case to ensure that the guilty are convicted and the innocent are not. The importance of this is explained by Gaines et al. (2000, p. 271): "In theory, each party in a courtroom dispute must have an equal chance to present its case and must be secure in the belief that no outside factors are going to influence the decision rendered by the court."

Keep in mind as you read this chapter that the people who work in the courts are very different from the people who are typically processed through the courts. Minorities and women are underrepresented in American courtroom workgroups (Bonsignore et al., 1998; Spire, 1990). Graham (2000) demonstrates how African Americans are underrepresented as attorneys and judges. Thus, much as legislators are not representative of Americans (see Chapter 3), those who work to convict or acquit suspected criminals also are not representative of Americans. Whether this is sufficient to explain injustice in the courts is unclear, but an unrepresentative courtroom workgroup is probably less likely to produce an outcome of justice than a representative workgroup.

Formal rules of procedure also are supposed to assist with objectivity. For example, "there are limitations as to how evidence may be introduced, what types of evidence may be admitted, and what types of questions may be asked" (Cox and Wade, 1998, p. 130). Later in this chapter I will return to whether the American criminal courts really act in an objective manner. First, I examine who works in the courts.

The **courtroom workgroup** is a term used to describe the main actors in this process within the criminal courts—the prosecutor, the defense attorney, and the judge (Cole and Smith, 2007; Cox and Wade, 1998; Schmalleger, 2006; Walker, 2005). A workgroup can be understood as a collective of individuals who interact, share goals, follow court norms, and develop interpersonal relationships (Fleming, Nardulli, and Eisenstein, 1992). This concept is important because it helps us understand why the workgroup's overriding concern is speeding up the process and getting rid of cases as efficiently as possible rather than "doing justice."

Ideally, each member of the courtroom workgroup plays its own roles and has its own goals. In reality, each member's main job is not to rock the boat in the daily operations of American courts, which are described as follows:

> Every day, the same group of courthouse regulars assembles in the same courtroom, sits or stands in the same places, and performs the same tasks as the day before. The types of defendants and the nature of the crimes they are accused of committing also remain constant. Only the names of the victim, witnesses, and defendants are different (Neubauer, 2007).

The Prosecutor

The **prosecutor**, as a representative of the court, fights for the "people" in an effort to "get justice" (as an outcome) for the crime victim and the community. His or her main job is to decide whether to press charges on the basis of the amount of quality evidence available to obtain a conviction. If the prosecution decides to press criminal charges, the next decision is to decide which charges to press. This decision will ultimately have a great effect on the resulting criminal sentence, as you will see in Chapter 8.

Criminal charges come in the form of an **indictment** (if the state uses a grand jury system) or an **information** (in cases of a preliminary hearing). The primary difference between grand juries and preliminary hearings is that grand juries are one-sided presentations by the prosecution, whereas preliminary hearings are adversarial in nature. Some have called the grand jury a "rubber stamp" for the prosecutor because grand juries almost never fail to return an indictment. Both grand juries and preliminary hearings result in a determination of whether there is enough evidence to pursue the case further (e.g., to a criminal trial).

A prosecutor must consider numerous factors when deciding either to accept a case for prosecution or to reject the case. Most cases that come before prosecutors' offices do not lead to a prosecution. In fact, just under half of arrests lead to prosecution. Despite what you may have heard about "legal technicalities," most cases are in fact dropped because of a lack of high-quality evidence. Of course, decisions to prosecute do not emanate from formal rules but from informal relationships with people such as the police, victims, and other community members. This is another reason that it is imperative that positive relationships be established and maintained among citizens, police, and other criminal justice officials.

Walker (2005) reviews the evidence or factors that influence prosecutors' decisions to accept cases for prosecution and concludes that the largest share of cases that are not prosecuted are dropped because of evidence problems—not enough high-quality evidence to obtain a conviction at trial. He claims that "due process problems—illegal searches or confessions—are not a major cause of rejections or dismissals." Thus, those who argue that "legal technicalities" should be disallowed may be off the mark. Pizzi (2000), in his book *Trials Without Truth,* claims that trials are too focused on winning and losing rather than on truth. One reform he advocates is eliminating the exclusionary rule as a means of convicting more guilty criminals. His reforms are aimed at achieving justice as an outcome rather than ensuring justice as a process. On the basis of the review of evidence in Chapter 6 I would disagree that the exclusionary rule should be abolished, but Pizzi is probably correct that trials are not really about truth.

The prosecutor also serves as **trial counsel for police** (fighting crime) and **house counsel for police** (giving legal advice) (Cole and Smith, 2007). Examples of the role of trial counsel for the police include zealously prosecuting suspected criminals and pursuing community crime control interests to achieve justice as an outcome. Examples of the role of house counsel for the police include "providing legal advice to [the police], providing training for police on criminal law and legal processes, preparing drafts of search warrants and wiretapping applications, participating in decisions regarding court administration, and engaging in a wide variety of public information and community relations programs" (Holten and Jones, 1982, p. 185). In both cases, the prosecutor can be accurately understood as a partner with the police in the fight against crime.

As a **representative of the court**, the prosecutor also must be concerned with justice as a process. A prosecutor is "obliged to protect the rights of the defendant" (Cox and Wade, 1998, p. 148), just as a police officer is obligated to uphold the constitutional rights of a suspect (Wrobleski, 2006). There is evidence, however, that many prosecutors ignore possible indications of innocence of defendants simply to gain convictions and clear cases.

Prosecutors have tremendous power in the criminal justice process. This power imbalances the court in favor of the state rather than the defendant. "Ideally, this power is balanced by a duty of fairness and a recognition that the prosecutor's ultimate goal is not to win cases, but to see that justice is done" (Gaines et al., 2000, p. 302). The American Bar Association (1993, 1997), for example, expects that prosecutors will "seek justice, not merely convict" criminals because they have the "responsibility of a minister of justice." Justice Sutherland wrote, in *Berger v. United States* (1935), that the prosecutor "may prosecute with earnestness and vigor—indeed he should do so. But, while he may strike hard blows, he is not at liberty to strike foul ones."

Yet most prosecutors are also elected officials, meaning that they will at times be concerned with what they perceive their community wants, as well as with the underlying philosophy of the voters (DeFrances and Steadman, 1998; Merlo and Benekos, 2000). Gershman (2000, p. 286) demonstrates that the typical jury is biased toward the prosecution, meaning that jurors will be more tolerant of misconduct by prosecutors than by defense attorneys, including promises made about evidence in opening statements of a trial but not delivered during the trial and purposeful mention of inadmissible evidence. Ensuring high conviction rates sends a signal to the community that the prosecutor is tough on crime. The desire to be tough on crime while simultaneously being fair and making sure that innocent people are not convicted seem to conflict.

Are prosecutors biased against any particular group of people? That is, is there any evidence that they are more likely to press charges against some groups of people? The *Harvard Law Review* (1988) suggested that prosecutors sometimes abuse their discretion by upgrading charges against minorities and downgrading them against Caucasians. More recent evidence is consistent with this assertion, at least in some jurisdictions (Walker, Spohn, and DeLone, 2006). In Chapter 10, you will see clear evidence of bias toward minorities in death penalty cases. The main source of this bias is prosecutor discretion.

The Defense Attorney

The **defense attorney** represents the "defendant" and has the main duty of being an advocate for the defendant. This is the main actor in the criminal justice process who is responsible for ensuring that constitutional protections of the accused are upheld and protected. Defense attorneys are the actors in the court process responsible for upholding the due process function of the court, protecting "individuals from the unfair advantages that the government—with its immense resources—automatically enjoys in legal battles" (Gaines et al., 2000, p. 271). Standard 4–1.2(b) of the American Bar Association's Standards for Criminal Justice (1991) states that the basic duty of the defense attorney is "to serve as the accused's counselor and advocate with courage and devotion, and render effective, quality representation." The ideal functions of defense attorneys include the following (Siegel, 1998, pp. 487–488):

- Investigating the facts of the case against his or her client
- Preparing his or her client's case for trial
- Submitting motions in favor of his or her client's case
- Representing the defendant at trial
- Negotiating the sentence with the prosecutor if the client is convicted
- Appealing convictions

The reality is that these functions may be carried out by some defense attorneys but not by others. It all depends on what type of defense attorney a person can afford. At the state level, defense attorneys include **nationally known attorneys**, other **private attorneys**, and **courthouse regulars** (e.g., public defenders) (Cole and Smith, 2007). There are generally three types of systems available to defend those who cannot hire their own attorneys:

- **public defender systems**—a salaried staff of government attorneys paid for by taxpayers
- **assigned counsel programs**—private attorneys assigned to particular cases by courts
- **contracting attorney programs**—private attorneys hired to defend a group of defendants for a specified period of time (Bureau of Justice Statistics, 2007)

In the nation's 100 most populous counties, 90 had public defender programs, 89 had assigned counsel programs, and 42 had contract programs (Bureau of Justice Statistics, 2007). Public defender offices in the nation's largest 100 counties employed 12,700 people in 1999. Defense attorneys for indigent clients handled 4.2 million cases in 1999, 80% of which were criminal cases. Public defenders handled 82% of these cases, followed by 15% by appointed attorneys and 3% by contract attorneys.

At the federal level, the following types of defense are available for the indigent.

- **Panel attorneys**—appointed by the court from a list of attorneys on a case-by-case basis
- **Community defender organization**—incorporated service lawyers under grant by the Administrative Office of the U.S. Courts

Panel attorneys were available in all 94 districts, whereas community defender organizations were available in 74 districts. Of federal defendants, 36% used panel attorneys and 30% used attorneys from the Federal Defender Organization.

These systems are necessary primarily because the majority of defendants in criminal cases are indigents, or people who cannot afford their own attorney. The Supreme Court, in *Gideon v. Wainwright* (1963), held that the right to fair trial was jeopardized if state court defendants were not granted assistance by defense. In *Mempa v. Rhay* (1967), the Supreme Court extended the right of indigents beyond trial to other critical stages of the criminal justice process, including arraignment, preliminary hearing, entering of the plea, sentencing, and first appeal.

The typical defendant is not a wealthy person out to beat the system. "The average defendant in a criminal proceeding is indigent and not capable of hiring the 'best attorney money can buy.'" Instead, he or she is assigned a courthouse regular, who is usually paid a very low salary, works in a depressing environment, and has very few support services available (Merlo and Benekos, 2000, p. 57). Harrigan (2000, p. 319) writes that "the quality of state-provided representation seldom equals the representation you would obtain if you could afford to hire your own criminal layer." This is in part because they are "often so overloaded with cases they find it impossible to devote much of their time or effort to any specific case." Also, "because assigned lawyers get paid on a per-case basis rather than on an hourly basis, they have a great incentive to speed up the cases as much as possible." This led Blumberg (1967) to call many defense attorneys "double agents" and "cons" often working against the interests of their clients (Uphoff, 2000). Others assert that public defenders do as well at defending their clients as private attorneys do (Hansom and Ostrom, 1993). In Chapter 10, you will learn how incompetent defense attorneys are one of the most significant problems in death penalty cases.

The Judge

The **judge**, as leader of the courtroom workgroup, has the goal of ensuring that proper legal procedures are followed as a case is processed through the courts. The roles of judges include **adjudicator** (passes sentence), **negotiator** (referee between parties), and **administrator** (keeps up the docket). Judges decide if arrests are based on probable cause, inform charged suspects of their rights, determine if bail will be granted to defendants, rule on motions filed by the prosecution and the defense, officiate trials to make sure they are fair, and impose sentences on the legally guilty.

Ideally, judges embody justice and ensure due process, but in reality, judges spend most of their time in the administrative role, which would include such activities as preparing budgets, scheduling cases, supervising employees, and maintaining court records (Cole and Smith, 2007; Cox and Wade, 1998). Because of the number of cases they must handle and because of the amount of time courthouse employees spend together, the group may generally share the overriding goal of disposing of cases as quickly as possible more often than they may fight for justice. As more and more citizens have "run-ins with the law"—that is, as more police are put on the street and as American police make more arrests—the courts suffer the consequences. Today, the courts are forced to handle too many cases. As a result, many cases are simply dismissed before they are even considered (Donziger, 1996). Walker (1998, p. 13) writes, "The justice system can only handle so much business. It does not 'collapse' like a building. It keeps on going, but only through adjustments that are often undesirable."

AN IMBALANCE OF POWER IN THE COURT: FROM JUDGE TO PROSECUTION

The intimate nature of the daily operations of American courts makes the courtroom workgroup a "community" (Nardulli et al., 1988) because the members develop shared understandings of what cases should be worth and "reach a general consensus about how different kinds of cases should be handled" (Walker, 1998, p. 51). This means that even though prosecutors and defense attorneys are supposed to be adversaries, they rarely act this way.

By examining the reality of courtroom interactions today, you can learn a great deal about American priorities. For example, it is clear that prosecutors have much more power in the criminal justice process than judges or defense attorneys (Davis, 2007). Power is the ability to influence actions of others (see Chapter 2). The judge is ideally the most powerful member of the court, in that he or she can decide matters of law that affect courtroom operations and in that he or she presides over trials: "Since they are deciding benefits, judges are political actors with power" (Marion, 1995). Yet, since the "final decision about whether an alleged offender will be brought to court rests with the prosecutor" exclusively, the prosecutor has an enormous amount of discretion and is clearly the most powerful member of the court. Cox and Wade (1998, p. 147) state, "The decision not to prosecute *(nollee prosequi)*, in addition to the discretion in determining the number and severity of charges, renders the prosecutor a very powerful figure in the court process." Stated plainly, if the prosecutor decides not to prosecute a case, the defense attorney and judge will in essence have no say in the outcome of that case. It is the discretion of the prosecutor to act or not to act that gives him or her so much power (Albonetti, 1987).

A former U.S. attorney general once claimed, "The prosecutor has more control over life, liberty, and reputation than any other person in America" (in Cox and Wade, 1998, p. 147). This is especially true when large numbers of cases are sent from the police to courts. As American courts have become bogged down with more cases, judges have lost significant power because they are even more reliant on prosecutors to determine which cases merit charges, trials, and justice (Marion, 1995). The power of judges also has been significantly reduced by new sentencing rules (see Chapter 8). Milovanovich (2000, p. 516) claims that the power of the prosecutor in the United States is essentially unchallenged. Davis (2007) concurs, showing that mandatory minimum sentencing laws increase prosecutorial control over how cases are disposed of.

Because of this imbalance of power in the court, justice is severely threatened. Ideally, if Americans value justice, due process, "innocent until proven guilty," constitutional protections, and equality before the law, it seems that defense attorneys would have more power and a greater share of resources to ensure that their clients are processed fairly through the criminal justice network. Because most criminal defense attorneys work for the government (e.g., as public defenders), they have heavy caseloads, limited resources to investigate the facts of a case, and little or no financial incentive to take a case to trial (Casper, 1972; Cole and Smith, 2007). This may result in unequal justice for the rich and the poor. "The general suspicion is that equal justice is not available to rich and poor alike . . . indigents receive a lower quality of legal service, which results in their being more likely to suffer harsher penal sanctions than similarly situated defendants who can afford to buy good legal talent" (Sterling, 1983, p. 166). Despite this suspicion, others assert that because public defenders are members of the courtroom workgroup, they have the advantage of assuring a reasonable sentence from prosecutors with whom they interact on a daily basis (Skolnick, 1967; Wice, 1985).

PRETRIAL PROCEDURES AND JUSTICE

Everything that goes on in the criminal justice process between arrest, booking, and the criminal trial is called the **pretrial phase** (Peoples, 2000; Stuckey, Robertson, and Wallace, 2001). The term can be misleading in that it is called "pretrial" whether or not a trial actually results. The pretrial phase contains two major decisions that must be made before a case can proceed to trial (or be disposed of through some other means). These two decisions concern the issuing of bail and whether a case gets plea bargained. Next, I examine each of these two processes and demonstrate how each severely threatens justice.

Bail as an Injustice

First, there is the decision about bail. After suspects are arrested and brought to court to make an **initial appearance** (where they are notified of the charges against them and advised of their rights), they may be released from the supervision of the court through the process of bail. **Bail** is a specified sum of money paid to the court for suspects' release, to be paid back if they return for their court date. That is, bail is not the same thing as a fine, because it is not meant to be a form of punishment. It is important to point out that people are not supposed to be punished unless they commit a crime (under the policy of *nulla poena sine crimine*). Instead, bail is meant to ensure the presence of the defendant at trial. The logic is that if suspects pay a sum of money to the court, they will come back to have the money returned.

Types of bail are highlighted in Box 7-1.

BOX 7-1

TYPES OF BAIL

- **Percentage bail:** The defendant must pay only a percentage of the bail amount set by the judge up front, with the rest due if the defendant does not show up for his or her next trial date.
- **Fully secured bail:** The defendant must pay the entire bail amount set by the judge up front.

- **Unsecured bail:** The defendant must not pay any of the bail amount set by the judge up front, but must pay the full amount if the defendant does not show up for his or her next trial date.

Bail is based on the premise that no one—since everyone is supposedly innocent in the eyes of the law at this point—should be unduly burdened by being held against his or her will until the trial date. Because many crimes are relatively minor, holding many offenders would be a waste of taxpayer money. It would not be fair to interrupt suspects' lives—to separate them from family or force them to stop working and lose important wages—just to ensure that the state has its right to prosecute someone who is accused of a criminal offense.

There are, however, cases in which bail is not granted to suspected offenders. In some cases, people are detained in jail until their trial dates. For example, ex–football star O. J. Simpson spent two of his birthdays in jail while awaiting trial and during his trial. He was detained because it was feared that if he were let out, he would **abscond** or **jump bail** and not return for his court date. It was also feared that he might be dangerous to the community, given that he was accused of two heinous murders. The fact that Simpson was later **acquitted** (found not guilty) led some to question whether he was entitled to any compensation for his time served.

The answer is no. According to the Bail Reform Act of 1984, accused criminals can be held in jail in **preventive detention** for two primary purposes: to prevent them from fleeing the state's jurisdiction, and to protect the community. Thus, judges may deny bail when there is either a flight risk or some potential danger to the community. The constitutionality of this practice was upheld by the Supreme Court in *U.S. v. Salerno* (1987).

Bail, however, cannot be "excessive," according to the Eighth Amendment to the U.S. Constitution, although there is no clear understanding of what excessive really means. Instead, prosecutors may ask for a certain amount of bail, defense attorneys may ask for a reduction, and judges ultimately decide what the acceptable bail amount will be. Ideally, defense attorneys ensure that bail is not excessive for their clients; in reality, however, they rarely challenge the amount (Gaines et al., 2000, p. 312). A **going rate** for particular crimes seems to develop over time so that a person charged with a particular crime may have a rough idea of what he or she will have to come up with to be granted bail. The nature of the charges; the defendant's prior record (if any); and extralegal factors such as employment status, ties to the community, and status in the community are also considered when bail is being determined (Nordulli, Eisenstein and Flemming, 1992).

The application of bail has several major problems. First, it is biased against certain groups in the United States. Erving and Houston (1991) found evidence of judges using excessive bonds against minorities. Spohn and DeLone (2000) found that pretrial detention was disproportionately used against African Americans and Hispanics in two cities and against African Americans in another. Other studies show biases against the poor and minorities (Ayers and Waldfogel, 1994; Harmsworth, 1996). Such findings suggest that the bail decision can be biased against certain Americans. Kappeler, Blumberg, and Potter (2000, p. 226) claim that "[b]ail itself is inherently discriminatory." Logically, people who cannot afford bail are less likely to come up with the money or property to make bail and thus are forced to sit in jail awaiting trial. This may explain why jails are considered the poorhouses of the twentieth and twenty-first centuries (Cole and Smith, 2000): They are filled with poor criminals and accused criminals who could not afford bail.

Second, bail flies in the face of "innocent until proven guilty"—how can persons be detained if they have not been found guilty by a jury of their peers for any criminal act? In reality, approximately half of the people in jail in any given year are awaiting trial and thus have not been convicted of any criminal offense; yet they are living away from their families, in the company of convicted criminals, mentally ill citizens, and homeless people detained for minor crimes.

Third, courtroom workgroups inflate bail amounts for those they want to detain, meaning that two people charged with the same crime or same type of crime may see drastically different bail amounts. This practice is contradictory to equal justice under the law.

Fourth, bail may encourage guilty pleas. After all, if accused of relatively minor crimes, many would likely take a guilty plea and receive probation or a fine rather than being forced to sit in jail awaiting trial.

Fifth, preventive detention may increase the likelihood that a defendant will be convicted and sentenced to prison. Walker (1998, p. 118) reports findings from the National Pretrial Reporting Program illustrating that defendants held in preventive detention were more likely to be convicted of both felonies and misdemeanors. Whether this is because detained citizens appear in court wearing "jail garb" and thus "look guilty," while freed clients appear wearing normal clothes, is unknown. Logically, it would seem that seeing a person wearing jail clothing and perhaps in handcuffs or shackles would suggest that "this person must be guilty if he or she is in jail." Another possible explanation of why detained suspects are more likely to be convicted is that when a suspect is in jail, he or she is far less able to gather evidence in his or her defense. If the defense attorney is a public defender, the defendant will not receive quality efforts from the attorney, as will be illustrated later in this chapter. In their study, Spohn and DeLone (2000) found that those offenders held in pretrial detention were somewhat more likely to be sentenced to incarceration. Of course, it is possible that pretrial detainees are more often convicted and sentenced to prison because they are actually guilty and perhaps committed more serious crimes.

Finally, preventive detention may not generally be necessary, because most people who are let out on bail do not commit another crime while awaiting trial (Walker, 1998, pp. 121–122). The bottom line is that it is impossible to predict who might be dangerous if let out. "There are no reliable methods for either measuring or predicting future offense rates" (Greenwood and Turner, 1987, in Walker, 1998, p. 126). As stated by Fagan and Guggenheim (1996, p. 445), "The accuracy of prediction of dangerousness during the pretrial period remains questionable." Some crime control model advocates might conclude that we should therefore keep all people in jail until trial to protect our communities from those few who might become dangerous. The other extreme is advocated by Fagan and Guggenheim, who conclude that "preventive detention appears to be unjustified" (p. 448).

Given these limitations, there are also alternatives available to judges, as outlined in Box 7-2.

In 2002, about one-third (34%) of defendants charged with felonies in the 75 most populated counties were released from jail at some point in the court process prior to the disposition of their case. Another 28% were released on their own recognizance (ROR), through conditional release, or through unsecured bail (Sourcebook of Criminal Justice Statistics, 2007). More than one-third (38%) of defendants charged with felonies in the 75 most populated counties were detained until the final disposition of their cases, including 6% who were denied bail and 32% who could not afford their bail.

Of all those released by state courts in 2002, 33% failed by either violating a condition of their release or getting arrested for committing a new crime. Most were not

BOX 7-2

BAIL ALTERNATIVES

- **Release on own recognizance (ROR):** The defendant is released on the basis of his or her promise to appear.
- **Release into third-party custody:** The defendant is released into the custody of another person (e.g., a parent), who agrees to ensure that the defendant will show up for his or her next court date.
- **Conditional release:** The defendant is released on the basis of his or her promise to follow certain rules while free.

arrested for committing a new crime (82%), but charged drug offenders were most likely to be rearrested for a new crime (21%) versus 19% of property offenders and 13% of violent offenders (Sourcebook of Criminal Justice Statistics, 2007).

In federal courts in 2003, 59% of defendants were released prior to the disposition of their cases, versus 41% who were detained. One in five (20%) defendants failed by either violating a condition of their release or getting arrested for committing a new crime. Only about 2% were arrested for committing a new felony.

Defendants charged with violent crimes by states were least likely to be released (55%), followed by property offenders (60%) and drug offenders (66%). Of all offenders, accused murderers were least likely to be released (7%). Defendants charged with fraud (80%) were most likely to be released. This same pattern is found in federal courts, as well. Since most cases in federal courts deal with drugs, it is interesting to note that 85% of drug offense defendants in 2003 were detained until the final disposition of their cases (Sourcebook of Criminal Justice Statistics, 2007). Nearly the same percentage of murder defendants (88%) in 2003 were detained until the final disposition of their cases, versus only 43% of property offenders (including 16% of those charged with embezzlement, 22% charged with tax fraud, 38% charged with bribery, and 46% charged with fraud). Thus, at both the state and federal levels, accused white-collar offenders are most likely to be released.

With America's "war on terror," the U.S. military and various investigative and intelligence agencies, such as the FBI and CIA, have rounded up hundreds of suspects (more than 600) and detained them in Guantanamo Bay, Cuba, at Camp X-Ray, which the British Broadcasting Corporation calls "an island, on an island, on an island. It is a sealed off zone within the US naval base at Guantanamo Bay, which is itself sealed." The BBC describes the camp this way: "It is a maze of chain-link fences, razor wire and guard towers. There are dog patrols and snipers. You can see into the prisoners' cell block quite clearly, as its walls are also made from chain-link. The cells are protected from the elements only by a metal roof . . . the prisoners in their bright orange jumpsuits spend most of their time in their cells, sitting on the floor or lying on foam sleeping mats, trying to keep cool in the incredible heat."

Although Defense Secretary Robert Gates has recently stated that he would like to see Camp X-Ray closed, as of this writing there is no indication this will occur in the near future. Several hundred people are still detained there. Further, the U.S. Supreme Court has approved of the use of "enemy combatant" status by the president, even against American citizens. This is discussed in the Box 7-3.

BOX 7-3

THE U.S. SUPREME COURT AND THE WAR ON TERROR

Hamdi et al. v. Rumsfeld et al. (October 2003)

Yaser Hamdi was born in Louisiana and moved to Saudi Arabia as a child, retaining his American citizenship. He was captured in Afghanistan by the Northern Alliance for allegedly taking up arms with the Taliban and declared an "enemy combatant" by the United States. This was after Congress passed the "Authorization for Use of Military Force" (AUMF), which empowered the president to "use all necessary and appropriate force" against "nations, organizations, or persons" that he determines "planned, authorized, committed, or aided" in the 9/11 attacks. Hamdi was detained in the Navy brig in Charleston, South Carolina.

Hamdi alleged his detention was in violation of the Fifth and Fourteenth Amendments. He said he went to Afghanistan to do relief work, that he was there less than 2 months prior to 9/11, and that he could not have received military training in this time. The government's evidence against Hamdi consisted entirely of the "Mobbs Declaration" (named after a Defense Department official). The Mobbs Declaration alleged details about Hamdi's trip to Afghanistan, his affiliations with the Taliban, and his surrender of an assault rifle.

The District Court found the Mobbs Declaration little more than the say-so of the government. It also ordered the government to turn over its materials for an in-court review and ordered the appointment of a public defender for Hamdi. The Fourth Circuit Court reversed and noted that Hamdi was captured in an active combat zone so no factual inquiry or evidentiary hearing is needed. It also said the AUMF is an act of Congress that allows Hamdi's detention. The Circuit Court ruled that Hamdi should be allowed only limited judicial inquiry into the legality of his detention under U.S. war powers.

The Supreme Court held 6–3 that the judgment of the Circuit Court should be vacated and the case remanded (O'Connor, Rehnquist, Kennedy, Breyer, Souter, Ginsburg versus Scalia, Stevens, and Thomas). It held that every citizen, absent a suspension of the writ of *habeas corpus*, has the right to *habeas corpus* relief.

O'Connor, Rehnquist, Kennedy, and Breyer proposed a middle-ground between Hamdi's release and indefinite detention. They wrote that, although Congress authorized Hamdi's detention in this case, due process demands that citizens held in the United States as enemy combatants be given a meaningful opportunity to contest the factual basis for their detention before neutral decision makers. Souter and Ginsburg said Hamdi's detention is unauthorized and that he should have the opportunity to offer evidence that he is not an enemy combatant. They also noted that his detention is not necessary because there are numerous criminal laws under which he could be charged. They also wondered whether Hamdi is a prisoner of war (POW) and whether his detention is in violation of the Geneva Conventions and military regulations. The plurality thus said American citizens can be held as enemy combatants, but only as long as there are active hostilities. Further, they do not have the right to a full criminal trial.

In the dissent, Scalia and Stevens said Hamdi should be tried as a traitor through the criminal process. They noted that the president cannot indefinitely detain a person, and that the president should ask Congress to simply suspend the right of *habeas corpus.* They claimed that the plurality's ruling is an invented solution, and is part of the "fix it" mentality that wants to make everything turn out right, whether it is legal or not.

Thomas is the only justice who supported the president's decision to detain enemy combatants as he sees fit. Thomas wrote that we must trust the government and the president, and in this case, the president has broad discretion to protect the country from harm.

Ultimately, Yaser Hamdi was released after 2 years of imprisonment. He gave up his citizenship and returned to Saudi Arabia.

Rumsfeld v. Padilla et al. (October 2003)

Jose Padilla is a U.S. citizen apprehended at an airport in Chicago after arriving from Pakistan. He was held as a material witness by a warrant issued for the District Court of the Southern District of New York as part of a grand jury investigation into 9/11.

Padilla made a motion to vacate the warrant and while it was pending, President Bush issued an order to then–Secretary of Defense Donald Rumsfeld to designate Padilla an "enemy combatant" and to detain Padilla in military custody. Padilla was then moved to a Navy brig in Charleston, South Carolina, and the warrant that was being used to hold Padilla was vacated by the Court at the request of the government.

Padilla's counsel filed a *habeas* petition in the Southern District and the respondents were President Bush, Secretary of Defense Donald Rumsfeld, and Melanie Marr (the brig commander). He alleged a violation of the Fourth, Sixth, and Fourteenth Amendments, as well as the Separation Clause. The government argued that only Marr was the appropriate respondent and thus the Southern District lacked jurisdiction.

The District Court held Rumsfeld's involvement made him a respondent and that it had jurisdiction over him under New York's long-arm statute. The Second Circuit Court agreed but reversed that the president has the authority to detain Padilla in military custody.

The Supreme Court held 5–4 (Rehnquist, O'Connor, Scalia, Kennedy, and Thomas versus Stevens, Souter, Ginsburg, and Breyer) that the Southern District lacks jurisdiction and Padilla should have filed in the District of South Carolina, and that Marr is the only appropriate respondent because she is the person who has custody of Padilla.

The case law cited suggests that only the person with immediate custody (i.e., the warden where the inmate is being held) can be the respondent in a *habeas* writ. Further, the court issuing the writ must have jurisdiction over the custodian. The logic of the ruling is that it prevents forum shopping by *habeas* petitioners. An interesting issue is this: Did Padilla's lawyer know where he was being held? Padilla claims the

(continued)

BOX 7-3 (*Continued*)

government gave no notice to vacate the warrant or he would have filed it elsewhere.

In the dissent, it was noted that special circumstances justify an exception to the rule, that the Secretary of Defense has legal control over Padilla, and that the question is one of venue not jurisdiction (pp. 11–12). Yet the dissent cited no case law.

Jose Padilla is still in U.S. custody. After more than 3 years, he was finally charged with a crime—conspiracy to commit terrorism—and awaits criminal trial. He was not charged with attempting or planning to set off a dirty bomb in a U.S. city, nor was he charged with attempting or planning to blow up apartment buildings (charges publicly leveled against him by then–Attorney General John Ashcroft). He has been held in a maximum security prison and has reportedly suffered severe psychological problems.

Rasul et al. v. Bush et al. (October 2003)

Fourteen detainees were captured in Afghanistan, including 12 Kuwaitis and two Australians. They were held in Camp X-Ray at Guantánamo, Cuba. This base is under U.S. lease from Cuba and a treaty that recognizes Cuba's ultimate sovereignty.

The men claimed they were captured for monetary reward by the Northern Alliance and Pakistan. They also claim they were not combatants against the United States, nor were they terrorists. The men asserted that they have not been charged with any wrongdoing, have not been given counsel, and have not been given access to justice of any kind.

The District Court dismissed the case for want of jurisdiction (because aliens outside U.S. sovereign territory may not seek *habeas* relief). The Court of Appeals affirmed the ruling.

The Supreme Court held 6–3 (Stevens, O'Connor, Souter, Ginsburg, Breyer, and Kennedy versus Scalia, Rehnquist, and Thomas) that U.S. courts have jurisdiction to consider challenges to legality of detention of foreign nationals captured abroad and incarcerated in Guantánamo Bay, Cuba. It held that if a person is held in violation of U.S. laws, the right extends to aliens held in territories over which the United States has jurisdiction and that the United States has complete jurisdiction and control over Camp X-Ray in Guantánamo, Cuba (because federal law does not distinguish between U.S. citizens and aliens held in federal custody).

The majority said there is a long history of federal courts granting *habeas* relief in a wide range of cases. It notes that since the District Court has jurisdiction of the men, nothing more is required. Kennedy concurred and said that Guantánamo, Cuba, is part of U.S. jurisdiction, and that it is U.S. territory far removed from any hostilities.

In the dissent, it was claimed that this is a violation of precedent and an irresponsible overturning of settled law. It claimed the District Court has no jurisdiction because Guantánamo Bay, Cuba, is not within any jurisdiction of any federal court. They called the ruling clumsy, monstrous, and judicial adventurism. Further, the ruling complicates the present war by extending the *habeas* statute to the four corners of the Earth, including to parts of Afghanistan and Iraq that have been captured and thus can lead to *habeas* appeals.

Some of the captives from Camp X-Ray have likely been released, as hundreds have. The first military tribunal started and was halted, but the government won its appeal and now can proceed.

Hamdan v. Rumsfeld (June 2006)

In 2001, Salim Ahmed Hamdan (a Yemeni national) was captured in Afghanistan and turned over to the U.S. military. He was subsequently sent to Camp X-Ray in Guantánamo Bay, Cuba. Almost 2 years into his captivity, President Bush deemed Hamdan eligible for trial by military commission even though Hamdan had not yet been charged with any specific offense.

Ultimately, Hamdan was charged with conspiracy "to commit . . . offenses triable by military commission." Hamdan asserted that "the military commission lacks authority to try him because no law by Congress supports trial by this commission for conspiracy and because the procedures adopted by the United States to try him violate basic tenets of military and international law.

The District Court granted *habeas* relief and concluded that the president's authority to establish military commissions extends only to offenders or offenses triable by such a commission under the law of war. It also held that the commission convened to try him was a violation of both the Uniform Code of Military Justice (UCMJ) and Common Article 3 of the Third Geneva Convention.

The D.C. Circuit (which included Justice John Roberts, who is now Chief Justice of the U.S. Supreme Court) reversed. It ruled that Hamdan was not entitled to relief because the Geneva Conventions are not judicially enforceable and that Hamdan's military tribunal would not violate the UCMJ or military regulations related to the Geneva Conventions.

The Supreme Court disagreed, and held 5–3 (Stevens, Souter, Ginsburg, Breyer, and Kennedy versus Scalia, Alito, and Thomas, with Chief Justice John Roberts not participating) that President Bush's authorization of military tribunals at Guantánamo Bay violates the Uniform Code of Military Justice and the Geneva Conventions.

As of this writing, Hamdan awaits military tribunal.

Summary

The net effect of these rulings is that President Bush (and all presidents) have limited power even in times of war. He cannot order people to be held as "enemy combatants" in secret, without access to lawyers, and with no legal or evidentiary hearing regarding their status. And those held can challenge their detentions in American courts.

Yet the rulings bolstered presidential power more than they limited it. The rulings mean the president can label American citizens as "enemy combatants" and hold them indefinitely, for as long as there is a war on terror. While they now can challenge the case against them, even American citizens are not entitled to regular criminal trials with normal rules of procedure and evidence. The president alone has the authority to decide how and when they will be tried, and what due process rules will be followed in their cases.

Congress then acted, in the Military Commissions Act of 2006, to give the president the authority he declared through executive order with regard to enemy combatants. According to the Center for Constitutional Rights (2006), the law authorizes:

- the suspension of *habeas corpus* for non-citizens, including legal permanent residents, in U.S. custody;
- the president to detain anyone, including U.S. citizens, without charge by designating them enemy combatants or unlawful enemy combatants;

(continued)

BOX 7-3 *(Continued)*

- the president to determine what constitutes torture;
- the use of evidence obtained by coercion;
- the use of hearsay evidence; and

- retroactive immunity for U.S military and intelligence officials for abuses that occurred at sites such as Abu Ghraib, Guantánamo, Bagram, and secret CIA facilities.

Plea Bargaining as an Injustice

The ideal of American justice is an "adversarial" process whereby prosecutors and defense attorneys fight for the truth and justice in a contest at trial. Yet "the reality is that an administrative system is in effect, with a high degree of consensus and cooperation" (Walker, 1998, pp. 51–52). Most cases are handled informally in hallways and offices rather than in courtrooms, as in a crime control model rather than a due process model. Instead of criminal trials in which prosecutors and defense attorneys clash in an effort to determine the truth and do justice for all concerned parties, the prosecutors, defense attorneys, and sometimes judges "shop" for "supermarket" justice through plea bargaining (Feeley, 1979).

Shockingly, more than 90% of felony cases in the United States in any given year are disposed of via **plea bargaining**. This led Cole and Smith (2007) to call trials the "exceptional case," and Cox and Wade (1998) to call trials a "great American myth." Criminal trials are a formalized means of determining the legal guilt of your fellow citizens. Meanwhile, plea bargaining is an informal process whereby defendants plead guilty to lesser charges in exchange for not taking up the court's valuable time or spending the state's money on trials. Clients give up their constitutional rights to cross-examine witnesses, to present a defense, to not incriminate themselves, to testify on their own behalf, and to appeal their convictions in exchange for a dismissal or reduction in charges, and/or a lesser sentence (Blumberg, 1967; Casper, 1972). Gaines et al. (2000, p. 294) write that this type of assembly-line justice, consistent with a crime control model, "implies injustice. The term suggests that defendants are being hurried through the process, losing the safeguards built into our criminal justice system in the blur."

There are three basic types of plea bargaining: horizontal, vertical, and charge bargaining. In **horizontal bargaining**, additional charges or counts are not filed against the accused in exchange for a guilty plea. **Vertical bargaining** involves reducing the severity of charges—for example, being charged with manslaughter instead of murder. Finally, **charge bargaining** suggests that some provable charges simply will not be pressed against the defendant on the basis of his or her guilty plea (Milovanovich, 2000).

Walker (1998, p. 157) claims that: "[v]irtually all of the studies of plea bargaining have found a high degree of regularity and predictability in the disposition of cases," meaning that the resulting sentence can be reliably predicted on the basis of the nature of the charges and the defendant's prior record (e.g., see Nardulli et al., 1988). Thus, another type of **going rate** is established for particular types of crimes committed by particular types of people, one that becomes established over time and is learned by each member of the courtroom workgroup. Plea bargains typically closely parallel this **going**

rate, and defendants charged with particular crimes can easily learn what sentence they likely face if they plead guilty.

Plea bargaining is a process driven by large numbers of caseloads, understaffed courts, an imbalance between the prosecution and defense, and the renewed emphasis on using law enforcement to solve drug use and public order offenses. Of the more than 2.4 million felony cases in 2005, prosecutors achieved only 3% of these convictions through jury trials (Bureau of Justice Statistics, 2006). There are so few trials partly because large prosecutor offices closed an average of 13,000 felony cases, medium offices closed about 3,000 felony cases, and small offices closed an average of 300 felony cases. There are simply too many cases to have trials and not enough personnel or money to handle them all, and most of criminal spending and employees are devoted to police and corrections (see Chapter 1).

In Chapter 1, you saw that the largest share of justice spending goes to law enforcement ($89 billion in 2005). This is followed by spending on corrections, which includes jails, prisons, probation, and parole ($62 billion). The smallest share of resources is spent on prosecution and other legal services ($43 billion). The average court budget accounts for less than 2% of all state budget appropriations. There are 2,344 state court prosecutor offices with about 78,000 staff and a median annual budget of $355,000. Total budgets for state prosecutor offices totaled more than $4.9 billion in 2005.

In 2004, local police departments spent $88.9 billion. Thus, we spend nearly $100 billion catching and prosecuting mostly street criminals, the vast majority of which are poor. Recent data on the amount of money spent defending the indigent are not yet available, but in 1999, Americans in the 100 most populous counties spent only $1.2 billion to provide criminal defense to indigent clients. Nearly three-fourths (73%) was spent on public defenders, and 21% was spent on assigned counsel programs, plus another 6% on contract defense. This figure of $1.2 billion made up only 3% of all local criminal justice expenditures used for police, courts, and corrections in these counties. We can confidently say that we spend far more money catching and prosecuting indigent defendants than defending them. While expenditures for judicial and legal costs increased 321% between 1982 and 2003 (versus 423% for corrections and 241% for police), the fact remains that most of the increase went to prosecutions rather than the defense in order to handle the increased caseloads that generate plea bargaining.

Not surprisingly, plea bargaining results in a bias against poor clients, who are typically minorities, as well as the uneducated, who may not even know what is being done to them in the criminal justice process (Gorr, 2000; Kaminer, 1999; Palermo, White, and Wasserman, 1998). Stephen Bright, director of Atlanta's Southern Center for Human Rights, says it this way: "If you're the average poor person, you are going to be herded through the criminal justice system about like an animal is herded through the stockyards" (in Herbert, 1998, p. 15).

Some may argue that no one would enter a guilty plea for a crime he or she did not commit, but a person living in conditions of poverty who is charged with a minor crime and refuses to plead guilty will only guarantee himself or herself a longer stay in jail awaiting a hearing—often longer than the likely sentence to be imposed upon conviction through a guilty plea (R. Miller, 1997). If a public defender is representing the case, chances are the defendant will not have much of a chance to win at trial even if he or she is innocent because "[i]n many jurisdictions, public defenders and state appointed attorneys are grossly underpaid, poorly trained, or simply lack the resources and time to prepare for a case—a pattern documented in cases ranging from the most minor to the most consequential, capital crimes" (Weitzer, 1996, p. 113).

The U.S. Supreme Court has granted the defendant the right to a defense attorney during the plea-bargaining process (*Brady v. United States*, 1969). It is also required that the defendant voluntarily give his or her guilty plea (*Boykin v. Alabama*, 1969). When prosecutors offer a particular sentence in exchange for a guilty plea, they must keep their promise related to the sentence (*Santabella v. New York*, 1971). Finally, when defendants enter a guilty plea, they are asked numerous questions by the judge to ensure that they understand that they are giving up many constitutional rights and that the guilty plea was not coerced.

Coercion is not clearly defined for the defendant in this process. Pleas might be understood as coerced if one considers the quality of defense provided by public defenders. Oftentimes, defendants plead guilty because of the threat of losing at trial and receiving a much more severe sentence. Langbein (2000, p. 27) claims that "the plea bargaining system operates by threat." In the face of threats by the prosecution, defense attorneys essentially may tell their clients, "So you want your constitutional right to jury trial? By all means, be our guest. But beware. If you claim this right and are convicted, we will punish you twice, once for the offense, and once again for having displayed the temerity to exercise your constitutional right to jury trial." In other words, the goal of the public defender is to coerce clients into surrendering their rights by threatening them with the possibility of greater sanctions.

The work environment of public defenders, who are responsible for defending the indigent (those who cannot afford their own attorneys), is typically depressing. Public defenders have large caseloads and limited resources relative to the prosecution, they work long hours, and they receive low pay (Cole and Smith, 2007). The indigent defendant must know that the likelihood of winning is remote. The result should not be surprising: "Some public defenders seem to have little interest in using every possible strategy to defend their clients. On numerous occasions, legal errors are made by prosecutors and judges to which the public defender raises no objection. In addition, appeals are sometimes not initiated by public defenders even when chances of successful appeal seem to be good" (Cox and Wade, 1998, p. 149).

Note that the U.S. Constitution does not guarantee a competent attorney. In *Strickland v. Washington* (1984), the Supreme Court set forth the standard for competence. In essence, a defendant must be able to prove that his or her sentence was directly affected by the conduct of the defense attorney—an impossible standard to prove.

Factual guilt is not determined in plea bargaining as it would be at a criminal trial. Guilt is assumed rather than established. Langbein (2000, p. 31) calls plea bargaining "condemnation without adjudication"—that is, sentencing without an establishment of guilt. Little investigation of the case against the defendant is conducted. Witnesses and victims are not present to see or approve of justice being meted out to the guilty. The question addressed by plea bargaining is not whether the defendant is actually guilty of the charges but, rather, what to do with the defendant. And one more thing—when guilty people plea bargain, they receive relatively lighter sentences than those convicted at trial for all crimes (Smith, 1986). This means people convicted at trial for murder, rape, robbery, aggravated assault, burglary, drug possession, and drug trafficking get longer sentences than people convicted through plea bargains. And victims of crime have no say in the matter.

For all of these reasons, everyone seems to be against plea bargaining. It is surprising, then, that it happens so often:

> Conservatives believe it is a major loophole through which criminals beat the system and avoid punishment. Liberals, meanwhile, believe that it is a source of grave injustices: prosecutors deliberately "overcharge"; defense attorneys make deals rather than fight for their clients; defendants are coerced into waiving their right to a trial; some defendants get much better deals than others. (Walker, 1998, p. 153)

Cox and Wade (1998, p. 139) write, "Victims, the public, and the police are frequently unhappy about this practice, but if it were to be discontinued, the delays would be unconscionable." Thus, the large number of cases before today's courts seems to be driving the American plea-bargaining binge. Bradley (2000, p. 507) writes that the original approval of plea bargaining by the Supreme Court in *Santobello v. New York* (1971) "was based largely on the pragmatic concern that the criminal justice system could not afford to accord every defendant his constitutional rights, rather than on a claim that such a practice was inherently desirable."

When we shine a light on the outcome of justice in the United States, we see that the reality of plea bargaining is not consistent with the American ideal of the criminal trial, which is mentioned in the Declaration of Independence, three amendments to the U.S. Constitution, and scores of Supreme Court cases. Remember the two conceptions of justice discussed in Chapter 1—justice as an outcome and justice as a process. Then ask yourself: Does plea bargaining achieve either of these forms of justice? Donziger (1996, p. 182) answers that plea bargaining bestows "lenient treatment on the guilty" and "coercive treatment on the innocent." Either way, it is unjust. Plea bargaining achieves neither justice as a process nor justice as an outcome.

THE UNEQUAL RIGHT TO A DEFENSE IN THE UNITED STATES: PUBLIC VERSUS PRIVATE ATTORNEYS

Think about the so-called dream team that O. J. Simpson employed during his double murder trial in 1995. Not only did Simpson enjoy the talents of one of the best attorneys in the world, he also enjoyed the talents of many of the best attorneys in the world, as well as some of the top expert witnesses. Yet the "overwhelming majority of people accused of crimes" cannot afford even one attorney, and certainly not even one expert witness. In such cases, a defendant is granted one attorney who will have few resources and thus little ability to subject the evidence against his or her client to any scrutiny. This explains how, in the face of evidence against their clients, public defenders see their clients as guilty anyway and thus not worthy of a trial (Cole and Smith, 2007), especially since they carry 350 cases or more at a time and they receive so little of the criminal justice resources in any given year (Donziger, 1996).

The American Bar Association calls the underfunding of defense attorneys for the indigent a "crisis of extraordinary proportions" (Tuohy, 1995). As explained by the National Criminal Justice Commission, "[t]he Constitutional right to an attorney is meaningful only to the extent that resources are available to adequately prepare a defense," which "includes access to investigators, expert witnesses, paralegals, and support staff, as well as time to research the law and prepare the legal motions" (Donziger, 1996, p. 189).

Everyone in the United States does have the right to counsel, as granted by the Sixth Amendment to the U.S. Constitution. And the U.S. Supreme Court granted indigents the right to a defense in felony cases in the case of *Gideon v. Wainwright* (1962). But although the poor thus have an equal right to counsel, they clearly do not have the right to equal counsel (Cole, 1999; Reiman, 2006). The average courthouse regular who is assigned by the court to indigent defendants has more than 1,000 cases a year to handle (Cole and Smith, 2007); he or she has no time to investigate the facts of a case and put on an appropriate and thorough defense. Compare this with prosecutors "who can draw on big police departments, teams of investigators and lawyers to prepare their cases." It's no wonder many prosecutors enjoy conviction rates of more than 90%. Even the "typical murder defendant has little money and is represented by an underpaid, overworked public defender" (Streisand, 1994, p. 63). Adding to the built-in bias against the typical criminal defendant in the United States is the fact that criminal defense attorneys are usually from "less prestigious law schools, have less training, and come from lower socioeconomic backgrounds" (Kappeler et al., 2000, citing Ladinsky, 1984).

Why would a public defender, who is ideally responsible for upholding the constitutional right to due process of law for the most vulnerable of all citizens—poor defendants faced with the incredible power of the government—take part in plea bargaining? Reiman (1998, p. 118) answers, "Because the public defender works in day-to-day contact with the prosecutor and the judge, the pressures on him or her to negotiate a plea as quickly as possible, instead of rocking the boat by threatening to go to trial, are even greater than those that work on court-assigned counsel."

Various court rulings also permit and often encourage judges to treat inadequate defense attorneys as effective even when they fail to investigate the facts of the case or to cross-examine crucial witnesses, fall asleep during testimony, or come to court drunk (Cole, 1999). Perhaps it is easy to understand the claim of Kappeler et al. (2000, p. 225) that public defenders are generally less likely than private attorneys to get cases against their clients dropped or to achieve an acquittal: "In essence, justice is correlated with the ability to pay by the hour."

According to surveys of state and federal inmates, about 75% of African Americans and Hispanics in any given year used public defense attorneys. Caucasians were only slightly less likely to use them. Among federal prison inmates, African Americans were the most likely to use public defense attorneys (about 66%), versus just over more than half of Hispanics and Caucasians. Those represented by public attorneys met with their attorneys later in the criminal justice process and less frequently than those represented by private attorneys (Bureau of Justice Statistics, 2003). This may lead you to believe that private attorneys must do a better job than public attorneys.

Yet when one compares the various outcomes of court processes when clients have publicly provided defense attorneys (such as public defenders) and private attorneys (at both the state and federal level), the following facts emerge:

- Defendants with private attorneys are more likely than defendants with public attorneys to be released prior to the disposition of their cases.
- Conviction rates of defendants with public and private attorneys are nearly identical.

- Defendants with private attorneys are less likely than defendants with public attorneys to be sentenced to prison for their crimes and more likely to be sentenced to probation.
- Of those defendants sentenced to prison, those with public attorneys are sentenced to shorter sentences than defendants with private attorneys (Bureau of Justice Statistics, 2003).

The Bureau of Justice Statistics asserts that the type of crime is most likely what determines the type of attorney one has and the likely outcome of the case (this means the relationship between attorney type and outcome is spurious or dependent on other factors). This does not deny a bias in the criminal justice process; it just means the bias is in the criminal law, which defines some harmful acts as more harmful and more serious than others. As you learned in Chapter 4, the acts of the poor are more likely to be defined as serious crimes. Since the poor are, by definition, indigent, they are more likely to be served by public attorneys. This means they will be less likely to be released until their cases are disposed of, more likely to sit in jail while their cases are processed, and more likely to be sentenced to prison for their crimes. The fact that they spend less time than those with private attorneys when sentenced to prison serves as evidence of the effects of the courtroom workgroups on American justice: Public counsel are part of the courtroom workgroup and can gain lower sentences for their clients through bargaining.

In federal courts, defendants charged with white-collar crimes are most likely to use private attorneys, including more than 60% of those charged with regulatory offenses and more than 40% charged with fraud. This means they will be more likely to be released until their cases are disposed of, less likely to sit in jail while their cases are processed, and less likely to be sentenced to prison for their crimes. So even though public defenders are "experts" in criminal practice, whereas private attorneys may not be, public attorneys are often "among the most inexperienced" lawyers, often recent law school graduates in "positions . . . typically characterized by low salaries and limited support services" (Merlo and Benekos, 2000, p. 57).

THE "EXCEPTIONAL CASE" OF TRIAL

Cases that are not dismissed by the prosecutor and are not plea-bargained end up going to trial. That is, a trial results only when other forms of case disposition are either not sought or not obtained (Schmalleger, 2006). As noted earlier, trials are the exception to the rule of plea bargaining. They are very rare.

There are significant problems with the American trial process, most notably how rarely trials occur. Aside from that, several stages of the criminal trial process seem to result in biases against the poor and people of color. Before I move on to those stages and outline the main problems associated with bias, I want to point out that Americans charged with crimes are "innocent until proven guilty" of their crimes at trials. Americans ideally enjoy this **presumption of innocence** before and during trials. Former U.S. Supreme Court Justice Thurgood Marshall once said that American "principles of justice declare that the defendant is as innocent on the day before his trial as he is on the morning after his acquittal" (in Gaines et al., 2000, p. 338). This is the ideal, but do all Americans equally enjoy this presumption?

Stages of the Criminal Trial

Stages of the typical American trial include **voir dire**, opening statements, the presentation of the prosecution's case, the presentation of the defense's case, the calling of rebuttal witnesses, closing arguments by the prosecution, closing arguments by the defense, and jury instructions by the judge. After these stages, the jury is given the case by the judge and the deliberations begin. Finally, the jury issues its verdict and, if the defendant is found guilty, the sentence is subsequently handed down by the judge (Peoples, 2000; Stuckey et al., 2001).

Voir Dire

Voir dire, meaning "to speak the truth" (Gaines et al., 2000, p. 343), is an examination of potential jurors to ensure a fair trial for the defendant. Its ideal purpose is to gain a cross-section of the community so that the defendant can have a jury of his or her "peers." Potential jurors must answer questions verbally and/or in writing about their potential biases. Ideally, *voir dire* will result in an impartial jury for the trial of the accused. We want juries "to have no axes to grind, no prejudgments about the people or issues they confront. We also want them to have the ability to empathize with others, to evaluate credibility, to know what is fair" (Minow, 2000, p. 365). Thus, an unlimited number of jurors can be eliminated through **challenges for cause**, if a potential bias is identified. A limited number also may be eliminated through **peremptory challenges**, where no cause needs to be identified. A person may be excused from the jury in a death penalty case for cause if he or she absolutely refuses to impose the death penalty on a convicted murderer under any circumstances (see Chapter 10). A person may be excused from a jury for cause if he or she has racist feelings and the case deals with an interracial crime.

There are at least three significant problems with the first stage of the criminal trial. First, some groups are underrepresented in jury pools. Second, peremptory challenges can be used against certain groups without explanation. Third, jury consultants can be used to help select sympathetic juries. Each of these problems results in a bias in favor of people with greater resources. I discuss these problems next.

Jury pools for state trials come mostly from voter registration, though some states select juries from other sources, such as motor vehicle registration, telephone directories, and tax rolls. Since voting lists are the primary source of jury pools, juries tend to be less representative of poor people, people of color, the young, and the uneducated, because these members of society are less likely to vote. As a result, poor people, people of color, and young people are less likely to be represented by juries who are like them. If this affects the outcomes of cases, it would likely do so in a manner biased against these groups. The *Capital Jury Project*, discussed more in Chapter 10, shows that Caucasian males are more likely to vote for a death sentence for a convicted murderer, in part because they are more likely to see future dangerousness in the convicted offenders. African American males are less prone to vote for a death sentence for a convicted murderer, in part because they are more likely to see remorse in the convicted offenders.

Prosecutors and defense attorneys can use peremptory challenges to eliminate potential jurors without any explanation. Thus, lawyers can reject people for jury service on the basis of their style of dress or their demeanor without giving any valid reason. Bradley (2000, p. 508) claims that "peremptory challenges are largely a matter of wild guesses about how jurors will decide the case based upon their answers to one or two questions in the voir dire." Even if this is true, peremptory challenges allow a very troublesome practice. As in the use of drug courier profiles by police, these challenges allow attorneys to eliminate people who they feel "look wrong" (Kennedy, 1997). Additionally, racial minorities can be, and often are, denied the opportunity to serve on juries, even though rejecting potential jurors on the basis of race is specifically illegal based on the Supreme Court case, *Batson v. Kentucky* (1986) (Bohm, 2007). Lawyers use race as a proxy to develop peremptory challenges, in part because of racial myths and stereotypes, in part because courts allow subjective qualifications for jury service, and in part because it simply benefits their cases (Kennedy, 1997). Minorities are simultaneously inhibited from jury service for a variety of other reasons, many intimately related to their social class, social status, and past run-ins with the law.

The reality of jury selection, very different from the ideal, is that neither the defense nor the prosecution actually seeks an impartial jury. Barber (1994) explains that each side seeks out a jury that is likely to be partial to their side of the story. The problem with this for justice is that poor people and people of color are less able to hire professional jury consultants to analyze potential jurors so that they can select a jury more likely to sympathize with the defendant (Smith, 1993; Varinsky, 1993). Wealthy individuals, such as O. J. Simpson, can afford to hire the best jury consultants that money can buy and, in essence, have a much greater chance that a jury sympathetic with the defendant will find reasonable doubt and thus vote to acquit (McElhaney, 1998; Smith, 1993; Varinsky, 1993). The jury in the O. J. Simpson case was hand-picked with the help of a millionaire jury consultant who surveyed thousands of people prior to *voir dire* in order to identify the type of person who would make a sympathetic jury. The defense was able to isolate eight questions from an 85-page questionnaire that would identify jurors sympathetic to the defense's argument (Miller, 1995). The final O. J. Simpson jury was made up entirely of people who did not regularly read the newspaper, 75% of whom thought that Simpson was not likely to have committed the murders because he excelled at football, and 42% of whom thought that it was acceptable to use force on a family member (Davis and Davis, 1995). Clearly, everything about the O. J. Simpson case was unusual. Yet it serves as an excellent example of how jury consultants can be used to create a jury that will find reasonable doubt.

The National Criminal Justice Commission outlines many other problems with the American jury system. Jurors are exposed to endless waiting, must put up with insensitive questioning, are sometimes sequestered from their families, may lose substantial income, and can be eliminated without just cause through peremptory challenge (Donziger, 1996, p. 184).

Opening Statements

After a jury is impaneled, both sides of the case (the prosecution and the defense) make **opening statements** to lay the foundation of their cases. Opening statements are not allowed to be argumentative and cannot be considered as evidence by the jury. Opening statements are road maps, laying out where each side intends to take its case.

Prosecution Presents Its Case

Because the prosecution has the burden of proving its case beyond a reasonable doubt, it presents its case first. Its goal is to present relevant facts to the jury that prove that the named defendant(s) committed the named crime(s). Ingraham (1994) explains that because defendants are innocent in the eyes of the law, they do not have to present a case unless they feel the prosecution can prove its case that they are guilty of crimes beyond a reasonable doubt. Rush (2000, p. 113) defines **reasonable doubt** as "[t]he state of mind of jurors in which, after the comparison and consideration of all the evidence, they cannot say that they feel an abiding conviction, a moral certainty, of the truth of a criminal charge against a defendant." Essentially, if another theory of the crime for which the defendant is accused is reasonably likely to be true, jurors are required by law to find the defendant not guilty of the crime, even if they think the person is actually guilty of the act(s). Why do we have such a high standard of proof to establish legal guilt at criminal trials? "This high standard of proof in criminal cases reflects a fundamental social value—the belief that it is worse to convict an innocent individual than to let a guilty one go free." At least, that is the ideal (Rush, 2000, p. 113).

The reality of the prosecution is that it is generally much more powerful and better equipped to present its case than the defense. Most accused criminals, who are indigent and thus cannot hire private attorneys, do not have the resources to subject the state's evidence to meaningful scrutiny. This means little or no investigation of the charges against the defendant, no expert witnesses to rebut or refute the prosecution's case, and very short trials. The presumption of innocence may be a myth for most criminal defendants in the United States.

Defense Presents Its Case

If the defense attorney feels the defense must answer the charges of the prosecution, the defense will present its own case. It is not required that the defense present a case. If the defense feels that the prosecution's case is weak, it can ask that the charges be dropped against the defendant through a **directed verdict**. If the defense puts on its case, it will either provide contrary evidence to the prosecution, offer an **alibi** (e.g., the accused was somewhere else at the time of the crime), or present an **affirmative defense** (which admits the defendant committed the act or acts of which he or she is charged but the defendant is nevertheless not guilty of a "crime"). The purpose of the defense presentation is to raise reasonable doubt so the defendant will not be convicted. Once again, wealthier clients who can afford better attorneys are more likely to ensure that reasonable doubt will be found because they are more likely to subject the evidence to independent examinations, to construct alternative theories of the crime, and to hire expert witnesses in their defense.

Rebuttal Witnesses

After each side has presented its primary case, both sides have the option of calling **rebuttal witnesses** to discredit the testimony of previous witnesses for the other side. Clearly, poor clients and people of color are generally at a disadvantage here because of their lack of resources and the quality of their attorneys.

Closing Arguments

At the end of each side's case, prosecutors and defense attorneys are permitted to make **closing arguments** to the jury that presents the facts in a manner that is most favorable to their side. Prosecutors might choose to ignore evidence pointing to the innocence of the defendant, and defense attorneys might choose to point out alternative theories of who committed the crime(s). Truth is irrelevant here; what counts are the strong points of each side's case. Obviously, attorneys with some incentive to argue vehemently for the benefit of their clients will make better closing arguments on their clients' behalf.

Jury Instructions

After closing arguments, the judge instructs the jury as to how the law bears on their decisions. At a minimum, the **jury instructions** will include a definition of "reasonable doubt" and will explain what elements of the crime or crimes must be established to show guilt of the defendant. Both sides will meet with the judge and hammer out the specific content and wording of the instructions. Because of the importance of jury instructions, "one would expect jury instructions to be carefully drafted to maximize juror comprehension, but they are not" (Steele and Thornburg, 2000, p. 118). Some research shows that jurors may not even understand jury instructions given to them, a frightening thought given that the jurors are expected to follow these instructions carefully when deliberating about the guilt or innocence of the accused (Dattu, 1998; Steele and Thornburg, 1991). Once again, private attorneys of powerful and wealthy citizens have a significant advantage here, as they can assure that the instructions are most favorable for their clients. In death penalty cases, there is disturbing evidence that juries often do not understand much of the jury instructions (see Chapter 10).

Jury Deliberations

Once juries are given the case by the judge, they may consider only the evidence entered into the trial to determine whether the person(s) charged with the crime(s) is/are legally guilty beyond a reasonable doubt. In almost every state, the verdict must be unanimous, or else the result is a **hung jury** or a **mistrial**. It is hard to know whether juries follow the law in making decisions because of the secrecy afforded to jury deliberations. Much research into jury deliberations (mainly from mock trials) shows that jurors consider a lot of what they are not supposed to consider, including the defendant's appearance, his or her past record, and other facts not admitted to trial but learned about from other sources (Devine, 1988). Postinterview verdicts with jury members, mock juries, a few televised jury deliberations, and even transcripts of jury deliberations on the Internet show that juries frequently consider evidence they should not consider (MacCoun, 1990; Kassin, 2000). This is why some argue that jury deliberations should be open to judicial review to make sure that justice is being done according to the law (e.g., see Ruprecht, 1997). Gershman (2000) maintains that jurors consider strong opening statements (which may include promises of evidence to be presented even when such evidence is not delivered during trial) and purposefully mentioned inadmissible evidence, which is not supposed to be considered by the jury.

CONCLUSION

Scholars have argued that no trial system is deserving of public respect if it cannot be trusted to acquit the innocent and convict the guilty, if it fails to treat those who come into contact with the system with respect, and if does not appropriate judicial resources wisely. The American court system, highly consistent with a crime control model of criminal justice, handles cases in an administrative manner rather than an adversarial manner. More resources are given to prosecutors than to defense attorneys, adding to the immense power of American prosecutors. The clear evidence of bias in plea bargaining and the use of bail and preventive detention, as well as the low quality of defense afforded to those most in need, provides further evidence that the criminal justice network fails to do justice as expected. In essence, the courts have been left to do the best they can with increasing numbers of cases and relatively fewer resources than police and corrections.

Issue in Depth—Wrongful Convictions

It is impossible to know how many innocent people are convicted of crimes they did not commit each year. Huff, Rattner, and Sagarin (1996, p. 53), in their book, *Convicted But Innocent: Wrongful Conviction and Public Policy*, write, "Quite clearly, there is no accurate, scientific way to determine how many innocent people are convicted, or put another way, how many of those convicted of crimes are innocent." Yet, given recent research, we know it happens quite often. For example, Christianson (2006), in his book, *Innocent: Inside Wrongful Conviction Cases*, documents 42 cases of innocent people who were wrongly convicted due to errors in eyewitness identification, ineffective defense counsel, as well as more troubling cases of coerced false confessions, fabrication of evidence, and official misconduct.

We also do not know how many innocent people are executed for crimes they did not commit. A recent analysis by Cohen (2003), in his book, *The Wrong Men: America's Epidemic of Wrongful Death Row Convictions*, claims more than 100 wrongful convictions for capital crimes due to faulty eyewitness testimony and police and prosecutorial misconduct. Thankfully, most people wrongly convicted of capital crimes are not actually executed. One study, published as the book, *In Spite of Innocence* (Radelet, Bedau, and Putnam, 1992), found that 400 persons were wrongfully convicted of capital crimes, but only 23 were actually executed (and 22 others came within 72 hours of being executed). I will revisit the issue of wrongful convictions in capital cases in Chapter 10.

What follows here is a brief discussion of some actual cases in which people have been wrongfully convicted of crimes, as well as the factors that produce wrongful convictions in the United States. Of most importance for the main argument of this book is that wrongful convictions are obviously a direct threat to justice—to justice as an outcome (because the factually guilty are not punished for their wrongdoings and because innocent people do not deserve to be punished) and to justice as a process (because wrongful convictions suggest that the criminal justice network is not fair and unbiased). Dinitz (1996, pp. xii–xiii) states it this way:

> Wrongful convictions, however infrequent, are anathema to the American due process system and to all who believe in the fairness of our law enforcement and judicial systems and the constitutional protections guaranteed individual citizens. Not only do such wrongful convictions violate trust in our system, but . . . such convictions undermine public safety by leaving the "true" positives—the guilty—in the community to commit future grave offenses.

So a lot is at stake when wrongful convictions occur. First, the "conviction of the innocent leaves the guilty free to commit more crimes, thus threatening public safety" and "each instance of the conviction of an innocent enhances the possibility that there will be more not-guilty verdicts against the truly guilty" (Huff, Rattner, and Sagarin, 1996, p. 12) because of a distrust in the government resulting from wrongful convictions.

As I have stated, no one can know for sure how often errors are made, but a statement by Huff and his associates (1996, p. xxii) suggests the significance of the problem. They write, "The American criminal justice system is so large and has so many arrests each year that even if the system were 99.5% accurate, it would still generate more than 10,000 wrongful convictions a year for the eight serious index crimes alone" and even more for relatively less serious crimes. Huff et al. mailed a survey to various actors in the Ohio criminal justice network to estimate how frequently wrongful convictions occur; they make what they call "a conservative prevalence estimation made by a largely conservative sample," mostly because the people they surveyed would have reasons to deny the wrongful conviction of the innocent (p. 55). After throwing out cases where there were serious and reasonable doubts about the innocence of the convicted parties, along with cases in which people were punished and subsequently released but their innocence was not clearly established, they were left with individual cases where actual innocence is known. Some of these cases are discussed below. The first of these would not be included by Huff, Rattner, and Sagarin for there is still some doubt about the convicted man's guilt; yet I include it because it points out the absurdity of how our criminal justice network sometimes operates.

- James Hicks was a 31-year-old man who had served 7 years of a 10-year sentence for the murder of his wife after she disappeared in Maine. He denied on the stand that he had killed his wife and also admitted to having been living for about 5 years with another woman, with whom he had fathered two children. After being sentenced to prison, he attempted to marry his girlfriend but was denied a marriage license because there was no death certificate for his presumed dead wife. Huff et al. (1996, p. 7) write, "So, although he was convicted of murdering his wife on the basis of evidence that convinced 12 men and women beyond a reasonable doubt, the authorities entertained some doubt that his wife was dead."

In the remaining cases, we know the wrong people were actually convicted and/or punished for crimes they did not commit:

- David Fedderson is a Caucasian man convicted of raping a woman he did not know in Dubuque, Iowa. The victim identified Fedderson as her attacker as he walked in a crowd of people after her attack. Fedderson was walking along a street he normally walked along, and he had no history of violent behavior; but he also had no alibi for his whereabouts at the time of the crime. Only one person, the victim, saw the attacker, so her eyewitness testimony alone led to his conviction for rape. When Fedderson rose to speak on his behalf after his conviction, he did not express remorse for his actions or sympathy for the victim, for he knew he was innocent of the crime. Fedderson spent 2 years in prison before he was finally able to convince all parties that he was in fact innocent. The same judge who convicted him now set him free and stated that the fact that an innocent man could be convicted "is scary."

- Nathaniel Carter was sentenced to life imprisonment after being convicted of the stabbing death of Clarice Herndon. His conviction was based almost solely on the testimony of the actual killer, his ex-wife, who was found by police at the scene with blood on her hands (they assumed she, too, had been attacked). After Carter had spent 2 years in prison, his ex-wife came forward, after being promised immunity from being prosecuted, and testified that she had committed the murder.
- Johnny Binder is an African American man convicted in Houston, Texas, for a robbery committed by a group of African Americans driving a yellow Cadillac similar to Binder's car. Binder lived in Houston but was in Dallas at the time of the crime. Binder had no criminal record and knew he was innocent of the crime, but after hearing about the make and color of the car involved in the crime, he voluntarily went to the police to tell them that he was not involved in the crime. Binder was arrested and convicted by an all-white jury, despite the fact that several eyewitnesses claimed that he was not involved. After Binder had spent 4 years in prison, the real criminals were discovered and Binder was taken back to court where, however, he could not be set free or given a new trial by the judge. Binder was returned to his cell. An appeal for a writ of *habeas corpus* was denied because "it was not the appropriate route to be taken when there is a claim for a new trial based on newly discovered evidence" (Huff et al., 1996, p. 18). Binder was eventually set free by the judge, even though she did not have the authority to do so, and the state granted him a special pardon that did not contain anything about Binder's actual innocence.
- Todd Neely was a young man in Florida convicted of raping one of his neighbors. A woman in Neely's apartment complex had been raped by a boy she described as no older than 16 who wore braces on his teeth. Neely was 18 years old, did not have braces, and was 11 miles away having dinner with his parents at the time of the rape. The victim picked out a photograph of Neely from a photo line-up, but the photograph was several years old and showed Neely at an age more similar to that of the attacker. It turned out that the real rapist was a 14-year-old boy who also lived in the complex and who had a history of exhibitionism and voyeurism in the neighborhood (he also had told friends that he was the one who committed the rape). Neely was eventually freed, after spending 92 days in jail, mostly because his family spent $300,000 of their own money investigating the case. This case shows what can happen when the police and prosecution zero in on a suspect and ignore obvious evidence of his or her innocence.

Given all of these shocking cases, you may wonder why such wrongful convictions occur. According to Huff et al. (1996), the most common cause, responsible for more than half of wrongful convictions, is eyewitness identification—that is, victims and witnesses who pick out the wrong person even though they may truly believe that the people they have identified are the real criminals. Also of significance is

police and prosecutorial overzealousness: the anxiety to solve a case; the ease with which one having such anxiety is willing to believe, on the slightest evidence of the most negligible nature, that the culprit is in hand; the willingness to use improper, unethical, and illegal means to obtain a conviction when one believes that the person at the bar is guilty. (p. 64, emphasis in original)

EYEWITNESS TESTIMONY

Consider the case of Jeffrey Streeter, convicted and sentenced to a year in jail for the assault of an elderly man. Streeter, who was uninvolved in the case, had been sitting outside the courtroom when the defense attorney asked him to come in and sit in the defendant's usual place. Although the defendant was also in the courtroom, three eyewitnesses to the assault picked Streeter as the man who had committed the crime, as if, because Streeter was sitting where the defendant normally sits, he must be guilty. Streeter spent one night in jail before the error was realized. As this defense attorney had set out to demonstrate, eyewitness testimony is patently unreliable. Yet many consider it to be undeniable proof of guilt, and cases lacking eyewitness identification are often dismissed as "purely circumstantial" and thus inherently weaker.

Research demonstrates that human brains (of witnesses and victims of crimes, for example) store information from environmental experiences in chemical bits and pieces. When attempting to recall events, our brains actually reconstruct these events from the fragments stored in our brains. During the stages of acquisition, retention, and retrieval, falsehoods are pulled into our memories so that we "remember" things that really did not happen (Loftus, 1979; Gerrie, Belcher, and Garry, 2006; Marsh, 2007; Wells, Memon, and Penrod, 2006). As one example, a victim of crime may retrieve pieces of information gleaned from discussions with friends and families, news clippings, and other sources, and may wrongly attribute these recollections to the criminal event. Buckhout (1974, p. 23) explains why eyewitness identification is inherently unreliable:

> Research and courtroom experience provide ample evidence that an eyewitness to a crime is being asked to be something and do something that a normal human being was not created to be or do. Human perception is sloppy and uneven, albeit remarkably effective in serving our need to create structure out of experience. In an investigation or in court, however, a witness is often asked to play the role of a kind of tape recorder on whose tape the events of the crime have left an impression. . . . Both sides, and usually the witness, too, succumb to the fallacy that everything was recorded and can be played back through questioning.

Yet, as noted by Wells et al. (2006, p. 45): "Analyses of DNA exoneration cases since 1992 reveal that mistaken eyewitness identification was involved in the vast majority of these convictions, accounting for more convictions of innocent people than all other factors combined."

As it turns out, the criminal justice process itself serves to reinforce the likelihood that innocent people will be wrongly convicted. For example, witnesses and victims may see a photo lineup or actual physical lineup of real people and then choose one as the offender. From that point on, the face of the person picked will be the offender, even if it is not the actual offender. When asked to pick out the offender at court, witnesses and victims will point to that person as the offender because his or her identity matches that of the person picked out from the lineup. The memory of the face from the crime may be replaced with the memory of the face from the lineup. That this may be the wrong face is not considered by the person who is convinced he or she has chosen the right person (e.g., see Brown, Defenbacher, and Sturgill, 1977).

As a college student, I was one of two witnesses to a failed burglary attempt. Ironically, I had just watched a video in one of my criminology classes about the unreliability of eyewitness identification. In the video, a college professor set up an experiment whereby a stranger walked into the classroom, took the professor's bag from the desk, and then ran away. After the offender had left, the professor said, "All I recall is that the man had a large nose." Many of the subjects noted to the police that they recalled the man having a distinctive nose (even though he did not). One witness (who was wearing a hat) said he remembered the man wearing a hat (even though he did not). Most of the students could not pick out the actual offender from a photo lineup when the offender's photo was included. When the actual offender's photo was not included, many of the student witnesses picked out an innocent person.

So, when I witnessed the burglary attempt, I made sure I was prepared to provide a perfect description to the police. Here's what happened: Late one night I was up sick, unable to sleep. I heard someone hanging around outside, checking the doors and window screens. After listening for a while, I heard someone trying to force his way into my next-door neighbor's bedroom window. I went outside to see what was going on, as did a neighbor on the other side of the apartment, and we scared the offender away. He ran right by me, so I got a great look at him. I followed him down the stairs and proceeded to watch him climb a fence to get away. As I watched him run away, I took mental notes about the offender's appearance.

When the police arrived, they asked me what he looked like. My description was very precise and included details about the offender's height, weight, hair color and style, approximate age, clothing, shoes—even shoelaces! About two hours later (around 4:00 A.M.), the police came back to my apartment to ask me to accompany them to the rear of an abandoned house, where they had apprehended someone who resembled the offender. Upon arriving, the police shone a bright spotlight on the man and asked me if this was the offender. This man had been tracked by police dogs from the scene of the attempted burglary (when he climbed the fence to get away, his watch, along with his scent, got stuck at the top of the fence). The apprehended man was exactly like the man I described, with one significant exception—he was slightly shorter and heavier than I remembered. The police asked me if I could be sure that this was the man (I could not ethically say that I was 100% sure it was he, even though it had to be based on the dogs tracking his scent). He was too stocky to be the offender I saw.

As we waited in a police squad car, I asked the other witness what he had told the police, and he said that he thought the offender was taller and thinner than the man they had apprehended. This made me very uncomfortable—how could it be that we both had been so wrong about what we thought the offender looked like, given that the man the police apprehended was wearing the same outfit, including the same shoes and even shoelaces, had the same hair color and braids as I had described, and was also a Hispanic male? As I have thought about that experience over the years, I realized that my run-in with the burglar was not unlike the experiences of most crime victims and witnesses: I saw the man very briefly, it was late at night, I was tired when I witnessed the crime, and so on. Why shouldn't I expect to be wrong about some details? More important, how can the criminal justice network be so dependent on eyewitness identifications such as this one when they are so unreliable? Yet prosecutors are more willing to press charges and pursue convictions in court when eyewitnesses are part of the case, and jurors are more likely to convict given eyewitness testimony, even given results like those in the cases described here. Cases lacking an eyewitnesses are often described as merely circumstantial in nature and therefore seen as less reliable.

OVERZEALOUSNESS

As for overzealousness by police and prosecutors, I restrict my comments to the following main point: We must expect our police and prosecutors to pursue arrests and convictions zealously (in the pursuit of justice as an outcome); it is the current "tough on crime" environment that makes overzealousness more likely. Huff et al. (1996, p. 71) write that such overzealousness

> might come from a desire to add points to a scorecard, to enhance a reputation as a tough and successful prosecutor because of an impending election, or to receive commendation and promotion in the police department for having nabbed a vicious criminal and solved a difficult case . . . may sometimes derive from the inability, unwillingness, or lack of funds and personnel available to police to make true and proper investigations . . . [and] might also conceal bigotry and racism, or sometimes greed.

Other sources of overzealousness may be "the inability, unwillingness, or lack of funds and personnel available to police to make true and proper investigations."

Partly because of the overzealousness of the police and prosecution, as well as because of the presumption of guilt that accompanies an arrest and the immense power of the prosecution relative to the typical defense attorney, many innocent people will plead guilty (and some even confess to the police) to crimes they did not commit. Many of these plea bargains result in immediate freedom for the accused, through either release for time served or a probation sentence. Remember—a plea of guilty is not necessarily an admission of guilt. It can be as much a strategy for avoiding punishment as a not guilty plea is by a factually guilty suspect.

Consider this case involving presumption of guilt: Willie Jones, a 33-year-old African American man with a criminal record involving many minor criminal acts, was arrested for using Connecticut subway tokens on the New York City subway system. Jones was remanded to jail awaiting his arraignment, referred to a public defender, and thereafter confronted with a long rap sheet of serious crimes and an outstanding warrant for jumping bail on another charge. Jones correctly pointed out that the rap sheet was not his, that it must belong to another Willie Jones. The other Jones had a file with no photo and no fingerprints, so the police and his own attorney did not believe that he was really "innocent." He spent 3 months in jail awaiting trial because he refused to plead guilty to the serious charge for which the other Jones was accused. On his trial date the mistake was realized and Jones was released. So much for "innocent until proven guilty."

I will concede that many of those wrongfully convicted, like Willie Jones, do in fact have criminal records. Some may assert that this gives the police reason to suspect them of future criminal activity. I want to point out the irony of this expectation: Society gets upset when criminals continue to offend after their punishment, even though we simultaneously seem to expect them to commit more crimes.

At the extreme end of overzealousness are false confessions. Police may occasionally resort to any and all tactics necessary to gain convictions of people they truly believe to be guilty so that the end—a conviction, or justice as an outcome—in their minds justifies the means, violating justice as a process. In fact, some early texts on criminal interrogations and confessions encourage trickery by police to encourage confessions, which is actually allowed by courts (e.g., see Inbau and Reid, 1967). Cases of false confessions abound in the United States.

The case of James Richardson, a poor African American farm worker with an IQ of only 77, stands out. Richardson confessed to poisoning seven of his own children and stepchildren and was imprisoned and sentenced to death in 1968. Richardson served 22 years before being freed for these crimes, which he did not commit. The prosecution, suggesting that Richardson laced his children's lunches with poison and planned their deaths in advance, showed evidence that Richardson had sought life insurance policies for his children right before their deaths (in fact, a door-to-door insurance salesman had visited the day before and simply left his card). The children's babysitter, who was ultimately admitted to medical care for Alzheimer's disease, admitted more than one hundred times that she had killed the children. Richardson said he had been beaten into confessing his crime. The sheriff's deputy who allegedly coerced the confession out of Richardson probably believed that Richardson was guilty, but his unjust means resulted in an unjust outcome.

Such cases serve as the ugliest incidents uncovered by the research of Huff et al. (1996), cases that "involved outright lying, the fabrication and alteration of evidence, the intimidation and coaching of witnesses, and perjury and the suborning of perjury" (p. 143). As I stated earlier, my assertion is that these tactics, and thus wrongful convictions, are more likely in the current get-tough attitude promoted by politicians and emphasized in media coverage of crime and criminal justice. The research shows that wrongful convictions often start with a presumption of guilt on the part of criminal justice actors (characteristic of a crime control model of justice) and are made more likely because of numerous system breakdowns (which occur more often in the assembly-line process of American criminal justice).

KEY TERMS

abscond	directed verdict	peremptory challenges
acquitted	dual court system	plea bargaining
adjudicator	fully secured bail	precedent
administrator	general jurisdiction	presumption of
affirmative defense	going rate	innocence
alibi	horizontal bargaining	pretrial phase
appellate courts	house counsel for police	preventive detention
assigned counsel programs	hung jury	private attorneys
bail	indictment	prosecutor
challenges for cause	indigents	public defender systems
charge bargaining	information	reasonable doubt
circuit courts	initial appearance	rebuttal witnesses
closing arguments	judge	release into third-party
coercion	jump bail	custody
community defender	jurisdiction	release on own recognizance
organization	jury instructions	representative of the court
conditional release	mistrial	specific or limited jurisdiction
contracting attorney	nationally known attorneys	*stare decisis*
programs	negotiator	trial counsel for police
courthouse regulars	opening statements	unsecured bail
courtroom workgroup	panel attorneys	vertical bargaining
defense attorney	percentage bail	voir dire

DISCUSSION QUESTIONS

1. Why is the U.S. court system called a dual court system?
2. Define the term *jurisdiction*.
3. Contrast trial courts with appellate courts.
4. List and discuss the key functions of U.S. courts.
5. Identify the main actors in the courtroom workgroup and discuss the main roles of each member.
6. What factors affect whether prosecutors decide to press charges against accused criminals?
7. What important decisions are made during the pretrial phase of courts?
8. What is bail?
9. What is meant by saying that bail is not intended to be punishment?
10. Identify the main types of bail and discuss alternatives to bail.
11. How is preventive detention justified?
12. What are some of the main problems associated with the administration of bail?
13. What is plea bargaining?
14. Explain how plea bargaining is inconsistent with the ideal of justice as a process, as well as justice as an outcome.
15. Do you think that guilty pleas are ever coerced? Why or why not?
16. Is there a difference in the quality of the defense offered by private versus public defense attorneys? Why or why not?
17. Given how rare trials are in the United States, does the typical defendant have a reasonable expectation of trial?
18. Identify and discuss the main stages of the criminal trial.
19. What are some problems with the stages of the criminal trial that may bias trials in favor of the government and against the defendant?
20. What factors produce wrongful convictions?

CHAPTER

8

PUNISHMENT: DOES IT WORK AND IS IT FAIR?

1. Introduction
2. An Introduction to Sentencing
a. Types of Sentences
   • Box 8-1.   Facts About Three-Strikes Laws
3. Methods of Punishment
   • Box 8-2.   Typical Rules of Probation
   • Box 8-3.   Some Types of Intermediate Sanctions
   a. Punishment Facts
4. Why Do We Punish?
   a. Retribution
   b. Incapacitation
   c. Deterrence
   • Box 8-4.   Deterrence in American Punishment
   d. Rehabilitation
   e. Toward Restoration
   f. Punishment: A Summary
   • Box 8-5.   Restorative Justice
5. Is Punishment Effective?
   a. What We've Learned from Offenders
   b. What We've Learned from Other Criminal Justice Research
      • Box 8-6.   What Works, What Doesn't, What's Promising
6. Bias in the Sentencing Process
   • Box 8-7.   Some Individuals Sentenced Under Three-Strikes Laws
7. Conclusion
8. Issue in Depth—C. Ray Jeffery Explains the Failure of American Punishment
9. Key Terms
10. Discussion Questions

INTRODUCTION

This chapter examines the posttrial phase of the criminal courts—sentencing of the guilty by the courts to some form of punishment. I illustrate types of sentences available to sentencing judges and methods of punishment in the United States, including probation, imprisonment, and intermediate sanctions. A detailed discussion of why we punish provides insight into what's wrong with the American approach to punishment. I also show what we have learned about the effectiveness of various types of punishment. The chapter concludes with an examination of bias in the sentencing process.

AN INTRODUCTION TO SENTENCING

A **sentence** is a penalty or sanction imposed on a person by a court upon conviction for a criminal offense (Rush, 2000, p. 295). For example, when a person is convicted of murder, he or she may be sentenced to the death penalty, life in prison, some other term of imprisonment, or, in rare cases, a long term of probation and/or house arrest.

A sentence, then, is any criminal sanction or punishment. Herbert Packer, in his book, *The Limits of the Criminal Sanction* (1968), defines **punishment** as inflicting pain or unpleasant circumstances for an offense against legal rules on an offender or alleged offender for his or her offense, intentionally administered by human beings within a legal system that grants authority to do so. He argued that the only valid justifications for punishment were deterrence and retribution on an offender whose moral responsibility had been established beyond a reasonable doubt. Deterrence refers to creating fear through punishment to make would-be offenders not commit crime. Retribution is punishment of offenders to give them what they deserve based on the wrongs they inflicted on society. Each term is discussed more later in the chapter. Similarly, Hart (1968, p. 4) defined punishment as the infliction of pain for offenses against legal rules, applied to the actual offender, that is intentionally administered by a legal authority (cited in Jeffery, 1990).

Types of Sentences

The three primary forms of sentences are determinate sentences, indeterminate sentences, and mandatory sentences. **Determinate sentences** set forth a specified criminal sanction for a particular type of crime. Based on the severity of the offense, determinate sentences are generally the same for each person convicted of a particular type of crime. Although determinate or **fixed sentences** are generally set by law, judges have limited discretion when it comes to passing each sentence, based on certain aggravating and mitigating factors. As defined by Rush (2000, p. 8), **aggravating factors** are "circumstances relating to the commission of a crime which cause its gravity to be greater than that of the average instance of the given type of offense." For example, any crime committed with a weapon is considered more serious than one without a weapon, so the presence of a weapon would be an aggravating factor at sentencing. Thus, a rape committed at gunpoint may lead to a greater sentence than a rape without a weapon. **Mitigating factors** reduce the perceived seriousness of crimes (Rush, 2000, p. 216). Any motives of the offender that may make crimes more understandable to the court may be considered as mitigating factors. For example, a bank robber who is unarmed, does not pretend to have a weapon, and is truly motivated by the hunger of his children may receive a less severe sentence than a ruthless, armed bank robber motivated only by monetary gain.

Indeterminate sentences are not fixed on the basis of the crime but are a function of characteristics unique to each offender. Thus, indeterminate sentences, or **minimum–maximum sentences**, establish a range within which each individual offender may be sanctioned, somewhere between the minimum and maximum allowable sentences allowed in the law. Indeterminate sentences give judges more discretion in establishing what any given offender may receive for his or her crimes. The advantage of indeterminate sentences is that they allow judges to take into account both aggravating and mitigating factors. One murder may be either more or less serious than other murders; indeterminate sentences allow judges to reflect this in the sentences they hand down. The main drawback of indeterminate sentences is that they allow judges to abuse their discretion. That is, there is at least the potential that longer sentences will be passed down against particular groups of people who are convicted of the same offenses as other groups. For example, judges may consciously or subconsciously treat African Americans more harshly than Caucasians for identical offenses, especially given that African Americans are not well represented in courtroom workgroups (see Chapter 7).

To address such concerns, many states and the federal government have passed **sentencing guidelines** that minimize the amount of discretion to which judges are entitled when considering sentences for convicted offenders. Judges weigh various factors in determining the most appropriate sentence. Generally, the most important factors include the seriousness of the offense and the offender's prior record; the more serious the offense and the longer the prior record, the more severe the sentence will be. Relying on offense seriousness and previous record allows for biases in the criminal law and policing to affect sentences.

Federal sentencing guidelines were put into effect in 1987. The range of possible sentences was reduced, meaning that judge discretion was minimized, and discretionary early release from prison was abolished. Generally speaking, prison terms increased as a result of such revisions. One fundamental problem with these federal sentencing guidelines is that those criminal offenders who have information on other crimes may get lesser sentences than those without. Prosecutors are allowed to use their discretion in charging to give breaks to cooperative defendants (Walker, 1998, p. 136). Given the definitions of justice in Chapter 1, such practices can be considered unjust, as small-time offenders who have no information to give to prosecutors may get more severe sentences than big-time offenders who simply know more. Recently, federal sentencing guidelines were struck down by the U.S. Supreme Court in the case of *U.S. v. Booker* (2005). They are now expected to serve as "guidelines" for sentencing judges rather than mandating requirements.

Mandatory sentences simply establish a minimum sanction that must be served upon conviction for a criminal offense. Thus, everyone who is convicted of a crime that calls for a mandatory sentence will serve that amount of time. As explained by Walker (1998, p. 130), "Mandatory sentencing usually means two things: mandatory imprisonment for a certain crime and/or a mandatory minimum prison term." Judges have no discretion in mandatory sentencing because, by definition, the sentence is mandatory. A specified imprisonment term must be given to the convicted offender by law. The war on drugs is responsible for a large share of mandatory sentences. Consider, for example, 20-year-old Nicole Richardson of Mobile, Alabama, who was dating a drug dealer. When approached by an undercover officer about where to buy some drugs, Nicole said to talk to her boyfriend. Her sentence was 10 years in prison with no possibility of parole; her boyfriend, who cooperated with authorities, received a 5-year imprisonment sentence (Donziger, 1996, p. 25). Sentencing judges, with no discretion in mandatory sentencing, are generally opposed to it: Sileo (1993) reports that 90% of federal judges and 75% of state judges do not support mandatory sentences. Gray (2001), a judge himself, also reports that most judges are against mandatory sentences.

Good examples of mandatory sentences are the so-called **three-strikes laws** that have been passed by more than half the states in the United States. These laws usually require that upon conviction for a third felony, offenders will be sentenced to a period of imprisonment for the remainder of their natural lives: "Neither the particular circumstances, nor the seriousness of the crimes charged, nor the duration of time that has elapsed between crimes is given consideration" in three-strikes laws (Beckett and Sasson, 2000, p. 180). These laws also mandate that judges must "ignore mitigating factors in the background of offenders, as well as their ties to community, employment status, potential for rehabilitation, and obligations to children." Tonry (1995) argues that mandatory sentences are unwise because they do not allow judges to consider mitigating factors such as economic deprivation.

I will discuss whether three-strikes laws make any sense at all later in this chapter. Box 8-1 highlights some important facts about these laws.

BOX 8-1

FACTS ABOUT THREE-STRIKES LAWS

- According to the Justice Policy Institute (2004), at least 25 states have passed three-strikes laws since 1993. In most of these states, the law requires three strikes for a mandatory sentence. In many of these states, at least one strike must be a violent felony. And in at least 12 of these states, the mandatory term of punishment is life without the possibility of parole.

- Now more than half the states have three-strikes laws, as does the federal government, although only a handful of states have used these laws to any real degree (led by California).

- California's law, which has been the most scrutinized, requires only that two of the offenses be serious felonies, whereas the last strike can be for any crime. This explains why one person was sentenced as a three-strikes offender for stealing four chocolate chip cookies from a restaurant (Elikann, 1996).

- The logic of three-strikes laws is to increase penalties for second offenses and to require life imprisonment without the possibility of parole for third offenses.

- Many states, such as California, passed laws that were intended primarily for violent offenders but that failed to specify this intent. Many nonviolent offenders are being incarcerated under this law.

- Three-strikes laws are based on a false premise that "an increasingly larger portion of serious crimes are committed by recidivating felons" (Welsh and Harris, 1999, p. xii).

- Three-strikes laws grew out of a crime hysteria or moral panic caused by a publicized violent crime in California, and the idea grew out of the National Rifle Association.

- Experts estimated that every single dollar of new money in the state would have to be used to pay for

(continued)

BOX 8-1   *(Continued)*

this effort, although the law has been less costly than expected, mostly because the law has not been fully implemented.

- The Justice Policy Institute claims the three-strikes law in California has cost at least $8.1 billion in prison and jail costs, including $4.7 billion in added costs for longer incarceration sentences.

- In California, at least 43,000 inmates have been sentenced under either a second- or third-strike offense, including 7,200 third-strikers.

- The average cost of a third-strike incarceration is $26,500 per inmate per year.

- Approximately 57% of third-strikers in California were sentenced for nonviolent or nonserious crimes.

- Approximately 65% of second- and third-strikers were sentenced for nonviolent offenses.

- Three-strikes inmates in California are far more likely to be African Americans than Caucasians—approximately 45% of all third-strikers are African American. The rate of incarceration under three-strikes laws is twelve times higher for blacks than for whites; for Hispanics it is 45% higher than for whites.

- One three-striker is Michael Garcia, who stole a $5.62 package of chuck steak from a grocery store after his mother's social security check failed to arrive on time (Schiraldi, Sussman, and Hyland, 1994). His previous strikes also were nonviolent offenses.

- Early in the implementation of the law, the California three-strikes law was about four times as likely to be used against a person for marijuana possession than for murder, rape, and kidnapping combined. Additionally, most sentenced inmates committed nonviolent offenses, including 672 drug offenders (versus 62 murderers, 199 rapists, and 279 people who committed assault with a deadly weapon).

- The number incarcerated for petty theft under three strikes is ten times higher than before three strikes.

- Although crime fell significantly after the three-strikes law in California, crime rates were already declining in the state prior to the passage of the law.

- Crime rates in counties that widely used the law had crime declines roughly equal to those counties that did not use the law.

- Crime rates in states without three-strikes laws had crime rate declines equal to those states that did have three-strikes laws.

- In California, three of four (75%) of second- and third-strikers are minorities.

- In California, African Americans make up less than 10% of the general population and more than 20% of arrests, but 36% of second-strikers and 45% of third-strikers.

- Most Americans support three-strikes laws.

SOURCES: http://www.justicepolicy.org/article.php?id=452; http://www.soros.org/initiatives/justice/articles_publications/publications/still_striking_20040305; http://www.cjcj.org/pubs/three_strikes/strikingout.html; http://www.rand.org/pubs/research_briefs/RB4009/index1.html; http://www.keep3strikes.org/CDAA_3x_WhitePaper.pdf; http://www.lao.ca.gov/2005/3_Strikes/3_strikes_102005.htm; http://www.threestrikes.org/.

Truth-in-sentencing laws are also examples of mandatory sentences. At least 29 states now have these laws on the books, and the first was imposed in 1984. Most of these states require inmates to serve at least 85% of their sentences. Many states have also abolished **parole** to reduce early release from prison or have abolished parole board release for some offenders, such as violent or felony offenders. Although truth-in-sentencing laws may sound logical, what they do is eliminate reductions in sentencing for good behavior and mandate that correctional facilities keep inmates in prison for longer periods of time than they would normally serve. In some states, these longer sentences have created an extraordinary burden because of the added expense to correctional budgets and the growth of overcrowding problems.

Walker (2005) concludes that mandatory sentences are responsible in part for the shift of power in the courts to prosecutors, as well as for "unduly harsh" punishments for some crimes. Tonry (1992, p. 243) states it very clearly: "Mandatory penalties do not work." The American Bar Association has concluded that no mandatory sentencing should be in effect for any category of offenses.

In 2003, the Supreme Court upheld California's three-strikes sentencing law in the cases of *Ewing v. California* (01-6978) and (*Lockyer v. Andrade* (01-1127) ruling 5–4 that long prison terms are constitutionally permissible even for minor offenders. The court upheld sentences of 25 years to life and 50 years to life for a thief who shoplifted clubs from a golf course and for a man who stole a handful of videotapes from Kmart, respectively. In the former case, Sandra Day O'Connor wrote, "We do not sit as a super-legislature to second-guess [the legislature's] policy choices. It is enough that the state of California has a reasonable basis for believing that dramatically enhanced sentences for habitual felons advances the goals of its criminal justice system in any substantial way." Only time will tell whether she was right or wrong. It should be noted that many eminent criminologists believe California's law is a major mistake and a burden on California rather than a blessing.

Although the longest time a person can actually serve is the term of his or her natural life, as in the case of mandatory life sentences, the longest sentence actually imposed by a court was 10,000 years! The sentence was imposed in Tuscaloosa, Alabama, on Dudley Wayne Kyzer, age 40, for a triple murder in 1981. Obviously, no one can ever serve such a sentence—they are handed down by judges who want to make political or moral statements. In fact, the longest sentence ever served for a crime was by Paul Geidel, convicted of second-degree murder in 1911 as a 17-year-old in New York City; he served 68 years, 8 months, and 2 days (Rush, 2000, p. 295).

METHODS OF PUNISHMENT

When you think of punishment, what do you see? Prisons? The death penalty? These are currently considered valid sentencing options for judges who are responsible for meting out punishments in the United States (death is available in 37 states, the federal government, and the U.S. military). However, prison and death are two punishments that are relatively infrequently administered. I say "relatively infrequently" not to suggest that their administration is not plagued with problems, but to make the point that, relative to probation, imprisonment and death are rare. In Chapters 9 and 10, I will take a close look at incarceration and the death penalty, respectively.

FIGURE 8-1   Continuum of American Punishments

Generally speaking, four main categories of punishment are used in the United States—including probation, incarceration, intermediate sanctions, and death. These are depicted along a continuum in Figure 8-1. Punishments (also known as **criminal sanctions**) on the left of this figure are generally less restrictive and less expensive than those to the right of the continuum.

Probation, the least restrictive of punishments depicted in the figure, is also the most commonly used criminal sanction in the United States. According to the U.S. Department of Justice, probation is the court-ordered community supervision of convicted offenders by a probation agency, requiring the adherence to specific rules of conduct while living in the community. Box 8-2 lists some of these requirements. If violated, probation can be revoked and the offender sent to prison or jail, whatever was stated in the original sentence by the judge.

Probation is not intended for serious, repetitive, violent criminals. Generally, it is not intended for people convicted on multiple charges, for people who were arrested while on probation or parole, for repeat offenders, for drug addicts, or for violent offenders (Petersilia and Turner, 1986). In fact, the offense most likely to lead to a sentence of straight probation or a split sentence between incarceration and probation has in recent history been simple drug possession, while the least likely is murder, followed by rape. For every type of crime, people sentenced to probation generally receive shorter sentences than those sentenced to prison.

BOX 8-2

TYPICAL RULES OF PROBATION

- Pay supervision fees.
- Pay fines.
- Pay court costs.
- Attend substance abuse treatment.
- Gain and maintain employment.
- Participate in drug testing.
- Pay victim restitution.

- Perform community service.
- Gain education and/or training.
- Have no contact with the victim.
- Remain drug-free.
- Attend counseling.
- Abide by driving restrictions.
- Abide by movement restrictions.

Walker (2005) claims that we use probation for various reasons. First, as noted, many crimes are relatively minor and thus do not warrant a term of incarceration. Second, there are not enough prison and jail cells for those we have already sentenced to incarceration, which is why U.S. prisons are operating above maximum capacity. Third, probation is much cheaper than prison. It costs about 35 times more to incarcerate an offender for a year in prison than it does to supervise someone on probation. Fourth, probation is no less effective than prison. In fact, probation is actually more successful than more severe sanctions at reducing recidivism.

Incarceration takes many forms, notably being sent to prison or jail. It involves having one's freedoms taken away while one is locked away from society. A **prison** is a state or federal correctional facility used to house those sentenced to more than one year of incarceration. A **jail** is a local correctional facility used to hold persons awaiting trial, awaiting sentencing, serving a sentence of less than one year, or awaiting transfer to another facility. Incarceration is used more for violent criminals than for property criminals and is a sanction supposedly intended for more severe offenders.

Unlike those on probation, people who are incarcerated are not allowed to live in the community. They are taken away from their families and loved ones and are subjected to numerous discomforts (see Chapter 9). Think of being locked away from free society, not being able to come and go as you please, being told what to do, when to do it, and how to do it. Does this sound like soft punishment?

Imprisonment costs approximately $30,000 per year per inmate. Since most offenders do not warrant incarceration, and because probation may not be tough enough for some offenders, a wide array of **intermediate sanctions** have become available to sentencing judges. Box 8-3 lists several of these.

BOX 8-3

SOME TYPES OF INTERMEDIATE SANCTIONS

- **Boot camps:** Usually intended for juveniles, these facilities are run as paramilitary organizations, attempting to instill discipline in wayward youth through hard work and exercise, and to increase educational and vocational skills.

- **House arrest:** This is intended for less severe offenders, who are required to stay within a certain distance of their actual residence.

- **Electronic monitoring:** This is usually used in conjunction with house arrest. An offender is monitored via an electronic device attached to his or her leg, which assures that the offender does not violate the terms of arrest.

- **Community service:** This is typically used for the least severe offenders, who are required to spend a specified number of hours serving their community by picking up garbage or performing other necessary tasks.

- **Day reporting center:** This is a facility where probationers are sent to attend treatment and counseling sessions each day.

Punishment Facts

In 2002, state and federal courts convicted just over 1 million adults of felonies, the vast majority of which were handled by state courts. Of these, only 19% were for violent crimes, versus 31% for property crimes, 32% for drug offenses, and the rest for other offenses. As you see in Table 8-1, of all felons convicted by state courts in 2002, 69% were sentenced to incarceration (41% to prison and 28% to jail), and 31% were sentenced to probation. Incarceration was more likely for violent offenses (77%) than drug offenses (66%) and property offenses (66%). The felony offense most likely to lead to incarceration was murder (95%), while the lowest were fraud, forgery, and embezzlement (59%).

At the federal level, 76% of convicted defendants were sentenced to prison in 2003, up from 65% in 1994. Almost all violent offenders (93%) and those convicted federal drug offenses (92%) were sentenced to prison in 2003. The least likely offenders to be sentenced to federal prison committed fraud (60%) and regulatory offenses (48%). Of those sentenced to prison, the average sentence for those convicted of violent felonies was 97 months, versus 84 months for weapons felonies and 81 months for drug felonies. The shortest sentences were for those convicted of regulatory offenses (33%) and fraud (25%). Even though average sentences fell from the mid-1990s, the average time served has actually significantly increased.

As you see in Table 8-2, the average sentences of these convicted felons in state courts in 2002 was 53 months for those sentenced to prison, 38 months for those sentenced to probation, and 7 months for those sentenced to jail. Prison sentences for convicted violent felons were longer (84 months) than for drug offenders (48 months) and property offenses (41 months). In 2002, murderers were sentenced to the longest average sentences (225 months in prison), whereas motor vehicle thieves were given the shortest average sentences (30 months), followed by those convicted of drug offenses (48 months in prison).

As for intermediate sanctions, additional sentences imposed by state courts on convicted felons included fines to courts (25%), restitution to victims (12%), community

TABLE 8-1 Types of Sentences Imposed on Convicted Felons (2002)			
	Prison	*Jail*	*Probation*
All offenses	41%	28%	31%
Violent offenses	52%	25%	23%
Murder/manslaughter	91%	4%	5%
Sexual assault/rape	59%	23%	18%
Robbery	71%	15%	14%
Aggravated assault	42%	29%	29%
Property offenses	38%	28%	34%
Burglary	46%	26%	28%
Theft	36%	31%	33%
Motor vehicle theft	37%	39%	24%
Fraud/forgery/embezzlement	31%	28%	41%
Drug offenses	39%	27%	34%

Source: Sourcebook on Criminal Justice Statistics (2006).

TABLE 8-2 Average Sentences Imposed on Convicted Felons (2002)			
	Number of Months		
	Prison	**Jail**	**Probation**
All offenses	53	7	38
Violent offenses	84	8	43
Murder/manslaughter	225	10	76
Sexual assault/rape	100	8	54
Robbery	91	11	52
Aggravated assault	54	7	39
Property offenses	41	7	37
Burglary	50	7	40
Theft	34	6	36
Motor vehicle theft	30	6	33
Fraud/forgery/embezzlement	38	6	36
Drug offenses	48	6	36

Source: Sourcebook on Criminal Justice Statistics (2006).

service (4%), treatment (3%), and other sentences (7%). These additional sentences were generally more likely to be handed down to property and drug offenders than violent offenders.

At the end of 2005, more than 7 million people were under some form of criminal justice supervision in the United States (i.e., probation, incarceration in jail or prison, or on parole). This represents 3.2% of all U.S. adult residents. State and federal prisons housed 1,446,269 inmates (1,259,905 in state custody and 179,220 in federal custody), and local jails housed 747,529 people either awaiting trial or serving a sentence (an additional 71,905 people were under jail supervision serving their sentence in the community). An additional 4.9 million adults were on probation or parole in 2005 (approximately 4,162,500 were on probation and 784,400 were on parole) (Bureau of Justice Statistics, 2007). Figure 8-2 shows the number of people under of each of these forms of correctional supervision.

The rate of incarceration (prisons and jails) at the end of 2005 was 737 per 100,000 residents, number one in the world. The rate of imprisonment (prisons only) was 491 per 100,000 people and the rate of jail incarceration was 252 per 100,000 people. The rate of imprisonment growth is alarming and unprecedented in our nation's history. The use of probation tripled from 1980 to 1997, a rate equal to the increase in the use of incarceration (Gaines, Kaune, and Miller, 2000, p. 420). As you see in Figure 8-3, the growth in probation outpaced all other forms of punishment in the United States.

You might think that because most convicted criminals do not go to prison, this is proof that the United States is "soft on crime." In fact, the United States leads the world in incarceration rates. Russia is now a distant second.

The rate of growth of the nation's prison population has gradually slowed over the past decade, but it has continued to increase. According to the Bureau of Justice

Source: Bureau of Justice Statistics (2006). Corrections Statistics. http://ojp.usdoj.gov/bjs/correct.htm.

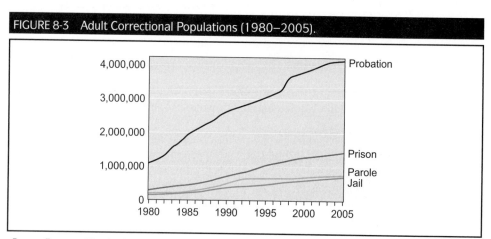

Source: Bureau of Justice Statistics (2006). Adult correctional populations. http://ojp.usdoj.gov/bjs/glance/corr2.htm.

Statistics (2007), "[b]etween yearend 1995 and yearend 2005, the incarcerated population grew an average 3.3% annually. Population growth during the 12-month period ending December 31, 2005, was lower in state prisons (up 1.3%) than in federal prisons (up 5.1%) and local jails (up 4.7%)."

At the end of 2005, state prisons were operating between 1% and 14% over capacity, and federal prisons were operating 37% over capacity. According to the Bureau of Justice Statistics, 23 states and the federal government were at or above capacity and 26 states were below capacity. Private prisons housed 7% of state and federal inmates in 2005.

WHY DO WE PUNISH?

Punishment is natural: "Parents punish children by taking away privileges. The punishment is often characterized as 'teaching a lesson.' Teachers discipline students who don't follow the rules; managers penalize unproductive employees" (Kappeler and Potter, 2004). Given that punishment is natural, it is unlikely that we can ever put a complete end to the use of punishment as a means to control crime. Yet many criminal justice scholars do believe that the United States is overrelying on punishment generally and on certain forms of punishment in particular.

Here I assess why American criminal justice administers punishment to offenders. John Stuart Mill (1859) argued that we should punish people only to prevent harms to others. Sir James Stephen (1883) disagreed with this position and stated that the purpose of punishment is to enforce the morality of the community—to allow the community to hate the criminal and to get revenge against him or her. Similarly, Immanuel Kant saw punishment as virtuous because the guilty deserve to suffer. However, Kant did not believe that punishment should be used to deter others who had not yet done anything wrong, nor did he believe in rehabilitation (cited in Jeffery, 1990, p. 63). The great legal scholar Oliver Wendell Holmes did not support vengeance; he believed the only justifications for punishment were deterrence and reform.

Lord Patrick Devlin (1959) attacked Mill's position and supported Stephen's view that punishment should be used to enforce morality. H. L. A. Hart (1968, p. 231) defended Mill and argued that the law could not successfully be used to enforce morality. Hart thought the only justification for punishment was the prevention of harm. Hart did support retribution, as well, and claimed that "the justification for punishing men (who have committed wickedness) is that the return of suffering for moral evil voluntarily done, is itself just or morally good."

Whatever your own personal beliefs, most criminal justice scholars agree that there are four primary justifications for criminal punishment.

- Retribution
- Incapacitation
- Deterrence
- Rehabilitation

Each of these justifications for punishment is discussed next, along with an additional justification that is gaining in popularity in the United States—restoration.

Retribution

Retribution implies "an eye for an eye, a tooth for a tooth." That is, when a criminal harms a victim, he or she deserves to suffer a similar if not identical harm. In Western societies, the notion of retribution has evolved out of religious convictions found in the Old Testament.

Retribution has two related meanings. The first deals with the natural human emotion of **vengeance**—the desire to give the offender his or her "just desserts." At various times in U.S. history, notable people have attempted to achieve such literal retribution. For example, Thomas Jefferson proposed to the legislature that for the crime of murder by poisoning, poisoning be the just penalty. For the crime of rape, he proposed castration of the rapist as retributive justice. For treason, he suggested that the offender be buried alive (Gottfredson, 1999, p. 3).

The second meaning of retribution deals with a more rational approach to justice. It assumes that when harm is committed against a victim, the offender gains an unfair advantage to which he or she is not entitled under the law. To balance the scales of justice, punishment must be administered to counteract the advantage gained through crime. In essence, when rules are broken, rule breakers must be punished. The basic differences between vengeance and retribution are as follows.

- Retribution is rooted in the law (and thus is legal) and vengeance is not.
- Retribution is public (i.e., decided by legislators, judges) and vengeance is private (i.e., carried out by family members of victims).
- Retribution is something the offenders pay back to society for their crimes (e.g., years of their lives, restitution to the victims), whereas vengeance is what society pays back to the offender (e.g., punishment, pain).
- Retribution is also about socialization (i.e., teaching people wrong from right), whereas vengeance is merely a human emotion.

With regard to the first meaning of retribution, Beckett and Sasson (2000, p. 164) claim that "those [victims of crime] who believe that revenge will bring them relief often discover that it does not" (e.g., see Prejean, 1993; Shapiro, 1997). When you or a loved one becomes a crime victim, the desire to get even with the offender is natural and easy to understand. Yet this does not mean that getting even will make you feel a sense of justice or relief. Given the long delays in the administration of justice, the fact that victims are not highly involved in this process, and the fact that punishment is so detached from the victim, it is just as logical to assert that the criminal justice network cannot effectively make victims feel better.

It is tough to argue against the logic of the second meaning of retribution. If people freely choose to commit crime, they deserve some form of punishment for the harms they have inflicted on society. After all, one conception of justice, discussed in Chapter 1, requires that the guilty be held accountable for their crimes to achieve justice as an outcome. Yet, as I have attempted to demonstrate throughout this book, we should not let our goal of punishing the guilty so interfere with our goal of being fair and impartial in the criminal justice process that humans become generally less free, especially when this burden is imposed on some groups in society more than on others.

One clear benefit of retribution administered by the criminal justice network is that it limits the likelihood that **escalation** will occur (Glaser, 1997). That is, if victims were allowed to get "justice" for themselves, without the assistance of their government, the desire for vengeance would not be limited by the law. Thus, a single murder might lead to two more deaths—the death of the guilty offender and perhaps also the death of someone standing next to the offender when the victim's family opens fire. This in turn could lead to a desire for vengeance on the part of the offender's family and the family of the innocent bystander. Without state-controlled retribution, where would the cycle of vengeance and escalation end?

Incapacitation

Incapacitation involves restricting the freedom of offenders so they cannot offend again. The logic of incapacitation is summed up by Friedman (1993, p. 237) as follows: "[A] burglar in jail can hardly break into your house. This effect is called 'incapacitation'. . . . If all the crooks are behind bars, they cannot rape and loot and pillage." Most people think of prisons and jails when they think of incapacitation, because they envision the offender being removed from society, but in fact the most typical form of incapacitation is not incarceration; probation is more commonly used to restrict the freedom of offenders, as you saw earlier.

Unless you believe in reincarnation, the ultimate form of incapacitation is death. When an offender is killed, he or she can no longer offend against society. Thus, incapacitation becomes a justification for the death penalty (see Chapter 10). Aside from death, however, we cannot be assured that offenders who are locked up behind bars will not continue to offend against society, and there is overwhelming evidence of crimes committed within prisons and jails against other inmates and correctional personnel. Because such crimes are not widely discussed or broadcast in the news, society can easily ignore them, but this does not make them any less real or harmful. It also does not deny that offenders who are locked away with other criminals will ultimately learn to be better offenders (see Chapter 9).

One thing we can conclude is that the United States is currently on an incarceration binge that is unprecedented in the history of the world. Yet Americans seem generally unconcerned with the long-term social and economic implications of this trend for the United States. Incapacitation, whether it be achieved through incarceration or through the death penalty, suggests an "I give up" attitude toward crime and criminals. If we are unwilling to treat those who are sick, unwilling to change those environments that are conducive to street crime, and unwilling to invest in long-term approaches to crime prevention, then the easiest alternative is simply to lock people away from society (or kill them) so that we do not have to think about them.

Incapacitation takes two main forms—general and selective (Walker, 2005). **General** or **collective incapacitation** occurs when society uses incarceration and other forms of incapacitation as a general punitive strategy for many forms of criminality. This type of incapacitation is aimed at all forms of criminality, regardless of the likelihood of **recidivism**, or repeat offending. It is based on the belief that incarceration and other forms of incapacitation are effective means of controlling crimes. **Selective incapacitation** occurs when these punishment mechanisms are reserved for the most dangerous offenders, those in most need of incapacitation because of their likelihood of repeating their criminality. Selective incapacitation is based on scientific research demonstrating that a small percentage of offenders commit a very large portion of all crimes (e.g., see Wolfgang, Figlio, and Sellin, 1972).

The main problem with general or collective incapacitation is that not every offender deserves or warrants it, especially given the enormous costs associated with incarcerating and executing offenders. Collective incarceration may make us feel safer, but incarcerating more people has a "limited capacity to actually make us safer" (Gottfredson, 1999, p. 431). As for selective incapacitation, the main problem is known as the "prediction problem" (Gottfredson and Gottfredson, 1994). Because we simply are unable to predict accurately which offenders pose the greatest risk of repeating their crimes, it is difficult to use selective incapacitation accurately (Walker, 2005). We do know that the most minor offenders are the ones who are most likely to reoffend. For example, thieves are more likely to commit more thefts after release than murderers are to commit more murders. Yet the costs of incarceration do not seem to be warranted for these minor offenders on the basis of the minor harms they are likely to inflict on society. Keeping thieves in jail or prison because of the likelihood that they will reoffend is not good criminal justice policy.

Deterrence

Deterrence is based on the logical notion that being punished for criminal activity will create fear in people so that they will not want to commit crime. There are two types of deterrence, special or specific deterrence and general deterrence. **Special** or **specific deterrence** means punishing an offender with the specific intent of instilling fear in offenders so they will not commit crimes in the future. **General deterrence** involves punishing offenders to instill fear in society generally so the rest of us will not want to commit crimes. Special or specific deterrence is aimed at stopping a known criminal offender from committing future crimes, whereas general deterrence is aimed at teaching the rest of us a lesson about what might happen to us if we were to commit crimes. Deterrence is evident in all that we do in the United States to fight crime, as discussed in Box 8-4.

Deterrence as a justification for punishment is based on several assumptions:

- Offenders are hedonistic or pleasure-seeking (e.g., crime provides various pleasures).
- Offenders seek to minimize costs or pains associated with crimes (i.e., they do not want to get caught and be punished).
- Offenders are rational (i.e., they choose to commit crime after weighing the potential costs or punishments and benefits or rewards).

BOX 8-4

DETERRENCE IN AMERICAN PUNISHMENT

- **Probation:** Offenders on probation are "hassled" by their probation officer and must follow many rules that they would not have to follow even in prison. Thus, they should be deterred from committing future crimes for fear that they might be put on probation again.

- **Incarceration:** Prisons and jails are horribly violent and repressive places. Any criminal who goes to prison ought to be afraid to go back. Additionally, all of society should fear suffering the pains of imprisonment. Thus, crime will be specially and generally deterred.

- **Boot camps:** Juvenile offenders sentenced to boot camps are forced to go to classes, work, and train

through various physical fitness activities. It is hoped that these juveniles will fear being forced to experience such conditions again in the future, so that boot camps will deter juvenile delinquency.

- **Chain gangs:** Forcing inmates to work on the side of the road doing hard labor will not only instill fear in those inmates, but also show others what can happen if they commit crimes. Thus, crime is both specially and generally deterred.

- **Death penalty:** Not only does the death penalty incapacitate the offender, it sends a message to all of society that anyone who commits murder can be executed for his or her offense.

Many criminologists believe human beings are rational and motivated by desire for personal pleasure and want to avoid pain (Bohm, 2007). Yet numerous human behaviors seem quite irrational. Most forms of criminality, it has been argued, are impulsive, short-sighted, stupid, and risky behaviors (see Robinson, 2004). Many types of crimes are committed with only short-term gain in mind and with little or no thought of likely outcomes. This is not consistent with the view of the rational criminal.

To deter would-be offenders effectively, punishment must be certain (or at least likely), swift (or at least not delayed by months or years), and severe enough to outweigh the pleasures associated with crimes. Of these requirements, the most important is the **certainty of punishment**. The more likely that punishment is to follow a criminal act, the less likely the criminal act will occur (Mendes, 2004; Nagin and Pogarsky, 2001; Pogarsky, KiDeuk, and Paternoster, 2005; Yu and Liska, 1993). Think of this example: If a lightning bolt were guaranteed to strike an offender who stole property, how many thefts do you think we would have each year? Probably not many. If it was absolutely certain that some higher being would strike you dead upon stealing someone else's property, then everyone would know this and would refrain from committing theft in order to remain alive.

Such punishment would be certain, swift, and severe. But this example is misleading. For deterrence to be effective, it must be certain and somewhat swift, but it has to be only severe enough to outweigh the pleasure gained by committing the offense. For most crimes, certain death by lightning strike is not required! The noted Italian criminologist Cesare Beccaria wrote, in *An Essay on Crime and Punishments* (1776):

> The certainty of punishment, even though it be moderate, will always make a stronger impression than the fear of one more severe if it is accompanied by the hope that one may escape that punishment, because men are more frightened by an evil which is inevitable even though minor in nature. Further, if the punishment be too severe for a crime, men will be led to commit further crimes in order to escape punishment for the crime. . . . It is essential that it be public, prompt, necessary, minimal in severity as possible under given circumstances, proportional to the crime, and prescribed by the laws.

Contemporary research supports Beccaria's original statement. For example, Blumstein (1995, pp. 408–409) writes: "Research on deterrence has consistently supported the position that sentence 'severity' (that is, the time served) has less of a deterrent effect than sentence 'certainty' (the probability of going to prison). Thus, from the deterrence consideration, there is clear preference for increasing certainty, even if it becomes necessary to do so at the expense of severity."

What do you think? Is American criminal justice doing a good job of providing certain, swift punishments that outweigh the potential benefits of committing crimes? The evidence says no.

For every 100 serious street crimes (as measured in the National Crime Victimization Survey), only about 40 are known to the police (as measured in the Uniform Crime Reports). Of these 40, only about 10 will lead to an arrest. Of those arrested, some will not be prosecuted, and some will be prosecuted but not convicted. Only about 3 of the original 100 crimes will lead to an incarceration. Punishment is anything but certain in the United States. Offenders know this. They tell criminologists that they know from personal experiences and from the experiences of fellow criminals that their risks of being apprehended by the police and convicted in court are very low (Cromwell, 1995).

Because there are only about 3 police officers in the United States for every 1,000 citizens (see Chapter 6), is this surprising?

What many offenders do tell us, and what is evident from their offending patterns, is that the great bulk of criminal behavior seems to be motivated by the desire to obtain short-term, immediate pleasures and gains. Long-term concern about potential punishment seems not to enter the minds of most offenders. If they thought there was a good chance of getting caught, after all, offenders would not likely engage in their criminal behaviors, especially if they are as rational as criminologists tell us. Further, there are numerous risk factors that increase the likelihood that individuals will choose crime (Robinson, 2004). This suggests rationality is not something possessed equally by all.

The main problem with deterrence as a justification for punishment is that it is impossible to demonstrate empirically that deterrence works. How can one prove the absence of criminal activity as a result of some criminal justice policy or program? This is why many criminal justice scholars argue that there is no empirical evidence supporting deterrence (Robinson, 2008).

Even if the threat of punishment does deter some would-be offenders from committing crimes, our common experiences also suggest that deterrence is a myth.

Rehabilitation

Rehabilitation, probably the least popular of all justifications for punishing people today, is justified to the degree that something within offenders or their environments causes them to commit crime. Rehabilitation is aimed at eliminating the causes of crime by making offenders "better"—restoring them to a healthy condition—or altering conditions in their "sick" environment. Rehabilitation would also include what Glaser (1997, p. 36) calls "anticriminal enculturation" ("[c]lassifying and separating inmates, promoting good staff–inmate relations, encouraging noncriminal visitors, providing law-abiding role models"), "retraining" ("[p]roviding academic and vocational instruction and employment during confinement, providing postrelease aid and personal counseling"), and "reintegrative shaming" ("[c]ondemning the offense but accepting the offender's apology, and granting public respect").

There is very little rehabilitation in American punishment today, mostly because of the widespread but false belief that we do not know what works or how best to use it. A major report by Martinson (2000, p. 23), a criminologist, stated that "with few and isolated exceptions, the rehabilitative efforts that have been reported so far have not had appreciable effect on rehabilitation." Such reports led to the decline of the rehabilitative ideal in the 1970s. In fact, some forms of *nurturant strategies* are likely to be highly effective at eliminating crime before it happens (see Robinson, 2004).

There is very little going on in the world of corrections today that we can call rehabilitation (Gottfredson, 1999, p. 420). This can be attributed, in part, to the use of crime as an election issue by politicians seeking to get elected and maintain power through law-and-order, get-tough-on-crime rhetoric. The shift from rehabilitative to law-and-order approaches coincided with the use of crime for national political gain, as discussed in Chapter 2. Beckett and Sasson (2000, p. 55) explain how the rehabilitative ideal collapsed in the United States

in the context of a growing chorus of criticism, from scholars and activists across the political spectrum, of "rehabilitation" as a primary justification for punishment.

Conservatives opposed rehabilitation on the grounds that punishment must be harsh and painful if it is to deter crime. Liberals also criticized policies associated with rehabilitation, arguing that the open-ended ("indeterminate") sentences designed to facilitate "correction" created the potential for the intrusive, discriminatory, and arbitrary exercise of power.

Dozens of reviews of the ineffectiveness of rehabilitation were published in the 1960s and 1970s (see Gottfredson, 1999, p. 423).

Walker (1998, p. 203) explains that we must, at least to some degree, still be committed to rehabilitation, because we still call the facilities that punish offenders "corrections" (which suggests that we hope to correct their behavior). Public opinion polls of Americans show that there is widespread support for rehabilitation, treatment, and crime prevention as alternatives to punitiveness (Roberts and Stalans, 2000). In fact, some treatment does work for some people (see Gottfredson, 1999, p. 434). In Chapter 13, I will argue that the future of criminal justice policy must be directed toward programs that are less punitive and more treatment-based.

Toward Restoration

One thing at which punishment of offenders is not very effective is healing crime victims, or restoring them to the state they were in prior to victimization. To restore generally means to give back or return (as in **restitution**), or to put something back into its original state (as in to *renew*). **Restorative justice** offers an alternative to punitive justice and is aimed at restoring both victims and offenders to the statuses they had prior to victimization and criminality (Aertsen, Daems, and Robert, 2005; De Gruchy, 2006; Elliott and Gordon, 2005; Johnstone, 2001; Johnstone and Van Ness, 2006; Sullivan, 2006; Zehr and Toews, 2004). Restorative justice is based on the assumption that criminal justice is very destructive—both to the offender and to the victim. Although it is not widely practiced nationwide yet, local restorative justice programs have been created all over the United States as a means to reduce the burden on criminal justice agencies as well as to better serve crime victims and their families. Box 8-5 summarizes some of the key principles of restorative justice.

Punishment: A Summary

The most severe sanctions are generally handed down for violent offenders and repeat offenders. Although judges ultimately hand down sentences to convicted offenders, the law is the instrument that sets forth minimum and maximum sentences. This gives legislators tremendous power in determining the direction of U.S. sentencing practices: "If lawmakers feel that the other two bodies—judges and officials of the executive branch—are being too lenient in their sentencing decisions, they can pass truth-in-sentencing laws that require convicts to serve the amount of time indicated in criminal codes" (Gaines et al., 2000, p. 382).

We can also conclude, by comparing punishment in the United States with that of other countries, that the United States is very "tough" on crime. In fact, the United States sentences convicted murderers and robbers roughly to the same length of incarceration as Canada and England (and we have the death penalty!); for relatively petty offenses, we sentence offenders to much longer terms of incarceration (Beckett and Sasson, 2000,

BOX 8-5

RESTORATIVE JUSTICE

According to Prison Fellowship International's Restorative Justice Center, restorative justice is "a theory of justice that emphasizes repairing the harm caused or revealed by criminal behavior. It is best accomplished through cooperative processes that include all stakeholders."

Three key principles are part of the foundation of restorative justice. First, "justice requires that we work to restore those who have been injured." Second, "those most directly involved and affected by crime should have the opportunity to participate fully in the response if they wish." Third, the role of government "is to preserve a just public order, and the community's is to build and maintain a just peace."

Restorative justice works by identifying and taking steps to repair harm, involving all important stakeholders, and transforming the traditional relationship between communities and their governments in responding to crime. Programs identified with restorative justice typically include:

- *Victim offender mediation*—entails meetings between the victim and offender with a trained mediator.
- *Conferencing*—similar to mediation, but also includes other relevant stakeholders such as families, employers, counselors, police, and so forth.
- *Circles*—similar to conferencing, but with broader participation by community members, each willing to talk and discuss healing of the victim and offender.
- *Victim assistance*—offers a variety of services to victims, such as legal, psychological, and social support.
- *Ex-offender assistance*—provides a similar set of services to offenders to assist them with re-integration into society.
- *Restitution*—includes monetary payments or payments through services to crime victims by offenders.
- *Community service*—entails making a payment to the community by completing local service projects.

Each of these programs allows victims and offenders to encounter one another along with other members of the community, allows offenders to make amends in an effort to repair harms, permits reintegration into society, and is inclusive. Each is aimed at building community by offering "a constructive framework to guide our responses to crime, conflict, offensive behavior, violations and injustices." Further, each values all people and seeks to "repair damages, (re)establish dignity, and (re)integrate all who were harmed and alienated."

SOURCES: Fresno Pacific University Center for Peacemaking and Conflict Studies (2007), Restorative Justice Project at http://peace.fresno.edu/rjp/; Prison Fellowship International (2007), Restorative Justice Online, Introduction, at http://www.restorativejustice.org/intro.

p. 29). Thus, the notion that the U.S. criminal justice network is lenient on criminals is simply a myth (Kappeler and Potter, 2004).

The bottom line is that punishment should be aimed toward the future, not the past. When we say, "Don't cry over spilled milk," we mean that it does very little good after the milk is spilled to cry about it. The milk should be cleaned up, and precautions should be taken so that no more milk will be spilled in the future. If this requires punishing the offender for being careless, reckless, or even intentionally spilling the milk, so be it. But it would not make much sense to punish the milk-spiller simply to get even with him or her. It would not get the floor clean (unless the punishment included cleaning the floor), it would not increase the likelihood that more milk would not be wasted in the future, and it might even be detrimental or destructive to the future of the milk-spiller, particularly if the punishment far exceeded the act. We wouldn't want to do anything that would make it more likely that the milk-spiller would spill more milk in the future, would we?

I argue that our system of punishment should be future based, aimed at crime prevention and restoration, and rooted in utilitarianism. **Utilitarianism** (based on the writings of John Stuart Mill, for example) holds that actions should be aimed at doing the greatest good for the greatest number of people. Some of what we do may ideally be based on utilitarian goals of crime prevention through deterrence, but most of what we do in the United States to punish criminals is based on retribution, which is backward looking: It aims to get even with the offender for past wrongs. The methods of punishment available to the U.S. network of criminal justice are not being best used to achieve the goals set forth in Chapter 1. Restorative justice is much more likely to be effective at achieving our goals.

IS PUNISHMENT EFFECTIVE?

There are several sources of information to consider when attempting to determine which types of punishment are effective. One valuable source is offenders themselves. Another is criminal justice research, which sheds some light on the effectiveness of various kinds of punishment. Next, I summarize what these sources suggest about the effectiveness of punishment in the United States.

What We've Learned from Offenders

Many scholars have spent time with known offenders, both incarcerated and free, to discover their motivations and mechanisms for committing crimes. Offenders report that they have learned from personal experience that their likelihood of getting punished is extremely low in the United States. Figure 8-4 illustrates the likelihood of being caught by the police, convicted by the courts, and sentenced to some form of incarceration (prison or jail) for various crimes. The numbers in the first column represent the percentage of criminal victimizations (NCVS) in 2002 that led to an incarceration in either prison or jail. The numbers in the second column represent the percentage of crimes known to the police (UCR) in 2002 that led to an incarceration in either prison or jail. As you can see, the only crime for which there exists a substantial risk of arrest, conviction, and imprisonment is murder and nonnegligent homicide. The risk of incarceration for murder and nonnegligent homicide in 2002 was 50%; the next highest risk

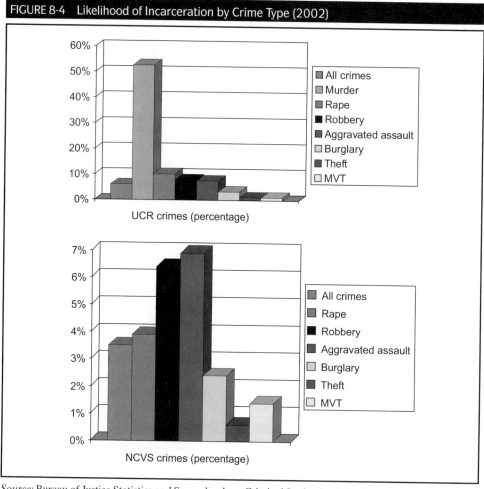

FIGURE 8-4 Likelihood of Incarceration by Crime Type (2002)

Source: Bureau of Justice Statistics and Sourcebook on Criminal Justice Statistics (2006).

was for sexual assault (8% of NCVS sexual assaults and 22% of UCR forcible rapes led to an incarceration). No other crime ever neared a 10% risk for incarceration.

The crime of burglary, committed by rational offenders who carefully choose their targets on the basis of certain environmental characteristics, provides an excellent example of how the threat of punishment can never deter would-be offenders (Wright and Decker, 1994). First, consider when burglars choose to commit their offenses. Many burglary studies show that residences are at highest risk for burglary when they are left unoccupied—that is, when no one is home. Both burglar interview studies (Cromwell and Olson, 2003; Maguire and Bennett, 1982; Walsh, 1980; Wright and Decker, 1994) and analyses of times of burglary (Reppetto, 1974; Waller and Okihiro, 1978; Winchester and Jackson, 1982) have demonstrated the importance of nonoccupancy in the occurrence of burglary. Scarr (1973) found in a study in Washington, D.C., that residential burglary occurred during the daytime and on weekends, following relatively regular patterns of nonoccupancy. Approximately half of all residential burglaries in Scarr's study occurred during the 6-hour period between 10:00 A.M. and 4:00 P.M. Rengert and Wasilchick (1985) also found that the occurrence of burglary corresponded with occupants' schedules, because burglaries occurred during times when dwellings were left unoccupied. Research by Robinson (1997, 1998, 1999) in Florida found similar results: Burglars targeted residences, often repeatedly, that were either unoccupied or where resident activity patterns did not allow for reliably predicting non-occupancy.

Offenders tell researchers that they prefer not to enter residences that are occupied (Cromwell, 1995). According to Cromwell, Olson, and Avary (1991, p. 37), 28 of the 30 burglars in their ethnographic study of breaking and entering indicated they would never intentionally enter an occupied residence. In Wright and Decker's (1994) study of residential burglary, occupancy served as the major risk factor associated with the decision not to enter a potential target residence. Thus, the major risk to burglars is not law enforcement, courts, and corrections but, instead, the threat of run-ins with residential occupants. Consider also what these offenders tell researchers about their likelihood of being punished by criminal justice agencies. They know from experience that this likelihood is very small. As many offenders have stated, "If I thought I was going to get caught, I wouldn't be doing it, now would I?" Criminal justice data confirm that the risk of getting caught and incarcerated is slim.

What We've Learned from Other Criminal Justice Research

Research shows that, overall, American punishment is highly ineffective at reducing crime. Regardless of the type of punishment, virtually every type of criminal sanction fails to reduce recidivism. One of the best explanations for why this is so is presented by Professor C. Ray Jeffery of the Florida State University in Issue in Depth at the end of this chapter.

According to the Bureau of Justice Statistics, "At least 95% of all state prisoners will be released from prison at some point; nearly 80% will be released to parole supervision." For example, in 2000, more than 570,000 inmates were released to community supervision after imprisonment. According to the data, most of these inmates will one day be back in trouble with the law. For example, a study of recidivism of prisoners released in 1994 from 15 states found that more than two-thirds (67.5%) were rearrested after 3 years and more than half (51.8%) returned to prison. Almost half (46.9%) were reconvicted of new crimes, and one-quarter (25.4%) were returned to prison with a new sentence (Sourcebook on Criminal Justice Statistics, 2003). Failure rates were highest for property and drug offenders, as well as for males and African Americans. According to The Sentencing Project (2003), about one-third of inmates were rearrested within 6 months, 44% were rearrested within the first year, 59% were rearrested by the second year, and 67.5% were rearrested by the third year.

As for inmates released from federal prisons in 1994, almost one-fifth (18.6%) were returned to prison within 3 years of their release. The highest rates of failure were for violent offenders at the federal level.

Most data on recidivism concern only the percentage of offenders who successfully complete the conditions of their release within the time period they are being supervised. These data are more suggestive of success, but they are not as accurate in terms of characterizing the widespread failure of probation and parole because they do not measure long-term change in offenders.

At the end of 2005, more than 682,000 adults were under state parole supervision and nearly 90,000 were under federal parole supervision. Of all those discharged in any given year, only about 40–55% will successfully complete their supervision term. The success rate for probationers is higher—about 60% of state probationers and 80% of federal probationers successfully complete their conditions of probation.

Failures are more common for violent offenders, and those most likely to violate probation and parole were those with a history of drug abuse, lower education backgrounds, and younger males. Thus, our most disadvantaged criminals are most likely to continue offending. Our approach to crime control does not address the root problems, so why should we expect success?

Given the horrors of prison life (see Chapter 9), it does not surprise many that prison fails so badly to stop repeat offenders. What is amazing to many is that even our most used criminal sanction—probation—appears to largely be a failure. Probation fails to stop recidivism about half the time (Walker, 2005).

A couple of important factors explain the failure of probation. First, only about one-tenth of the corrections budget in any given year is allocated to probation, even though two-thirds of people under the supervision of corrections are on probation (Petersilia, 1998). Also, even though probation populations have grown since 1980, funding for probation has remained virtually unchanged (Langan, 1994). Further, individual probation officers have large caseloads, making their jobs difficult if not impossible. Given that offenders spend very little or no time being supervised by probation officers and that this form of punishment does nothing to change the social conditions that produce criminality, maybe we should not expect probation to be effective.

In terms of other punishment strategies, many have been reviewed for their effectiveness at preventing crime. For example, Sherman et al. (1997) published a congressionally mandated evaluation of state and local crime prevention programs funded by the U.S. Department of Justice. The study, titled *Preventing Crime: What Works, What Doesn't, What's Promising,* clearly laid out the few programs we know work to reduce crime, the many more that we know don't work, and the largest share that appear to be promising.

The authors proceeded from the assumption that crime prevention means "any practice shown to result in less crime than would normally occur without the practice." Programs aimed at crime prevention, including reducing drug abuse and youth violence, were assessed and placed in the "seven local institutional settings in which these practices operated": in communities, in families, in schools, in labor markets, in places, by police, and by courts and corrections (p. 2).

The authors identified the hundreds of programs operated under U.S. Department of Justice funding and then developed the "Maryland Scale of Scientific Methods" to determine the effectiveness of each study. As mentioned before, each type of crime prevention program was categorized as either something that works, something that does not work, something that is promising, or something that is unknown. These terms are defined as follows:

- **What works:**   Programs the authors believe are "reasonably certain" to prevent crime or reduce risk factors for crime
- **What doesn't work:**   Programs the authors believe are "reasonably certain" to fail to prevent crime or reduce risk factors for crime

- **What's promising:** Programs for which the level of certainty is too low to make firm conclusions, but for which, on the basis of the limited evidence, there is some reason to expect some successful reduction in crime
- **What's unknown:** Programs the authors could not classify into one of these categories because of a lack of studies testing the programs' effectiveness

Box 8-6 presents the main findings from the study.

BOX 8-6

WHAT WORKS, WHAT DOESN'T, WHAT'S PROMISING?

According to the authors, the following worked:

- *For older male ex-offenders*: Vocational training reduces repeat offending.
- *For high-risk repeat offenders*: Monitoring by specialized police units reduces the crimes committed by repeat offenders on the streets. Incarceration of high-risk offenders keeps them from committing crime on the streets.
- *For drug-using offenders in prison*: Therapeutic community resident programs reduce repeat offending after release.

According to the authors, the following did not work:

- *Correctional boot camps* using traditional military basic training
- *"Scared Straight" programs* whereby minor juvenile offenders visit adult prisons
- *Shock probation, shock parole,* and *split sentences* adding jail time to probation or parole

- *Home detention with electronic monitoring*
- *Intensive supervision on parole or probation*
- *Rehabilitation programs using vague, unstructured counseling*
- *Residential programs for juvenile offenders using challenging experiences in rural settings*

According to the authors, the following can be considered promising:

- *Prison-based vocational education programs* may be beneficial for adult inmates in federal prisons.
- *Drug courts* may reduce repeat offending.
- *Drug treatment in jails followed by urine testing in the community* may reduce subsequent drug use.
- *Intensive supervision and aftercare of juvenile offenders* may reduce repeat offending.
- *Fines* may reduce repeat crimes.

SOURCE: Sherman, L., et al. (1997). *Preventing Crime: What Works, What Doesn't, What's Promising.* Washington, DC: United States Department of Justice.

BIAS IN THE SENTENCING PROCESS

Recall from Chapter 1 that for a criminal justice process such as sentencing to be just, it must be fair and "not be affected by extraneous factors, such as race, gender, or socio-economic status" (Kappeler, Blumberg, and Potter, 2000, p. 228). Instead, sentences should be based on legal factors such as seriousness of offense and prior criminal record. The use of legal factors to determine appropriate sentence, though obviously less troublesome than sentencing based on extralegal factors, is still problematic. Using prior record and seriousness of offense to determine sentence allows biases of the criminal law and police behavior to come into play.

According to Kappeler et al. (2000, p. 28), "The empirical research done by criminal justice scholars has demonstrated with remarkable regularity that minority group members (particularly African Americans) and the poor get longer sentences and have less chance of gaining parole or probation, even when the seriousness of the crime and the criminal record of the defendants are held constant." Pratt (1998) illustrates how race will continue to play a role in sentencing into the twenty-first century. Such conclusions would lead you to believe that power has a direct influence on justice because relatively less powerful groups in the United States don't receive equal justice. For example, a study of incarceration in Florida found that the people most likely to be imprisoned were unemployed African American males, even when the seriousness of the offense and the prior record of the defendant were held constant (Chiricos and Bales, 1991).

Walker, Spohn, and DeLone (2006, p. 280) conclude that sentencing in the 1990s was characterized by discrimination because they found evidence of bias in many court jurisdictions in various areas related to sentencing. They write:

> Judges in some jurisdictions continue to impose harsher sentences on racial minorities who murder or rape whites, and more lenient sentences on racial minorities whose victims are of their own racial or ethnic group. Judges in some jurisdictions continue to impose racially biased sentences in less serious cases; in these "borderline cases" racial minorities get prison, whereas whites get probation. In jurisdictions with sentencing guidelines, judges depart from the presumptive sentence less often when the offender is African American or Hispanic than when the offender is white. Judges, in other words, continue to take race into account, either explicitly or implicitly, when determining the appropriate sentence.

It is in borderline cases, then, the only cases in which discretion can come into play, where discretion does come into play. In other words, race and class biases affect sentencing when it is possible for them to do so Fortunately, what mandatory sentencing has done for us, through sentencing guidelines and truth-in-sentencing laws, is make it harder for prosecutors, judges, and juries to be discriminatory in sentencing matters.

If one were to look at sentencing nationally without distinguishing between types of offenses, sentencing generally does not appear to be biased against any race of people; that is, African Americans and Caucasians appear to receive the same sentences within the same categories of offenses. An earlier review of sentencing and race by the National Academy of Sciences claimed that factors other than racial discrimination in sentencing account for most of the disproportionate representation of blacks in

U.S. prisons, although "racial discrimination in sentencing may play a more important role in some regions or jurisdictions, for some crime types, or in the decisions of individual participants" (Blumstein et al., 1983, p. 13).

The average prison sentences imposed on convicted felons by state courts are virtually identical for African Americans and Caucasians for violent, property, drug, weapons, and other felonies. Yet there is evidence of clear sentencing bias against African Americans and Hispanics at the federal level, particularly with regard to drug offenses (Albonetti, 1997).

African Americans also are no more likely than Caucasians nationally to be sentenced to a term of imprisonment by state courts for violent crimes and are even less likely to be sentenced to imprisonment for property offenses. African Americans are, however, more likely than Caucasians to be sentenced by state courts to incarceration in prison for drug offenses. Finally, there is evidence of discrimination against people of color, because there are patterns of discrimination in some cities (Walker et al., 2006).

It is unclear why African Americans appear to be discriminated against when sentenced to imprisonment for drug felonies but not for violent and property felonies. It is also not clear why African Americans are sentenced to longer jail terms than Caucasians but not prison terms generally. With regard to drugs, African Americans probably receive longer average sentences than Caucasians because of prior record, which thus reflects a bias—not a court bias, but a policing bias—as African Americans are more likely to be arrested for drug offenses (see Chapter 11). The use of discretion by prosecutors in the charging phase of the criminal justice process probably explains the apparent biases against African Americans in jail terms. In serious felonies that will likely result in substantial prison terms, it would be very difficult for prosecutors to use their discretion in a biased manner. It would, however, be substantially easier for them to be biased in relatively minor felonies, where they have substantially more discretion to charge defendants with more or less severe offenses. The same would be true for judges, whose discretion is limited when sentencing for major felonies but substantially wider in less serious felonies that may lead to jail time rather than imprisonment.

This may be why some studies have found sentencing bias against minorities for crimes where the nature of the crime and the offender's prior record do not point clearly to the appropriate sentence (e.g., see Unnever and Hembroff, 1988). Such findings suggest that in at least some jurisdictions, when prosecutors and judges have discretion, they may be more likely to be biased against minorities than Caucasians. Other studies, in larger states and in areas where income inequality is higher, have found sentencing disparities based on race, even after controlling for legal factors (e.g., see Bridges and Crutchfield, 1988; Myers, 1987; Petersilia, 1995).

There is also evidence of discrimination in sentences to probation. Caucasians are overrepresented among probationers, leading Walker et al. (2006) to suggest that the less severe sentence of probation is more likely to be reserved for Caucasians, especially in borderline cases where either probation or a short sentence of incarceration are both options.

Some court clients are subjected to sentencing laws that are clearly biased. For example, the three-strikes laws introduced earlier in this chapter disproportionately are aimed at relatively nonserious minority offenders. Harvard Medical School researcher William Brownsberger claims they are "wasting prison resources on non-violent, low-level offenders and reducing resources available to lock up violent offenders" (quoted in National Center on Institutions and Alternatives, 1999). Walker (1998, p. 137) writes that three-strikes laws "have been almost universally condemned by criminologists and other experts on sentencing.

As noted earlier in the chapter, researchers confidently conclude that the laws cost billions of dollars, cause lengthy delays in the criminal justice process, and are biased against members of the poor and racial minorities. Although crime fell in California, the cost has been significant.

And who is getting caught? The shocking fact is that most offenders sentenced are not repeat violent murderers, rapists, and robbers. After the first 5 years in California, only 25% of third-strikers were convicted of violent offenses, including 294 murderers, 241 child molesters, and 136 rapists. The largest category of "violent" third-strikers was robbers, and most of these committed their crimes to get drugs and/or did not actually hurt anyone. After 10 years, the picture is much the same, as the majority of three-strikers are not serious, violent felons. Instead, they are burglars, arsonists, drug possessors, and robbers (a violent crime aimed at property gain). Box 8-7 lists some people sentenced under three-strikes laws. You should note that several of these individuals probably *need* to be in prison given their long criminal histories; others likely do not, given their crimes.

BOX 8-7

SOME INDIVIDUALS SENTENCED UNDER THREE-STRIKES LAWS

- Kenneth Parnell—Since 1951 Parnell has committed sexual predatory crimes against children. At the age of 19, Parnell kidnapped and sodomized a 9-year-old boy. In 1972, he kidnapped 7-year-old Steven Stayner and held him hostage as his "son" for more than 7 years. In December of 2002, Parnell attempted to purchase a 4-year-old boy for $500. Pursuant to the three-strikes law, Parnell was sentenced to 25 years to life in prison. If the current form of the three-strikes law were not in effect, Parnell would be released from prison in approximately January 2005.

- Jose Arreola—In 1982, Arreola received his first felony conviction for burglary. In 1983, he was convicted of sexually abusing a child. While on probation, Arreola was convicted of child molestation and sentenced to 8 years in prison. In 1995, Arreola was charged with felony possession of a controlled substance and hit-and-run. The trial court reduced Arreola's charge to a misdemeanor, disqualifying him from the three-strikes sentence, and placed him on probation. In 1999, Arreola pleaded guilty to two counts of forcible lewd acts upon a child in connection with his molestation of three of his relatives for more than a 5-year period. He admitted to mutual oral copulation and sodomy on boys ages 7, 8, and 10. Finally, pursuant to three-strikes, Arreola was sentenced to 50 years to life in prison.

- Cladius Johnson—Johnson was convicted for his role in gang-raping a woman at gunpoint in 1979. In

1985, he was convicted of robbery. Three years later, Johnson was convicted of carrying a loaded automatic machine gun; he was sentenced to 16 months in prison. If the three-strikes law were in effect at the time, Johnson likely would have been sentenced to 25 years to life in prison. Months after being paroled in 1989, Johnson was arrested and later convicted of assault with a deadly weapon, for which he served less than 6 years in state prison. Again, if three-strikes had been in effect at the time, Johnson likely would have been sentenced to 25 years to life in prison. Finally, in 1995 Johnson beat and choked his wife into unconsciousness during a child's birthday party. The trial court sentenced Johnson under the three-strikes law to 25 years to life in prison.

- Kenneth Fuller—Fuller was convicted in 1980 of attempted murder and felony child molestation causing great bodily injury. In 1992, he violated the conditions of his parole by living with a woman who had children and was returned to prison. In 1994 he was convicted of failing to register as a sex offender. Fuller again failed to register as a sex offender in 1997 when he moved to a new address. The trial court sentenced Fuller under the three-strikes law to 25 years to life in prison.

- Ervin Cole—Since 1984, Cole has been convicted of robbery using a firearm, burglary, and assault with a deadly weapon. He also violated parole five times. Cole was convicted in 1999 for evading arrest, car theft, and felony hit-and-run. Pursuant to the three-strikes law, Cole was sentenced to 25 years to life in prison.

- John Bunyard—For a 20-year period starting in 1955, Bunyard was convicted of 10 felonies. In 1973 he embarked on a crime spree including the murders of two women and the rapes, robbery, assaults, and kidnappings of many others from San Francisco to Lake Tahoe. For his crimes, he was sentenced to a prison term of 19 years. Bunyard was later released and in 1992 was convicted for possessing a billy club, a felony for which he could have received a 25-year-to-life sentence had the three-strikes law been in effect. Instead, Bunyard was placed on probation. In 1996 Bunyard solicited a 14-year-old girl who was walking to a store in San Jose. He offered the girl money so that he could "look" at her. Bunyard was arrested and convicted of attempting to commit a lewd and lascivious act on a minor. He was finally sentenced under the three-strikes law to 28 years to life in prison.

- Michael Cepeda—In the early 1980s, Cepeda was convicted of two residential burglaries. In 1989, he violated parole by being under the influence of drugs and later was convicted of robbery. In 1994, he was convicted of possessing cocaine; the trial court used its discretion to strike two of the prior three-strikes conviction allegations. Cepeda was sentenced under the two-strikes provision, receiving a total of 8 years in prison.

- Manuel Morales—In 1993, Morales was convicted of two counts of felony child molestation. In March of 2001 he was convicted by a jury of three

(continued)

BOX 8-7   *(Continued)*

counts of annoying or molesting a child. At sentencing, the trial court dismissed one of the prior strike convictions in furtherance of justice and sentenced Morales to 12 years, double the standard prison term pursuant to the two-strikes provision in the three-strikes law.

- Jerry Williams—The "Pizza Thief," Williams was made famous by many press accounts. Between 1980 and 1990 Williams was arrested 14 times. In July 1994, Williams approached four children who were sitting on the Redondo Beach pier eating pizza. Williams, who is 6 feet 4 inches tall and weighed 220 pounds, demanded a slice of pizza from the children. After the children said no to Williams, he confronted them and took a slice of the pizza. He was convicted of committing petty theft with prior robbery-related strike convictions. The trial court eventually dismissed one of Williams's strike convictions and sentenced him under the two-strikes provision to 6 years in prison.

- Steven Mathews—From 1969 to 1987 Mathews was convicted of kidnap, robbery (twice), murder, assault with intent to commit murder, and attempted murder (twice). If the three-strikes law were in effect in 1979, Mathews could have been sentenced to 25 years to life in prison at that time. Instead, he was released on parole and in 1987 was convicted of the rape and forcible oral copulation of his mother. In 2003, Mathews was stopped by law enforcement officers for drinking in public. Found inside his jacket was a two-foot long machete and a

geological hammer. The hammer had the words, "fag finder reminder" inscribed on its handle. Mathews was convicted of felony weapons possession and sentenced to 25 years to life in prison pursuant to the three-strikes law.

- Leandro Andrade—From 1982 to 1995 Andrade suffered nine convictions, including five felony residential burglaries and several drug-trafficking offenses. He had an addiction to heroin since 1977 and stole to support his habit. On two separate occasions in San Bernardino County in 1995, Andrade stole a total of nine videotapes valued at $153 from a department store. Andrade was convicted of two counts of felony theft and was sentenced by the trial court to two consecutive 25-years-to-life prison terms. The United States Supreme Court found the sentence to be constitutional.

In addition to these cases, provided by the California District Attorney's association, other offenders sentenced under three-strikes laws include:

- A woman who bought $20 worth of cocaine 14 years after her second conviction

- A robber of a sandwich shop in Washington who stole $151 (his two previous robberies netted $460) (Walker, 1998, p. 139)

- A teenager sentenced to life for stealing a cellular phone (Domanick, 1997)

- A man sentenced to 25 years to life for stealing a bottle of vitamins from a grocery store (Gaines et al., 2000, p. 394)

- A man convicted of stealing a carton of cigarettes from Target, with prior offenses 15 years earlier of burglary and assault
- A woman who gained $5 in a cocaine sale, whose prior offenses included robbery, burglary, and prostitution
- A man convicted of receiving stolen property (a 1985 car), whose prior offenses included burglary, drug possession, and a robbery that involved a pack of cigarettes from another inmate

- A homeless man, whose only possession was a bicycle, charged with stealing a $2 bicycle lock
- A severely retarded 34-year-old woman who was homeless and living in a park, charged with possession of a $5 rock of cocaine
- A man who allegedly bought a crushed macadamia nut from the police, charged with attempting to possess drugs (Dodge and Harris, 2000, pp. 355–356)

Many three-strikers are drug offenders, including those who were convicted and sentenced simply for possessing drugs. Meanwhile, the Rand Corporation claims that mechanisms such as drug treatment, parent training, delinquent supervision, and graduation incentives are up to seven times more effective at reducing recidivism than mandatory prison terms, and are more cost-effective as well (Robinson, 2000). Three-strikes laws have shifted the power in courts from judges to prosecutors, have led to backlogs in court dockets, have led to more pretrial detention for inmates charged with a third-strike offense (because they are considered a high flight risk), sentence length has increased (but only for minor crimes), prisons are overcrowded, funding for social services has been cut, and racial and class-based disparities have worsened.

Although street crime is down in California since the laws were implemented, criminologists have attributed such declines to factors beyond the scope of criminal justice (see Chapter 4). Further, crime was already declining prior to the passage of the laws, crime declined in other states without the laws, and crime declined more in the counties that used the laws less than in those that used it more.

When drug offenses are included in mandatory sentencing, such sentencing laws become a major source of criminal justice bias. For example, in 2004, African Americans were only slightly more likely than whites to report having used any illicit drug in the past month. Yet they made up more than one-third of arrests for drug abuse violations. Earlier data showed that African Americans made up more than half (55%) of convictions for drug offenses and almost three of four (74%) prison sentences for drug offenses (Mauer and Huling, 1995a). Additionally, whereas 39% of crack users were African American, 89% of people sentenced for federal crack crimes were African American. Throughout the United States, convicted drug offenders are disproportionately low-income minorities. And according to the Bureau of Justice Statistics (2003), African Americans are sentenced to prison more than half the time for drug offenses, whereas Caucasians are sentenced to incarceration only about one-third of the time for the same offenses. From 1990 to 1996, the number of African Americans in federal prisons for violent and property crimes decreased by 726 persons, but for drug offenses the number increased by 12,852!

The impact of sentencing laws on minorities (especially African Americans) is greatest at the federal level. Thus, the number of federal inmates in 1980 who were minorities was 8,085 (33%), but this increased to 65,000 (64%) by 1995 (Coalition for Federal Sentencing Reform, 1999). Such bias counters the myth that the criminal justice network is fair. Some even suggest that the war on drugs amounts to genocide "because African Americans constitute a disproportionate number of those subjected to arrest, prosecution, and incarceration for illicit drug trafficking" (e.g., see Meddis, 1993).

Federal sentencing against drug dealers demonstrates clear evidence of bias against people of color. One study, for example, found that African American and Hispanic drug offenders received longer sentences than Caucasian drug offenders, even after controlling for relevant legal factors (Albonetti, 1997), and that Caucasian defendants received more benefit from departures from federal sentencing guidelines. Albonetti concludes that her findings "strongly suggest that the mechanism by which the federal guidelines permit the exercise of discretion operates to the disadvantage of minority defendants" (p. 818).

In the wars against drugs and violence, federal sentencing has become much more complex. And the prosecutor, who decides what to charge and how many counts to charge (among the thousands of offenses in the federal criminal code), thereby effectively determines the likely sentence. Such concentration of power creates bias in favor of the government and against the client who is supposedly innocent until proved guilty. Also, judges have little oversight in the process, and only prosecutors can reward suspects for turning state's evidence against other suspects.

Federal sentencing is also viewed as unfair. For example, Judge Gray (2001) reports that most judges want to modify guidelines to increase their sentencing discretion. A 1992 survey of judges found they believed only one in four sentences imposed under guidelines is appropriate (Coalition for Federal Sentencing Reform, 1997). A particularly striking unfair pattern is the 100:1 ratio for sentences for crack cocaine and powder cocaine, meaning that to receive a mandatory sentence of 5 years' imprisonment, a person would need 100 times as much powder cocaine as crack (500 grams of powder versus 5 grams of crack). No one can say for sure if this discrepancy is racially motivated, but, in the late 1990s, African Americans accounted for 39% of crack cocaine users (and for only 13% of the general population) but 89% of those sentenced for federal crack crimes (Coalition for Federal Sentencing Reform, 1999). Media portrayal of crack use reinforces the stereotype or myth that it is an "African American drug" (e.g., see Reeves and Campbell, 1994). Because harms associated with crack cocaine (e.g., "crack babies") were so broadly portrayed and discussed, not even a single African American member of Congress spoke out against the sentencing disparities between crack and powder cocaine at the time that the law was originally proposed and debated (Kennedy, 1997).

Of course, bias in sentencing can be found when we look at crimes committed by the wealthy. As noted by Kappeler et al. (2000, p. 230), this is where the courts tend to be "kinder and gentler." Compare people in one study who were convicted for grand theft versus those convicted of fraud in the health care industry, for example. This study (Tillman and Pontell, 1992) showed that those who were convicted of fraud were only half as likely as those convicted of grand theft to be sentenced to prison even though the damages they caused were 10 times greater. The average sentence given to offenders in the savings and loan crisis in the 1980s was 36 months, versus 38 months for people who committed auto theft and 56 months for burglars (Pontell, Calavita, and

Tillman, 1994). The average sentences for white-collar and corporate offenders in the most recent cases have been modest, as well, relative to the damages they have inflicted on society. Failing to sentence the guilty simply because of their social class and skin color is as unjust as sentencing a small group of the guilty more harshly because of their social class or skin color. Elite deviance (see Chapter 4) is one place where Justitia, the Lady Justice, truly is not blind. Instead, she knowingly shrugs off the harms caused by wealthy Caucasian criminals.

CONCLUSION

Sentencing is the process whereby a person who has been convicted of a crime or crimes is sanctioned for his or her wrongdoings by a court. In the United States, we punish offenders because we want them to suffer (vengeance), we want them to pay us for the harms they inflicted on us (retribution), and we want to scare them from committing crimes in the future (deterrence). Yet most of what we do to fight crime does not "get even" with offenders and does not prevent future criminality. American criminal justice is dedicated to sentencing criminals to punishments that have clearly been proven ineffective, particularly imprisonment. Meanwhile, punishment in the United States is also biased in some ways against poor people, people of color, and women. Although biases in sentencing are not institutional, there is clear evidence of sentencing disparities based on class, race, and gender. These biases serve as further evidence of unjust practices in the U.S. criminal justice network.

Issue in Depth—C. Ray Jeffery Explains the Failure of American Punishment

Professor C. Ray Jeffery (1990), on the basis of psychological theories of behavior, outlined significant reasons that American punishment does not work to reduce crime and may, under certain circumstances, actually increase crime. His main points include the following.

- To be successful, the time lag between the behavior and punishment must be short . . . punishment must be swift. . . . Punishment is anything but swift with long delays between the crime, arrest, conviction, sentencing and imprisonment. Today, it may take years before a criminal is punished.
- To be successful, punishment must be certain. In our system of criminal justice we have many unknown and unreported crimes, which can run as high as five unreported crimes for one reported crime. Of those crimes reported, few arrests are made, few convictions are made, and few criminals are sentenced to prison. . . . For the same crime the sentence can vary in many ways. . . . To be effective, punishment must overcome positive reinforcement. . . . When a reinforcer such as money can be gotten by an illegal response, the person can weigh the risk of punishment versus the monetary gain. Since the risk of punishment is low, the criminal has the odds in his/her favor as he/she commits a crime. The prospect of gaining money immediately outweighs the threat of punishment in the distant future.

- To make punishment effective, we must provide the person with alternative means for reinforcement. If a person is offered an alternative to the punished response, the punished response will be diminished or eliminated. This implies the establishment of crime prevention programs that block the illegal opportunities structure, as well as behavioral programs that create legitimate opportunities.

- Punishment can become a conditioned stimulus for positive reinforcement. If a child is spanked and then given candy, the child will misbehave to get candy. If the only time a child is noticed by the parent is when the parent is punishing the child, the child will act in an antisocial manner to get attention.

- Punishment creates escape and avoidance behaviors. . . . A person does not learn through punishment to obey the law; rather, he or she learns how to commit crimes and to escape punishment. Criminals can avoid punishment by avoiding detection and arrest; if arrested, they can give an alibi or hire lawyers; if charged, they can falsify statements and attempt to win an acquittal; if found guilty, they can tell the social worker a story that may result in probation; if sentenced, they can try to manipulate the prison community to gain privileges and an early release. The criminal justice system is one huge escape and avoidance conditioning system. Rather than conditioning people to legal behavior, it conditions them to escape and avoid the law.

- Punishment creates aggression in those who are punished. This aggression can be operant—that is, against the aggressor, to remove the aggression—or reflexive. Reflexive aggression occurs when pain is administered to a person and the person strikes out against any object or person in the environment. When we put people in prison, we make them more vicious and hateful than before. This is a major failure of our prison system to rehabilitate.

- Any stimulus associated with punishment can become a conditioned stimulus (CS) for punishment. A child who avoids or hates a parent or teacher may run away from home or become a truant from school. Many delinquent careers start with such behavioral problems at home or in school. The use of punishment to control behavior creates major behavioral problems of its own.

- If an animal is conditioned to receive unavoidable shocks, with no possibility of escape or avoidance, the animal will not learn to avoid shock later when the shock is avoidable. This is called learned helplessness, and it is also an important aspect of psychological depression. Punishment of prisoners can create learned helplessness. The ability to control one's environment is an important aspect of healthy adaptive behavior; criminal behavior, by contrast, can reflect learned helplessness, a trust in fate, and a loss of control over the environment.

- The punisher (lawyer, parent, teacher, police officer) may be angry or hostile toward the person punished. Aggression rewards those doing the punishing. It allows for a feeling of power over others, it releases feelings of revenge and hatred, and it allows one to be aggressive in a legitimate manner. Aggression can be either lawful or unlawful. The criminal justice system continues to punish and execute criminals not because of the impact of punishment on the criminal but because of the impact of punishment on those doing the punishing, including you and me.

- Punishment, then, is not a successful way to control criminal behavior, because it is so disruptive to other, lawful behaviors.

C. Ray Jeffery's main point is that we ought not to expect American punishment to reduce crime, given the many ways in which it may actually encourage people to initiate and maintain criminal careers. Jeffery has always advocated a more rational and preventive approach to crime reduction, one that identifies the risk factors that increase the likelihood of antisocial behavior in children. Ultimately, if we can reduce one's exposure to these risk factors, we should see less juvenile delinquency and ultimately less adult criminality.

KEY TERMS

aggravating factors	general deterrence	rehabilitation
boot camps	general incapacitation	renew
certainty of punishment	house arrest	restitution
chain gangs	incarceration	restorative justice
collective incapacitation	indeterminate sentences	retribution
community service	intermediate sanctions	selective incapacitation
criminal sanctions	jail	sentence
day reporting center	minimum–maximum sentences	sentencing guidelines
death penalty	mitigating factors	special deterrence
determinate sentences	parole	specific deterrence
deterrence	prison	three-strikes laws
electronic monitoring	probation	truth-in-sentencing laws
escalation	punishment	utilitarianism
fixed sentences	recidivism	vengeance

DISCUSSION QUESTIONS

1. What is sentencing?
2. Identify and discuss different types of sentences.
3. Identify some of the drawbacks to determinate and indeterminate sentences.
4. Why do you think judges are generally opposed to mandatory sentences?
5. What types of crimes generally receive the longest sentences? Why?
6. Identify and discuss the main justifications for punishment.
7. Why has the U.S. criminal justice network largely given up on rehabilitation?
8. Identify and discuss the main methods of punishment in the United States.
9. Which type of punishment is the most used? Which is the least used? Why?
10. Why are some people sentenced to probation and others sentenced to terms of incarceration, even though they are convicted for the same crimes?
11. Why is the administration of punishment in the United States so ineffective at reducing crime?
12. Why is American punishment a failure, according to C. Ray Jeffery?
13. Identify the main sources of bias during the sentencing process.
14. How does criminal sentencing reflect biases of the criminal law and policing?
15. Identify and discuss the main problems with the so-called three-strikes laws.
16. Why do you think the criminal justice network pursues crime prevention strategies that have been proved ineffective?
17. Why did the U.S. Supreme Court strike down federal sentencing guidelines? Was it the right decision? Explain.

CHAPTER

9

INCARCERATION: LOCK 'EM UP AND FORGET ABOUT 'EM

1. Introduction
2. The Organization of Corrections in the United States
3. America's Incarceration Rate
   a. What It Costs
4. Who's in Prison and Jail?
5. What Happens in Prison? Pains of Imprisonment
   a. Loss of Liberty
   • Box 9-1.   Myths About Florida Prisons
   • Box 9-2.   Twenty-Four Hours in the North Carolina Department of Correction Division of Prisons
   b. Loss of Autonomy
   c. Loss of Security
   d. Deprivation of Heterosexual Relationships
   • Box 9-3.   Jose Padilla
   e. Deprivation of Goods and Services
   f. Loss of Voting Rights
   g. Loss of Dignity
   h. Stigmatization
   i. Summary: Pains of Imprisonment
6. Forgiving the Offender: Why Harass Parolees?
7. How and Why Corrections Reflects Criminal Justice Bias
8. Conclusion
9. Issue in Depth—The Convict School of Criminology
10. Key Terms
11. Discussion Questions

INTRODUCTION

The end result of the criminal justice process is our corrections system. The corrections system in the United States is made up of a group of agencies and programs that are responsible for administering punishment to people accused and convicted of criminal offenses. As discussed in the last chapter, forms of punishment include incarceration in prisons and jails, probation in the community, and a wide array of intermediate sanctions. This chapter gives separate attention to incarceration, and mostly to imprisonment, because it is one of the most destructive and expensive forms of punishment in the United States. It is also a method that clearly does not achieve the ideal goals of the criminal justice network.

THE ORGANIZATION OF CORRECTIONS IN THE UNITED STATES

Currently in the United States there are thousands of agencies of **institutional corrections**, including more than 1,000 state prisons, 80 federal prisons, and countless jails operated by local governments. Additionally, there are thousands of agencies of **community corrections**, typically governed by counties that run probation and parole services and some forms of intermediate sanctions. Together, these correctional agencies supervise more than 7 million Americans who were convicted of criminal offenses. As you saw in previous chapters, **prisons** are run by states and the federal government, and are intended for people convicted of "serious" crimes and sentenced to more than one year of incarceration. **Jails** are typically run by cities and are intended for people convicted of less serious crimes and sentenced to 1 year or less of incarceration. Jails also hold some people waiting to have their cases heard in court, as well as people picked up by the police for disturbing the peace or awaiting transfer to other institutions. **Probation** is a sentence imposed by the court for relatively minor offenses that requires inmates to complete a term of supervision in the community under certain rules. **Parole** is similar to probation but it is not a sentence imposed by the court; rather it is a term of supervision to be served after release from incarceration. Finally, **intermediate sanctions**, which are not widely used in the United States, are more restrictive than probation but less restrictive than incarceration.

AMERICA'S INCARCERATION RATE

As you saw in Chapter 8, the United States has the highest rate of incarceration in the world, and more than five times greater than most industrialized nations (Beckett and Sasson, 2000; Irwin and Austin, 1997). This is due to massive increases in incarceration in the last 35 years (e.g., see Beck, 1998). Just how many people are incarcerated in the United States? If we took all the people who are incarcerated and put them in one place, it would be the fourth largest city in the country! Table 9-1 lists the cities with the top populations in 2005, along with the incarcerated population in the United States. As you saw in the last chapter, the rate of incarceration (prisons and jails) at the end of 2005 was 737 per 100,000 residents, number one in the world. When only considering prisons, the rate of imprisonment was 491 per 100,000 people.

TABLE 9-1 Most Populous Cities in the United States (Including the Incarcerated Population)	
New York, NY	8.1 million
Los Angeles, CA	3.8 million
Chicago, IL	2.8 million
American inmates	**2.2 million**
Houston, TX	2.0 million
Philadelphia, PA	1.5 million
Phoenix, AZ	1.5 million
San Antonio, TX	1.3 million
San Diego, CA	1.3 million
Dallas, TX	1.2 million

The National Criminal Justice Commission writes, "Since 1980, the United States has engaged in the largest and most frenetic correctional buildup of any country in the history of the world" (Donziger, 1996, p. 31). While the increases slowed in the early twenty-first century, they continue to climb slowly. This is true for incarceration in prisons and jails and also for probation and parole populations. Collectively, these correctional populations have swelled to more than 7 million people, including more than 2.2 million people incarcerated.

Think about the irony of this. Professor Todd Clear, an expert on corrections, writes the following in the foreword to Irwin and Austin's (1997) book, *It's About Time: America's Imprisonment Binge.*

> As Americans, we think of ourselves as a free people. And we think that our freedoms are central to what sets us apart from the rest of the world. . . . It is ironic, then, that in America more people are denied these freedoms by law than in any other Western nation: we lock up more citizens per capita than any other nation that has bothered to count its prisoners. (p. xiii)

Without much doubt, the U.S. imprisonment rate alone (which does not include jail populations) stands as a testament to how far our nation's leaders are willing to go to fight crime—or, more accurately, to fight some types of crime committed by some types of people.

Walker (2005) describes recent crime control efforts in the United States as "an imprisonment orgy." Figure 9-1 documents the unprecedented explosion of *imprisonment* in the United States from the early twentieth century through the early twenty-first century. First, note how the U.S. imprisonment rate was historically relatively constant. It fluctuated over the years, but never until the 1970s did it consistently and dramatically increase. In fact, scholars had written about the *stability of punishment* because there was so little fluctuation in the nation's incarceration rate for so long (Blumstein and Cohen, 1973). Second, note how the imprisonment explosion began in the early 1970s. Between the early 1970s and the mid-1990s, there was approximately

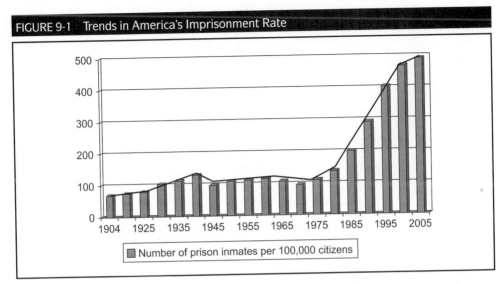

FIGURE 9-1   Trends in America's Imprisonment Rate

a 6.5% increase each year (Blumstein, 2000, p. 6). As you learned in Chapter 8, the rate of growth slowed significantly recently.

According to Kappeler, Blumberg, and Potter (2000, p. 161), the number of sentenced prisoners in both state and federal prisons increased almost seven times from 1972 to 1998 alone. The United States now has more than twice the number of prisoners per 100,000 citizens as any other democracy, and more than five times the rate of democracies such as Canada, England, Germany, and France (The Sentencing Project, 1997). Also, jail, probation, and parole populations in the United States have tripled since 1980.

Figure 9-2 shows the key years during the imprisonment explosion and identifies some key events. You see in the figure the years that public concern peaked over violent crime and drugs. Keeping in mind what you learned about the media in Chapter 5, you should remember that the public did not become concerned about these crimes and demand more imprisonment. In part, it is logical to expect that increased media coverage of crime and of mass imprisonment actually made people more afraid, which then led to an even greater criminal justice response.

Much of the increase in prisons is due to drug convictions (including a 478% increase in drug offenders sentenced to state prisons and a 545% increase in drug offenders sentenced to federal prisons from 1985 to 1996). From 1980 to 1993, the percentage of prisoners in state prisons serving sentences for drug offenses more than tripled; in federal prisons, it more than doubled (Welch, 1999, p. 52). Meanwhile, drug treatment in prison is insufficiently funded, although it is supported by most Americans (Welch, 1999, p. 62). According to the Bureau of Justice Statistics, between 1990 and 2000, violent offenders accounted for 53% of the growth in prison populations, whereas drug offenders made up 20%, public-order offenders made up 15%, and property offenders made up 12%. From 1995 until 2003, the proportion of violent offenders increased from 47% to 52%, whereas the proportion of property offenders decreased from 23% to 21% and the proportion of drug offenders decreased from 22% to 20%. Given that when Americans think about crime, they think about violent crime, most

FIGURE 9-2   Key Events in America's Imprisonment Boom

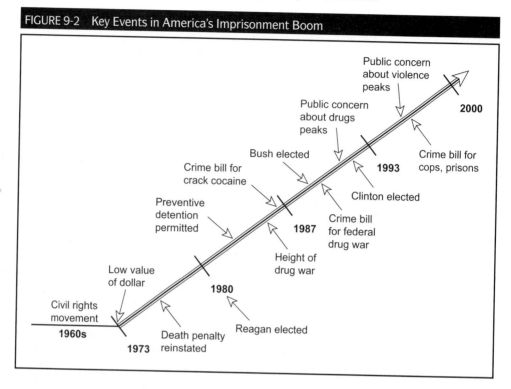

would probably be surprised to learn that only about half of the increase of the prison population is because of violent offenders.

Does sound, scientific evidence suggest that mass imprisonment will work to make us safer? My answer would be, "To a small degree, temporarily." As you saw in Chapter 3, most of the reasons for the crime drop were due to noncriminal justice factors such as economic improvements and an aging population, although mass imprisonment and other criminal justice factors also played some role.

May (2000, p. xvi), editor of a series of essays on prison titled, *Building Violence,* suggests that "[t]he United States is conducting a social experiment unparalleled in its size and implications" and that "[c]riminological research has not been able to demonstrate convincingly that the incarceration of more people, and longer sentences, ultimately provide more security." Given the conclusion from Sherman et al. (1997) that incarceration of repeat offenders "works" to reduce crime, it seems honest to conclude that some of the decline in street crime in the 1990s was attributable to locking up some of the "right offenders." The problem is that a lot of offenders we have locked up are probably not the "right offenders." Additionally, any gains in crime reduction must be understood as temporary given that about 95% of prisoners will one day be released (Bureau of Justice Statistics, 2007). If these offenders are angry and want revenge, we should expect them to commit more crime later.

Let me state unequivocally that the dramatic upward shift in the U.S. imprisonment rate is not attributable to increases in street crime. In Chapter 4, you saw that property crime (the vast majority of street crime) started to decline in the early 1970s. The murder rate was relatively constant prior to and after the boom in incarceration, although it fell precipitously in the 1990s. One trend that corresponds with the increased use of imprisonment as a criminal sanction is an upward shift in income, documented nicely by Phillips (1991) in *The Politics of Rich and Poor* and by Barlett and Steele (1992) in *America: What Went Wrong?* These authors demonstrate how, during the 1980s, the wealthiest Americans got richer while most Americans actually lost ground. In an environment of corporate-friendly legislation, including the deregulation efforts and tax breaks of Presidents Reagan and Bush, many more Americans found themselves living in conditions conducive to criminality. For example, from 1977 to 1988, the average after-tax family income for Americans in the bottom 10% declined nearly 11%, while for the upper 10% it increased almost 25%, and for the top 1% it increased almost 75%. Also, compensation for CEOs of corporations increased more than 100%, and the number of millionaires and billionaires increased by 250%. Do you think that any of these figures are relevant for understanding why the United States is incarcerating so many people?

If you compare these rising imprisonment rates to crime rate declines since the early 1970s, you might conclude that incarceration is an effective means of reducing crime. But this conclusion would be, at best, incomplete and, at worst, wrong. First, there has not been a dramatic drop in crime during this same time period, as you would expect given that incarceration rates are nearly four times what they were 20 years ago (Blumstein, 2000). Second, according to the experts, the modest declines in crime rates are more likely due to noncriminal justice interventions. One major reason street crime rates have declined in the United States is that Americans have gotten older. Street crime is generally a young male phenomenon, so an older population means less crime. Irwin and Austin (1997, p. 144) attribute 60% of the decline in U.S. crime rates between 1980 and 1988 to reductions in the size of the population aged 15 to 24 years old.

Todd Clear, in the foreword to Welch's (1999, p. ix) *Punishment in America: Social Control and the Ironies of Imprisonment,* claims that the U.S. incarceration rate has little to do with crime rates in the United States: "Prison populations continue to grow, despite five consecutive years of falling crime; indeed, since 1975, we have had 10 years of declining crime rates and then 13 years of increasing crime rates—but prison populations have gone up every year regardless." Welch (1999) claims that prison populations are being driven more by economic and market forces than by crime. He claims that

> political leaders, rather than simply treating lawbreakers firmly but fairly, are becoming increasingly intolerant and vindictive. In a sense, the state appears to have crossed the line from "getting tough" to "getting rough" by encouraging institutions and authorities to bully individuals lacking the power to defend themselves adequately against an ambitious and overzealous criminal justice system. (p. xix)

An analysis by King, Mauer, and Young (2005) is particularly revealing. They note, "Advocates of increased use of incarceration have contended that the significant growth in incarceration has been the primary factor responsible for this reduction. The two-pronged approach of tougher sentences and restrictive release patterns are the primary cause, proponents claim, of this sustained crime drop" (p. 1). For example, they point out that violent crime declined by 33% and property crime decreased by 23% between 1994 and 2004. During this same period, rates of incarceration increased by 24%. "Some commentators draw upon these two trends to support the conclusion that incarceration 'works' to reduce crime. The reality is far more complex" (p. 3).

An analysis of different time periods from 1984 to 1998 illustrates the less than clear relationship between incarceration and crime rates. From 1984–1998, "incarceration rates rose consistently, by 65% in the first seven-year period of 1984–91, and then by 47% from 1991–98. Yet crime rates fluctuated in this period, first increasing by 17% from 1984–91, then declining by 22% from 1991–98" (p. 3). Further, an analysis of the changes in incarceration and crime in all 50 states "reveals no consistent relationship between the rate at which incarceration increased and the rate at which crime decreased. . . . Between 1991 and 1998, those states that increased incarceration at rates that were *less* than the national average experienced a *larger* decline in crime rates than those states that increased incarceration at rates higher than the national average" (p. 3).

The authors conclude, "While incarceration is one factor affecting crime rates, its impact is more modest than many proponents suggest, and is increasingly subject to diminishing returns. Increasing incarceration while ignoring more effective approaches will impose a heavy burden upon courts, corrections and communities, while providing a marginal impact on crime. Policymakers should assess these dynamics and adopt balanced crime control policies that provide appropriate resources and support for programming, treatment, and community support" (p. 8).

The U.S. imprisonment binge is ironic given that numerous scholars and organizations have demonstrated that incarceration is destructive to the United States and that our war on crime "has made things worse: that it has not deterred [much] crime, that it is racially biased, and that it has contributed to the destruction of inner-city communities" (Walker, 1998, pp. 10–11). Currie (1998, pp. 56–57) demonstrates that there is not clear evidence showing that states and countries that incarcerate more people have lower crime rates. Irwin and Austin (1997, p. 146) show that states that incarcerate more people do not necessarily have lower crime rates; in fact, the opposite is true overall, although the differences between states are inconsequential. Within the academic disciplines of criminology and criminal justice, a consensus has emerged against overrelying on incarceration, and yet we continue to lock up more and more people. You will recall from earlier chapters that crime is a political issue that can be "sold" to voters and viewers of the mass media, and that politicians must appear "tough on crime" to get elected and stay in office (see Chapter 5). Nevertheless, criminal justice policies motivated by politics are not in line with the scientific knowledge generated within the academic disciplines of criminology and criminal justice.

Irwin and Austin (1997, pp. xvii–xviii) discuss the main tenets of the political agenda that justifies more and more prisons, which include the following.

- The War on Poverty, which sought to fight crime through education, job training, and rehabilitation in the 1960s and 1970s, was a total failure.
- Dangerous criminals repeatedly go free because of liberal judges or decisions made by the liberal Supreme Court that help the criminal but not the victim.
- Swift and certain punishment in the form of more and longer prison terms will reduce crime by incapacitating the hardened criminals and making potential lawbreakers think twice before they commit crimes.
- Most inmates are dangerous and cannot be safely placed in the community.
- In the long run, it will be far cheaper for society to increase the use of imprisonment.
- Greater use of imprisonment since the 1980s has in fact reduced crime.

Chances are you'll still hear politicians promoting such ideas about crime and criminal justice on any given day in the United States.

What It Costs

It is difficult to put a price tag on the U.S. corrections system, because the cost of building and maintaining prison cells varies from state to state. Additionally, true costs of building prisons cannot be known unless one considers the added costs of interest over time on loans to build prisons. When these costs are added, a fair estimate of the true cost is $1 million per inmate for a 30-year term (Ambrosio and Schiraldi, 1997; Irwin and Austin, 1997).

The approximate cost of incarcerating one inmate in prison for 1 year is $30,000, although this varies by state (and is higher for those inmates held in maximum security facilities, as well as for aging inmates). With 1.4 million inmates in state and federal prisons, the cost of prisons in the United States is more than $40 billion annually. To accommodate new correctional clients, dozens of federal prisons were built in the 1980s and 1990s, and states continue to build new prisons to keep up with the new inmates being sentenced each year. State and federal prisons are now regularly over their maximum allowable capacity.

Additional costs come in the form of cuts in educational funding, student loans, libraries, work incentives, opportunity-creating programs, employment programs, and highway repair and construction (J. Miller, 1997). As such programs were being cut, in the 1980s alone, federal, state, and local expenditures for police grew 416%, for courts they increased 585%, for prosecution and legal services they grew by 1,019%, for public defenders they grew 1,255%, and for corrections they increased 986%. Federal justice spending overall increased 668%, county justice spending increased by 711%, and state spending increased 848% (Miller, 1998). More recently, the statistics show that growth for justice spending has increased significantly, with a majority of the money going to law enforcement and corrections (see Chapter 1).

The evidence suggests that the U.S. war on crime is not only costing us dearly now, but will continue to do so in the future. Ironically, crime funding may actually exacerbate criminogenic factors. Less money for education means less access to education. Less education can lead to less opportunity for legitimate success, leading in turn to conditions of strain, which historically have been linked to increased risk for criminality (Agnew, 1993; Merton, 1938a). "If education has historically been an investment in the future of society, then the cuts in education to finance prison represent a *dis*investment in the future" (Walker, 1998, p. 13; emphasis in original). According to the National Association of State Budget Officers (1996, pp. 77, 98), the total cost of state-issued bonds to build prisons surpasses the total issued to build colleges. Also, as the burdens of imprisonment fall disproportionately on some communities, incarceration creates a condition known as **social disorganization**, which has been associated with higher rates of street crime (Robinson, 2004).

WHO'S IN PRISON AND JAIL?

Why do we lock up so many more of our citizens than other countries do, even though we have no more crime overall? One primary reason is that criminal justice in the United States is much harsher toward relatively minor criminals than in other countries

(Donziger, 1996, p. 10). In fact, for a large part of our history, the majority of people in our nation's jails and prisons were convicted of nonviolent offenses. This may explain why many prison wardens feel that up to half of the offenders under their supervision could be released without making the country any less safe (Simon, 1994). Ingley (2000, p. 21) summarizes who's in prison:

> Today's corrections reality is such: the fastest growing [prison] populations are those captured from our "war on drugs," the deinstitutionalization of our mental health system, and mandatory minimum sentencing policies. . . . [T]he majority of our prisoners are chronic substance abusers, functionally illiterate, indigent, or possess few, if any, job skills.

In fact, according to the Bureau of Justice Statistics, at the end of 2003, 52% of prison inmates were serving time for violent offenses, followed by 21% for property offenses, 20% for drug offenses, and 7% for public-order offenses. As shown in Figure 9-3, the number of drug offenders matched the number of property offenders starting in 1999.

As you can see in Figure 9-4, 54% of all federal prison inmates were incarcerated for drug crimes at the end of 2004, versus only 12% for weapons offenses, 11% for immigration offenses, 10% for violent offenses (including robbery), 5% for property offenses, 5% for white-collar offenses (including extortion, fraud, and bribery), and 3% for other offenses. The number of drug offenders in federal prisons rose 41% between 1990 and 2000, but the fastest growth was for immigration offenses (691% increase) and weapons offenses (247% increase).

So a significant portion of state and federal prisoners has been incarcerated for nonviolent crime. What has happened in the United States has been likened to a bait-and-switch scam, because politicians have talked tough about violent criminals and promised tougher punishment for them, yet many of the people being sent to prison are not violent offenders (Donziger, 1996, p. 18). This works because Americans see

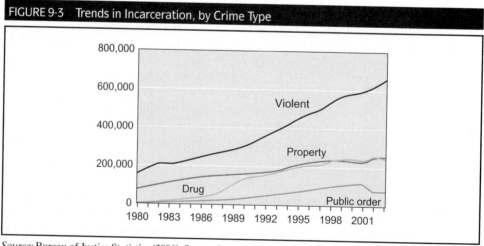

FIGURE 9-3   Trends in Incarceration, by Crime Type

Source: Bureau of Justice Statistics (2006). State prison populations. http://ojp.usdoj.gov/bjs/glance/corrtyp.htm.

FIGURE 9-4   Trends in Federal Drug Imprisonment

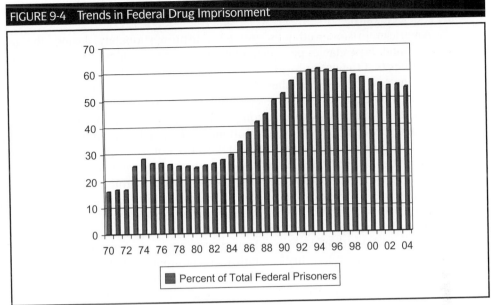

Percent of Total Federal Prisoners

Source: Sourcebook on Criminal Justice Statistics (2006).

"crime" and "violence" as essentially the same thing (Zimring and Hawkins, 1997). Most incarcerated criminals are not violent criminals, nor are most incarcerated criminals "career criminals" (Irwin and Austin, 1997). Americans may support imprisonment as punishment for repeat, violent criminals. It is doubtful they would support it for relatively minor offenders. It is, after all, their money that pays for prisons. Yet mass releases of prisoners will certainly not occur, even with the realization that it may be cost effective and relatively safe to release nonviolent and drug offenders from prison to serve probationary parole sentences (Bureau of Justice Statistics, 1995).

A possible danger of incarcerating relatively minor offenders is that as Americans become aware of this, some may begin to disrespect law generally. Rold (2000, p. 45) claims, "People are more likely to follow laws when they agree with them and respect the legitimacy of the community and agency administering the laws." Because prisons are used against many relatively harmless offenders, what is threatened is "the fabric of our social order and our view of ourselves as a compassionate nation." This is also the argument of Packer (1968), whose crime control and due process models of criminal justice were discussed in Chapter 1. Packer suggested that victimless crimes (such as drug use and prostitution) should be decriminalized because their illegal status led to disrespect for the law generally.

Recall from Chapter 2 the discussion of alternative goals of the criminal justice network. I suggested that the criminal justice network may be serving limited interests by controlling certain segments of the population. Politicians benefit from the incarceration boom by getting elected to office. Additionally, private companies lobby and make hundreds of thousands of dollars in political contributions to maintain a stranglehold on criminal justice. An irony is that as the nation's economy provides substantially more wealth to the richest of Americans, more of the rest of us support more prisons simply because they provide us with jobs that allow us to enjoy some of the benefits of the good economy.

American prisons and jails are used disproportionately against the nation's "riffraff" and those classes perceived to be dangerous (Shelden, 2007). Williams (2000, p. 72) writes that the nation's "lost souls find their only productive social role is as fodder for the ever-growing number" of prisons and jails. Irwin and Austin (1997, p. 8) write that what explains the U.S. reliance on incarceration as a means to control serious crime is "the American people's strong desire to banish from their midst any population of people who are threatening." Rothman (1971) makes a similar point in his book, *The Discovery of the Asylum*, by analyzing the history of American corrections. Rothman shows that the United States has always set aside the poor, mentally retarded, and mentally ill under the guise of corrections. A study by del Carmen and Robinson (2000) shows how both tuberculosis and crime prevention efforts used at the turn of the century in the nation's big cities were aimed primarily at poor immigrants.

It is estimated that roughly one in ten of the nation's prisoners is mentally ill (Weisman, 2000, p. 105), although some suggest that the figure may be more like 40% (Torrey et al., 1992). The Bureau of Justice Statistics (2006) reports that in mid-year 2005, more than half of all inmates had a mental health problem of some kind, including 705,600 state prison inmates, 70,200 federal prisoners, and 479,900 local jail inmates. The incidence of mental illness is even more pronounced for people spending life in prison.

These numbers are of particular concern considering that correctional facilities are ill-equipped to provide safety and appropriate treatment for mentally ill persons. Prisons are dangerous and debilitating for inmates with mental illnesses, who often are victimized by other prisoners. Moreover, symptoms of mental illness are often misinterpreted by correctional staff as disruptive behavior, which can lead to additional punishment and disciplinary actions that may extend the length of an individual's sentence (Mauer, King, and Young, 2004, p. 15).

The mentally ill are in jail largely because the nation's mentally ill populations were released from state hospitals in the expectation that they would be able to get treatment in their communities. But community treatment programs are not available in many communities; in places where such programs are available, systems are not in place to ensure that people who need them will obtain treatment. Over the past two decades, hundreds of new prisons have opened and nearly every state mental hospital was closed. Thus, "[j]ails and prisons have become the de facto providers of mental health services in this country" (Weisman, 2000, p. 106). In most states, the largest provider is the prison system; the nation's largest provider is the Los Angeles County Jail.

Jail may represent the largest waste of resources on offenders: Most people in county jails who were convicted of crimes committed very minor crimes, and the average sentence they will serve is a few days. Prisoners, by contrast, will serve longer sentences because of the perceived severity of their offenses. I have focused on prisons in this chapter because of the prolonged stay of their inmates. Yet jail populations serve as further evidence of who we pursue through our agencies of criminal justice, so I briefly mention them here. Welch (1999, p. 89) calls the jailing of offensive but nondangerous populations a form of "social sanitation" reserved mostly for the urban underclass or our nation's "rabble" (Irwin, 1985). People in jail are generally "either members of the working poor or permanent members of the underclass," with low educational attainment and "limited means to survive economically" (Welch, 1999, p. 94).

Do Americans really support these policies? Public opinion research has consistently shown that Americans prefer that inmates in the nation's prisons be granted access to rehabilitation (Roberts and Stalans, 2000). It is doubtful, too, that many Americans truly understand who is in prison. The typical prisoner, as you have seen, is not a repetitive, violent criminal. Rather, he or she (most likely a "he") is typically a property or drug offender. Slightly less than half of Irwin and Austin's (1997, p. 40) sample of incarcerated prisoners were characterized as "career criminals." Of those, about 60% were imprisoned for what Americans view as "petty crimes." Of the 25% of their sample who were serving lengthy sentences, many did not warrant these sentences on the basis of the relative nonseriousness of their offenses.

Thus, Irwin and Austin (1997, p. 57) write: "Most crimes are much pettier than the popular images promoted by those who sensationalize the crime issue (such as politicians and the media). More than half of the persons sent to prison committed crimes that lacked any of the features the public believes compose a serious crime." Even the high-risk inmates, the career criminals, are typically uneducated, unskilled, and underemployed. From public poll results, Irwin and Austin claim that if Americans knew this, they would not likely support the massive use of incarceration as a means to reduce crime.

Then consider an alarming possibility about U.S. prisons: One of their functions may be to warehouse a significant portion of the population that is not employable. Most convicted offenders sentenced to a term of imprisonment are poor, uneducated, and underemployed. To the degree that people are targeted, then, one function served by incarceration is a reduced need to provide social services to those people. In fact, virtually everyone in prison is poor (Shelden, 2007).

Table 9-2 illustrates that many people in prison were underemployed (i.e., not employed full-time) in the year prior to their incarceration, that most offenders in prison earned less than $10,000 per year, and that the vast majority of offenders in prison did not go to college. These statistics prove that the war on crime disproportionately affects poor people. Americans view street crimes (committed by the poor) as "our problem," when in reality it is mostly "their problem" (because criminal victimization is disproportionately directed at the poor). Our criminal justice reactions, particularly imprisonment, aimed at

TABLE 9-2 Characteristics of American Inmates	
Male	93%[1]
Black	40%[1]
Hispanic	20%[1]
Sentenced for nonviolent crimes	48%[1]
Did not complete high school	68%[2]
Earning less than $1,000 per month	64%[3]
Under influence of drugs at time of crime	60%[3]
Unemployed	36%[3]

Source: Bureau of Justice Statistics (2003, 2006).

[1] All prison inmates, 2005.

[2] State prison inmates, 1997.

[3] Jail inmates, 1996.

TABLE 9-3 African Americans Among Correctional Populations	
	Percentage Black
Prisoners	40% (2005)
Jail inmates	39% (2005)
Probationers	30% (2005)
Death row inmates	42% (January 2007)

Source: Sourcebook on Criminal Justice Statistics (2006).

making it better for "us," actually make it worse for "them." This is another ironic, unintended consequence of U.S. criminal justice practices (Walker, 2005).

As noted throughout this book, incarceration also disproportionately affects people of color. Is this a recent phenomenon? According to Cahalan (1986), we can confidently say that prison populations have been disproportionately made up of African Americans since 1926, the first year that national prison statistics were collected. In that year, African Americans made up 9% of the population but 21% of the prison population. At the end of 2005, African Americans made up about 12% of the U.S. population but 40% of all inmates in state and federal prisons, versus 35% Caucasians. According to Harrison and Beck (2005, p. 8) 60% of state and federal inmates at the end of 2005 were black or Hispanic. More specifically, black males (547,200) outnumbered white males (459,700) and Hispanic males (279,000) among inmates with a sentence of more than 1 year, as shown in Table 9-3. Thus, about 8.1% of black males age 25 to 29 were in state or federal prison, compared to 2.6% of Hispanic males and 1.1% of white males in the same age group.

The first time that more African Americans were admitted to U.S. prisons than non–African Americans was in the late 1980s, during the height of the war on drugs. Even worse, only about 10% of those seeking college degrees are African American (Walker, Spohn, and DeLone, 2000, p. 260).

The picture in American jails is very similar, as Caucasians made up 45% of inmates at the end of 2005, African Americans made up 40%, and Hispanics made up 15%. This means the majority of jail inmates were people of color. I will return to the issue of bias at the end of this chapter, but first I will dispel some myths about what it is like to be in prison.

WHAT HAPPENS IN PRISON? PAINS OF IMPRISONMENT

Most people who are in prison will one day get out (see the section on parole later in the chapter). It may be easy to lock up criminals and believe that we are somehow safer for it. But 9 out of 10 inmates will one day be released. Thus, Americans must realize that their own safety depends on what happens to prisoners while they are incarcerated. And prison, contrary to popular belief, is a horrendous place.

Contrary to the mythical view of the comfortable prison, American prisons are terribly hot, loud, and violent places to live (and work—keep in mind that many people in prison simply work there). The myth of "country club" prisons has led state lawmakers to pass some laughable legislation and make startling threats. The National Criminal Justice Commission reports the following examples:

- A Mississippi law forbidding individual air conditioners, even though no inmate actually had an individual air conditioner
- A Louisiana law forbidding inmates from taking martial arts classes, even though such classes were not currently available
- A complaint by the governor of Connecticut about the landscaping outside a prison, even though the plantings were made at the request of residential neighbors (Donziger, 1996, p. 45)

Add to these examples efforts by state lawmakers to take away inmates' cigarettes (which contain the addictive drug nicotine and are used as a form of currency within prisons), other efforts to prevent inmates from lifting weights or watching television, the resurgence of chain gangs in many southern states, and other efforts to humiliate inmates by making them wear orange, pink, or striped jumpsuits. All these efforts to make prison less pleasant negate the general impression that prison is a pretty easy place to be. In fact, because of the numerous **pains of imprisonment** (Sykes, 1958), the typical prison is far from anything like a country club.

Gresham Sykes (1958), in his groundbreaking work *The Society of Captives,* outlined the major pains of imprisonment:

- Loss of liberty
- Loss of autonomy
- Loss of security
- Deprivation of heterosexual relationships
- Deprivation of goods and services

To these, I add three more:

- Loss of voting rights
- Loss of dignity
- Stigmatization

I will discuss each of these in turn.

Loss of Liberty

First and foremost, prisoners suffer from a **loss of liberty**. Many Americans seem to conceive of prisons as comfortable places where offenders watch television free of charge, eat three square meals per day at no cost, enjoy various extracurricular activities such as weight lifting and basketball, and get a free education. Most of these conceptions are false. The Florida Department of Corrections maintains a web page where myths about its prisons are disputed, as shown in Box 9-1.

Prisons in most states are similar in their conditions. For example, Box 9-2 describes a day in the North Carolina Department of Correction Division of Prisons.

Although recreation is permitted and even encouraged within most U.S. prisons, it is allowed for the safety of correctional personnel. And funding for educational, vocational training, and treatment programs within prisons has been slashed dramatically. In part, treatment is lacking because of prisoners' protections from government intervention. McLaughlin (2000, p. 24) states, for example, "Federal regulations for the Protection of

BOX 9-1

MYTHS ABOUT FLORIDA PRISONS

1. *Inmates don't work.* On March 2, 2007, there were 90,679 inmates in the Florida prison system. Private prisons housed 5,353 inmates and the remaining 85,326 were in Department of Corrections (DC) facilities. On March 2, 2007, 81.9% of the inmates in institutions and facilities were assigned to work, assigned to participate in a substance abuse program or vocational education or adult education program, or were assigned to some other program activity. The remaining 18.1% were medically unable to work, or were participating in the reception and orientation process, assigned to a disciplinary work squad as a result of rule infractions, assigned to a restricted labor squad, or were in some type of confinement for management purposes, including death row.

   Inmate labor is used to perform work on farms and gardens managed by the department, construct new correctional facilities, perform repairs and renovations to facilities, and otherwise support and maintain the ongoing operation of correctional institutions. Inmates also prepare and serve all meals, maintain prison grounds, participate in sanitation and recycling processes, and work in Prison Rehabilitative Industries and Diversified Enterprises or Prison Industry Enhancement work programs. Additionally, inmates are assigned to Community Work Squads provided by the department. These inmates perform services under agreements with the Department of Transportation, other state agencies such as the Division of Forestry, counties, cities, municipalities, and nonprofit organizations. In fiscal year (FY) 2005–06, the DC's Community Work Squad Program saved Florida taxpayers more than $44.5 million through inmate labor—a $2.5 million increase from the prior fiscal year.

2. *Inmates have cable television and satellite dishes.* There are no correctional facilities with cable television. The 33 prisons that have satellite dishes use them for staff training as part of the Corrections Distance Learning Network (CDLN). The CDLN saves money by training staff throughout the state simultaneously. Most prisons have televisions available to inmates for use when inmates are not working. The televisions are located in dormitory dayrooms for group viewing. Most of the department's televisions were paid for by proceeds from sales to inmates from the inmate canteens. However, state law now prohibits the purchase of televisions for recreational purposes.

3. *Why don't inmates grow their own food and save taxpayers some money?* Inmates do grow some of their own food, and expansion of the Bureau of Institutional Support's edible crops program continues. In FY 2005–06, the Bureau cultivated approximately 1,700 acres and harvested approximately 4.1 million pounds of produce, including

watermelons and cantaloupe. The number of inmates assigned to the edible crops program continues to increase, due largely to the expanded use of close custody inmates supervised by Field Force Officers. Field Force Officers, mounted on horseback, supervise close custody inmates who are assigned to work in the fields cultivating the edible crops. Usually the squad is made up of four mounted, armed officers and one unarmed (on the ground) supervisor who control up to 75 close custody inmates. There are currently 225 of these inmates in Field Force Squads at the following institutions: Apalachee Correctional Institution (CI), New River CI, "O" Unit, and Desoto Annex. There are an additional 400 inmates also assigned to the farm program. "With the privatization of food service in our department, the edible crops program is moving toward more centralized operations on our large-scale farms, thus allowing greater efficiency in processing and distributing harvested products."

4. *The Department of Corrections determines how long inmates serve in prison.*   The Department of Corrections does not determine the length of prison sentences or the length of time inmates serve in prison. Judges and juries, in accordance with state laws and sentencing guidelines, make these decisions. The department is solely responsible for the care and custody of offenders under its jurisdiction. In FY 2005–06, the average sentence length for all prison admissions was 4.4 years for whites, 4.7 years for blacks, and 5.0 years for all others.

The average sentence length for all offenders admitted in FY 2005–06 was 4.6 years.

5. *Inmates still aren't serving most of their sentences.*   Offenders who committed their offenses on or after October 1, 1995, are required to serve a minimum of 85% of their court-imposed sentences prior to their release. Offenders released in January 2007 served an average of 86.4% of their sentence. The average percentage of sentence served for released offenders has significantly increased in the last 10 years (January 1997, 67.7% versus January 2007, 86.4%). A downloadable brochure on Time Served by Florida inmates is also available.

6. *Prisons are air-conditioned.*   Only 10 of the major state-managed prisons in Florida have air-conditioning in some portion of the facility housing inmates, and many of these are located in South Florida. The following correctional institutions have air-conditioning in the areas indicated: Lancaster (confinement area); Union (13 dorms); Youthful Offender institution Brevard (all dorms); Lake and Zephyrhills (air conditioning installed in Mental Health areas in 1997 at Lake and 1995 at Zephyrhills); female institutions at Broward, Hillsborough, and Homestead (all dorms); Dade (Mental Health area); and Charlotte (Mental Health area air conditioned in FY 1994–95). The five Florida prison facilities built under the privatization contract are also air-conditioned.

7. *Inmates who get life sentences don't really stay in prison for life.*   Since

(*continued*)

BOX 9-1 *(Continued)*

1995, anyone sentenced to life in prison is serving a life term with no possibility of parole. On June 30, 2006, there were 628 Florida parolees and 1,526 parolees from other states under supervision in Florida. Offenders sentenced to life for noncapital crimes committed between 1983 and 1993 are serving life sentences without any chance for release. Ironically, offenders sentenced to life for capital crimes committed between 1983 and 1993 are parole eligible after serving

25-year mandatory sentences. These sentencing provisions appear reversed, but they are correct. This anomaly in the law lasted from 1983 to 1994. Since 1995, anyone sentenced to life in prison is serving a life term with no possibility of parole. On March 3, 2007, there were 10,412 inmates in prison serving life sentences. A total of 5,923 were serving life with the possibility of parole and 4,489 were serving life sentences without the possibility of parole.

SOURCE: Florida Department of Corrections. Online: http://www.dc.state.fl.us/oth/myths.html.

Human Subjects . . . are extended to prisoners due to past abuses and the concern that prisoners may be limited in their ability to give truly informed consent." Many, if not all, medical treatments are discouraged because of these strict requirements. In essence, the criminal justice network can stick a needle in a person's arm for punishment, but not for treatment. At the same time, "[b]ehavioral interventions . . . are developed and conducted frequently by people with little or no training in the area, no monitoring or thought as to the potential damage that an intervention may cause, and no informed consent" (McLaughlin, 2000, pp. 24–25). Although somewhere between 70% and 85% of inmates need substance abuse treatment, only about 15% actually receive it (National Center on Addiction and Substance Abuse, 1998; Robinson and Scherlen, 2007; Simpson, Knight, and Pevoto, 1996). This is true even though studies have proved how much more effective drug treatment is than expanding the use of prisons in reducing recidivism (Caulkins et al., 1997; MacCoun and Reuter, 2000).

Some Americans might prefer to throw inmates into freshly dug holes in the ground and provide them with nothing but the bare minimum to survive. Others would like to "make 'em break rocks" (McGinnis, 2000, p. 35). Former Massachusetts governor William Weld publicly stated that life in prison should be "akin to walking through the fires of hell" (in McGinnis, 2000, p. 35). But these people misconceive the purpose of imprisonment. We send people to prison as punishment, not for punishment. As explained by Ingley (2000, p. 20), "The incarceration itself [is] supposed to be the punishment, not an occasion for the state to arbitrarily inflict additional punishment." In other words, the main part of the punishment is losing one's freedom. Individual freedom may be the most cherished part of being American. Prisoners, because they are locked up, away from friends and family, have lost their liberty. This means they are not free to do all the things you and I can do as we see fit. Their activities are decided by others.

BOX 9-2

TWENTY-FOUR HOURS IN THE NORTH CAROLINA DEPARTMENT OF CORRECTION DIVISION OF PRISONS

	Type of Facility		
Hour	Minimum	Medium	Close
Morning			
5:00	Sleep	Wake up	Sleep
6:00	Wake up	Breakfast	Wake up
7:00	Breakfast	Travel to work site	Breakfast
	Travel to work site	Work	Go to work in prison
8:00–10:00	Work		
11:00	30 minutes for lunch	30 minutes for lunch	Work
Afternoon			
12:00	Work	Work	30 minutes for lunch
1:00–2:00	Work	Work	Work
3:00	Work	Work	Work day ends
	Travel to prison	Travel to prison	Time on prison yard
		Off duty	
4:00	Off duty time on prison yard	Time on prison yard	Return to cell
5:00	30 minutes for supper	30 minutes for supper	30 minutes for supper
Evening			
6:00–7:00	Time for specialized programming such as religious services, Narcotics Anonymous, anger management		
8:00	Return to dorm	Return to dorm	Return to cellblock
9:00–10:00	Remain in housing area		
11:00	Lights out; sleep	Lights out; sleep	Lights out; sleep
12:00–4:00	Lights out; sleep	Lights out; sleep	Lights out; sleep

Close-Custody Inmates at Central Prison

In close-security prisons, inmates remain in the prison 24 hours a day and have no assignments outside the prison. Movement from one area of the prison to another is restricted. Armed correctional officers man security towers to stop escape attempts.

At 3:30 A.M. the first inmates are awakened. They are the kitchen workers who get up to prepare the morning meal.

These inmates live and work together. Correctional officers escort them to the kitchen as a group. Each worker is thoroughly frisk-searched before entering the kitchen. The first-shift kitchen workers arrive at the kitchen for duty at 4 A.M. to begin preparing for breakfast and the day's meals.

All inmates are awakened by 6 A.M. for the formal inmate count. Correctional staff count and recount inmates over and over throughout the day. Around 7 A.M.

(continued)

BOX 9-2 *(Continued)*

the feeding of breakfast begins. All inmate workers report to their jobs at 7:30 A.M. Second-shift inmate workers may use the gyms, recreation yard, and canteens.

Inmates work in the kitchen, license tag plant, or laundry or perform maintenance or janitorial tasks during the day.

Around 3 P.M. inmates usually check their mail and spend some time on the recreation yard prior to returning to the dining hall for the evening meal at 4 P.M. After the evening meal, inmates will have access to the gym, auditorium, or recreation yard. Depending on the day of the week, they may be involved in some organized recreational activities. On Wednesdays, Fridays, Saturdays, and Sundays, there is noncontact visitation with individuals who are on the inmates' approved visitors list. The visits are usually from 1 hour to 1.5 hours in duration.

At approximately 6:30 P.M. inmates may attend classes in the school or take part in other activities such as Alcoholics Anonymous, Narcotics Anonymous, Freedoms Journey Classes, or Jaycees. At 8:30 P.M. another formal count is conducted. At 9 P.M. inmates return to their housing area and are allowed to watch television, write letters, or play checkers, chess, or cards.

At 11 P.M. the inmate is locked into his cell and the lights are dimmed for the night.

Medium-Custody Inmates Working on a Road Squad at Pender Correctional Institution

In medium-security prisons, most inmates remain in the prison 24 hours a day. Armed correctional officers supervise squads of inmates who leave the prison to work on road squads, cutting brush or working the fields at the state prison farm. Armed correctional officers man security towers to stop escape attempts.

Inmates wake up at 5:30 A.M. and have 45 minutes to shower, clean up, and make their bed. They go to the dining hall and eat breakfast in shifts beginning at 6:15. The inmates assemble for the count, search, and assignment to the road squads at 8 A.M. and over the next 30 minutes travel to their work site. The squads work in Pender and three surrounding counties. Travel time may vary, but all squads are busy at work by 9 A.M.

Squads work until noon when they get a 30-minute break for lunch. They continue the work until around 3 P.M. As they arrive at the prison at 3:30, each inmate must be searched.

Inmates get cleaned up and prepare for dinner, which begins at 4:30 P.M. Afterwards, they may exchange clothing at the prison clotheshouse, report to staff for counseling or medical appointments, or go to the prison yard.

Inmates are locked into the dormitory at 7 P.M. They may leave only to take part in religious, education, or other programs in the prison's chapel, education center, or programs building.

All programs end at 9:30 P.M. and inmates return to their dorms to be counted. At 10 P.M. lights are dimmed in the sleeping area and inmates may remain in adjacent dayroom space. The inmates may watch television or play cards or table games. The 32 inmates on each dorm wing share a television and watch programming selected by inmates and preapproved by staff.

At 11:30 P.M. inmates are required to go to their dormitory beds and lights are dimmed.

Minimum-Custody Inmates Working on a Community Work Squad at Umstead Correctional Center

Inmates must be within 5 years of release to enter minimum custody. Minimum security prisons prepare inmates for return to the community. While those entering minimum custody are assigned to jobs and remain at the prison, inmates in later phases leave the prison for work assignments. In the final stage of minimum custody, inmates may take part in work release jobs, family visits, and community volunteer visits where they leave the prison in the custody of an employer, family member, or volunteer.

One of the many work assignments for minimum custody inmates is the community work squad, where inmates are supervised by a correctional officer in a short-term manual-labor job for local governments or public agencies.

At 6 A.M. inmates are awakened and have time to shower, dress, make up their beds, and prepare for breakfast. They eat in the dining hall at 6:45 and then prepare for the day's work.

A correctional officer assembles the community work squad inmates who prepare their equipment and travel by prison van to their work site. By 8 A.M. the inmates are hard at work. They work on short-term manual-labor jobs like clearing brush from ditches, painting public buildings, or improving community parks. The work crews get 30 minutes to eat a bag lunch prepared by inmate kitchen workers.

The squads may work up to 5 P.M. if the job requires. Normally, they wrap up work and return to the prison around 3–4 P.M. They get cleaned up and attend to any unit duties they may have. At 5 P.M. they go to the dining hall for dinner. After dinner, they may have some time on the prison yard. Between 7 and 9 P.M. they may participate in specialized or religious programming such as Bible studies or Narcotics Anonymous.

By 9 P.M. inmates return to the dormitory they share with up to 150 other inmates. They may talk, play cards, or watch the dorm's one television. At midnight, dorm lights go out and inmates are required to stay in their bunks.

Correction officers, constantly watching, patrol the dorms.

Inmates repeat this routine day after day after day.

SOURCE: North Carolina Department of Correction. Online: www.doc.state.nc.us/dop/hours24.htm.

Loss of Autonomy

Related to loss of freedom is the **loss of autonomy** that accompanies being incarcerated. Inmates do not decide for themselves when or where to sleep, wake up, shower, eat, engage in recreation, or live. They are told when and how to do virtually everything they do. Thus, prisoners lose the capacity and, some argue, the ability to govern their own lives and behaviors. What are the implications of this for society? If we want people to be responsible for themselves, their lives, their families, their children, wouldn't it make sense to equip them with the ability to live in the free world? Is our desire to make prisoners suffer more important than protecting us from their future acts of crime and violence?

May (2000, p. xvii) claims that incarceration can "foster dependency" and, for some, actually "becomes a way of life—even a generational phenomenon." For them, the criminal justice network "becomes their only source of social support, structure, discipline, validation, and even power and respect." These people typically have family and friends who have been processed through the criminal justice agencies and live in communities where incarceration is simply an expected part of life.

Loss of Security

Prisoners are subjected to numerous forms of victimization that are much more prevalent in correctional facilities than outside in the free world, and thus suffer from a **loss of security**. Prisoners are subjected to psychological victimization, economic victimization, social victimization, physical victimization, and sexual victimization. May (2000, p. 134) describes prisons this way:

> Prisons are violent places, and prisons teach violence. Anyone walking into a prison for the first time can feel the tension. The concrete and steel walls and floors serve to echo and intensify the noises of chains, steel doors slamming, yelling, cursing, and beatings. For an inmate who must make the prison his or her home, whether for months, years, or even a lifetime, avoiding a violent attack becomes a daily concern. The need to maintain constant vigilance creates stress, tension, and chronic anxiety. Even in their sleep, they do not feel safe. They almost instinctively react to provocation with violence, as adjustments to this sense of vulnerability.

Page (2000, pp. 138, 141) claims that "[v]iolence is a dominant and defining thread running through the fabric of jail and prison life" and describes facilities of incarceration as "factories of rage and pain."

As explained by the National Criminal Justice Commission, "Inmates learn to strike first and seek strength in gangs often comprised of dangerous offenders. Sexual assaults are frequent and usually go unpunished" (Donziger, 1996, p. 43). Rather than being a deterrent to future criminality, the commission concludes that "the violent subculture of the correctional facility increasingly acts as a vector for spreading crime in our communities" (Donziger, 1996, p. 44). Ironically, then, imprisonment escalates the very behavior it is intended to deter (Marx, 1981) because it increases violence instead of decreasing it (Poporino, 1986; Welch, 1999).

American criminals who are imprisoned are locked away in overcrowded warehouses and forced to live in closet-sized rooms (Clark, 1994). Most are subjected to some type of physical abuse and many to sexual abuse (Donaldson, 1995). Violence inflicted for the purpose of causing pain or as punishment is illegal and prohibited by the American Correctional Association (Martin, 2000, p. 114). Additionally, many of the inmates who become victims in prison were convicted of relatively minor acts—acts that many of us may have committed at one time in our lives. And remember, most of these inmates will one day get out of prison. Some of these include inmates who have gone on to earn their doctoral degrees and now teach in criminology and criminal justice. They are now known as the **Convict School of Criminology** and are examined in Issue in Depth at the end of this chapter.

Human rights violations are commonplace in prison. As examples, Welch (1999) discusses chain gangs, inhumane prison conditions, and the use of political imprisonment in the United States. He writes: "American prisons are neither *civilized* nor *civilizing*. Simply put, inmates are subjected to a degrading prison environment, then returned to the community" (p. 199; emphasis in original).

Deprivation of Heterosexual Relationships

Although not everyone is heterosexual, most Americans are. Incarceration means being forced to suffer from a **deprivation of heterosexual relationships**. This is likely worst for married couples who are separated by imprisonment. But for any heterosexual person, being imprisoned generally means living without sexual contact with a member of the opposite sex. Consequently, heterosexuals may have to abstain completely from sexual encounters, turn to self-gratification, or engage in homosexual encounters. Even if a prisoner chooses to abstain, there is, of course, the risk of being forced to engage in homosexual relations because of the threat of rape in prison. And even though prison administrators know that rapes occur within the walls of American prisons, these attacks generally are not pursued nor prevented (Mariner, 2000, p. 129).

A growing number of American prisoners are being deprived of virtually all relationships, including contact with other people. One reason is that more and more prisons are being built in rural areas, far from the offenders' family members and significant others. Prisons are promoted in rural communities as a blessing—a source of jobs to boost the local economy. Another reason is that the United States has begun incarcerating some of its most dangerous offenders in **supermaximum** or **supermax prisons**. These facilities restrict inmate contact with other inmates and with correctional personnel. Many inmates are locked in their cells for most of the day, in stark cells with white walls. Cells have completely closed front doors, no windows, and bright lights on at all hours of day and night.

Examples of supermax facilities include Marion (Illinois) and Pelican Bay (California). Welch (1999, p. 200) describes the conditions in these prisons:

> [In Marion] all prisoners are confined to their cells for 23 hours per day, granted 1 hour of exercise outside of their cell, and allowed to shower 2 or 3 days a week. Handcuffs are fastened to inmates while they are transported within the facility . . . [and they are chained] "long-term . . . to their beds."
>
> [In Pelican Bay] [i]nmates are confined to their 8- by 10-foot cells, where the temperature registers a constant 85 to 90 degrees, for twenty-two and a half hours per day. The unrelenting heat produces headaches, nausea, and dehydration and drains the inmates of their mental and bodily energy.

Human rights violations in supermax facilities, of course, are hidden from the public. When abuses of prisoners in other types of prisons become known, Americans do not become concerned because state-controlled media outlets do not construct these harms as social problems (Welch, 1999, p. 208). The Pelican Bay facility in California was built at a cost of $278 million for 2,080 maximum security inmates. That's $134,000 per inmate! The organization Human Rights Watch calls these expensive facilities "a clear violation of human rights" and a breach of an international treaty implemented by the United States in 1992 (Weinstein, 2000, p. 120). Yet Americans are generally unaware or unconcerned over human rights violations against convicted criminals. Box 9-3 describes life in a supermax facility for one American citizen.

BOX 9-3

JOSE PADILLA

One well-known case of an American citizen being held in a supermax prison is that of Jose Padilla. Jose Padilla, who was born in New York City and who lived in Chicago, Illinois, was arrested in Chicago on May 8, 2002. He was first detained for a month as a material witness until President Bush declared him an enemy combatant, a status he held for more than 4 years.

Bush Administration officials publicly commented that Padilla was plotting a "dirty bomb" attack against a major U.S. city, and it was alleged that he planned to firebomb apartment buildings in the United States. Padilla was thus claimed to be a major terrorist. Yet Padilla was never charged with any such offense. After years of protests and legal challenges to President Bush's detention of Padilla without any criminal charges, Padilla was finally charged in a criminal court with conspiracy to commit terrorism in January 2006.

Although Padilla had been a member of a street gang in Chicago and had been arrested several times, as well as convicted for aggravated assault in an attack that killed another gang member, there was little to indicate that he was a terrorist threat against the United States. Padilla had befriended some people who were allegedly "linked" to al Qaeda and had traveled throughout the Middle East. There, he allegedly attended a "terrorist training camp," although the U.S. government has never publicly released evidence to this effect.

In November 2005, Padilla was indicted for conspiracy to murder, kidnap, and maim people overseas. Padilla's role in the alleged conspiracy was relatively minor; supposedly he attended a terrorist training camp but was never directly involved in any plans to carry out terrorist attacks in the United States or elsewhere. Since his capture, Padilla has allegedly been subjected to torture, including sensory and sleep deprivation and being forced to sit in various stressful positions for extended periods of time. He also has been held in solitary confinement in a supermax prison, forced to sleep on a steel bed with no mattress, and is allegedly suffering from Post Traumatic Stress Disorder (PTSD). Padilla's attorneys claim he was threatened with physical attacks and even execution.

Padilla's case is highly unusual; not many American citizens have been declared enemy combatants in the war on terror. However, Padilla's experience in a supermax prison is similar to that of other inmates held in like conditions.

Deprivation of Goods and Services

Another significant loss associated with imprisonment is the **deprivation of goods and services**. Imagine all of your worldly possessions being inaccessible to you, along with virtually every service and product that a free person can enjoy. This would be a major loss associated with having your freedom taken away. More and more, prison life is becoming a boring, uniform routine with what inmates consider to be "chickenshit rules" (Irwin and Austin, 1997, p. 75). Some prisoners may become **prisonized** and unable to make it in the real world (Clemmer, 1940).

Loss of Voting Rights

According to The Sentencing Project (2007), 48 states and the District of Columbia prohibit inmates from voting while incarcerated for a felony offense; 35 states prohibit felons from voting while they are on parole (30 of these states also exclude felony probationers); 2 states deny the right to vote to all ex-offenders (including those who have completed their sentences); 9 states disenfranchise certain categories of ex-offenders and/or permit application for restoration of rights for specified offenses after a waiting period.

The Bureau of Justice Statistics maintains that all states impose some form of **collateral damage** on inmates. Although you may not consider the **loss of voting rights** an important loss, especially if you do not currently vote, it is inconsistent with the goal of integrating ex-convicts into free society. Members of free society have the right to vote and thus to help shape the direction of their lives, as well as that of their families and communities. In a representative democracy, when a person cannot vote, by definition, that person's voice cannot be heard and he or she is not represented.

According to The Sentencing Project (2007), about 5.3 million Americans have lost their rights to vote because of felony convictions. In the United States, the loss of the right to vote is a burden disproportionately imposed on poor people and people of color. Statistics show that 1.4 million African American men (13% of all black men) are disenfranchised. The rate for black males is seven times the national average. The Sentencing Project reports that, "[i]n five states that deny the vote to ex-offenders, one in four black men is *permanently* disenfranchised. . . . Given current rates of incarceration, three in ten of the next generation of black men can expect to be disenfranchised at some point in their lifetime. . . . In states that disenfranchise ex-offenders, as many as 40% of black men may permanently lose their right to vote." Further, more than 2 million white Americans are disenfranchised, and more than 675,000 women currently cannot vote because of a felony conviction.

Loss of Dignity

Associated with each of the losses described here is a **loss of dignity**. Prisoners are not treated as individual human beings, but as numbers. At worst, they lose respect for themselves because of this treatment. They come to be dependent on the government to live their lives. They are also subjected to various labels, such as "convict," "ex-convict," "criminal," "dangerous," and "antisocial." According to Robinson (2004), when such labels are applied to offenders and would-be offenders in a destructive, mean-spirited manner, their risk of offending actually increases rather than decreases. This is predicted by the theory of **reintegrative shaming**.

Stigmatization

As I showed earlier in this chapter, most people in U.S. prisons are truly disadvantaged: poor; uneducated; underemployed. Irwin and Austin (1997) illustrate that the typical offender enters prison with a tenth-grade education and leaves with a tenth-grade education plus the stigma of being an "ex-con." Most inmates "leave prison with all their previous disadvantages plus the additional stigma of a felony conviction" (Kappeler et al., 2000, p. 251). Perhaps this is why estimates suggest that inmates will lose about 70% of the income level they were accustomed to prior to entering a prison (The Sentencing Project, 1998), a level that already was low relative to the national average. Not surprisingly, then, when prisoners are released, the pain of **stigmatization** (e.g., the "ex-con" label) makes it difficult for them to find places to live and work.

   Labeling theory asserts that when people are labeled by the criminal justice network as "criminals," "convicts," or "offenders," the label can affect how these offenders view themselves, thus potentially changing their self-concepts. Once they begin to see themselves as "deviant" or "different," they will continue committing crime to live up to the expectations that society has set forth for them (Bohm, 2001). Sampson and Laub (1997) suggest that employers use the ex-con label as a warning against hiring former offenders. According to Bushway (2000, p. 144), "Federal legislation explicitly denies ex-felons employment in *any* job in the financial sector, as well as in other areas such as child care and private investigations. Most states also have legislation mandating screening on the basis of criminal history records for literally hundreds of jobs" (emphasis in original).

   Irwin and Austin (1997, p. 82) summarize the issue this way:

> The disturbing truth is that growing numbers of prisoners are leaving our prisons socially crippled and profoundly alienated. Moreover, they understand that they will be returning to a society that views them as despicable pariahs. They are also aware that they will have major difficulty finding employment than formerly, and consequently their expectations are low.

Shouldn't we be able to expect more out of a system of "corrections"? As May (2000, p. xvii) correctly points out, the term *corrections* is really a misnomer.

Summary: Pains of Imprisonment

Given these pains of imprisonment, it's no wonder that most prisoners will end up back in prison in the future. As Irwin and Austin (1997, p. 62) explain, "Because most will be released within two years, we should be deeply concerned about what happens to them during their incarceration." We have to decide, as states and as a nation, what we think is most important—punishing offenders for retribution or preventing their future crime. If we want to make inmates mad at society and want to create a sense of vengeance in them, we should continue doing what we are doing. If we want them to become part of legitimate U.S. society, we must witness a change of direction in punishment.

   For the past several decades, U.S. prisons did little more than warehouse inmates. Irwin and Austin (1997, p. 62) describe it this way:

> Convicted primarily of property and drug crimes, hundreds of thousands of prisoners are being crowded into human (or inhuman) warehouses where they are increasingly deprived, restricted, isolated, and consequently embittered and alienated from conventional worlds and where less and less is being done to prepare them for their eventual release. As a result, most of them are rendered incapable of returning to even a meager conventional life after prison.

Simultaneously, as indicated earlier, opportunities for education, vocational training, and recreation have substantially decreased in the prevailing punitive environment of American punishment. Irwin and Austin (1997, p. 80) suggest that fewer than 20% of all prisoners are enrolled in any type of educational program.

Incarceration also hurts more than the criminal. Effects of imprisonment on families can be tremendous. Obviously, imprisonment runs counter to the goal of maintaining a two-parent family. The National Criminal Justice Commission writes:

> For many young women in the inner city, there is a scarcity of available men of marriage age because so many are going in and out of jails and prisons. . . . In some inner-city areas, virtually every resident has a close relative and over 50 percent have a parent who is in prison, on probation, on parole, in jail, or hidden because there is a warrant out for their arrest. (Donziger, 1996, p. 47)

Whitehead (2000, p. 87) reports that in a study of inner-city women, some African American females (15 to 19 years old) reflected on this situation in their comments on dating. They were asked, "What recommendations would you have for other young women your age, who have met a new boy with whom they are thinking of entering into a relationship?" Some of their answers included: "Make sure the police isn't looking for him" and "Make sure he didn't recently get out of jail" (Whitehead, 1997). Think of the irony of politicians speaking of the value of two-parent families while simultaneously promoting policies that split them up. Is it any wonder that about 60% of prisoners have been there before and will end up there again?

Given that prison is such an awful place, does imprisonment reduce crime? That is, is it a deterrent to future criminal activity? I explained earlier that most of the recent declines in crime are not attributable to massive increases in imprisonment. Research findings do not support politicians' claims that imprisonment is an effective method of reducing crime rates and making people safer. Politicians, in essence, promote a failing means of crime reduction to Americans who have sworn an allegiance to it, even though it does not work. Even if you believe that imprisonment is a special deterrent (a punishment that instills fear in the offender, making it less likely that he or she will commit crimes in the future), consider this possibility: For individuals who see no promising options in the legitimate economy, for whom life in the street is very risky anyway, and who have not been effectively socialized against committing crimes, the prospect of spending time in prison, perhaps with others they know, of being assured meals and a bed (even if far from luxurious), may not deter them from criminal activity. Prison may not be a very attractive option, but its increment of pain is likely to be far less than it is to middle-class populations (Blumstein, 2000, p. 10).

There is also substantial evidence that prisons serve as **colleges of crime**. Think about it: A logical outcome of placing large numbers of convicted criminals together is that they will teach one another new tricks of the trade! Amazingly, although we know that having criminals live in close proximity to one another will ultimately produce more crime, for this reason and others, we still continue to build more and more facilities to house more and more inmates. Politicians who claim that crime is down because of increased use of imprisonment are, at best, misinformed and shortsighted. The long-term effects of mass imprisonment will be disastrous and costly.

Walker (1998, p. 14) shows how the United States' fight to reduce crime by means such as imprisonment parallels efforts of some overweight people to lose weight: "Just as people go on crash diets, lose weight, put it all back on, and then take up another diet fad a year later, so we tend to 'binge' on crime control fads." Many people fail to recognize that fighting fat through fad diets will never work, and that weight-loss fads result in billions of dollars of profit each year for those who misrepresent even the most bizarre programs and products. It is ironic that people who want to lose weight are most likely to try approaches that actually increase their weight. Similarly, reducing crime cannot be achieved through fad crime control policies that are proposed for purely symbolic reasons by politicians and inadequately designed by criminal justice policymakers. Even though they are enormously profitable for some, prisons do not significantly reduce crime in the long run. There is no "miracle cure" for crime. Reducing crime, like losing weight, requires dedication and time. In Chapter 13, I will explore some criminal justice options that might work to reduce crime in the United States.

Yet we continue with our "crime control theology," rooted not in empirical evidence and sound scientific argument but rather, in shared beliefs and common sense. As discussed in Chapter 2, politicians have pledged to put more police on the streets and put more people in prison. Even though these measures are only a temporary fix, they are widely supported by the public (Walker, 1998, p. 75). Irwin and Austin (1997) suggest that imprisonment is rooted in a false image of the typical offender, created by politicians and by media attention to violent crimes, and rooted in what they call "voodoo criminology." They write that

> the idea that increased penalties will reduce crime is based on a simplistic and fallacious theory of criminal behavior [that] starts with the idea that every person is an isolated, willful actor who makes completely rational decisions to maximize his or her pleasure and to minimize his or her pain. . . . If penalties for being caught are small or nonexistent, then many persons who are not restrained by other factors . . . will commit crimes . . . a lot of crimes. Only by increasing the certainty and severity of punishment, this thinking goes, will people "think twice" and be deterred. (p. 156)

These are fallacious assumptions about the motivations for criminal behavior. It's no wonder prison fails so consistently.

After some period of confinement in a prison, offenders typically are not yet off the hook. Even after their term of imprisonment is reduced (or when they are released early), they typically will still be under some form of criminal justice supervision. In the next section, I address how one such mechanism—parole—can increase the risk of repeat offending.

FORGIVING THE OFFENDER: WHY HARASS PAROLEES?

Parole means conditional release to community supervision, whether by parole board decision or by mandatory conditional release after serving a prison term. At the end of 2005, 784,400 were on parole. More than 682,000 adults and about 90,000 children/teenagers were supervised by the federal government. According to the Bureau of Justice Statistics, about half of those entering parole in 2005 were **mandatory releases** from prison rather than **discretionary releases**. Mandatory releases occur because of a sentencing statute or good-time provision in the law. Discretionary releases are granted by parole boards. Parolees are subject to being returned to jail or prison for rule violations or other offenses. This is because parole can be revoked when a person either commits another criminal act or violates one of the rules of release.

If rearrest is a sign of parole failure, then parole is a failure. Irwin and Austin (1997, p. 113) write, "In general, most inmates are rearrested at least once after being released from prison." This does not mean that they committed new crimes, only that they either were suspected of having committed a new crime or violated some rule of their parole. In some ways, police harassment of parolees makes sense.

When a crime is committed in the vicinity of a known offender, especially one that fits his or her modus operandi (M.O.), the ex-con becomes a logical suspect. Yet some feel that once an offender has paid his or her debt to society, police should not automatically assume that an "innocent" person is guilty of a crime.

In fact, most people who fail parole fail not because they committed new crimes but because of **technical violations**. As you saw in Chapter 8, most state and federal parolees do not successfully complete their supervision term. At both levels of government, failures were more attributable to technical violations rather than new crimes. Irwin and Austin (1997, pp. 116, 123) attribute parole failures to increased supervision capacities of parole officers and to an increased focus on the law enforcement function of parole as opposed to its social service function. Parolees are typically required to follow the same general rules of those on probation, including obeying all laws, reporting to their parole officers, permitting their parole officers to visit them, remaining in the jurisdiction, maintaining employment, abstaining from associating with known felons, paying fines and court costs, engaging in community service, and participating in treatment and/or training.

Irwin and Austin (1997) lay out the main reason that people who go to prison are likely to eventually end up back there after release. They suggest that, in addition to the pains of imprisonment discussed earlier and the harassment of parolees by the police, the following reasons make it easy to understand why the prison experience followed by parole fails to reform prisoners.

- Reentering society is literally a shock to offenders who are used to the routine of prison life lived under government-controlled rules and orders.
- Finding a job is next to impossible, given ex-prisoners' lack of employment skills, educational deficits, and criminal record.

In essence, prisons are not really supposed to make people better; they are just supposed to warehouse criminals for only short-term benefit to society. Given this, it may seem logical for police and corrections officials to monitor those released on parole from prison. Yet doing so assures that a high rate of offenders will fail and thus return to prison.

HOW AND WHY CORRECTIONS REFLECTS CRIMINAL JUSTICE BIAS

Because corrections represents the end of the criminal justice process, it is the ideal place to look for **disparities** that suggest injustices in the law, media coverage of crime, police activity, and court processes. Imagine if small biases existed within each of these institutions. The outcome would probably be large disparities in correctional populations.

Clearly, U.S. prisons reflect a significant disparity in punishment in the United States. This led Irwin and Austin (1997, p. 164) to write, "In effect, we are gradually putting our own apartheid into place." According to The Sentencing Project (2007), the characteristics of those in prisons at the end of 2005 include the following: 93% were male; 40% were black; 20% were Hispanic; 76% were sentenced to prison for nonviolent crimes, including 31% for drug offenses and 29% for property offenses. Additionally, the typical prisoner has not completed high school, was underemployed (i.e., unemployed, employed part-time, or making very little money in a full-time job), was earning less than $1,000 per month at the time of arrest, and was under the influence of drugs at the time of their offenses.

African American males are disproportionately likely to be under all forms of correctional supervision. According to The Sentencing Project (2007), African American males have a 32% chance of serving time in prison at some point in their lives, versus 17% of Hispanic males and 6% of Caucasian males.

The war on crime is clearly having its greatest effects on young African American males. For example, the Bureau of Justice Statistics reports that at the end of 2005, one in eight (12%) black males aged 25 to 29 was in prison or jail, versus 1 in 26 (3.9%) Hispanic males and 1 in 59 (1.7%) white males. Thus, young African American males are six times more likely than young Caucasian males and two times more likely than young Hispanic males to be in prison. Amazingly, African American males in their 20s and 30s make up approximately 30% of all people locked up in America!

Figure 9-5 shows the rates of sentenced prisoners for various groups in the United States. The higher the number, the greater the number of people per 100,000 people in that group in society are incarcerated. I have shaded the highest numbers to illustrate the focus of imprisonment in America.

Blakemore (1998, p. 4) asserts that the prison industry is being built "on the backs of blacks." In fact, there are more African American males incarcerated than enrolled in higher education. The racial disparities in prison are generally getting worse and worse as time goes by.

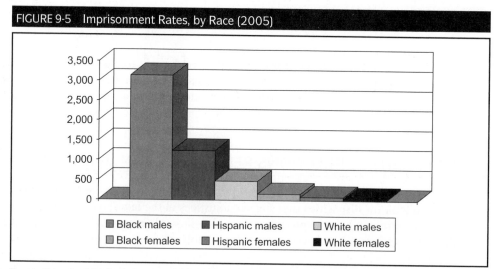

FIGURE 9-5   Imprisonment Rates, by Race (2005)

Black males | Hispanic males | White males
Black females | Hispanic females | White females

Source: Bureau of Justice Statistics (2006). Prisoners in 2005. Available at http://ojp.usdoj.gov/bjs/abstract/p05.htm.

As noted earlier, at the end of 2005, Caucasians made up 45% of inmates, versus 40% African Americans and 15% Hispanics. So African Americans are also overrepresented among jail inmates.

As for probation, at the end of 2005, men made up 77% of probationers and women made up 22%. Caucasians made up 55% of probationers, African Americans made up 30%, and 13% were Hispanics. Here, men and African Americans are overrepresented.

Parolees at the end of 2005 were 88% men and 12% women. Caucasians made up 41% of parolees, 40% were African Americans, and Hispanics made up 18%. Here again, men and African Americans are overrepresented, as are Hispanics (but only slightly).

From these statistics, it is clear who is suffering most from our current criminal justice policies. Young, poor, minority men (and increasingly women) are most affected by mass imprisonment and other forms of punishment.

The result of such disparities is devastating. As noted earlier, 1.4 million African American men (13% of all black men) cannot vote because of felony convictions. This is seven times higher than the national average. Additionally, about 80% of African American males can expect to have been arrested by age 35 (National Center on Institutions and Alternatives, 1999; see also Miller and Holman, 1992; Tillman, 1987).

Miller (1997a) claims that contact with the criminal justice network is now a "rite of passage" for young African American men. As a result,

> it is now a sad reality that most of the young African American men can anticipate being at least briefly ushered through a series of hothouses for sociopathy: prisons, jails, detention centers, and reform schools—all of which nurture those very characteristics that can subsequently be labeled as pathological.

Blakemore (1998, p. 5) calls contact with the criminal justice network a "badge of honor" for some African American males, and claims that punishment thus loses its deterrent effect for them. Also, criminal justice network targeting of minorities exacerbates problems such as single parenthood and unemployment (Blakemore, 1998), which undoubtedly increases the likelihood of criminality. For example, in 1999, more than 1.5 million minor children had parents in prison. More than 640,000 state inmates and nearly 80,000 federal inmates were parents to children under the age of 18 years. In 1997, 55% of inmates said they had minor children and 45% reported living with their children at the time of their admissions. These numbers have grown as the criminal justice network has caught more and more women over the past decade.

Other minorities and disenfranchised groups suffer as well. For example, the percentage of Hispanics in state and federal prisons doubled between 1980 and 1993, to more than 14% (Mauer and Huling, 1995b). At the end of 2005, Hispanics made up 20% of all inmates. The greatest increase in incarceration between 1989 and 1994 was 78% for African American women (Mauer and Huling, 1995b). From 1986 to 1991, the number of African American women incarcerated for drug offenses in state prisons increased 828% (Mauer and Huling, 1995b). More and more African American women are being incarcerated, partly because they do not have anything to offer the prosecutors who are looking for "bigger fish," and so the "small fish" in the drug markets go to prison (Miller, 1997a).

At the end of 2005, only 7% of state and federal prison inmates were women. Yet since 1995, the number of female inmates grew faster than the number of male inmates. This accelerated growth has disproportionately affected minority women and a significant portion is attributable to the war on drugs. Thus, since 1990, 33% of the total growth in female inmates is for drug offenses, versus only 19% for male inmates. Similarly, drug offenses account for the greater growth among African American inmates (27%) than of Caucasian inmates (15%) or Hispanic inmates (7%).

There has been a dramatic increase in drug offender imprisonment, as drug offenders now make up 54% of all federal inmates (Sourcebook of Criminal Justice Statistics, 2006). As explained earlier, at least half of state prison inmates were convicted of crimes that are considered petty by the American public. Drug offenders made up 1 in 11 offenders in 1983, but now make up about 1 in 5 inmates nationally, costing billions of dollars per year, in part because the probability of imprisonment for drug offenses has increased 500% since 1980 (Beck, 1999).

So there is clearly a correlation between punitiveness in the United States generally, the U.S. wars on crime and on drugs in particular, and racial disparities in the criminal justice network. Whether intended or not, our nation's crime control efforts disproportionately affect poor people and people of color. Perhaps part of these disparities can be explained by differences in offending patterns (see Chapter 12). But most of them cannot. Thus, the most valid explanation of these disparities is discrimination in the criminal justice network, beginning with bias in the criminal law, reinforced by the media, and continuing with the police and courts. Discrimination in the criminal justice network makes criminal justice operations incompatible with its ideal goal of being fair, neutral, unbiased, and nondiscriminatory. In other words, correctional populations serve as evidence of an unjust U.S. criminal justice network.

CONCLUSION

This chapter illustrated how the use of imprisonment will ultimately add to the crime problem in the United States, even if it temporarily locks some criminals away from society. Imprisonment, a main component of the unprecedented U.S. incarceration rate, has increased dramatically since the early 1970s. This chapter demonstrated that this increase had little or nothing to do with crime, is incredibly expensive, and is very unlikely to make Americans safer. In fact, given that most people in prisons are not repeat, violent offenders, many have claimed that we are wasting too much money on relatively harmless offenders such as drug criminals. This chapter also demonstrated that, contrary to the myth of the comfortable prison, prisons in the United States are rough places to stay and serve as more than sufficient punishments for most crimes. Because of these pains of imprisonment and because we harass parolees after they complete their sentences, it is very difficult for street criminals to "go straight" upon their release. Thus, we are guaranteeing our failure by choosing to imprison so many of our citizens. Most important for the theme of the book, imprisonment serves as a clear example of how the U.S. criminal justice network fails to meet its ideal goal of doing justice. Plainly stated, the use of imprisonment in the United States is biased against the poor and people of color.

Issue in Depth—The Convict School of Criminology

The *Convict School of Criminology* was formalized in 2001 with the appearance of a journal article and in 2003 with the publication of the book, *Convict Criminology* (Ian and Richards, 2003). This new "school of thought" within the discipline of criminology came about when a handful of criminologists with criminal records met over time in their graduate school programs, at academic conferences, and through correspondence via e-mail and telephone.

As criminologist John Irwin (2003, p. xvii) notes, "It seemed to me that convicts were springing up like toadstools in the clear and pure fields of academe; one of the unintended consequences of laws recently casting a larger and larger net and catching, in addition to the usual suspects, a whole bunch of more educated and educable felons." As explained by Ian and Richards (2003), convict criminology

> consists primarily of essays and empirical research conducted and written by convicts or exconvicts, on their way to completing or already in possession of a Ph.D., or by enlightened academics who critique existing literature, policies, and practices, thus contributing to a new perspective on criminology, criminal justice, corrections, and community corrections. This is a "new criminology" . . . led by exconvicts who are now academic faculty. These men and women, who have worn both prison uniforms and academic regalia, served years behind prison walls, and now, as academics, are the primary architects of the movement.

John Irwin's (2003) case is particularly interesting, one that he describes quite well:

> I served five years for armed robbery in the mid-1950s at Soledad Prison in California. Soledad was planned to be the model rehabilitative prison in the California system. We prisoners were forced to participate in educational and vocational training programs. I repeated many high school courses . . . and earned 24 college units from the University of California Extension Division. Though after release I was discouraged by parole authorities, I immediately entered San Francisco State College, then transferred to UCLA and earned a B.A. in sociology. (p. xx)

Upon graduating with his bachelor's degree, Irwin was encouraged to go to graduate school by another notable criminologist, with whom Irwin would ultimately go on to publish. He then received financial assistance and a position with the help of yet another notable criminologist, and ultimately earned his Ph.D. at the University of California, Berkeley, and was hired to be a sociologist who would study crime by yet another criminologist at San Francisco State University.

Irwin (2003) explains the significance of all this: "The point is, I made my transition from the life of a thief, drug addict, and convict to one of a 'respectable' professional during a period when there was growing tolerance toward us condemned wrongdoers. The doors were opening. Then, in the mid-1970s, they slammed shut again" (p. xx). Yes, as I claim in Chapter 9 of this book, prisons are horrible places with few opportunities for rehabilitation.

Among the explicit claims of convict criminologists are the following.

- Prisons are being used as a solution to a social problem that does not respond to prison.
- America's prisons and correctional agencies are clearly flawed.
- Efforts to reform America's prisons have failed.
- The level of incarceration in the United States is at its highest level ever.
- The major justifications for America's unprecedented prison expansion are unwarranted.
- Every cell built in a new prison costs approximately $100,000 and is money that is not spent on other vital social services such as education.
- Prisons do not reduce crime.
- Prison expansion has disproportionately affected people of color.
- One dramatic result of mass imprisonment is that as many as 2 million people of color currently are denied the right to vote.
- Prison expansion has disproportionately affected the nation's poor, especially poor men of color, who are seen as marginal to America's political economy.
- Most people have not noticed how rapidly the prison population has grown, in part because the people who have the greatest voice in today's culture are not largely affected by the expansion of prisons.
- Prisoners are extremely demonized and marginalized despite being human beings.
- Vocational programs have been reduced in prisons as privileges simultaneously were reduced so that there is virtually no rehabilitation in American prisons.
- The treatment of prisoners inside is permitted mostly because people (including the academic criminologists who study crime for a living) do not understand what it is like to be inside and the culture that is unique to prisoners.
- Most inmates are normal, relatively harmless people who made bad decisions and committed relatively harmless but bothersome crimes.
- Not only are too many people incarcerated but they are also generally held for too long.
- Even the motivations of serious offenders in prison can typically be understood without invoking negative personality traits or character flaws (this is not to justify their behavior, however, but rather to explain it).
- When released, prisoners reenter a society that fears and loathes them, and do so with meager resources and virtually no preparation.

In essence, most of the claims of convict criminologists match what I have written in this chapter about America's prisons and its imprisonment boom. What is most unique about convict criminologists is their insight into prison life and their way of telling their stories that so clearly cast grave doubts on our entire method of punishment in the United States.

Although convict criminologists appear to be taken seriously within the academic discipline of criminology, it is hard to say how a group of current and former prison inmates (even with doctoral degrees) would be viewed by legislators and general members of society. Given the politicization and intense media coverage of crime, and America's overall fear of both criminals and the unknown, it is unlikely that any reforms suggested by convicts and ex-convicts would be taken seriously. Thus, other conditions in society must be changed prior to implementing the reforms suggested by convict criminologists. For more on such recommendations, see Chapter 13.

Convict criminologists advocate at least the following reforms.

- Reduce the number of people in prison through diversion to probation and other community sanctions.
- Close large prisons where thousands of inmates are warehoused and forced to live in conditions like animals at the slaughterhouse, and replace them with smaller and safer prisons with individual cells.
- Increase the quality of food and clothing of prisoners to reduce resentment and violence within prisons.
- Better fund prison programs, including those for employment, vocational training, higher education, and family skills training.
- Restore voting rights for all ex-convicts.
- Provide voluntary drug education therapy.
- Provide inmates with 3 months of pay for food and rent upon release to give them a fair chance at reform.
- Use victim-offender reconciliation programs and other forms of restorative justice to relieve some of the burden on criminal justice.
- End the drug war.

I advocate many of these same reforms given the research presented in Chapter 9. The drug war is discussed in Chapter 11.

KEY TERMS

collateral damage
colleges of crime
community corrections
convict school of criminology
deprivation of heterosexual
    relationships
deprivation of goods and
    services
discretionary releases
disparities

institutional corrections
intermediate sanctions
jails
labeling theory
loss of autonamy
loss of dignity
loss of liberty
loss of security
loss of voting rights
mandatory releases

pains of imprisonment
parole
prisonized
prisons
probation
reintegrative shaming
social disorganization
stigmatization
supermax prisons
technical violations

DISCUSSION QUESTIONS

1. Why is the United States incarceration rate so high compared with rates for other countries?
2. Differentiate between prisons and jails.
3. Do you think there is a link between crime rates and incarceration rates? Why or why not?
4. Identify the claims of politicians that would justify building more prisons.
5. What are some of the costs associated with imprisonment?
6. In what ways might imprisonment increase crime?
7. Describe the typical prisoner.

8. Why do you think politicians have passed laws that have led to a removal of educational, vocational, and drug treatment opportunities within prisons?
9. Think back over the course of your life and try to recall any crimes you may have committed that could have led to your own imprisonment. What made you commit those crimes?
10. What is parole?
11. What are the typical conditions required of parolees?
12. Outline the ways in which imprisonment can be considered a failure.
13. Briefly discuss the issue of racial disparities in imprisonment and criminal justice generally. Why are African Americans and Hispanics more likely than whites to be incarcerated?
14. What is the convict school of criminology? What are its main criticisms of crime fighting and of prison in particular?

PART

IV

FAILING CRIMINAL JUSTICE POLICY AND HOPE FOR THE FUTURE

Chapter 10   The Ultimate Sanction: Death as Justice?

Chapter 11   The "War on Drugs": Focusing on the Wrong Drugs?

Chapter 12   The War on Crime as a Threat to Equality: Innocent Bias Against the Poor, People of Color, and Women

Chapter 13   Summary, Conclusions, and Recommendations for the Future

CHAPTER

10

THE ULTIMATE SANCTION: DEATH AS JUSTICE?

1. Introduction
2. A Brief History of Capital Punishment
   - Box 10-1.   A Broken System
3. Death Penalty Facts
   - Box 10-2.   Is Lethal Injection Cruel and Unusual?
   - Box 10-3.   Death Penalty Offenses at the State Level
   - Box 10-4.   Death Penalty Offenses at the Federal Level
4. Public Support for Capital Punishment
   - Box 10-5.   The Marshall Hypothesis
5. Justifications for Capital Punishment: Logical or Not?
   a. Vengeance
   b. Retribution
   - Box 10-6.   Capital Punishment in the Bible
   c. Deterrence
   d. Incapacitation
6. What's Wrong with the Death Penalty? Alleged Problems with the Administration of Death
   - Box 10-7.   Inmates Executed Despite Doubts About Their Guilt
7. Conclusion
8. Issue in Depth—Expert Opinion on Capital Punishment
9. Key Terms
10. Discussion Questions

INTRODUCTION

The death penalty, also known as **capital punishment**, is the ultimate punishment imposed by any society. America has had a long and sordid history with this criminal sanction, including both state-sanctioned killings and the murders of African American men through lynchings carried out in the name of "punishment" for alleged wrongdoings.

This chapter briefly examines this history and then turns to the issue of whether the death penalty achieves its goals. The questions of whether capital punishment is moral or immoral, right or wrong, good or bad, necessary or unnecessary, just or unjust, and so forth, have been asked and answered numerous times throughout history. There is no one answer to which all people agree, but most of us have made up our own minds as to what side of the debate we are on. However you feel about the death penalty personally, capital punishment is a highly emotional issue. As you read this chapter, you should attempt to put your personal opinions aside and understand that your personal opinion may not be supported by empirical evidence. In this chapter, I critically analyze the justifications for the death penalty and conclude with a discussion of what's wrong with the application of capital punishment in the United States.

A BRIEF HISTORY OF CAPITAL PUNISHMENT

The earliest recorded execution in America was in 1608, of Captain George Kendall, a member of the Virginia colony. His punishment was for the crime of spying for Spain (Espy and Smykla, 1987). Since that time, nearly 25,000 people have been executed in America (Bohm, 2007). Another 10,000 or so were lynched in the nineteenth century (Bedau, 1982).

Most of those executed have been men—only 2% were women—and the largest share of those executed were put to death prior to 1866 (Schneider and Smykla, 1991). Originally, death sentences were mandatory for certain crimes, such as murder, but this began to change in 1838 when Tennessee enacted a discretionary death sentence (Acker and Lanier, 1998). Today, mandatory death sentences are considered unconstitutional. In the case of *Woodson v. North Carolina* (1976), the Supreme Court ruled 5–4 that the death penalty statutes in question were "cruel and unusual." In essence, the Supreme Court found that mandatory death sentences violated the evolving standards of respect for human life implicit in the Eighth Amendment to the Constitution. Robinson (2008, p. 73) explains the Court held that "society has evolved away from mandatory sentences . . . mandatory sentences do not eliminate arbitrariness."

According to Costanzo (1997, pp. 13–15), there have been four consistent trends in the application of the death penalty over the past two centuries:

- A dramatic shrinking in the number and types of crimes punishable by death
- Attempts to lessen the cruelty of executions
- Attempts to ensure that death sentences are imposed fairly and rationally
- Efforts to sanitize executions by making them private

As you will see in this chapter, the combined effect of these death penalty trends is a freakish experience with executions in America.

Figure 10-1 illustrates trends in executions in the United States. The decade that saw the largest number of executions was the 1930s, when the average number of executions per year was 167 (Schneider and Smykla, 1991). In the 1940s, 1,289 people were executed. In the 1950s, 715 were executed. From 1960 through 1976, only 191 were executed. The U.S. witnessed a **moratorium** on executions from 1968 to 1976. After the moratorium on executions ended, 120 people were killed through 1989. In the 1990s, 478 people were executed. Between 2000 and 2006, the United States has executed 459 people.

FIGURE 10-1   Trends in American Executions

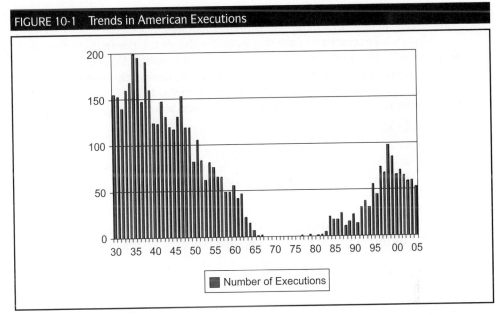

Source: Bureau of Justice Statistics (2006).

   Throughout U.S. history, many states have temporarily abolished the death penalty, and the United States as a whole briefly witnessed a moratorium, as noted above. Cases heard by the U.S. Supreme Court about racial discrimination in the administration of capital punishment, particularly cases of alleged rapes of Caucasian women by African American men, led to an "unofficial suspension" of the death penalty after June 1967 (Bohm, 1999, p. 13). The Supreme Court formally prohibited capital punishment with *Furman v. Georgia* (1972) but later ruled it constitutional with *Gregg v. Georgia* (1976). I discuss each of these cases later in the chapter.

   The first person executed after the death penalty was reinstated in 1976 was Gary Gilmore, who requested to be killed by the state of Utah (Bohm, 1999, p. 13). Gilmore insisted that he be put to death by the state, and he was, in 1977 by shooting squad. Gilmore's brother now discusses how ironic it is that his brother's last gift to humankind, created by his own push to be executed as rapidly as possible, was a return to capital punishment in the United States.

   The United States is the only Western, industrialized country still practicing the death penalty. Most of our European allies abolished capital punishment after the horrors of World War II (Zimring and Hawkins, 1986). This may suggest that American respect for life is less than in other countries. In 1961, the law professor Gerald Gottlieb wrote that "the death penalty was unconstitutional under the Eighth Amendment because it violated contemporary moral standards, what the U.S. Supreme Court in *Trop v. Dulles* . . . referred to as 'the evolving standards of decency that mark the progress of a maturing society'" (Bohm, 1999, p. 11). In the case of *Weems v. United States* (1910), the Supreme Court held that punishments are excessive only if they violate "evolving social conditions." The fact that we administer the death penalty in the United States must mean that the courts do not believe our country has evolved enough socially to warrant a cessation of capital punishment. Public opinion shows widespread support for capital punishment generally.

Although we continue to use the death penalty, its use began to decline after World War II as our allies moved to abolish it. The trends shown in Figure 10-1 are illustrative of what first appeared to be a moving away from the death penalty. Yet the United States witnessed a rebirth of capital punishment in the 1990s. Here is some evidence of the resurgence of capital punishment in the United States during the 1990s:

- In 1992, Robert Alton Harris was the first person executed in California in a quarter century.
- Presidential candidate Bill Clinton interrupted his 1992 campaigning to fly back to Arkansas to preside over two executions.
- In 1993, Wesley Allan Dodd became the first person executed in Washington in almost 30 years.
- In 1994, Maryland carried out its first execution in more than 30 years, Nebraska killed its first citizen in 35 years, and Idaho began executing citizens again after 36 years.
- In 1995, New York reinstated the death penalty.
- In 1996, Congress passed a law allowing death row inmates only one federal appeal unless new evidence proves clearly and convincingly that the person is innocent. In that same year, Oregon carried out its first execution in 34 years.
- In 1997, Arkansas executed three prisoners in one night (Costanzo, 1997, p. 1).

Since 2000, the number of executions has significantly declined, as have the number of death sentences and even the size of our death penalty populations. Figure 10-2 shows that the number of people on death row began to increase in the 1970s as our nation moved more toward a crime control model of criminal justice.

As I mentioned earlier, the case of *Furman v. Georgia* (1972) led to a temporary abolition of capital punishment in the United States. William Henry Furman, a 25-year-old

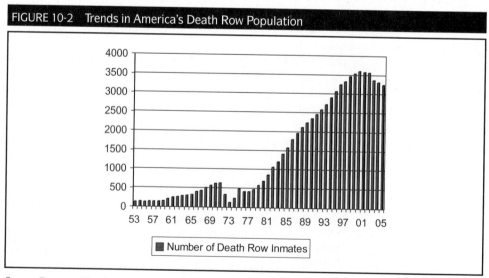

FIGURE 10-2   Trends in America's Death Row Population

Number of Death Row Inmates

Source: Bureau of Justice Statistics (2006).

African American with an IQ of only 65, was convicted of the murder of Wiliam Micke, Jr., a Coast Guard petty officer in Georgia who was also the father of four children and the stepfather of six others. This case, in which Furman was convicted of killing his victim in a failed burglary attempt, was not the stereotypical killing in the United States. Most murders are intraracial—that is, committed against a person of the same race as the murderer—and, historically, most have been committed by persons known to the victims rather than by strangers. Because Furman was an African American and a stranger, and his victim was a Caucasian as well as a family man who served in the military, Furman's chance of not receiving the death penalty was slim, especially in a southern state with a history of racial unrest.

Furman's attorneys argued to the Supreme Court that capital punishment in Georgia was unfair because capital trials essentially gave the jury unbridled discretion about whether to impose a death sentence on convicted defendants. The *Furman* case was only one of three heard by the Supreme Court at the same time, all dealing with death sentences imposed against African American men. The other two cases specifically involved rapes of Caucasian women by African American males (Coyne and Entzeroth, 1994), a crime that has been a primary source of discriminatory punishment in American history.

The *Furman* case led to nine separate opinions by each of the justices of the Supreme Court, and the ruling was 5–4 that the death penalty statutes in question were "cruel and unusual" because they violated the Eighth and Fourteenth Amendments of the U.S. Constitution. In essence, the Supreme Court found that capital punishment was being imposed "arbitrarily, infrequently, and often selectively against minorities" (Bohm, 1999, p. 23). So it was not the death penalty itself that was at issue; it was how this penalty was being applied arbitrarily and disproportionately to some groups of people.

Bohm (citing Anderson, 1983) writes: "A practical effect of *Furman* was the Supreme Court's voiding of 40 death penalty statutes and the sentences of 629 death row inmates." The Supreme Court, however, did not conclude that the death penalty per se was unconstitutional. It was only unconstitutional to the degree that is was imposed arbitrarily and unfairly. Thus, "36 states proceeded to adopt new death penalty statutes designed to meet the Court's objections" (p. 24). States, concerned with their image as much as with the public safety of their citizens, quickly passed death penalty laws that would be considered constitutional by the Supreme Court.

Nearly one-third of states enacted mandatory death sentences for some crimes (Acker and Lanier, 1998), taking the issue of discretion of judges and juries out of the picture. Most states passed "guided discretion" statutes that would give juries and sentencing judges some guidelines to follow when considering death sentences (Bohm, 1999, p. 25). The mandatory death sentence statutes were rejected 5–4 by the Supreme Court as unconstitutional in *Woodson v. North Carolina* (1976), but in the case of *Gregg v. Georgia* (1976), the Court ruled by a 7–2 vote that guided discretion statutes were acceptable in death penalty cases. The Court also upheld the use of bifurcated trials, where guilt or innocence would be decided in the first phase and sentencing decided in the second, as well as automatic appellate review of convictions and sentences and, finally, proportionality reviews to compare sentences of particular cases against similar cases to ensure just sentencing practices. Thus, suggestions made in 1959 by the American Law Institute's Model Penal Code and aimed at making the death penalty fairer were finally put into place.

Almost all of the 36 states that still practice the death penalty provide an automatic appeal of all death sentences, whether the defendant wanted it or not (Snell, 1997). The use of appeals supposedly makes it less likely that a death sentence will be inappropriately handed down. Automatic appeals do not, however, lessen the likelihood that an innocent person will be wrongfully executed, for evidence pointing to the defendant's innocence may arise or be discovered only years later. Contrary to popular belief, many discretionary appeals initiated by defendants are not frivolous. In fact, since 1976, there have been more than 2,000 cases in which defendants have either had their convictions overturned or had their sentences reduced by appeals courts. Using such statistics, Bohm (1999, p. 45) estimated that approximately 21% to 32% of imposed death sentences "have been found faulty" by appeals courts for reasons such as ineffective counsel, prosecutors referring to defendants' refusal to testify (as if this is a sign of guilt rather than a constitutional right), denial of an impartial jury, and use of bad evidence such as coerced confessions of guilt (Freedman, 1998). A more recent report shows an even higher incidence of serious reversible error. Box 10-1 discusses serious errors in capital cases according to a shocking report titled "A Broken System."

BOX 10-1

"A BROKEN SYSTEM"

An alarming study was recently published by James S. Liebman, Jeffrey Fagan, and Valerie West. Part I of the study was titled, *A Broken System: Error Rates in Capital Cases, 1973–1995*. These authors undertook "the first statistical study ever undertaken of modern American capital appeals (4,578 of them in state capital cases between 1973 and 1995)" and found that capital trials end up placing people on death row who do not belong there (either because serious errors were made during their cases or because they were innocent of the crimes of which they were charged), and that it takes a long time to carry out sentences of death in the United States because of the numerous errors in the process. According to the findings of this report, "American capital sentences are so persistently and systematically fraught with error" that their reliability is seriously undermined. The authors claim that capital punishment in the United States is "collapsing under its own mistakes . . .

a system that is wasteful and broken and needs to be addressed."

Here are some of the key findings of this report.

- Nationally, the overall rate of prejudicial error was 68% — that is, "courts found serious, reversible error in nearly 7 of every 10 of the thousands of capital sentences that were fully reviewed during the period."

- Serious error was "error substantially undermining the reliability of capital verdicts."

- "Capital trials produce so many mistakes that it takes three judicial inspections to catch them—leaving grave doubt whether we *do* catch them all" (emphasis in original). State courts dismissed 47% of death sentences because of errors, and a later federal review dismissed 40% of the remaining cases.

- The most common errors found in the cases were (1) egregiously incompetent defense attorneys who missed evidence of the defendant's innocence or evidence that he or she did not deserve a death sentence and (2) suppression of evidence by police and prosecutors.

- Eighty-two percent of those whose death sentences were overturned by state courts were found to be deserving of less than a death sentence, and 7% were found to be innocent of the crimes for which they were convicted.

- Serious errors have been made in every year since the death penalty was reinstated, and more than half of all cases were found to be seriously flawed in 20 of the 23 study years.

- Serious errors are made in virtually every state that still executes people, and more than 90% of these states make errors more than half of the time.

- "In *most cases,* death row inmates wait for years for the lengthy review procedures needed to uncover all this error. Then their death sentences are reversed" (emphasis in original).

- "This much error, and the time needed to cure it, impose terrible costs on taxpayers, victims' families, the judicial system, and the wrongly condemned. And it renders unattainable the finality, retribution and deterrence that are the reasons usually given for having a death penalty."

- The death penalty ranges from 2.5 to 5 times as expensive as life imprisonment without parole. When you add the costs of posttrial reviews, executions become about 24 times as expensive as life imprisonment without parole. The death penalty is so much more expensive than life imprisonment because of the high rates of error that occur at each stage and the persistence of high error rates over time and across the nation, which mandate multiple expensive judicial inspections.

- The death penalty is rarely applied— of the 5,760 state death sentences handed down between 1973 and 1995, only 313 (5.4%) led to an execution during this time. Additionally, since 1984 when post-*Furman* executions began in earnest, we have executed only about 1.3% of our nation's death row inmates each year. This makes "the retributive and deterrent credibility of the death penalty" very low.

- Homicide rates were slightly higher in death sentencing states than in non-death-sentencing states during the study years.

From their findings, the authors conclude that the administration of capital punishment in America is nothing less than irrational. They note: "Death penalty states sentenced 22 times more defendants per 1,000 homicides than they executed. And they sentenced 26 times more defendants per 100,000 population than they executed" (p. 45). I would characterize these types of findings as bizarre. Consider this: "There is no relationship between death-sentencing and execution rates" (p. 92). It is as if death sentences really have nothing to do with justice, but more to do with politics.

In fact, the study found a not-so-surprising relationship between politics

(continued)

BOX 10-1   *(Continued)*

and the death penalty—that political pressure plays a role in capital punishment. The authors explain as follows.

> In general, the more electoral pressure a state's judges are under, the higher the state's death-sentencing rate, but the lower the rate at which it carries out its death sentences. [This] suggests that political pressure tends to impel judges—or to create an environment in which prosecutors and jurors are impelled—to impose death sentences, but then tends to interfere with the state's capacity to carry out the death sentences that are imposed . . . a desire to curry favor with voters may lead elected prosecutors and judges to cut corners in an effort to secure that premium—simultaneously causing death-sentencing rates, and error rates, to increase. (p. 103)

Part II of the study, titled *A Broken System II: Why There Is So Much Error in Capital Cases,* attempted to assess the causes of the errors in America's capital punishment processes. According to the study's authors,

> This study uncovered a number of conditions related to error in capital cases, including politics, race, crime control and the courts. But running through all the data was a simple finding—the more a state or county sentences people to death, the more often they make mistakes. . . . Everything else being equal, when death sentencing increases from the lowest to the highest

rate in the study, the reversal rate increases six-fold, to about 80%. The more often states and counties use the death penalty for every, say 10 or 100 homicides, the more likely it is that any death verdict they impose will later be found to be seriously flawed, and the more likely it is that the defendant who was found guilty and sentenced to die will turn out to be not guilty.

Additionally, the authors found that there are four key factors that lead to errors:

> homicide risk to whites and blacks; the size of the black population; the rate at which police catch and punish criminals; and politically motivated judges. . . . Everything else being equal, when the risk of a white person getting murdered is high relative to the risk of an African-American getting murdered, twice as many appeals are reversed than where that risk is low. . . . When whites and other influential citizens feel threatened by homicide, they put pressure on officials to punish as many criminals as severely as possible—with the result that mistakes are made, and a lot of people are initially sentenced to death who are later found to have committed a lesser crime, or no crime at all.
>
> The more African Americans there are in a state, the more likely it is that serious mistakes will be made in death penalty trials. This could be because of fears of crime driven by racial stereotypes and economic factors. . . . It is disturbing that race plays a role in the outcome of death penalty cases, whatever the reasons.

Despite the implementation of numerous reforms, little has changed in the outcome of death penalty cases. Steiker and Steiker (1998, p. 70) claim:

> The Supreme Court's death penalty law, by creating an impression of enormous regulatory effort, while achieving negligible effects, effectively obscures the true nature of our capital sentencing system. The pre-*Furman* world of unreviewable sentencer discretion lives on, with much the same consequences in terms of arbitrary and discriminatory sentencing patterns.

In other words, the death penalty still does not pass constitutional muster in practice.

Yet the last time the death penalty was seriously challenged, the Court failed to abolish capital punishment once and for all. In *McCleskey v. Kemp* (1987), the Supreme

Court heard testimony from a sociologist (Dr. Baldus) who showed that the death penalty was applied disproportionately to African Americans in Georgia. The study used a multiple regression analysis including 230 variables likely to affect the outcome of death penalty cases to test the hypothesis that race of defendant and race of victim played a role in death penalty sentences. This study found that only 1% of Caucasians received the death penalty in homicide cases between 1973 and 1979, whereas 11% of African Americans received the death penalty. Additionally, the study found that 22% of African Americans who killed Caucasians received death sentences, versus only 3% of Caucasians who killed African Americans. The Court recognized the validity of these findings and even acknowledged a general pattern of discrimination in the application of death sentences in Georgia. Yet the Court held that an individual defendant must demonstrate discrimination in his or her specific case for the case to be considered unconstitutional. That is, he or she must be able to demonstrate that the prosecutor acted in a discriminatory fashion in the individual case or that the legislature intended to make discriminatory law. Can this standard ever be met by an individual person?

Bohm (2007) reviews executions in Georgia since the *McCleskey* decision and finds that racial disparities still exist. Specifically, killers of Caucasians are far more likely than killers of African Americans to be sentenced to the death penalty, especially when African Americans are convicted of killing Caucasians.

The point is this: We know, and the Supreme Court even acknowledged in this case, that the death penalty is disproportionately applied to African Americans who harm Caucasians, yet the Court failed to use this evidence to overturn the death penalty. A majority of Americans still say that they support the use of capital punishment.

DEATH PENALTY FACTS

In early 2007, the 36 states with the death penalty and the federal government held 3,350 prisoners who had been sentenced to death. The state of New Jersey abolished the death penalty at the end of 2007. The 3,350 people on death row in 2007 included less than 10 from New Jersey. Of these men and women (mostly men) who sit on the nation's death rows, some have been there only months while others have been there for more than 20 years. Although I will discuss the issue of deterrence and the death penalty later in this chapter, it is impossible not to point out at the beginning that the death penalty is rarely administered in the United States. The rare nature of capital punishment calls into question its effectiveness as a potential deterrent.

Between 1976—when capital punishment was reinstated by the U.S. Supreme Court—and 2006, there were approximately 575,000 murders and nonnegligent homicides. These led to only 7,072 death sentences and 1,063 executions. Thus, only 1.2 percent of killings from 1977 to 2006 led to death sentences, and only 0.18 percent of killings have led to an execution so far. Why do we kill so few of our nation's killers? First, thirteen states and the District of Columbia do not have the death penalty. Second, only **aggravated murders** are eligible for the death penalty. Third, even most death penalty states rarely carry out executions, primarily because prosecutors are unwilling to seek it, juries are unwilling to impose it, and states are unable to pay for it with any greater frequency (Robinson, 2008).

What is perhaps most surprising is that, even during the 1930s (the decade with the most executions), only about 20% of all death-eligible offenders were executed

(Bohm, 2007). How can it be that our nation, supposedly devoted to justice, tolerates a punishment that is, and always has been, so arbitrarily applied? Bowers, Pierce, and McDevitt (1984, p. 188) calls the application of the death penalty "an occasional product of chance—an unpredictable occurrence." Even after the modifications to the death penalty after the *Furman* ruling, its application is still "rare," "uncommon," and "freakish" (Bohm, 1999, p. 146).

Death row inmates constitute far less than 1% of the nation's correctional inmates. Of death row inmates, most are Caucasians, but minorities are overrepresented. As shown in Figure 10-3, in early 2007, there were 1,517 Caucasians (45%), 1,397 African Americans (42%), 359 Hispanics (11%), and 77 people of some "other" race (2%) on death row. The increase in Americans on death row since 1990 has been higher for African Americans than for Caucasians and other ethnic groups. Almost all (98%) of death row inmates are males. The average age of death row inmates is less than 30 years. I'll visit the issue of bias in the application of the death penalty in the United States later in this chapter.

In 2006, 53 people were executed in 14 states. The average time on death row for those executed was nearly 11 years—hardly proof of a swift system. Table 10-1 illustrates which states executed people in 2006. As you can see, Texas leads the nation in executing its killers, proving once again, "Don't Mess with Texas!" Between 1977 and 2006, Texas executed 37% of all people put to death by capital punishment in the United States! Executions are so infrequent in most states (even in Texas) that it is almost laughable to assert that the death penalty deters would-be murderers. But if there should be a deterrent effect anywhere, it should be in Texas! Yet the murder rate in Texas in 2005 was 6.2 per 100,000 people, higher than the national average of 5.6 per 100,000 and ranked number 14 in the country.

You might expect that California would have a low murder rate as well, given that it has more death row inmates than any other state. Yet the murder rate in California in 2005 was 6.9 per 100,000 people, also higher than the national average, and ranked

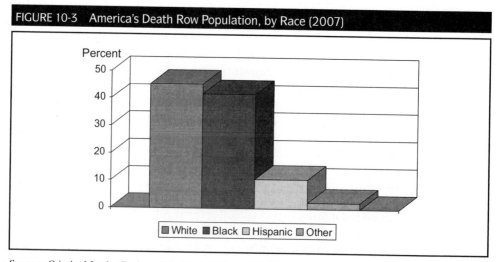

FIGURE 10-3   America's Death Row Population, by Race (2007)

Sources: Criminal Justice Project of the NAACP Legal Defense and Educational Fund (2007). Death Row USA. http://www.naacpldf.org/content/pdf/pubs/drusa/DRUSA_Winter_2007.pdf.

TABLE 10-1 Executions in the United States (2006)	
Texas	24
Ohio	5
Florida	4
North Carolina	4
Oklahoma	4
Virginia	4
Alabama	1
California	1
Indiana	1
Montana	1
Mississippi	1
Nevada	1
South Carolina	1
Tennessee	1
Total	53

Source: Death Penalty Information Center (2007).

number 8 in the country. Table 10-2 shows the states with the most death row inmates in 2006. Again, there is Texas, trying to displace California as the nation's leader. Jurisdictions without the death penalty include the District of Columbia, Alaska, Hawaii, Iowa, Maine, Massachusetts, Michigan, Minnesota, New Jersey, New York, North Dakota, Rhode Island, Vermont, West Virginia, and Wisconsin.

Most people executed today will be killed by lethal injection. Table 10-3 documents the method of execution of all those offenders executed between 2000 and 2006. As you can see, the vast majority were killed using lethal injection, although a handful were executed with the electric chair, including one in 2006. There has been a move to make the death penalty as sanitary and "clean" as possible, so that allegations of cruel and unusual punishment will be harder to prove against states that use capital punishment. Yet many have recently claimed that even lethal injection might be cruel and unusual. Box 10-2 discusses this issue.

Methods of capital punishment have changed with evolving standards of decency; that is, as beliefs about what is acceptable punishment have changed, so too have methods of capital punishment. Bohm (2007) notes that hanging has been the most common form of capital punishment in American history, although electrocution was the most commonly used form of the death penalty in the twentieth century. It is likely that the future will see new forms of capital punishment developed; until then, lethal injection is likely to be the most popular from of capital punishment in the United States in the twenty-first century. Currently authorized options for methods of executions include lethal injection (36 states), electrocution (10 states), lethal gas (5 states), hanging (3 states), and firing squad (2 states). The U.S. government and the U.S. military use lethal injections, as well. Most of these states use lethal injection only because the other methods are typically authorized for people convicted of capital crimes under previous statutes; in some cases, inmates have the choice among available methods.

TABLE 10-2 Death Row Populations in the United States (2006)	
California	660
Florida	397
Texas	393
Pennsylvania	226
Alabama	195
Ohio	191
North Carolina	185
Arizona	124
Georgia	107
Tennessee	107
Louisiana	88
Oklahoma	88
Nevada	80
South Carolina	67
Mississippi	66
Missouri	51
U.S. Government	44
Kentucky	41
Arkansas	37
Oregon	33
Indiana	23
Idaho	20
Virginia	20
Delaware	18
New Jersey	11
Illinois	11
Kansas	9
Nebraska	9
U.S. Military	9
Utah	9
Washington	9
Connecticut	8
Maryland	8
South Dakota	4
Colorado	2
Montana	2
New Mexico	2
Wyoming	2
New York	1

Source: Death Penalty Information Center (2007).

Prior to the *Furman* decision, individual methods of punishment were considered cruel and unusual only if they involved torture, unnecessary cruelty, or lingering death due to inhuman and barbarous punishments (Bohm, 2007). Of course, human beings have historically been subjected to executions that today would be considered cruel

TABLE 10-3 Method of Executions							
	2000	2001	2002	2003	2004	2005	2006
Lethal injection	80	66	70	64	58	60	52
Electrocution	5	0	1	1	1	0	1

Source: Death Penalty Information Center (2006). Executions in the United States. [Online]. Available at http://www.deathpenaltyinfo.org/article.php?did=414&scid=8.

BOX 10-2

IS LETHAL INJECTION CRUEL AND UNUSUAL?

Lethal injection is now under attack by abolitionists and human rights activists, and with at least some justification. Death row inmates have recently challenged the constitutionality of lethal injection, contending that lethal injection constitutes cruel and unusual punishment because the chemicals used in the execution process can cause pain (Wilson, 2006). An editorial by the *New York Times* (2006) explains:

In lethal injection, three different chemicals are administered in sequence. The first is an anesthetic, another paralyzes the muscles and stops breathing, and a third stops the heart. Improper administration of the anesthetic can have the ghoulish effect of leaving the prisoner able to feel the tremendous pain of being killed by the poison that is injected into him while rendering him unable to communicate his agony by sound or gestures.

In North Carolina, Willie Brown, Jr., was put to death by lethal injection for the 1983 killing of Vallerie Ann Roberson Dixon. He was the first person executed in the United States using a "bispectral index (BIS) monitor, that measures brain waves and ranks . . . level of consciousness from a scale of zero to 100" (Weigl, 2006). The BIS monitor was used in an attempt to alleviate concerns raised by Brown's attorneys that if he were not fully sedated before the second and third drugs were injected into his body, he might be awake to experience an excruciating death.

Brown's appeal that the BIS monitor was inappropriate for this purpose was denied by a U.S. District Court judge and affirmed by two federal appeals court judges. One of the federal judges ruled in Brown's favor. When Brown's lawyer asked the full court of 14 judges to consider their appeal, it was not considered. The U.S. Supreme Court also refused to hear his case. Shockingly citizens in North Carolina learned that the doctor involved in Brown's execution never did monitor the BIS, as required by state law.

Another inmate who challenged lethal injection was Clarence Hill, who killed police officer Larry Bailly in Pensacola, Florida, in 1982. Twenty-four years after his crime, he was strapped to a gurney and awaiting his execution in April 2006 when the U.S. Supreme Court granted Hill a stay of execution. This incident caused Governor Jeb Bush of Florida to stop signing death row warrants until the case is resolved (Word, 2006). Eventually, Hill was executed.

Another inmate, Marvin Bieghler, was executed in Indiana in January 2006 for killing Tommy Miller and his pregnant wife, Kimberly Jane Miller back in 1981. The U.S. Supreme Court overturned a stay of execution granted to him by a

(continued)

BOX 10-2 *(Continued)*

lower federal court just 90 minutes earlier. Bieghler, unlike Hill, had already unsuccessfully challenged the execution method at the state level. When about to be executed, Bieghler said: "Let's get it over with" (Wilson, 2006).

Then, in May 2006, Joseph Clark was executed in Ohio for the 1984 murder of David Manning as part of a drug-induced robbery (Clark also killed another man, Donald Harris, during the same crime spree). After officials worked to find a suitable vein in one arm for 90 minutes, the lethal injection process started, but one of Clark's veins collapsed, prompting Clark to sit up and tell prison officials: "It's not working. It's not working." Clark did not challenge his execution or ask for it to be stopped. Instead, Clark was executed after officials inserted the needle into his other arm (CNN, 2006).

The point of these three cases is that even lethal injection—probably the most humane method ever devised of killing murderers—is not perfect, nor is it free from legitimate legal challenges. In fact, one inmate successfully argued to the U.S. Supreme Court (in a unanimous decision in the case of *Nelson v. Campbell,* 2004) that he should be able to challenge a procedure known as a "cut-down procedure" as cruel and unusual punishment. Since Nelson's veins are badly damaged, it is likely impossible to insert a needle into his arm without first cutting into his arm, which could cause him pain, bleeding, and even problems with his heart.

Denno (2003, p. 715), who has testified numerous times in trials dealing with lethal injection, raises the possibility that lethal injection itself might meet the definition of "cruel and unusual punishment." She notes that: "Sodium thiopental— an 'ultra short' acting drug ... —typically

wears off very quickly; other similar drugs, such as pentobarbital, endure far longer. The 'fast acting' aspect of sodium thiopental can have horrifying effects if the inmate awakens while being administered the other two drugs." Yet, since the inmate is paralyzed there is a "calm scene" even though the "inmate may be conscious and suffering."

Further, since prison officials typically have discretion about capital punishment procedures, they may "ignore each prisoner's physical characteristics (for example, age, body weight, health), even though these factors strongly affect an individual's reaction to the chemicals as well as the condition of their veins" (Denno, 2003, p. 721). Individual physical characteristics are related to the amount of sodium thiopental an inmate would need to be asleep, and if the amount is insufficient, the inmate would be awake through his or her own death, which could lead to excruciating pain as the other drugs flow through the body.

Another interesting issue with lethal injection is that doctors have resisted participating in capital punishment through this "medical" method. In response to a challenge to lethal injection in Missouri, state officials sent letters to 298 certified anesthesiologists that resided near the state's death chamber in Boone Terre, and all of them turned the state's offer to participate in executions down. Both the American Medical Association and the American Society of Anesthesiologists have issued statements saying that doctors should never participate in executions since it is a violation of their basic oath to do no harm. The challenge was initiated in response to reports of a dyslexic Missouri surgeon who participated in lethal injections in Missouri that often improvised the process of executions by giving the condemned smaller doses of the anesthesia used to reduce the pain of the lethal drugs than required by state policy. As noted above, this could lead to intense pain on the part of the condemned inmate who is paralyzed and thus cannot react to the pain (Davey, 2006).

According to the Death Penalty Information Center (2007), at least 14 states have temporarily halted their use of lethal injection due to challenges by inmates and/or doctors. My state of North Carolina provides a good example of some of the relevant issues. A federal judge ordered that all executions be monitored by medically trained personnel. The state had already agreed to have a physician observe a machine meant to monitor the condemned inmate's degree of consciousness, and at least one inmate was executed using this monitor.

Then a North Carolina Superior Court judge granted stays of execution to several condemned inmates after the state's execution protocols were modified without the approval of the Council of State (a board made up of the heads of different state agencies, most of which have nothing to do with criminal justice or capital punishment). Approval of the Council of State is required by state law. The state did not appeal the ruling, meaning that in effect, all scheduled executions are stayed. North Carolina Governor Mike Easley then declared that, essentially, a moratorium on executions in the state was in effect.

The Council of State eventually approved a lethal injection process that requires doctors to be present and to monitor the possible suffering of the inmate being executed. However, the North Carolina Medical Board issued a statement saying that medical personnel (i.e., doctors and nurses) should not participate in executions. Therefore, the informal moratorium remains in effect as of this writing. Several bills are currently before the state's General Assembly (legislature) that could eventually resolve the issue. A majority of state citizens approve of a moratorium, according to several polls (Robinson, 2008).

Perhaps for all these reasons, the U.S. Supreme Court will hear arguments in 2008 about the constitutionality of the three drug cocktail used in lethal injection. The chances of the Court finding this method of death unconstitutional are slim given that the Court has never found any method of death to be unconstitutional.

and unusual. Bedeau (1982, p. 14) writes about some historical examples of methods of execution, including "flaying and impaling, boiling in oil, crucifixion, pulling asunder ... burying alive, and sawing in half."

One highly recognized example of a brutal execution is that of Robert-François Damiens, who in 1757 attempted to assassinate King Louis XV of France. His execution is described by Jones (1987a, p. 26):

> At seven o'clock in the morning of his execution day, Damiens was led to the torture chamber, where his legs were placed in "boots" that were squeezed gradually as wedges were inserted. A total of eight wedges were inserted, each at fifteen-minute intervals, until the attending physicians warned that an additional wedge could (prematurely) provoke [Damiens's death]. Thereupon, Damiens was removed to the place where he would be executed. . . . The condemned man was placed on a scaffold,

where a rope was tied to each arm and leg. Then, Damiens' hand was burned with a brazier containing burning sulphur, after which red-hot tongs were used to pinch his arms, thighs, and chest. Molten lead and boiling oil were poured onto his open wounds several times, and after each time the prisoner screamed in agony. Next, four huge horses were whipped by attendants as they pulled the ropes around Damiens' bleeding wounds for an hour. Only after some of the tendons were cut did two legs and one arm separate from Damiens' torso. He remained alive and breathing until the second arm was cut from his body. All parts of Damiens' body were hurled into a nearby fire for burning.

Executions often were public spectacles of excess. Adler, Mueller, and Laufer (1995, p. 56) write that, at the execution of Damiens, so many people wanted to watch the hour-long killing that window seats overlooking the site were sold at high prices. Criminal defendants in Europe were stretched on their backs, in public, and had large rocks or iron weights placed on their chests until they confessed or died.

Early methods of execution included stoning, "death by a thousand cuts," hanging, being drawn and quartered, being "parboiled" (cooked in salt and cumin seed), being drowned, being beaten to death, beheading, "breaking on the wheel," being pressed to death, and burning at the stake (Costanzo, 1997).

Even in the United States, executions have been carried out in public. Costanzo (1997, p. 7) describes how public executions in America were similar to those in Europe: "The condemned was forced to take a slow wagon ride to the gallows, often sitting atop the very coffin he or she would soon occupy. The rowdy crowds who witnessed the hangings often numbered in the thousands." Bohm (1999, p. 4) notes that the first state to "hide executions from the public" was Pennsylvania, in 1834. The last public execution in the United States was in Galena, Missouri, in 1937, before a crowd of nearly 20,000 (Costanzo, 1997, p. 9). Since this time, executions have occurred in the nation's prisons, in isolated rooms, inaccessible to the general public, late at night, without much attention by the media. This is to prevent or reduce the "public disorder, rioting, and even murder," as well as public knowledge of botched executions and disappointment associated with last-minute reprieves, that accompanied public executions (Bowers, 1984, p. 8; Denno, 1994, p. 564).

You may imagine that executions should be public as a deterrent to would-be criminals, but there is no evidence to support this assertion. In fact, when executions were public in Europe just prior to the French Revolution, large crowds of witnesses would attract pickpockets, who would steal from witnesses watching the public spectacle. Yet theft was a crime punishable by death (Adler et al., 1995)! I'll return to the issue of deterrence later in this chapter.

As I have mentioned, most people executed today will be executed after being convicted for aggravated murders. Box 10-3 lists specific death penalty offenses at the state level.

At the federal level, the situation is much the same. Most crimes punishable by death involve murder. Laws such as the 1994 crime bill discussed throughout this book and the 1996 *Anti-Terrorism and Effective Death Penalty Act* specifically increased the number of crimes punishable by death to more than 50, but only 4 of them do not involve the crime of murder. Box 10-4 lists specific death penalty offenses at the federal level.

BOX 10-3

DEATH PENALTY OFFENSES AT THE STATE LEVEL

- Alabama: Intentional murder with 18 aggravating factors (Ala. Stat. Ann. 13A-5-40[a][1]-[18])

- Arizona: First-degree murder accompanied by at least 1 of 10 aggravating factors (A.R.S sec 13-703[F])

- Arkansas: Capital murder (Ark. Code Ann. 5-10-101) with a finding of at least 1 of 10 aggravating circumstances; treason

- California: First-degree murder with special circumstances; train wrecking; treason; perjury causing execution

- Colorado: First-degree murder with at least 1 of 17 aggravating factors; treason

- Connecticut: Capital felony with 8 forms of aggravated homicide (C.G.S. 53a-54b)

- Delaware: First-degree murder with aggravating circumstances

- Florida: First-degree murder; felony murder; capital drug trafficking; capital sexual battery

- Georgia: Murder; kidnapping with bodily injury or ransom when the victim dies; aircraft hijacking; treason

- Idaho: First-degree murder with aggravating factors; aggravated kidnapping; perjury resulting in death

- Illinois: First-degree murder with 1 of 21 aggravating circumstances

- Indiana: Murder with 16 aggravating circumstances (IC 35-50-2-9)

- Kansas: Capital murder with 8 aggravating circumstances (KSA 21-3439)

- Kentucky: Murder with aggravating factors; kidnapping with aggravating factors (KRS 532.025)

- Louisiana: First-degree murder; aggravated rape of victim under age 12; treason (La. R.S.14:30, 14:42, and 14:113)

- Maryland: First-degree murder, either premeditated or during the commission of a felony, provided that certain death eligibility requirements are satisfied

- Mississippi: Capital murder (97-3-19[2]MCA); aircraft piracy (97-25-55[1] MCA)

- Missouri: First-degree murder (565.020 RSMO 2000)

- Montana: Capital murder with 1 of 9 aggravating circumstances (46-18-303 MCA); capital sexual assault (45-5-503 MCA)

- Nebraska: First-degree murder with a finding of at least 1 statutorily defined aggravating circumstance

- Nevada: First-degree murder with at least 1 of 15 aggravating circumstances (NRS 200.030, 200.033, 200.035)

- New Hampshire: Six categories of capital murder (RSA 630:1, RSA 630:5)

- New Mexico: First-degree murder with at least 1 of 7 statutorily defined aggravating circumstances (Section 30-2-1 A, NMSA)

- New York: First-degree murder with 1 of 13 aggravating factors (NY Penal Law sec 125.27)

- North Carolina: First-degree murder (NCGS sec 14-17)

(continued)

BOX 10-3   *(Continued)*

- Ohio: Aggravated murder with at least 1 of 10 aggravating circumstances (O.R.C. Secs. 2903.01, 2929.02, and 2929.04)
- Oklahoma: First-degree murder in conjunction with a finding of at least 1 of 8 statutorily defined aggravating circumstances
- Oregon: Aggravated murder (ORS 163.095)
- Pennsylvania: First-degree murder with 18 aggravating circumstances
- South Carolina: Murder with 1 of 11 aggravating circumstances (sec 16-3-20[C][a])
- South Dakota: First-degree murder with 1 of 10 aggravating

- circumstances; aggravated kidnapping
- Tennessee: First-degree murder with 1 of 15 aggravating circumstances (Tenn. Code Ann. sec 39-13-204)
- Texas: Criminal homicide with 1 of 8 aggravating circumstances (TX Penal Code 19.03)
- Utah: Aggravated murder (76-5-202, Utah Code Annotated)
- Virginia: First-degree murder with 1 of 13 aggravating circumstances (VA Code sec 18.2-31)
- Washington: Aggravated first-degree murder
- Wyoming: First-degree murder

Source: U.S. Department of Justice, Office of Justice Programs, Bureau of Justice Statistics, Bulletin, Capital Punishment, 2004. November 2005, NCJ 211349. [Online]. Feb 1, 2006. Available at http://www.ojp.usdoj.gov/bjs/pub/ascii/cp04.txt.

BOX 10-4

DEATH PENALTY OFFENSES AT THE FEDERAL LEVEL

- Assassination or kidnapping resulting in the death of the President or Vice President: 18 U.S.C., Section 1751 (by reference to 18 U.S.C., Section 1111).
- Bank-robbery-related murder or kidnapping: 18 U.S.C., Section 2113.
- Civil rights offenses resulting in death: 18 U.S.C., Sections 241, 242, 245, 247.
- Crimes against persons in the United States resulting in death, committed by a person engaged in conduct

- transcending national boundaries: 18 U.S.C., Section 2332(b).
- Death resulting from aircraft piracy: 49 U.S.C., Section 46502.
- Death resulting from offenses involving transportation of explosives, destruction of government property, or destruction of property related to foreign or interstate commerce: 18 U.S.C., Sections 844(d), (f), (i).
- Destruction of aircraft, motor vehicles, or related facilities resulting in death: 18 U.S.C., Sections 32, 33, 34.

- Death resulting from aggravated sexual abuse, sexual abuse, sexual abuse of a minor or ward, or abusive sexual conduct: 18 U.S.C., Sections 2241, 2242, 2243, 2244, 2245.
- Espionage: 18 U.S.C., Section 794.
- First-degree murder: 18 U.S.C., Section 1111.
- Genocide: 18 U.S.C., Section 1091.
- Mailing of injurious articles with intent to kill or resulting in death: 18 U.S.C., Section 1716.
- Murder by a federal prisoner: 18 U.S.C., Section 1118.
- Murder by an escaped federal prisoner already sentenced to life imprisonment: 18 U.S.C., Section 1120.
- Murder committed by the use of a firearm during a crime of violence or a drug trafficking crime: 18 U.S.C., Section 924(j).
- Murder committed during a drug-related drive-by shooting: 18 U.S.C., Section 36.
- Murder committed at an airport serving international civil aviation: 18 U.S.C., Section 37.
- Murder committed during an offense against a maritime fixed platform: 18 U.S.C., Section 2281.
- Murder committed during an offense against maritime navigation: 18 U.S.C., Section 2280.
- Murder committed in a federal government facility: 18 U.S.C., Section 930.
- Murder during a hostage taking: 18 U.S.C., Section 1203.
- Murder during a kidnapping: 18 U.S.C., Section 1201.
- Murder for hire: 18 U.S.C., Section 1958.
- Murder involved in a racketeering offense: 18 U.S.C., Section 1959.
- Murder involving torture: 18 U.S.C., Sections 2340, 2340(A).
- Murder of a court officer or juror: 18 U.S.C., Section 1503.
- Murder of a federal judge or law enforcement official: 18 U.S.C., Section 1114.
- Murder of a foreign official: 18 U.S.C., Section 1116.
- Murder of a member of Congress, an important executive official, or a Supreme Court Justice: 18 U.S.C., Section 351 (by reference to 18 U.S.C. 1111).
- Murder of a state or local law enforcement official or other person aiding in a federal investigation; murder of a state correctional officer: 18 U.S.C., Section 1121.
- Murder of a U.S. national in a foreign country: 18 U.S.C., Section 1119.
- Murder related to a carjacking: 18 U.S.C., Section 2119.
- Murder related to a continuing criminal enterprise or drug trafficking offense, or drug-related murder of a federal, state, or local law enforcement officer: 21 U.S.C., Section 848(e).
- Murder related to sexual exploitation of children: 18 U.S.C., Section 2251.
- Murder with the intent of preventing testimony by a witness, victim, or informant: 18 U.S.C., Section 1512.
- Retaliatory murder of a member of the immediate family of law

(*continued*)

BOX 10-4   *(Continued)*

enforcement officials: 18 U.S.C., Section 115(b)(3) [by reference to 18 U.S.C., Section 1111].

- Retaliatory murder of a witness, victim, or informant: 18 U.S.C., Section 1513.

- Terrorist murder of a U.S. national in another country: 18 U.S.C., Section 2332.

- Treason: 18 U.S.C., Section 2381.
- Use of a weapon of mass destruction resulting in death: 18 U.S.C., Section 2332(a).
- Use of chemical weapons resulting in death: 18 U.S.C., Section 2332(c).
- Willful wrecking of a train resulting in death: 18 U.S.C., Section 1992.

Source: Capital Defense Network. Federal Capital Offenses by Topic. [Online]. February 1, 2006. Available at http://www.capdefnet.org/fdprc/contents/fed_cap_off/fed_cap_right_frame.htm.

PUBLIC SUPPORT FOR CAPITAL PUNISHMENT

According to public opinion polls, most people in the United States support the death penalty. In fact, the percentage of Americans who report that they support capital punishment increased consistently since the 1960s, but leveled off in the 1990s. A poll in 2006 showed that 67% said they favored capital punishment for those convicted of murder.

Results from the Harris poll question, "Do you believe in capital punishment, that is, the death penalty, or are you opposed to it?" suggest that, although a majority of Americans still say they support the death penalty, the percentage who say they do declined somewhat recently.

Gallup polls show that when asked, "What do you think should be the penalty for murder—the death penalty, or life imprisonment with absolutely no possibility of parole?" less than half of Americans favor the death penalty. As you can see in Figure 10-4, support for capital punishment is far from universal. A study by Sandys and McGarrell (1995) found that only about 9% of respondents in their survey of Indiana residents could be categorized as universally supportive of the death penalty. Their findings suggest that many Americans may simply accept capital punishment without actually supporting it. Consistent with this idea are findings that support for the use of the death penalty becomes more ambiguous when citizens are provided with alternatives; the percentage of Americans who say they support the death penalty for convicted murderers declines when the option of life imprisonment without parole (LWOP) is given as a sentencing option. When restitution to the victim's family is added in, support for capital punishment falls even farther below 50%.

What has been well established is that support for capital punishment is highest for Caucasians, males, older citizens, the wealthy, Republicans, people who consider themselves to be "conservatives," people living in the South and the West, Protestants (among religious denominations), and people who do not attend religious services regularly. In terms of religion, some research shows that fundamentalists (who believe strongly in free will and personal responsibility) and who take the Bible literally are more likely to support the death penalty, while evangelicals (who believe in compassion for others) are less likely to support it (Young, 2002).

FIGURE 10-4   Public Support for Capital Punishment

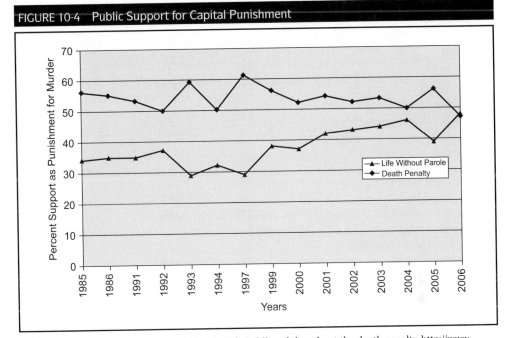

Source: Death Penalty Information Center (2007). Public opinion about the death penalty. http://www.deathpenaltyinfo.org/article.php?did=209&scid=23.

The death penalty is also more supported by people who fear crime, who think courts treat people leniently, and who do not know actual sentences imposed by courts. Support for capital punishment is also directly related to racial animosity (Cochran and Chamlin, 2006). Support is highest among people who (wrongly) believe the death penalty meets its goals and is cheaper than alternatives such as life imprisonment (Haney, 2005). Table 10-4 shows some diversity in death penalty support by different groups of Americans.

Finally, support for capital punishment is inversely related to level of education, so that the most educated people are the least supportive of the punishment. This might explain the fact that support for capital punishment is found to decrease with knowledge about realities of the death penalty—especially problems with it, such as racial bias and innocence.

From all this information, a fair characterization of public opinion of the death penalty in the United States is that it is wide but not deep (Sandys and McGarrell, 1995). Death penalty scholar Franklin Zimring (2003) claims Americans are quite ambivalent about the death penalty because we claim to support it but we are also deeply troubled by its very real problems. Robert Lifton and Greg Mitchell (2000, p. 12) write that "ambiguity around this issue abounds. Nearly everyone feels that there is *something* wrong about capital punishment, perhaps it violates our fundamental commitment to life without claiming to uphold it."

Finally, it is possible that Americans, who are largely ignorant of the realities of capital punishment practice, may not be highly in favor of executions but instead may only support the death penalty in the abstract. The Marshall hypothesis, discussed in

TABLE 10-4   Public Support for Capital Punishment by Demographics

	In favor	Not in favor	Don't know/refused
Sex			
Male	70%	24%	6%
Female	59%	34%	7%
Race			
White	69%	26%	5%
Black	35%	56%	9%
Age			
18–29 years	60%	36%	4%
30–49 years	64%	29%	7%
50–64 years	69%	25%	6%
65+ years	61%	31%	8%
Education			
College post graduate	54%	41%	5%
College graduate	62%	34%	4%
Some college	69%	24%	7%
High school graduate or less	66%	27%	7%
Income			
$75,000+	64%	29%	7%
$50,000–74,999	68%	26%	6%
$30,000–49,999	68%	29%	3%
$20,000–29,999	67%	26%	7%
Under $20,000	57%	33%	10%
Community			
Urban area	59%	33%	8%
Suburban area	66%	29%	5%
Rural area	67%	25%	8%
Region			
East	59%	35%	6%
Midwest	64%	30%	6%
South	68%	25%	7%
West	65%	29%	6%
Politics			
Republican	77%	18%	5%
Democrat	56%	37%	7%
Independent	63%	31%	6%

Source: Sourcebook of Criminal Justice Statistics (2006). Table 2.52. Attitudes Toward the Death Penalty for Persons Convicted of Murder, by Demographic Characteristics, United States, 2005. [Online]. Available at http://www.albany.edu/sourcebook/pdf/t2522005.pdf.

Box 10-5 suggests that if Americans knew more about how capital punishment was actually administered in the United States, they would be less supportive of it.

Table 10-5 shows reasons that Americans gave in 2006 for favoring the death penalty. More than half said they support the death penalty because of retribution

BOX 10-5

THE MARSHALL HYPOTHESIS

As noted earlier, the U.S. Supreme Court temporarily suspended capital punishment by invalidating arbitrary death penalty statutes in *Furman v. Georgia*, 408 U.S. 238 (1972). In his opinion as part of the five justice plurality, Justice Thurgood Marshall examined the issue of what is cruel and unusual punishment and related it to the evolving standards of decency in a maturing society. He suggested that a punishment would be cruel and unusual if it met any of four conditions: (1) It causes too much physical pain or is excessive; (2) it has not been practiced prior; (3) it serves no valid purpose or it is unnecessary; and (4) popular sentiment is against it or it is immoral.

In Marshall's *Furman* opinion—which to this day remains one of the most significant anti–death penalty arguments— he dismissed all justifications for capital punishment by suggesting that the death penalty as practiced does not actually serve retribution, deterrence, or incapacitation, and that it is more expensive than life imprisonment.

The most significant part of the Marshall opinion is what became known as the Marshall hypothesis. Marshall wrote that "the question with which we must deal is not whether a substantial proportion of American citizens would today, if polled, opine that capital punishment is barbarously cruel, but whether they would find it so in the light of all information presently available." Marshall put forth what he viewed as the reality of capital punishment and suggested that people would not support it if they knew this reality.

Marshall wrote: "I believe the following facts would serve to convince even the most hesitant of citizens to condemn death as a sanction: Capital punishment is imposed discriminatorily against certain identifiable classes of people; there is evidence that innocent people have been executed before their innocence can be proved; and the death penalty wreaks havoc with our entire criminal justice system." According to Marshall, if Americans knew of these realities, they would reject capital punishment. However, although he believed that support for capital punishment would vary inversely with knowledge about the punishment and that greater attainment of knowledge about the realities of capital punishment would lead to lessened support, Marshall also stated that support for capital punishment would not be reduced among those who favor the punishment due to retributive reasons.

Perhaps the strongest evidence that the Marshall hypothesis is correct comes from anecdotal evidence. Justice Harry Blackmun wrote in his dissent to deny *certiorari* in *Callins v. James* (1994):

From this day forward, I no longer shall tinker with the machinery of death. For more than 20 years, I have endeavored—indeed, I have struggled—along with a majority of this Court, to develop procedural and substantive rules that would lend more than the mere appearance of fairness to the death penalty endeavor. Rather than continue to coddle the Court's delusion that the desired level of fairness has been achieved and the need for regulation eviscerated, I feel morally and intellectually obligated simply to concede that the death penalty experiment has failed. It is virtually self-evident to me now that no combination of procedural rules or substantive regulations ever can save the death penalty from its inherent

(continued)

BOX 10-5 *(Continued)*

constitutional deficiencies. The basic question—does the system accurately and consistently determine which defendants "deserve" to die?—cannot be answered in the affirmative. It is not simply that this Court has allowed vague aggravating circumstances to be employed . . . relevant mitigating evidence to be disregarded . . . and vital judicial review to be blocked . . . . The problem is that the inevitability of factual, legal, and moral error gives us a system that we know must wrongly kill some defendants, a system that fails to deliver the fair, consistent, and reliable sentences of death required by the Constitution.

Blackmun had voted to uphold capital punishment in *Furman and Gregg* and was considered a capital punishment supporter on the Court. His first-hand experience with the realities of capital punishment apparently led him to change his mind.

Some tests of the Marshall hypothesis and death penalty opinion find little support for Marshall's main idea and/or have offered different conclusions. For example, some studies find that gaining increased information about the death penalty can polarize opinions, so that those who support it before, support it more afterward and those who oppose it before, oppose it more afterward (Ellsworth and Ross, 1983; Lord, Ross, and Lepper, 1979). Other studies suggest that when people become emotional about capital punishment—for example, because of reading or learning about heinous murders—they may be more likely to indicate support for capital punishment in such cases even though they may not generally support the death penalty (Durham, Elrod, and Kinkade, 1996).

In spite of such findings, most studies of the Marshall hypothesis offer at least qualified support—regardless of the nature of the testing—but significant caveats exist. Studies testing the Marshall hypothesis tend to ask subjects about their opinions on the death penalty before and after they read scripts or short essays containing facts about the administration of capital punishment in the United States (Sarat and Vidmar, 1976; Vidmar and Dittenhoffer, 1981). Other studies were based on first-day and last-day surveys of students who were taking death penalty classes (Bohm, 1989, 1990; Bohm, Clark, and Aveni, 1990, 1991; Bohm and Vogel, 1994, 2002; Bohm, Vogel, and Maisto, 1993).

Death penalty expert Robert Bohm (2003, p. 265) conducted many of the latter types of studies. He summarizes the findings of his tests by saying

In sum, results of this research provided at least qualified support for all three of Marshall's hypotheses. Subjects generally lacked knowledge about the death penalty and its administration prior to exposure to the experimental stimulus but were more informed following it. To the degree that retribution provided the basis for support of the death penalty, knowledge had little effect on opinions. The hypothesis that an informed public would generally oppose the death penalty was supported in one test but not in others.

Even though more students reported being against capital punishment after taking death penalty classes than before, a follow-up with the students 2, 3, and 10 years later found that their support for capital punishment had rebounded to about its original levels. Bohm (2003, p. 266) suggests that the changed opinions "do not appear to be a function of a loss of knowledge, the irrelevancy of the death penalty class, or the influence of the instructor." It may be because "death penalty opinions are based primarily on emotion rather than on cognition and that, in the long run, cognitive influences on death penalty opinions give way to emotional factors."

A recent test of the Marshall hypothesis found that death penalty supporters were somewhat less informed than death penalty opponents, that increased knowledge of realities of capital punishment was associated with increased opposition to the punishment (Chamlin and Cochran, 2006). However, those who based their support on retribution were no less likely to change their minds than those who based their support on other justifications. The study found that half of the students in the class either stopped supporting the punishment, supported it less, or opposed it more. Students were also more likely to support life imprisonment without the possibility of parole at the end of the course than before it.

While it is not clear what an effective strategy for spreading information about the realities of American capital punishment is, I speculate that if Americans knew and truly understood the problems with the death penalty, they would be far less likely to support the death penalty than they currently do.

Haney (2005, p. 68) suggests that

Public support for capital punishment . . . has depended on a *lack* of understanding about . . . how the death penalty actually operates in our society. The more people know about what really happens in the overall administration of capital punishment, the less inclined they are to support it. Thus, preserving our system of death sentencing depends in some ways on preserving the public's lack of accurate knowledge about how it actually functions.

Conversely, reforming (or abolishing) capital punishment will likely require informing people about the realities of capital punishment in the United States.

Some may wonder whether the American way of execution—hiding executions from the public and conducting them at night—is intended to keep the death penalty invisible. If so, why? Two possible explanations are that Americans don't support capital punishment strongly enough to actually see it, and the invisibility of America's death penalty practice maintains our ignorance (Dow, 2002). I don't know if either or both of these explanations are true, but each is logical enough given what we know about capital punishment.

(an eye for an eye; they took a life; punishment fits the crime; fair punishment; biblical reasons; to serve justice). Another small portion supported it for its deterrent value or for incapacitation (they will repeat their crime; keeps them from repeating it; don't believe they can be rehabilitated; life sentences don't always mean life sentences). Other Harris polls show that less than half of Americans answer affirmatively to the question, "Do you feel that executing people who commit murder deters others from committing murder, or do you think such executions don't have much effect?"

Let me now turn to the issue of whether these beliefs of Americans are justified on the basis of either logic or empirical evidence. If you support the death penalty, I think you will be surprised by much of what you will read.

TABLE 10-5 Reasons for Supporting Capital Punishment (2006)	
Retribution (61%)	
An eye for an eye/they took a life/fits the crime	37%
They deserve it	13%
Biblical reasons	5%
Serve justice	4%
Would help/benefit families of victims	2%
Deterrence (11%)	
Deterrent for potential crimes/set an example	11%
Incapacitation (10%)	
They will repeat their crime/keep them from repeating it	7%
Don't believe they can be rehabilitated	2%
Life sentences don't always mean life in prison	1%
Other (28%)	
Save taxpayers money/cost associated with prison	11%
Depends on the type of crime they commit	4%
Fair punishment	3%
If there's no doubt the person committed the crime	3%
Support/believe in the death penalty	2%
Relieves prison overcrowding	1%
Other	4%
No opinion	2%

Source: Sourcebook of Criminal Justice Statistics (2006). Table 2.56. Reported Reasons for Favoring the Death Penalty for Persons Convicted of Murder, United States, 1991, 2000, 2001, and 2003. [Online]. Available at http://www.albany.edu/sourcebook/pdf/t255.pdf.

Note: Percentages do not add up to 100% because respondents could offer more than one answer.

JUSTIFICATIONS FOR CAPITAL PUNISHMENT: LOGICAL OR NOT?

Why do we have a death penalty? There seem to be only four possible justifications: vengeance, retribution, incapacitation, and deterrence. Vengeance and retribution are the most commonly cited reasons for support of the death penalty; incapacitation is the second most often stated justification for supporting the death penalty. Americans today rarely mention deterrence as a reason for supporting capital punishment, and most criminologists and criminal justice scholars no longer think capital punishment is a deterrent to murder.

Vengeance

Costanzo (1997), in his book by the same name, suggests that the death penalty is *Just Revenge*. **Vengeance** is a "vengeful, aggressive act . . . performed in cold blood, after the damage has been done, and . . . is not a defense against immediate danger . . . which is of great intensity, often crude, vicious, and insatiable" (Marongiu and Newman, 1987, p. 2; citing Erich Fromm). You can see how the death penalty fits this definition of vengeance in that the penalty is administered years after the criminal offense has been done. The death penalty also is not administered in the face of any immediate danger: Once an offender is properly confined in custody, he or she no longer poses a threat to society.

This may be one limitation to vengeance as a justification for punishment. As stated by the criminologist Frederic Faust (1995), "No other species will expend the energy to kill the enemy after it is clear that it has already won." Yet once a person has been arrested and convicted for murder and is thus no longer capable of killing another free member of society, we may still kill the person.

What needs to be understood about vengeance is that it is a human emotion. Nothing is wrong with feeling the desire to get even with someone who hurts you; indeed, this is probably natural. The problem arises when we try to justify a state response to crime based only on a human emotion. Since crimes are acts against the state, including murder, the emotional state of the victim and his or her family is not relevant for deciding the proper punishment. The punishment in a rational system of punishment must be based on reason rather than emotion.

Retribution

One major reason we administer capital punishment in the United States is to do to offenders what they have done to someone else, to get even with offenders or, stated differently, to give offenders their *just desserts*. This is related to vengeance, except that retribution is a rational desire to have offenders pay something back to society to rebalance the scales of justice.

A benefit of state-sanctioned **retribution** is that it limits the emotional aspects of vengeance, which often prompt retaliation on the part of victims and ultimately lead to escalation rather than resolution of the situation. For example, when a murder has been committed, only the state has the legal authority to seek justice for the harm inflicted. In the absence of this formal system of justice, victims would be left to seek out revenge for their loved ones and would likely end up killing not only the offender, in the name of justice, but whoever happened to be with the offender when the vengeance was carried out. This would ultimately lead to the killing of even more people in the name of justice for the new victims, with little hope of a successful ending to the killing. Mahatma Gandhi said that the problem with "an eye for an eye" is that it leads the whole world blind.

State-sanctioned retribution, ideally, does provide the advantage of preventing retaliation and escalation that is produced by vengeance. Without punishment of the guilty, "there [would] exist the typical progression or spiraling process by which each offense [would be] countered by another offense more severe until the complete destruction of one of the parties [would be] achieved. It is the establishment of a social order that attempts to break this cycle of destruction" (Marongiu and Newman, 1987, p. 4). There is certainly evidence of such escalation in history, which may justify state-sanctioned and state-administered vengeance. In ancient tribes, before the establishment of the Magna Carta in A.D. 1215 and the philosophy on which it was based (*lex talionis,* or an "eye for an eye"), retaliation threatened the social order as a result of "blood feuds." As stated by Jeffery (1990, p. 61), "tribal law was based on revenge and the blood feud. The offended group carried out revenge against the offending group until some form of restitution was made by the offending group." If one individual offended against another, retaliation ensued, which would lead to escalation, clearly a destructive force. The only solution to this problem, according to Marongiu and Newman (1987, p. 5) is the development of an acceptable formal means of social control, such as a criminal justice network.

By limiting retaliation to an "eye for an eye," no more than one "eye" could be paid to right a wrong. The process of escalation should effectively be wiped out by punishing a guilty party for his or her acts. As explained by Jeffery (1990, p. 62):

> Legal systems emerged . . . to control the blood feud and private vengeance. The law said, "You cannot kill another person in retaliation for an injury to you or your tribe." However, the political state proceeded to establish criminal law based on the basis of public vengeance; that is, the state arrested, convicted, and killed the offender through legal procedures. Although the victim or his family is not allowed to kill the offender, the state is. Public vengeance replaced private vengeance.

This is an important point to remember when considering the validity of any punishment. But why do we have to kill people rather than subject them to some other form of punishment? "An eye for an eye" does not mandate plucking an eye from one who plucks an eye from you; it means that this is the most you can possibly do to the offender (Johnson, 2000). Similarly, when one person kills another, we do not have to kill the offender, we just cannot do more to the offender (e.g., torture and kill the offender).

That is, retribution does not mandate an eye for an eye (Erez, 1981). The state could easily administer some other punishment to achieve retribution. After all, the state does not rape rapists, burn the property of arsonists, or assault people who assault others (Amsterdam, 1982).

One reason people support the death penalty as a form of retribution is the perception that it is supported by the Bible. In fact, among the earliest justifications for the death penalty in Colonial America were religious passages, quoted in early criminal statutes (Bohm, 1999, p. 1). Costanzo (1997, p. 11) writes:

> Early justifications for killing wrongdoers rested on religious authority. Religious leaders insisted that executions were means of carrying out the will of God. According to the laws of Moses, the death penalty was a way to appease God and avert famines, plagues, and other misfortunes that might result from "God's fierce anger" against any community that failed to punish sinners.

Box 10-6 provides a summary of the death penalty and the Bible by a criminal justice scholar. His analysis shows less support for capital punishment than one might think.

BOX 10-6

CAPITAL PUNISHMENT IN THE BIBLE

Johnson (2000) focuses on instances where the Bible either mandates, explicitly acknowledges, or implies a state-sponsored execution. He writes: "People often cite specific verses of the Bible to justify a particular position on capital punishment, but these passages are frequently acontextual, failing to consider the significance of the passages containing these verses or the Bible as an entire document" (p. 15). Because the Bible is more ambiguous on the death penalty than one might believe, both supporters and opponents can find evidence supporting their arguments in the Bible.

Consider that "[t]he majority of biblical statements that support capital punishment are found in the Old Testament, more specifically the first five books of the Old Testament . . . the Pentateuch . . . the books of Genesis, Exodus, Leviticus, Numbers, and Deuteronomy." These are the oldest books of the Bible and they "clearly mandate the use of the death penalty for premeditated homicide" (p. 17). They also allow for capital punishment for the crimes of blasphemy and sacrifice to false gods, dishonoring parents, disrespecting priests or elders, adultery, incest, and homosexuality!

The New Testament, a more recent testimony to God, "provides no overt statement in which Jesus or New Testament authors endorse the use of death as a punishment for crimes" and "also fails to reveal any overt rejection of capital punishment," although death was clearly used as a state-sanctioned punishment during this time (p. 23). Yet the New Testament "also contains many passages that seem to refute the death penalty" (p. 26). For example, the Bible at times argues against taking revenge and seems to advocate forgiveness. Jesus even says:

> You may have heard that it was said, "An eye for an eye and a tooth for a tooth." But I tell you to resist an evil person . . . whoever slaps you on your right cheek, turn the

other also. . . . You have heard that it was said, "You shall love your neighbor and hate your enemy." But I say to you, love your enemies, bless those who curse you, do good to those who hate you, and pray for those who spitefully use you or persecute you. (Matthew 5: 38–45).

Perhaps the clearest example of ambiguity about the death penalty in the Bible comes in the form of the outcomes of people who committed murder in the Bible. Johnson (2000, p. 29) identifies 22 murderers in the Bible, only 4 of whom (18%) are executed by the state (see Table 10-6). As explained by Johnson: "It seems difficult to suggest that the Bible sincerely endorses state sponsored capital punishment, when so few murderers in the Scriptures receive the death penalty" (p. 31).

Considering the lack of a clear mandate for executions in the Bible, Bohm (1999, p. 182) poses an interesting question: How can people, "particularly people whose lives are governed by the Bible . . . endorse revenge, support or oppose capital punishment, and use the Bible as a basis of their support or opposition, when they know the Bible is ambiguous on the subject"?

Even though the Bible may not provide the answer, consider that the "leaders of most organized religions in the United States no longer support the death penalty and actually openly favor its abolition" (Bohm, 1999, p. 177). This includes Pope John Paul II and the National Conference of Catholic Bishops, who suggested that death by execution is "uncivilized," "inhumane," "barbaric," and "assaultive of human life" (Gow, 1986, p. 80).

(continued)

BOX 10-6 (*Continued*)

TABLE 10-6 Murderers From the Bible and Their Punishments		
Name	*Verse of Crime*	*Outcome*
Cain	Genesis 4:8	Marked by God
Ehud	Judges 3:21	Liberates Israel from Moabites
Gideon	Judges 8:22	Nothing
Abimelech	Judges 9:5	Killed in military defeat
Rechab & Baanah	Samuel 4:6	Executed by King David
David	Samuel 11:15	Cursed by God to always have strife
Absalom	Samuel 13:29	Killed by Joab
Joab	Samuel 3:27	Executed by King Solomon
Baasha	Kings 15:28	Cursed by God
Zimri	Kings 16:10	Commits suicide
Jezebel	Kings 21:8–10	Killed by her eunuchs
Hazael	Kings 8:12–15	Becomes King of Aram
Jehu	Kings 9:24	Nothing
Athaliah	Kings 11:2	Executed by Jehoiada, High Priest
Jozachar & Jehozabad	Kings 12:20–21	No further mention
Shallum	Kings 15:10	Killed by Menahem
Menahem	Kings 15:14	Serves as King of Israel
Pekah	Kings 15:25	Killed by Hoshea
Hoshea	Kings 15:30	Imprisoned by King of Assyria for later crime
Amon's servants	Kings 21:23	Executed by leaders of Judah
Jehoram	Chronicles 21:4	Cursed by God
Ishmael	Jeremiah 41:2	Escapes to Ammonites
Herodias	Matthew 14:8–11	No further mention

Source: Johnson, S. (2000). The Bible and the death penalty: Implications for criminal justice education. *Journal of Criminal Justice Education* Vol. 11(1): 15–33.

Since human life is precious, shouldn't we mourn the loss of any human life, including that of the offender? Keep in mind that when a person is executed, his or her family is victimized by the loss of their own loved one. In many ways, the loss of the convicted killer is just as bad as the loss of the innocent victim. Consider these points by Vandiver (1998, p. 486):

- The families of condemned prisoners know for years that the state intends to kill their relatives and the method that will be used. They experience a prolonged period of anticipatory grieving, complicated by the hope that some court or governor will grant relief.

- Their relatives' deaths will come about as the result of actions by dozens of respected and powerful persons. Their deaths are caused not by a breakdown in social order, but by a highly orchestrated and cooperative effort of authority.
- Their relatives are publicly disgraced and shamed; they have been formally cast out by society and judged to be unworthy to live.
- The deaths of their relatives are not mourned and regretted as other violent deaths are; rather, the death is condoned, supported, and desired by many people and actively celebrated by some.

Whatever the case, all acts of retribution and vengeance are motivated by concerns for equality, justice, and reciprocity, as well as the safety of society (Marongiu and Newman, 1987). This means that people who support capital punishment seek to achieve legitimate and positive goals for society. Even the U.S. Supreme Court, in the case of *Gregg v. Georgia* (1976), recognized that retribution is a legitimate purpose of administering capital punishment; the Court even suggested that executing the guilty serves the purpose of satisfying the feelings and needs of the public for revenge (Bedau, 1987). A significant drawback to their reasoning is that family members who survive murder victims are not well served by the execution of their loved ones' killers. Vandiver (1998) shows that there are many reasons that family members of murder victims do not want the killers executed, including the following.

- They do not support capital punishment.
- An execution would diminish the memory of their relative.
- They do not want to be forced to have prolonged contact with criminal justice agencies.
- They do not want the condemned killer to have any added public attention for his or her wrongdoing.
- They prefer the finality of a sentence of life imprisonment without the possibility of parole and the obscurity of prisoners over the continued uncertainty and publicity of the death penalty.
- They want the offender to reflect on his or her wrongdoing for life and to feel remorse.
- They may hope to develop, from the offender, a sense of understanding of why he or she committed the act.

There are many limits to retribution as a justification for punishment. For example, Jeffery (1990, p. 64) writes, "Retribution perpetuates the human urge for revenge, and it brutalizes societies and individuals by its use. . . . Although retribution is justified as a moral position, it is an immoral, vulgar, and self-defeating response to human behavior." Such statements are representative of those who feel that getting even to make us feel better is, simply stated, evil.

Others point to the hypocritical assertion that we can teach people that killing people is wrong by killing people who kill people: "[Some may] reap revenge in order to cancel out an offense, yet those same persons are perpetrating the very same behavior that they wish to avenge" (Marongiu and Newman, 1987, p. 3). As asked on the bumper stickers you might have seen on cars, "Why do we kill people who kill people to show them that killing people is wrong?" The idea that the death penalty is hypocritical was also put forward by the British criminologist Jeremy Bentham, who claimed that the state could no more justly take the life of a person than could an individual person. In essence, the crime and the punishment become indistinguishable.

Obviously, not everyone feels that the death penalty is evil or hypocritical, given Americans' support of capital punishment. Virtually every politician claims to support the death penalty, at least publicly. To be against the death penalty today is virtually to ensure that you will not get elected. Many philosophers have claimed that retribution is a valid justification for punishment by positing that offenders who harm others are deserving of punishment. By killing, killers give up their right to life.

Other supporters of the death penalty claim that it is the only form of justice to which individual victims are entitled. For example, Ernest Van den Haag states that punishment is a "collective reaction aimed at the satisfaction of the desire for retaliation by the injured party" (cited in Marongiu and Newman, 1987, p. 3). Perhaps this is so, but the question remains: Could we more effectively and humanely achieve retribution through some alternative method of punishment?

Deterrence

Another supposed reason for administering capital punishment is to achieve **deterrence**—to stop would-be murderers from committing murder. I should point out from the outset that most people probably no longer really believe that the death penalty is a deterrent to murder. It is currently the least mentioned reason for supporting the death penalty.

Recall from Chapter 8 that there are two types of deterrence—**special or specific deterrence** aimed at preventing one offender from committing future crimes, and **general deterrence** aimed at preventing members of society from engaging in criminality by making examples of criminals who already have. Some assert that the death penalty is at the very least a special deterrent, but this is an incorrect statement based on a misunderstanding of the meaning of special deterrence. Special deterrence implies that convicted offenders will fear punishment for future offenses after their punishment and will thus refrain from committing crimes in the future. Since an execution results in the death of an offender, it is not a special deterrent because it does not create fear in the offender. Instead, it kills the offender, meaning he or she is incapacitated.

So, is the death penalty a general deterrent? That is, when a person is executed, does it create a sense of fear in other Americans so that they will refrain from committing murder? If so, the death penalty would save lives (Costanzo, 1997, p. 12). Logically, when Americans learn of executions, they should get the clear message: "SEE WHAT CAN HAPPEN TO YOU IF YOU GET CAUGHT COMMITTING SUCH AN OFFENSE!" Recall that much of what we do to punish criminals is based on logic. It appeals to our common sense that the death penalty should deter would-be murderers. The problem with common sense is that it is often more "common" than "sense." Common sense would suggest, for example, that the sun revolves around the earth, but we know that the opposite is true (Costanzo, 1997, p. 95).

A significant problem comes from the assumption about murderers on which the death penalty is based. As explained by Costanzo (1997, p. 104), when we elect to impose a death sentence on murderers, we assume "that potential killers engage in a dispassionate weighing of the costs and benefits of killing." In other words, we assume that offenders choose to commit murder because the pleasure outweighs the potential pains associated with committing murder; thus, if we can somehow make the potential pains outweigh any benefits gained from committing murder, would-be murderers would not choose to commit murder. Costanzo claims: "This assumption is simply wrong." Most people who kill another do not carefully weigh the pleasures and pains associated with committing a murder; most, instead, act in the heat of the moment, without much thought about getting caught, convicted, and punished for their acts. In 2004, 66% of murders were firearm related. How long does it take to grab a gun and pull the trigger? Is it likely that these murderers even think of the death penalty in the short time it takes to pull the trigger?

Van den Haag (1982, p. 326) sums up the logic of deterrence by suggesting that since "our penal system rests on the proposition that more severe penalties are more deterrent than less severe penalties," logic would dictate that "the most severe penalty—the death penalty—would have the greatest deterrent effect." Bohm (1999, p. 84) responds by saying that this assertion" is based on a debatable assumption and a testable proposition with no scientific evidence to support it." Van den Haag's assumption that the death penalty is more severe than life imprisonment is debatable and has been contested for hundreds of years. Perhaps it is far worse to have to live in prison for the rest of your life than to be executed after spending only 10 years on death row. However you feel about this issue personally, the fact remains that "[t]here is no evidence that capital punishment deters more than an alternative noncapital punishment, such as life imprisonment without opportunity for parole. Instead, statistics indicate that capital punishment makes no discernible difference on homicide or murder rates" (Bohm, 1999, p. 85).

It does not matter if one compares states with and without the death penalty, nations with and without the death penalty, or jurisdictions before and after executions—all methods show no valid empirical evidence that the death penalty deters murderers. In fact, more studies show a **brutalization effect** of the death penalty—that is, that capital punishment increases the rate of murder rather than decreasing it (Bailey, 1998; Cochran, Chamlin, and Seth, 1994; Robinson, 2008).

Some recent studies found evidence consistent with deterrence of murder by capital punishment (e.g., Brumm and Cloninger, 1996; Cloninger and Marchesini, 2001, 2005; Dezhbakhsh, Rubin, and Shepherd, 2003; Dezhbakhsh and Shepherd, 2003; Mocan and Gittings, 2003; Shepherd, 2004; Zimmerman, 2004); yet, when replicated, the results have not been supported (Berk, 2004; Donohue and Wolfers, 2005; Fagan, 2005; Goertzel, 2004). In fact, on at least one occasion the opposite finding was the result: Each execution was associated with more murders rather than less (Robinson, 2008).

The brutalization hypothesis suggests that the death penalty shows people that killing is an acceptable means to settle disputes; thus, when an execution is held, murders actually increase for a short period of time. Although effects on homicide tend to be relatively small, the point is that homicides seem to increase in the short term after an execution, rather than decreasing. Even if these findings turn out to be false, there still is absolutely no valid, scientific evidence showing a deterrent effect on homicides. It may be that the death penalty has no effect, overall, on murders in the United States (Bohm, 2007).

Bowers et al. (1984, p. 90) write:

> The evidence that capital punishment has no deterrent advantage over imprisonment is now stronger and more consistent than when the Court last considered this issue. . . . Indeed, a comprehensive review of previous studies and recent analyses of refined statistical data both support the contention that the death penalty has a "brutalizing" rather than a deterrent effect—that executions can be expected to stimulate rather than to inhibit homicides.

Supporters of capital punishment typically draw cautious conclusions about the evidence. For example, Pojman (1998, p. 38) says, "We must conclude that we lack strong statistical evidence that capital punishment deters.... There is no such evidence for nondeterrence either. The statistics available are simply inconclusive." And Van den Haag (1997, p. 449) says: "Statistics have not proved conclusively that the death penalty does or does not deter murderers more than other penalties." After an exhaustive review of the deterrence literature, Bailey and Peterson (1997, p. 155) make a more assertive claim. They write, "We feel quite confident in concluding that in the United States a significant general deterrent effect for capital punishment has not been observed, and in all probability, does not exist."

Why might we expect the death penalty to increase rather than decrease murders? In effect, the would-be murderers see that killing is an acceptable means of righting a wrong against someone who has offended them, so that the lesson of capital punishment may be that lethal vengeance is acceptable.

Perhaps this is one reason that the American Society of Criminologists—the largest association of crime experts in the United States—passed a resolution calling for the abolition of the death penalty in 1989. Further, a survey of 67 current and past presidents of the top three criminology professional organizations—the American Society of Criminology, the Academy of Criminal Justice Sciences, and the Law and Society Association—found the following.

- 84% say the death penalty is not a deterrent to homicide.
- 93% say the threat of the death penalty is not a greater deterrent to murder than long prison terms.
- 87% say abolishing the death penalty in a state would have no significant effects on murder in that state.
- 0% say the death penalty significantly reduces homicide.
- 100% say politicians support the death penalty to appear tough on crime.
- 87% say debates about the death penalty distract law makers from focusing on real solutions to crime problems (Radelet and Akers, 1996).

The American Society of Criminology's National Policy Committee concludes that there is "little evidence that the death penalty has a deterrent effect on violent crimes. A comparison of homicide rates both pre- and post-death-penalty eras have not shown a deterrent effect, either within a single state or between states." Also opposed to the death penalty are medical organizations and the American Bar Association (Costanzo, 1997).

A more recent study of capital punishment experts—discussed in Issue in Depth at the end of this chapter—finds that the vast majority of capital punishment experts do not believe the death penalty is a deterrent to crime. Generally, they are adamant that the research is clear on this point.

The rarity of the application of the death penalty alone, as I have mentioned, suggests that it can never deter offenders. Recent legislative initiatives have increased the number of offenses punishable by death in an effort to increase its application, presumably to send a message to criminals that "crime does not pay." Yet the reality is, and always will be, that most murderers are not even charged with capital offenses and therefore do not receive the death penalty.

Despite all this, supporters of capital punishment rely on what they call the best-bet hypothesis and rely on anecdotal evidence of deterrence. The **best-bet hypothesis** suggests that if we do not know that the death penalty is a deterrent, we should bet that it is. They say it would be better to assume there is a deterrent (when there is not) and use the death penalty than to assume there is not a deterrent (when there is) and not use the death penalty. In the former case, we would only be unnecessarily killing guilty murderers, whereas in the latter case, we would be allowing innocent victims to die. **Anecdotal evidence** of deterrence comes from offenders who claim they did not commit murder (when they could have) because of the fear of the death penalty. If these stories are true, no one can deny that the death penalty may deter some people, perhaps even more than life in prison. But given the weight of the evidence, it is safe to conclude that there is virtually no deterrent value to capital punishment. And it is no wonder, given that we rarely execute anyone.

Incapacitation

Without question, the death penalty achieves the goal of **incapacitation** of the offender. Once an offender has been executed, there is no chance that he or she will commit another crime, unless you believe that people get another go-round on the planet because of reincarnation. Yet because the death penalty is so rare, we only incapacitate about 1% of killers (i.e., those who commit murder and nonnegligent manslaughter).

The question is: Can we achieve incapacitation with a form of punishment other than the death penalty? The answer is yes: Incapacitation can be achieved with life imprisonment without the possibility of parole.

Luckily for taxpayers, the costs associated with life imprisonment without the possibility of parole for one offender are actually less than the costs associated with an execution of the same offender. Administering this alternative punishment would also eliminate the possibility of killing innocent people, as we now know has been done.

The alternative I would likely advocate would be life imprisonment without the possibility of parole, plus restitution (LWOP+R)—that is, where people convicted of aggravated murders would spend the rest of their lives behind bars and be required to work to pay for part of their incarceration costs and repay families of victims of their crimes. Costanzo (1997, p. 163) claims that "detailed surveys of attitudes toward the death penalty show that Americans favor LWOP+R because it reduces the cost of incarceration, provides some form of restitution to victims, and is more likely to teach murderers to accept responsibility for their crimes." Since most jurors are reluctant to impose death sentences (regardless of their general support of capital punishment), because errors are inevitable, and because appeals in death penalty cases are numerous, LWOP+R sentences would be swifter, surer, and more final, and we would never again have to worry about killing an innocent person.

WHAT'S WRONG WITH THE DEATH PENALTY? ALLEGED PROBLEMS WITH THE ADMINISTRATION OF DEATH

There are many reasons that the application of capital punishment is unjust (Nelson and Foster, 2001). Streib, in the Foreword to *Death Watch* (2001), suggests, "We have given capital punishment ample opportunity to prove whether or not it can reduce violent crime. It has made us only more violent and less sensitive to human suffering. We now must put this barbaric practice behind us and confess our shame at having used it for so many centuries before seeing the light."

Some view the death penalty as wrong. For example, the National Coalition to Abolish the Death Penalty (NCADP) asserts that the death penalty is wrong because it is plagued by racial disparities, costs more than life in prison, and is used against innocent people, the mentally retarded, and potentially people who committed their crimes as juveniles (although the U.S. Supreme Court abolished the execution of juveniles in the case *Roper v. Simons* (2005) and of the mentally retarded in the case of *Atkins v. Virginia* (2002). Bedau (1997, p. 101) agrees, saying, "I think it is unnecessary for deterrence or incapacitation . . . [is] arbitrary and discriminatory in the retribution it inflicts . . . and therefore [is] an affront to our civilized sensibilities."

Others view capital punishment as cruel and unusual punishment. For example, Bedau (1997, p. 103) suggests that the application of capital punishment violates due process and equal protection of the law, rights he claims are "not forfeitable and cannot be waived. . . . Individuals cannot do anything that . . . nullifies his or her 'moral worth' or standing as a person."

Regardless of how you feel about capital punishment in theory, it only exists in practice. Therefore, we should assess its practice—the reality of capital punishment in America. When we do this, we do see the following problems.

• *The Death Penalty Is a Political Process More Than a Criminal Justice Process*

Capital punishment is an issue that serves one significant purpose in America's political system: It gives politicians something to talk tough about. Seriously, when was the last time you heard a politician speak out against the death penalty? Taking a tough stand on crime by supporting capital punishment is easy and has no risks.

The last time I recall a serious presidential candidate speak out against the death penalty was Governor Michael Dukakis of Massachusetts in the 1988 presidential debates. When asked the question, "Governor, if [your wife] Kitty Dukakis were raped and murdered, would you favor an irrevocable death penalty for the killer?" he answered: "No, I don't. . . . And I think you know that I've opposed the death penalty all of my life. I don't see any evidence that it's a deterrent, and I think there are better and more effective ways to deal with violent crime. We've done so in my own state." Dukakis lost the election to George Bush (the first).

Then, in the 2000 presidential debates, both George W. Bush (the second) and Al Gore were asked about their support for capital punishment. Bush answered: "I believe it saves lives. . . . I'm proud that violent crime is down in the state of Texas." Gore said: "I think it is a deterrence [sic] . . . I know that's a controversial view but I do think it's a deterrence [sic]." With a follow-up question about whether the death penalty deters murderers, Bush answered: "I do. It's the only reason to be for it. . . . I don't think you should support the death penalty to seek revenge. I don't think that's right." Gore also said: "Yes. If it was not, there would be no reason to support it."

Given there was virtually no difference between Bush and Gore on any issue, it is not surprising that the election was so close. What is sad is that neither Bush nor Gore seemed to know that virtually every expert on capital punishment does not think that the death penalty is a deterrent to crime. That is, the views of Bush and Gore are not consistent with the scientific evidence. Since this is a political issue, it does not seem to matter.

We have to be concerned with the political nature of capital punishment because politics is not supposed to decide issues such as who lives and who dies. Ideally, murders that receive the death penalty and those that do not should be decided based on legal factors such as the presence of **aggravating factors** and **mitigating factors** (state laws require that aggravating factors outweigh mitigating factors for a death penalty sentence to be imposed). Unfortunately, research suggests that death penalty murders and non-death-penalty murders are typically not distinguishable based on legal factors but rather can only be distinguished based on extra-legal factors, or factors outside the law (Robinson, 2008).

For example, whether one heinous murder receives death or not is often determined by factors such as the county where the crime occurred, the state where the crime occurred, the region of the country where the crime occurred, the racial make-up of the jury, the race of the defendant and his or her victim (Bedau, 1997), as well as the quality of the defense attorney. In an ideal system of punishment, such factors would be irrelevant for justice.

Because of the way our courts operate, it is entirely up to the discretion of the prosecution whether a murder case leads to a capital trial or a non-capital trial. Research shows that prosecutors in the southern United States, particularly in Texas, are tougher on crime. For example, the Death Penalty Information Center (DPIC) reports that between 1976 and 2006, 82% of all executions occurred in the South, about two-thirds occurred in five states (Texas, Virginia, Oklahoma, Missouri, and Florida), almost half occurred in just two states (Texas and Virginia), and nearly 40% occurred in Texas alone. In 2006, the state of Texas carried out 45% of all executions.

Should where a crime occurs determine whether murderers live and die? When it plays a role, ultimately we see a **geographic disparity** in the administration of capital punishment. The best justification for this problem is that state laws vary and murderers ought to be smarter than to commit their crimes in states that are tougher on crime.

• *The Death Penalty Is Arbitrarily Applied and Is Discriminatory in Nature*

Because the death penalty is not mandatory, is so rare, is decided by discretion, and because of the problem of inadequate representation for the indigent (see Chapter 7), its application is necessarily **arbitrary**. This means it is not decided by legal factors but is more a matter of random chance. We see the arbitrary nature of capital punishment in the numerous forms of **disparity** based on factors such as gender, class, and race.

Recall from Chapter 1 that for something to be just, it must be fair. Justice requires that all persons will be treated equally in the eyes of the law. Injustice is present when any group is singled out for differential treatment by the law. Using this definition, the application of the death penalty in the United States is clearly unjust (McAdams, 1998).

According to Nakell and Hardy (1987, p. 16), **discrimination** is deliberate, whereas disparities may not be (see Chapter 12 for more). There is no doubt that capital punishment in the United States is applied in a disparate fashion. The question is, Is this disparity intentional? When it comes to deaths intentionally caused by the government, perhaps it shouldn't really matter. Injustice does not require intentional discrimination by police, courts, and correctional personnel. As I have argued throughout this book, it can also arise out of innocent biases created in the criminal law and reinforced by media coverage of crime.

Beginning with gender, women make up more than 10% of all murder arrests in any given year but only about 2% of all death sentences imposed, less than 2% of people on death row, and only about 1% of all executions (Robinson, 2008). The death penalty is highly unlikely to be used against women for no other reason than they are not men.

As for social class, states almost never execute wealthy killers, in part because their forms of killing typically are either not illegal or are not viewed as serious crime (see Chapter 4), but also because prosecutors are less likely to seek death and achieve death sentences when clients have private attorneys and numerous resources at their disposal to win lesser sentences from juries. In fact, approximately 95% of death row inmates were represented by public defenders (Bedau, 1997). While every American ideally has the right to a competent defense attorney, in fact not every American can really afford a high-quality defense. Recall from Chapter 7 the distinctions between private and publicly appointed attorneys. Costanzo (1997, p. 75) claims, "The sad, shameful fact is that money makes the difference between life and death for many defendants." This is true because publicly appointed attorneys are often inexperienced at capital cases and have limits on how much they can spend to prepare their defense.

As for race, we see clear disparities in both the federal and state capital punishment systems. Of those inmates awaiting executions in the federal system at the end of 2006, 53% were African Americans. According to the study, "The Federal Death Penalty System: A Statistical Survey, 1988–2000," 50% of all defendants approved for death penalty prosecution were African Americans and 75% were minorities. According to the study, "Racial Disparities in Federal Death Penalty Prosecutions, 1988–1994," "Racial minorities are being prosecuted under federal death penalty law far beyond their proportion in the general population or the population of criminal offenders." A more recent study of the federal death penalty system from 1995 to 2000 found no evidence of racial bias in the stage where cases are recommended for death penalty prosecution. The study, conducted by the RAND Corporation, illustrated that the death penalty was more sought after when defendants killed white victims than when defendants killed black victims. Yet the factor that explained the disparity was the characteristics of the crime (e.g., the heinousness of the murder, such as when a person was brutally murdered and when there was more than one victim). The authors of the study assert that the findings should not be generalized to earlier or later time periods, and they admit that bias could still be present at other points in the criminal justice process at the federal level.

Within the military death penalty system, 66% of inmates awaiting executions are African American (six out of nine inmates). The last time a person was executed by the U.S. military was 1961.

The picture is somewhat different at the state level. Caucasians make up the largest share of death row inmates in the United States (45.5%), African Americans make up 41.7%, Hispanics make up 10.4%, and members of other races make up only 2.3% of death row inmates (NAACP-LDF, 2006).

As for executions, the majority (58%) of those executed from 1976 through March 2006 were Caucasian (Death Penalty Information Center, 2006). Yet African Americans are overrepresented among those executed (34%, followed by 6% Hispanics, and

2.3% other). If one looked only at these numbers, one might conclude that capital punishment is biased against Caucasians. Although they are underrepresented among death row populations and executions relative to their share of the U.S. population, they are overrepresented based on their share of arrests and convictions for murder. The opposite is true with regard to African Americans. At first glance, the death penalty appears least likely to be used against them. Although they are overrepresented among death row populations and executions relative to their share of the U.S. population, they are underrepresented based on their share of arrests and convictions for murder.

There are at least two possible explanations for this. First, it is possible that the ways in which Caucasians and African Americans commit murder are different. Perhaps Caucasians are more likely than African Americans to commit murders that are aggravated in nature and thus eligible for the death penalty (Scheidegger, 2003). Another possibility, related to the first, is that what matters is *who* is killed.

Evidence suggests that about 90% of murders are intraracial (committed by a person of one race against a person of the same race). Since whites tend to kill whites and blacks tend to kill blacks, one possible explanation as to why whites are more often sentenced to death and executed than blacks is the race of the victims killed.

According to the data, between 1976 and March 2006, 80% of all people executed in the United States killed white victims. Only 14% of people executed during these years killed blacks, 4% killed Hispanics, and 1.9% killed someone from another race (Death Penalty Information Center, 2006).

More telling is an examination of interracial murders (murders between members of different races) since 1976. After excluding cases involving multiple victims of several different races, the remaining 221 cases (5%) involved a white defendant and black victim in only 12 cases, versus 209 (95%) cases of black defendants and white victims. Looking even farther back, a study of 15,978 executions since 1739 found only 30 cases in which a Caucasian was put to death for a crime against an African American (Radelet, 1989).

Perhaps the most comprehensive study of race and capital punishment at the state level is "Race and the Death Penalty in North Carolina," which assessed how race affected all capital sentences between 1993 and 1997. It found that the odds of receiving a death sentence were 3.5 times greater for killers of Caucasians (Unah and Boger, 2001).

A review of 28 similar studies conducted by 21 sets of researchers with 23 data sets by the U.S. General Accounting Office found "a pattern of evidence indicating racial disparities in the charging, sentencing, and imposition of the death penalty" (Bedau, 1997, p. 271). The study concluded that "in 82 percent of the studies, race of victim was found to influence likelihood of being charged with capital murder or receiving the death penalty . . . race of victim influence was found at all stages of the criminal justice system process" even after controlling for legally relevant variables.

Such disparities are not proof of discrimination. In fact, there are various forms of discrimination (discussed in Chapter 12). Yet we know that the application of the death penalty is plagued by significant disparities, some of which are based on race of the defendant and race of the victim.

Rather than stemming from overt racism, the problem today lies in abuse of discretion. The entire network of criminal justice agencies is "saturated with discretion" that works to the disadvantage of people of color and the poor (Black, 1974, pp. 90–91). When deciding to arrest or not, police discretion is at issue; when deciding to charge or not, to plea bargain or go to trial, or to seek the death penalty or not, prosecutor discretion is at issue; when conviction or acquittal and sentencing are at hand, discretion of the jury and/or judge is at issue; and so on. The accumulated effects of these discretionary decisions results in the discriminatory application of the death penalty in the United States.

The death penalty, because it is applied in a discriminatory fashion, threatens justice. If you look up the word *discrimination* in any dictionary, you will find definitions suggesting that it means "distinguishing" or "differentiating." Human beings, who assign blame and punishment, distinguish and differentiate on the basis of their own perceptions and preferences. This means that all punishments, including the death penalty, will inevitably be applied in a discriminatory fashion. The significant problem with the death penalty is that it is final: Once it is administered, it cannot be "taken back" or undone.

In studies, most racial bias is found to come from prosecutorial discretion, meaning it is up to the whim of the prosecutor as to which heinous murderers deserve to die and which deserve to live. Apparently, in our nation's courts, killers of Caucasians are more deserving of death than killers of minorities. According to the research, part of this problem also stems from problems with capital juries.

• *Death Penalty Juries Are Often Confused, Incompetent, and Are Not Representative of the Population*

As you saw in this chapter, most Americans say they are in favor of capital punishment, generally, and for aggravated murders specifically. When juries are faced with making decisions about whether convicted murderers ought to live the remainder of their natural lives in prison or be executed by the government, these juries are not representative of the general population. First, the groups least likely to be represented on juries are the ones most likely to be processed through the criminal justice network. This is also true for capital juries.

Equally important, jurors who refuse to consider death as a valid option at sentencing are routinely denied service on capital juries. Bohm (2007) and Robinson (2008) cite research indicating that *death-qualified juries*, as they are called, are more conviction prone and more likely to recommend a sentence of death (Dillehay and Sandys, 1996; Ellsworth, 1991; Luginbuhl and Burkhead, 1994; Robinson, 1993). Defendants accused of capital crimes are at a significant disadvantage when the jurors who will determine their fate are more likely to hold crime control values consistent with the goals of the prosecution rather than due process values more in line with the defense. Stated differently, capital juries are more likely to be concerned with justice as an outcome (i.e., giving the alleged offender what he or she deserves) rather than justice as a process (i.e., making sure that the trial is fair).

A continuing study sponsored by the National Science Foundation, known as the *Capital Jury Project*, has shown us a great deal about how capital juries function. Researchers have conducted interviews with 1,115 jurors from 340 capital cases in 14 states. This study shows that juries are a significant cause of arbitrary sentencing. Capital juries often do not understand fundamental legal issues such as the meaning of aggravating and mitigating factors and how to weigh them to decide if a convicted defendant lives or dies (see Bedau, 1997). The study shows capital juries often engage in premature decision making (e.g., they may determine a defendant should be executed during the guilt phase of a trial) and they often do not understand jury instructions and misperceive their sentencing responsibility (e.g., they may mistakenly believe that upon agreement of the presence of an aggravating factor they are required to vote for death and/or that a judge will overrule their sentence if he or she feels the jury made a mistake). Although jury instructions do explain to capital jurors the meaning of aggravating and mitigating factors, juries are typically instructed to "weigh" these factors. Many scholars conclude that this type of setup is confusing to juries, given that judges are "loath to offer any clarification beyond the vague charge of the jury instructions." Therefore, it is likely that jurors will have tremendous difficulty assessing which convicted people deserve death and which do not (Costanzo, 1997, p. 36).

Race of the capital juries matters greatly to trial outcomes. Research shows that African American males are more sympathetic toward defendants and are more likely to sense remorse that justifies lesser sentences, whereas Caucasian males are less sympathetic toward defendants and are more likely to see signs of future dangerousness that warrant death sentences. As noted earlier, race of the victim also matters. When the victim is Caucasian, capital juries are more likely to return death sentences. Finally, we also know that juries make critical mistakes. This leads us to the issue of innocence.

• *The Death Penalty Is Sometimes Used Against the Innocent*

Recall the logic of the due process model of criminal justice, discussed in Chapter 1. The most important values in this model are liberty, individual freedom, and the protection of constitutional rights from unnecessary government intervention. Proponents of the due process model would argue that it is far better to let guilty people go free than to punish even one innocent person. The killing of even one innocent individual, especially when it is state-sanctioned and carried out by state officials, is the ultimate evil. It might also be considered unacceptable to kill people who acted because of biological brain disorders (the mentally ill) or who cannot develop the full mental capacity or intent to be held accountable for their actions (the mentally incompetent).

The U.S. Supreme Court ruled in *Herrera v. Collins* (1993) that a claim of actual innocence is not relevant for decisions about whether new hearings should be granted in federal courts (Bohm, 1999, p. 37). Because only issues of law are decided by appeals courts, issues pertaining to factual guilt or innocence are not relevant for these courts. Only when state courts violate constitutional procedures are federal appeals courts really able to correct wrongful convictions. This leaves the wrongfully convicted with little hope of being set free other than executive clemency, which, for political reasons, is rarely granted.

How often are the innocent actually executed? With the recent renewal of debate about the death penalty in the United States, many politicians have claimed that there is absolutely no evidence that a single innocent person has been executed in the United States. Yet Espy (reported in Bohm, 1999, p. 125) estimates that of the 19,000 executions since 1608, 5% have been of innocent persons: About 950 wrongful executions have been carried out.

The famous (or infamous, depending on one's perspective) list compiled by the Death Penalty Information Center includes 117 individuals wrongly convicted and freed from death row between 1976 and February 2006. The Death Penalty Information Center notes that it "uses the traditional objective criteria that have determined innocence since the founding of this country. In order to be included on the list, defendants must have been convicted and sentenced to death, and subsequently either: a) their conviction was overturned and they were acquitted at a re-trial, or all charges were dismissed; or b) they were given an absolute pardon by the governor based on new evidence of innocence." A description of each case is presented on the website of the Death Penalty Information Center.

Between 1976 and early 2006, 117 people have been released from death row, while only 1,070 have been executed. This means for every 8 or 9 people we execute, we release one from death row! We do not know for sure whether all of these people are truly innocent, but the answer is a function of how innocence is defined. The largest study ever on wrongful convictions, *In Spite of Innocence* (Radelet, Bedau, Putnam, 1994), found that at least 400 people have been wrongly convicted. Of these, 23 were executed and 22 were freed within 72 hours of execution. Since this study, approximately 5 wrongful convictions have been discovered each year! More specifically, "In the 25 years from 1973 to 1998, there were an average of 2.96 exonerations per year. In the five years since 1998, [through] 2003, that average has risen to 7.60 exonerations" (Death Penalty Information Center, 2006). Given that most mistakes are discovered by luck or chance based on the work of student groups and people in the media, it is unlikely that we catch them all.

There is no question that our country has wrongly convicted and executed innocent people. In my state of North Carolina, for example, between 1910 and 1961, the state executed 71 rapists (87% African American) and 11 burglars (100% African American). These are crimes for which eyewitness identification is inherently unreliable (see Chapter 8), and no DNA tests were available during this time. Thus, it is certain that some of these executions were of innocent people, especially in the cases where African Americans were alleged to have raped Caucasian women.

It is, of course, hard to say how likely it is today that we will execute an innocent person. But executions of the innocent are less likely under **super due process**. Bohm (1999, p. 131) claims, "As many as a dozen people (and likely more) may have been executed in error in the United States since 1976 and the implementation of super due process. That represents nearly three percent of all executions through April 1, 1998." A study conducted by the Columbia Law School found that at least 7% of all death penalty cases appealed between 1973 and 1995 were found to be innocent (see Issue in Depth at the end of this chapter).

There is no way to know for sure how many innocent people we have executed. Part of this is because politicians do not seem to want to know. For example, consider the cases in Box 10-7, excerpted from information described by the Death Penalty Information Center.

BOX 10-7

INMATES EXECUTED DESPITE DOUBTS ABOUT THEIR GUILT

- **Ruben Cantu** (executed in Texas, 1993)—He was 17 years old when he was charged with capital murder for shooting a man during an attempted robbery. Both the prosecutor and the jury forewoman have expressed doubts about Cantu's guilt, and a key eyewitness in the state's case against Cantu and Cantu's co-defendant have come forward to say that Texas executed an innocent man. Juan Moreno, an eyewitness in the case, said that it was not Cantu who shot him and that he only identified Cantu as the shooter because he felt pressured and was afraid of the authorities. Moreno said that he twice told police that Cantu was not his assailant, but that the authorities continued to pressure him to identify Cantu as the shooter after Cantu was involved in an unrelated wounding of a police officer. David Garza, Cantu's co-defendant, signed a sworn affidavit saying that he allowed Cantu to be accused and executed even though he wasn't with him on the night of the killing. Garza stated, "Part of me died when he died. You've got a 17-year-old who went to his grave for something he did not do. Texas murdered an innocent person." Miriam Ward, forewoman of the jury, said, "With a little extra work, a little extra effort, maybe we'd have gotten the right information. The bottom line is, an innocent person was put to death for it. We all have our finger in that."

- **Larry Griffin** (executed in Missouri, 1995)—A man injured in the same drive-by shooting that claimed the life of Quintin Moss says Griffin was not involved in the crime, and the first police officer on the scene has given a new account that undermines the trial testimony of the only witness who identified Griffin as the murderer. Based on its findings, the NAACP has supplied the prosecution with the names of three men it suspects committed the crime, and all three of the suspects are currently in jail for other murders.

- **Joseph O'Dell** (executed in Virginia, 1997)—New DNA blood evidence has thrown considerable doubt on the murder and rape conviction of O'Dell. In reviewing his case in 1991, three Supreme Court Justices said they had doubts about O'Dell's guilt and whether he should have been allowed to represent himself. Without the blood evidence, there is little linking O'Dell to the crime. . . . O'Dell asked the state to conduct DNA tests on other pieces of evidence to demonstrate his innocence but was refused.

- **David Spence** (executed in Texas, 1997)—Spence was alleged to have been hired by a convenience store owner to kill a girl but killed three others by mistake. The convenience store owner, Muneer Deeb, was originally convicted and sentenced to death, but then was acquitted at a retrial. The police lieutenant who supervised the investigation of Spence, Marvin Horton, later concluded, "I do not think David Spence committed this crime." Ramon Salinas, the homicide detective who actually conducted the investigation, said, "My opinion is that David Spence was innocent. Nothing from the investigation ever led us to any evidence that he was involved." No physical evidence connected Spence to the crime. The case against Spence was pursued by a zealous narcotics cop who relied on testimony of prison inmates who were granted favors in return for testimony.

- **Leo Jones** (executed in Florida, 1998)—Jones was convicted of murdering a police officer. He had

(*continued*)

BOX 10-7 (*Continued*)

signed a confession after several hours of police interrogation, but he later claimed the confession was coerced. In the mid-1980s, the policeman who arrested Jones and the detective who took his confession were forced out of uniform for ethical violations. The policeman was later identified by a fellow officer as an "enforcer" who had used torture. Many witnesses came forward pointing to another suspect in the case.

- **Gary Graham** (executed in Texas, 2000)—He was 17 when he was charged with the robbery and shooting of Bobby Lambert outside a Houston supermarket and "was convicted primarily on the testimony one witness, Bernadine Skillern, who said she saw the killer's face for a few seconds through her car windshield, from a distance of 30–40 feet away. Two other witnesses, who worked at the grocery store and said that they got a good look at the assailant said that Graham was not the killer, but they were never interviewed by Graham's court-appointed attorney, Ronald Mock, and were not called to testify at trial. Three of the jurors who voted to convict Graham signed affidavits saying they would have voted differently had all of the evidence been available.

- **Cameron Willingham** (executed in Texas, 2004) Willingham was

convicted for starting a fire in his own home that killed his three children. Later, four national arson experts concluded that the original investigation of Willingham's case was flawed and it is possible the fire was accidental. They found that prosecutors and arson investigators used arson theories that have since been repudiated by scientific advances. Arson expert Gerald Hurst said, "There's nothing to suggest to any reasonable arson investigator that this was an arson fire. It was just a fire." Former Louisiana State University fire instructor Kendall Ryland added, "[It] made me sick to think this guy was executed based on this investigation. They executed this guy and they've just got no idea—at least not scientifically—if he set the fire, or if the fire was even intentionally set." Among the only other evidence presented by prosecutors during the trial was testimony from jailhouse snitch Johnny E. Webb, a drug addict on psychiatric medication, who claimed Willingham had confessed to him in the county jail. Coincidentally, less than a year after Willingham's execution, arson evidence presented by some of the same experts who had appealed for relief in Willingham's case helped free Ernest Willis from Texas's death row. The experts noted that the evidence in the Willingham case was nearly identical to the evidence used to exonerate Willis.

SOURCE: Death Penalty Information Center (2006). Available at http://www.deathpenaltyinfo.org/article.php?scid=6&did=111#executed.

Even if you still doubt that innocent people have been executed, remember that we also know that more than 100 wrongfully convicted Americans have been set free from death row since 1976. Consider these two cases:

- In 1996, Rolando Cruz was freed after 11 years on death row. He had been convicted of the rape and murder of a 10-year-old Chicago girl on the basis of phony evidence invented by the police. The real murderer confessed to the crime 8 years prior to Cruz's release, but Cruz was not released until a DNA test proved he had not committed the crime.
- In 1993, Walter McMillan was released from death row in Alabama after the state admitted that it had withheld evidence that an eyewitness had lied. Kirk Bloodworth was also released that year in Alabama after a DNA test proved him to be innocent.

Wrongly convicted Americans typically will have spent about 10 years in prison for crimes that they did not actually commit, in isolation from their families and even from other inmates. More than 100 such cases can be read about online at the Death Penalty Information Center. Bohm (1999, p. 126) writes that these inmates would have been executed if "not for sheer luck." Politicians who use these cases as evidence that the system works to (eventually) set free the innocent, while simultaneously promoting policies to speed up the system and limit appeals of death row inmates, are hypocritical and a threat to justice in the United States.

Why are innocent people wrongfully convicted of capital crimes, even with all the protections put into place by states to ensure that this does not occur? The answers are straightforward and not surprising. The bottom line is that errors are inevitable. To not make mistakes is beyond the capabilities of human beings. Many wrongful convictions stem from errors made by eyewitnesses to crimes (Huff, Rattner, and Sagarin, 1986). Think of the recent execution of Gary Graham in Texas. Graham was convicted on the basis of the eyewitness identification of one person. Another five people claim that Graham was not the actual offender, but did not testify to the court.

Another major reason that people are wrongfully convicted of capital crimes is the incompetence of their defense attorneys. In the Graham case, two of his attorneys reportedly never made an effort to interview or call to the stand the witnesses who claimed that Graham was not the offender. A 1990 study found that many capital defense attorneys "had never handled a capital trial before, lacked training in life-or-death cases, made little effort to present evidence in support of a life sentence, or had been reprimanded, disciplined, or subsequently disbarred" (Bohm, 1999, p. 134). The standard for a competent attorney in capital cases is very low and is inconsistent with justice as a process. According to the standard set forth in *Strickland v. Washington* (1984), an individual defendant must show that his or her attorney was deficient in performance and that this deficiency contributed to the outcome of the case. Given that virtually every capital defendant lacks the resources necessary to prove such deficiencies, this is an impossible standard to meet.

Apparently, Americans are not bothered enough by the thought of executing the innocent to diminish their overwhelming support of capital punishment. A Gallup poll found that, if they knew for a fact that the death penalty resulted in the wrongful execution of 1% of people subjected to it, three-fourths reported that they would still support the death penalty for people convicted of murder. This serves as evidence that Americans value justice as an outcome rather than justice as a process, and prefer crime control values over due process ones.

Research suggests that mistakes are made more likely the more we carry out capital punishment, when cases are politicized, when police and prosecutors zealously pursue executions, and when we limit appeals. In Issue in Depth at the end of this chapter, you'll see that, unfortunately, these factors continue to produce wrongful convictions.

• *The Death Penalty Costs More Than Life Imprisonment*

Administering the death penalty to a convicted murderer costs 2.5 to 5 times as many taxpayer dollars as locking up an offender for life without the possibility of parole. When you add the costs of posttrial reviews, executions become about 24 times as expensive as life imprisonment without parole. The death penalty is so much more expensive than life imprisonment because of the high rates of error that occur at each stage and the persistence of high error rates over time and across the nation, which mandate multiple, expensive judicial inspections (Liebman, Fagan, and West, 2000).

Consider these statistics:

- Taxpayers in California could save about $90 million each year if the state abolished the death penalty (Magagnini, 1988).
- California spent more than $1 billion on its death penalty system between 1977 and 1996 but executed only five people, one of whom asked to be killed (Costanzo, 1997, p. 61).
- In Florida, the average cost of an execution is $3.2 million (Von Drehle, 1988).
- Texas capital cases cost about $2.3 million (Hoppe, 1992).
- In North Carolina, capital cases cost taxpayers an additional $2.16 million, added onto the costs of the typical murder case (Cook, Slawson, and Gries, 1993).

The added costs mount simply by maintaining an elaborate system of capital punishment. When they do result, capital trials are more complex and time-consuming, and appeals are costly. Costanzo (1997, p. 66) reviews these statistics and concludes, "Massive resources are squandered, courts and prisons are strained, just so that, eventually, a few condemned prisoners can be killed." Thus, he concludes that the death penalty is an elaborate, costly charade.

The social costs are harder to identify, but the bottom line is this: The death penalty does not teach Americans that killing is wrong; it teaches them that killing is acceptable under certain circumstances. Humankind says, through its criminal law, that killing is sometimes acceptable; only murder is wrong. Killing of humans is not always wrong, but "no matter if done by a legitimate authority such as the state under the term of 'retribution' or if done by a private citizen in the name of 'vengeance,' the act of killing becomes no more moral, only more legitimate" (Marongiu and Newman, 1987, p. 6).

The United States stands out as a shining example of injustice, ironic given that this country is supposed to be a beacon of justice and freedom for the rest of the world. In fact, by continuing to administer capital punishment, we place ourselves in the company of other countries such as China, Iran, Saudi Arabia, Pakistan, Yemen, Vietnam, Jordan, Mongolia, Singapore, and Iraq, countries whose civil rights violations we deplore.

CONCLUSION

America's long and sordid history with capital punishment has provided plenty of rationale for abolishing the death penalty, something that many states have in fact done. The United States briefly witnessed a moratorium on the death penalty in the face of overwhelming evidence that it was being applied in an arbitrary and discriminatory fashion, but capital punishment has since been reinstated and is now being increasingly used despite the evident bias and inequity in its application. One exception is the state of Illinois, which temporarily instituted a moratorium on executions after realizing that 13 innocent people had been freed from death row since 1977, while only 12 persons had been executed. Based on careful study and a complete understanding of the realities of capital punishment in the state, the legislature of New Jersey recently voted to abolish the death penalty, and the governor of the state signed the bill. This makes New Jersey the first state in the modern era to abolish capital punishment. Public support for capital punishment, though apparently widespread, is not as clear-cut as it may seem from opinion polls, and without doubt is lessening. With knowledge that the death penalty does not achieve its goals of retribution and deterrence, and that incapacitation can be achieved more fairly, humanely, and cheaply through life imprisonment without the possibility of parole, public support for capital punishment will likely dwindle in the years to come.

ISSUE IN DEPTH—Expert Opinion on Capital Punishment

A national survey of capital punishment scholars—those who have spent their careers teaching and conducting research on the death penalty—examined whether the death penalty actually achieves its goals, and whether there are "fatal flaws" to the death penalty. The goal of the survey was to capture the realities of capital punishment as it is actually practiced in the United States.

Dictionary.com (2006) defines the word *expert* as "[a] person with a high degree of skill in or knowledge of a certain subject." Wikipedia (2006) defines an expert as "someone widely recognized as a reliable source of knowledge, technique, or skill whose judgment is accorded authority and status by the public or their peers. Experts have prolonged or intense experience through practice and education in a particular field." The two definitions of *expert* are combined as "A capital punishment expert is a person with a high degree of knowledge of capital punishment, someone who is widely recognized as a reliable source of knowledge due to prolonged experience through practice and education related to the death penalty, whose judgment is accorded authority and status by the public or their peers" (Robinson, 2008, p. 109).

A sample of experts from all capital punishment scholars who had published books and articles on the death penalty between 2001 and 2005 was selected. The sample was made up of 94 of the most prominent capital punishment experts, 48% of whom responded to the survey.

The study's main conclusions were that the death penalty fails to meet its goals of retribution, incapacitation, and deterrence, and that the application of the death penalty in the United States is plagued by serious problems including racial and class biases, a significant risk of being used against the innocent, as well as other problems. For these reasons, the vast majority of experts were opposed to capital punishment, favored alternatives to the punishment, and thought abolition of capital punishment was justified.

TABLE 10-A   Expert Opinion on Whether Capital Punishment Achieves Retribution

Does capital punishment, as actually practiced in the United States, achieve retribution (i.e., provide justice for murder victims, their families, and society at large)?

Yes	31%
No	36%
Unsure	33%

N = 42

As shown in Table 10-A, the largest portion of capital punishment experts (36%) responded that they did not think the death penalty achieves retribution, but a sizable portion of death penalty experts (31%) indicated that capital punishment provides justice for murder victims, their families, and society at large (retribution). Another third of the experts (33%) said they were unsure.

Respondents who said that the death penalty achieves retribution indicated that for some crime victims' families, execution produces some sense of relief and justice; those who said that the death penalty does not achieve retribution tended to indicate that crime victims' families typically do not feel a sense of relief or justice after an execution. Further, respondents who answered yes suggested that the length of time it takes to carry out executions in the era of super due process serves to draw out the process of healing after a murder. Perhaps most important is that, when judged by the standard of whether capital punishment generally leads to retribution, the experts indicated that capital punishment does not achieve the goal of retribution because of the rare nature of the punishment. That is, nearly all murder victims' families do not see the killer of their loved one sentenced to death and ultimately executed. Finally, the experts suggested that retribution can be accomplished through alternatives to capital punishment such as long terms of imprisonment or life imprisonment without the possibility of parole (LWOP).

As shown in Table 10-B, only a small fraction of death penalty experts (9%) indicated that capital punishment prevents future murders by causing fear in would-be murderers so they do not commit murder (deterrence). The largest portion of capital punishment experts (79%) responded that the death penalty achieves deterrence, and 12% said they were unsure.

Respondents who said the death penalty achieves deterrence referred to recent econometric studies that purport to show a deterrent effect of executions on murder. Respondents who said the death penalty does not achieve deterrence were adamant that

---

TABLE 10-B   Expert Opinion on Whether Capital Punishment Achieves Deterrence

Does capital punishment, as actually practiced in the United States, achieve deterrence (i.e., prevent future murders by causing fear in would-be murderers so they do not commit murder)?

Yes	9%
No	79%
Unsure	12%

N = 43

TABLE 10-C   Expert Opinion on Whether Capital Punishment Achieves Incapacitation

Does capital punishment, as actually practiced in the United States, achieve incapacitation (i.e., prevent future murders by killing murderers who would murder again)?

Yes	64%
No	24%
Unsure	12%

N = 41

executes do not deter murder and they referred both to historical and contemporary evidence (including replications of the econometric studies) that the executions do not deter murder. The main reason capital punishment does not deter murder, according to the experts, is that executions are extremely rare relative to the number of murders.

As shown in Table 10-C, most death penalty experts (64%) indicated that they think capital punishment prevents future murders by killing murderers who would murder again (incapacitation). Yet a sizable portion of capital punishment experts (24%) responded that they did not think the death penalty achieves incapacitation, and 12% said they were unsure.

Respondents who said the death penalty achieves incapacitation indicated that for those murderers who are executed, they are certainly incapacitated and therefore unable to commit future murders. Yet even a majority of experts who said that executions achieve incapacitation stated that most murderers do not murder again and thus need not be executed. Even those who indicated that executions incapacitate offenders commonly noted its rare nature, calling into question is incapacitative value. Further, they noted that predicting future dangerousness is impossible and that incapacitation can be achieved through other means such as life imprisonment without the possibility of parole. Respondents who said the death penalty does not achieve incapacitation indicated that the penalty is used too infrequently to meaningfully impact murder rates. Finally, they noted that incapacitation through capital punishment also poses enormous costs, including financial costs and a significant risk of executing the innocent.

As shown in Table 10-D, a very large majority of capital punishment experts (84%) believes that the death penalty is "plagued by a racial bias" of some kind. Some respondents (7%) do not think that the death penalty is "plagued by a racial bias" of some kind, and a few respondents (9%) suggested that they were unsure.

Respondents who said the death penalty is racially biased indicated overwhelmingly their belief that the racial bias in capital punishment does not pertain to race of

TABLE 10-D   Expert Opinion on Whether Capital Punishment Is Racially Biased

Is American capital punishment plagued by a racial bias of any kind?

Yes	84%
No	7%
Unsure	9%

N = 43

TABLE 10-E   Expert Opinion on Whether Capital Punishment Is Class Biased

Is American capital punishment plagued by a social class bias of any kind?

Yes	80%
No	4%
Unsure	16%

N = 45

defendant but rather to race of victim, so that killers of white victims are far more likely to be executed than killers of black victims. A few respondents also suggested that killers of white females are most likely to be executed. Respondents who said the death penalty is not racially biased discussed the waning significance of race of defendant effects.

As shown in Table 10-E, a significant majority of capital punishment experts (80%) believes that the death penalty is "plagued by a social class bias" of some kind. Some respondents (4%) do not think that the death penalty is "plagued by a social class bias" of some kind, and more (16%) suggested that they were unsure.

Respondents who said the death penalty is class biased indicated overwhelmingly their belief that the main problem in terms of social class is inadequate legal representation for the poor in capital cases, although some respondents suggested there is a class bias in all of criminal justice. The respondent who said the death penalty is not class biased did not provide any explanation for his or her answer.

As shown in Table 10-F, a clear majority of capital punishment experts (76%) indicated that they thought the death penalty had been used against the innocent, but many were also unsure (22%). Only one respondent (2%) indicated that he or she thought the death penalty had never been used against the innocent.

Respondents who said the death penalty is used against the innocent tended to discuss the long list of those wrongly convicted and sentenced to death, created by groups like the Death Penalty Information Center and the Innocence Project, although some respondents also discussed individual cases of executions of individuals they thought to be innocent. The respondent who said the death penalty is not used against the innocent refuted the lists and pointed out that many of the alleged innocent are actually guilty.

In response to the open-ended question as to whether there were any other problems with the way capital punishment was administered, most death penalty experts

TABLE 10-F   Expert Opinion on Whether Capital Punishment Is Used Against the Innocent

Is American capital punishment ever used against the innocent?

Yes	76%
No	2%
Unsure	22%

N = 42

TABLE 10-G   Expert Opinion on Whether Capital Punishment Has Other Problems

In your opinion, are there any other problems (not addressed in Tables 10-A to 10-F) with the way capital punishment is practiced in the United States?

Yes	80%
No	10%
Unsure	10%

N = 39

(80%) said yes. In fact, only 10% said no. An additional 10% responded with unsure. Table 10-G illustrates these values.

Respondents who said the death penalty has other problems indicated a long list of other problems, including its excessive costs; the length of time it takes to complete the appeals process; problems with jury selection, jury instructions, and interpreting how to weigh aggravating and mitigating circumstances; the problematic nature of victim impact statements; ineffectiveness of counsel; politics; geographic disparities; its arbitrary nature; a lack of proportionality; judicial and appeals review; inadequate resources and representation for the poor; the unwillingness of parole boards or governors to grant clemency in deserving cases; improper application when the victim is culpable; conditions of death row and the length of confinement; the effects of the death penalty on families of defendants; the potential for a brutalizing effect; and executing the mentally ill. Others reiterated that they felt the punishment is immoral, that methods of execution are inhumane (e.g., with botched executions), and that the reputation of the United States is suffering as a result of continuing to appply capital punishment. Respondents who said the death penalty does not have other problems tended not to provide any justifications for their answers.

As shown in Table 10-H, a very large majority of death penalty experts in this study (80%) indicated that they are opposed to capital punishment. Only 9% of experts who responded to the survey expressed support for capital punishment; 11% said they were not sure.

Respondents who said they believe in the death penalty indicated that the punishment fit the crime of murder and that as long as it is a legal punishment voted on by the people, it is consistent with justice in a democracy. Respondents who said they do not believe in the death penalty referred to their beliefs that the death penalty does not meet its goals of retribution, deterrence, and incapacitation and that it is plagued by

---

TABLE 10-H   Degree of Support by Experts for Capital Punishment

Do you believe in capital punishment/the death penalty, or are you opposed to it?

Believe in	9%
Opposed	80%
Unsure	11%

N = 44

TABLE 10-I   Expert Opinion on the Appropriate Sentence for Convicted Murderers

What is the most appropriate punishment for someone convicted of first-degree murder?

Death sentence	0%
Life without parole	37%
Other	63%

N = 43

serious problems like race and class bias, a serious risk of executing the innocent, and other problems.

When asked what the most appropriate punishment is for someone convicted of first-degree murder, *all* capital punishment experts who participated in this study answered "life imprisonment without parole" (37%) or "other" (63%). As shown in Table 10-I, no experts (0%) indicated capital punishment. Other punishments specified by respondents included life imprisonment with the opportunity for parole, 25 years' imprisonment to life, and other terms of imprisonment (e.g., a long term of imprisonment with parole consideration after 10 years, life with the possibility of parole after 20 years, life imprisonment with the possibility of parole after 25 years, 50 years with the possibility of parole after 25 years).

Respondents who said the most appropriate punishment was LWOP indicated that it achieves the goal of incapacitation without the risk of executing the innocent, as well as saving society money. Those respondents who answered "other" tended to suggest very long terms of imprisonment dependent on the nature of the crime and the defendant. They explained that LWOP was not acceptable to them because such a sentence interfered with a chance at redemption and was inconsistent with maturation away from crime and violence due to aging.

As shown in Table 10-J, the vast majority of death penalty experts (79%) answered in the affirmative to the question, "Do you personally favor a temporary halt to executions (moratorium) in the United States while the practice of American capital punishment is studied?" Another 14% of experts answered no and 7% said they were not sure.

As shown in Table 10-K, the vast majority of death penalty experts (84%) also answered in the affirmative to the question, "Does capital punishment, as actually practiced in the United States, have problems that are serious enough to make it unacceptable as a government-sanctioned punishment (so that states should permanently stop

TABLE 10-J   Degree of Support by Death Penalty Experts for a Moratorium on Executions

Do you personally favor a temporary halt to executions (moratorium) in the United States while the practice of American capital punishment is studied?

Yes	79%
No	14%
Unsure	7%

N = 44

TABLE 10-K   Degree of Support by Death Penalty Experts for Abolition of Capital Punishment

Does capital punishment, as actually practiced in the United States, have problems that are serious enough to make it unacceptable as a government-sanctioned punishment (so that states should permanently stop executing convicted murderers)?

Yes	84%
No	14%
Unsure	2%

N = 44

executing convicted murderers)?" Another 14% of experts answered no and only one respondent (2%) indicated uncertainty.

Respondents who favored abolition justified their answers again based on the ineffectiveness of capital punishment and the very real problems with its application in the United States. Respondents who did not favor abolition referred to their core belief in the punishment, as well as the fact that it is supported by the public.

Conclusion

Expert opinion is solidly opposed to capital punishment, not just for theoretical and philosophical reasons, but also based on an awareness created through scholarship and teaching that the death penalty is a failed policy. According to the experts, capital punishment fails for two primary reasons. First, most experts indicated that the death penalty does not achieve retribution—defined as providing justice for murder victims, their families, and society at large. A very large majority indicated that the death penalty does not achieve deterrence of murder or other crimes. Although most capital punishment experts indicated that capital punishment achieves incapacitation, many concluded that the size of the effect was small (due to the infrequency with which executions actually occur in America), that the incapacitative effect was not without significant costs, and that incapacitation could be achieved through other means, such as LWOP.

Second, most experts indicated that the application of the death penalty is plagued by significant problems. The experts say the death penalty is racially and class biased and likely to be used against the innocent. Further, a large majority of capital punishment experts in the study listed other problems with the reality of capital punishment in America, including excessive costs; the length of time it takes to complete the appeals process; problems with jury selection, jury instructions, and interpreting how to weigh aggravating and mitigating circumstances; the problematic nature of victim impact statements; ineffectiveness of counsel; politics; geographic disparities; a lack of proportionality; judicial and appeals review; inadequate resources and representation for the poor; the unwillingness of parole boards or governors to grant clemency in deserving cases; improper application when the victim is culpable; the immoral nature of the punishment; inhumane methods of execution; and that the reputation of the United States is suffering as a result of continuing to apply capital punishment.

Based on the belief that capital punishment is a failed policy, the experts are opposed to capital punishment and unanimously favor alternatives to capital punishment for convicted first-degree murderers, such as life imprisonment without the opportunity for parole and other very long prison sentences depending on the nature of the offender and the offense. Although 78% of capital punishment experts who responded to this survey stated their opposition to capital punishment, not a single expert (0%) answered that the most appropriate sentence for convicted murderers was death. The vast majority of death penalty experts also said they supported a permanent end to capital punishment due to problems that were serious enough to make capital punishment "unacceptable as a government-sanctioned punishment."

Robinson (2008, p. 239) concludes "[i]f criminal justice policies like capital punishment should be influenced by empirical evidence, and if the opinions of the experts in this study reflect this empirical evidence, the only justifiable policy is to abolish capital punishment. This is a conclusion based not on theoretical or philosophical arguments but instead on empirical evidence as captured through the opinion of the experts who study it for a living."

KEY TERMS

aggravated murders	deterrence	mitigating factors
aggravating factors	discrimination	moratorium
anecdotal evidence	disparity	retribution
arbitrary	expert	special or specific deterrence
best-bet hypothesis	general deterrence	super due process
brutalization effect	geographic disparity	vengeance
capital punishment	incapacitation	

DISCUSSION QUESTIONS

1. What are the main means of execution in the United States?
2. Why do you think more men are executed than women?
3. Why do you think so many of our allies have abolished the death penalty?
4. Why do you think that executions declined in the United States between the 1930s and the 1970s?
5. What are the main factors that lead to legal errors in death penalty cases?
6. Why didn't the Supreme Court abolish the death penalty with the case of *McCleskey v. Kemp*?
7. Why do so few murders lead to executions in the United States?
8. Why do the vast majority of executions take place in the southern states?
9. Is there any evidence that suggests that public executions would deter murderers?
10. Discuss why most Americans say they support the death penalty.
11. Identify and discuss the main justifications for capital punishment.
12. Is there support for the death penalty in the Bible? Why or why not?
13. Does the death penalty deter murderers? Why or why not?
14. In your opinion, do the errors in American capital punishment warrant a halt in executions? Explain.

CHAPTER

11

THE "WAR ON DRUGS": FOCUSING ON THE WRONG DRUGS?

1. Introduction
2. The War on Drugs
   a. Goals of the Drug War
   b. Elements of the Drug War
   c. Drugs and Crime
   d. A Brief History of the Drug War
3. What Is a Drug?
4. Types of Drugs
   - Box 11-1. Examples of Major Drugs
5. Extent of Drug Use in the United States
6. Harms Associated with Drugs
   - Box 11-2. Marijuana Versus Cigarettes
7. Legal Status of Each Drug: Why Are the Most Harmful Drugs Legal While Some Relatively Harmless Drugs Are Illegal?
   a. The Role of the Media in Drug Scares
   - Box 11-3. Community Epidemiology Work Group (CEWG) Field Quotes About Crack Cocaine
8. Harms Caused by the Drug War
9. Alternatives to the Drug War: Legalization and Decriminalization
   - Box 11-4. How America's Drug War Is a Success
   - Box 11-5. Harm Reduction
10. Conclusion
11. Issue in Depth—Drug War Lies?
12. Key Terms
13. Discussion Questions

INTRODUCTION

This chapter introduces you to the U.S. war on drugs. The drug war is a prime example of a war on crime that serves limited interests and is used to control certain segments of the U.S. population, notably the poor and people of color. This chapter shows who is most affected by the nation's drug war and how ineffective the war is for reducing illicit drug use. In this chapter, you will learn what a drug is, how prevalent drug use is in the United States, and harms associated with various drugs. An interesting issue arises: Why are the most harmful drugs legal while some relatively less harmful drugs are criminalized? I conclude the chapter with an assessment of legalization and decriminalization as strategies for American criminal justice. The chapter concludes with an assessment of claims made by the federal agency responsible for the drug war: the Office of National Drug Control Policy (ONDCP).

THE WAR ON DRUGS

The **war on drugs** is the phrase used to describe the American approach to reducing drug use and abuse in the United States. President George Bush (the first) declared in a nationally televised message that drug abuse was "our nation's most serious domestic problem" (Beckett, 1997, p. 6). Earlier, President Reagan had diverted more than $700 million from education, treatment, and research to law enforcement programs to fight the war on drugs. Reagan also gave more money to prisons and to the Drug Enforcement Administration, the federal agency responsible for preventing illicit drug use (Kraska, 1990, p. 117). Now, our federal government spends more than $20 billion fighting the drug war (this figure does not include state and local government costs).

Figure 11-1 depicts federal dollars spent on the war on drugs over the years. Note that federal and state governments actually spend far more on the drug war than shown on the chart. Beginning in 2003, the Office of National Drug Control Policy (ONDCP)

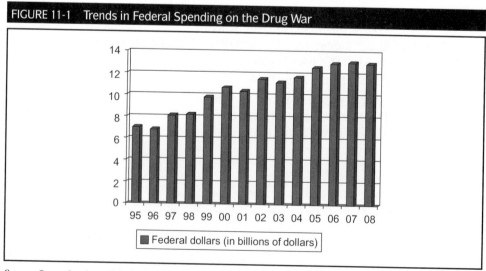

FIGURE 11-1   Trends in Federal Spending on the Drug War

Federal dollars (in billions of dollars)

Source: Sourcebook on Criminal Justice Statistics (2006).

changed the way it presented its budget to the American people. The net effect of this war was the appearance that the drug war was less costly than it is in reality. Issue in Depth at the end of this chapter discusses the issue of honesty and dishonesty in the drug war more thoroughly.

Goals of the Drug War

For what are Americans spending more than $20 billion? The Office of National Drug Control Policy (ONDCP) stated the goals of the war in 2000:

- To educate and enable America's youth to reject illegal drugs as well as alcohol and tobacco (reduce drug use)
- To increase the safety of America's citizens by substantially reducing drug-related crime and violence (reduce crime)
- To reduce health and social costs to the public of illegal drug use (reduce harm)
- To shield America's air, land, and sea frontiers from the drug threat (border control)
- To break foreign and domestic drug sources of supply (eradicate and interdict)

In 2002, the ONDCP put forward some revised goals, including:

- Stopping drug use before it starts; education and community action (reduce drug use)
- Healing America's drug users; getting treatment resources where they are needed most (reduce harm)
- Disrupting the market; attacking the economic basis of the drug trade (eradicate and interdict)

The three goals above remain the stated goals of the drug war today. Given these goals, the key questions to assess America's war on drugs are:

- Is drug use down?
- Is crime down?
- Are health and social costs down?
- Are drug users more healthy?
- Are drugs less available?
- Is treatment more available?
- Are our borders secure?

If the answers to these questions are yes, America's drug war has succeeded.

Unfortunately, most scholars suggest the answers to the above questions are no. Take, for example, this statement from Glaser (1997, p. 116):

> Narcotics are the bane of our criminal justice system, and control efforts have been much more extensive than for any vice except possibly alcohol use during Prohibition. Attempts to diminish the use of drugs by punishment have been tremendously costly, but usually seem to have no effect on the prevalence of drug abusers and their predations.

In this chapter, I assess our nation's performance in its war on drugs and show that the answer to most of the questions above is no. Additionally, I demonstrate that the war has probably caused more harm than it has prevented.

Elements of the Drug War

The main elements of the war on drugs include three policies: crop eradication efforts, interdiction efforts, and street-level drug enforcement (Kappeler and Potter, 2004). **Crop eradication** is aimed at destroying crops before they can be cultivated and sold as illicit drugs. **Interdiction** efforts include border control and strategies aimed at intervening in countries where drugs are grown and harvested. **Street-level drug enforcement** includes undercover drug busts and seizures of drugs. **Treatment** of drug abusers and drug **prevention** education are also involved in the drug war, but these efforts have received far less funding over the years. Finally, **asset forfeiture** involves the seizure by police of cash profits and property generated by drugs.

The majority of American drug war spending is reactive supply side rather than proactive or preventive (demand side), as shown in Figure 11-2. The statistics in the figure pertain to 2008 drug war budget requests from ONDCP.

Table 11-1 shows what the war on drugs looks like, using data from various government sources. It illustrates how many people are arrested, charged, and sent to some form of correctional supervision for drug offenses. It also illustrates how many drugs are seized in the United States.

The Sentencing Project (2003) summarizes what the drug war has looked like:

Arrests for drug offenses nearly tripled from 580,900 in 1980 to 1,579,566 by 2000. Nearly 315,000 persons were sentenced in state courts for a drug offense in 1998. Of these, 43% were sentenced to prison, 26% to jail, and 32% to probation and/or treatment. The number of inmates incarcerated for drug offenses at all levels—state and federal prisons and local jails—has skyrocketed by more than 1,000% from 40,000

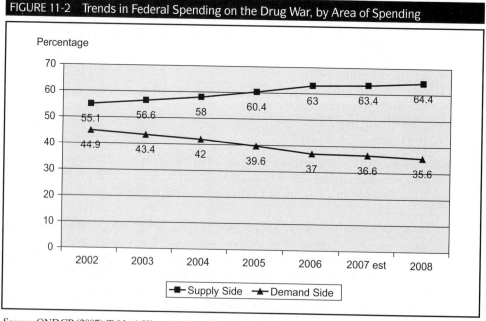

FIGURE 11-2 Trends in Federal Spending on the Drug War, by Area of Spending

Source: ONDCP (2007). Table 4. Historical Drug Control by Function. Available at http://whitehousedrugpolicy.gov/publications/policy/08budget/tbl_4.pdf.

TABLE 11-1 Key Facts of the War on Drugs	
Drug arrests, 2005	1,034,844 (12.5% of all arrests)
Most common arrest, 2005	Possession of drugs (82% of all drug arrests)
Marijuana arrests, 2005	444,983 (43% of all drug arrests, 88% for possession)
State court drug convictions, 2002	340,330 (32.3% of all felony convictions)
Federal drug court cases, 2005	29,251 (44.4% of all cases filed)
Federal drug convictions, 2005	26,588 (34.4% of all convictions, 23% for marijuana)
Drug offenders in corrections	State prisons, 2003 — 250,900 (20% of all state prisoners)
	Federal prisons, 2004 — 154,706 (54% of federal prisoners)
	Jails, 2002 — 154,002 (22% of jail inmates)
	State probation, 2005 — 1,165,510 (28% of probationers)
	State parole, 2005 — 290,230 (37% of all parolees)

Source: Sourcebook of Criminal Justice Statistics (2006).

in 1980 to 453,000 by 1999. At that point, there were 251,200 drug offenders in state prisons incarcerated at a [conservative] cost of about $5 billion annually.

According to a study by the U.S. Sentencing Commission, most people sentenced to time in federal prisons for drug offenses are low-level (55%) or mid-level dealers (34%). Further, according to The Sentencing Project, three-fourths of state prison inmates were convicted of drug and/or nonviolent crimes, and most sentenced drug offenders in state and federal prisons (58%) have no history of violence or high level drug activity. Additionally, more than one-third (35%) of drug inmates have criminal histories that are limited to drug offenses and 21% are first-time offenders. Finally, four out of every five drug offenders are African American (56%) and Hispanic (23%).

Virtually every law enforcement agency has a drug budget, including federal agencies, 3 out of 4 state level agencies, and more than 9 out of 10 local agencies. In 2005, police officers made 1.9 million arrests, 13.1% of all arrests that year. Most (82%) were for simple possession of drugs, and 43% were for marijuana crimes (38% of the drug arrests were for marijuana possession) (see Chapter 6). Although data are not yet available for state court convictions for the same year, roughly one-third of all convictions in any given year are for drug offenses. The picture is much the same in federal courts, where about 40% of all people charged in any given year are alleged drug offenders (see Chapter 7). Now, drug offenders make up more than half of all federal prisoners and about 20% of all inmates in the state and federal prisons. They also make up roughly one quarter of all people in jail and those on probation (see Chapter 9).

Each year our nation spends tens of billions of dollars on drug law enforcement and incarceration. As a nation, we have spent hundreds of billions of dollars on the war on drugs since 1980 (Merlo and Benekos, 2000, p. 19). The cost of the drug war increased sixfold between 1986 and 1996, and most of this money went to domestic law enforcement at the local and state levels of government (Gaines, Kaune, and Miller, 2000, p. 610). Domestic social programs were cut dramatically to pay for the war on drugs (Goetz, 1996).

Between FY 2002 and FY 2008, spending for supply side mechanisms grew from 55.1% of the total drug war budget to 64.4%, while spending for demand side efforts shrank from 44.9% to 35.6%. Additionally, much of the 35.6% is for prevention and treat-ment research rather than actual prevention programs and treatment services. The gap between reactive and proactive drug war measures has increased under the Bush Admin-istration, despite claims by ONDCP that the drug war is balanced and compassionate.

Consider this irony: Police departments in the United States have begun to profit from drug seizures and asset forfeitures of drug dealers. American police can seize assets accumulated as a result of illicit drug trafficking and keep a share of the proceeds to fund training and equipment (Gaines et al., 2000). If the police have come to need these funds for their own operating budgets, what would happen if they completely eliminated illicit drugs from our society?

Drugs and Crime

The drug war is aimed at stopping **drug-related crimes** (e.g., acts of violence caused either by the pharmacological effects of drugs on people or by the need to obtain money to buy drugs), **crimes associated with a drug-using lifestyle** (e.g., drug use itself), and crimes committed because of coming into contact with drug dealers and other users (Walker, 1998). In similar terms, Beckett and Sasson (2000, p. 40), discuss types of drug-related homicides, including **psychopharmacological homicides** caused directly by effects of drugs on the brain. Ironically, the war on drugs also creates **drug-defined crimes**, such as possession and sale of drugs, which obviously would not be "crimes" if drugs were not illegal (Office of National Drug Control Policy, 2002).

Despite the common image of a drug-crazed criminal, most crimes committed by people involved with drugs are not caused by the pharmacological effects of the drugs on behavior (Robinson and Scherlen, 2007). Some criminal justice statistics promote this myth about the overall harmfulness of drugs. For example, research by the National Center on Addiction and Substance Abuse at Columbia University (1998) found that 80% "of prisoners in the United States were involved with alcohol or other drugs at the time of their crimes." This sounds like clear proof of the link between drug use and crime. But consider what this research actually means: "that is to say, 80 percent were either under the direct influence of alcohol or other drugs while committing the crime, had a history of drug abuse, committed the crime to support a drug habit, or were arrested for violating drug or alcohol laws" (Gaines et al., 2000, p. 51). Considering all that being "involved with drugs" includes, it is hard to imagine any prisoner who is not "involved with" alcohol or other drugs at the time of his or her crimes.

Drug-related crimes include what Beckett and Sasson (2000) call **economic com-pulsive homicides**—murders motivated by the need to obtain money to buy high-priced drugs. Others are **systemic homicides,** such as turf war killings aimed at protecting illicit drug markets. In essence, the illegal status of drugs creates **criminal subcultures,** such as gangs, that develop their own norms: being tough, getting respect, and making money through illicit activity. Reiman (2006) calls such crimes **secondary crimes,** which could be virtually eliminated if drugs were not illegal. Inciardi (2002, p. 193) lists several types of systemic violence, including "territorial disputes between rival drug dealers; assaults and homicides committed within dealing and trafficking hierarchies as means of enforcing normative codes; robberies of drug dealers, often fol-lowed by usually violent retaliations; elimination of informers; punishment for selling phony, adulterated, or otherwise bad drugs; retribution for failing to pay one's debts; and general disputes over drugs and drug paraphernalia."

A Brief History of the Drug War

Although the United States has always engaged in wars against drugs, the current drug war really started in the 1970s under President Richard Nixon. In 1973, Nixon created the Drug Enforcement Agency (DEA) within the Department of Justice as the federal government's lead agency for suppressing drugs in the United States (Lyman and Potter, 1998). Since that time, drug use has been blamed for "the dramatic rise in the murder rate in the 1980s [and] gang violence." The resulting focus on drugs by U.S. criminal justice agencies, however, has produced something perhaps more disastrous—"the soaring prison population, the worsening crisis in race relations, and the steady erosion of individual rights in the Supreme Court" (Walker, 1998, p. 243).

Walker links these outcomes directly to U.S. drug policy, which he calls "nonsensical." Sensible discussion about drugs, Walker claims, does not occur because of the public hysteria accompanying our war against drugs. The national outcries over "reefer madness" in the 1930s and "crack babies" in the 1980s, to be discussed later in this chapter, are prime examples of hysterias that led politicians to promote myths about drug use and crime and to talk tough about how to reduce use of drugs by Americans. The result has been our war on drugs.

Judge James Gray, who served a career as a judge fighting the war on drugs, wrote a book that condemns the war as a failure. In his book, *Why Our Drug Law Have Failed and What We Can Do About It* (2001), Gray argues that there are actually two sets of Bills of Rights now in place, one for the war on drugs and one for everything else. In his book, Gray provides numerous examples of how the Constitution has been eroded to allow the nation's police to fight the drug war, despite its continued failures.

Why, then, have Americans supported the addition of police and prisons in efforts to stop drug use, which is mostly "casual and recreational and does not lead to either addiction or criminal activity" (Walker, 1998, p. 247)? Why has the war on drugs become such a powerful force in the United States? Gaines and Kraska (1997, p. 4) claim:

> Most people do not question the political/media cries to do something about our "drug problem"; to wage wars on "drugs"; or that "drug use" destroys a person's or even an entire community's well-being. Drug war ideology lulls us into assuming a number of properties about drugs. We refer to certain drugs . . . as if they were little demons committing crimes. Waging war on drugs—as if the drugs themselves constitute our "drug problem"—allows us to overlook the underlying reasons why people abuse these substances. . . . The language of ideology fools us into thinking that we're waging war against drugs themselves, not real people. . . .

These authors describe our war on drugs as "hypocritical, exploitative, and dangerously misleading" (p. 5).

Best (1999, p. 144) explains the value of the war metaphor:

> Declaration of war on social problems are dramatic events; they call for society to rally behind a single policy, against a common foe. Typically, the initial pronouncements receive favorable attention in the mass media; the press details the nature of the problem and outlines the efforts designed to wage war against it. Usually, the enemy . . . has no one speaking on its behalf. There is the sense that society is united behind the war effort. Declaring war seizes the moral high ground.

According to Jensen and Gerber (1998, p. ix), misguided drug policies result from at least three factors: political opportunism, media profit maximization, and desire among criminal justice professionals to increase their spheres of influence. Politicians create concern about drug use to gain personally from such claims; they achieve this largely by using the media as their own mouthpiece.

Jensen and Gerber suggest that concern over drugs typically occurs in a cycle whereby some government entity claims the "existence of an undesirable condition" and then legitimizes the concern, garnering public support through the media by using "constructors" (similar to what Gans [1995] has called "counters") who provide evidence of the problem. Claims-makers "typify" the drug problem by characterizing its nature (Best, 1989). For example, drugs are typified as "harmful" even if they are being used recreationally. They are characterized as bad regardless of the context in which they are being used. Any drug use is wrong even if it is not abuse (Jensen and Gerber, 1998, p. 5). Most troubling, drugs are connected to other social problems to make them seem worse. Recently, illicit drugs were tied to acts of terrorism in television commercials and print ads paid for by taxpayers. I return to the specific role that the media have played in creating public concern about drugs later in this chapter.

Several myths about drugs exemplify this typification. For example, the "dope fiend mythology" promulgated by the U.S. government in the early 1900s contained these elements: "the drug addict is a violent criminal, the addict is a moral degenerate (e.g., a liar, thief, etc.), drug peddlers and addicts want to convert others into addicts, and the addict takes drugs because of an abnormal personality" (Lindesmith, 1940, p. 8). Another example typified the use of marijuana, as indicated in a pamphlet circulated by the Bureau of Narcotics in the 1930s:

> Prolonged use of Marihuana frequently develops a delirious rage which sometimes leads to high crimes, such as assault and murder. Hence Marihuana has been called the "killer drug." The habitual use of this narcotic poison always causes a marked deterioration and sometimes produces insanity. . . .
>
> While the Marihuana habit leads to physical wreckage and mental decay, its effects upon character and morality are even more devastating. The victim frequently undergoes such moral degeneracy that he will lie and steal without scruple. (Quoted in Bonnie and Whitebread, 1974, p. 109)

The propaganda circulated by the Bureau of Narcotics included the story of a "murder of a Florida family and their pet dog by a wayward son who had taken one toke of marijuana" (Kappeler, Blumberg, and Potter, 2000, p. 9). Evidence about the relative harmlessness of marijuana was ignored.

Amazingly, the federal government recently called marijuana more dangerous than all other illegal drugs combined! The ONDCP now claims that aggressive antisocial behavior among youth is linked to frequency of marijuana use and that marijuana use is linked to cutting class, stealing, and property crime.

The main effects of the war on drugs have included pressure on police to arrest drug violators, the use of drug assets for police benefits (what Jensen and Gerber [1998] call "policing for profit"), and increased militarization of police departments (Kraska and Kappeler, 1997). As the soldiers in the war on drugs, police departments have been encouraged by policies first instituted by President Reagan in the 1980s to pursue drug offenders; as a reward, they are allowed to confiscate and keep some drug-related assets

(Gray, 2001). Again, think of the irony of law enforcement officials coming to rely on drug assets to purchase equipment and conduct training so that police can exterminate drug use (Rasmussen and Benson, 1994). It may be startling to realize that the majority of law enforcement agencies in the United States have such asset forfeiture programs in place (Jensen and Gerber, 1998; McAnamy, 1992).

According to Webb and Brown (1998), such "wars" on drugs as inanimate objects "tend to be concerned less with the drugs they purportedly target than with those who are perceived to be the primary users of the drugs (Morgan and Signorielli, 1990)" (p. 45). For example, the war on opium in the late 1800s and early 1900s was focused on Chinese laborers who represented unwanted labor competition. Thus, the Harrison Act of 1914, which forbade importation and manufacture of opium by Chinese, excluded the "Chinese living in the United States from fully participating in the labor market" (p. 46). The war on marijuana in the 1930s was grounded in racism against Mexican immigrants, who were characterized as "drug-crazed criminals" taking jobs away from Americans during the Great Depression (Sandor, 1995, p. 48). Finally, "the use of crack by the urban poor provided political leaders (in the 1980s) with a convenient scapegoat for both diverting attention from pressing social and economic problems and blaming a specific powerless group for social disaster" (Belenko, 1993, p. 9).

Other effects of wars on drugs include overloaded court systems, increased punitiveness in the form of stiff mandatory sentences for drug offenses, exploding prison populations, and ultimately a worsening of racial disparities in criminal justice (Jensen and Gerber, 1998, pp. 1–2). This chapter examines the American war on drugs in an effort to determine if such effects are justified.

In the next section, I examine what a drug is and discuss types of drugs. Then, I explore the extent of drug use in the United States and document harms associated with each type of drug.

WHAT IS A DRUG?

What do you think of when you hear the word **drug**? The meaning of the word really depends on who is asked. To a doctor or pharmacist, for example, a drug is something very different than it is to a homeless person living on the street (Liska, 2000).

The term drug does have a clear definition. Lyman and Potter (1998, pp. 59–60) begin their examination of drugs in American society with a discussion of the dictionary definition of the term. Liska (2000, pp. 3–4) writes that drugs are used to fight infection, reverse a disease process, relieve symptoms of illness, restore normal functioning of human organs, aid in diagnosing sickness, inhibit normal body processes, and maintain health. This is the relatively positive view of drugs.

Have we as a nation declared a war on substances that help fight disease and maintain health? Clearly not. Obviously, there must be another meaning of drugs. Lyman and Potter (1998, p. 60) define a drug as "any substance that causes or creates significant psychological and/or physiological changes in the body." Liska (2000, p. 4) defines a drug as "any absorbed substance that changes or enhances any physical or psychological function in the body." But these definitions of a drug would include coffee, tea, and cigarettes—in fact, virtually any substance. Have we declared war on these substances? Obviously not.

Merriam-Webster's Collegiate Dictionary (2007) includes as its last acceptable definition of the word *drug*, "something and often an illegal substance that causes addiction, habituation, or a marked change in consciousness." Is this the focus of our war on drugs? Clearly, it is. Our American "war on drugs" is being waged against illegal forms of drug use and the activities that permit it (manufacturing, distribution, sales, possession, etc.).

All drugs, whether legal or illegal, affect the brain by interacting with naturally occurring brain chemicals known as **neurotransmitters** (such as dopamine): "The major drugs of abuse—e.g., narcotics like heroin or stimulants like cocaine—mimic the structure of neurotransmitters, the most powerful mind-altering drugs the human body creates" (Lyman and Potter, 1998, pp. 60–61). By altering the brain's chemistry, drugs alter people's behavior. When their effects are dangerous or simply unintended, such as interfering with a person's family, work, or social relations, drugs can be harmful to the user (Lyman and Potter, 1998, p. 60). In fact, every drug—from legal drugs such as aspirin to illegal drugs such as cocaine—is potentially harmful.

The effects of any drug depend on numerous factors, including the type of drug, its potency and quantity, the method in which it is ingested, the setting in which it is ingested, the frequency of use, the mood of the user, and the user's biological and psychological makeup (Gaines and Kraska, 1997; Lyman and Potter, 1998; Robinson and Scherlen, 2007). Effects of particular types of drugs will be discussed later.

Keep in mind the clear distinction between **drug use** and **drug abuse**. Drug use is generally understood as any consumption of a drug, including recreational or occasional use. Remember President Bill Clinton explaining, as a candidate in 1992, that he had tried marijuana in college, didn't inhale it, and didn't like it? That's drug use, as is the alleged cocaine use of President George W. Bush (the second).

Drug abuse implies a problematic level of use, or overuse, of drugs. Lyman and Potter (1998, p. 60) define drug abuse as "illicit drug use that results in social, economic, psychological or legal problems for the drug user." They also note that the Bureau of Justice Statistics defines drug abuse as "the use of prescription-type psychotherapeutic drugs for nonmedical purposes or the use of illegal drugs."

Drug use, even of illegal substances, is not the same as drug abuse. It is possible to use illegal drugs without abusing them, although this is a lesson that seems to be lost on U.S. criminal justice agencies. We treat drug use as a crime rather than a recreational habit and do not recognize that most people who use drugs do not abuse them. In fact, most drug-related arrests are for simple possession, not for manufacturing, distributing, or selling drugs (Beckett and Sasson, 2000, p. 172).

Drug abuse varies by individual: "Abuse occurs when the use of the drug—whether aspirin, beer, caffeine, cigarettes, marijuana, diet pills, or heroin—becomes a psychological, social, or physical problem for the user" (Gaines and Kraska, 1997, p. 6). Only a small portion of drug users, somewhere between 7% and 20% depending on the type of drug in question, actually become drug abusers (Kraska, 1990). The Office of National Drug Control Policy (ONDCP) has stated the risk of abuse at between 10% and 33% (Robinson and Scherlen, 2007). In fact, depending on one's definition of a drug, we all use drugs as part of our everyday lives: "Some form of drug use is an everyday part of living for most Americans" (Lyman and Potter, 1998, p. 11).

Drugs are useful because they can alter our moods, create feelings of pleasure, stimulate brain activity, or aid in sedation or enhanced physical and psychological performance (Lyman and Potter, 1998). Some suggest that drug use is innate or natural, as much as the need for food or sex. Weil (1998, p. 4) writes, "The use of drugs to alter consciousness is nothing new. It has been a feature of human life in all places on the earth and in all ages of history." Hamid (1998, p. vii) suggests that "the human use of psychoactive drugs is both primordial and nearly universal. In almost every human culture in every age of history, the use of one or more psychoactive drugs was featured prominently in the contexts of religion, ritual, health care, divination, celebration (including the arts, music, and theater), recreation, and cuisine." People use drugs in certain rituals in groups, such as during "Happy Hour" or at parties with friends. People may use drugs to relieve boredom (Glassner and Loughlin, 1987), to alter their moods, to inspire creativity, and sometimes for medicinal and religious purposes. College students drink large amounts of alcohol during certain nights of the week, on weekends, at parties, tailgating before and after sporting events, and during "spring break."

For numerous reasons, then, people use drugs without experiencing significant problems associated with drug abuse. This does not mean that drug use should be promoted or supported by government, but it does raise the question of why we spend so many physical and financial resources fighting something that is considered normal by most people at some point in their lives, is relatively harmless, and is not likely to be stopped through criminal justice mechanisms. I would argue that drug abuse (which is only a small portion of all drug use) should be of concern to our government because of its possible outcomes, regardless of whether the drug being abused is legal or not.

Lyman and Potter (1998, p. 62) list several outcomes of drug abuse:

- **Physical dependence:** The user becomes increasingly tolerant of a drug's effects, so that increased amounts of the drug are needed to prevent withdrawal symptoms.
- **Psychological dependence:** The user develops a craving for or compulsive need to use drugs because they provide him or her with a feeling of well-being and satisfaction.
- **Tolerance:** The user who continues regular use of a drug must administer progressively larger doses to attain the desired effect, thereby reinforcing the compulsive behavior known as drug dependence.
- **Withdrawal:** The user experiences a physical reaction when deprived of an addictive drug, characterized by increased excitability of the bodily functions that have been depressed by the drug's habitual use.

These outcomes suggest that drug abuse is maladaptive and thus potentially dangerous. Still, whether the U.S. government should wage a war on drug abuse is debatable, given that drug abuse is more likely to respond to medical treatment. It is clear, however, that our investment in stopping simple drug use is costing us far more than it is returning. Kappeler and Potter (2004) conclude that illicit drug-related deaths are infrequent and that they are actually more likely to occur because of the effects of drug laws.

TYPES OF DRUGS

Drugs can be categorized according to their principal effects on brain function and hence on human behavior. The major general categories of drugs include **stimulants, depressants, hallucinogens**, and **narcotics/opiates** (Inciardi and McElrath, 1998; Liska, 2000). Lyman and Potter (1998) also add **inhalants** (drugs that are drawn into the body by breathing in) as a separate category because of their use among young people in particular. Inciardi and McElrath (1998) add **analgesics** (painkillers), **sedatives** (which produce calm and relaxation), and **hypnotics** (depressants that produce sleep).

As defined by Inciardi and McElrath (1998, pp. xii–xiii), these substances are as follows.

- *Stimulants:* Drugs that stimulate the central nervous system (CNS) and increase the activity of the brain and spinal cord.
- *Depressants:* Drugs that act to lessen the activity of the CNS, diminishing or stopping vital functions.
- *Hallucinogens:* Drugs that act on the CNS to produce mood and perceptual changes varying from sensory illusions to hallucinations.
- *Narcotics:* A category of illegal drugs including opium and opium derivatives, as well as their synthetic versions.

Box 11-1 gives some examples of drugs that fall into each category. Note that some of the substances within each category are legal; others are illegal. Thus, the nature of the drug does not determine its legal status.

As you might guess, stimulants stimulate brain activity. The most common stimulants in the United States are legal—caffeine (in coffee) and nicotine (in cigarettes). These drugs make people feel stronger, alert, decisive, and even exhilarated. Depressants, as you also might guess, depress brain activity. Users become sluggish, have impaired judgment and slurred speech, and suffer from loss of motor coordination. Hallucinogens distort perceptions of reality through the auditory (hearing), tactile (touch), and visual (sight) systems. Narcotics, which produce feelings of euphoria in users, can be accompanied by undesirable effects including nausea, vomiting, drowsiness, apathy, respiratory depression, loss of motor coordination, and slurred speech.

Another way of categorizing drugs is by the government classification system. The Controlled Substances Act (CSA), Title II of the Comprehensive Drug Abuse Prevention and Control Act of 1970, consolidated many laws regulating the manufacture and distribution of narcotics, stimulants, depressants, hallucinogens, steroids, and chemicals used in the illicit production of controlled substances. This law classified drugs into the following five categories.

BOX 11-1

EXAMPLES OF MAJOR DRUGS

- *Stimulants:* Caffeine, nicotine, cocaine, amphetamines, methamphetamine, Ecstasy
- *Depressants:* Alcohol, barbiturates, gamma hydroxy butyrate (GHB), Rohypnol

- *Hallucinogens:* Marijuana, lysergic acid diethylamide (LSD), phencyclidine (PCP), psilocybin mushrooms, peyote cactus, Ecstasy, ketamine
- *Narcotics:* Opium, heroin

- *Schedule I:*   These drugs or other substances have a high potential for abuse and have no currently accepted medical use in treatment in the United States. There is a lack of acceptance for use of the drug or other substance under medical supervision. Examples include heroin, LSD, marijuana, and methaqualone.
- *Schedule II:*   The drug or other substance has a high potential for abuse but has a currently accepted medical use in treatment in the United States or a currently accepted medical use with severe restrictions. Abuse of the drug or other substance may lead to severe psychological or physical dependence. Examples include morphine, PCP, cocaine, methadone, and methamphetamine.
- *Schedule III:*   The drug has less potential for abuse than the substances in Schedules I and II and has a currently accepted medical use in treatment in the United States. Abuse of the drug or other substance may lead to moderate or low physical dependence or high psychological dependence. Examples include anabolic steroids, codeine and hydrocodone with aspirin or Tylenol, and some barbiturates.
- *Schedule IV:*   The drug has a lower potential for abuse than the substances in Schedule III and has a currently accepted medical use in treatment in the United States. Abuse of the drug or other substance may lead to limited physical dependence or psychological dependence relative to the drugs or other substances in Schedule III. Examples include Darvon, Talwin, Equanil, Valium, and Xanax.
- *Schedule V:*   The drug or other substance has a low potential for abuse relative to the drugs or other substances in Schedule IV and has a currently accepted medical use in treatment in the United States. Abuse of the drug or other substances may lead to limited physical dependence or psychological dependence relative to the drugs or other substances in Schedule IV. Over-the-counter cough medicines with codeine are classified in Schedule V.

This classification system is useful for reference later in the chapter when we examine which drugs are targeted by criminal justice agencies. The higher the level of a drug (nearer to Schedule I), the more vigorously it is pursued, regardless of whether it is being used for recreational purposes or is being abused.

Recently, scientists have proposed a new classification system for twenty different drugs, one based not on history or politics but instead on actual evidence related to the degree of nine different categories of social and physical harms caused by drugs, as well as their risk for dependence. In this proposed system, hard drugs like heroin and cocaine would be ranked at the top of the system, while alcohol and tobacco would be ranked fifth and ninth, respectively. Marijuana ranks at number eleven, followed by LSD at number fourteen and Ecstasy at number eighteen (Nutt and Blakemore, 2007). This new classification system, if ever adopted by our government, would significantly change America's drug war.

EXTENT OF DRUG USE IN THE UNITED STATES

Table 11-2 lists several sources of drug use data available in the United States. The most important sources of drug use data include (1) the *National Survey on Drug Use and Health* (NSDUH), formerly the National Household Survey on Drug Abuse,

TABLE 11-2	Sources of Data on Drug Use

1. National Survey of Drug Use and Health (NSDUH)
   By Substance Abuse and Mental Health Services Administration (SAMHSA), yearly since 1976
   Survey of people age 12 years and older
2. Monitoring the Future (MTF) Survey
   By National Institute on Drug Abuse (NIDA), yearly since 1972
   Survey of high school students in 8th, 10th, and 12th grades
3. Survey of Health Related Behavior Among Military Personnel
   By Department of Defense, every three years since 1980
   Survey of military personnel
4. Drug Abuse Warning Network (DAWN)
   By National Institute on Drug Abuse (NIDA), yearly since 1972
   Mentions of drug use by patients in emergency rooms
5. Survey of Inmates in State Correctional Facilities
   By Bureau of Justice Statistics (BJS), every five years since 1974
   Survey of inmates
6. Arrestee Drug Abuse Monitoring (ADAM)
   By National Institute on Justice (NIJ), yearly since 1997
   Survey and drug testing of arrestees in 34 cities

conducted by the Substance Abuse and Mental Health Services Administration (SAMHSA), which is a survey of people age 12 years and older; (2) the *Monitoring the Future Survey* (MTF), conducted by the National Institute on Drug Abuse (NIDA), which is a survey of high school students in 8th, 10th, 12th grades; and (3) the *Drug Abuse Warning Network* (DAWN), conducted by the National Institute on Drug Abuse (NIDA), which collects total mentions of drug use by patients in emergency rooms. These sources of drug use data give us a pretty good picture of drug use in the United States.

Arrestee Drug Abuse Monitoring (ADAM), conducted by the National Institute on Justice (NIJ), is a survey on drug testing of arrestees in 34 cities. The *Survey of Inmates in State Correctional Facilities,* conducted by the Bureau of Justice Statistics (BJS) every 5 years, is a survey of inmates. The *Survey of Health Related Behavior Among Military Personnel,* conducted by the Department of Defense every 3 years, is a survey of military personnel. These sources allow us to see drug use trends in the military and among our nation's arrestees and inmates.

Figure 11-3 shows how many people use each type of drug in the United States. The most commonly used drugs are legal substances such as caffeine, nicotine, and alcohol. More than 100 million Americans use caffeine (in the form of coffee) and consume alcohol, meaning that about half of the U.S. adult population consumes caffeine in coffee and drinks alcohol. Another 10 million people under the age of 21 years admit to drinking alcohol. There were almost 70 million users of nicotine (through some form of tobacco use).

The 2005 NSDUH found that 19.7 million Americans aged 12 or older, or 8.1% of the U.S. population, were current (previous month) illicit drug users. Further, 46.1% admitted to having tried an illicit drug at least once in their lives. Marijuana was the

FIGURE 11-3   Extent of Drug Use in the United States (2005)

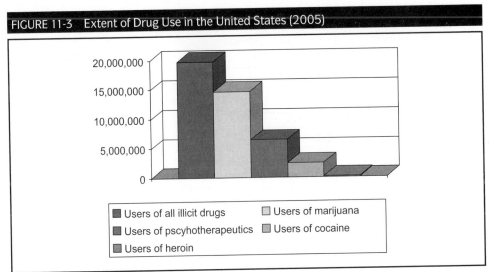

- Users of all illicit drugs
- Users of marijuana
- Users of pscyhotherapeutics
- Users of cocaine
- Users of heroin

Source: U.S. Department of Health and Human Services. Office of Applied Statistics. 2005 National Survey on Drug Use and Health. Available at http://oas.samhsa.gov/nsduh/2k5nsduh/2k5Results.htm#TOC.

most commonly used illicit drug (14.6 million previous-month users, or 6% of the population), followed by nonmedical use of prescription drugs. There were 6.4 million current users (or 2.6% of the U.S. population) who used prescription-type psychotherapeutic drugs nonmedically. Of these, 4.7 million used pain relievers, 1.8 million used tranquilizers, 1.1 million used stimulants, and 272,000 used sedatives. There were also about 2.4 million current cocaine users (1% of the population). Hallucinogens were used by 1.1 million persons (0.4% of the population), including 502,000 (0.2% of the population) who had used Ecstasy.

Are legal drugs more widely used by Americans because they are less harmful than those that are currently illegal, such as marijuana, cocaine, and heroin? Actually, no. I return to this issue later in this chapter.

Figure 11-4 shows drug use trends in the United States according to NSDUH. The figure illustrates that drug use trends are largely unchanged since ONDCP was created to lead the drug war. That is, drug use among adults has not declined since the founding of ONDCP in 1988. ONDCP goes to great lengths to ignore this fact, as I show in Issue in Depth at the end of this chapter.

Figure 11-5 illustrates drug use trends among the nation's youth according to the MTF. The figure shows that while some forms of drug use have declined recently among young people, others have increased. Further, youth drug use is higher today than when ONDCP was created.

Figure 11-6 illustrates the percentage of high school seniors who say that they can easily or very easily obtain drugs. The figure shows that the availability of most illicit drugs is unchanged since the founding of ONDCP.

Figure 11-7 depicts emergency room mentions of drug use in the United States according to DAWN. Figure 11-8 shows deaths attributable to illicit drugs in the United States. These figures show that more people are dying and getting ill each year from illicit drug use.

FIGURE 11-4   Trends in Drug Use (NSDUH)

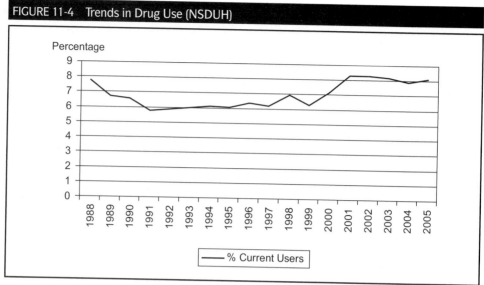

Source: Sourcebook of Criminal Justice Statistics (2006).

FIGURE 11-5   Trends in Drug Use (MTF)

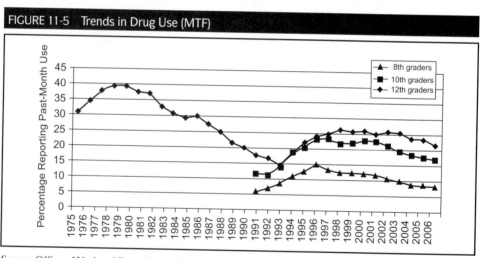

Source: Office of National Drug Control Policy (2007). National Drug Control Strategy, p. 2.

Examining these figures allows us to return to some of the key questions to assess the effectiveness of the drug war:

- First, is drug use down? No. According to NSDUH data, there is virtually no change among adults in the percentage of previous-month drug users in the United States since the founding of ONDCP. There is virtually no change in the number of previous-month marijuana or heroin users in the United States during

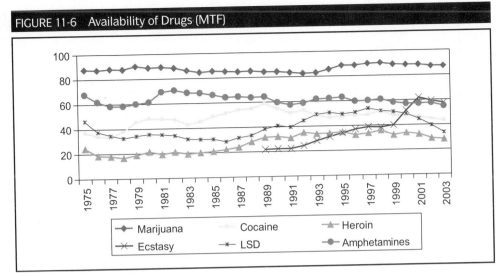

FIGURE 11-6   Availability of Drugs (MTF)

Source: Monitoring the Future (2003).

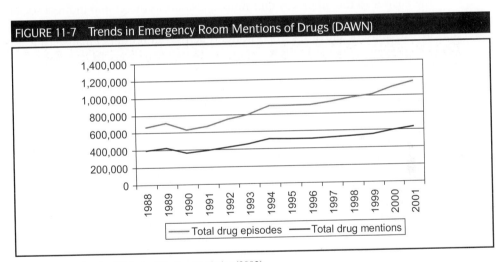

FIGURE 11-7   Trends in Emergency Room Mentions of Drugs (DAWN)

Source: Sourcebook of Criminal Justice Statistics (2003).

this time, nor is there any significant change in the number of previous-month cocaine users in the United States. According to MTF data, previous-month drug use among high school students has increased since the founding of ONDCP. New drug initiates have increased for many drugs, including prescription drugs.

- Second, are drug users more healthy? No. Mentions of drug use in emergency rooms have increased in the United States since ONDCP's founding. And drug-related deaths have increased in the United States, as well.
- Third, are drugs less available? No. The war on drugs has not made illegal drugs hard to obtain for young people in the United States.

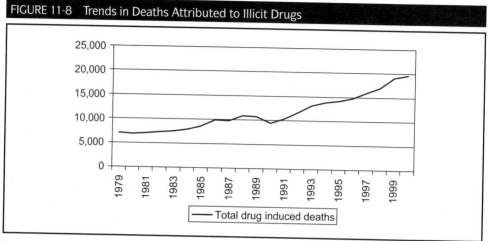

FIGURE 11-8   Trends in Deaths Attributed to Illicit Drugs

Source: Sourcebook on Criminal Justice Statistics (2003).

The answer to the other key questions is also no, as direct and indirect social costs of drug abuse have increased every year through the 1990s, treatment is no more available to drug abusers, and drugs still flow freely across our borders. Finally, crime is down, yet as you saw in Chapter 4, this is not due to the war on drugs. In fact, a study reports that drug offenders sentenced to prison have higher rates of recidivism than those sentenced to probation, and tend to re-offend more quickly (Spohn and Halleran, 2002). Thus, it appears that the drug war has mostly failed to meet its goals.

HARMS ASSOCIATED WITH DRUGS

Every drug, legal or illegal, is at least potentially harmful. In the section that follows, I examine the relative harms of nicotine (found in tobacco) and tetrahydrocannabinol or THC (found in marijuana), two drugs that are consumed through smoking. Box 11-2 contains the U.S. government's "official line" on the dangers of marijuana versus those of cigarettes. Which sounds worse to you?

Nicotine is a drug. It is the substance in tobacco that keeps smokers smoking. Since nearly one-fourth of all Americans smoke, nicotine is the most prevalent psychoactive drug—that is, affecting the mind and mental processes—used in the United States. Nicotine is the second most abused drug in the United States, behind alcohol. This is attributable to many factors, including the legal status of the drug, the numerous social contexts in which smoking nicotine is acceptable and even expected, and the advertising campaigns of the tobacco industry. Given the highly addictive nature of nicotine, tobacco use is thus considered a legal form of substance abuse. According to the Boston University Medical Center, each cigarette delivers about 6 to 8 milligrams of nicotine. It was recently discovered that major tobacco companies increased nicotine levels in cigarettes.

The most likely future nicotine addicts are teens targeted by tobacco industry advertisers. Children are about twice as likely as adults to smoke the three most advertised

BOX 11-2

MARIJUANA VERSUS CIGARETTES

SHORT-TERM EFFECTS OF USING MARIJUANA

- Sleepiness
- Difficulty keeping track of time, impaired or reduced short-term memory
- Reduced ability to perform tasks requiring concentration and coordination, such as driving a car
- Increased heart rate
- Potential cardiac dangers for those with preexisting heart disease
- Bloodshot eyes
- Dry mouth and throat
- Decreased social inhibitions
- Paranoia, hallucinations

LONG-TERM EFFECTS OF USING MARIJUANA

- Enhanced cancer risk
- Decrease in testosterone levels for men; also lower sperm counts and difficulty having children
- Increase in testosterone levels for women; also increased risk of infertility
- Diminished or extinguished sexual pleasure

- Psychological dependence, requiring more of the drug to get the same effect

RISKS ASSOCIATED WITH SMOKING CIGARETTES

- Diminished or extinguished sense of smell and taste
- Frequent colds
- Smoker's cough
- Gastric ulcers
- Chronic bronchitis
- Increase in heart rate and blood pressure
- Premature and more abundant face wrinkles
- Emphysema
- Heart disease
- Stroke
- Cancer of the mouth, larynx, pharynx, esophagus, lungs, pancreas, cervix, uterus, and bladder
- Cigarette smoking is perhaps the most devastating preventable cause of disease and premature death.
- Smoking is particularly dangerous for teens because their bodies are still developing and changing and the 4,000 chemicals (including 200 known poisons) in cigarette smoke can adversely affect this process.

SOURCE: Substance Abuse and Mental Health Services Administration, an agency of the U.S. Department of Health and Human Services (2000).

brands. According to a recent study, tobacco advertising has increased every year since 1998, the year big tobacco companies signed an agreement with Congress to stop target-ing children. Nicotine addiction occurs when a person has a compulsive need for nicotine, as discussed earlier. Smokers thus feel a persistent craving for a cigarette, which is, in essence, what the Food and Drug Administration calls "a delivery system for an addictive drug" (Centers for Disease Control and Prevention, 1994).

The large majority of smokers begin smoking before the age of 18 (Robinson, 1998). Every day, thousands of new young people begin to smoke. Teenagers see smoking as "cool" or "sexy," images created by the tobacco industry and reinforced by peers in social situations. The amount of nicotine used and the frequency of use start small but increase over time as the user becomes addicted to nicotine. People continue to use nicotine even after they learn of the health risks associated with smoking. Smokers claim they cannot quit because they experience irritability, lowered concentration, weight gain, cravings for nicotine, and even tremors. These effects suggest nicotine is being used to avoid physical withdrawal symptoms (Boston University Medical Center, 2000).

Nicotine is smoked because it is most rapidly absorbed into the body in this way. About 90% is absorbed into the lungs, oral cavity, and gastrointestinal system. Nicotine particles act on every cell and thus on every organ of a user's body, including the heart, kidneys, skin, and brain. According to the Boston University Medical Center, nicotine increases salivation, stomach acid and motility, heart rate, and blood pressure, and reduces circulation in the blood. It also can lead to impotence in as little as 10 years of prolonged use.

Nicotine can be used more safely through alternative methods of ingestion, for example, through an inhaler. Tobacco companies developed such a mechanism, similar to that used by asthmatics, but ultimately rejected it because it was inconsistent with their portrayals of cigarettes as harmless and nonaddictive products (Glantz et al., 1996).

When inhaled by smoking, nicotine becomes a very dangerous drug. For example, cigarettes contain more than 70 known carcinogens as well as thousands of other harmful chemicals. Cigarettes include various amounts of the following materials: acetic acid (a caustic solvent found in vinegar), acetone (a poisonous solvent found in nail polish removal), acrolein (an aquatic herbicide), ammonia (a cleaning agent and poisonous gas), aniline (an industrial solvent), butane (cigarette lighter fluid), cadmium (as in rechargeable batteries), carbon dioxide (as in global warming), carbon monoxide (as in auto exhaust), catechol (a tanning and dyeing agent), DDT/deildrin (insecticides), ethanol (alcohol), formaldehyde (the fluid used to embalm bodies), formic acid (a caustic solvent), glycolic acid (a metal cleaning agent), hexamine (barbecue lighter), hydrazine (a rocket fuel chemical), hydrogen cyanide (as in rat poison and the poison used in the gas chamber), hydroquinone (a photographic developing agent), lactic acid (a caustic solvent), methane (as in swamp gas), methyl chloride (a poisonous refrigerant), methylamine (a tanning agent), nicotine (an addictive drug and insecticide), methylpyridine (an insecticide solvent), napthalene (from mothballs), nitrobenzene (a gasoline additive), nitrous oxide phenols (a disinfectant), phenol (a toilet disinfectant), polonium-210 (a radioactive element), pyridine (a poisonous solvent), quinoline (a specimen preservative), stearic acid (candle wax), succinic acid (an agent in lacquer manufacturing), toluene (an industrial solvent in explosives), vinyl chloride (used to make PVC), and zinc (an anticorrosion coating for metals).

Not surprisingly, then, smoking kills about 25 times as many people as murder each year through lung diseases such as cancer, emphysema, chronic mucus secretion and air flow blocks, bronchitis, and respiratory and bacterial infections. It also causes heart disease because of cholesterol buildup, which restricts blood flow (the same thing that causes impotence). Smoking causes stiffness in the artery walls, high blood pressure, blood clots, and oxygen demand in muscles (Boston University Medical Center, 2000).

Lung cancer is not the only type of cancer caused by smoking, which is also a major cause of cancer of the lips, tongue, salivary glands, mouth, larynx, esophagus, stomach, bladder, renal pelvis, uterine cervix, and pancreas. Secondhand smoke also kills thousands (Robinson, 1998), mainly because it contains dozens of dangerous chemicals (Centers for Disease Control and Prevention, 1997). Thus, nonsmokers (such as children of smokers) suffer chronic ear infections, coughing because of phlegm buildup, and acute respiratory illnesses such as bronchitis and pneumonia.

What about marijuana? Does this illegal substance cause the same problems as tobacco, which is legal? Virtually every expert who has studied this issue answers a resounding "no."

Let us start by dispelling some myths about marijuana, which come from Zimmer and Morgan's (1997) book, *Marijuana Myths, Marijuana Facts*:

- Marijuana is relatively harmless. The British medical journal *Lancet* concluded in 1995 that "the smoking of cannabis, even long term, is not harmful to health."
- Most people who smoke marijuana do not smoke it regularly. Only about 1% of users smoke the drug daily.
- Marijuana does not lead to physical dependence or addiction.
- Smoking marijuana does not lead to use of hard drugs (the so-called gateway drug hypothesis). Because marijuana is the most popular illegal drug in the United States, the majority of people who use other drugs have also used marijuana at one time. Most marijuana users, however, never use another illicit drug, and, in fact, virtually every illicit drug user started with tobacco and alcohol.
- Marijuana offenders are not dangerous. The effects of marijuana use are relatively mild. About 80% of those arrested for marijuana in any given year are arrested for mere possession of the drug, not for growing or selling it.

In 1988, Francis Young, a judge affiliated with the DEA, reached the following conclusions about marijuana (in Kappeler et al., 2000, p. 152):

- Among the 70 million Americans who have used marijuana, there has never been a reported overdose.
- Marijuana in its natural form is one of the safest therapeutically active substances known to humans.
- In strict medical terms, marijuana is far safer than many foods we commonly consume.

Still, the THC in marijuana is a drug and it is harmful. It is the substance in marijuana that is addictive. The use of marijuana as a psychoactive drug is far less prevalent than nicotine use, for many reasons: Marijuana is illegal; there are fewer social contexts in which smoking marijuana is as acceptable as smoking cigarettes, and it is not advertised by any corporate industry.

Smoking marijuana is typically a behavior associated with young people. Whereas smoking tobacco increases over time as the user becomes addicted to nicotine, smoking marijuana is consistently limited to relatively small amounts. Effects of marijuana begin immediately upon ingesting the substance into the body, so there is no need to smoke greater and greater amounts over time. As explained by the National Institutes of Health (NIH) (1997):

> THC is quite potent when compared to most other psychoactive drugs. An intravenous (IV) dose of only a milligram or two can produce profound mental and physiologic effects. Large doses of THC delivered by marijuana or administered in the pure form can produce mental and perceptual effects similar to drugs usually termed hallucinogens. . . . However, the way marijuana is used in the United States does not commonly lead to such profound mental effects.

THC is smoked because it is more rapidly absorbed into the body in this way, much like nicotine. THC particles are absorbed within seconds and delivered to the human brain immediately, and they also act on every cell and thus on every organ of a user's body, including the heart, kidneys, skin, and brain.

Marijuana contains over 400 chemicals, including THC and other cannabinoids, which are the psychoactive chemicals in the plant. Yet it has "remarkably low lethal toxicity" (NIH, 1997). Whereas one in three smokers of cigarettes will die from a smoking-related illness, marijuana use rarely kills anyone (less than one person a year dies from marijuana in the United States). The effects of marijuana on the user are numerous, including the following:

> [A] sense of well-being (often termed euphoria or high); feelings of relaxation; altered perception of time and distance; intensified sensory experiences; laughter; talkativeness; and increased sociability when taken in a social setting; impaired memory for recent events; difficulty concentrating; dreamlike states; impaired motor coordination; impaired driving and other psychomotor skills; slowed reaction time; impaired goal-directed mental activity; and altered peripheral vision are common associated effects. (Adams and Martin, 1996; Fehr and Kalant, 1983; Hollister, 1988; cited in NIH, 1997)

Other adverse effects can include anxiety, panic, depression, delusions, and hallucinations (Adams and Martin, 1996; Fehr and Kalant, 1983; Hollister, 1988). Such effects usually present themselves rapidly and last only 2 to 3 hours. Although marijuana use can heighten the effects of mental illnesses such as schizophrenia and bipolar affective disorder, it is not a significant cause of these illnesses, which are thought to be biologically based (Raine, 1993). Use of the drug can, however, lead to temporary lessening of motivation and impaired educational performance (Pope and Yurgelun-Todd, 1996).

The physical effects of smoking marijuana include temporary increases in heart rate and blood pressure, as well as lowered body temperature, which has not "presented any health problems for healthy and relatively young users" (NIH, 1997). However, chronic use can lead to bronchitis, pharyngitis, and increased frequency of pulmonary and respiratory illnesses because of suppressed antibody formation and resistance to infection from bacterial and viral infections. Still, "[c]onclusive evidence for increased malignancy, or enhanced acquisition of HIV, or the development of AIDS, has not been associated with marijuana use" (NIH, 1997).

From this comparison, we can confidently conclude the following:

- Cigarettes contain nicotine, a physically addictive drug that produces dependence and withdrawal symptoms when ceased.
- Smoking cigarettes is a highly deadly form of drug use.
- Marijuana contains THC and other cannabinoids, which are psychologically addictive drugs that do not cause dependence or physical withdrawal symptoms when ceased.
- Smoking marijuana is a potentially harmful form of drug use.
- Smoking cigarettes is far more dangerous than smoking marijuana.

Nevertheless, smoking cigarettes is generally legal, while smoking marijuana is generally illegal. Even though there are only one-sixth as many marijuana users as nicotine users, smoking kills about 430,000 people each year, and marijuana kills about one. Alcohol kills approximately 110,000 people per year. The death rate for tobacco users in any given year (430,000 deaths per year divided by 67 million users) is 0.66%, meaning in any given year, 1 in 152 tobacco users will die from the drug. The death rate for alcohol (110,000 deaths per year divided by 109 million users) is 0.1%, meaning 1 in 990 alcohol users will die from the drug. The death rate for illicit drugs (26,000 deaths divided by 19.1 million users) is 0.14%, meaning 1 in 714 illicit drug users will die from the drugs. Keep in mind that most of those who die from illegal drugs die from prescription drug abuse. This means at the very least, tobacco use is 3.7 times more deadly than illicit drug use, yet tobacco is legal. The death rates for illicit drugs and alcohol are nearly identical, yet alcohol is legal.

Government-funded studies in the 1970s, as summarized by Hamid (1998, pp. 47–51), were far more pessimistic and alarmist in their conclusions with regard to marijuana. These studies found evidence of what Hamid calls amotivational syndrome, cannabis psychosis, mental and physical deterioration, brain damage, and escalation to harder drugs. Evidence from more recent studies shows that these effects were, at best, grossly overstated. A new study, the largest of its kind, found that smoking marijuana (even regularly and heavily) was not found to lead to lung, head, or neck cancer (Hashibe et al., 2007). Additionally, since marijuana contains THC, smoking marijuana and ingesting the substance may kill aging cells and keep them from developing into cancer.

Use and abuse of other illicit drugs include adverse health consequences (Jensen and Gerber, 1998; Liska, 2000). In 2005, for example, nearly 1.5 million people visited emergency rooms and mentioned some form of drug use, including 448,481 cocaine visits; 242,200 marijuana visits; 164,572 heroin visits, and 138,950 stimulants visits (Department of Health and Human Services, 2007). Long-term health consequences of opiates include hypotension, allergies, and insomnia; overdose can cause fatal convulsions and seizures. Cocaine's adverse effects include death via seizures and strokes (Fishbein and Pease, 1996). Most deaths from cocaine are caused by smoking the drug in the form of crack (Goode, 1999); these deaths are not attributable to the dangers of cocaine itself but, rather, to the fact that there are fewer quality controls on street-level crack than on powder cocaine.

Even relatively harmless drugs such as marijuana produce smoke that is carcinogenic, and chronic smokers of marijuana suffer from "toxic effects on several organs, including the brain, heart [and] lungs" (Fishbein and Pease, 1996, p. 310). Of course, these outcomes are not as severe as those suffered by users of legal drugs such as tobacco and alcohol. Using the harmfulness of illegal drugs to justify their illegal status while simultaneously ignoring the harms of these legal drugs is hypocritical at best.

Glaser (1997, p. 117) describes the hypocrisy of the nation's drug war when he writes: "The law prohibits marijuana, cocaine, and the opiates but allows our intake of items that can be equally disabling, including whiskey, wine, and beer, as well as tranquilizers, sedatives, analgesics, stimulants, and antidepressants sold in drug stores, some without prescription." At the same time, "[r]elatively affluent users (and abusers) of illicit drugs are able to engage in their habits with impunity. They are likely to be able to insulate themselves from criminal justice activity. If they are in need of medical assistance, they are likely to arrange for private care and are likely to have health insurance that covers such treatment." By contrast, poor people who live in urban areas are the most likely to suffer from the horrible side effects of illegal drugs, are most likely to be discovered because of their limited access to medical care, and are most likely to suffer whatever violent crime does result from drug use and abuse (p. 199).

LEGAL STATUS OF EACH DRUG: WHY ARE THE MOST HARMFUL DRUGS LEGAL WHILE SOME RELATIVELY HARMLESS DRUGS ARE ILLEGAL?

Given that illegal drugs (such as marijuana) are typically less dangerous than legal drugs (such as tobacco), why are these drugs illegal? One primary reason is the fear that illegal drug use is associated with an increased risk for criminality.

According to Nuro, Kinlock, and Hanlon (1998, p. 221), "Evidence of criminal activity among narcotics users is longstanding and abundant; however, it is apparent that relationships among the important variables involved are much more complex than were initially believed." These authors suggest that prevalence and diversity of criminality among narcotics users are high, but that most crime committed by drug users is for the purpose of supporting drug use. Higher levels of drug use, then, tend to be associated with higher involvement in criminality. For heavy users of drugs and persistent criminals, initiation into both criminality and drug use begins at early ages (p. 225).

The smallest portion of criminality among drug users is violent crime (p. 227), and most crime is petty, nonviolent crime (Goldstein, 1998, p. 246), but amounts and types of crimes vary by individual (Nuro, Kinlock, and Hanlon, 1998, p. 229). Drug research thus supports the claims of legalization proponents that alternative approaches to the drug war would reduce overall criminality in the United States (Robinson and Scherlen, 2007).

The drugs most relevant for a psychopharmacological violence effect are alcohol, stimulants, barbiturates, and PCP (e.g., see Asnis and Smith, 1978; d'Orban, 1976; Ellingswood, 1971; Feldman, Agar, and Beschner, 1979; Gerson and Preston, 1979; Glaser, 1974; Tinklenberg, 1973; Virkunnen, 1974). The suspected and sometimes asserted link between opiates and marijuana and violence has been discredited (e.g., see Finestone, 1967; Greenberg and Adler, 1974; Inciardi and Chambers, 1972; Kozel,

Dupont, and Brown, 1972; Kramer, 1976; Schatzman, 1975). In fact, these drugs may actually "ameliorate violent tendencies. In such cases, persons who are prone to acting violently may engage in self-medication, in order to control their violent tendencies" (Goldstein, 1998, p. 245). Heroin users will refrain from committing violent crimes to acquire money to buy their drug if alternatives exist (e.g., see Cushman, 1974; Goldstein and Duchaine, 1980; Goldstein, 1979; Gould, 1974; Johnson et al., 1985; Preble and Casey, 1969; Swezey, 1973).

There is obviously violence in the drug business, so what causes it? According to Reuter (1998, p. 315), "[t]he violence, overdoses, and massive illegal incomes that are such a prominent part of our current concerns with psychoactive drugs are not consequences of the nature of the drugs themselves, but rather of the conditions of use that society has created." In other words, violence typically does not stem from drug use per se but, rather, from the fact that drug use is illegal and violence is required to protect business interests of drug dealers. This is systemic violence rather than psychopharmacological violence.

James Inciardi, a notable expert on the drug war, agrees. In his book, *The War on Drugs III* (2002, p. 193), he writes, "The economic compulsive model of violence best fits the aggressive behavior of contemporary heroin, cocaine, and crack users." This means that many, if not most, violent crimes committed by users of these drugs are aimed at obtaining resources to buy their drugs, rather than by the influence of the drugs on their brains. In fact, Inciardi concludes that there is more evidence of a crime–drugs connection (drug use intensifies criminal careers) than a drugs–crime relationship (drug use produces crime).

In numerous drug scares throughout U.S. history, this fact has escaped the public. Each drug scare has centered on some type of illicit drug use. Beckett (1997, pp. 45–46) briefly outlines several of these, including the antiopium movement in California in the late 1870s, the temperance (antialcohol) movement of the Women's Christian Temperance Union (WCTU) in the 1890s, the cocaine scare of the post-Reconstruction South, the "killer weed" antimarijuana movement in the southwestern United States in the 1930s, and the crack cocaine scare of the 1980s. Each of these drug scares blamed all sorts of societal evils on "outsiders" (Becker, 1963) or on poor minority groups, from Chinese immigrants (opium smoking in the 1870s) to Mexicans (marijuana in the 1930s) to African Americans (cocaine and crack). As explained by Beckett and Sasson (1998, p. 37), crime and drug problems were typified as "'underclass' problems resulting from insufficient social control."

Traditionally, drug use becomes characterized as problematic only when it involves particular groups of people (Jensen and Gerber, 1998, p. 3). In essence, this serves as a form of "institutional racism" (p. 21). Drug use by targeted groups is characterized as a source of other societal problems (Reinarman, 1994), while institutional sources of poverty and crime are ignored. The nation's drug war meets the definition of **institutional discrimination** proposed by Walker, Spohn, and DeLone (2006), because race and class are not explicitly stated as valid factors for using criminal justice agencies selectively against drug offenders. Yet racial and ethnic disparities appear in criminal justice outcomes that result from the application of racially neutral factors. In the drug war, the racially neutral factor is the fallacious notion that "their drugs" are more harmful than "our drugs." In the case of crack versus powder cocaine, this spurious belief is built directly into the written criminal law.

Because such drug scares are focused on relatively powerless groups such as minorities, immigrants, and lower-class people, you may be wondering whether the drug scares are actually aimed at lowering drug use and abuse rates or whether their legislative intent is aimed at other outcomes. Recall from Chapter 2 the difference between intended goals and functions served by particular criminal justice policies (policies can serve functions without being intentional). By examining the role of the media in portraying drug scares, you may get a sense of the functions they serve for powerful members of society.

The Role of the Media in Drug Scares

As discussed in Chapter 5, the media, in what they portray and in what they choose not to portray, reinforce moral boundaries in society. At various times, the media have created **moral panics** focused on drug use. The crack cocaine scare is the most recent of those discussed earlier. As Potter and Kappeler write, "The media—particularly news magazines, television, and newspapers—and the state engaged in a frenzied attempt to create a moral panic in the form of a drug scare as a means of continuing and extending the 'War on Drugs' begun in the Reagan administration" (1998, p. 9). As noted by Merlo and Benekos (2000, p. 16), images and stories in the media (especially about crack cocaine) spread fear that drug use was a major source of the nation's problems, especially crime.

Claims by field sources from the Community Epidemiology Work Group (CEWG), established by the National Institute on Drug Abuse to provide community-level surveillance of drug abuse in 20 metropolitan areas, show the concern about crack cocaine in American inner cities. Box 11-3 contains some quotes from field sources in the early 1980s.

Public demand did not create this "war on drugs." Beckett (1997, pp. 55, 58) reports that in 1981 more Americans believed that reducing unemployment would be more effective in curbing drug use than cutting the drug supply. Only about 2% of Americans at that time felt that drug abuse was the nation's most important problem (also see Roberts, 1992). In fact, public concern over drugs increased only after President George Bush (the first) made the nationally televised speech mentioned at the beginning of this chapter. After Bush said on national television, "All of us agree that the gravest domestic threat facing our nation today is drugs" (Bertram et al., 1996, pp. 113–114), media coverage of problematic drug use increased, as did concern about drugs among Americans. Thus, public concern did not start the drug war.

Reinarman and Levine (1989a) outline this 1980s drug scare, in which all sorts of societal problems were blamed on crack cocaine. These authors argue that media portrayals of crack cocaine were highly inaccurate. The scare began in late 1985, when the *New York Times* ran a cover story announcing the arrival of crack in the city. In 1986, *Time* and *Newsweek* magazines ran five cover stories each on crack cocaine. *Newsweek* and *Time* called crack the largest issue of the year (Beckett, 1997). In the second half of 1986, NBC News featured 400 stories on the drug. In July 1986 alone, the three major networks ran 74 drug stories on their nightly newscasts (Potter and Kappeler, 1998). Drug-related stories in the *New York Times* increased from 43 in the second half of 1985 to 92 and 220 in the first and second halves of 1986 (Beckett, 1997), and thousands of stories about crack appeared in magazines and newspapers (Reinarman, 1995).

BOX 11-3

COMMUNITY EPIDEMIOLOGY WORK GROUP (CEWG) FIELD QUOTES ABOUT CRACK COCAINE

- Boston: "Cocaine is a massive problem."
- Miami: "Cocaine is more available than ever before."
- Newark: "Cocaine is gaining rapid popularity."
- New Orleans: "Cocaine appears to be dominating the drug scene."
- Philadelphia: "There is a significant increase in availability and use."
- Phoenix: "Large quantities are available through Miami; prices have dropped."
- Seattle: "Cocaine is the county's most important problem."
- Buffalo: "There has been a marked increase in cocaine use."
- Chicago: "Cocaine is the only drug to have shown consistently increasing patterns of abuse."
- Denver: "It's the major drug of abuse in the state."

- Detroit: "Cocaine use continues to increase."
- Los Angeles: "Cocaine use has reached epidemic levels."
- New York City: "Cocaine activity continues to increase."
- St. Louis: "Cocaine is readily available throughout the metropolitan area."
- Washington, DC: "Cocaine use continues to rise."
- Dallas: "Pushers are selling cocaine in capsules in African American lower income communities. Cuban cocaine traffickers were arrested."
- Newark: "African Americans are dealing large amounts of cocaine."

These quotes from field sources suggest that crack cocaine was becoming a significant problem for American cities. As a result, a war was launched to stop crack cocaine.

After the *New York Times* coverage, CBS produced a 2-hour show called *48 Hours on Crack Street,* and NBC followed with *Cocaine Country*. In April 1986, the National Institute on Drug Abuse (NIDA) released a report called "Cocaine: The Big Lie," and 13 public service announcements that aired between 1,500 and 2,500 times on 75 local networks. This was followed by 74 stories on crack cocaine on ABC, CBS, and NBC in July 1986 alone. In November 1986, approximately 1,000 stories appeared about crack in national magazines, where crack was called "the biggest story since Vietnam," a "plague," and a "national epidemic."

As media coverage of drugs increased, people were paying attention. Consumers of media information are more likely to recognize issues as the "most important problems" when they receive a lot of notable attention in the national news (Bennett, 1980; Iyengar and Kinder, 1987; Leff, Protess, and Brooks, 1986; McCombs and Shaw, 1972). Drug coverage in the media was more extensive in the 1980s than at other times. The CBS program *48 Hours on Crack Street* obtained the highest rating of any news show of this type in the early 1980s (Reinarman and Levine, 1989a, pp. 541–542).

Once the media and public were all stirred up, laws were passed aimed at toughening sentences for crack cocaine. For example, the *Anti-Drug Abuse Act of 1986* created the 100:1 disparity for crack and powder cocaine (5 grams of crack would mandate a 5-year prison sentence versus 500 grams of powder cocaine). Additionally, the *Anti-Drug Abuse Act of 1988* lengthened sentences for drug offenses and created the Office of National Drug Control Policy (ONDCP). The U.S. Sentencing Commission recommended to Congress that this disparity be eliminated, yet Congress rejected this (which was the first time Congress ever rejected the Commission).

The intense media coverage of crack cocaine is problematic because it was invented, inaccurate, and dishonest. News coverage did not reflect reality, as crack cocaine use was actually quite rare during this period (Beckett, 1994; Orcutt and Turner, 1993; Walker, 1998) and, according to research from NIDA, was in fact declining at this time. According to NIDA, most drug use peaks occurred between 1979 and 1982, except for cocaine, which peaked between 1982 and 1985 (Jensen and Gerber, 1998, p. 14). Media coverage of cocaine use increased in the late 1980s even after drug use had already begun to decline.

The crack war was dishonest and the media failed to report this. The war was aimed at getting tough on crime and maintaining the status quo approaches to fighting drugs. The public was not concerned about drugs until after the media coverage captured its attention. Jensen and Gerber (1998, p. 17) suggest that President Reagan's declaration of war against drugs in August 1986 created an "orgy" of media coverage of crack cocaine, and public opinion about the seriousness of the "drug problem" changed as a result. According to Clymer (1986), in mid-August 1986, drugs became the most important problem facing the nation in public opinion polls. By late August 1986, 86% of Americans said "fighting the drug problem" was "extremely important" (*U.S. News & World Report,* 1986).

This coverage of drugs in the media typified social problems as stemming from the pharmacological properties of drugs such as crack cocaine, when in reality most of the associated violence stemmed from volatile crack cocaine markets (Beckett and Sasson, 2000, p. 28). News stories were also generally inaccurate and/or misleading in the way they characterized addiction to crack cocaine as "instantaneous," as if everyone who tried crack would become addicted immediately (Reinarman, 1995). As a teenager in the 1980s, I recall, adults warned me that one-time use of crack cocaine would lead to inevitable addiction. Without personal experience to rely on, these adults were likely relying on information supplied by the media. In fact, very few of those who use cocaine will become addicted: Fewer than 3% of users will ever become problem users (Kappeler and Potter, 2004). Cocaine does not produce physical dependence as, say, tobacco does, and thus is not considered a physically addictive drug.

The addictive nature of nicotine in tobacco received relatively little if any attention in the 1980s (Reeves and Campbell, 1994), although for every cocaine-related death in that decade, there were 300 tobacco-related deaths and 100 alcohol-related deaths (Potter and Kappeler, 1998), facts that escaped widespread media coverage. Although there is much more media focus on tobacco these days, the negligent and reckless actions of tobacco companies were not discussed widely until the mid- and late 1990s.

Finally, the coverage of crack in the news did not accurately portray the racial composition of people involved in drugs. The Sentencing Project reports that about two out of every three crack users are Caucasians, even though in 1994, 84.5% of people convicted in federal courts for crack possession and 88.3% of those convicted for crack trafficking were African Americans.

Even though half of all television news stories about drugs show African Americans using or selling drugs (Reed, 1991), the majority of drug users are white; African Americans are not overrepresented among users (Walker, 1998). This does not imply that the media are racist in their coverage of drug issues but, rather, that the media, like most Americans, were duped by the focus of criminal justice agencies on particular types of drugs and drug users. Harrigan (2000, pp. 137–138) suggests that most Americans

> lead lives that are far removed from the pictures of their lives portrayed on television. They go to work regularly, pay most of their taxes, try to raise their children as best they can, are faithful to their spouses for years on end, do not steal from their employers, have no connection with drug traffickers or organized crime, and live from paycheck to paycheck without margin for economic setbacks.

Because these facts do not make for sensational "news," they are ignored. The stereotypical image of the poor person or the African American person as lazy or criminal results from such ignorance.

Beckett (1997) reviewed media depictions of drug-fighting strategies and found that two types of "frames" for drug issues were most often used. She calls these the "Get the Traffickers" and "Zero Tolerance" frames. Criminal justice policies aimed at reducing drug use do not necessarily have to reflect a "law and order" perspective (see Issue in Depth at the end of this chapter). Yet, according to Beckett, stories that depict drug raids and tough sentences for drug runners dominate the media. These depictions create and reinforce public support for get-tough measures and hence a "war on drugs," despite the tremendous harms that result.

The influence of drug policies on people's perceptions of drugs, crime, and the proper role of government in intervening in lives of drug users is an example of how "[p]olicy-making is a form of reality construction" (Brownstein, 1996, p. 59). Although criminal justice policy perhaps should be the primary source of information for policymakers (Barak, 1988; Brownstein, 1991; Burnstein and Goldstein, 1990), criminal justice policy today is neither rational nor orderly. Instead, it is driven by "competition and collaboration of claimsmakers as they strive to advise and influence policymakers [where] . . . lobbyists, political constituents, and anyone else with a vested interest argues in this arena for their own favored position" (Brownstein, 1996, p. 61).

Even when research clearly shows that crack-related homicides are mostly systemic (because they are related to volatile, illicit crack markets) rather than due to the pharmacological effects of the drug, laws tend to get tough on crack users for fear they will become violent (Brownstein, 1996, p. 65). And even when disparities in sentencing for crack versus powder cocaine were demonstrated to Congress to be unjustified, given that crack cocaine is no more addictive or dangerous than powder cocaine (Lockwood, Pottieger, and Inciardi, 1996; Moore, 1995), lawmakers voted to reduce the disparities but nevertheless to maintain them. The National Criminal Justice Commission claims that "evidence of meaningful pharmacological differences between crack and powder cocaine is exceedingly thin" and that "violence associated with crack stems more from turf battles between police and crack dealers, and among crack dealers battling between themselves to control lucrative markets, than from the narcotic effect of crack itself" (Donziger, 1996, p. 119). Perhaps this is why many judges in the United States do not agree with sentencing disparities between crack and powder cocaine (Gray, 2001).

The drug war has been aimed at disrupting, dismantling, and destroying the illegal market for drugs (Brownstein, 1996, p. 45). Of course, a war can be conducted only against people, as noted, not against an abstract target such as "drugs." A "declaration of war suggests an imminently threatening national crisis or open conflict requiring the use of extraordinary power and authority, and the mobilization of massive resources to curb the threat and vanquish the enemy" (Merlo and Benekos, 2000, p. 17). The real enemy in this war has unquestionably been poor minorities, as indicated by the prison populations in the United States today (see Chapter 9). In fact, more than half of prison admissions for drug offenses are African Americans and Hispanics (Donziger, 1996), largely because of the focus of law enforcement in minority communities (Tonry, 1995). Not surprisingly, the majority of people convicted and sentenced for crack cocaine offenses are African American (Robinson, 2000).

Imagine if Presidents Nixon, Reagan, Bush (the first), Clinton, and Bush (the second) had declared war directly against poor people or minorities? Such a thing would have alarmed the media and would have been rejected by Americans as unacceptable, intolerant, and downright bigoted, especially after the struggles of the civil rights movement. A more indirect war against the same people, however, apparently is acceptable.

Imagine also a president suggesting that we take away individual constitutional rights of all Americans to stop some from using drugs. The media would have featured such a story on the front page of every magazine and newspaper in the United States. Americans of all political persuasions—from members of the National Rifle Association (NRA) to members of the American Civil Liberties Union (ACLU)—would join forces to fight such a move. Yet the declared war on drugs in the 1980s has led to increased use of law enforcement actions that infringe upon Second, Fourth, Fifth, and Sixth Amendment rights. "Taking away rights of criminals" is how such infringements are sold to Americans, even though all of us enjoy less freedom today. Apparently, we see such sacrifices as necessary to stop drug abuse (Treaster, 1990). Each of these is a cost of the drug war, which I discuss below.

HARMS CAUSED BY THE DRUG WAR

The war on drugs not only fails to meet its own goals, it also creates or exacerbates significant harms. These include the following

• *The Drug War Leads to Overburdened Criminal Justice Agencies*

As you saw in this chapter, our police, courts, and corrections spend a significant portion of their time and resources dealing with drug offenses. Robinson and Scherlen (2007) show that the proportion of arrests for drug offenses as a share of all arrests has consistently increased during the drug war, as have the number of people convicted and imprisoned for drug crimes. Every minute and every dollar spent fighting the war on drugs is a minute and a dollar not spent fighting those acts that most threaten us, including violent crime and elite deviance. Since many drug offenders are sentenced through mandatory sentences, when correctional facilities are overburdened, drug offenders cannot be released early. Instead, more serious offenders are released early, including violent criminals. Thus, the war on drugs can create crime.

• *The Drug War Leads to Crime and Violence*

Since drugs are illegal, crimes such as theft, prostitution, and other secondary crimes are committed to support drug habits. Drug offenders are also involved in gangs, drive-by shootings, and murders for the right to sell drugs. Internationally, we see that the drug war creates money laundering, funds revolutionary groups, and provides money for the training of terrorists (Gray, 2001). Systemic violence caused by drugs was discussed earlier in the chapter.

Some drug users also commit crimes to support their habits. Hamid (1998, p. 106) claims, "The greater the police presence on the streets, the greater the resort to risky behaviors on the part of users." These risky behaviors include stealing, selling sex for money, breaking and entering, robbery, and even murder. Vigorous drug enforcement by police may actually lead to more rather than less "organized, professional and enduring forms of criminality" (p. 109, citing Dorn and Smith, 1992).

Currently, "because [drug] criminal entrepreneurs operate outside of the law in their drug transactions, they are not bound by business etiquette in their competition with each other. . . . Terror, violence, extortion, bribery, or any other expedient strategy is relied upon by these criminals" (Goldstein, 1998, p. 249, citing Glaser, 1974).

There is a positive relationship between a drug's perceived seriousness by government and the price at which it sells. That is, as a drug is made illegal and especially as it is labeled a serious threat to the community, it becomes more expensive to buy, even though production costs for most illicit drugs are comparable to those for many legal drugs. As noted by Nadelmann (1991, p. 29), "most of the price paid for illicit substances is in effect a value-added tax created by their criminalization which is enforced and supplemented by the law-enforcement establishment, but collected by the drug traffickers." This amounts to a subsidy by the government (i.e., taxpayers) paid to the black market drug offenders. Herbert Packer (1968) called it a **crime tariff** paid to those individuals and groups who must be willing to take tremendous risks to succeed in the drug business. Essentially, as the risks associated with drug offenses increase, so too will the rewards that drug offenders will expect. The American drug war, aimed at deterrence through increased risk, seems simultaneously to achieve higher rewards for those willing to engage in the drug trade.

Wisotsky (1991, p. 107) claims that the war on drugs has made things worse by spinning a "spider's web of black market pathologies," including homicides and other street crimes and widespread governmental corruption. Wisotsky claims that these pathologies were foreseeable because of the laws of supply and demand inherent in the market for an illicit substance that is in high demand. The crime tariff is the result. It is "what the seller must charge the buyer to monetize the risk he takes in breaking the law, in short, a premium for taking risks" (p. 107).

• *The Drug War Erodes Constitutional Protections and Privacy*

In addition to creating crime, the drug war erodes our freedoms. As explained by Wisotsky (1991, p. 108), the U.S. drug war has led to greater levels of pretrial detention resulting from a statutory bias in favor of such detention for those facing certain drug offense charges. Second, within the political framework of the war on drugs, the Supreme Court has eroded defendants' rights not to have illegally seized evidence used against them in a court of law (Gray, 2001). Wisotsky (1991, p. 109) outlines some of these erosions:

- Establishing the authority of police officers to stop, detain, and question people who fit the "profile" of drug couriers in airports, even without probable cause
- Permitting travelers' luggage to be sniffed by dogs without probable cause
- Making searches of automobiles without a warrant
- Searching ships in inland waterways without probable cause
- Obtaining warrants based on informants' tips
- Establishing the "good-faith exception" for police who use flawed warrants
- Permitting warrantless searches of open fields and barns adjacent to residences
- Enlarging the authority of police to stop motorists on the road without probable cause
- Permitting warrantless aerial searches over private residences and of motor homes used as residences
- Allowing warrantless searches of public high school students' purses

Police also can claim exigent circumstances to justify gathering and using unlawful evidence, including evidence that was in their plain view or within reach. Also, police can seize a person's property through asset forfeiture programs based on suspicion of drug activity. The burden of proof falls on the accused to prove that he or she is not involved in the drug trade; even when this is accomplished, the government can keep up to 30% of the property for administrative purposes. This is inconsistent with the presumption of innocence and due process, as defined in Chapter 1.

• *The Drug War Is a Significant Source of Corruption*

Related to increased powers of police and prosecutors, the war on drugs is a significant source of corruption in agencies of criminal justice. The amount of money involved in the drug trade is a source of unbelievable temptation, leading to numerous highly publicized cases of corruption in law enforcement (Gray, 2001). Recent cases include the Dallas Police Department (Texas) and the Tulia Police Department (Texas) where minorities were arrested after officers planted evidence and invented cases against innocent individuals (see Chapter 6).

• *The Drug War Leads to Death and Illness Among Drug Users*

Ironically, the drug war ends up causing death and illness among users (Gray, 2001). Addicts are less likely to seek medical attention and treatment because of fear of criminal sanctions (MacCoun and Reuter, 2001). Deaths are directly attributable to high prices of illegal drugs and, as you saw in this chapter, emergency room mentions of drugs and deaths due to illicit drugs are actually increasing.

Robinson and Scherlen (2007) compared the death rate of illicit drug users in 1979 (the peak of drug use in the United States) with 2000 and found drug users in 2000 were four times more likely to die, meaning that illicit drugs in 2000 were four times more dangerous than illicit drugs in 1979. Even as use fell, users were far more likely to die from drug use.

The Food and Drug Administration (FDA) does not have the jurisdiction to regulate illicit drugs (or to regulate nicotine in tobacco, according to the Supreme Court in

2000). This means the levels of active ingredients in drugs are typically not known and certainly not intentionally managed as is alcohol content. "Imagine that Americans could not tell whether a bottle of wine contained 6%, 30%, or 90% alcohol, or whether an aspirin tablet contained 5 grams or 500 grams of aspirin" (Nadelmann, 1991, p. 33). Also imagine if manufacturers of legal drugs like alcohol were permitted to add far more dangerous substances to their products, as in the case of cocaine and heroin. The drug war makes even relatively harmless recreational drug use much more dangerous than it would be if drugs were legal and regulated for quality control.

• *The Drug War Leads to Financial Cutbacks for Other Social Services*

Every dollar we spend fighting the war on drugs is a dollar not spent on other social services. This ultimately harms Americans. For example, since the 1970s, spending on the war on drugs has increased tremendously, as you saw in this chapter. Now that state budgets are in crisis, it is nearly impossible to cut back funding for operations of police, courts, and corrections as they fight the war on drugs. Yet funding for social service functions has been cut, including education, mental health treatment, and welfare assistance, as have basic investments in vital infrastructures needed to run communities effectively.

• *The Drug War Heightens Racial Disparities*

As you saw earlier in this chapter, minorities disproportionately suffer criminal justice processing when it comes to the war on drugs. According to Hamid (1998, p. 122), "minority persons who have been arrested for drug offenses and other crimes far outnumber European Americans." The penalties they receive are frequently harsh and unfair. Figure 11-9 illustrates that even though Caucasians account for a higher percentage of

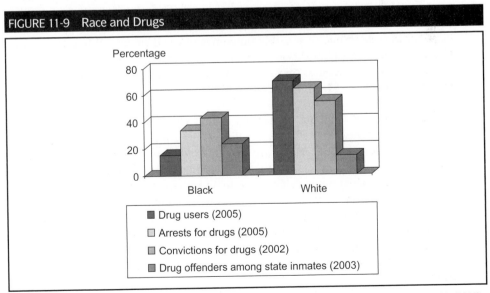

FIGURE 11-9   Race and Drugs

Sources: Sourcebook on Criminal Justice Statistics (2006), National Survey on Drug Use and Health (2005), and U.S. Census (2006).

drug users and people arrested for drugs, minorities account for the majority of inmates convicted of drug offenses and sentenced to the nation's prisons.

• *The Drug War Causes Environmental Damage*

Many harms associated with the war on drugs are rarely considered because they tend to be felt most by those who reside in **producer countries** (e.g., Colombia, Afghanistan) and **transporter countries** (e.g., Mexico) rather than **consumer countries** (such as the United States). One of the harms is the destruction of crops, the soil in which it is grown, and the drinking water that surrounds it by the use of pesticides and other means by the U.S. government (and foreign governments in cooperation with the U.S. government). Crop eradication is one means by which the war on drugs is fought. Yet according to our very own ONDCP, total cultivation of illicit drugs is unchanged: As one spot is eradicated, another pops up elsewhere, which is a form of displacement.

• *The Drug War Threatens the Sovereignty of Other Countries*

Another harm of our drug war is that we threaten the sovereignty of other nations. Countries such as Mexico and Colombia have had numerous disagreements with the United States government over our threats to **decertify** them if they do not cooperate with our war on drugs. This causes resentment among the people of these countries because it interferes with their ability to govern themselves as they see fit.

ALTERNATIVES TO THE DRUG WAR: LEGALIZATION AND DECRIMINALIZATION

This chapter concludes with an examination of the relative merits of drug legalization and decriminalization as policy alternatives to America's drug war. First, I address how our current prohibition efforts are doomed to fail. Then, I address the relative merits of legalization and decriminalization.

Consider the range of possible outcomes of the drug war. When law enforcement agencies invade a neighborhood or community to interfere with drug activity, any combination of three outcomes may result. These outcomes are depicted in the three models shown in Figure 11-10. These models are ideals and are not necessarily mutually exclusive.

Model 1, which I call the **subterfuge model**, characterizes all neighborhoods where drug-related activity exists. Because selling drugs is illegal, drug dealers must hide their activity from the police. Police are at a distinct disadvantage in the war on drugs because they must identify, locate, and apprehend drug offenders who are typically very good at concealing and disguising their activities. For example, street-level crack cocaine dealers utilize numerous strategies to avoid detection by the police. Two strategies involve moving transactions from street corners to apartment buildings and frisking potential buyers for wires (Gaines et al., 2000, p. 611). In the subterfuge model, when police efforts are directed at a particular neighborhood, drug dealers use lookouts to warn them of police presence. This makes preventing or controlling drug sales very difficult.

It is illogical to assume that police agencies can ever stem the flow of the tide of illicit drug dealing in the United States. There are currently only about 3 police officers

FIGURE 11-10   Possible Outcomes of Policing Drugs

per 1,000 U.S. citizens. Given the amount of illicit drug use among these 1,000 people, it would be impossible for the police to be able to stop enough of it to make much of a difference. Additionally, given that drugs can be grown virtually anywhere, and given that growers of drugs "camouflage and protect" their operations from detection efforts (Nadelmann, 1991, pp. 22–23), national and international efforts to stem the production of drugs in the United States and the flow of drugs into the United States are doomed to fail. Nadelmann (1991, p. 22) suggests: "In the final analysis, the principal accomplishment of most domestic drug-enforcement efforts is not to reduce the supply or availability of illegal drugs, or even to raise their price; it is to punish the drug dealers who are apprehended, and cause minor disruptions in established drug markets.

In Model 2, the **displacement model**, drug dealers are literally scared away by the police into other neighborhoods and communities. In the presence of zero-tolerance policing, police intervene in even the most minor of criminal infractions and attempt to eliminate "social incivilities" such as the visibility of homeless and mentally ill people on the streets. Street sweeps of the homeless and mentally ill are merely means of "sweeping such problems under the rug," so to speak, rather than dealing with them more effectively and, some would say, more humanely. Likewise, efforts to capture and arrest street-level drug dealers, under the umbrella of zero-tolerance laws, is a very ineffective method of attempting to eliminate drug use and abuse in the United States.

Zero-tolerance laws are based on the following assumptions:

- If there were no drug abusers, there would be no drug problem.
- The market for drugs is created not only by availability, but also by demand.
- Drug abuse starts with a willful act.
- Drug users are not powerless to act against the influences of drug availability and peer pressure.
- Most illegal drug users can choose to stop their drug-taking behaviors and should be held accountable if they do not.

- Individual freedom does not include the right to self-destruction and societal destruction.
- Public tolerance for drug abuse must be reduced to zero. (Inciardi, 1991, p. 11)

With zero-tolerance laws, drug dealers are theoretically deterred from engaging in drug-related crimes in the presence of police. But rather than giving up their illegal and immensely profitable livelihoods, drug offenders simply move their criminal operations elsewhere.

In Model 3, the **replacement model**, law enforcement efforts are temporarily successful. In neighborhoods and communities where police efforts result in numerous arrests of drug offenders, drug dealers are temporarily put out of business. Yet, as suggested by the title of this model, when drug dealers are taken off the street, others simply take their place in the illegal drug market. This is because of the "push-down/pop-up" nature of urban drug markets (Nadelmann, 1991, p. 23)—when one market is shut down, another simply "pops up" in its place. Glaser (1997, p. 119) claims, "Arrest of any individual involved in drug production usually impairs the drug supply only briefly, because the trade consists of many independent entrepreneurs in diverse roles, in all types of illegal drug distribution, and most getting the highest income from it. Others hurry to replace anyone removed from the industry by arrest."

Because the new drug dealers will be aware of the increased risks of apprehension, they will be better prepared to avoid detection and arrest. They may also be better armed and more ruthless than the previous drug dealers so that they can better battle the police. Skolnick (1997, p. 412) calls this the "Darwinian trafficker dilemma" whereby only the "fittest" drug dealers survive.

So we are left with this result: When drug dealers are taken off the street, others simply step in and take their place. We are left with the same number of drug dealers on our streets, but more inmates in our prisons. There are no fewer drugs available, but we're spending more of our money. The National Criminal Justice Commission puts it this way:

> Somebody else almost always steps in to take the place of the dealer when he or she goes to prison. Incarcerating the second drug dealer costs just as much as incarcerating the first. By the time the criminal justice system has passed through several generations of drug dealers, billions of dollars have been spent and the corner is still scattered with empty vials of crack cocaine. (Donziger, 1996, p. 61)

As noted, these models represent ideals, so any neighborhood or community with any amount of drug-related problems and any level of law enforcement presence will experience some of each outcome. That is, to some degree, subterfuge, displacement, and replacement will occur as police attempt to prevent and control illicit drugs. This means that the likely results of the American drug war are arrests, convictions, and punishment of some but not most drug dealers, the entrenchment of new drug dealers to replace those who are removed from the market, and displacement of drug offending dealings to areas where law enforcement presence is not as great. Do you consider this a success?

For these reasons, success in the war on drugs is not likely. In fact, I argue that because of the effects of subterfuge, displacement, and replacement, it is impossible to win the war on drugs. This is why American drug control efforts, though they may be well intended, are futile at best. Whether this provides a valid rationale for legalizing drugs is debatable, but it does suggest that the United States should abandon its war on drugs—unless, of course, you believe that the war really is successful at something else entirely. Box 11-4 briefly shows how the war on drugs could be considered a success.

Given the findings of this chapter, some alternative to the American drug war may be justified, including **legalization** and **decriminalization**. *Legalization* calls for eliminating drug offenses from the criminal statutes and thus could lead to a complete government withdrawal from drug-related issues. In a commercialized, capitalistic society,

---

BOX 11-4

HOW AMERICA'S DRUG WAR IS A SUCCESS

Failure in the war on drugs may actually amount to success if, as pointed out in Chapter 2, the goal is really not to succeed. Erickson and Butters (1998, p. 177) assert that if we look at the war on drugs as a policy aimed at reducing harm, then prohibition is a failure. If we look at it as an ideology (an orientation that characterizes the thinking of a group), then it is "one of the great success stories of the twentieth century." That is, as a means to shift control to the political right and lock people up for political gain, the war on drugs is working. It is pretty clear who benefits from the failing drug war and who is most harmed by it. While the incarceration boom may be beneficial for those with vested financial interests, it disproportionately affects poor people and minorities. Given the resulting disparities based on race and class, by definition the drug war is not just. This is why the war on drugs provides evidence that American criminal justice agencies are not blind. Instead, they seem to have poor people of color clearly in their sight. Tonry (1995, p. 105) writes, "Urban African-Americans have borne the brunt of the War on Drugs. They have been arrested, prosecuted, convicted, and imprisoned at increasing rates since the early 1980s, and

grossly out of proportion to their numbers in the general population or among drug users." Now that we know this to be fact, how can we allow it to continue?

Results of the war on drugs have included "enormous profits for drug dealers and traffickers, overcrowded jails, police and other government corruption, a distorted foreign policy, predatory street crime carried on by users in search of the funds necessary to purchase black market drugs, and urban areas harassed by street-level drug dealers and terrorized by violent drug gangs." Astonishingly, efforts to prevent drugs from coming into the country stop only about 10% of illicit drugs such as marijuana and cocaine from entering the United States (Inciardi, 1991, p. 12). Inciardi, a staunch opponent of drug legalization, nonetheless admits that interdiction efforts aimed at reducing the passage of drugs into the United States have failed and that more drug abuse treatment is needed (p. 75). Finally, the nation's drug war is a major source of police and criminal justice corruption (Lyman and Potter, 1998). This led Kappeler et al. (2000, p. 166) to call the drug war a "government-sponsored subsidy to organized crime."

advertisers would push substances and inevitably increase drug use (MacCoun and Reuter, 2001). *Decriminalization* does not take the government out of drug prevention efforts. Instead, decriminalization involves limiting the use of drugs and taxing and limiting their production, promotion, sales, and use. Further, profits from drug use would be used to treat those who are involved in harmful drug abuse (Kleiman, 1997). Decriminalization simply calls for eliminating or reducing the penalties for the recreational use of illicit substances.

The main argument in favor of decriminalization is that the drug war fails so miserably in controlling drug use (which is mostly recreational in nature) and drug abuse (which is in essence a medical problem). The main argument against decriminalization is that drug use and abuse will increase and cause unimaginable harms.

Most Americans may think that any alterative to our current approach of prohibition would be "an invitation to drug infested anarchy" (Nadelmann, 1991, p. 18), but this does not have to be the case. Even the staunchest drug legalization advocates acknowledge that use of certain substances might increase if they were legalized, not only because they would be more readily available but also because the deterrent effect of the criminal sanction would no longer apply. No one will argue that more drug use would actually be a good thing, but it may not be as bad a thing as you might imagine. The harms associated with increased use would depend on the specific drug legalization proposal. For example, if the government decided to legalize all drugs and then regulated their quality and availability and also restricted their use to competent, mature adults, increased recreational drug use might actually be a cost-effective alternative to the American drug war.

No, decriminalization is not sure to be a success (e.g., see Wilson, 1998), for "[n]o one knows for certain the extent to which it would increase the number of addicts. . . . Few would deny . . . that the greater availability of, and easier access to, drugs would increase drug use (and addiction) beyond current levels" (Nuro, Kinlock, and Hanlon, 1998, p. 230). This seems a logical and fair conclusion.

Nadelmann (1998) does suggest that drug legalization would increase the availability of drugs, lower their prices, and remove whatever deterrent effect the law has currently, which might suggest increased drug use. Price is a function of supply and demand (Reuter, 1998): When demand for drugs is high, prices are low, and when prices are low, demand may be high. As long as drugs are illegal, sellers can artificially inflate the price to whatever levels they see fit—whatever price warrants the inherent risks associated with being in the illicit drug business.

Could we at least consider decriminalization of illicit drugs as a policy possibility, especially given that current interdiction efforts "have shown little success in stemming the flow of cocaine and heroin into the United States" (Nadelmann, 1998, pp. 289–290)? Law enforcement cannot ever possibly "go to the root of the problem" (Reuter, 1998, p. 315). Making some drugs illegal "has proven highly costly and counterproductive in much the same way that the national prohibition of alcohol did" (Nadelmann, 1998, p. 290).

Nadelmann writes that legalization is not a "get out of jail free card" for drug dealers. Rather, it is a way to put them out of the drug business and to remove much of the criminality surrounding drugs, as well. It is also not an excuse for irresponsible use or abuse of drugs. What I propose, echoing the sentiments of Nadelmann, is that the government make currently illicit substances legally available to adults, while simultaneously regulating their production, distribution, and sale. In conjunction with these efforts, the government must provide drug-related education about the true harms associated with all drug use, including the use of currently legal drugs such as tobacco and alcohol (Jonas, 1991, p. 172). It must also offer drug treatment programs for people who are addicted to or abuse any drugs.

I believe criminal justice agencies should get out of the drug war business for a number of reasons. As you saw in this chapter, the drug war fails to achieve its goals, including to reduce illicit drug use and abuse. Additionally, our drug control efforts are highly costly, both financially and socially. For example, you saw that the criminalization of drugs creates crime through an illegal black market—which actually encourages people to get into the illicit drug business; that our drug reduction efforts have led to an erosion of constitutional protections; and that because drugs are illegal, there are no quality controls in place to ensure safe use.

• *The Drug War Is Hypocritical*

Without doubt, one primary purpose of the criminal law is to promote morality (see Chapter 3). Thus, a primary function of the government is "the promotion of moral behavior and good health practices among its citizens" (Rouse and Johnson, 1991, p. 185). To focus on some drugs and characterize them as immoral, while virtually ignoring others that cause more harm, seems illogical at best.

As discussed earlier in this chapter, far more harms are associated with legal drugs like tobacco and alcohol than with illicit drugs such as marijuana, cocaine, and heroin. Even relative to their levels of use in the United States, some legal drugs are far more deadly and dangerous than many illicit drugs (Jonas, 1991). So Nadelmann (1991, p. 25) concludes:

> There is little question that we could reduce the health costs associated with use and abuse of alcohol and tobacco if we were to criminalize their production, sale, and possession. But no one believes that we could eliminate their use and abuse, that we could create an "alcohol-free" or "tobacco-free" country. Nor do most Americans believe that criminalizing the alcohol and tobacco markets would be a good idea.

As explained by Nadelmann, criminalizing legal drugs is a bad idea because of two primary beliefs of Americans: "that adult Americans have the right to choose what substances they will consume and what risks they will take; and that the costs of trying to coerce so many Americans to abstain from those substances would be enormous."

Still, we have identified and isolated some drugs that, even when used recreationally or when merely possessed, are criminalized on the basis of their likelihood of causing harm. This focus seems hypocritical, given that a shift from casual alcohol use to the recreational use of marijuana would likely lead to a decrease in violence in the United States (Nadelmann, 1991, p. 31). Yet Americans overwhelmingly support the drug war and draw a "moral line in the sand" between unlawful and lawful substances. However, just because "the American people simply do not want it" (Inciardi, 1991, p. 66), that does not mean that legalization of drugs is wrong. To the degree that

Americans base their opinions about crime and justice on media information and public stances of politicians (see Chapter 5), it is not surprising that they tend to oppose decriminalization.

• *Drug Abuse Would Not Likely Increase if Illicit Drugs Were Decriminalized*

As noted earlier in this chapter, most drug use in the United States is recreational. It is intimately linked to American culture as a whole and to particular subcultures within the larger society, and it is typically limited to certain social situations and social groups. Because most drug users do not become drug abusers, any increase in drug use resulting from decriminalization would not likely lead to very large levels of drug abuse. Experimentation with relatively minor drugs such as marijuana would also not likely lead to the use of "harder" drugs such as cocaine and heroin, as proponents of the "gateway hypothesis" suggest. In fact, most people who use marijuana recreationally do not use or abuse harder drugs; the gateway to illicit drugs is found in legal drugs such as tobacco and alcohol (Casement, 1987; Schoenborn and Cohen, 1986; Trebach, 1997). Even the federal government and the ONDCP admit that the first steps of drug use are tobacco and alcohol, yet these drugs are not criminalized. Tobacco and alcohol users are far more likely, according to the ONDCP, to use illicit drugs.

As predispositions to drug abuse continue to be discovered, it is likely that we soon will be able to identify those individuals most susceptible to drug addiction and dependence and be able to focus our drug use education programs and drug abuse prevention programs directly at these individuals. Perhaps drug use would become more socially acceptable if all drugs were not criminalized. This could be counteracted with effective education programs that make drug use socially undesirable except in very specific circumstances.

Another reason to doubt that drug abuse would increase is that drugs are already widely available to most people (Inciardi, 1991, p. 56). Legalization might make it easier to obtain drugs for use, but Americans can already easily obtain illicit substances as they wish. Inciardi cautions that once illicit drugs become legal, the market economy will take over or at least become heavily involved in maintaining drug use. This may be true, given corporate involvement in the U.S. alcohol and tobacco industries. But again, nothing mandates that the government has to permit this.

Interestingly, legalization opponents such as Inciardi argue against all forms of legalization, in part because they hold that drug legalization would be a "program of social management and control that would serve to legitimate the chemical destruction of an urban generation and culture" (Inciardi, 1991, p. 65). Why? Because disenfranchised segments of the population might end up using more drugs, Inciardi posits that drug legalization would be a racist and elitist policy. I conclude the opposite, that the war on drugs currently results in alarming criminal justice disparities based on race and class, and that these disparities would be lessened if drug offenses were decriminalized. This would make criminal justice more just and thus more in line with its ideal goals.

Wisotsky (1991, pp. 108–109) concludes that the American drug war "makes a net negative contribution to the safety, well-being, and national security interests of the American people." If this is true, as I believe it is, then the criminal justice network, by waging a war against drugs, is not only failing to meet its goal of reducing crime but may in fact be exposing U.S. citizens to greater threats to their personal safety.

• *Drug Abuse Is a Medical Problem, Not a Criminal Justice Problem*

Decriminalization would also deemphasize the use of criminal justice resources to deal with the medical problem of drug abuse (Nadelmann, 1998). Our money might be better spent dealing with tobacco and alcohol use and abuse, as well as serious violent crimes. As Nadelmann (1998, p. 294) points out, "The standard refrain regarding the immorality of drug use (such as that in Nancy Reagan's 'Just Say No' campaign) crumbles in the face of most Americans' tolerance for alcohol and tobacco use."

Research shows that treatment works to reduce drug abuse and to alleviate the harms associated with it (Gray, 2001; MacCoun and Reuter, 2000; Robinson and Scherlen, 2007). According to the RAND Corporation, drug treatment is 7 times more cost effective than law enforcement, 11 times more than interdiction, 23 times more than drug eradication (Gray, 2001). According to NIDA, "Most people don't believe treatment works, and they're wrong" (MacCoun and Reuter, 2001). And according to Benekos (2007), rearrest rates are lower for people involved in special drug court programs than those handled in normal court processes.

The war on drugs has allowed American policing to get bigger and meaner, resulting in numerous tragic abuses of human rights. Growing use of undercover operations and electronic surveillance may infringe upon our freedoms, and the growing use of informants flies in the face of crime control goals. Says Nadelmann (1998, p. 195):

> Overzealous enforcement of the drug laws risks undermining the ethic of tolerance toward those who are different but do no harm to others and propagating in its place a society of informants. Indeed, enforcement of the drug laws makes a mockery of an essential principle of a free society, that those who do no harm to others should not be harmed by others, and particularly not by the state.

Decriminalization would allow people to engage in drug-using behaviors that are relatively harmless while simultaneously leading to the development of possible mechanisms to identify and treat drug abusers medically. Criminal justice responses to drug use and abuse do not allow for this.

• *Alternatives to the War Would Be Much More Effective at Reducing Drug Use and Abuse, and Would Reduce Overall Harms*

According to MacCoun and Reuter, in their exhaustive book, *Drug War Heresies* (2001), many alternative drug reduction and harm reduction programs have proven to be effective in European nations. These include needle exchange programs, which save lives by reducing HIV and AIDS infections but do not seem to lead to increased use. Needle exchange programs are endorsed by the Centers for Disease Control and Prevention, the National Academy of Sciences, and numerous health and medical organizations. Other successful programs include drug treatment programs (which have been proven more effective at reducing drug use and abuse than prisons), methadone maintenance programs (which allow drug users to lead functional lives with a much lower risk of overdose or death as a result of their use), and marijuana decriminalization (which has kept use rates lower in the Netherlands than the United States). The Dutch have also not seen increases in use of harder drugs and have also saved money on not incarcerating marijuana offenders—the United States currently incarcerates at least 50,000 marijuana offenders.

According to Nadelmann (1998, p. 299), decriminalization of drugs would accomplish the following:

- Shift control of drug manufacturing and distribution to the government.
- Afford consumers opportunities to make more informed decisions about drug use.
- Lessen the degree of harms associated with impure substances.
- Correct the hypocritical and dangerous message that legal drugs are harmless.
- Allow government to shape drug consumption patterns.

The bottom line is that the U.S. war on drugs creates far more harm than it stops. MacCoun and Reuter (2001, p. 386) conclude, as I have in this chapter, that our policies "have failed to eliminate drug dependence, have at best only moderately reduced drug use, and have left its harms largely intact" and that our policies themselves are a source of many drug-related harms. They also point out that, although the U.S. government claims one of its goals is harm reduction, there is not one specific program aimed at achieving that goal!

An alternative to waging war on drugs would be a policy of **harm reduction**, which "is the emphasis on the reduction of adverse consequences rather than the elimination of drug use. Harm reduction is a framework from which policy and program strategies are conceptualized, developed, and implemented with the outcome goal being the reduction or minimization of harm (without requiring user abstinence or less consumption)" (MacCown and Reuter, 2001, p. 179). It is aimed at reducing adverse physical, social, and economic consequences of drug use. Harm reduction is discussed in Box 11-5.

A more effective antidrug strategy would thus be characterized by the following (Jensen and Gerber, 1998):

- A focus on harm reduction
- No mention of war or war-related rhetoric, which create enemies
- Less criminal justice spending
- Honesty and research-informed policy

For such an approach to be effective, it must be "accompanied by the view of users as mainstream or potentially functional members of society rather than marginal deviant misfits." Also, truths about drug use must emerge, meaning myths of drug use must be overcome (p. 189). One example is that most of the population of virtually every nation never tries cocaine. Of those who do, most do not become addicted. In fact, only 5% to 10% of cocaine users use the drug frequently (Erickson, 1993). Imagine politicians and the media trying to sell the war against cocaine to Americans in the face of these facts.

MacCoun and Reuter (2001, p. 409) challenge U.S. policy makers to at least consider the evidence. They say, "We earnestly believe that, ignoring specific proposals, the desirability of major reform has a reasonable empirical and ethical basis. To scorn discussion and analysis of such major change, in light of the extraordinary problems associated with current policies, is frivolous and uncaring."

I conclude by echoing the sentiment of Kappeler et al. (2000, p. 167), whom I think speak for most within the disciplines of criminology and criminal justice when they

BOX 11-5

HARM REDUCTION

Harm reduction approaches are not necessarily aimed at reducing drug use. Based on the realization that some drug use is inevitable, harm reduction strategies are simply aimed at reducing harms associated with recreational drug use.

Some alternative harm reduction programs have proven to be effective in other nations. These include *needle exchange programs*, which save lives by reducing HIV and AIDS infections but do not seem to lead to increased use. Needle exchange programs are endorsed by the Centers for Disease Control and Prevention, the National Academy of Sciences, and numerous health and medical organizations.

Other successful programs include *methadone maintenance programs*, which allow drug users to lead functional lives with a much lower risk of overdose or death as a result of their use, and *depenalization* of marijuana, which has kept use rates lower in the Netherlands than the United States. The Dutch have saved money by not incarcerating marijuana offenders while *not* witnessing increases in the use of harder drugs (MacCoun and Reuter, 2001).

There is fear among policy makers that harm reduction approaches might increase drug use and abuse. There is some evidence that legalization would increase use and abuse, as noted earlier. Yet there is no such evidence that a policy of depenalization would lead to more use. In this approach, possession of small amounts for personal use would be legal but manufacturing and selling would still be illegal, as would marketing and privatization of the drug trade.

Even assuming that drug use and abuse would be higher if the United States pursued alternatives to its drug war, this does not mean that the policy would do more harm than good. There is much evidence, even in ONDCP's annual National Drug Control Strategy, that harms associated with the war on drugs clearly outweigh the gains. Some of these harms would be eliminated through the pursuit of alternatives to the drug war. That is, since many of the harms associated with the prohibition of drugs would be eliminated and/or reduced, we still would witness greater overall savings in financial costs, social costs, criminal justice costs, and so forth.

write, "Drug control policy has not failed for lack of resources, funding, legal powers, or adequate personnel. It has failed because the problem is not amenable to a criminal justice solution." We know this. Failing to correct it produces outcomes inconsistent with the ideal goals of the U.S. criminal justice network.

CONCLUSION

American history is dotted with wars on drugs. In these wars, which we seem to conduct every so often against drugs perceived to be used by problematic populations, we generally ignore the lessons of the past. The criminal justice network remains blind to its own illogical drug war. Even though actual harms attributed to use of illicit drugs pale in comparison to the harms caused by legal drugs, we seem content to use law enforcement and military efforts to try to solve problems associated with the medical problem of drug abuse. Although our recent efforts have had no appreciable effect on drug use or abuse in the United States, our nation's prisons and jails are filling up with poor street criminals, many of whom are people of color, who have committed very minor drug crimes. The media continue to fall prey to politicians' efforts to wage war against these people in the name of the war on drugs rather than independently asserting how the nation's drug war is a massive failure. More violence is attributable to the nation's drug war than to the actual use of drugs. Thus, decriminalization seems to be a legitimate alternative worth pursuing.

Issue in Depth—Drug War Lies?

A study of the White House agency in charge of the nation's drug war found evidence of distortion and manipulation of statistical and visual information in order to "sell the drug war" to citizens and policy makers in spite of its consistent failures. The Office of National Drug Control Policy (ONDCP)—"the accountable agency" in the nation's drug war according to its director, John Walters—fails to live up to basic standards of accountability by consistently producing flawed reports regarding the drug war.

Robinson and Scherlen (2007) studied seven consecutive versions of ONDCP's *National Drug Control Strategy,* a document that "directs the Nation's anti-drug efforts and establishes a program, a budget, and guidelines for cooperation among Federal, State, and local entities" (ONDCP, 2006). Its purpose is *not* to showcase ONDCP or the antidrug efforts of any presidential administration; rather, it is meant to direct the nation's drug control policy and to provide a fair and honest evaluation of associated efforts.

Since its inception, the drug war has pursued the goals of reducing drug use, disrupting drug markets so that illicit drugs will become less available, healing drug users through treatment, and reducing health and social costs of drug abuse. According to the study, ONDCP has failed to meet any of these goals. Since ONDCP's founding, drug use has not declined, drugs are still widely available, the vast majority of people who need drug treatment do not get it, and more people are getting sick and dying from drug-related causes.

Perhaps this explains why ONDCP does not present statistics in an honest and transparent manner. Robinson and Scherlen (2007) found that ONDCP consistently misrepresents the truth, "spinning the data" to suggest success. For example, ONDCP generally focuses on short-term trends that show recent declines in youth drug use while ignoring the long-term trends that illustrate higher overall drug use since the founding of ONDCP. ONDCP presents visual information showing drug use trends beginning in 1979 (the peak in drug use) or 1985 (prior to its founding) to assure that trends will suggest the appearance of declines even when trends since its founding have remained constant or increased.

The study also shows that ONDCP generally ignores statistics that counter its claims of success. For example, it does not discuss increasing adult drug use trends, rising death rates attributed to illicit drugs, falling drug prices, increasing drug purity, and mostly steady availability of illegal drugs. These statistics run directly counter to the goals of the drug war.

At times, it is a subtle manipulation of statistics used by ONDCP to suggest a conclusion that is not warranted based on the data. For example, Figure 11-11 shows a figure from ONDCP's 2006 strategy.

You notice that ONDCP combines drug use trends for eighth, tenth, and twelfth graders from the data source Monitoring the Future (MTF) rather than reporting them independently. This is interesting for several reasons. First, ONDCP's 2001 strategy set a goal of "[a] 10 percent reduction in current use of illegal drugs by eighth, tenth, *and* twelfth graders." Further, the same goal of reducing current use of illegal drugs by eighth, tenth, *and* twelfth graders is stated in the 2002 and 2003 strategy reports. Second, in previous and subsequent strategy reports, ONDCP reported on these trends individually rather than combining them. For example, in the 2003 strategy, ONDCP reported declines of 11.1%, 8.4%, and 1.2% for eighth, tenth, and twelfth graders, respectively.

Robinson and Scherlen (2007) noted that combining the trends lines possibly masks important trends specific to each grade. After examining the trends independently, Robinson and Scherlen found MTF data show 2-year declines in previous-month drug use among eighth graders (20.6%), tenth graders (16.4%), and twelfth graders (6.6%). In other words, when broken down by grade level, ONDCP had *not* achieved its 2-year goal of reducing drug use by 10% for twelfth graders. ONDCP combined the data to arrive at a single statistical trend for all grades to claim it has met its goal, which it had not.

At other times, ONDCP's manipulation of statistics is much more pronounced and obvious. A clear example comes from the 2003 and 2006 strategy reports. In the 2003 strategy report, ONDCP boldly presents visual evidence that previous efforts of

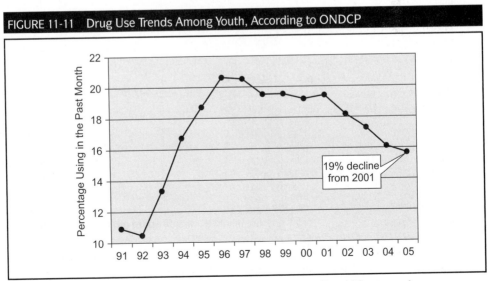

FIGURE 11-11   Drug Use Trends Among Youth, According to ONDCP

Source: Office of National Drug Control Policy (2006). National Drug Control Strategy, p. 1.

the drug war (prior to the creation of the ONDCP) did in fact work. For example, it says:

> The data on the prevalence of drug use shows the steep reductions in use that followed the national mobilization started in 1985 by Nancy Reagan's "Just Say No" campaign. Like smoking and other social pathologies, drug use is a problem that responds to societal pressure; when we push against this problem, it gets smaller.

In fact, the figure presented as evidence shows that marijuana use had already begun to decline in 1979, six years prior to Nancy Reagan's campaign, and that cocaine use was already lower in 1985 than it was in 1979. The Substance Abuse and Mental Health Services Administration (SAMHSA) reports that overall cocaine use peaked in the early 1980s and then declined through 1991. Perhaps this is why the ONDCP figure only shows trends among 18–25 year olds (rather than all users), which appear in the figure to begin to decline in 1985. Further, ONDCP does not assess the role of other factors in declining cocaine use, such as the waning of the crack cocaine epidemic. Figure 11-12 depicts this.

FIGURE 11-12   ONDCP Promotes "Just Say No"

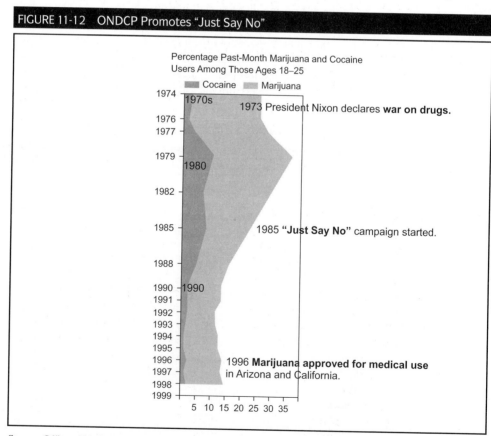

Source: Office of National Drug Control Policy (2003). National Drug Control Strategy, p. 10.

It is unclear why ONDCP would show drug use trends drawn from statistics of drug use among only 18–25 year olds, given that Nancy Reagan's "Just Say No" campaign was aimed at children and adolescents more so than adults. Robinson and Scherlen (2007) looked up two sets of statistics to check ONDCP's figure and claims regarding the "Just Say No" campaign. NHSDA statistics for adolescents (aged 12–17 years) and for all people 12 years and older suggest that:

- Past-month use of any illicit drug declined from 14.1% in 1979 to 12.1% in 1985 (the year "Just Say No" started), and continued to decline to 5.8% in 1992. The percentage remained relatively constant thereafter but rose to 6.4% in 1997 and 6.2% in 1998.
- Past-month use of marijuana declined from 13.2% in 1979 to 11.5% in 1985 (the year "Just Say No" started), and continued to decline to 4.6% in 1994. The percentage remained relatively constant thereafter but rose to 5.1% in 1997 and 5% in 1998.
- Past-month use of cocaine declined from 2.6% in 1979 to 2.4% in 1985 (the year "Just Say No" started), and then increased to 3% in 1988. Afterwards, past-month use declined to 0.7% in 1993 and remained at about that rate until 1998.

The statistics for those aged 12–17 years (adolescents) suggest that:

- Past-month use of any illicit drug declined from 16.3% in 1979 to 13.2% in 1985 (the year "Just Say No" started), and continued to decline to 5.3% in 1992. The percentage began to rise thereafter, reaching 11.4% in 1997 and 9.9% in 1998.
- Past-month use of marijuana declined from 14.2% in 1979 to 9.9% in 1985 (the year "Just Say No" started), and then increased to 10.2% in 1988. Afterwards, past-month use declined to 3.4% in 1993 and then rose thereafter, reaching 9.4% in 1997 and 8.3% in 1998.

These statistics show that drug use for all people 12 years and older, as well as for those aged 12–17 years (adolescents) began to decline prior to "Just Say No" and did not universally decline from 1985 through 1988 (after "Just Say No" began). This NHSDA example alone demonstrates that ONDCP selectively uses statistics to prove a point, even when an examination of all drug use statistics (and especially the most relevant) does not warrant the conclusion. Robinson and Scherlen (2007) say they did not know why ONDCP chose to highlight the "Just Say No" campaign as an effective one, but other examples in the same strategy report provide hints.

For example, ONDCP highlights the "major reductions in smoking that followed the 1964 Surgeon General's report linking cigarettes with health problems, and the imposition of federal restrictions on tobacco sales in 1992." A figure on the same page, using statistics for all people 18 years and older (rather than only for 18–25 year olds), visually demonstrates that for adults, two government efforts—one educational in 1964 and the other legal in 1972—resulted in reductions in cigarette smoking. ONDCP attempts to link the "Just Say No" campaign to similar reductions in illicit drugs. Yet, for illicit drugs, it presents data only for 18–25 year olds, even though the "Just Say No" program was aimed at kids. This is a selective and inappropriate use of statistics.

A cursory review of MTF data, which are available for twelfth graders during the 1980s, shows that the Nancy Reagan effort was not effective. For example, for twelfth graders:

- Past-month use of any illicit drug declined from a high of 38.9% in 1979 to 37.2% in 1980, 36.9% in 1981, 32.5% in 1982, 30.5% in 1983, 29.2% in 1984, 29.7% in 1985, and 27.1% in 1986.
- Past-month use then declined every year thereafter until 1992, when it reached 14.4%. After that, it increased every year until 1997 when it reached 26.2% and then leveled off and slightly declined until 2004 when it was 23.4%.
- Past-month use of marijuana declined from a high of 37.1% in 1978 to 36.5% in 1979, 33.7% in 1980, 31.6% in 1981, 28.5% in 1982, 27% in 1983, 25.2% in 1984, 25.7% in 1985, and 23.4% in 1986. Past-month use then declined every year thereafter until 1992, when it reached 11.9%. After that, it increased every year until 1997 when it reached 23.7% and then leveled off and slightly declined until 2004 when it was 19.9%.
- Past-month use of cocaine declined from a high of 5.8% in 1981 to 5% in 1982, and 4.9% in 1983. After that past-month use rose again between 1983 and 1985 when it reached 6.7%, a new high. After 1985, past-month use declined every year until 1993 when it reached 1.3%. After that, it increased every year until 1999 when it reached 2.6% and then leveled off and slightly declined until 2004 when it was 2.3%.

Of all these trends, the only one that is consistent with the claim by ONDCP that "Just Say No" was effective is the declines in past-month use of cocaine among twelfth graders, which began to decline between 1985 and 1986 and consistently declined thereafter for more than a decade. MTF statistics for eighth and tenth graders were not available until 1991, but "Just Say No" did not cause declines among twelfth graders. Nor is there evidence it did so for adolescents, according to NHSDA statistics from that time period. ONDCP's claims regarding the effectiveness of the "Just Say No" campaign simply fly in the face of statistics.

Interestingly, ONDCP also presents a figure concerning total alcohol consumption through the twentieth century. In the figure, the years 1919–1933 are identified as the years of Prohibition. During these years, total alcohol consumption is depicted as rapidly increasing. Not surprisingly, in spite of making claims about both tobacco use and illicit drug use, ONDCP makes no claim about alcohol use. The careful strategy reader would wonder why ONDCP makes no claims about the significance for the drug war of rising alcohol consumption during alcohol prohibition.

Amazingly, in the 2006 strategy, ONDCP presented a similar figure based on the same data—drug use by 18 to 25 years old—and the trend line in marijuana use is noticeably different than the same figure from 2003. In the 2003 strategy, the figure showed trends in illicit drug use among those aged 18–25 years from 1974 to 1998. The 2006 figure shows trends in illicit drug use among those aged 18–25 years from 1974 to 2004. Whereas the 2003 strategy figure showed that cocaine use began to decline in the year of the initiation of the "Just Say No" campaign (1985), the 2006 strategy figure

FIGURE 11-13   ONDCP's Data Show "Just Say No" Did Not Reduce Drug Use

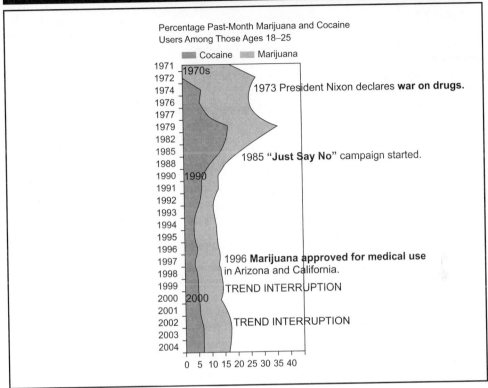

Source: Office of National Drug Control Policy (2006). National Drug Control Strategy, p. 15.

(which is based on the same data) shows that cocaine use had already begun to decline in 1979 with no noticeable increase prior to 1985. In other words, the two figures, each based on the same statistics, show two different trends and lead to two very different conclusions (see Figure 11-13).

In the 2003 strategy, ONDCP commented on its figure and claimed that the "Just Say No" campaign caused drug use to go down. In the 2006 strategy, ONDCP merely presents the figure but makes no such claim (probably because the data don't, and never did, justify this conclusion). The discrepancy in the two figures is deeply troubling given that ONDCP used the figure in the 2003 strategy to try to prove the effectiveness of the "Just Say No" educational campaign.

In conclusion, Robinson and Scherlen (2007) recommend terminating ONDCP and replacing it with an independent federal agency aimed at honestly evaluating the drug war annually based on its stated goals and utilizing all available data. Robinson and Scherlen (2007, p. 206) note, "American citizens expect accuracy, honesty, transparency, and efficacy from government agencies. And citizens deserve more from government than its opposite."

KEY TERMS

analgesics
asset forfeiture
consumer countries
crime tariff
crimes associated with a drug-using lifestyle
criminal subcultures
crop eradication
decertify
decriminalization
depressants
displacement model
drug
drug abuse
drug use

drug-defined crimes
drug-related crimes
economic compulsive homicides
hallucinogens
harm reduction
hypnotics
inhalants
institutional discrimination
interdiction
legalization
moral panics
narcotics/opiates
physical evidence
prevention

producer countries
psychological dependence
psychopharmacological homicides
replacement model
secondary crimes
sedatives
stimulants
street-level drug enforcement
subterfuge model
systemic homicides
tolerance
transporter countries
treatment
war on drugs
withdrawal

DISCUSSION QUESTIONS

1. What is the war on drugs?
2. Identify and discuss the main elements of the drug war in the United States.
3. Can a war really be fought against inanimate objects like drugs? Why or why not?
4. What are the main goals of our nation's drug wars?
5. Do you think we need a war on drugs? Why or why not?
6. Identify examples of how wars on drugs have been declared on powerless groups in the United States.
7. What is a drug?
8. Contrast drug use with drug abuse.
9. Discuss some of the potential outcomes of drug abuse.
10. Make a list of the major categories of drugs and discuss the effects they have on those who use them.
11. Differentiate the five schedules of drugs.
12. Do you think drug use would increase if drugs were not illegal? Why or why not?
13. Why do you think more people smoke cigarettes than marijuana?
14. According to the evidence discussed in the chapter, which is more harmful to smoke, cigarettes or marijuana? Why?
15. Is there a link between drugs and crime? If so, what are some of the relationships?
16. Discuss the role of the media in promoting drug scares.
17. Outline and compare the main arguments for and against legalization of drugs.
18. Identify the main arguments in favor of decriminalization. Do you agree with them or not? Explain.
19. Identify and discuss three possible outcomes of drug intervention, including subterfuge, displacement, and replacement.
20. Do you think zero-tolerance laws are a logical approach to fighting drugs? Why or why not?
21. List and discuss some examples of how the Office of National Drug Control Policy (ONDCP) "lies" with statistics to justify continuing the drug war.

12

THE WAR ON CRIME AS A THREAT TO EQUALITY: INNOCENT BIAS AGAINST THE POOR, PEOPLE OF COLOR, AND WOMEN

1.   Introduction
2.   Is the War on Crime a War on the Poor?
     • Box 12-1.   Functions Served by the War on Crime
     a. The Rich Are Getting Richer and the Poor Are Getting Poorer
3.   Is the Criminal Justice Network Biased Against People of Color?
     • Box 12-2.   Race and Criminality According to Sources of Crime Data
     a. Race, Ethnicity, and Social Class
     b. Race, Ethnicity, Government Policy, and Criminal Justice
4.   Gender and Criminal Justice
5.   Conclusion
6.   Issue in Depth—The Greatest Threat to Civil Rights Is the Criminal Justice Network
7.   Key Terms
8.   Discussion Questions

INTRODUCTION

Consider the following facts established in previous chapters:

• The law is made by people who are not representative of the general public.
• Lawmakers are voted for by people who are not representative of the general public.
• Most people do not regularly vote.
• Lawmaking is influenced by special interests.

- Who spends the most money in political campaigns is virtually guaranteed to win.
- Money for political candidates and political parties does not come from normal, everyday citizens but instead from wealthy donors, lobbyists, and political action committees (PACs).
- Crime is not a label used to identify the most serious threats to our lives and property.
- "Serious" crimes are those crimes committed on the streets of America; far more dangerous acts of elite deviance are not generally considered or pursued by criminal justice agencies as serious crimes.
- Media coverage of crime is focused disproportionately on street crime, especially violent crimes committed by poor people and people of color.
- The police, because they are predominantly located in the inner cities of America and focused on street crime almost exclusively, are disproportionately likely to stop, question, arrest, and use force against the poor and minorities.
- The power among courtroom workgroups is imbalanced in favor of prosecutors, and both pretrial (bail and plea bargaining) and trial processes are inherently biased in favor of the wealthy and against the poor and members of minority groups.
- The poor and minorities are disproportionately likely to be sentenced to probation, jail, prison, and other criminal sanctions through mandatory sentences, and they make up the majority of people under correctional supervision in the United States.
- The administration of capital punishment is biased in favor of the wealthy, against killers of Caucasians, and against the poor.
- The war on drugs disproportionately affects the poor and minorities.

Given these facts, a safe conclusion is that the criminal justice network fails to achieve its goals of reducing crime and doing justice. Moreover, it is reasonable to assume that the criminal justice network as a whole is biased against certain groups in society. In this chapter, I revisit some key findings from previous chapters and try to make sense out of why agencies of criminal justice seem focused so squarely on some people and some acts but ignore others. The key question addressed in this chapter is, Do the above facts warrant the conclusion that the criminal justice network is biased against certain groups, as suggested in Chapter 2?

IS THE WAR ON CRIME A WAR ON THE POOR?

Recall from Chapter 2 that Jeffrey Reiman (2006) argues that criminal justice operations are biased against the poor at every step of the process, beginning with the law. Reiman, in his book, *The Rich Get Richer and the Poor Get Prison,* demonstrates that the criminal law essentially ignores harmful acts committed by the powerful, such as those committed in white-collar jobs and by corporations. As discussed in Chapter 4, these acts are either not illegal (such as the manufacture and sale of tobacco), or are against the law but not seen as "serious" and thus not widely pursued by law enforcement agencies (e.g., manufacturing and selling defective products).

The label of criminality is almost always reserved for the poor, even though criminality is not a function of social class. After reviewing the alleged links between social class and crime, Robinson (2004) concludes that social class only predicts the types of crime people are likely to commit. For example, poor people tend to acquire wealth through crimes such as theft and robbery. Middle class and wealthy individuals tend not to rob people, stores, and banks. Instead, they steal through means such as embezzlement and fraud. This is not to say that everyone steals, but most people do (at least occasionally)!

Yet we are filling up our prisons with poor street criminals and building more prisons to accommodate the growing number of convicted street criminals as though only some forms of crime warrant our attention. So is the war on crime a war on the poor?

Herbert Gans (1995) analyzes antipoverty policies in the United States and outlines the main components of what he calls *The War against the Poor* throughout American history. Gans analyzes U.S. government policy generally, but his analysis speaks volumes to how the criminal justice network in the United States operates. Keep in mind that politics and criminal justice cannot be separated (see Chapter 2). Thus, some government attempts to reduce poverty may have implications for criminal justice, and vice versa.

Gans uses the term **underclass** to refer to a segment of the poor who supposedly refuse to "behave in the 'mainstream' ways of the numerically or culturally dominant middle class" (p. 2). William Julius Wilson (1987) used the same term to explain how a small segment of the United States has become socially isolated and "truly disadvantaged," although he has subsequently replaced this term with **ghetto poor**. Wilson writes that the poor become socially isolated when they are detached from middle-class role models who successfully moved out of poor areas. Singh (1991, p. 509) concurs, claiming: "Unemployment and growing isolation from the mainstream economy have led to unwed parenting, dependency, lawlessness, joblessness, and school failure."

Gans (1995) argues that the label of *underclass* is a term used to describe a culture supposedly unique to poor people. This historical view of the poor suggests that the underclass are to blame for their own problems because of their questionable morality and deteriorating values. "The labeling of the poor as moral inferiors . . . blames them falsely for the ills of the American society and economy, reinforces their mistreatment, increases their misery, and further discourages their moving out of poverty" (p. 1). In essence, application of the underclass label amounts to an accusation against people who are seen as undeserving of assistance because of their bad values and moral deficiencies. Lauer and Lauer (2000, p. xi) call such depictions of the poor as flawed individuals "simplistic." Simplistic understandings of complex problems—rooted in individuals' own assumptions about human nature and general perspectives about the world rather than in empirical evidence or scientific facts—lead to simplistic and ineffective solutions to social problems such as poverty and crime.

Gans (1995) explores how the United States has always been involved in a war against the poor, which, he argues, has worsened since the 1980s. Incidentally, this is the same time when the country's entrenchment with the crime control model of criminal justice became so evident, as discussed in Chapter 2. Given the increasingly punitive nature of U.S. criminal justice policy since the 1980s directed at street criminals, it becomes easy to see the war on crime as really a war on crimes committed by the poor. Gans argues that this is the result of how Americans have come to see the poor as "deserving" of their poverty and suffering, and "undeserving" of assistance.

Gans (pp. 6–7) lays out four aspects of the "undeserving" nature of the poor (and thus the criminal). He argues:

- If poor people do not behave according to the rules set by mainstream society, they must be undeserving . . . because they believe in and therefore practice bad values, suggesting that they do not want to be part of mainstream America culturally or socially. As a result of bad values and practices, undeservingness has become a major cause of contemporary poverty. If poor people gave up these values, their poverty would decline automatically, and mainstream Americans would be ready to help them, as they help other, "deserving" poor people.
- The men among the undeserving poor are lazy or unable to learn the cultural importance of work and its requirements; in some cases, their bad values turn them into street criminals. If they really wanted to work, jobs would be available for them, and they would be able to earn their own income like other Americans.
- The women among the undeserving poor have an unhealthy and immoral taste for early sexual activity and for having babies as adolescents. If they would wait until they were older, sufficiently mature, and ready to find work as well as husbands who wanted to work, they and their children would not need to be poor, and poverty might even end with the current generation.
- If the deserving poor do not alter their values and practices voluntarily, they must be forced to do so, for example by ending welfare payments, placing illegitimate children into foster care or orphanages, and by other forms of punishment.

The deserved forms of punishment include criminal sanctions such as imprisonment. Of course, as you saw in Chapter 3, criminal sanctions are specified by the criminal law, which is not made by or informed by poor people.

This is particularly true given that the umbrella label of underclass encompasses other labels such as criminal. I illustrate this in Figure 12-1. This visual is meant to depict that our war against the poor encompasses many forms, the most significant of which may be our war against crime. As you saw in Chapter 11, the war on drugs is a major component of our war on crime. These wars on the poor, the criminal, and those involved in the drug trade lead to massive increases in incarceration, in addition to scores of other destructive outcomes for the underclass. Americans seem to be unconcerned with these outcomes, perhaps because they perceive criminal justice as something that only affects "them"—the poor.

The American view of the poor suggests they are different from the rest of us. This is similar to the conception of criminals versus noncriminals: They deserve what they get, including punishment, for their wrongdoings. The American notion of "just desserts" or vengeance for punishment is rooted in the assumption that criminals choose to commit crimes and therefore deserve whatever punishment they get (see Chapter 8). When criminals are poor, our view of the poor is reinforced: "See, they are so lazy and immoral they would rather commit crimes than work!" Given that most people who are processed through the criminal justice network are poor, crime is seen

FIGURE 12-1   The Wars on Crime, Drugs, and the Poor

as a problem of the poor. Both "underclass" and "criminality" are seen as deserved labels, oftentimes applied to the same people.

This is not to say that only the poor are "bad apples"; in fact, bad apples exist at all levels. As noted by Gans (1995, p. 4), "As one moves up the socioeconomic ladder, however, the bad apples and their questionable behavior become less visible." In Chapter 4, you saw that the crimes considered serious by the federal government are those that are committed primarily by the poor; in Chapter 5 you saw that these are the same acts covered disproportionately in the media. As a result, these are the most visible crimes to Americans, meaning that we fear them the most and support measures that deal with these acts through any and all means possible. Not surprisingly, police, courts, and corrections are most focused on these acts.

As noted in Figure 12-1, one means of dealing with these people is through incarceration, often even for relatively minor offenses (see Chapter 9). This raises the question: Does incarceration serve the function of population control, as suggested in Chapter 2? Gans writes, "In an economy in which there may no longer be enough decent jobs for all who want to work, the people who are labeled as undeserving can be forced out of the economy so as to preserve the jobs of the deserving citizens" (p. 8). If the underclass cannot find decent work, they may commit property and drug crimes for income. In these cases, the corresponding views of the poor as undeserving of government assistance and the criminal as deserving of punishment make criminal justice intervention certain.

But is all of this intended? As noted in Chapter 2, not necessarily. Functions of a war against the poor or the criminal may not be intended. Rather, they may be so beneficial to those in positions of power that there may exist little incentive to change. Gans outlines the functions served by the war on the poor. In Box 12-1, I apply these same functions to the war on crime.

To the degree that these functions are actually served by U.S. criminal justice processes, the criminal justice network is biased against the poor and failing to do justice. How can it be, in the "land of the free and the home the brave," that our criminal justice processes are biased against those who are least able to protect themselves? To

BOX 12-1

FUNCTIONS SERVED BY THE WAR ON CRIME

- *Reducing risk:* If we can identify those who are dangerous and deserving of intervention, we can minimize the likelihood that we will have contact with them. In particular, if we lock them up in prison, we do not even have to think about them.

- *Supplying objects of revenge and repulsion:* By identifying them as wrongdoers, we gain the right to punish them, even in a system of justice in which victims play little role in the criminal justice process. In essence, victims regain the right to be involved in the punishment of the guilty, even if their involvement is limited to an emotional one.

- *Creating jobs for the better-off population:* The behaviors of the lower class must be modified so they will act in socially approved ways. This means they must be policed and processed through the system. In Chapter 2, you saw how many jobs are provided by the existence of crime.

- *Staffing the reserve army of labor:* In the case of criminal justice, the government obtains a means of very cheap labor in offenders who work when they are locked away from society.

- *Forcing the poor out of the labor force:* What better way to lower the unemployment rate than to take a large portion of the unemployable off the streets?

- *Value reinforcement:* How would we know what was wrong if people didn't show us by pushing the limits of acceptable behavior? Crime serves the function of demonstrating what is not acceptable behavior.

- *Legitimating values:* The same laws that determine what is illegal also define what is law-abiding. Numerous forms of harmful behaviors are either not considered criminal, or are against the law but not considered serious (see Chapter 4). This undeniably serves the interests of dangerous upper-class citizens and corporations.

- *Creating popular cultural villains:* The poor as undeserving and criminals in general are depicted as the enemy in the wars against the poor and against crime. Those who fight these wars are seen as important and even heroic.

- *Scapegoating institutions:* Focusing on the shortcomings of certain groups in society all but guarantees that no attention will be paid to the real problems of poverty and criminality, which are more complex in nature than depicted.

- *Reproducing stigma and the stigmatized:* As we fight our wars against poverty and crime, we virtually guarantee that we will continue to see an enemy to target. In the current era of U.S. crime control and drug reduction policies, for example, more resources have gone toward reactive law enforcement and corrections approaches than to preventive approaches, thereby ensuring failure and guaranteeing that a future segment of the population will commit crime and use drugs.

- *Shifting power to conservatives:* By focusing on crime and poverty through a law-and-order approach, conservative crime control economic

campaigns can be launched and strengthened by public support. The result is a shift to a crime control model of justice and a diminishing of due process rights for all Americans.

understand this, it is important to recall an important lesson from Chapter 2. Criminal justice agencies are political in nature, meaning they operate first and foremost in the interests of the powerful. As shown in Chapter 3, this begins with the definition of some behaviors as crimes and "serious crimes," while others (more harmful acts) are downplayed or entirely ignored.

The Rich Are Getting Richer and the Poor Are Getting Poorer

Since the 1980s, the effects of politics on poor people and on U.S. crime control policy have been particularly startling. Harrigan (2000) demonstrates how the past 20 years have produced higher incomes for the top 40% of wage earners in the United States, while the bottom 60% actually earn a smaller share of the total national income today. Since 1974, the wealthy have captured more of the national income, while the rest of us have received less. The top 20% of wage earners earn 50% of the nation's income; the bottom 20% earn only 3% (U.S. Census, 2006). In fact, the top 1% of the wealthy now own an astounding 40% of the nation's wealth.

The result is **income inequality**, a reference to the gap between the rich and the poor (Kuttner, 2003). Now, the ratio of top 5% of wage earners to bottom 20% of wage earners is nearly 20:1, the largest gap in the United States' recorded history. The average household income of the top 1% of households is about $650,000, versus about $8,500 for the lowest 20% of the population and about $34,000 for the middle 20% of the population (Phillips, 2003). What is most troubling about these figures is that the average household income of the bottom and middle 20% of households has remained unchanged since 1979, while the average income of the top 1% has grown 150%. Further, the gap between the rich and the poor has increased 4.2% from 1995 to 2005 (U.S. Census, 2006).

Alan Greenspan, the former Federal Reserve Board chairman, claims that this type of income inequality could pose a "major threat to national security" (*U.S. News & World Report,* 2000, p. 43). As the nation's poor are more and more likely to live together in conditions of "social isolation" (as discussed by Wilson, 1987), they are more likely to be aware of their oppression and logically be less happy about it. They are also disproportionately exposed to increased rates of depression and other forms of mental illnesses, asthma, heart disease, and cancer, as well as joblessness, family disruption, and community instability (Pearson, 2000). The nation's poorest are minorities, who also are exposed to more pollution and toxic waste, what Maher (2000, p. 147) calls **environmental racism** (also see Boer, Pastor, and Sadd, 1997). Krahn, Hartnagel, and Gartrell (1986) suggest that countries with higher levels of inequality also have higher rates of murder (also see Land, McCall, and Cohen, 1990; Messner and Tardiff, 1986; Sampson, 1987). This is one source of the incredibly high U.S. murder rate.

In general, people living in conditions of extreme and concentrated poverty are exposed to more violence. In fact, about half of all murders in the United States occur in large cities that are inhabited by less than one-fifth of the population. Within cities, rates of homicide are twenty times the national average in areas where poverty is highly concentrated (Sherman et al., 1997). Politicians are either unaware of these concentrated criminal victimizations or unable to understand their implications. Because of their lack of action, politicians appear unconcerned and unwilling to prevent them. This is one indication that the criminal justice network fails to reduce crime and do justice adequately.

Levy (1988) documents the upward shift of income and suggests that the middle class is falling behind the well off and that the poor are falling even further behind. This supports at least part of Reiman's (2006) contention that "the rich get richer" as discussed in Chapter 2. Harrigan (2000, p. 215) explains growing income inequality as a function of tax policies passed by Congress that benefit the wealthy, along with cuts in domestic programs that traditionally have benefited poorer people. Taxation has also shifted from corporations to individual citizens. In the 1940s, for example, corporations paid one-third of all taxes; today they pay only about 15%. Simon (1999) illustrates that about 90,000 U.S. corporations pay no taxes each year! At the same time, the poorest of the poor have been left "surrounded by other poor people . . . physically removed from the suburban areas of dynamic job growth, and . . . out of personal contact for the most part with middle-class America." Hence, they "lack the skills, knowledge, and behavioral habits with which to improve their situations" (Harrigan, 2000, p. 16). Yes, the poor are getting poorer and thus are more likely to end up in prison, supporting the other part of Reiman's argument.

In her book, *Pigs at the Trough*, Arriana Huffington (2003) demonstrates how wealthy CEOs of corporations now indicted for widespread fraud and abuse made out like bandits while their employees lost unimaginable amounts of money. For example, she reports that the "CEOs of 23 large companies under investigation by the SEC and other agencies" (such as World Com and Enron) earned $1.4 billion between 1999 and 2001. Yet since January 2001 "the market value of these 23 companies nosedived by over $500 billion, or roughly 73%, and they have laid off over 160,000 employees."

According to Huffington, K Mart CEO Charles Conaway received $23 million in compensation over 2 years, after which K Mart filed for bankruptcy, 283 stores closed, and 22,000 people lost their jobs. Tyco CEO Dennis Kozlowski received $467 million in compensation over 4 years, after which Tyco's stockholders lost $92 billion. Enron CEO Kenneth Lay earned more than $100 million the year before Enron's collapse, after which Enron lost $68 billion, 5,000 people lost their jobs, and workers lost $800 million. Huffington claims that corporate executives earned $66 billion by selling company stocks "even while their companies crashed and burned." Some companies forbade their employees from selling their stocks even after they started losing value.

Harrigan (2000), in his book, *Empty Dreams, Empty Pockets: Class and Bias in American Politics,* analyzes American political institutions and argues that the "main institutions of politics today have a significant bias against the economic interests of lower-status people" (p. xii). Harrigan argues that "American government and politics are not neutral. When government acts, or does not act, some groups of people get most of the benefits, while other groups get most of the costs" (p. 1). Although there are more jobs for the poor and the middle class, especially in the low-paying service sector, "there are still millions of people without health insurance, without secure jobs, and just as economically desperate today as they were at the beginning of the decade before the boom began" (p. xiii). At the same time, the move toward conservative politics and greater crime control efforts has diluted the influence of the nonwealthy. Is any of this consistent with the United States' supposed devotion to justice?

Political and criminal justice policy and practice can be biased and thus unjust both by what they do and by what they do not do. Currently, there are about 47 million Americans without health insurance, meaning that at least 15% of Americans are not insured (U.S. Census, 2006). The burden falls, not surprisingly, on the poor and people of color. Harrigan illustrates, for example, that one-third of families who earned more than twice the poverty level in 1991 had no medical insurance, whereas only 6% of those with incomes four times the poverty level lacked health insurance. Because the poor are disproportionately African American and Hispanic, it is not surprising to see that they also suffer from high rates of noncoverage. Simultaneously, politicians enjoy excellent health care benefits. And efforts to guarantee all Americans high-quality, affordable health care, spearheaded in the early 1990s by President Bill Clinton and First Lady Hillary Clinton, were defeated after the health care industry lobbied Congress to vote against it and created the illusion through advertising that a national health care plan would not allow citizens to choose their own doctors. In other words, the efforts were defeated by politics (Hagan, 1998). It is ironic that government policies that harm the poor and people of color simultaneously make it more likely that these groups will live in conditions conducive to criminal activity and thus in need of intervention by the criminal justice network.

IS THE CRIMINAL JUSTICE NETWORK BIASED AGAINST PEOPLE OF COLOR?

With all this focus on the poor, what is the role of race and ethnicity in criminal justice processes? Numerous scholars claim that the criminal justice network is in essence racist because of its built-in biases against people of color (Mann, 1993). Consistent with this view is the claim by Gans (1995, p. 16) that, "Although most labels for the poor are literally neutral with respect to ethnicity and race, they have actually been meant mainly for immigrants and dark-skinned people in the United States." Figure 12-2 illustrates one's relative risk, based on race and class, for becoming involved in the criminal justice network.

As you can see, poor people and people of color are at the greatest risk for criminal justice involvement. The highest risk is for poor men of color. The criminal justice system disproportionately arrests, convicts, and punishes poor people and people of color. But does this mean that the criminal justice network is biased against these groups?

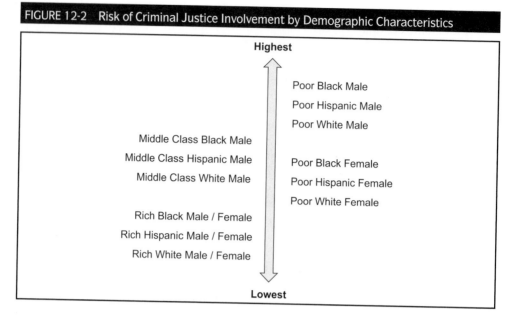

FIGURE 12-2   Risk of Criminal Justice Involvement by Demographic Characteristics

Walker, Spohn, and DeLone (2006), in their book, *The Color of Justice,* conclude that American criminal justice is characterized by what they refer to as *contextual discrimination,* defined in Figure 12-3. These authors write:

> We believe that the criminal justice system is characterized by obvious disparities based on race and ethnicity. It is impossible to ignore the disproportionate number of minorities arrested, imprisoned, and on death row. Some of the decisions that produce these results involve discrimination. . . . After considering all of the evidence, we conclude that the U.S. criminal justice system is characterized by *contextual discrimination.* (2000, p. 287; emphasis in original)

Contextual discrimination implies that there is discrimination based on race and/or ethnicity at some places and at some times under certain circumstances in the United States. Walker et al. explain that contextual discrimination is different from **systematic discrimination**, which they define as "discrimination at all stages of the criminal justice system, at all times, and all places" or **institutional discrimination**, defined as "racial and ethnic disparities in outcomes that are the result of the application of racially neutral factors such as prior criminal record, employment status, demeanor, etc." (p. 16). Note that the presence of contextual discrimination suggests that the problem is more complicated than discrimination resulting from behaviors of particular individuals, and that pure justice does not exist in the United States. The authors argue that the "salience of race and ethnicity varies from jurisdiction to jurisdiction" in part because "the major racial and ethnic minority groups are not evenly distributed across the country" (p. 14). The important point for this book is that since race and ethnicity play some role in the criminal justice process across the United States, the criminal justice network by definition is failing to achieve its ideal goal of doing justice (which assumes that race and ethnicity play no role).

FIGURE 12-3   Degrees of Discrimination

- *Systematic:*   Discrimination at all stages of the criminal justice network, at all times, and all places
- *Institutionalized:*   Racial and ethnic disparities in outcomes that are the result of the application of racially neutral factors such as prior criminal record, employment status, demeanor, etc.
- *Contextual:*   Discrimination found in particular contexts or circumstances
- *Individual:*   Discrimination that results from the acts of particular individuals but is not characteristic of entire agencies or the criminal justice network as a whole
- *Pure justice:*   No racial or ethnic discrimination at all

Source: Walker, Spohn, and DeLone (2000).

The racial disparities in American criminal justice are stunning. As you saw in Chapter 9, 8.1% of black males age 25 to 29 were in state or federal prison, compared to 2.6% of Hispanic males and only 1.1% of white males in the same age group. Further, when adding in jails, one in eight (12%) black males aged 25–29 was incarcerated, versus 1 in 26 (3.9%) Hispanic males and 1 in 59 (1.7%) white males. Black males in their 20s and 30s make up roughly 30% of all people locked up in America! So the war on crime is clearly having its greatest effects on young African American males.

The U.S. network of justice agencies consistently catches, punishes, and convicts people who are both poor and of color, so it is difficult to establish whether social class or race and ethnicity are driving criminal justice activity (Weitzer, 1996). Walker et al. (2000, p. 60) claim that both "[r]ace discrimination and social and economic inequality have a direct impact on crime and criminal justice, accounting for many of the racial disparities in the criminal justice system."

Walker et al. also attribute some racial and ethnic disparities to legal factors such as offense seriousness and offender prior record. This implies that African Americans and Hispanics commit more than their share of criminality. Box 12-2 addresses the relationship between race and crime.

Given the box discussion, African Americans do commit more than their fair share of some forms of crime (mostly due to differential economic strain and greater opportunity to commit certain kinds of acts). However, this does not suggest that African Americans are more dangerous than Caucasians. In fact, acts committed disproportionately by Caucasians (e.g., elite deviance) are far more dangerous than the street crimes disproportionately committed by people of color, as shown in Chapter 4.

Even if legal factors such as greater involvement in some forms of street criminality explain some racial and ethnic disparities in the criminal justice network, some disparities are explained by extralegal factors based on race, ethnicity, social class, and so forth. In other words, even if it were true that people of color committed disproportionately more crime than we might expect—given their percentage in the population—their proportion of arrests, convictions, and make-up of correctional populations cannot be explained by their criminality alone. What, then, explains the overrepresentation of minorities in America's criminal justice network? A careful analysis of statistics relating to race, ethnicity, and social class and their relationships with crime and criminal justice may lead to some answers.

BOX 12-2

RACE AND CRIMINALITY ACCORDING TO SOURCES OF CRIME DATA

Some believe that the notion of a racist criminal justice network is a myth (Wilbanks, 1987) and/or that skin color is declining in importance when it comes to criminal justice activity (DeLisi and Regoli, 1999). For example, some claim that the criminal justice network is not focused on race, ethnicity, or class, but that it processes the poor and people of color disproportionately because of their higher levels of involvement in criminality (DeLisi and Regoli, 1999; Wilbanks, 1987). The data suggest differently.

As discussed in Chapter 4, sources of crime data include the Uniform Crime Reports (UCR), National Criminal Victimization Survey (NCVS), and self-report studies. Remember that the UCR is a measure of crimes known to the police, crimes cleared by arrests, and arrests. UCR data do not contain detailed information about ethnicity and crime, and "therefore do not tell us anything about rates of offending" (Walker et al., 2000, p. 13).

Official rates of offending based on the UCR are in fact higher in poor, minority communities and for African Americans generally (Kennedy, 1997; Tonry, 1995). Yet relying on the UCR and other such official statistics for discovering offender characteristics is flawed and can create misconceptions about who is dangerous and who should be feared.

Miller (1997, p. 29) writes, "Relying on 'experience' emanating from the justice system is dicey even in the best of circumstances. Its rituals and procedures distort social realities and feed stereotypes at virtually every step." The UCR is a more valid measure of police experience than of crime because it measures the behavior of police rather than that of criminal offenders; therefore, it is not surprising that over 40% of every 100 individuals who are arrested for felonies are never prosecuted, or have their cases dismissed at first appearance (Miller, 1997).

UCR arrest statistics tend to create myths about who is dangerous and who is guilty. If we relied on arrest statistics to develop composites of "dangerous classes," we would not get an accurate picture of those who most threaten us (see Chapter 6 for a lengthier discussion of arrest rates and their meaning). Walker et al. (2000, p. 37) comment, "The picture of the typical offender that emerges from official arrest statistics may be racially distorted. If police target enforcement efforts in minority communities or concentrate on crime committed by racial minorities, then obviously racial minorities will be overrepresented in arrest statistics."

Russell (1998, p. 114) calls the stereotypical criminal in the United States the **criminalblackman**. Consider the following quote from the Reverend Jesse Jackson, a long-time civil rights activist who also happens to be an African American: "There is nothing more painful for me at this stage in my life than to walk down the street and hear footsteps and start to think about robbery and then to look around and see if it's somebody white and feel relieved" (Kennedy, 1997, p. 15). The truth is, people fear African Americans and other minorities and perceive them to pose significant threats to their personal safety (e.g., see Hurwitz and Peffley,

1997; Miethe, 1995; Peffley and Hurwitz, 1997; Skogan, 1995; St. John and Heald-Moore, 1996).

"Blackness," in particular, is treated as a sign of increased risk of criminality (Kennedy, 1997, p. 387). As illustrated by the Jesse Jackson example, this is a normal phenomenon, which results not from individual racism or bias but, rather, from deep-seated myths about race and crime that are created and reinforced by official sources of crime data such as the UCR, as well as media portrayals of crime and criminal justice.

Recall that the NCVS is a measure of self-reported victimizations, including both crimes reported to the police and those not reported to the police. The NCVS, generally thought to be a more valid measure of criminal behavior than the UCR, shows that households headed by African Americans and Hispanics have higher rates of victimization than Caucasian households. Also, African Americans and Hispanics are more likely than Caucasians to suffer from personal criminal victimization. Finally, one's lifetime risk of being victimized by certain violent street crimes is highly correlated with one's race.

According to the Bureau of Justice Statistics, in 2005, for every 1,000 persons, 27 African Americans, 20 Caucasians, and 14 persons of other races were victimized by a violent crime. While blacks and whites experienced similar rates of simple assault and about the same rates of rapes and sexual assaults, the rate of victimization of blacks for serious violent crimes (i.e., homicide, rape, robbery, and aggravated assault) was 13.6 per 1,000 people, versus only 6.5 for whites. Further, according to the FBI's Uniform Crime Reports, approximately 49% of murder victims were white and 49% were black,

suggesting that blacks are overrepresented among murder victims.

Because most street crimes are intraracial in nature, logic would dictate that African Americans are disproportionately committing street crimes against their own households and persons. Yet according to the Bureau of Justice Statistics (2005), higher victimization rates are partially a function of social class and living in inner cities.

For the purpose of this examination, I assume that people of color commit more street crime (but not more crime, generally) than one would logically expect given their proportion of the population. For example, the NCVS also shows that victims report a higher percentage of victimizations at the hands of African Americans than one would expect given their percentage of the population (Kennedy, 1997, p. 23). "African Americans are overrepresented as offenders for all of the offenses" of the NCVS (Walker et al., 2000, p. 42). Assuming that NCVS data are valid in this regard is questionable, because NCVS researchers must rely on victims' perceptions of their offenders. Whatever the case, the real question for the issue of whether disparities in the criminal justice network stem from higher involvement in criminality by minorities is whether the very small differences in offending suggested by the NCVS can account for the observed disparities in official arrest, conviction, and incarceration statistics. Virtually no one thinks they can.

Why are African American males more likely to be incarcerated for crimes than other groups? According to the NCVS, the proportion of violent street crimes committed by African American males has remained steady since the 1980s, yet the disproportionate use of imprisonment has worsened since then

(continued)

BOX 12-2 (*Continued*)

(Tonry, 1995, p. 4). Steffensmeir, Ulmer, and Kramer (1998, p. 789) call this the "high cost of being black, young, and male." Spohn and Hollerman (2000, p. 281) suggest that convicted criminals who happen to be young, male, and African American will pay an added "incarceration penalty" on top of the sentence given to other groups in America.

In support of the notion that observed disparities in official arrest, conviction, and incarceration statistics cannot be explained by differences in offending behaviors, Reiman (2006, p. 105) compares criminal victimization statistics of the NCVS and arrest statistics of the UCR. He concludes that "police are arresting blacks almost two times more frequently that the occurrence of their perceived offenses. Because arrest determines the pool from which charged, convicted, and imprisoned individuals are selected, this suggests that deep bias persists throughout the criminal justice system." This is why Kappeler et al. (2000, p. 223) write, "Comparisons of UCR and NCVS statistics offer clear evidence of racism." A similar conclusion is reached by Walker et al. (2000, p. 42): "African Americans are represented in arrest figures in much higher proportions than the perception of offenders from victim interviews suggest."

Tonry (1995) argues that African American males are more involved in crimes that are punishable by imprisonment. To prove this, Tonry examines various sources of data (UCR arrest data, NCVS victim identification records, self-report studies) and concludes that arrests by police and sentences by prosecutors are not discriminatory or biased. For example, Tonry shows that crime victims are only slightly less likely to identify African Americans as their assailants in robbery and aggravated assault cases than one might expect given trends in black arrests for these crimes.

Unfortunately for Tonry's argument, he does not even address the question of whether the law is biased. If the law has disproportionately criminalized what poor people do and if African Americans tend to be poor, then the law is where one needs to look to see bias against African Americans. An example is seen in the case of robbery, a crime committed by the poor. NCVS data show that African Americans are perceived to be offenders in about half of robberies but in no more than 30% of any other violent offense. UCR data show that African Americans make up about 56% of people arrested for robbery crimes (Sourcebook on Criminal Justice Statistics, 2006). African Americans are disproportionately involved in robberies. Given that monetary gain is the primary motive for robbery, it is not a stretch to conclude that it is the offenders' social class that explains their involvement in the crime of robbery. Rich people do not have to stick a gun in your face to get your money, nor do they have to rob a bank to steal money from it. Instead, they can and do steal money through fraud and embezzlement, as in the case of the savings and loan (S&L) scandals, which produced more financial losses than all the bank robberies in the history of the United States. Yet such crimes have not been treated as "serious" throughout our country's history. Even now when fraud and embezzlement are treated roughly as seriously as theft, law enforcement resources are not adequate to fight fraud and embezzlement. In fact, most American police officers, who work for city and county governments, are not involved in investigating and apprehending acts of elite deviance (see Chapter 6). Instead, they are on the streets, fighting the types of thefts committed primarily by the poor, such as robbery.

You might argue that robbery is more serious than similar acts of elite deviance because, technically, it is violent in nature (that is, it implies that some force or weapon was used to achieve the theft). But robbery is clearly aimed at property gain, just like fraud and embezzlement. The primary difference is that rich people

do not have to resort to robbery to acquire wealth illegally—they have the luxury of illegitimate opportunities to engage in other, less risky forms of theft.

So, although Tonry suggests that African Americans actually commit proportionally more felonies than Caucasians, he does acknowledge a potential bias when he writes, "Whatever their race, most felony defendants are poor, badly educated, un- or underemployed, and not part of a stable household" (p. 101). These are America's enemies in the war on crime.

Race, Ethnicity, and Social Class

There is an intimate relationship among race, ethnicity, and social class in the United States. Specifically, racial and ethnic minorities are disproportionately likely to be poor and to be exposed to harmful environmental conditions. This means that some racial disparities in criminality as well as criminal justice processing may in fact be explained by economic factors.

Walker et al. (2006) note three important facts that implicate economic factors as major sources of criminal justice bias against people of color: an economic gap between the rich and the poor, regardless of race or ethnicity; an economic gap between Caucasian Americans and people of color; and a growing segment of the population that is very poor. Differences in social class standing among racial and ethnic groups can be explained on the basis of income, wealth, employment, and poverty rates (Walker, Spohn, and DeLone, 2006). **Income**—how much money a family earns in a year—is highly influenced by race. For example, African Americans ($30,858) and Hispanics ($35,967) make far less on average than Caucasians ($50,784) (U.S. Census, 2006).

Wealth—a measure of all assets accumulated—is nearly 11 times lower for African Americans than for Caucasians and about 8 times lower for Hispanics. Meanwhile, the **unemployment** rate is more than twice as high for African Americans and almost twice as high for Hispanics than for Caucasians. **Poverty** rates are also higher for African Americans (24.9%) and Hispanics (21.8%) than for Caucasians (8.3%) (U.S. Census, 2006). In American slums, where there is far greater despair and deterioration than in the suburbs and rural areas, nearly 7 out of every 8 people are minorities (Beckett and Sasson, 2000, p. 37). Finally, child poverty rates are more than two times higher for African Americans and Hispanics than for Caucasians.

Underemployment is also higher for people of color than for Caucasians (Bluestone and Rose, 2000). Being underemployed means one is either not employed full-time or is not making enough money on which to live. The so-called **poverty wage** (Jennings, 1999, p. 25) is a major source of poverty. Earning a minimal amount of money for a full-time job leaves people poor and is thus a form of "inclusive exclusion"; that is, these workers are included in the workforce but excluded from enjoying the benefits of full-time, well-paying jobs (George, 1999, p. 202). According to Kim (1999, p. 307), "the working poor constitute one of the fastest growing segments of the impoverished population." These "forgotten Americans" cannot make more money, cannot work more hours, and hence are still poor because of factors beyond their own control (Quan, 2000).

Ehrenreich (2001), in her book, *Nickel and Dimed*, demonstrates how difficult it is to make it in the working world of America's service economy for many people. In 1998, Ehrenreich moved across three states, working as a waitress, maid, cleaning woman, aide to a nursing home, and a sales clerk for Wal-Mart. She shows that it is impossible to have a residence earning only $6 to $7 per hour and that service-type jobs are not highly valued or rewarding jobs in our society. Yet these are the jobs that have grown the fastest in our economy. Similarly, Shipler (2005), in his book, *The Working Poor: Invisible in America*, shows what life is like for the millions of people in America who are employed full-time but are nevertheless poor.

Disparities in employment are greatest for young, male minorities, that segment of the population most likely to have encounters with the police (see Chapter 6). Regular wages are also lower for minorities and women than for Caucasians and men (Weinberger, 2000).

In addition to these factors, widespread patterns of **residential segregation** still exist. Those residents stuck in our nation's inner cities "find it extremely difficult both to learn about job opportunities and to travel to and from work. Public transportation systems are either weak or nonexistent in most cities" (Walker et al., 2000, p. 69). Inner-city residents are also less likely to have the necessary contacts to attain jobs. In case you think that anyone who wants to can move away from the inner cities, keep in mind that real estate agents and banking personnel play major roles in maintaining residential segregation by discriminating against poor people and people of color.

Criminologists and sociologists claim that being socially isolated in inner cities leads to an increased risk of criminality because these residents have less contact with good role models and less ability to participate in controlling institutions (Skogan, 1990; Wilson, 1987). Increased crime in inner-city neighborhoods lowers the quality of life, as well. Thus, many government policies in the United States promote criminality among the nation's poor and people of color.

Why do people of color have lower average household incomes and lower levels of net worth than Caucasians (Beckett and Sasson, 2000, p. 34)? There are two competing explanations. According to Smith (1995, p. 107), **cultural perspectives** "emphasize the values, beliefs, attitudes, and lifestyles" of the poor, whereas **structural perspectives** "emphasize enduring features of the economic and social systems." The cultural view "sees" the problem as coming from within the poor people themselves; the structural view "sees" the problem as originating outside the poor people. Murray and Herrnstein (1994), supporters of the cultural perspective, posit that the United States will be "dumbed down" as a result of illegitimate children being born to those with lower IQs.

Even if there is a culture unique to people of color or the poor, it may emerge from the U.S. capitalist economy. Such is the claim of Marxist and conflict criminologists, who hold that crime is a reaction by those at the bottom of the capitalist economy to oppression and domination (e.g., see Greenberg, 1993; Lynch, 1997). Unemployment is a key factor in accounting for this culture or way of life, which has always been higher for African Americans and Hispanics than for Caucasians. Unemployment is associated with murder, suicide, mental illness, divorce, separation, child abuse, and drug abuse (Smith, 1995, pp. 131–132).

The cultural explanation of poverty ignores poverty's structural correlates. Kushnick and Jennings (1999, p. 1) explain that poverty is produced by structural factors such as the "increasing imbalance in the distribution of wealth, with the rich continually becoming richer; the unbridled mobility of capital, both in finance and in production; and the prevalence of low wages coupled with levels of relatively high unemployment of certain groups." When "national policies . . . allow corporate leaders to pursue profits without consideration of the social costs incurred by their strategies," things only get worse.

Poverty is usually framed in politics as a "lack of work ethic" or a "failure of personal responsibility" among poor people. The media then "racialize" poverty by depicting poverty as a "minority thing," which then diverts attention from the real problems associated with the U.S. economic system. The role of the wealthy and the state in creating and reinforcing inequality is thus virtually ignored (Dill, Zinn, and Patton, 1999, p. 263). Given the corporate ownership of the media (see Chapter 5), this is not surprising. One example is that African American criminals are depicted as "thoughtless, sadistic, and callous" individuals who commit random crimes (Franklin, 1999, p. 128). Additionally, in the 1990s, the media "saturated the public with stories and pictures about African American teenager birth rates, African American illegitimate birth rates, and African American female AIDS rates (Franklin, 1999, p. 130, citing Jackson, 1988). Typically, these images and stories feature members of the poor "African American underclass," who represent less than 1% of the population and who live in the nation's largest urban areas.

The media also "socialize the entire population, mainstream and minority, young and old, by the way they depict and discuss minorities" (Chaffee and German, 1998, p. 311; also see Reed, 1993). "The kind of coverage, positive or negative, may also impact the nature of treatment, beneficial or negative, accorded to minorities in the political system" (Chaffee and German, 1998, p. 312). Overall, positive views of minorities are lacking in media portrayals, and African Americans receive most minority-related news coverage.

American politicians go on to depict poor individuals as being born with a unique "ethos" that reflects immorality, a lack of hard work, and low levels of intelligence (Banfield, 1973), as well as being psychologically and programmatically dependent (Murray, 1984). Since the 1980s, politicians have talked about a "lack of family values" as responsible for the "significant decline in living standards for African Americans" in the 1980s (George, 1999, p. 198). High unemployment rates are thus blamed on lazy people.

Katz (1999, p. 63) argues that one reason African Americans in particular experience such tremendous poverty is that they historically have lacked an ethnic niche in employment: "Every time African Americans gained a modest presence in a promising trade, discrimination undercut their efforts, and whites replaced them." **Strain theory** predicts that African Americans thus have been forced either into **retreatism** (unemployment and drug use) or into **innovation** (selling African American market goods, including drugs). Innovation involving illegitimate activity is a means to overcome strain (Merton, 1938b) and **differential opportunity** (Cloward and Ohlin, 1961). When African Americans turn to illegal activity to tilt the scales in their favor, they become more likely to have run-ins with the law.

Another option for the poor is to seek government assistance in the form of welfare. Although the U.S. government has been willing to assist its own poor to varying degrees throughout its history, antipoverty programs have become anti–poor people efforts since the early 1970s. People who are in trouble are characterized as "people who make trouble" (Beckett and Sasson, 2000, p. 155). In the 1990s, the U.S. government passed laws that limit the total time period a person can be on welfare over the course of his or her life to 5 years. The attack on welfare rights during the 1980s and 1990s "has served the interests of corporate capital and its political and media allies" (Kushnick, 1999, p. 147). As the attack against the poor was stepped up, the code words for welfare dependency became "big government," and right-wing political leaders such as Ronald Reagan, Pat Buchanan, and Newt Gingrich began to call for "smaller government." In reality, the majority of Americans did not vote for the Congress that passed this type of reform: "The majority of Americans either voted for candidates who lost or, even more telling, did not bother to vote at all." Nevertheless, some of the harshest social policies we have seen in generations are being carried out in the name of the American people (Ransby, 1999, p. 327). Ironically, these same leaders share responsibility for increasing the size and strength of criminal justice agencies in the United States, all of which are funded and operated by the government. That is, these self-styled opponents of big government are responsible for creating big government in the form of the U.S. criminal justice network.

Meanwhile, according to the U.S. Census (2006), in 2005 17.6% of all American children lived in poverty. According to the Children's Defense Fund (2006), a disproportionate number of minority children live in poverty. More than 1 in 3 black children live in poverty, versus nearly 1 in 3 Hispanic and nearly 1 in 10 white children. Poor children have worse nutrition, are at a heightened risk of stunted growth, receive a poorer education, will earn lower incomes, and are at greater risk for child abuse and neglect. Poor children are also disproportionately minorities and living in single-parent households. Obviously, criminal justice officials are not equipped to address these social facts. What is clear is that every dollar invested by the U.S. government in criminal justice is a dollar not invested in social programs that can assist in alleviating childhood poverty rates in the United States.

Even though most poor, single, childbearing women are not African American (Sidel, 1996), "family breakdown is often a thinly veiled attack on the African American urban underclass" and "single mother" is often used as a code word to mean "African American single mother" (Dill et al., 1999, p. 269). Given that the 1996 welfare reform law all but eroded the notion that Americans are "entitled" to assistance from their own government, it is easy to imagine how Americans have come to see African Americans as unentitled, even though "they live in one of the richest countries in the world" and most of them have paid taxes to the federal government (Ransby, 1999, p. 332).

During the same time, corporate perks grew. Former secretary of labor, Robert Reich, spoke critically of benefits enjoyed by corporate elites because of government policies (Ransby, 1999, p. 324). For example, corporate taxes accounted for about one-third of federal revenues in the 1950s, but only about 10% in the 1990s. In essence, taxation became more of a burden on individual Americans and their families, while corporations pay virtually no taxes today. Corporate profits have increased as a result, but this has not stopped companies from downsizing and even moving overseas or south of the border for cheaper labor costs.

Race, Ethnicity, Government Policy, and Criminal Justice

From the previous review of the relationship among race, ethnicity, and social class, it is apparent that many of the criminal justice biases against minorities in the United States are at least partly attributable to social class. Of course, one's social class standing is affected by many other factors, including race, ethnicity, and historical and contemporary discrimination against people of color. After hundreds of years of discrimination against minority groups, there is still not a level playing field for all races in the United States.

Race and ethnicity also play significant roles in government policy and the criminal justice process. The result is discrimination in numerous government policies and overwhelming disparities throughout the criminal justice network. Mann (1993) calls this *Unequal Justice*. The result for young minority males has been *Lock 'Em Up and Throw Away the Key* (Mauer, 1998) because of what some call a *Search and Destroy* mission by the criminal justice network (Miller, 1998). Although racial disparity does not necessarily imply racial discrimination (Walker et al., 2006), if the disparity is harmful, the intent is really not important, especially if we know about it but do nothing to stop it (Kennedy, 1997).

Some studies do not find evidence of racial bias in the criminal justice network. For example, most studies examining sentencing severity find that length of sentence is typically determined by legal factors such as seriousness of offense and prior record (see Chapter 8). However, if the law is biased, then seriousness of offense is a function of the bias in the law rather than bias in the courts. An offender's prior record would also be affected by criminal justice factors such as presence of police in one's neighborhood. This means that discrimination in criminal justice cannot be dismissed even in the face of findings that legal variables account for offenders' sentences. Other studies that do not appear at first glance to show evidence of bias may also show bias on closer examination. For example, as discussed in Chapter 10, numerous studies of the death penalty process find that prosecutors are actually less likely overall to seek the death penalty against African Americans (unless they kill whites).

Some may use such studies to show that criminal justice activities are clearly not biased against African Americans. However, as you learned in Chapter 10, careful analysis shows that the bias is still against African Americans, and is most apparent in interracial crimes.

Racism today is less overt—no more fire hoses and police dogs being used to suppress minorities, as was common during the civil rights movement—and is intertwined with legitimate government activity. For example, crime control is a legitimate state goal, yet "law and order" and "tough on crime" are phrases that are used to conjure up images of dangerous people of color. They are thus "code words," words that refer indirectly to minorities but appear not to revolve around racial themes (Omi and Winant, 1986). Do not be fooled, however. Punitiveness is partially "a manifestation of hostility toward African Americans" (Beckett and Sasson, 2000, p. 135). Is it a coincidence that American punitiveness is disproportionately directed at minorities, particularly African Americans? At the very least, because African Americans are disproportionately poor and are socially isolated in poor communities, they become more susceptible to criminal justice focus. In essence, they live where the police are most likely to patrol, making it more likely that they will be arrested and become involved with the criminal justice network.

Still, most scholars agree that our nation has made great strides to become less biased since the civil rights movement of the 1960s. For example, Walker et al. (2006) demonstrate that American schools are less segregated today than they were in the 1960s, that more voters and elected officials are minorities, and that minorities are more likely to work in the criminal justice network and serve on juries. These authors write, "The civil rights movement eliminated *de jure* segregation and other blatant forms of discrimination, but pervasive discrimination in society and the criminal justice system continues" (p. 77; emphasis in original). The evidence supports this statement. Changes in the law and in attitudes of individuals within the criminal justice network have made systematic discrimination against African Americans much less likely. But even though the civil rights movement led to rapid changes for people of color, economic inequality of racial and ethnic groups has not been widely addressed. The result is that institutional racism is still with us.

Robert Smith, in *Racism in the Post–Civil Rights Era: Now You See It, Now You Don't* (1995), convincingly argues that institutional racism is alive and well in the United States. Smith (citing Carmichael and Hamilton, 1969), defines **institutional racism** as "the predication of decisions and policies on considerations of race for purpose of **subordinating** a racial group and maintaining control over that group" (p. 2; emphasis in original). Smith provides evidence of racism in several American institutions, including employment, education, housing, health, and consumer services. Disparities in such institutions produce injustice in the United States and may explain the greater criminal justice involvement of African Americans. Ironically, we don't see higher street crime rates in minority neighborhoods as a product of racial and ethnic discrimination, but as indicators that the residents of those neighborhoods are simply different from (and inferior to) us.

Smith does not claim that institutional racism is necessarily intentional; rather, he suggests that "whenever one observes policies that have the intent or effect of subordinating a racial group, that phenomenon is properly identified as racism" (p. 29). Institutional racism occurs when the "normal, accepted, routine patterns and practices of society's institutions have the *effect or consequence* of subordinating an individual or group . . ." (p. 33; emphasis in original). Because African Americans are disproportionately affected by criminal justice processes, Smith might claim that the U.S. criminal justice network is involved in institutional racism.

Smith does not address this issue directly, although he does briefly mention the war on drugs as an example of racist U.S. policy. Rather, he examines how institutional racism has evolved from individual racism and become entrenched in the contemporary United States. Beckett and Sasson (2000, p. 39) claim that racial segregation of housing, for example, is a product of racial discrimination. Massey and Gross (1990) call housing discrimination a form of "American apartheid" that undoubtedly leaves African Americans living in ghettos where jobs and legitimate opportunities for success are scarce.

When people are not working and may be committing crimes, it becomes easy to characterize them as lazy, inferior, and bad, even though the real villain may be downsizing in corporations and the restructuring of the American workforce from manufacturing to service jobs. The myth of a free economy creates the illusion of equal opportunity for all Americans, which appears to prove that people who do not make it are to blame. Smith documents the historical notion of "black inferiority" among Americans, which has been used to justify both slavery and colonization of other countries. One need only look around to find "official" evidence of African American inferiority — in unemployment rates, relative housing conditions, and educational attainment of various groups, and in rates of family dissolution, out-of-wedlock births, alcohol abuse, and crime. The fact that African Americans are disproportionately likely to be unemployed, live in poor housing conditions, lack formal education, be single parents, abuse some drugs, and commit street crime is used as proof of African Americans' inferiority to Caucasians.

Although Caucasians are less likely now to express openly beliefs in African American inferiority, public opinion polls such as the General Social Survey (GSS) still illustrate high levels of negative views of African Americans. Almost half of Americans believe that African Americans tend to be lazy. More than half think African Americans are violence-prone, and nearly one-third think African Americans are unintelligent (Smith, 1995, p. 39).

According to Beckett (1997, p. 84), beliefs about crime and punishment are "highly correlated with race and racial attitudes." For example, those who most strongly believe in a law-and-order approach to crime fighting tend to be more racist and not to support equal rights for minorities. They believe African Americans are inferior to Caucasians and thus are deserving of punitive sanctions when they violate the law. Further, people who have hostilities toward African Americans are more likely to support the death penalty (see Chapter 10).

In reality, African Americans cannot be inferior to Caucasians simply because of their skin color or ethnicity, because race is a societal-level variable rather than an individual-level variable. Race cannot be used, for example, as evidence of inborn differences between Americans of African and European descent in terms of intelligence or willpower. Genetic variation is higher within the races than between them (Jeffery, 1990; Robinson, 2004). Smith (1995) claims that anti–African American stereotypes were worse in the 1990s than in the 1970s. Smith blames this, as well as increased racist violence in the 1980s, on the political dogma generated by Presidents Reagan and Bush (the first), particularly with regard to crime control issues — for example, the use of the Willie Horton incident to make early prison release a campaign issue, as discussed in Chapter 2. Smith writes, "The use by the 1988 Bush campaign of the now infamous Willie Horton ad was an indirect, subtle appeal to this racist stereotype" of the libidinous, dangerous African American male. "For twenty-eight days during the 1988 fall campaign an ad [showed] a picture of Horton, a person very dark in skin color and in a photograph that he himself said pictured him as 'depraved and maniacal' and as the 'devil incarnate' (Horton says at the time the photograph was taken he had not been permitted a shave or haircut for six months or more)" (p. 21).

The fact that Horton was accused of raping a Caucasian woman allowed politicians to tap into deeply held fears that characterize African American males as sexually aggressive and dangerous. In reality, most rapists are Caucasian males, and most people out on temporary prison release do not commit crimes, although these facts are not reflected in public opinion polls (Anderson, 1995).

But then, Willie Horton was also poor. Whether the ad campaign was intended to create fear of African Americans or of poor criminals is not entirely clear and perhaps not actually important. As noted, untangling the effects of race and social class is very difficult. As explained by Smith (1995, p. 34), "any policy having an adverse impact on blacks should not be conceptualized as institutionalized racism because of the intersection of race and class in the United States. African Americans in the United States are disproportionately lower class, and in any class-stratified society most institutional arrangements have an adverse impact on the poor and dispossessed whatever their race." So, "much of what may appear to be institutional racism is simply the effects of routine class bias in a market economy" (p. 53).

An example of negative consequences suffered disproportionately by African Americans is poor health, which has "substantially deteriorated" in the post–civil rights era. Smith (1995) demonstrates that infant mortality rates are nearly twice as high for African Americans as for Caucasians, and that life expectancy is shorter. He writes, "Much of the data suggest that the vast differentials in African American and white health are to be explained on the basis of social class and public policy; in terms of the latter, primarily because of the absence of a comprehensive national health insurance program" (p. 69).

Nevertheless, Smith believes that class-related disparities in health have likely resulted from hundreds of years of individual racism and the institutions created by racists; thus, he includes them as a form of institutional racism. Figure 12-4 depicts five forms of institutional discrimination facing the poor and racial minorities, as well as the likely outcomes, in the areas of employment, education, housing, health, and consumer services. This results in an increased likelihood of exposure by African Americans to criminogenic conditions such as unemployment, underemployment, lack of formal education, poverty, environmental pollution, and violence. Such conditions lead not only to increased physical and financial harms, but also to lower levels of self-esteem among African Americans living in conditions of severe poverty, expressed through the American polity, church, media, schools, and popular culture.

Smith argues that, because of the negative meanings of the word *black*—which has been "associated with discouragement, despair, depression, coldness, the unknown, the haunting shadow and nightmare" (Anderson and Cromwell, 1977, p. 76)—some African Americans see themselves as violent, dependent on government assistance, and to a

FIGURE 12-4   Forms of Institutional Discrimination

Forms of Discrimination	Likely Effects
Employment	Criminogenic conditions
Education	Criminal victimization
Housing	Disproportionate governmental focus
Health	
Consumer services	

lesser degree, lazy and unintelligent. He writes that "a significant minority of African Americans (ranging from 10 to 25 percent depending on the survey and the question) continue to tell survey researchers that they hold negative images of the race" (p. 95). It is not surprising that the militant "Black Power" movement of the mid- to late 1960s became the focus of criminal justice agencies. In essence, when African Americans began to rise up in an effort to assert their rights and be recognized as good people—reflected in the slogan "black is beautiful," for example—their actions were criminalized by the dominant Caucasian power structures in southern criminal justice agencies. If they were not jailed and/or threatened with bodily violence, they were beaten during riots initiated by the police, even though they are no more criminal than other groups in society.

GENDER AND CRIMINAL JUSTICE

Gender bias is also prevalent in the U.S. criminal justice network (Boritch, 1992). Gottfredson and Jarjoura (1996, p. 49) state it this way, "Extreme racial (and gender) disproportionalities have existed in America's prison and jail populations for at least 175 years." Gender bias includes decisions that favor or harm individuals on the basis of gender. Overall, criminal justice activities seem to be less punitive toward women. We can call this a bias against men, who are responsible for a much larger portion of street crime and violence in general than women (Jeffery, 1990). This may be due to what Belknap (1996, pp. 69–70) calls the **chivalry or paternalism hypothesis**. For example, you saw in Chapter 10 that, although women commit more than 10% of all murders in any given year, they make up less than 2% of all people on death row and 1% of all executions.

Generally speaking, women are less likely to be victimized by crime, less likely to commit it, less likely to be arrested, less likely to be convicted, less likely to be sentenced to prison or jail, and generally are sentenced to less time than men. Starting with victimization, Catalano (2006, p. 8) notes that, in 2005, "Males were victims of overall violent crime, robbery, total assault, aggravated assaults and simple assault at rates higher than females. Females were more likely than males to be victims of rape or sexual assault." Table 12-1 shows that, in 2005, the rate of criminal victimization was lower for women than men for every crime except sex offenses. The rate of female victimization was lower than the rate of male victimization for violent crimes (17.1 per 1,000 people versus 25.5 per 1,000 people), simple assault (11.2 per 1,000 people versus 15.9 per 1,000 people), robbery (1.4 per 1,000 people versus 3.8 per 1,000 people), and aggravated assault (3.1 per 1,000 people versus 5.6 per 1,000 people). Rates of sexual assault victimization were higher for women than men (1.4 per 1,000 people versus 0.1 per 1,000 people).

Table 12-2 shows the percentage of arrests that were men and women in 2005 for various types of crimes. As you can see, women (who make up 51% of the U.S. population) are underrepresented among arrestees for every category of crime except for prostitution and commercialized vice offenses (66.4%). Women made up only 23.8% of all arrests in 2006, including 17.9% of violent crime arrests and 32% of property crime arrests (Sourcebook on Criminal Justice Statistics, 2006).

According to the Sourcebook on Criminal Justice Statistics (2006), women are underrepresented among court clients, as well. Table 12-3 (see page 436)shows that, of all

TABLE 12-1 Rates of Criminal Victimization by Gender (2005)	Men	Women
All personal offenses	28.0 per 1,000	23.9 per 1,000
Violent offenses	25.5 per 1,000	17.1 per 1,000
Murder/manslaughter	8.5 per 1,000	2.6 per 1,000
Sexual assault/rape	0.1 per 1,000	1.4 per 1,000
Robbery	3.8 per 1,000	1.4 per 1,000
Simple assault	15.9 per 1,000	11.2 per 1,000
Aggravated assault	5.6 per 1,000	3.1 per 1,000
Theft	0.8 per 1,000	1.0 per 1,000

Source: Bureau of Justice Statistics (2006). Criminal Victimization 2005. Available at http://ojp.usdoj.gov/bjs/pub/pdf/cv05.pdf.

people convicted of felonies in state courts in 2002, only 17% were women, including 11% of convicted violent felons, 25% of convicted property felons, and 17% of convicted drug offenders. The crime category for which their percentage of convictions is most similar to their representation in society is "fraud, forgery and embezzlement" (42%).

In federal courts, the picture is very similar. Table 12-4 (see page 437) shows that women made up a minority of people convicted of crimes in federal district courts in 2003. Women made up 13.2% of those convicted of all crimes, 7.6% of those convicted of violent crimes, 26.6% of those convicted of property crimes, 12.6% of those convicted of drug offenses, 11.9% of those convicted of public-order offenses, 3.6% of those convicted of weapons offenses, and 4.8% of those convicted of immigration offenses.

Women are also underrepresented among sentences to prison and jail for most crime at the state and federal level of courts. For example, 72% of males were sentenced to incarceration in 2000 for felony convictions, versus only 57% of women. Males were more likely than women to be sentenced to incarceration for violent offenses (81% versus 65%), for property offenses (70% versus 52%), and for drug offenses (70% versus 61%). Simultaneously, women convicted of felonies in state courts were more likely than men to be sentenced to probation for all offenses (38% versus 24%), for violent offenses (31% versus 17%), for property offenses (42% versus 26%), and for drug offenses (34% versus 26%).

At the federal level, the picture is much the same. In 2003, women were less likely than men to be sentenced to incarceration for all offenses (57.5% versus 82.8%), for violent offenses (76.4% versus 95%), fraud (48% versus 63.6%), and drug offenses (82.3% versus 93.6%).

Female convicted felons at the state level also tend to receive shorter sentences than men. Women receive shorter sentences than men for all offenses (23 months versus 28 months), for violent offenses (44 months versus 70 months), for property offenses (19 months versus 29 months), and for drug offenses (19 months versus 30 months). These patterns generally hold true for both incarceration sentences and probation sentences.

TABLE 12-2 Arrests by Gender (2005)	Men	Women
All offenses	76.2%	23.8%
Violent offenses	82.1%	17.9%
Murder/manslaughter	89.0%	11.0%
Forcible rape	98.5%	1.5%
Robbery	88.9%	11.1%
Aggravated assault	79.2%	20.8%
Property offenses	68.0%	29.9%
Theft	61.4%	38.6%
Motor vehicle theft	82.4%	17.6%
Burglary	85.5%	14.5%
Forgery/counterfeiting	60.3%	39.7%
Fraud	54.5%	45.5%
Embezzlement	50.0%	50.0%
Prostitution/commercialized vice	33.6%	66.4%

Source: Sourcebook on Criminal Justice Statistics (2006).

At the federal level, women also generally receive shorter sentences than men. The average sentences in 2003 were shorter for women than men for violent offenses (65 versus 98.4 months), fraud (18.3 versus 25.7 months), and drug offenses (49.5 versus 84.5 months).

It is generally thought that courts are more lenient to convicted female felons than convicted male felons because of legal factors—that is, women generally cause less damage through their criminality and typically have shorter criminal records. But when comparing sentences for certain types of crimes, women are sometimes sentenced at a rate closer to men. For example, African American females convicted of drug offenses—both possession and trafficking—are more likely to be sentenced to prison than Caucasian men and Caucasian women. Given the biases in policing (see Chapter 6) and the biases of the drug war (see Chapter 11), it is highly likely that some of these disparities are attributable to biases in the law rather than actual behavior differences. This is discussed more in Issue in Depth at the end of the chapter.

As of 2005, men made up 95% of all inmates in state and federal prisons while women made up only 5%. The rate of imprisonment for males is more than 13 times higher than the female rate of imprisonment. Men also made up 87.3% of all adults incarcerated in jails in 2005. Yet the number of female inmates in both jails and prisons has increased at a much faster rate since the 1970s. As you have seen throughout this book, this is attributable to the explosion of get tough policies, including the war on drugs, that regularly catch small-time and nonviolent offenders who tend to increasingly be women.

There is some evidence of what Belknap (1996) calls the **evil woman hypothesis**, which posits that women will be treated more harshly for similar crimes than men. Morgan-Sharp (1999, p. 384) suggests that the criminal justice network is tougher on women when they "do not adhere to prescribed gender roles." This suggests that

TABLE 12-3 Convictions by State Courts by Gender (2002)

	Men	*Women*
All offenses	83%	17%
Violent offenses	89%	11%
Murder/manslaughter	90%	10%
Sexual assault	97%	3%
Robbery	92%	8%
Aggravated assault	85%	15%
Property offenses	75%	25%
Burglary	91%	9%
Theft	75%	25%
Motor vehicle theft	89%	11%
Fraud, forgery, embezzlement	58%	42%
Drug offenses	83%	17%

Source: Sourcebook on Criminal Justice Statistics (2006).

women may be reacted to more harshly by courts when they do things that are not generally expected of them (Chesney-Lind and Pasko, 2004).

According to the National Criminal Justice Commission, even though the vast majority of people punished in the United States are men, "women are the fastest-growing category of prisoners nationwide" (Donziger, 1996, p. 146). For example, in the 1980s the rate of female incarcerations increased more than the rate of male incarcerations in every year except one. The commission attributes this fact to changes in sentencing policy that have overcome traditionally lenient sentences for women compared to men (Daly, 1994; Steffensmeir, Ulmer, and Kramer, 1998) and to the war on drugs, which I discussed in depth in Chapter 11. From 1990 to 1996, the number of female prisoners per 100,000 people in Florida increased by 65%; for male inmates, the increase was only 45% (Crawford, 2000, p. 263). Crawford writes, "Although the Florida system is extremely reluctant to classify women as habitual offenders, there is a notable and disturbing exception based on offenders' race and drug-related crimes" (p. 277). Crawford (2000) found evidence of a sentencing bias against minority women in Florida. His research suggests that the state's habitual offender statute was disproportionately being used against African American women, even after controlling for legal factors such as prior criminal record and crime seriousness. More recent research supports this conclusion (Belknap, 2006; Muraskin, 2006).

The increasingly punitive response of our criminal justice agencies to female offenders does not owe itself to a female crime wave. Instead, women are simply more likely to be sent to prison for offenses that typically did not receive imprisonment in the past. According to Bureau of Justice Statistics figures cited by the National Criminal Justice Commission, increases in female arrests and incarcerations were mostly due to relatively minor, nonviolent charges such as shoplifting, check forgery, welfare fraud, and drug crimes (Donziger, 1996, p. 149). Some female incarcerations for drug offenses stemmed from mandatory sentences, which give judges no discretion in setting punishment. Thus,

TABLE 12-4 Sentences Under Federal Sentencing Guidelines by Gender (2003)		
	Men	*Women*
All offenses	86.7%	13.3%
Murder	85.2%	14.8%
Manslaughter	91.7%	8.3%
Sexual abuse	97.7%	2.7%
Robbery	91.3%	8.7%
Assault	86.9%	13.1%
Burglary	87.5%	12.5%
Theft	62.0%	18.0%
Motor vehicle theft	96.7%	3.3%
Fraud	70.5%	29.5%
Embezzlement	46.0%	54.0%
Forgery/counterfeiting	76.7%	23.3%
Drug trafficking	87.8%	12.2%

Source: Sourcebook on Criminal Justice Statistics (2006).

judges cannot consider factors such as the subordinate role women may have played in criminal offenses, the fact that women are less likely to commit more crimes after release, or women's child care needs (Raeder, 1993). For these reasons, women are hurt more than men by mandatory sentencing.

Most women in prison, like their male counterparts, can be considered "truly disadvantaged." For example, in the 1990s, "[t]wo-thirds of women in prison are minorities, about half ran away from home as youths, a quarter had attempted suicide, and a sizable number had serious drug problems. Over half had been victimized by physical abuse and over a third reported sexual abuse. Most had never earned more than $6.50 an hour" (Donziger, 1996, p. 150). Perhaps the saddest aspect of female incarceration is that almost three out of every four female inmates are mothers.

When we punish mothers for relatively minor crimes, it increases the harms associated with the mothers' criminality. Children of incarcerated mothers are more likely to be incarcerated later in their lives (Dressel and Porterfield, 1998). These children suffer from "traumatic stress, loneliness, developmental regression, loss of self-confidence, aggression, withdrawal, depression, interpersonal violence, substance abuse, and teenage pregnancy" (Donziger, 1996, p. 153). The vast majority of incarcerated mothers are not permitted to see their children. About three out of four of the children end up living with relatives other than the natural father, or even in foster care. All of this may be considered punishment for the mothers, but it is also harmful to the children. Why would Americans want to separate mothers from their children and increase the likelihood that the children also will come under the supervision of criminal justice agencies in the future?

Simultaneously, women are not protected by the criminal justice network from the crimes that most threaten them—domestic violence and sexual assault. According to the Centers for Disease Control and Prevention, more women seek hospital treatment from domestic violence incidents than from all muggings, car accidents, and rapes combined (Donziger, 1996, p. 146). No one knows how many women are abused in their own homes at the hands of domestic or "intimate" violence, but it is estimated that somewhere between 2 and 27 million women are beaten every year (Donziger, 1996, p. 156). In fact, the U.S. Surgeon General has ranked abuse by intimates as the leading cause of injuries to women ages 15 to 44 years (Feder, 2000; Gosselin, 2000; Miller, 2000). Although the National Criminal Victimization Survey (NCVS) (2005) suggests that domestic violence affects about 1 million people per year, most acts of domestic violence are never reported. The NCVS suggests about 18% of all violent acts against females are committed by "intimates." The National Criminal Justice Commission claims, "All things considered, women in this country are nine times more likely to be a victim of crime in the home than out on the streets" (Donziger, 1996, p. 156).

The criminal justice network does very little to assist women with leaving their abusive husbands and partners, even though women are more likely to be murdered when attempting to leave than at any other time (Browne, 1993). And it does very little to prevent domestic violence even though reducing crime is one of its ideal goals. Given that domestic violence occurs in a cycle—since rationalization for and techniques of behavior are learned—when we fail to prevent it in one generation, we are guaranteeing that it will occur again in the next. Children from violent homes are more likely to become violent and abusive, to commit crimes, and to commit suicide than children from nonabusive homes (Robinson, 2004).

In terms of sexual assault, there is evidence that law enforcement officers and prosecutors are less likely to pursue cases where the victim knows the attacker and where the victim has had an active sex life or was dressed in a way thought to provoke the attack. Additionally, judges may set lower bail for alleged rapes where the offender is known to the victim.

These are a few ways in which the American criminal justice network operates based on gender. It is evident that most of the "clients" of the U.S. criminal justice network are men, even above and beyond their representation in the criminal population, Yet with the war on drugs and the advent of mandatory sentences for some types of drug offenders, more and more women, who are usually poor and of color, are being processed through criminal justice agencies.

CONCLUSION

In this chapter, I demonstrated how the criminal justice network is biased against the poor and people of color, as well as against women in some situations. It is difficult to say why discrimination against people of color persists in the United States, but one thing is certain: It does persist. The findings of this chapter suggest that the U.S. criminal justice network is failing to meet its goal of doing justice, because it is inherently unfair in its treatment of some groups. Thus, the reality of justice in the United States is that it is not blind, as it is ideally thought to be. Although it is not clear that the criminal justice network is intentionally biased against any group, it is obvious that various functions are served for people in positions of power by the fact that the criminal justice network fails to live up to its ideal goal of being just.

ISSUE IN DEPTH—The Greatest Threat to Civil Rights Is the Criminal Justice Network

An organization formed by the Leadership Conference on Civil Rights and the Leadership Conference Education Fund published a study (2000) called *Justice On Trial: Racial Disparities in the American Criminal Justice System* (www.civilrights.org). The major claim of this chilling report is, "Racial disparity in the criminal justice system is the most profound civil rights crisis facing America in the new century. It undermines the progress we have made over the past five decades in ensuring equal treatment under the law, and calls into doubt our national faith in the rule of law."

As the authors of this report explain:

> In the half century since a tired seamstress named Rosa Parks refused to give up her seat on the bus, the United States has made significant progress toward the objective of ensuring equal treatment under law for all citizens. The right to vote and the right to be free from discrimination in employment, housing and public accommodations are enshrined in statute. The number of minorities in positions of authority in public and private life continues to grow. America's minorities now enjoy greater economic and educational opportunities than at any time in our history. While it certainly cannot be said that the United States has achieved complete equality in these areas, we continue to make slow but steady progress on the path toward that goal.
>
> But in one critical arena—criminal justice—racial inequality is growing, not receding. Our criminal laws, while facially neutral, are enforced in a manner that is massively and pervasively biased. The injustices of the criminal justice system threaten to render irrelevant fifty years of hard-fought civil rights progress.

When Martin Luther King, Jr. was assassinated in 1968, many major achievements had been realized by the Civil Rights Movement. Yet since then, these gains have being rescinded through criminal justice processes. For example, according to www.civilrights.org:

- In 1964 Congress passed the Civil Rights Act prohibiting discrimination in employment. Yet today, three out of every ten African American males born in the United States will serve time in prison, a status that renders their prospects for legitimate employment bleak, and often bars them from obtaining professional licenses.
- In 1965 Congress passed the Voting Rights Act. Yet today, 31 percent of all black men in Alabama and Florida are permanently disenfranchised as a result of felony convictions. Nationally, 1.4 million black men have lost the right to vote under these laws.
- In 1965 Congress passed the Immigration and Nationality Act, which sought to eliminate the vestiges of racial discrimination in the nation's immigration laws. Yet today, Hispanic and Asian Americans are routinely and sometimes explicitly singled out for immigration enforcement.
- In 1968 Congress passed the Fair Housing Act. Yet today, the current housing for approximately 2 million Americans—two-thirds of them African American or Hispanic—is a prison or jail cell.

- Our civil rights laws abolished Jim Crow laws and other vestiges of segregation, and guaranteed minority citizens the right to travel and utilize public accommodations freely. Yet today, racial profiling and police brutality make such travel hazardous to the dignity and health of law-abiding black and Hispanic citizens.

The main argument of this report is that the U.S. Constitution's guarantees of equal treatment under the law have been eroded because of criminal justice: "Unequal treatment of minorities characterizes every stage of the process. Black and Hispanic Americans, and other minority groups as well, are victimized by disproportionate targeting and unfair treatment by police and other front-line law enforcement officials; by racially skewed charging and plea bargaining decisions of prosecutors; by discriminatory sentencing practices; and by the failure of judges, elected officials and other criminal justice policy makers to redress the inequities that become more glaring every day."

This report claims that the biases begin with police: "The disparate treatment of minorities in the American criminal justice system begins at the very stage of that system: the investigation of suspected criminal activity by law enforcement agents." In fact, the problem clearly starts with the law (see Chapter 3). This report discusses several examples of biased laws, including the disparate treatment of crack and powdered cocaine (see Chapter 11), and various Supreme Court rulings, including the decision of *McCleskey v. Kemp* (1987), where the Supreme Court refused to overturn capital punishment in the face of overwhelming evidence of racial disparities that could not be explained away by legal factors (see Chapter 10).

The main problems with policing, according to this report, include:

- The use and abuse of discretion by police, which allows and even encourages under legal techniques (such as pre-textual traffic stops and stop and frisk searches), to use racial profiling to disproportionately stop African Americans with little evidence of wrongdoing
- Immigration practices that disproportionately detain and deport Hispanics
- Department policies and laws that permit and encourage police to respond to flight by citizens as suspicious behavior, which increases the risk of use of force and use of lethal force by police against people not involved in criminal activity
- Police brutality and corruption, each of which disproportionately affects minorities
- The disparate enforcement of open air drug markets (which disproportionately occur in inner cities where minority residence is high) rather than markets that are better hidden and tend to involve the people who are most likely to deal drugs—Caucasians.

I discussed most of the issues in Chapters 6 and 11 of this book. With the exception of brutality and corruption, these are forms of **innocent bias** and do not require "bad cops" to occur. In fact, this organization concurs that police brutality and corruption are made more likely in an environment characterized by a "get tough on crime" approach where police officers find ways to justify behaviors they normally would not condone or commit because of the fact that most police officers are "good cops."

The main problems with courts, according to this report, include:

- The unchecked discretion of prosecutors in deciding whom to prosecute, what charges to press, and what sentences to pursue, which generally benefits Caucasian defendants (except in death penalty cases).

- The discretion of federal prosecutors to decide in some cases to pursue some cases (especially drug cases) in federal courts rather than state courts, where sentences are generally harsher. With drug cases, this disproportionately occurs when cases involve alleged minority defendants.
- The disproportionate use of preventive detention for African Americans and the poor rather than granting bail, as well as the use of inflated bail amounts to deny the poor freedom while awaiting the disposal of their cases.
- Mandatory sentencing laws (such as three-strikes laws) are disproportionately used to harm minorities, especially when it comes to drug laws, by tying the hands of judges and not allowing them to use their own discretion to impose more rational sentences for relatively minor offenders.
- Death sentences are more routinely handed down for cases involving Caucasian murder victims, especially Caucasian victims murdered by minorities.

Most of these issues were discussed in Chapters 7, 8, 10, and 11 of this book. I showed that the pretrial phase of courts, including charging, bail, and plea decisions are inherently biased against people of color and the poor. The authors of this report did not discuss trial procedures, but did point out some of the same sentencing biases that I discussed. The authors of the report write, "As an empirical matter, it is undeniable that prosecutors exercise their discretion in ways that have racially disproportionate impacts, even if their intent is race neutral. Such unfairness may ultimately be more dangerous than explicitly racist behavior, since it is harder to detect . . . and harder to eradicate. . . ." In other words, the authors of this report have identified the same types of *innocent bias* that I concluded characterize American courts, and agree that race has effects on sentencing when it can.

The main problems with corrections, according to this report, include:

- The abolition of parole at the federal level and in some states, which lengthens time served in prison and worsens correctional overpopulation
- A massive increase in minority incarceration above and beyond their actual involvement in crime
- Generally longer sentences for minority males and females for drug offenses
- The increased imprisonment of nonviolent offenders, who are disproportionately likely to be minority males and increasingly minority females.

I discussed most of the issues in Chapters 9, 11, and 12 of this book. Each of these outcomes is the result of America's get tough on crime attitude. This report shows how this general approach to crime most directly affects minorities and the poor.

According to the authors of the report, the following are consequences of America's get tough on crime and minorities approach:

- Disenfranchising minorities convicted of criminal offenses (e.g., the loss of voting rights)
- Destabilizing communities by routinely removing large numbers of African American males and females from certain neighborhoods over decades
- Compromising of the entire criminal justice apparatus by reducing respect for the law generally
- Reducing the willingness of minorities to assist police with investigations and crime prevention through community policing, because of perceived racial bias

- Reducing the willingness of minorities to serve on juries because of perceived racial bias
- Reducing funding for education and other social services, which also disproportionately affects the poor and people of color
- Increasing exposure to harmful conditions, including illnesses and violence in overcrowded prisons
- Increasing economic strain on American society by reducing the size of the American work force and tax base
- Reducing America's standing in the world by harming our human rights image

The authors of the report conclude, "If the American criminal justice system were a corporation, it would be found to violate the civil rights laws so extensively that it might well be shut down. But for several reasons, racial inequality in the criminal justice system cannot be eradicated easily." This is because there truly is no "criminal justice system" (see Chapter 1), so changing the conditions that produce these problems requires changing laws and practices within thousands of agencies at various levels of governments. Also, "racial disparities emerge from deeply rooted, self-fulfilling stereotypes and assumptions" that are hard to root out. Finally, the political nature of crime and criminal justice in America is not conducive to honesty (see Chapter 2).

Overall, the authors of the study conclude that the U.S. criminal justice network is one of the greatest threats to civil rights in our country: "The criminal justice arena is an especially critical battleground in the continued struggle for civil rights. Current disparities in criminal justice threaten fifty years of progress toward equality." Because "[c]riminal justice reform is a civil rights challenge that can no longer be ignored," the authors of the report put forth several recommendations for overcoming the problems they outlined. Many of these correspond nicely to the 50 recommendations I put forth in Chapter 13.

KEY TERMS

underclass	unemployment	innovation
ghetto poor	poverty	differential opportunity
income inequality	underemployment	institutional racism
environmental racism	poverty wage	subordinating
systematic discrimination	residential segregation	chivalry or paternalism
institutional discrimination	cultural perspectives	hypothesis
criminalblackman	structural perspectives	evil woman hypothesis
income	strain theory	innocent bias
wealth	retreatism	

DISCUSSION QUESTIONS

1. Who are the underclass?
2. In what ways is the war on crime a war on the poor?
3. What functions are served for U.S. society by the war on crime?
4. List some major sources of income inequality in the United States.
5. How do you think income inequality produces crime?

6. Do you think it is "right" that more than 40 million Americans do not have health insurance? Why or why not?
7. What is the difference between race and ethnicity?
8. Which groups in the United States have the greatest risks of involvement with the criminal justice system? Why do you think this is true?
9. Define contextual discrimination.
10. Discuss the apparent relationships among race, ethnicity, and social class.
11. Identify some possible reasons that people of color are more likely to be poor.
12. How have minorities made progress since the civil rights movement?
13. In what ways do you think the criminal justice system is biased against people of color?
14. Do people of color commit more crime than Caucasians? Why or why not?
15. Should the crime of robbery (a Part I offense of the UCR) be considered more serious than crimes such as fraud and embezzlement (Part II offenses of the UCR)? Why or why not?
16. How are the responses of the criminal justice system affected by gender?
17. Discuss the "chivalry or paternalism" hypothesis.
18. Discuss the "evil woman" hypothesis.
19. How is American criminal justice a threat to civil rights?

13

SUMMARY, CONCLUSIONS, AND RECOMMENDATIONS FOR THE FUTURE

1. Introduction
2. Summary: The Criminal Justice Network Fails to Achieve Justice and Reduce Crime
3. Where to Go from Here: Alternatives to Current Criminal Justice Practice
   a. General Recommendations About Government and Informing Citizens
   b. Recommendations About Reforming the Law and Crime
   c. Recommendations About the Media
   d. Recommendations About the Police
   e. Recommendations About the Courts and About Sentencing
   f. Recommendations About Corrections
4. Likelihood of Success
5. Conclusion
6. Issue in Depth—Toward Social Justice: Groups Doing the Work Now
7. Discussion Questions

INTRODUCTION

This final chapter summarizes the main arguments made throughout the book. I illustrate precisely how agencies of criminal justice fail to achieve their goals of doing justice and reducing crime. I then provide recommendations to overcome the factors that produce injustice in American criminal justice. My hope is that the reality of criminal justice in America can move closer to the ideals of criminal justice in America if these recommendations are adopted and implemented. I end the chapter with a discussion of how likely it is that the recommendations will be adopted.

SUMMARY: THE CRIMINAL JUSTICE NETWORK FAILS TO ACHIEVE JUSTICE AND REDUCE CRIME

In Chapter 1, I showed that there is no such thing as a criminal justice system, because the numerous agencies of criminal justice do not work together in an efficient, coordinated, harmonious way to fight crime or assure justice. Yet I showed that the U.S. criminal justice network (the collective of thousands of criminal justice agencies) is ideally aimed at doing justice and reducing crime. Our agencies of criminal justice fight crime in a mostly reactive way, to control crime rather than to prevent it. I illustrated clearly that politicians in the United States have allocated resources and employees disproportionately to law enforcement and corrections, at the expense of American courts. I argued in this chapter that the United States has shifted toward a crime control model of justice since the 1970s at the expense of due process rights of citizens. Ironically, this shift has not made Americans safer from the harms that most threaten them.

In Chapter 2, I suggested some alternative goals of criminal justice, including controlling certain segments of the population to serve limited interests. I suggested that, most likely, these functions are not intended but rather are inevitable because of the role that politics and ideology play in American criminal justice. In our system of government, politics equals power, and politicians define acts as crimes and especially serious crimes when they are committed by the relatively powerless groups in our society. The policies that result from our get tough on street crime mentality are unplanned and thus unlikely to reduce crime before they are even implemented. Part of the problem, as our culture has been greatly influenced by large corporations, is that our agencies of criminal justice have now become McDonaldized, as I showed in Chapter 2. Thus, much of our crime fighting efforts are aimed at efficiency, calculability (more for less), predictability, and control rather than justice.

Injustice in American criminal justice most greatly affects poor people and people of color. In recent years, the groups most likely to suffer at the hands of criminal justice processes are poor women of color. Figure 13-1 summarizes criminal justice bias in the United States. The diagram is organized around the areas discussed in the book: the law, the media, the police, the courts, and corrections.

All criminal justice activity stems from the law, so bias in the criminal justice process begins with the law. As I showed in Chapter 3, the law in the United States does not represent all Americans. Specifically, legislators at the federal and state levels are not representative of Americans in demographic terms, voters are not representative of Americans in demographic terms, and most people do not vote. Additionally, I illustrated how monied interests assert their influence on lawmakers through lobbying and donations to elections and political parties in the form of hard money and soft money from wealthy donors and political action committees (PACs). These facts lead to the possibility that the criminal law does not label the most dangerous acts as the most serious crimes.

Chapter 4 illustrated that crimes do not exist until they are invented by human beings who write down the law. Perhaps because U.S. lawmakers and others are not demographically representative, American criminal law does not define as crimes those acts that are most threatening to the safety and well-being of Americans—acts of elite deviance. Instead, it labels as the most serious crimes those acts that are committed primarily by the poor and by people of color. Our criminal justice focus is squarely focused

FIGURE 13-1   Sources of Bias in American Criminal Justice

Law	Media	Police	Courts	Corrections	Other
Legislators not representative	Owned by large corporations	Discretion	Courtroom workgroups not representative	Probation	War on drugs
Most people do not vote	Run for profit	Profiling		Incarceration	Poverty
		Location by place			Income inequality
Voters not representative	Inaccurate reporting		Differential power of prosecutor	Death penalty	Unemployment
Money drives politics (PACS, wealthy donors)	Focus on street crimes	Focus on street crimes	Charging		
	Focus on violent, bizarre crimes	War on drugs	Bail and preventive detention		
	No context provided		Plea bargaining		
	Rely on crime control officials for information		*Voir dire*		
			Private attorneys		
			Expert witnesses		
			Mandatory sentencing		
			Drug crimes		

on those acts, while we virtually ignore other acts that are more dangerous and costly. This is not consistent either with doing justice or with reducing crime.

As I showed in Chapter 5, the media promote stereotypes about crime and criminal justice by focusing on the most violent, bizarre, and random types of crime in the United States, which ultimately increases fear of crime and support for crime control values rather than due process values. The media, which are largely for-profit institutions owned by large corporations, serve the interests of wealthy and powerful members of society by providing inaccurate reports about crime and criminal justice that lack critical context. The media also misrepresent crime trends and promote moral panics, mostly for ratings. Most troublesome, the media give relatively little attention to acts of elite deviance, even though these acts are much more damaging to society as a whole than common street crimes. They also focus little on misguided criminal justice policies that are not only costing us now but will continue to do so in the future. The inner ring of the media has the greatest impact on the news and the trend in media ownership is toward further monopolization of the news by larger and larger corporations. As illustrated in

Chapter 5, the causes of media inaccuracies include the way that mainstream media institutions are organized for profit, the peer culture of journalism, a lack of basic criminological education, and the politics of crime and criminal justice.

The police, as gatekeepers of the criminal justice network and soldiers on the front lines of the American wars on crime and drugs, are biased against poor people and people of color. This is not because of bad police officers (although they clearly exist) but because of what I termed *innocent bias* in Chapter 6. This innocent bias—a function of enforcing bad law—comes in many forms. Because police are able to use discretion— to act according to their own personal judgments—stereotypes about groups of people are allowed to seep into policing. Police profiling based on fallacious stereotypes of dangerous groups, the concentration of police in the United States' inner cities, and the focus on street crimes all explain why poor people and people of color are disproportionately likely to be stopped, questioned, and arrested by law enforcement officers. They are also more likely to be victims of excessive force by the police. The criminal law and the organization of policing in the United States combine to create unjust outcomes. In their daily jobs, police do not spend most of their time fighting crime and drugs. When they do, the opportunities are too great for some to ignore, leading to corruption and abuses unimaginable to most Americans. The main problem of policing, however, is that it is focused almost exclusively on street crime and is disproportionately found in the inner cities of America. The most significant bias of policing is thus structural in nature.

Courts are also biased against the poor and against people of color. The bias occurs in all three phases of the court process, the pretrial, trial, and post-trial phases. Most of the criminal justice bias occurs in the pretrial phase behind closed doors, where decisions about bail and charging are made. The bail process, by definition, is biased against people without money. Poor people and people of color are less likely to be offered bail and thus are more likely to be detained in jail awaiting their trial dates. As illustrated in Chapter 7, more than 90% of felony court cases are disposed of through plea bargaining, so most people charged with crimes do not have a reasonable expectation of a criminal trial. When cases go to trial, poor people and people of color are less likely to receive justice as an outcome because of biases in the *voir dire* process, such as the use of peremptory challenges to exclude minorities and the use of jury consultants by those with money. Poor people are underrepresented among jury pools and also are less able to afford private attorneys and hire expert witnesses; thus, their voices are less heard in jury deliberations and they receive less competent defenses when charged with crimes.

Sentencing, the subject of Chapter 8, is biased in some places against poor people, people of color, and women—meaning it is characterized by contextual discrimination. Overall, minorities in the United States receive no more severe sanctions than Caucasians for most crimes, but they are disproportionately sentenced to imprisonment for drug felonies. African Americans also are sentenced to longer jail terms than Caucasians. I tied these findings to false conceptions of dangerousness created in the criminal law and media coverage of crime and criminal justice. Examples of biased sentencing practices include mandatory sentences such as the three-strikes laws that are almost universally condemned by criminologists and criminal justice experts. Clearly, American punishment is driven mostly by the desire for retribution (getting even with offenders), incapacitation (warehousing offenders), and deterrence (creating fear in people to prevent future crime). Yet a majority of Americans report that they support rehabilitation (eliminating the factors that produce crime), which is now largely absent in American criminal justice. Our criminal justice network practices punishments that have been shown by research to be ineffective on the very offenders we try to catch—more evidence that the network fails to meet its ideal goals. Further, there is very little attention paid to mechanisms of restorative justice, which has the potential to better serve crime victims as well as restore offenders to a more healthy state.

Currently, the U.S. courts are overloaded with more than 2 million felony cases per year, a significant portion of which are drug crimes. Almost all of these cases are pursued against the poor and a significant portion are against minorities, the very people who are least represented in courtroom work groups. Meanwhile, prosecutors now enjoy the most power in the court process, thereby assuring wrongful convictions in our crime control model of criminal justice. Although there is little evidence of sentencing disparities, when sentencing disparities do occur, they tend to be found in borderline cases. That is, discretion is abused by prosecutors in the cases when they can abuse discretion.

Corrections, the last phase of the criminal justice process, was addressed in Chapter 9 (imprisonment) and Chapter 10 (the death penalty). The U.S. incarceration rate has exploded since the early 1970s, at a tremendous cost to American taxpayers and to the residents of our inner cities. The United States now leads the world in its rate of imprisonment. The incarceration binge did not result from increased crime rates, was not called for by Americans, and has not resulted in large declines in crime. Surprisingly, most offenders in our nation's prisons are not repeat violent offenders as one might expect given tough talk by politicians and media coverage of crime and criminal justice. In fact, a large share of our nation's prisoners are nonviolent property and drug offenders who are suffering the tremendous pains of imprisonment discussed in Chapter 9. In essence, we seem intent on making prisoners suffer enormous hardships in hopes that they will somehow be turned into law-abiding citizens. Yet most offenders enter prison uneducated, unskilled, and underemployed (and thus poor) and leave prison the same way, yet also with the stigma of being ex-convicts. Offenders return to the same criminogenic environments that produced them, and police and parole officers harass parolees, increasing the likelihood that they will end up back in prison. Indeed, prison is a massive failure, yet politicians have sworn an allegiance to it. We now spend more money building prisons than on higher education. In Chapter 9, I also showed clear evidence of disparities in all forms of American punishment.

In Chapter 10, I discussed the use of capital punishment, the rarest of all criminal sanctions. In essence, the death penalty is a punishment that is applied so arbitrarily that it is freakish and clearly unjust. I illustrated how and why the death penalty is disproportionately used against the nation's poor and people of color (especially when they murder whites) and why we are likely to execute even the innocent, with the apparent acceptance of Americans. Given the irrefutable evidence that the death penalty is biased against particular groups in the United States and that executions do not deter crime, its practice is the clearest proof that the criminal justice network does not meet its ideal goals of doing justice and reducing crime. The main problems with capital punishment, as applied in the United States, include its political nature, numerous flaws with capital juries, and its enormous financial costs. The error rate is so high in capital cases that it is outrageous that we still practice this punishment.

Capital punishment experts agree, saying that the death penalty does not meet its goals and is plagued by serious problems. The experts—who study the death penalty for a living—are best equipped to speak to the realities of capital punishment in the United States.

Drug crimes, a major focus of criminal justice in the past few decades, have led to major increases in the incarcerated populations in the United States. In Chapter 11, I demonstrated that our criminal justice network punishes people for being involved in the illicit drug trade—mostly for simple possession—even though the illegal drugs involved are relatively less harmful than such legal drugs as alcohol and tobacco. On the basis of this evidence, the nation's drug war cannot be considered a valid means of either doing justice or reducing crime. Furthermore, my assessment of the nation's war on drugs demonstrates that we fail to meet our stated goals of reducing drug use, crime, and harms associated with drugs, and interrupting the flow of drugs into the country. Instead, drug use is largely unchanged, more drug users are dying, and drugs are still very easily obtainable by young people. Additionally, the war on drugs causes far more harm than it prevents, especially to the poor and people of color and to the freedoms that we as Americans supposedly enjoy.

Research reported in Chapter 11 shows that the federal agency in charge of the nation's drug war—the Office of National Drug Control Policy (ONDCP)—is aware of its failures. Yet ONDCP attempts to hide drug war failures by manipulating statistical information and visual graphs, a practice that is clearly not aimed at honesty and transparency in government.

I illustrated in Chapter 12 that the criminal justice network as a whole is focused almost exclusively on crimes perceived to be the acts of the poor and people of color. Thus, the criminal justice network is characterized by discrimination against these groups. Although this discrimination is not typically intentional, criminal justice processes are nevertheless biased against poor people, people of color, and in some cases women. Most of this bias is "innocent"; that is, it comes from the criminal law rather than from the intentional actions of "bad apples" working in criminal justice. But because the biases are functional for powerful segments of society, efforts aimed at overcoming them are typically resisted. As you saw in Chapter 12, some of the biases result from class-related issues such as poverty, income inequality, unemployment, etc., and some are institutionalized or rooted in legitimate government policies such as our criminal laws.

WHERE TO GO FROM HERE: ALTERNATIVES TO CURRENT CRIMINAL JUSTICE PRACTICE

This book has shown you that the U.S. criminal justice network fails to achieve its goals of doing justice and reducing crime. Of course, it is easy to criticize people, institutions, and policies without attempting to suggest alternatives. This seems to be the American way: We know how to criticize but are less well equipped to offer alternatives for our own failed policies.

To counter this, in this chapter I provide 50 recommendations for creating positive change within the U.S. criminal justice network. Each recommendation suggests an alternative to the current direction of criminal justice policy in the United States. Because the recommendations stem directly from the literature reviewed in this book, I arrange them in a manner consistent with the overall organization of the book. Thus, I offer recommendations in the following areas: general recommendations about government and informing citizens; recommendations about law and crime; recommendations about the media; recommendations about police; recommendations about the courts and sentencing; and recommendations about corrections.

I firmly believe that we can change the direction of American criminal justice to make it more just and more effective at reducing crime. These recommendations are a step in that direction. In the next section, I offer suggestions for preventing crime and promoting justice in the United States. I believe our only hope lies in the careful creation of criminal justice policies that strive to move away from the reactive, carelessly constructed criminal justice policies of the late twentieth century.

General Recommendations About Government and Informing Citizens

1. Our government should write clear statements reflecting the goals of American criminal justice.   Given the importance of justice as a process, due process values should be emphasized over crime control values. At every step of the criminal justice process, we must ensure that every individual's constitutional rights are protected and that innocent people are not wrongfully subjected to criminal justice processes. In other words, we must act in ways consistent with the ideal of "innocent until proven guilty." The first step is to reorganize the thousands of criminal justice agencies into something more like a system.

2. Our government should develop clearly stated policies of government aimed at not discriminating on the basis of race, social class, and gender.   If justice is to be blind, and thus fair, we must first state clearly that we will not, under any circumstances, tolerate discrimination based on factors such as race, class, and gender. These values should be codified and exhibited by government for all to see.

3. The government should also make a commitment to evaluate the performance of our criminal justice agencies at regular periods of time, to assess how well we are achieving our stated goals.   How can we know how well we are doing unless we assess our performance carefully? Evaluation can be relatively inexpensive. Given the importance of the goal of providing justice, an evaluation of the criminal justice network's performance on a regular basis is warranted. Criminologists and criminal justice experts should be involved in this regular evaluation.

4. To be more effective at reducing crime, our government must encourage a fundamental shift away from punitiveness toward prevention, treatment, and restoration.   Conditions in communities and society that produce criminality must be eliminated, sick people who commit crimes must be treated, and both victims of crime and criminal offenders must work together toward restoration of each to noncriminal and nonvictim status. For this to happen, we must commit ourselves to forgiveness rather than vengeance. Forgiveness is the only mechanism proven to produce peace for victims of crime. Thinking outside the box allows us to imagine forms of community and restorative justice, staffed by normal people trained in conflict and dispute resolution and mediation of common problems.

5. Our government must shift its focus from criminal justice responses to violence toward medical, public-health models to treat violence as an epidemic in the United States.   As I explained in this book, violence is the main problem in the United States when it comes to crime. Crime rates are not exceedingly high relative to other similar countries. Yet we suffer from alarmingly high rates of violent victimization, especially murder. We must shift our focus away from criminal justice approaches toward public-health approaches to reducing violence by treating violence as the epidemic that it is.

6. *Our government should also stop "shooting itself in the foot" by hurting its own citizens. For example, we need to reinvest in American labor—to stop engaging in practices such as downsizing and outsourcing to increase profits and cap CEO/CFO earnings to limit conditions of income inequality.* Government should regulate businesses by requiring victim impact statements when decisions affecting a company's workers will be made. Politicians who talk about the importance of families should not tolerate the practice of maximizing profits by moving jobs overseas and south of the border at the expense of American workers and families. Sudden unemployment has been related to many adverse consequences, including depression, family instability, and domestic violence. When corporations plan to make decisions that will affect American workers and their families, criminal justice implications should be considered.

7. *Other legitimate opportunities must be developed for citizens who find themselves living in conditions of poverty.* On the basis of a review of evidence, street crimes are not the most harmful types of crime committed. Yet street crime is tremendously harmful and disproportionately affects poor people. Politicians claim that poor people choose to commit criminal acts to maximize pleasure, gain rewards, earn money, and so forth. Our response, based on this premise, has been to increase the punishments and other pains associated with choosing crime. An alternative to this futile approach would be to increase the benefits associated with choosing noncriminal acts. People should be rewarded for abiding by the law, going to work, and raising their families. One means of addressing this is by instituting a guaranteed living wage for anyone working full-time.

8. *Overall, Americans must insist that politics be taken out of crime and criminal justice issues.* Politicians have created cynicism in Americans by using partial facts and distorted truths about crime that have made developing sensible policy impossible. Recall the Willie Horton example discussed in the book. Horton had been out on furlough eight times in Massachusetts without committing any apparent criminal acts. On his ninth release, he committed a rape and aggravated assault. The 1988 presidential candidate, George Bush (the first), used the image of Horton as evidence that his opponent, Michael Dukakis (who was then governor of Massachusetts), was soft on crime. This was, at the least, dishonest of the Bush campaign; at worst, it was deceitful and racist. Politicians promote criminal justice policies that they should know do not and cannot work, and Americans and our media should call them on it rather than giving politicians a free pass to say whatever they want.

9. *A rational system of planned change should be used to reduce crime in the United States.* Currently, criminal justice policy seems to be made based on subjective decisions, characterized by unreliability, low validity, bias, and variability among decision makers (Gottfredson, 1999, p. 443). According to Walker (1998, p. xxi), most American crime control policies simply do not work: "They are nonsense." Walker critically assesses U.S. criminal justice policy, including both conservative "get tough"

approaches and liberal efforts at "rehabilitation," and concludes that almost none of them are effective. Neither conservative nor liberal approaches are carefully planned. The conservative approach has traditionally involved more police, more prisons, and swifter, harsher punishment, whereas the liberal approach has focused more on rehabilitation and treatment. As noted in Chapter 2, both conservatives and liberals now support more police, more prisons, and the death penalty as effective means of fighting crime. Planned change was introduced in Chapter 2 and is aimed at carefully studying crime problems and responding to them with carefully planned efforts to address the root causes of criminality (Welsh and Harris, 2004). This is a very promising alternative to quick-fix, feel-good, short-term approaches to reducing crime in the United States.

10. The nation's crime experts must strive to educate citizens about injustice in American criminal justice and about their true risks of victimization. It is highly unlikely that many Americans are aware of how the criminal law is biased against particular groups of people in the United States. Given our devotion to justice, it is likely that when Americans become aware of injustice, they will revolt against it and demand change, as they did during the civil rights movement. Victims of other forms of culpable harmful acts, such as victims of elite deviance, often do not know they have been victimized and when they do, often do not know where to turn for help (Friedrichs, 1995). If we truly want to stop victimization, we must make sure people know they are being victimized, and then increase and clarify their options for law enforcement assistance.

Recommendations About Reforming the Law and Crime

11. As the criminal law currently is not made by people who are representative of the population, it should not be a surprise that the criminal law does not serve the interests of most Americans. Thus, we need to make the law more representative by increasing the representativeness of lawmakers. This would entail increasing informed voting behavior by educating citizens about crime and criminal justice, as well as minimizing and equalizing the funding of elections, candidates, and parties by special interests and lobbying groups. One way to achieve this would be to subsidize elections by providing equal resource support to each candidate running for major political office.

12. We must shift our focus from criminalization to harm reduction. Americans and their leaders apparently think that we can stop people from engaging in harmful behaviors by criminalizing them. In fact, the most effective controls may very well be informal in nature—that is, instilled by families, peers, churches, and schools rather than by police, courts, and corrections. Instead of criminalizing behaviors to reduce harms, we ought to encourage policies of harm reduction, aimed at preventing harms associated with behaviors such as drug use and abuse. Rather than punishing drug users and sellers, for example, treatment options ought to be available for addicts, and alternative means of employment ought to be made available for sellers, especially once we put them out of business.

13. The government must define crimes based on degree of harm caused. To the degree that the criminal law is necessary, acts ought to be as serious as the harms they cause. This entails careful study (much of which has already been done and is discussed in this book) about which behaviors are really most likely to kill, injure, and result in property loss for Americans. Behaviors that are most harmful ought to be called the most "serious" and should be the focus of law enforcement, courts, and corrections.

14. "Victimless" crimes such as drug use and possession ought to be decriminalized. American police spend a disproportionate amount of time and resources on some "victimless" street crimes, called this not because they are truly harmless but because they are engaged in by consenting adults so that no one involved feels victimized. The best example is the war on drugs. As explained in this book, law enforcement focus on drug crimes and mandatory sentencing laws that call for longer minimum sentences for drug offenders explain the United States' unprecedented overreliance on imprisonment. Many of those we are incarcerating are first-time, low-level drug dealers or people who simply were found in possession of marijuana. Meanwhile, victims of other forms of harms are virtually ignored. Drug use can be a normal behavior that occurs in various recreational contexts, and government can decriminalize drug use while simultaneously discouraging people from using drugs. Criminalizing drug use will not deter our children from experimenting. In fact, the illegal status of drugs is precisely what leads to much drug use, as well as a lot of crime and violence in the United States.

15. Create and administer a national source of data on elite deviance. To discover more accurately how much damage is caused by these types of acts, our government must create a measure to gather valid data on acts of elite deviance, much as it does on street crime. If we are to shift our focus toward the acts that cause the most harm in society, we must first commit ourselves to collecting data on the acts. Creating a national source of data on elite deviance will be a major impetus toward national recognition that such acts are in fact "serious" crimes.

Recommendations About the Media

16. Educate the media about crime and criminal justice through planned workshops. The nation's crime experts can no longer afford to sit on the sidelines, watching the media continue to get it wrong. We seem to know how and why the media are misinforming citizens about the true nature of crime and criminal justice in the United States. It is our responsibility to ensure that this misinformation stops, especially given that most Americans get their crime information from media outlets. Part of the educational effort would be aimed at separating mainstream media from corporate ownership.

17. Insist that the media get it right by reducing consumer demand for sleazy news. We must encourage citizens to pursue alternative forms of education and news rather than crime shows and sensational news. Research shows that crime entertainment and news promote a "siege mentality" among some viewers, who become more likely to stay inside and to fear the poor and people of color rather than wanting to help them achieve legitimate success. The news media should develop and broadcast clear statements reflecting their intention to cease broadcasting sleazy, sensationalized crime stories.

18. Develop a network of contacts between criminal justice scholars and the media. Every criminologist and criminal justice expert owes it to the nation to insert himself or herself into the media when stories about crime and criminal justice are discussed. We cannot afford to allow politicians and the police to be the primary sources of information about crime and criminal justice in the United States, given their clear biases in favor of the status quo, and because we study crime and criminal justice for a living.

19. Utilize, advertise, and celebrate independent media outlets.   One thing we can all do, including criminologists and their students, is use independent media outlets that are not privately owned and that operate with the interests of the people in mind. We ought to tell our colleagues and students and everyday people to turn off the television unless they are watching public television, or to at least boycott television shows and networks that sell us crime and criminal justice and harm the nation in so doing.

Recommendations About the Police

20. Reorganize police resources (including the numbers of law enforcement officers allocated to each level of government, the types of behaviors they focus on, and the ways in which they use their time) so that victims of all culpable harmful acts, whether legal or illegal, will be served by law enforcement.   Policing in the United States is organized in a manner that mandates that officers focus almost exclusively on street crime victimization. Simultaneously, U.S. police officers spend most of their time doing work not related to crime or victimization. This must change so that police can serve all victims of culpable harms.

To correct this, we must do the following:

21. Reallocate policing resources away from local government to states and, to a lesser degree, to the federal government.

22. Increase training of local, state, and federal police on matters related to elite deviance.

23. Reallocate policing resources to better assist victims of all culpable, harmful acts.   We must reeducate police officers about forms of victimization other than street crimes because state and federal officers are currently best equipped, given their special training, to provide assistance to victims of other forms of harm. To ensure that victims of such acts receive sufficient attention, police agencies at the state and federal levels must be granted more resources, including both employees and funding, relative to local police. Local police must be educated about forms of culpable harm other than street crime, particularly to the degree that they will likely be called on to assist with victims of such harms. City and county law enforcement assistance would not be possible unless allocation of local police personnel by location and time was systematically changed from urban areas, where street crime is perceived to occur, to areas where other forms of culpable harms occur. That is, for local police to provide their traditional services to a more diverse set of victims, the times and places they patrol would also change. Since police "tend to respond most emphatically to . . . events that they perceive as conforming to legal definitions of serious crimes" (Sacco and Kennedy, 1996, p. 65), they would be unlikely to sympathize with victims of culpable behaviors other than street crimes, unless such acts were recognized as serious crimes by society and treated as such by criminal justice agencies.

Police should devote free time to forms of victimization other than street crimes committed by individuals against individuals. We might also decide as a society to let police exclusively fight victimization, and leave service functions to other agencies. Perhaps we could also redesign our social service agencies to operate on a 24-hour basis, so that police could devote themselves exclusively to fighting victimization and/or crime through their law enforcement function. Given the amount of time police at all levels of government spend on service functions, it is apparent that this time is not being allocated to victim assistance, although it is difficult to ascertain how much police service time is spent on precisely this function. Additionally, many criminal victimizations are never discovered, and virtually all noncriminal victimizations are ignored. From these facts, we can confidently conclude that police are not very effectively serving victims of culpable harms.

24. Increase educational qualifications for American police officers to a minimum of a bachelor's degree. The Police Executive Research Forum claims that education benefits the police and the community. Through education, police gain greater maturity and increase their knowledge base about criminal justice and American government, as well as an increased understanding and appreciation of people of different cultures (Carter and Sapp, 1993). These factors, along with high intelligence, flexibility, and honesty, have been shown to be related to better policing.

25. Recruit police officers in high school and college whose personalities are consistent with the Law Enforcement Code of Conduct. Individuals who are willing and appear able to follow the ethical mandates for police work specified by the International Association of Chiefs of Police should be identified and recruited into police work starting in high school. Candidates at the high school level should be sponsored for college work and academy training. Individuals willing to serve the community, protect the innocent, keep the peace, and strive to ensure the rights of all to liberty, equality, and justice should be recruited, as long as they are likely to honestly, impartially, and with dignity carry out these vital roles for society.

26. Increase police officer pay to reduce police corruption. It is understandable that some good cops will "go bad" when they are paid very little and see huge amounts of money exchanged regularly in criminal enterprises. To reduce the likelihood that police will steal cash from offenders, we must pay our police officers more and create other mechanisms to show our appreciation for the valuable services they provide to Americans.

27. Develop mandatory multicultural educational efforts within police academies. As evidence shows that police disproportionately hassle ethnic minorities and people of color, police should be exposed to more educational materials about other cultures to increase their understanding of, and appreciation for, people unlike themselves, especially given that most police are Caucasians.

28. Outlaw the use of police profiling based on race and ethnicity. There is no valid justification for this practice. Even if profiling results in more arrests, more seizures of evidence related to criminal activity, and so on, the ends cannot be justified by the means. Recall that justice as a process is what criminal justice agencies in America ideally value. Police profiling is an ugly practice that should never be tolerated. We should require police to gather statistics about interactions with citizens and then evaluate each jurisdiction for evidence of racial profiling. When racial profiling is found, departments must be punished accordingly.

29. Develop police–community partnerships and problem-oriented policing where they are needed most.   Community policing, the buzzword in policing for the past three decades or so, has not been beneficial to the communities where it is needed most. Inner cities and high-crime areas have witnessed the highest lack of respect for police and the least police involvement in community policing. These are the areas where community policing strategies must be stepped up. Additionally, problem-oriented policing offers great promise for crime prevention. Police agencies around the country should work toward implementing strategies aimed at eliminating community-specific problems before they become crimes.

Recommendations About the Courts and About Sentencing

30. Reallocate criminal justice resources so they are more equitable, particularly to "courthouse regular" defense attorneys.   This book has shown that most money spent on criminal justice is allocated to law enforcement and then to corrections. In essence, we spend more money trying to catch criminals and punish them than making sure that we have caught the right ones. Is it any wonder, given the presumption of guilt inherent in plea bargaining, that sometimes we end up punishing the wrong people for crimes they did not commit? If we truly believe in due process and "innocent until proven guilty," we must give defense attorneys the resources necessary to defend their clients adequately. Ideally, each side must be assured of the resources necessary to take cases to trial.

31. Increase representation by racial and ethnic minorities in courtroom work groups.   As was shown, people of color are underrepresented as members of the courtroom work group. Here, the government could assist by providing targeted scholarships to people of color to attend law school, with the stipulation that they will serve a minimum number of years working for the government as officers of the court.

32. Reassign sentencing discretion to judges instead of prosecutors.   The current move to allow prosecutors to decide sentences through the charging process has resulted in an imbalance in the court. Sentencing discretion must reside in the hands of judges, not prosecutors. Judges tell researchers that they do not support mandatory sentences such as three-strikes laws because of their inability to consider mitigating factors when sentencing some of the nation's truly disadvantaged. Prosecutors, as elected officials, are more likely to be concerned about their image as "tough on crime" and to maintain high conviction rates at virtually any cost. Their discretion must be reduced if we want to ensure that justice is done. This can be accomplished by abolishing mandatory sentences at least for relatively harmless acts.

33. Prohibit preventive detention based on the criterion of "to protect the community," and permit it only when a significant flight risk exists.   Stated plainly, there is no justification for locking up people who have yet to be convicted of criminal offenses.

Only under rare circumstances, as when officers witness a person in the act of committing violence or when a person is found to be mentally unstable and violent because of a severe brain disorder (e.g., schizophrenia), can we justify locking up a person who is supposedly "innocent until proven guilty." Yet approximately half of the people now in our nation's jails have not been convicted of any crimes. These people are being punished without conviction. When preventive detention is used, all efforts must be made to speed up the criminal justice process for these cases in particular and to provide treatment for those with mental illnesses.

34. Create a system of structured bail based on how much the accused can afford to pay and assess bail outcomes regularly to ensure that bail is not being used to discriminate against any group of persons. If bail is simply to be used to ensure the presence of the defendant at trial, and not as punishment, unreasonably high bails for the poor cannot be tolerated. Many poor citizens are forced to sit in jail even for accusations of relatively minor criminality because they cannot afford bail. Given the evidence showing biases in bail against the poor and people of color, something must be done to correct bail biases. At regular intervals, bail outcomes should be evaluated to ensure that unreasonably high bail is not being used disproportionately against any group. If bail is found to be differentially applied, mandatory and equal bail amounts should be established by independent assessors of the courts.

35. Prohibit plea bargaining. The plea bargaining process does not address the guilt or innocence of the accused. Rather, the issue addressed by plea bargaining is what to do about the defendant, who is assumed to be guilty by everyone involved in the criminal justice process. Neither justice as an outcome nor justice as a process is achieved through this process. Decriminalization initiatives would aid in the effort to ensure that court caseloads do not grow to the point where it would be impossible to hold a trial for each criminal case. Frankly, it might be wise to discourage arrests for any matter that is not likely to lead to trial. The only way to eliminate plea bargaining is to reduce the number of cases entering the criminal justice process in the first place.

36. Insist that indigent clients be given quality counsel by creating incentives to represent poor clients zealously. Part of this incentive should be financial. Courthouse regulars who make their living defending the poor ought to be able to afford to investigate the charges against their clients thoroughly and to mount an adequate defense. Nothing less than justice depends on fair court processes.

37. Jurors ought to be selected from sources other than voter lists, for a majority of people in the United States do not vote. Voters tend to be unrepresentative of the nation's population, so biases will result against those who do not vote. Alternative jury lists must be created from other sources such as lists of people with driver's licenses or other sources that will assure greater representation.

38. Prohibit the use of peremptory challenges in jury selection. There is no valid reason to allow any challenge to a juror without adequate cause being stated to (and supported by) a judge. Because peremptory challenges are used to disqualify people of color and people who "look suspicious," the jury process has been corrupted by the use of these challenges.

39. Encourage citizens to participate in jury duty by providing adequate financial compensation.   Jurors provide a valuable service to the country. They are supposed to be the backbone of the criminal justice network, ensuring that arbitrary and overzealous governments do not unnecessarily interfere in the lives of American citizens. Thus, they should be paid a reasonable amount to compensate for their lost wages and service to the government and people of the United States. Jury duty should not be something Americans dread.

40. Prohibit the use of jury consultants during voir dire.   The use of jury consultants clearly biases the trial phase in favor of those clients who can hire individuals to hand-pick a jury sympathetic to their case. The poor and, often, people of color do not enjoy this privilege. As long as justice is to be related to fair processes and fair outcomes, paid jury consultants are not consistent with the ideal of American justice.

41. Allow jurors to ask questions and take notes during the trial phase.   Currently, jurors must listen to long trials and complex testimony and other forms of evidence without being able to write anything down or ask questions for clarification. This likely gives more credence to opening and closing arguments than to the actual evidence presented during trial.

42. Make jury instructions understandable.   Research clearly shows that jury instructions cannot be understood by many Americans. They should be written with the lay person in mind, and examples of major terms should be provided to help the jury make just decisions. Sample jury instructions can be tested on everyday Americans to make sure they can be understood.

43. Acknowledge that deterrence is a myth and not a likely outcome of criminal sentencing.   Very few criminal sanctions provide a deterrent effect, especially for those most likely to commit street crimes. Those with little legitimate opportunity for success—a "stake in conformity"—are far less likely to be scared into crime-free lifestyles when other means of earning income are so restricted and unavailable to them.

44. Eliminate three-strikes laws unless it is assured that they will be used only against repeat violent felons (that is, who actually hurt people).   We will inevitably need to lock some criminals away from society for our own protection, but many relatively minor offenders do not warrant such severe sentences. Mandatory sentences are not a cost-effective way to punish these offenders. These sanctions also contribute to the "get tough" approach that permeates much of U.S. society, a major impediment to effective change within the criminal justice network. These laws should be used only against offenders who have committed more than one violent offense, at least one of which led to some actual injury.

Recommendations About Corrections

45. Increase the use of intermediate sanctions as cost-effective alternatives to prison.   These sanctions are not necessarily any more effective than prison, but they are certainly less expensive. Many such sanctions are at least considered promising by criminologists and criminal justice experts, but they are not used widely enough to demonstrate how well they work. For relatively minor offenders likely to end up in prison, these sanctions seem to be a better investment.

46. Humanize prisons—minimize the pains of imprisonment. Those criminals who simply must be kept away from society for our protection should not be subjected to unnecessary forms of punishment while incarcerated. Instead, they should be humanely incapacitated and treated as human beings, not as wild animals. Remember, virtually all of them will be released one day.

47. Insist on educational and vocational skill development in prison as a criterion for release. Prisoners should be required to demonstrate that they will likely make it in the free world before they are released. This means correctional facilities must do more than simply warehouse offenders. Imprisoned offenders ought to be encouraged to work, study, make decisions for themselves, and be prepared to live in the free world. This may be unpopular with Americans who want to see the guilty suffer, but it likely will be more effective in preventing future crimes than brutal punishment. Vocational and educational opportunities must be made available to inmates for their benefit, but especially for ours.

48. Shift the role of probation and parole officers to social service functions rather than supervisory, law enforcement functions. Probationers and parolees are currently sent to prison for violating rules not imposed on free people. This must stop. Those who are charged with supervising the progress of such offenders ought to be rewarded for successes and urged to help offenders make it in the free world by assisting their clients with necessary vocational, educational, and medical rehabilitation.

49. Provide more resources for probation and parole officers. Currently, it is impossible for probation and parole officers to supervise their large caseloads. A society as wealthy as the United States ought to be able to afford to pay for enough officers to ensure successful integration of offenders into society during and after punishment.

50. Abolish the death penalty. The United States is the only industrialized Western nation that still practices capital punishment, a shameful practice that is applied so rarely and arbitrarily that its use is clearly unjust. It is so evidently biased against the poor and minorities that one wonders how it can possibly be legal. There is no valid evidence showing that the death penalty deters crime, and there is some evidence that an opposite effect may occur. Given that we cannot administer the death penalty enough to make it effective, capital punishment should be replaced by an ultimate sanction of life imprisonment without possibility of parole, plus restitution for victims (LWOP+R). An alternative, which most Americans already support, is an immediate moratorium on executions while we determine whether our administration of capital punishment can be fixed.

LIKELIHOOD OF SUCCESS

I do not pretend that these reforms will be rapidly accepted and implemented in the United States. In fact, considering past efforts by criminologists and criminal justice scholars to make criminal justice processes more just, it may be unwise to expect many of these reforms to be adopted in the immediate future. Yet change is possible and, on the basis of the evidence presented in this book, change is necessary. American criminal justice policy is misconceived and dangerous. We must invest in prevention rather than more prisons (Greenwood, 1998; Welsh and Farrington, 2005).

Most change is gradual, but gradualism can lull us all to sleep. As Americans, we must insist that the criminal justice network achieve justice as both an outcome and a process. The debate over the death penalty is now raging across the country, so it is possible that capital punishment will soon be stopped in several states (probably through a temporary moratorium, but perhaps through a permanent abolition). Some discussion has occurred with regard to police profiling and abuse of power by criminal justice professionals, but less debate is occurring with regard to many of the other issues addressed in this book. I hope this book serves as a starting point for such debate.

Vila (1997) has pointed out how ironic it is that as knowledge about what works to reduce crime becomes clearer, we live in a time when effective or promising efforts are less likely to be implemented. His research, like that presented here, suggests that the media, politicians, and public impatience will be significant barriers to effective change. I advocate a team approach, based on consensus building among the media, politicians, and the public, to bring about effective change. And you, the reader of this book, have a tremendous opportunity to work from within agencies of criminal justice to bring about positive change. What ideas can you come up with to help create the changes needed to make American criminal justice more just and more effective? Further, how can we assure that the changes I have suggested are actually pursued?

CONCLUSION

This chapter summarized the main findings of *Justice Blind?* and put forth recommendations for overcoming injustice in the United States. Our criminal justice network is supposed to do justice and reduce crime, but according to the findings reported in this book, we fail miserably at both. Since the 1970s, we have chosen a crime control model of justice at the expense of due process rights of citizens. Ironically, this shift has not made Americans safer from the harms that most threaten them. As I demonstrated in this book, injustice in American criminal justice most greatly affects poor people and people of color, and it has begun to affect poor, minority women at a rate higher than that for men. The late Martin Luther King, Jr., would be saddened to know that injustice in America is more prevalent now than at any time during his life. For example, the percentage of African American males in our nation's prisons and jails has increased consistently since King's death. In effect, the war on crime is one of the nation's leading causes of segregation. The Issue in Depth that follows considers an alternative approach to justice, called social justice, that we should pursue if we are ever to realize the goals of Dr. King.

Issue in Depth—Toward Social Justice: Groups Doing the Work Now

Is justice blind? The obvious answer is no. In this book, I have outlined numerous ways in which police, courts, and corrections fail to produce justice as a process. I hope this troubles you as much as it does me. After all, the United States is supposed to be devoted to the notion of blind justice, based on the U.S. Constitution, the American

CHAPTER 13 *Summary, Conclusions, and Recommendations for the Future* 461

Declaration of Independence, and the figure of a blindfolded woman holding scales that adorns many of our courthouses and legislative buildings.

Supposedly, Americans will not support criminal justice processes that fail to punish those who deserve it. Ideally, they will not support criminal justice processes that wrongfully convict the innocent or are biased against any group. Why, then, do we tolerate the shortcomings of our criminal justice agencies?

In this last chapter, I outlined numerous recommendations to make our criminal justice network more just. I hope that these recommendations are taken into account as criminal justice reforms are debated now and in the future. I want to conclude by drawing your attention to an important point about justice: that injustice in criminal justice is a threat to social justice.

Social justice is perhaps the broadest conception of justice. It is bigger than the criminal justice network and exists when all forms of culpable harmful behaviors are abhorred, opposed, denounced, combated, and abolished (Barak and Henry, 1999, p. 152). It exists when all people are treated equally under the law.

Although equality is undeniably part of social justice, the meaning of social justice is actually much broader. Further, "equal opportunity" and similar phrases such as "personal responsibility" have been used to diminish the prospective for realizing social justice by justifying enormous inequalities in modern society (Berry, 2005). The most recent theories of and scholarly statements about social justice illustrate the complex nature of the concept. Two of the most prominent statements about social justice, each of which posits its own theory of social justice, are John Rawls's (2003) *Justice as Fairness* and David Miller's (2003) *Principles of Social Justice*. While neither of these theories can be considered an exhaustive treatment of the subject matter, each offers a complex theory of social justice that illustrates its broad meaning. Both conceptions of social justice are similar, so there is significant overlap between the main ideas of the theorists; this is likely because they are founded on like principles and based on previously posited theories from significant historical political philosophers (Brighouse, 2005).

John Rawls's theory of social justice is referred to as "justice as fairness." It can be summarized with two primary principles. They are:

1. Each person has the same indisputable claim to a fully adequate scheme of equal basic liberties, which scheme is compatible with the same scheme of liberties for all; and
2. Social and economic inequalities are to satisfy two conditions: first, they are to be attached to offices and positions open to all under conditions of fair equality of opportunity; and second, they are to be to the greatest benefit of the least-advantaged members of society (Rawls, 2003, pp. 42–43).

According to Rawls, these principles are ordered, meaning the first principle (the "equal liberties principle") should be achieved before efforts to achieve the second principle are attempted. Further, the first part of the second principle (the "equal opportunity principle") precedes the second part (the "difference principle"). The ordering of the principles suggests that, to Rawls, equality is the most important element of social justice. Equality means a fair distribution of each of the capacities needed "to be normal and fully cooperating members of society over a complete life" (Rawls, 2003, p. 18). Rawls explains that the "priority [of equality] means . . . that the second principle (which includes the difference principle as one part) is always to be applied within a setting of background institutions that satisfy the requirements of the first principle (including the requirement of securing the fair value of the political liberties). . . ." (Rawls, 2003, p. 46). Background institutions refer to basic structures of society (e.g., family, school, religion, economy, polity), which, when just, can be referred to as "background justice" (Rawls, 2003, p. 10).

Just because Rawls's conception of social justice values equality, this does not mean that equal outcomes will be achieved in society, or that they can be. In fact, Rawls's second principle asserts that inequalities in society are acceptable as long as they meet two conditions. First, as per the "equal opportunity principle," inequalities are acceptable if every person in society has a reasonable chance of obtaining the positions that lead to the inequalities. An example would be equal opportunity to achieve any job. Rawls (2003, p. 43) specifies that "fair equality of opportunity" requires "not merely that public offices and social positions open in the formal sense, but that all should have a fair chance to attain them." The disparities in income and wealth identified in Chapter 12 are just because there is not equal opportunity for success in the United States, even today.

Second, as per the "difference principle," inequalities in society must be organized so that they are to the greatest benefit of the least advantaged members of society. After explaining that today's economic inequalities are simply not acceptable, Rawls (2003, pp. 59–60) explains the difference principle this way: "To say that inequalities in income and wealth are to be arranged for the greatest benefit of the least advantaged simply means that we are to compare schemes of cooperation by seeing how well-off the least advantaged are under each scheme, and then to select the scheme under which the least advantaged are better off than they are under any other scheme." With two competing arrangements of incomes in a society, the fairer of the two—and therefore the more just of the two—is the one that is to the greatest benefit of the least advantaged. For example, if in one arrangement, the most well-off class (e.g., chief financial officers) received compensation in the amount of $10 million per year while the least well-off (e.g., average workers) were paid a salary of $14,000, and in another the most well-off received compensation in the amount of $3 million per year while the least well-off were paid a salary of $30,000, the second arrangement would be to the greatest advantage of the least advantaged and thus the most just.

By the least advantaged, Rawls is referring to those who lack what he calls "primary goods" (2003, p. 53). Primary goods, according to Rawls, include "things needed and required by persons seen in the light of the political conception of persons, as citizens who are fully cooperating members of society, and not merely as human beings apart from any normative conception. These goods are things citizens need as free and equal persons living a complete life; they are not things it is simply rational to want or desire, or to prefer or even to crave" (2003, p. 58). Such goods include:

- The basic rights and liberties: freedom of thought and liberty of conscience, and the rest
- Freedom of movement and free choice of occupation against a background of diverse opportunities, which opportunities allow the pursuit of a variety of ends and give effect to decisions to revise and alter them
- Powers and prerogatives of office and position of authority and responsibility

- Income and wealth, understood as all-purpose means (having an exchange value) generally needed to achieve a wide range of ends, whatever they may be
- The social bases of self-respect, understood as those aspects of basic institutions normally essential if citizens are to have a lively sense of their worth as persons and to be able to advance their ends with self-confidence (Rawls, 2003, pp. 58–59)

It should also be noted that Rawls (2003, p. 13) acknowledges the importance of "human rights" as well. He writes, "A just world order is perhaps best seen as a society of peoples, each people maintaining a well-ordered and decent political (domestic) regime, not necessarily democratic but fully respecting basic human rights." Human rights are expansive and include rights in many areas (Donnelly, 2002; Buergenthal, Shelton, and Stewart, 2002). We can use Rawls's theory of "justice as fairness" to determine if any process or outcome is consistent with social justice. When a process or outcome does not comport with any of Rawls's principles, we can conclude that it is not consistent with social justice. That is, something is not consistent with Rawls's conception of social justice if it interferes with any person's indefensible claims to equal basic liberties (the "equal liberties principle"), or if inequalities in society are not attached to offices and positions open to all under conditions of fair equality of opportunity (the "equal opportunity principle"), or if inequalities in society are not arranged to the greatest benefit of the least-advantaged members of society (the "difference principle").

David Miller's theory comprises a wider range of concepts than that of John Rawls. Meant to be pluralistic and circumstantial, the theory is built around those principles of justice that people actually hold. First, the theory can be considered pluralistic or circumstantial because different parts of his conception of social justice are more or less relevant depending on the circumstances (Miller, 2003, pp. 62–63). Second, Miller's (2003, p. ix) goal was to discover those principles people actually use when judging whether parts of society are just or unjust. Miller created his theory from public opinion polls and studies of public opinion with regard to different elements of justice. He does this in part because—while social justice must be "critical" in nature so that changes toward more fairness in society can be achieved—it must not be utopian.

To Miller, social justice deals with the distribution of good and bad in society, and more specifically with how these things should be distributed within society. Miller (2003, p. 1) explains that when "we attack some policy or some state of affairs as socially unjust, we are claiming that a person, or more usually a category of persons, enjoys fewer advantages than that person or group of persons ought to enjoy (or bears more of the burdens than they ought to bear), given how other members of the society in question are fairing."

Given this conception of social justice, it is not surprising that Miller's theory focuses on the concepts of need, desert, and equality. Need is a claim that one is lacking basic necessities and is being harmed or is in danger of being harmed and/or that one's capacity to function is being impeded (Miller, 2003, pp. 207, 210). Desert is a claim that one has earned reward based on performance, and that superior performance should attract superior recognition (Miller, 2003, pp. 134, 141). Equality refers to the social ideal that society regards and treats its citizens as equals, and that benefits such as certain rights should be distributed equally (Miller, 2003, p. 232).

Miller's (2003, p. 25) theory asserts that whether need, desert, or equality takes precedence depends on which "mode of human relationship" is being considered. This is because "we can best understand which demands of justice someone can make of us by looking first at the particular nature of relationship." A "mode of human relationship" refers to the different kinds of relationships that people have with one another.

Miller (2003, p. 26) specifies three basic modes of human relationships, including the solidaristic community, instrumental associations, and citizenship. A solidaristic community "exists when people share a common identity as members of a relatively stable group with a common ethos" (e.g., family relations). In this mode of human relationships, the principle of distribution according to need is most relevant: "Each member is expected to contribute to relieving the needs of others in proportion to ability, the extent of liability depending upon how close the ties of community are in each case. . . . Needs will be understood in terms of the general ethos of the community. Each community embodies, implicitly or explicitly, a sense of the standards that an adequate human life must meet, and it is in terms of this benchmark that the much-contested distinction between needs, which are matters of justice, and mere wants is drawn" (Miller, 2003, p. 27).

Instrumental associations exist when "people relate to one another in a utilitarian manner; each has aims and purposes that can best be realized by collaboration with others" (e.g., economic relations). In this mode of human relationships, the principle of distribution according to desert is most relevant: "Each person comes to the association as a free agent with a set of skills and talents that he deploys to advance its goals. Justice is done when he receives back by way of reward an equivalent to the contribution he makes. A person's deserts, in other words, are fixed by the aims and purposes of the association to which she belongs; these provide the measuring rod in terms of which relative contributions can be judged" (Miller, 2003, p. 28).

Finally, citizenship refers to "members of a political society" in "modern liberal democracies" who "are related not just through their communities and their instrumental associations but also as fellow citizens. Anyone who is a full member of such a society is understood to be the bearer of a set of rights and obligations that together define the status of citizen." In this mode of human relationship, the principle of distribution according to equality is most relevant because everyone in the society is deemed equal in terms of certain rights (Miller, 2003, p. 30).

Because of the citizenship mode, rights play a significant role in Miller's theory of social justice, as they also did in Rawls's theory. Miller (2003, p. 13) explains that "a central element in any theory of justice will be an account of the basic rights of citizens, which will include rights to various concrete liberties, such as freedom of movement and freedom of speech . . . an extensive sphere of basic liberty is built into the requirements of social justice itself." The meaning of human rights is well understood, and includes rights in dozens of areas.

Miller does not build a theory of social justice that requires one to emphasize either need, desert, or equality over the others; rather, he presents a theory whereby the three are in balance with one another. Because people's views about justice are pluralistic and "very often people decide what a fair distribution consists of by balancing claims of one kind against claims of another," it follows that "the social context in which the distribution has to be made—or more precisely how that context is perceived by those making the judgment—will determine which principle stands out as the relevant principle of justice" (Miller, 2003, p. 63).

A significant issue, though, is which should take precedence when there are conflicting demands and expectations for processes that aim to accommodate need, desert, and equality, as well as for outcomes that satisfy need, desert, and equality. Miller prioritizes need above desert, and desert above equality, although he also points out that at times desert can take precedence over need (as in the case where the needy are not seen as deserving) (Miller, 2003, pp. 76–78). Although Miller spends most of his time discussing desert or merit (in part because it is likely the most complicated), he is careful to point out that "[m]erit of any sort should only be allowed to govern the distribution of a certain range of goods and services, and in particular *not* those goods and services that people regard as necessities, such as health care" (Miller, 2003, p. 200, emphasis added). To the degree that access to knowledge is such a necessity, claims based on need ought to take priority over claims based on desert.

Similar to Rawls, Miller holds that inequalities in society are at times just. There are at least two reasons for this. First, economic inequalities that motivate people to strive for more can sometimes be justified. Second, inequalities may result from differential claims on merit. That is, those individuals who are more meritorious because of their performances deserve more than those who are less meritorious because of their education, skills, and performances (Miller, 2003, pp. 68–70). Yet Miller (2003, p. 70) agrees with Rawls that today's economic disparities are not acceptable.

We can use Miller's pluralistic theory of social justice to determine if any process or outcome is consistent with social justice. When a process or outcome does not comport with any of Miller's principles, we can conclude that it is not consistent with social justice. That is, something is not consistent with Miller's conception of social justice if it interferes with one's necessities or hurts one's capacity to function, if it interferes with claims based on desert, or if it impedes equal opportunity or treatment.

Criminal justice is not necessarily aimed at achieving social justice, nor must it be. According to Arrigo (1999, pp. 9, 253), the goals of criminal justice (to do justice and to reduce crime) may be completely separate and distinct from the goal of achieving social justice. In fact, the way our agencies of criminal justice are organized may actually make it harder to achieve social justice (Barak and Henry, 1999).

I believe that one goal of the criminal justice network should be to achieve social justice—that is, "to advance principles of fairness, equity, reasonableness, and so forth, through police, court, and correctional practices" (Arrigo, 1999, p. 253). In other words, I believe that the criminal justice network not only must seek to achieve justice as an outcome and justice as a process, but also must never be allowed to interfere with the realization of social justice. Our criminal justice agencies must, in their operations, remain anchored in "fairness, equity, proprietorship, due process, and so forth" (Arrigo, 1999, p. 9). Otherwise, social justice will not be possible.

Many of the impediments to realizing social justice exist outside criminal justice. Achieving social justice may not be possible simply by adopting the recommendations made in this chapter. It may require making changes to the basic structure of the United States' governments. One example is suggested by Reiman (2006), who, in *The Rich Get Richer and the Poor Get Prison*, advocates a redistribution of wealth as a means of reducing the conditions of poverty that produce much of the street crime in the United States. He does not suggest handouts to the poor but, rather, writes that our government needs to give the poor more of a helping hand to achieve the so-called American Dream. Reiman does not specifically lay out how this would be achieved, leading many to wonder how this can be achieved without socializing our government.

I do not seriously believe that the fundamental structure of American government will soon, if ever, be changed in such a way. Instead of advocating such structural changes, I advocate an approach that seeks change from within. That is, you, who may one day work within some agency of criminal justice in the United States (or, at least, most likely will live in this country as an American), will be called upon to put into practice the changes required to make the criminal justice network more just. It will be up to you to achieve social justice in America.

Crime victims must be involved in achieving the goal of social justice. Further, groups working for social justice ought to work just as hard to reduce violence in society, not only because social justice requires that people be safe but also because social justice advocates will gain significant credibility among "conservatives" concerned with law and order and crime control for doing so.

Consider the growing list of organizations who feel the same way. For example, visit these websites:

- Campaign for Effective Crime Policy: http://www.crimepolicy.org/
- Center for Justice and Reconciliation: http://www.restorativejustice.org/
- Center for Restorative Justice and Peacemaking: http://ssw.che.umn.edu/rjp/
- Centre for Social Justice: http://www.socialjustice.org/
- Coalition for Federal Sentencing Reform: http://www.sentencing.org/
- Crime Victims for a Just Society: http://www.crimevictims.net/index.html
- Criminal Justice Policy Foundation: http://www.cjpf.org/
- Death Penalty Information Center: http://www.deathpenaltyinfo.org/
- Drug Policy Alliance: http://www.drugpolicy.org/homepage.cfm
- Families Against Mandatory Minimums: http://www.famm.org/index2.htm
- Journey of Hope: http://www.journeyofhope.org/
- Murder Victims Families for Reconciliation: www.mvfr.org
- National Center on Institutions and Alternatives: http://www.ncianet.org/
- National Coalition to Abolish the Death Penalty: http://www.ncadp.org/
- People of Faith Against the Death Penalty: http://www.pfadp.org/
- Restitution Incorporated: http://www.restitutioninc.org/
- Sentencing Project: http://www.sentencingproject.org/
- Stop the Drug War: http://stopthedrugwar.org/
- Stopviolence.com: http://stopviolence.com/
- Tolerance.org: http://www.tolerance.org/index.jsp
- Victim Offender Mediation Association: http://www.voma.org/

Each of these organizations, along with so many others, is currently doing work to achieve social justice. Thus, there is hope. And there is something you can do.

This book has demonstrated that the U.S. criminal justice network fails to achieve any of these conceptions of justice. And so we've come full circle, returning to the first words of the book:

"Injustice anywhere is a threat to justice everywhere."
—Martin Luther King, "Letter from Birmingham Jail"

As I wrote in the preface, injustice anywhere in the United States is a threat to all persons living in the United States. And injustice in America is every American's business. Now that you understand the many ways in which the American criminal justice network is unjust, let's get down to the business of making it more just.

DISCUSSION QUESTIONS

1. Do you agree with the overall assessment of the U.S. criminal justice network as it was summarized in this chapter? Explain.
2. Explain each step of planned change.
3. Are the U.S. criminal justice network's efforts to reduce crime consistent with planned change? If so, how? If not, why not?
4. Which of the recommendations discussed in this chapter do you think is most likely to be implemented in the near future? Explain.
5. What is social justice? How is it related to criminal justice?

REFERENCES

Acker, J., and C. Lanier. (1998). Death penalty legislation: Past, present, and future. In J. Acker, R. Bohm, and C. Lanier, eds., *America's experiment with capital punishment: Reflections on the past, present and future of the ultimate penal sanction.* Durham, NC: Carolina Academic Press.

Adams, I., and B. Martin. (1996). Cannabis: Pharmacology and toxicology in animals and humans. *Addiction* 91 (11): 1585–1614.

Adler, F., G. Mueller, and W. Laufer. (1995). *Criminology.* New York: McGraw-Hill.

Aertsen, I., Daems, T., and L. Robert. (2005). *Institutionalizing restorative justice.* UK: Willan.

Agnew, R. (1993). An empirical test of general strain theory. *Criminology* 30:475–99.

Agnew, R. (2007). *Why do criminals offend? A general theory of crime and delinquency.* New York: Oxford University Press.

Agron, J., and L. Anderson. (2000). School security by the numbers. *American School and University* 72 (9): 6–11.

Akers, R. (1996). *Criminological theory: Introduction and evaluation.* Los Angeles: Roxbury.

Akers, R., and G. Jensen. (2007). *Social learning theory and the explanation of crime.* Edison, NJ: Transaction.

Albonetti, C. (1987). Prosecutorial discretion: The effects of uncertainty. *Law and Society Review* 21:291–313.

Albonetti, C. (1997). Sentencing under the federal sentencing guidelines: Effects of defendant characteristics, guilty pleas, and departures on sentencing outcomes for drug offenses, 1991–1992. *Law and Society Review* 31:789–822.

Alpert, G., Dunham, R., and M. Smith. (2007). Investigating racial profiling by the Miami-Dade Police Department: A multimethod approach. *Criminology & Public Policy* 6 (1): 25–55.

Altheide, D. (1984). TV news and the social construction of justice: Research issues and policy. In R. Surette, ed., *Justice and the media.* Springfield, IL: Charles C Thomas.

Altheide, D. (2004). Consuming terrorism. *Symbolic Interaction* 27:289–308.

Altheide, D. (2006). *Terrorism and the politics of fear.* Lanham, MD: AltaMira Press.

Alvarado, M., and O. Boyd-Barrett. (1992). *Media education: An introduction.* London: Milton Keynes.

Ambrosio, T., and V. Schiraldi. (1997). *From classrooms to cell blocks: A national perspective.* Washington, DC: The Justice Policy Institute.

American Academy of Pediatrics. (2002). Online: www.aap.org.

American Bar Association. (1993, 1997). Online: www.abanet.org/crimjust/standards/home.html.

Amsterdam, A. (1982). Capital punishment. In H. Bedau, ed., *The death penalty in America.* New York: Oxford University Press.

Anderson, C., and R. Cromwell. (1977). Black is beautiful and the color preferences of Afro-American youth. *Journal of Negro Education* 46:76.

Anderson, E. (1995). *Streetwise: Race, class and change in an urban community.* Chicago: University of Chicago Press.

Anderson, K. An eye for an eye. *Time* 24 (January 1983): 28–39.

Angolabahere, S., R. Behr, and S. Iyengar. (1993). *The media game: American politics in the television age*. New York: Macmillan.

Arrigo, B., ed. (1999). *Social justice/criminal justice: The maturation of critical theory in law, crime, and deviance*. Belmont, CA: Wadsworth.

Asnis, S., and R. Smith. (1978). Amphetamine abuse and violence. *Journal of Psychedelic Drugs* 10:317–77.

Ayers, I., and J. Waldfogel. A market test for race discrimination in bail setting. *Stanford Law Review* 46 (May 1994): 987.

Bagdikian, B. (2004). *The New Media Monopoly*. Boston: Beacon Press.

Bailey, W. (1998). Deterrence, brutalization, and the death penalty: Another examination of Oklahoma's return to capital punishment. *Criminology* 36:711–33.

Bailey, W., and R. Peterson. (1997). Murder, capital punishment, and deterrence: A review of the literature. In H. Bedau, ed., *The death penalty in America: Current controversies*. New York: Oxford University Press.

Baker, R., and F. Meyer. (1980). *The criminal justice game: Politics and players*. Lexington, MA: D. C. Heath.

Banfield, E. (1973). *Unheavenly city*. Boston: Little, Brown.

Barak, G. (1988). Newsmaking criminology: Reflections on the media, intellectuals, and crime. *Justice Quarterly* 5:565–87.

Barak, G. (1994). *Media, process, and the social construction of crime*. New York: Garland.

Barak, G. (1995). Between the waves: Mass-mediated themes of crime and justice. *Social Justice* 21 (3): 133–47.

Barak, G., and S. Henry. (1999). An integrative-constitutive theory of crime, law, and social justice. In B. Arrigo, ed., *Social justice/criminal justice: The maturation of critical theory in law, crime, and deviance*. Belmont, CA: Wadsworth.

Barber, J. (1994). The jury is still out. *American Criminal Law Review* 31:1225–52.

Barclay, G., and C. Tavares. (2002). *International comparisons of criminal justice statistics 2000*. London: Home Office.

Barkan, S. (1997). *Criminology: A sociological understanding*. Upper Saddle River, NJ: Prentice Hall.

Barlett, D., and J. Steele. (1992). *America: What went wrong?* Olympia, WA: Democratic Media Services, House of Representatives.

Barnett, C. (2003). The measurement of white-collar crime using Uniform Crime Reporting (UCR) data. Online: www.fbi.gov/whitecollarforweb.pdf.

Bayley, D. (1994). *Police for the future*. New York: Oxford University Press.

Beccaria, C. (1776). *Dei delitti e della pena* [An essay on crime and punishments], 6th ed.

Beck, A. (1998). Trends in United States corrections population. In K. Haus and G. Alpert, eds., *The dilemmas of corrections*. Prospect Heights, IL: Waveland Press.

Becker, H. (1963). *Outsiders*. New York: The Free Press.

Beckett, K. (1994). Setting the public agenda: "Street crime" and drug use in American politics. *Social Problems* 41:425–47.

Beckett, K. (1997). *Making crime pay: Law and order in contemporary American politics*. New York: Oxford University Press.

Beckett, K., and T. Sasson. (1998). *The politics of injustice*. Thousand Oaks, CA: Sage.

Beckett, K., and T. Sasson. (2000). *The politics of injustice: Crime and punishment in America*. Thousand Oaks, CA: Pine Forge Press.

Beckett, K., and T. Sasson (2003). *The politics of injustice: Crime and punishment in America*, 2nd ed. Thousand Oaks, CA: Sage.

Bedau, H., ed. (1982). *The death penalty in America*, 3rd ed. New York: Oxford University Press.

Bedau, H. (1987). *Death is different: Studies in the morality, law, and politics of capital punishment*. Boston: Northeastern University Press.

Bedau, H. (1997). *Capital punishment in America: Current controversies*. New York: Oxford University Press.

Bedau, H., and M. Radelet. (1987). Miscarriages of justice in potentially capital cases. *Stanford Law Review* 40:21–179.

Belenko, S. (1993). *Crack and the evolution of the anti-drug policy*. Westport, CT: Greenwood Press.

Belknap, J. (1996). *The invisible woman*. Belmont, CA: Wadsworth.

Belknap, J. (2006). *The Invisible Woman: Gender, Crime, and Justice*, 3rd ed. Beverly Hills, CA: Wadsworth.

Belzman, J. Congressional pork includes some real stinkers. *MSNBC* (April 5, 2006). Online: http://www.msnbc.msn.com/id/12169524/.

Benjamin, D., and R. Miller. (1991). *Undoing drugs: Beyond legalization*. New York: Basic Books.

Bennett, L. (1980). *Public opinion in American politics*. New York: Harcourt Brace Jovanovich.

Berk, R. (2004). New claims about execution and general deterrence: Deja vu all over again? *Journal of Empirical Legal Studies*. Online: http://preprints.stat.ucla.edu/396/JELS.pap.pdf.

Berry, B. (2005). *Why social justice matters*. Cambridge, England: Polity Press.

Berry, J. (1984). *The interest group society*. Boston: Little, Brown.

Bertram, E., M. Blachman, K. Sharpe, and P. Andreas. (1996). *Drug war politics: The price of denial*. Berkeley: University of California Press.

Best, J. (1999). *Random violence*. Berkeley: University of California Press.

Biskupic, J. (1991). Letter writing and campaigns. *Congressional Quarterly Weekly Report* 49:171–74.

Bittner, E. (1970). The police and the "war on crime." In *The functions of police in modern society*. Washington DC: U.S. Government Printing Office.

Black, C. (1974). *Capital punishment: The inevitability of caprice and mistake*. New York: Norton.

Black's law dictionary, 6th ed. (1991). St. Paul, MN: West.

Blakemore, E. (1998). The effect of mandatory minimum sentencing on black males and black communities. Online: www.udayton.edu/~race/annotate/s98blake.htm.

Blount, E. (2002). *Occupational crime: Deterrence, investigation, and reporting in compliance with federal guidelines*. New York: CRC.

Bluestone, B., and S. Rose. (2000). Overworked and underemployed. In R. Lauer and J. Lauer, eds., *Troubled times: Readings in social problems*. Los Angeles: Roxbury.

Blumberg, A. (1967). The practice of law as confidence game: Organizational cooption of a profession. *Law and Society Review* 4:115–39.

Blumstein, A. (1993). Racial disproportionality of U.S. prison populations revisited. *University of Colorado Law Review* 64:743–60.

Blumstein, A. (1995). Prisons. In J. Wilson and J. Petersilia, eds., *Crime*. San Francisco: San Francisco Institute for Contemporary Studies.

Blumstein, A. (2000). The connection between crime and incarceration. In J. May, ed., *Building violence: How America's rush to incarcerate creates more violence*. Thousand Oaks, CA: Sage.

Blumstein, A., and J. Cohen. (1973). A theory of the stability of punishment. *Journal of Criminal Law and Criminology* 35 (1): 133–75.

Blumstein, A., J. Cohen, S. Martin, and M. Tonry, eds. (1983). *Research on sentencing: The search for reform*. Washington, DC: National Academy Press.

Blumstein, A., and J. Wallman, eds. (2000). *The crime drop in America*. New York: Cambridge University Press.

Boer, J., M. Pastor, and J. Sadd. (1993). Is there environmental racism? The demographics of hazardous waste in Los Angeles County. *Social Science Quarterly* 78 (4): 793–810.

Bohm, B. (1989). The effects of classroom instruction and discussion on death penalty opinions: A teaching note. *Journal of Criminal Justice* 17:123–31.

Bohm, B. (1990). Death penalty opinions: Effects of a classroom experience and public commitment. *Sociological Inquiry* 60:285–97.

Bohm, B., L. Clark, and A. Aveni. (1990). The influence of knowledge on death penalty opinions: An experimental test, *Justice Quarterly* 7:175–88.

Bohm, B., L. Clark, and A. Aveni. (1991). Knowledge and death penalty opinion: A test of the Marshall hypotheses. *Journal of Research in Crime and Delinquency* 28:360–87.

Bohm, B., and R. Vogel. (2002). More than ten years after: The long-term stability of informed death penalty opinions. Paper presented at the annual meeting of the Academy of Criminal Justice Sciences, Los Angeles.

Bohm, B., R. Vogel, and A. Maisto. (1993). Knowledge and death penalty opinion: A panel study. *Journal of Criminal Justice* 21:29–45.

Bohm, R. (1999). *Deathquest: An introduction to the theory and practice of capital punishment in the United States*. Cincinnati, OH: Anderson.

Bohm, R. (2001). *A primer on crime and delinquency,* 2nd ed. Belmont, CA: Wadsworth.

Bohm, R. (2003). *Deathquest II: An introduction to the theory and practice of capital punishment in the United States,* 2nd ed. Cincinnati, OH: Anderson.

Bohm, R. (2007). *DeathQuest III: An introduction to the theory and practice of capital punishment in the United States,* 3rd ed. Cincinnati, OH: Anderson.

Bohn, K. Patriot Act report documents civil rights complaints. *CNN* (July 31, 2003). Online: http://www.cnn.com/2003/LAW/07/21/justice.civil.liberties.

Bonnie, R., and C. Whitebread. (1974). *Marihuana conviction: A history of marihuana prohibition in the United States.* Charlottesville: University of Virginia.

Bonsignore, J., E. Katsh, P. D'Errico, R. Pipkin, S. Arons, and J. Rifkin. (1998). *Before the law: An introduction to the legal process,* 6th ed. Boston: Houghton Mifflin.

Boritch, H. (1992). Gender and criminal court outcome: An historical analysis. *Criminology* 30:293–325.

Boston University Medical Center. (2000). Online: www.bmc.org.

Bowers, W., G. Pierce, and J. McDevitt. (1984). *Legal homicide.* Boston: Northeastern University Press.

Bradley C. (2000). Reforming the criminal trial. In G. Mays and P. Gregware, eds., *Courts and justice: A reader,* 2nd ed. Prospect Heights, IL: Waveland Press.

Bridges, C., and R. Crutchfield. (1988). Law, social standing, and racial disparity in imprisonment. *Social Forces* 66:699–724.

Brigham, J. (2005). "Anti-anti terror: Color coding and the joke of "Homeland Security." *New Political Science* 27 (4): 481–496.

Brighouse, H. (2005). *Justice (key concepts).* Cambridge, England: Polity Press.

Brown, E., K. Defenbacker, and W. Sturgill. (1977). Memory for faces and the circumstance of encounters. *Journal of Applied Psychology* 62:311–18.

Browne, A. (1993). Family violence and homelessness: The relevance of trauma histories in the lives of homeless women. *American Journal of Orthopsychiatry* 63:370–84.

Brownstein, H. (1991). The social construction of public policy: A case for participation by researchers. *Sociological Practice Review* 2:132–40.

Brownstein, H. (1996). *The rise and fall of a violent crime wave: Crack cocaine and the social construction of a crime problem.* Albany NY: Harrow and Heston.

Brumm, H., and D. Cloninger. (1996). Perceived risk of punishment and the commission of homicides: A covariance structure analysis. *Journal of Economic Behavior and Organization* 31 (1): 1–11.

Brunk, G., and L. Wilson. (1991). Interest groups and criminal behavior. *Journal of Research in Crime and Delinquency* 28:157–73.

Buckhout, R. (1974). Eyewitness testimony. *Scientific American* 231:23–31.

Buergenthal, T., D. Shelton, and D. Stewart. (2002). *International human rights in a nutshell.* Belmont, CA: West.

Bureau of Justice Assistance. (1993). Online: www.ojp.usdoj.gov/bja.

Bureau of Justice Statistics. (1995, 1996, 1997, 2000, 2003, 2006, 2007). Online: www.ojp.usdoj.gov/bjs.

Burnstein, H., and P. Goldstein. (1990). Research and the development of public policy. *Journal of Applied Psychology* 7:77–92.

Bushway, S. (2000). The stigma of a criminal history record in the labor market. In J. May, ed., *Building violence: How America's rush to incarcerate creates more violence*. Thousand Oaks, CA: Sage.

Cable News Network (CNN). Killer executed the hard way. (May 2, 2006). Online: http://www.cnn.com/2006/LAW/05/02/lethal.injection.reut/index.html.

Caffrey, A. (2003). FBI takes up heavy load of corporate fraud probes. Online: www.truthout.org.

Cahalan, M. (1986). Historical corrections statistics in the United States, 1850–1984. Washington, DC: Bureau of Justice Statistics, U.S. Department of Justice.

Campaign for America's Future. (2006). Online: http://home.ourfuture.org.

Carlson, J., and T. Williams. (1993). Perspectives on the seriousness of crimes. *Social Science Research* 22:190–207.

Carmichael, S., and C. Hamilton. (1969). *Black power*. New York: Vintage Books.

Carter, D., and A. Sapp. (1993). Police response to street people: A survey of perspectives and practices. *FBI Law Enforcement Bulletin* 62:5–10.

Casement, M. (1987). Alcohol and cocaine. *Alcohol and Health Research World II* 4:18–25.

Castellano, T., and E. McGarrell. (1991). The politics of law and order: Case study evidence for a conflict model of the criminal law formation process. *Journal of Research in Crime and Delinquency* 28 (3): 304–29.

Catalano, S. (2006). Criminal Victimization, 2005. Online: http://www.ojp.gov/bjs/pub/ascii/cv05.txt.

Caulkins, J., C. Rydell, W. Schwabe, and J. Chiesa. (1997). *Mandatory minimum drug sentences*. Santa Monica, CA: Rand Corporation.

Cavender, G. (2004). Media and crime policy: A reconsideration of David Garland's *The Culture of Control*. *Punishment and Society* 6:335–48.

Center for Media and Public Affairs. (1997). *Media Monitor*. Washington, DC: Center for Media and Public Affairs.

Center for Media and Public Affairs. (1999). In K. Owens, *The world of the child*. New York: Macmillan.

Center for Media and Public Affairs. (2000). Online: www.cmpa.com/factoid/agenda.htm.

Center for Media Education. (2000). Online: www.cme.org.

Center for Public Integrity. (2007). Online: http://www.publicintegrity.org/default.aspx.

Centers for Disease Control and Prevention. (1994a). Changes in brand preference of adolescent smokers in the United States, 1989–1993. *Morbidity and Mortality Weekly Report* 43:577–81.

Centers for Disease Control and Prevention. (1994b). Cigarette smoking among adults in the United States, 1994. *Morbidity and Mortality Weekly Report* 45:588–90.

Centers for Disease Control and Prevention. (1994c). *Preventing tobacco use among young people: A report of the surgeon general*. Atlanta, GA: U.S. Department of Health and Human Services.

Centers for Disease Control and Prevention. (1997). *CDC's tobacco use prevention program: Working toward a healthier future*. Atlanta, GA: U.S. Department of Health and Human Services.

Chaffee, R., and D. German. (1998). New frontiers in political socialization research. In K. Hufer and B. Wellie, eds., *Sozialwissenschaftliche und bildungstheoretische Reflexionen: Fachliche und didaktische Perspektiven zur politisch-gesellschaftlichen Aufklarung*. Cambridge, MA: Galda and Wilch Verlag.

Chairs-Sims, L. (1991). Long-range planning to minimize the negative effects of downsizing in an organization. National-Louis University.

Chambliss, W. (2000). *Power, politics, and crime*. Boulder, CO: Westview Press.

Chamlin, M., and J. Cochran. (2005). Ascribed inequality and homicide in modern societies. *Homicide Studies* 9:3–29.

Champion, D. (1997). *The Roxbury dictionary of criminal justice*. Los Angeles: Roxbury.

Chapper, J. A., and R. A. Hanson. (1990). *Intermediate appellate courts: Improving case processing.* Williamsburg, VA: National Center for State Courts.

Chermak, S. (1994). Crime in the news media: A refined understanding of how crime becomes news. In G. Barak, ed., *Media, process, and social construction of crime: Studies in news making criminology.* New York: Garland.

Chesney-Lind, M., and L. Pasko. (2004). *The Female Offender: Girls, Women, and Crime.* Thousand Oaks, CA: Sage Publications.

Children's Defense Fund. (2006). Online: http://www.childrensdefense.org/site/PageServer.

Chiricos, T. (1995). The moral panic of the drug war. In M. Lynch, ed., *Race and criminal justice.* Albany, NY: Harrow and Heston.

Chiricos, T., and W. Bales. (1991). Unemployment and punishment: An empirical assessment. *Criminology* 29:701–24.

Chiricos, T., and M. DeLone. (1992). Labor surplus and punishment: A review and assessment of theory and evidence. *Social Problems* 39:421–46.

Chiricos, T., and S. Eschholtz. (2002). The racial and ethnic typification of crime and the criminal typification of race and ethnicity in local television news. *Journal of Research in Crime and Delinquency* 39 (4): 400–20.

Chiricos, T., S. Eschholz, and M. Gertz. (1997). Crime, news and fear of crime: Toward an identification of audience effects. *Social Problems* 44:342–57.

Christianson, S. (2006). *Innocent: Inside wrongful conviction cases.* New York: New York University Press.

Christie, N. (2000). *Crime control as industry.* New York: Routledge.

Christopher, W. (1991). *Report of the Independent Commission on the Los Angeles Police Department.* Los Angeles: The Commission.

Citizens Against Government Waste. (2007). 2007 Pig Book Summary. Online: http://www.cagw.org/site/PageServer?pagename=reports_pigbook2007.

Clark, C. Prison overcrowding. *Congressional Quarterly Researcher* 4 (February 1994): 100.

Clear, T., G. Cole, and M. Reisig. (2005). *American Corrections,* 5th ed. Beverly Hills, CA: Wadsworth.

Clemmer, D. (1940). *The prison community.* Boston: Christopher.

Clinard, M., and P. Yeager. (2005). *Corporate Crime.* Edison, NJ: Transaction.

Cline, A. (2002). Agnosticism/Atheism. Online: www.about.com.

Cloninger, D., and R. Marchesini. (2001). Execution and deterrence: A quasicontrolled group experiment. *Applied Economics* 33 (5): 569–76.

Cloninger, D., and R. Marchesini. (2005). Execution moratoriums, commutations and deterrence: The case of Illinois. Online: http://www.cjlf.org/deathpenalty/IllStudyRevised.pdf.

Cloward, R., and L. Ohlin. (1961). *Delinquency and opportunity: A theory of delinquent gangs.* London: Routledge.

Clymer, A. Public found ready to sacrifice in drug fight. *New York Times* (September 2, 1986): A1, D16.

Coalition for Federal Sentencing Reform. (1997). Online: www.sentencing.org.

Coalition for Federal Sentencing Reform. (1999). Online: www.sentencing.org.

Cochran, J., and M. Chamlin. (2006). The enduring racial divide in death penalty support. *Journal of Criminal Justice* 34 (1): 85–99.

Cochran, J., M. Chamlin, and M. Seth. (1994). Deterrence or brutalization? An impact assessment of Oklahoma's return to capital punishment. *Criminology* 32:107–34.

Cohen, M. (1991). Some new evidence on the seriousness of crime. *Criminology* 26:343–53.

Cohen, S. (1972). *Folk devils and moral panics: The creation of the mods and the rockers.* London: Macgibbon and Kee.

Cohen, S. (2003). *The wrong men: America's epidemic of wrongful death row convictions.* New York: Carroll & Graf.

Cohen, S., and S. Solomon. (2005). How *Time* magazine promoted a cyberhoax. Online: www.fair.org/media-beat/950719.html.

Cohen, S., and J. Young, eds. (1981). *The manufacture of news.* Newbury Park, CA: Sage Publications.

Cole, D. (1999). Conditional sentencing: Recent developments. In J. Roberts and D. Cole, eds., *Making sense of sentencing.* Toronto: University of Toronto Press.

Cole, G., and C. Smith. (2006). *The American system of criminal justice,* 11th ed. Beverly Hills, CA: Wadsworth.

Coleman, J. (1990). *The criminal elite,* 2nd ed. New York: St. Martin's Press.

Coleman, J. (1998). *The criminal elite,* 4th ed. New York: St. Martin's Press.

Common Cause. (1999). Online: www.commoncause.org/laundromat/results.html.

Community Epidemiology Work Group. (1999). *Identifying and monitoring emerging drug use problems: A retrospective analysis of drug abuse data/information.* Bethesda, MD: National Institute on Drug Abuse.

Congress Link. (2003). Online: www.congresslink.org.

Congressional Quarterly. (1999). New Congress is older, more politically seasoned. *Congressional Quarterly* (January 9): 60–3.

Conklin (2002). *Why crime rates fell.* Boston: Allyn & Bacon.

Cook, P., D. Slawson, and L. Gries. (1993). *The cost of processing murder cases in North Carolina.* Raleigh: North Carolina Administrative Office of the Courts.

Costanzo, M. (1997). Just revenge: *Costs and consequences of the death penalty.* New York: St. Martin's Press.

Cox, S., and J. Wade. (1998). *The criminal justice network: An introduction.* New York: McGraw-Hill.

Coyne, R., and L. Entzeroth. (1994). *Capital punishment and the judicial process.* Durham, NC: Carolina Academic Press.

Crawford, C. (2000). Gender, race, and habitual offender sentencing in Florida. *Criminology* 38 (1): 263–80.

Cromwell, P. (1995). *In their own words.* Los Angeles: Roxbury.

Cromwell, P., and J. Olson. (2003). *Breaking and entering: Burglars on burglary.* Belmont, CA: Wadsworth.

Cromwell, P., J. Olson, and D. Avary. (1991). *Breaking and entering.* London: Sage.

Cronin, F., T. Cronin, and M. Milakovich. (1981). *The U.S. versus crime in the streets.* Bloomington: Indiana University Press.

Cullen, F., B. Link, and L. Travis. (1985). Consensus in crime seriousness: Empirical reality or methodological artifact? *Criminology* 23:99–118.

Culverson, D. (1998). Stereotyping by politicians: The welfare queen and Willie Horton. In C. Mann and M. Zatz, eds., *Images of color, images of crime.* Los Angeles: Roxbury.

Cunningham, B. Re-thinking objectivity. *Columbia Journalism Review* (July/August 2003): 24–32.

Currie, E. (1998). *Crime and punishment in America.* New York: Holt.

Curtis, D., and J. Resnick. (1987). Images of justice. *Yale Law Journal* 96:1727–72.

Cushman, P. (1974). Relationship between narcotic addiction and crime. *Federal Probation* 38:38–43.

Daly, K. (1994). Gender, crime, and punishment. New Haven, CT: Yale University Press.

Dattu, F. Illustrated jury instructions. *Judicature* 82 (September–October 1998): 79.

Davey, M. (2006). Missouri says it can't hire doctor for executions. *New York Times.* Online: http://www.nytimes.com/2006/07/15/us/15lethal.html?ex=1310616000&en=a36c6cb76aa3ccc3&ei=5088&partner=rssnyt&emc=rss.

Davis, A. (2007). *Arbitrary justice: The power of the American prosecutor.* New York: Oxford University Press.

Davis, J., and T. Smith. (1996). *General Social Surveys, 1972–1996.* Chicago: National Opinion Research Center.

Davis, M., and K. Davis. (1995). Star rising for Simpson jury consultant. *ABA Journal* 81:14.

Davis, R., and S. Meddis. Random killing hit a high. *USA Today* (December 5, 1994): 1a.

Death Penalty Information Center. (2006, 2007). Online: http://www.deathpenaltyinfo.org.

DeFrances, C., and G. Steadman. Prosecutors in state courts, 1996. *Bureau of Justice Statistics Bulletin* (July 1–10, 1998) Washington DC: U.S. Department of Justice.

De Gruchy, J. (2006). *Reconciliation: Restoring justice.* Minneapolis, MN: Augsburg Fortress Publishers.

del Carmen, A., and M. Robinson. (2000). Crime prevention through environmental design and consumption control in the United States. *Howard Journal of Criminal Justice* 39 (3): 267–89.

DeLisi, M., and B. Regoli. (1999). Race, conventional crime, and criminal justice: The declining importance of skin color. *Journal of Criminal Justice* 26 (6): 549–57.

Democracy North Carolina. (2003). Online: www.democracy-nc.org.

Denno, D. (1994). Is electrocution an unconstitutional method of execution? The engineering of death over the century. *William and Mary Law Review* 35:551–692.

Denno, D. (2003). Lethally humane? The evolution of execution methods in the United States. In J. Acker, B. Bohm, and C. Lanier, eds., *America's experiment with capital punishment: Reflections on the past, present, and future of the ultimate penal sanction.* Durham, NC: Carolina Academic Press.

Department of Health and Human Services (2007). Drug abuse warning network. Online: http://www.oas.samhsa.gov/DAWN/2k5ed.cfm.

Der Derian, J. (2002). The war of networks. *Theory and Event* 5. Online: http://muse.jhu.edu/journals/theory_and_event/v005/5.4derderian.html.

Devine, F. (1988). Inside the jury room: Deliberations of a mock jury. *Trial* 24:74–8.

Devlin, P. (1959). *The enforcement of morals.* London: Oxford University Press.

Dezhbakhsh, H., Rubin, P., and J. Shepherd (2003). Does capital punishment have a deterrent effect? New evidence from postmoratorium panel data. *American Law & Economics Review* 5 (2): 344–76.

Dezhbakhsh, H., and J. Shepherd. (2003). The deterrent effect of capital punishment: Evidence from a "judicial experiment." Department of Economics, Emory University. Working Paper No. 03-14. Online: http://people.clemson.edu/~jshephe/CaPuJLE_submit.pdf.

Dictionary.com (2006). Entry for "expert." Online: http://dictionary.reference.com/browse/expert.

Dill, B., M. Zinn, and S. Patton. (1999). Race, family values, and welfare reform. In L. Kushnick and J. Jennings, eds., *A new introduction to poverty: The role of race, power, and politics.* New York: New York University Press.

Dillehay, R., and M. Sandys. (1996). Life under Wainwright v. Witt: Juror dispositions and death qualification. *Law and Human Behavior* 20: 147–65.

Dinitz, S. (1996). Foreword. In R. Huff, A. Rattner, and E. Sagarin, eds., *Convicted but innocent: Wrongful conviction and public policy.* Thousand Oaks, CA: Sage.

Dodge, M., and Harris, J. (2000). Calling a strike a ball: Jury nullification and three strikes cases. In L. May and P. Gregware, eds., *Courts and justice: A reader.* Prospect Heights, IL: Waveland Press.

Dominick, J. (1997). Dumb kid: Petty crimes: A life term? *Los Angeles Times* (July 24): B9.

Donaldson, S. (1995). *Rape of incarcerated prisoners: A preliminary statistical look.* New York: Stop Prison Rape, Inc.

Dong, L., Block, G., and S. Mandel. (2004). Activities contributing to total energy expenditure in the United States: Results from the NHAPS study. *International Journal of Behavioral Nutrition and Physical Activity* 1:4.

Donnelly, J. (2002). *Universal human rights in theory and practice,* 2nd ed. Ithica, NY: Cornell University Press.

Donohue, J., and J. Wolfers. (2005). Uses and abuses of empirical evidence in the death penalty debate. *Stanford Law Review* 58:791–846.

Donziger, S., ed. (1996). *The real war on crime: The report of the National Criminal Justice Commission.* New York: HarperPerennial.

D'Orban, P. (1976). Barbiturate abuse. *Journal of Medical Ethics* 2:63–7.

Dorn, N., and N. Smith. (1992). *Traffickers.* London: Routledge.

Douglas, J., and J. Johnson. (1977). *Official deviance—Readings in malfeasance, misfeasance, and other forms of corruption.* Philadelphia: Lippincott.

Dow, D. (2002). How the death penalty really works. In D. Dow, and M. Dow, eds., *Machinery of death: The reality of America's death penalty regime.* New York: Routledge.

Dreschel, R. (1983). *News making in the trial court.* New York: Longman.

Dressel, P., and J. Porterfield. (1998). Mothers behind bars: Incarcerating increasing numbers of mothers has serious implications for families and society. *Corrections Today* 60 (7): 90–4.

Drug Policy Alliance. (2007). Police corruption. Online: http://www.drugpolicy.org/law/police.

Durham, A. (1992). Observations on the future of criminal justice education: Legitimating the discipline and serving the general university population. *Journal of Criminal Justice Education* 3 (1): 35–52.

Easton, D. (1953). *The political system.* New York: Knopf.

Edelman, M. (1988). *Constructing the political spectacle.* Chicago: University of Chicago Press.

Edsall, T., and M. Edsall. (1991). *Chain reaction: The impact of race, rights, and taxes on American politics.* New York: Norton.

Ehrenreich, B. (2001). *Nickel and dimed.* New York: Owl Books.

Eley, T. (2005). Did Big Oil participate in planning the invasion of Iraq? Online: http://www.globalresearch.ca/index.php?context=viewArticle&code=ELE20051211&articleId=1444.

Elikann, P. (1996). *The tough on crime myth.* New York: Insight.

Ellenius, A., and European Science Foundation. (1998). *Iconography, Propaganda, and Letigitimation.* New York: Oxford University Press.

Ellingswood, E. (1971). Assault and homicide associated with amphetamine use. *American Journal of Psychiatry* 127:90–5.

Elliott, E., and R. Gordon. (2005). *New directions in restorative justice: Issues, practice, evaluation.* UK: Willan.

Ellsworth, P. (1991). To tell what we know or wait for Godot? *Law and Human Behavior* 15:77–90.

Ellsworth, P. C. (1991). Unpleasant facts: The Supreme Court's response to empirical research on the death penalty. In K. Haas and J. Inciardi, eds., *Challenging capital punishment.* Newbury Park, CA: Sage.

Ellsworth, P., and L. Ross. (1983). Public opinion and capital punishment: A close examination of the views of abolitionists and retentionists. *Crime and Delinquency* 29:111–69.

Epperlein, T., and B. Nienstedt. (1989). Reexamining the use of seriousness weights in an index of crime. *Journal of Criminal Justice* 17 (5): 343–60.

Erez, E. (1981). Thou shalt not execute: Hebrew law perspective on capital punishment. *Criminology* 19:25–43.

Erickson, P. (1993). Prospects of harm reduction for psychostimulants. In N. Heather, A. Wodak, A. Nadelmann, and P. O'Hare, eds., *Psychoactive drugs and harm reduction.* London: Whurr.

Erickson, P., and J. Butters. (1998). The emerging harm reduction movement: The de-escalation of the war on drugs? In E. Jensen and J. Gerber, eds., *The new war on drugs: Symbolic politics and criminal justice policy.* Cincinnati, OH: Anderson.

Ericson, R. (1995). *Crime and the media.* Brookfield, VT: Dartmouth University Press.

Ericson, R., P. Baranek, and J. Chan. (1989). *Negotiating control: A study of news sources.* Toronto: University of Toronto Press.

Erman, M., and R. Lundman. (2001). *Corporate and governmental deviance: Problems of organizational behavior in contemporary society,* 6th ed. New York: Oxford University Press.

Erving, J., and B. Houston. Some judges punish people without benefit of a trial. *Hartford Courant* (June 17, 1991): A1.

Eschholz, S. (1997). The media and fear of crime: A survey of the research. *University of Florida Journal of Law and Public Policy* 9 (1): 37–59.

Espy, M., and J. Smykla. (1987). Executions in the United States, 1608–1987: The Espy file. Machine-readable data file. Ann Arbor, MI: Inter-University Consortium for Political and Social Research.

Evans, D. (1997). Exploring police–probation partnerships. *Corrections Today* 59:86.

Evans, S., and R. Lundman. (1987). Newspaper coverage of corporate crimes. In M. Erdman and R. Lundman, eds., *Corporate and government deviance: Problems of organizational behavior in contemporary society.* New York: Oxford University Press.

Fagan, J. Public policy choices on deterrence and the death penalty: A critical review of new evidence. Testimony before the Joint Committee on the Judiciary of the Massachusetts Legislature on House Bill 3934, July 14, 2005. Online: http://www.deathpenaltyinfo.org/MassTestimonyFagan.pdf.

Fagan, J., and M. Guggenheim. (1996). Preventive detention and the judicial prediction of dangerousness for juveniles: A natural experiment. *Journal of Criminal Law and Criminology* 86 (2): 415–48.

Faust, F. (1995). Personal communication, August 14.

Feagin, J. (2000). *Racist America.* New York: Routledge.

Feder, L. (2000). Likelihood of an arrest decision for domestic and nondomestic assault calls: Do police underenforce the law when responding to domestic violence? In R. Muraskin, ed., *It's a crime: Women and criminal justice,* 2nd ed. Upper Saddle River, NJ: Prentice Hall.

Federal Bureau of Investigation. (2006). Uniform Crime Reports. Online: http://www.fbi.gov/ucr/ucr.htm.

Federal Bureau of Prisons. (1996, 1998). Online: www.bop.gov.

Feeley, M. (1979). *The process is the punishment.* New York: Russell Sage Foundation.

Fehr, A., and H. Kalant. (1983). Behavioral effects of prolonged administration of delta 9-tetrahydrocannabinol in the rat. *Psychopharmacology* 80 (4): 325–30.

Feldman, H., M. Agar, and G. Beschner, eds. (1979). *Angel dust: An ethnographic study of PCP users.* Lexington, MA: Lexington Books.

Felling, M. (2004). Terrorists' visual warfare uses the media as weapon. *Christian Science Monitor,* August 4. Online: http://www.csmonitor.com/ 2004/0804/ p09s02-coop .html?s=ent.

Fields, C., and B. Jerin. (1999). The media and the criminal justice system. In R. Muraskin and A. Roberts, eds., *Visions for change: Justice and the twenty-first century.* Upper Saddle River, NJ: Prentice Hall.

Finestone, H. (1967). Narcotics and criminality. *Law and Contemporary Problems* 22:60–85.

Fishbein, D., and S. Pease. (1996). *The dynamics of drug abuse.* Boston: Allyn & Bacon.

Fishman, M. (1978). Crime waves as ideology. *Social Programs* 25:531–43.

Flemming, R., P. Nardulli, and J. Eisenstein. (1992). *The craft of justice: Politics and work in criminal court community.* Philadelphia: University of Pennyslvania Press.

Frank, N., and M. Lynch. (1992). *Corporate crime, corporate violence.* Albany, NY: Harrow and Heston.

Franklin, R. (1999). White uses of the black underclass. In L. Kushnick and J. Jennings, eds., *A new introduction to poverty: The role of race, power, and politics.* New York: New York University Press.

Freedman, E. (1998). Federal habeas corpus in capital cases. In J. Acker and C. Lanier, eds., *America's experiment with capital punishment: Reflections on the past, present and future of the ultimate penal sanction.* Durham, NC: Carolina Academic Press.

Friedrichs, D. (1983). Victimology: A consideration of the radical critique. *Crime and Delinquency* 29 (2): 283–94.

Friedrichs, D. (1995). *Trusted criminals: White collar crime in contemporary society.* Belmont, CA: Wadsworth.

Friedrichs, D. (2006). *Trusted criminals: White collar crime in contemporary society,* 3rd ed. Beverly Hills, CA: Wadsworth.

Fukurai, H., E. Butler, and R. Krooth. (1993). *Race and the jury: Racial disenfranchisement and the search for justice.* New York: Plenum Press.

Fuller, F. (2005). *Criminal justice: Mainstream and crosscurrents.* Upper Saddle River, NJ: Prentice Hall.

Fyfe, J. (1983). The NIJ study of the exclusionary rule. *Criminal Law Bulletin* 19:253–60.

Fyfe, J., J. Greene, W. Walsh, O. Wilson, and R. McLaren. (1997). *Police administration,* 5th ed. New York: McGraw-Hill.

Fyfe, J., and J. Skolnick. (1993). *Above the law: Police and excessive use of force.* New York: The Free Press.

Gaines, L., M. Kaune, and R. Miller. (2000). *Criminal justice in action.* Belmont, CA: Wadsworth.

Gaines, L., and P. Kraska, eds. (1997). *Drugs, crime, and justice.* Prospect Heights, IL: Waveland Press.

Gans, H. (1979). *Deciding what's news.* New York: Vintage Books.

Gans, H. (1995). *The war against the poor.* New York: Basic Books.

Garland, D. (2001). *The culture of control: Crime and social order in contemporary society.* Chicago, IL: University of Chicago Press.

Gaynes, E. (1993). The urban criminal justice system: Where young + black + male = probable cause. *Fordham Urban Law Journal* 20:621.

Gebotys, R., and B. Dasgupta. (1987). Attribution of responsibility and crime seriousness. *Journal of Psychology* 121:607–13.

Gebotys, R., J. Roberts, and B. Dasgupta. (1988). News media use and public perceptions of crime. *Canadian Journal of Criminology* 30:3–16.

Geller, W., and M. Scott. (1992). *Deadly force: What we know.* Washington, DC: Police Executive Research Forum.

Geller, W., and H. Toch, eds. (1995). *And justice for all.* Washington, DC: Police Executive Research Forum.

George, H. Jr. (1999). Black America, the underclass, and the subordination process. In L. Kushnick and J. Jennings, eds., *A new introduction to poverty: The role of race, power, and politics.* New York: New York University Press.

Gerbner, G. (1994). Television voice: The art of asking the wrong question. *Currents in Modern Thought* (July): 385–97.

Gerbner, G., et al. (1980). The mainstreaming of America: Violence profile No. 11. *Journal of Communications* 30:10–29.

Gerrie, M., L. Belcher, and M. Garry. (2006). Systematic eyewitness false memories occur in the absence of external suggestion. *Applied Cognitive Psychology* 20:689–96.

Gershman, B. (2000). Why prosecutors misbehave. In G. Mays and P. Gregware, eds., *Courts and justice: A reader,* 2nd ed. Prospect Heights, IL: Waveland Press.

Gerson, L., and D. Preston. (1979). Alcohol consumption and the incidence of violent crime. *Journal of Studies on Alcohol* 40:307–12.

Gerth, H. (1992). Crisis management of social structures: Planning, propaganda and societal morale. *International Journal of Politics, Culture and Society* 5:337–559.

Gest, T. (2001). *Crime and politics.* New York: Oxford University Press.

Gilbert, C. (2003). Chairman: PATRIOT powers eternalized 'over my dead body.' *Akron Beacon Journal,* April 17, 2003. Online: http://www.ohio.com/mld/ohio/news/politics/5657664.htm.

Gilmer, W., Jr. (1986). *The law dictionary,* 6th ed. Cincinnati, OH: Anderson.

Glantz, S., J. Slade, L. Bero, P. Hanauer, and D. Barnes. (1996). *The cigarette papers.* Berkeley: University of California Press.

Glaser, D. (1974). Interlocking dualities in drug use, drug control, and crime. In J. Inciardi and C. Chambers, eds., *Drugs and the criminal justice system.* Beverly Hills, CA: Sage Publications.

Glaser, D. (1997). *Profitable penalties: How to cut both crime rates and costs.* Thousand Oaks, CA: Pine Forge Press.

Glassner, B. (1999). *The culture of fear: Why Americans are afraid of the wrong things.* New York: Basic Books.

Glassner, B., and J. Loughlin. (1987). *Drugs in adolescent worlds: Burnouts to straights.* New York: St. Martin's Press.

Goertzel, T. (2004). Capital punishment and homicide: Sociological realities and econometric illusions. *Skeptical Enquirer Magazine.* Online: http://www.deathpenaltyinfo.org/article.php?scid=12&did=1176.

Goetz, E. (1996). The U.S. war on drugs as urban policy. *International Journal of Urban and Regional Research* 20:539–49.

Gold, S. (1990). *The state fiscal agenda for the 1990s.* Denver, CO: National Conference of State Legislatures.

Goldstein, H. (1975). *Police corruption: A perspective on its nature and control.* Washington, DC: Police Foundation.

Goldstein, H. (1990). *Problem-oriented policing.* New York: McGraw-Hill.

Goldstein, P. (1979). *Prostitution and drugs.* Lexington, MA: D. C. Heath.

Goldstein, P. (1998). The drugs/violence nexus: A tripartite conceptual framework. In J. Inciardi and K. McElrath, eds., *The American drug scene: An anthology,* 2nd ed. Los Angeles: Roxbury.

Goldstein, H. (2001). Reported in Center for Problem-Oriented Policing. Online: http://www.popcenter.org/about-whatisPOP.htm.

Goldstein, P., and N. Duchaine. (1980). Daily criminal activities of street drug users. Paper presented to the annual meeting of the American Society of Criminology.

Goode, E. (1999). *Drugs in American society,* 5th ed. New York: Knopf.

Goode, E., and N. Ben-Yehuda. (1994a). Moral panics: Culture, politics, and social construction. *Annual Review of Sociology* 20:149–71.

Goode, E., and N. Ben-Yehuda. (1994b). *Moral panics: The social construction of deviance.* Cambridge, MA: Blackwell.

Gorr, M. (2000). The morality of plea bargaining. *Social Theory and Practice* 26 (1): 129–51.

Gosselin, D. (2000). *Heavy hands: An introduction to the crime of domestic violence.* Upper Saddle River, NJ: Prentice Hall.

Gottfredson, D. (1999). *Exploring criminal justice: An introduction.* Los Angeles: Roxbury.

Gottfredson, S., and D. Gottfredson. (1994). Behavioral prediction and the problem of incapacitation. *Criminology* 32 (3): 441–74.

Gottfredson, S., and G. Jarjoura. (1996). Race, gender, and guidelines-based decision making. *Journal of Research in Crime and Delinquency* 33:49–69.

Gould, L. (1974). Crime and the addict: Beyond common sense. In J. Inciardi and C. Chambers, eds., *Drugs and the criminal justice system.* Beverly Hills, CA: Sage.

Gove, W., M. Hughes, and M. Geerken. (1985). Are uniform crime reports a valid indicator of the index crimes? An affirmative answer with minor qualifications. *Criminology* 23:451–501.

Gow, H. (1986). Religious views support the death penalty. In B. Szumski, L. Hall, and S. Bursell, eds., *The death penalty: Opposing viewpoints.* St. Paul, MN: Greenhaven.

Graber, D. (1980). *Crime news and the public.* Westport, CT: Praeger.

Graber, D. (1996). The new media and politics: What does the future hold? *Political Science and Politics* (March): 33–6.

Graham, B. (2000). Judicial recruitment and racial diversity on state courts: An overview. In G. Mays and P. Gregware, eds., *Courts and justice: A reader,* 2nd ed. Prospect Heights, IL: Waveland Press.

Gray, J. (2001). *Why our drugs laws have failed and what we can do about it.* Philadelphia: University of Temple Press.

Gray, M. (1998). *Drug crazy.* New York: Random House.

Greenberg, E. (1993). *The American political system: A radical approach,* 5th ed. Glenville, IL: Scott, Foresman.

Greenberg, S., and F. Adler. (1974). Crime and addiction: An empirical analysis of the literature, 1920–1973. *Contemporary Drug Problems* 3:221–70.

Greenwood, P. (1998). *Diverting children from a life of crime: Measuring costs and benefits.* Santa Monica, CA: Rand Corporation.

Greenwood, P., and S. Turner. (1987). *Selective incapacitation revisited: Why the high rate offenders are hard to predict.* Santa Monica, CA: Rand Corporation.

Gurevitch, M. (1982). *Culture, society, and the media.* London: Methuen.

Gusfield, J. (1967). Moral passage: The symbolic process in public designations of deviance. *Social Problems* 15:175–88.

Hagan, J. (1989). Why is there so little criminal justice theory? Neglected macro- and micro-level links between organization and power. *Journal of Research on Crime and Delinquency* 26 (2): 116–35.

Hagan, J. (1998). *Political crime, ideology, and criminality.* Boston: Allyn & Bacon.

Hall, J. (1992). *Deadly force: The common law and the Constitution.* Washington, DC: Federal Bureau of Investigation, U.S. Department of Justice.

Haltom, W. (1998). *Reporting on the courts: How the mass media cover judicial elections.* Chicago: Nelson-Hall.

Hamid, A. (1998). *Drugs in America: Sociology, economics, and politics.* Newbury Park, CA: Sage.

Haney, C. (2005). *Death by design: Capital punishment as a social psychological system.* New York: Oxford University Press.

Hansen, D. (1999). Answer to question about origin of lady of justice. Online: www.commonlaw.com/Justice.html.

Hansom, R., and B. Ostrom. (1993). Litigation and the courts: Myths and misconceptions. *Trial* 29:40–4.

Harmsworth, E. (1996). Bail and detention: An assessment and critique of the federal and Massachusetts systems. *New England Journal on Criminology and Civil Confinement* 22:213.

Harrigan, J. (2000). *Empty dreams, empty pockets: Class and bias in American politics.* New York: Addison-Wesley Longman.

Harris, D. (1999). *Driving while black: Racial profiling on our nation's highways.* New York: American Civil Liberties Union.

Harrison, P., and H. Beck. (2005). Prisoners in 2005. Online: http://www.ojp.usdoj.gov/bjs/pub/ascii/p05.txt.

Harriston, K., and M. P. Flaherty. (1994). Law and disorder—The District's troubled police. *Washington Post,* August 28–31.

Hart, H. (1968). *Punishment and responsibility.* New York: Oxford University Press.

Harvard Law Review. (1988). Developments in the law—Race and the criminal process. *Harvard Law Review* 101:1496.

Hashibe, M., H. Morgenstern, Y. Cui, D. Tashkin, Z. Zhang, W. Cozen, T. Mack, and S. Greenland. (2006). Marijuana use and the risk of lung and upper aerodigestive tract cancers: Results of a population-based case-control study. *Cancer epidemiological biomarkers and prevention* 15 (10): 1829–34.

Heath, L., and K. Gilbert. (1996). Mass media and fear of crime. *American Behavioral Scientist* 39:379–86.

Henderson, J., and D. Simon. (1994). *Crimes of the criminal justice system.* Cincinnati, OH: Anderson.

Herman, E., and N. Chomsky. (1988). *Manufacturing consent.* New York: Pantheon.

Herman, E., and N. Chomsky. (2002). *Manufacturing conesnt: The political economy of the mass media.* New York: Pantheon.

Hess, K., and H. Wrobleski. (1997). *Police operations,* 2nd ed. St. Paul, MN: West.

Hess, S. (1981). *The Washington reporters.* Washington, DC: Brookings Institution.

Hilgartner, S., and C. Bosk. (1988). The rise and fall of social problems: A public arenas model. *American Journal of Sociology* 94:53–78.

Hollinger, R., and L. Lanza-Kaduce. (1988). The process of criminalization. *Criminology* 26:101–26.

Hollister, L. (1988). Cannabis—1988. *ACTA Psychiatrica Scandinavica Supplementum* 345:108–18.

Holten, G., and M. Jones. (1982). *The system of criminal justice,* 2nd ed. Boston: Little, Brown.

Hoppe, C. (1992). Life in jail, or death? Life term is cheaper. *Charlotte Observer,* March 22:12A.

Huff, C., A. Rattner, and E. Sagarin. (1986). Guilty until proven innocent: Wrongful conviction and public policy. *Crime and Delinquency* 32:518–44.

Huff, C., A. Rattner, and E. Sagarin. (1996). *Convicted but innocent: Wrongful conviction and public policy.* Thousand Oaks, CA: Sage.

Huffington, A. (2003). *Pigs at the trough.* New York: Random House.

Hurwitz, J., and M. Peffley. (1997). Public perceptions of race and crime: The role of racial stereotypes. *American Journal of Political Science* 41 (2): 375–401.

Ian, J., and S. Richards. (2003). *Convict Criminology.* Belmont, CA: Wadsworth.

Inciardi, J., ed. (1991). *The drug legalization debate: Studies in crime, law, and justice.* Newbury Park, CA: Sage.

Inciardi, J. (2002). *The war on drugs III.* Boston: Pearson Education.

Inciardi, J., and C. Chambers. (1972). Unreported criminal involvement of narcotic addicts. *Journal of Drug Issues* 2 (2): 57–64.

Inciardi, J., and K. McElrath, eds. (1998). *The American drug scene: An anthology,* 2nd ed. Los Angeles: Roxbury.

Ingley, S. (2000). Corrections without corrections. In J. May, ed., *Building violence: How America's rush to incarcerate creates more violence.* Thousand Oaks, CA: Sage.

Ingraham, B. (1994). The right of silence, the presumption of innocence, the burden of proof, and a modest proposal. *Journal of Criminal Law and Criminology* 85:59–95.

Institute on Money in State Politics. (2005). Online: http://www.followthemoney.org.

International Chiefs of Police. (2002). Police use of force in America, 2001. Online: http://www.theiacp.org/documents/pdfs/Publications/2001useofforce%2Epdf.

Iraq Study Group Report. (2006). Online: http://www.usip.org/isg/index.html.

Irwin, J. (1985). *The jail: Managing the underclass in American society.* Berkeley: University of California Press.

Irwin, J. (2003). Preface. In Ian and Edwards, eds., *Convict criminology.* Belmont, CA: Wadsworth.

Irwin, J., and J. Austin. (1997). *It's about time: America's imprisonment binge.* Belmont, CA: Wadsworth.

Iyengar, S., and D. Kinder. (1987). *News that matters: Television and American opinion.* Chicago: University of Chicago Press.

Jackall, R. (1999). *Propaganda.* New York: New York University Press.

Jackson, D. Politician crime rhetoric. *Boston Globe* (October 21, 1994): 15.

Jackson, J. Aging black women and public policies. *Black Scholar* (May–June, 1988): 33.

Jackson, P. (1997). *Minority group threat, crime and policing: Social context and social control.* New York: Praeger.

Jeffery, C. (1990). *Criminology: An interdisciplinary approach.* Beverly Hills, CA: Prentice Hall.

Jennings, J. (1999). Persistent poverty in the United States: A review of theories and explanations. In L. Kushnick and J. Jennings, eds., *A new introduction to poverty: The role of race, power, and politics.* New York: New York University Press.

Jensen, E., and J. Gerber, eds. (1998). *The new war on drugs: Symbolic politics and criminal justice policy.* Cincinnati, OH: Anderson.

Johnson, B., P. Goldstein, E. Preble, J. Schmeidler, D. Lipton, B. Sprunt, and T. Miller. (1985). *Taking care of business: The economics of crime by heroin abusers.* Lexington, MA: Lexington Books.

Johnson, S. (2000). The Bible and the death penalty: Implications for criminal justice education. *Journal of Criminal Justice Education* 11 (1): 15–33.

Johnstone, G. (2001). *Restorative justice: Ideas, practices, debates.* UK: Willan.

Johnstone, G., and D. Van Ness. (2006). *Handbook of Restorative Justice.* UK: Willan.

Jonas, S. (1991). The United States drug problem and the United States drug culture. In J. Inciardi, ed., *The drug legalization debate: Studies in crime, law, and justice.* Newbury Park, CA: Sage.

Jones, D. (1987a). *History of criminology: A philosophical perspective.* New York: Greenwood.

Juarez, J. (2004). *Brotherhood of corruption: A cop breaks the silence on police abuse, brutality, and racial profiling.* Chicago, IL: Chicago Review Press.

Justice Policy Institute. (2004). Still striking out: Ten years of California's three strikes. Online: http://www.justicepolicy.org/reports/three%20strikes_9.04.pdf.

Kaminer, W. (1999). Games prosecutors play. *American Prospect* 46:20–26.

Kappeler, V., M. Blumberg, and G. Potter. (1996) *The mythology of crime and criminal justice.* Prospect Heights, IL: Waveland Press.

Kappeler, V., M. Blumberg, and G. Potter. (2000). *The mythology of crime and criminal justice,* 3rd ed. Prospect Heights, IL: Waveland Press.

Kappeler, V., and G. Potter. (2004). *The mythology of crime and criminal justice,* 4th ed. Prospect Long Grove, IL: Waveland.

Karmen, A. (1996). *Crime victims: An introduction to victimology,* 3rd ed. Belmont, CA: Wadsworth.

Kassin, S. (2000). The American jury: Handicapped in the pursuit of justice. In G. Mays and P. Gregware, *Courts and justice: A reader,* 2nd ed. Prospect Heights, IL: Waveland Press.

Katz, M. (1999). Reframing the underclass debate. In L. Kushnick and J. Jennings, eds., *A new introduction to poverty: The role of race, power, and politics.* New York: New York University Press.

Kelling, G., T. Pate, D. Dieckman, and C. Brown. (1974). *The Kansas City preventive patrol experiment: A summary report.* Washington, DC: The Police Foundation.

Kellner, D. (2003). *From 9/11 to terror war: The dangers of the Bush legacy.* Lanham, MD: Rowman & Littlefield.

Kellner, L. (1988). Narcotics-related corruption. In *Prosecution of public corruption cases* (pp. 39–53). Washington, DC: U.S. Department of Justice.

Kennedy, D. (1997). Pulling levers: Chronic offenders, high crime settings, and a theory of prevention. *Valparaiso University Law Review* 31 (2): 449.

Kennedy, R. (1997). *Race, crime and the law.* New York: Vintage.

Keve, P. (1995). *Crime control and justice in America: Searching for facts and answers.* Chicago: American Library Association.

Kim, M. (1999). The working poor: Lousy jobs or lazy workers? In L. Kushnick and J. Jennings, eds., *A new introduction to poverty: The role of race, power, and politics.* New York: New York University Press.

King, R., M. Mauer, and M. Young. (2005). Incarceration and crime: A complex relationship. Online: http://www.sentencingproject.org/Admin/Documents/publications/inc_iandc_complex.pdf.

Kitsuse, S., and M. Spector. (1973). Toward a sociology of social problems: Social condition, value judgments, and social problems. *Social Problems* 20:407–19.

Kittel, N. (1986). Police perjury: Criminal defense attorneys' perspectives. *American Journal of Criminal Justice* 11:1.

Kleiman, M. (1997). Neither probation nor legalization: Grudging toleration in drug control policy. In M. McShane and F. Williams, eds., *Drug use and drug policy.* New York: Garland.

Klockars, C. (1991). The rhetoric of community policing. In J. Greene and S. Mastrofski, eds., *Community policing: Rhetoric and reality.* New York: Praeger.

Koning, H. (1993). *The conquest of America: How the Indian nations lost their continent.* New York: Monthly Review Press.

Kooistra, P., J. Mahoney, and S. Westervelt. (1999). The world of crime according to "COPS." In G. Cavender and M. Fishman, eds., *Entertaining crime: Television reality programs.* Hawthorne, NY: Aldine de Gruyter.

Kowalski, B., and R. Lundman. (2007). Vehicle stops by police for driving while Black: Common problems and some tentative solutions. *Journal of Criminal Justice* 35 (2): 165–81.

Kozel, N., R. Dupont, and B. Brown. (1972). A study of narcotic involvement in an offender population. *International Journal of the Addictions* 7:443–50.

Krahn, H., T. Hartnagel, and J. Gartnell. (1986). Income inequality and homicide rates: Cross-national data and criminological theories. *Criminology* 24: 269–93.

Krajicek, D. (1998). *Scooped! Media miss real story on crime while chasing sex, sleaze, and celebrities.* New York: Columbia University Press.

Kramer, J. (1976). From demon to ally—How mythology has and may yet alter national drug policy. *Journal of Drug Issues* 6: 390–406.

Kraska, P. B. (1990). The unmentionable alternative: The need for, and the argument against the decriminalization of drug laws. In R. Weisheit, ed., *Drugs, crime, and the criminal justice system.* Cincinnati, OH: Anderson.

Kraska, P., and V. Kappeler. (1997). Militarizing American police: The rise and normalization of paramilitary units. *Social Problems* 44 (1): 1–17.

Kull, S., C. Ramsay, S. Subias, E. Lewis, and P. Warf. (2003). Misperceptions, the media, and the war on Iraq. Online: www.pipa.org/OnlineReports/Iraq/Media_10_02_03_Report.pdf.

Kushnick, L. (1999). Responding to urban crisis: Functions of white racism. In L. Kushnick and J. Jennings, eds., *A new introduction to poverty: The role of race, power, and politics.* New York: New York University Press.

Kushnick, L., and J. Jennings, eds. (1999). *A new introduction to poverty: The role of race, power, and politics.* New York: New York University Press.

Kuttner, R. Sharing America's wealth. *The American Prospect* (Summer, 2003): A3–A5.

Lab, S. (2004). *Crime prevention: Approaches, practices and evaluations,* 4th ed. Cincinnati, OH: Anderson.

Ladinsky, J. (1984). The impact of social background of lawyers in legal practice and the law. In J. Bonsignore et al., eds., *Before the law.* Boston: Houghton Mifflin.

Land, K., P. McCall, and L. Cohen. (1990). Structural co-variates of homicide rates: Are there any invariances across time and space? *American Journal of Sociology* 95:922–63.

Langan, P. (1994). No racism in the criminal justice system. *Public Interest* 117:48–51.

Langbein, J. (2000). On the myth of written constitutions: The disappearance of criminal jury trial. In G. Mays and P. Gregware, eds., *Courts and justice: A reader,* 2nd ed. Prospect Heights, IL: Waveland Press.

Lapley, R., and M. Westlake. (1988). *Film theory: An introduction.* Manchester, England: Manchester University Press.

Lasswell, H. (1936). *Politics: Who gets what, when, how.* New York: McGraw-Hill.

Lauer, R., and J. Lauer, eds. (2000). *Troubled times: Readings in social problems.* Los Angeles: Roxbury.

Lazarus, E. (2000). How Miranda really works and why it matters. Online: http://writ.news.findlaw.com/lazarus/20000605.html.

Leadership Conference on Civil Rights and the Leadership Conference Education Fund. (2000). Justice on trial: Racial disparities in the American criminal justice system. Online: www.civilrights.org.

Leff, D., D. Protess, and S. Brooks. (1986). Crusading journalism: Changing public attitudes and policy-making agendas. *Public Opinion Quarterly* 50:300–15.

Levitt, S., and S. Dubner (2005). *Freakonomics.* New York: William and Morrow.

Levy, F. (1988). *Dollars and dreams: The changing American income distribution.* New York: Norton.

Lewis, D. (1981). Crime in the media: Introduction. In D. Lewis, ed., *Reactions to crime.* Beverly Hills, CA: Sage Publications.

Lichtenberg, I. (2006). Driving while black (DWB): Examining race as a tool in the war on drugs. *Police Practice & Research,* 7 (1): 49–60.

Lichter, S. (1988). Media power: The influence of media on politics and business. *Florida Policy Review* 4:35–41.

Lichter, S., L. Lichter, and S. Rothman. (1994). *Prime time: How TV portrays American culture.* Washington, DC: Regnery.

Liebman, J., J. Fagan, and V. West. (2000). *A broken system: Error rates in capital cases, 1973–1995.* New York: Columbia University Law School.

Lifton, R., and G. Mitchell. (2000). *Who owns death? Capital punishment, the American conscience, and the end of executions.* New York: William Morrow.

Lilly, J., and P. Knepper. (1993). The corrections-commercial complex. *Crime and Delinquency* 39:150–66.

Lindesmith, A. (1940). *Opiate addiction.* Bloomington, IN: Principia Press.

Lindsell-Roberts, S. (1994). *Loony laws and silly statutes.* New York: Sterling Publications.

Liska, K. (2000). *Drugs and the human body,* 6th ed. New York: Macmillan.

Livingston, J. (1996). *Crime and criminology,* 2nd ed. Upper Saddle River, NJ: Prentice Hall.

Lockwood, D., A. Pottieger, and J. Inciardi. (1996). Crack use, crime by crack users, and ethnicity. In D. Hawkins, ed., *Ethnicity, race, and crime.* Albany: State University of New York Press.

Loewen, James. (1995). *Lies my teacher told me.* New York: Touchstone.

Loftus, E. F. (1979). *Eyewitness testimony.* Cambridge, MA: Harvard University Press.

Lord, C., L. Ross, and M. Lepper. (1979). Biased assimilation and attitude polarization: The effects of prior theories on subsequently considered evidence. *Journal of Personality and Social Psychology* 37:2098–2109.

Lowi, T., and B. Ginsburg. (1990). American government: *Freedom and power.* New York: Norton.

Luginbuhl, J., and M. Burkhead. (1994). Sources of bias and arbitrariness in the capital trial. *Journal of Social Issues* 103.

Lule, J. (2002). *Daily news, eternal stories: The mythological role of journalism.* New York: Guilford Publications.

Lyman, M., and G. Potter. (1998). *Drugs in society.* Cincinnati, OH: Anderson.

Lynch, M. (1997). *Radical criminology.* Brookfield, VT: Aldershot.

MacCoun, R. (1990). The emergence of extralegal bias during jury deliberation. *Criminal Justice and Behavior* 17:303–14.

MacCoun, R., and P. Reuter. (2001). *Drug war heresies: Learning from other vices, times, and places.* New York: Cambridge University Press.

Magagnini, S. (1988). Closing death row would save state $90 million a year. *Sacramento Bee* (March 28, 1988): 1.

Maguire, M., and T. Bennett. (1982). *Burglary in a dwelling.* London: Heinemann.

Maher, T. (2000). Environmental racism. In R. Lauer and J. Lauer, eds., *Troubled times: Readings in social problems.* Los Angeles: Roxbury.

Mann, C. (1993). *Unequal justice.* Bloomington: Indiana University Press.

Manning, P. (1997). *Police work: The social organization of policing,* 2nd ed. Prospect Heights, IL: Waveland Press.

Mariner, J. (2000). Body and soul: The trauma of prison rape. In J. May, ed., *Building violence: How America's rush to incarcerate creates more violence.* Thousand Oaks, CA: Sage.

Marion, N. (1995). *A primer in the politics of criminal justice.* Albany, NY: Harrow and Heston.

Marion, N., and W. Oliver. (2005). *The Public Policy of Crime and Criminal Justice.* Upper Saddle River, NJ: Prentice Hall.

Marongiu, P., and G. Newman. (1987). *Vengeance: The fight against injustice.* Totowa, NJ: Rowman and Littlefield.

Marsh, E. (2007). Retelling is not the same as recalling: Implications for memory. *Current Directions in Psychological Science* 16 (1): 16–20.

Marsh, H. (1991). A comparative analysis of crime coverage in newspapers in the United States and other countries from 1960–1989: A review of the literature. *Journal of Criminal Justice* 19:67–80.

Martin, S. (2000). Sanctioned violence in American prisons. In J. May, ed., *Building violence: How America's rush to incarcerate creates more violence.* Thousand Oaks, CA: Sage.

Martinson, R. (2000). What works? Questions and answers in prison reform. *The Public Interest* 35:22–55.

Marx, G. (1981). Ironies of social control: Authorities as contributors to deviance through escalation, nonenforcement, and covert facilitation. *Social Problems* 28:221–46.

Massey, D., and A. Gross. (1990). *A pessimistic interpretation of recent declines in black residential segregation.* Chicago: Ogburn-Stouffer Center.

Mauer, M. (1998). "Lock 'em up and throw away the key": African Americans and meals and the criminal justice system. In K. Haas and G. Alpert, eds., *The dilemma of corrections.* Prospect Heights, IL: Waveland Press.

Mauer, M., and T. Huling. (1995a). One in three young black men ensnared in justice system. *Overcrowded Times* 6:1–10.

Mauer, M., and T. Huling. (1995b). *Young black Americans and the criminal justice system: Five years later.* Washington DC: The Sentencing Project.

Mauer, M., R. King, and M. Young. (2004). *The meaning of "life": Long prison sentences in context.* Washington DC: The Sentencing Project.

May, J., ed. (2000). *Building violence: How America's rush to incarcerate creates more violence.* Thousand Oaks, CA: Sage.

Mayhew, P., and J. Van Dijk. (1997). *Criminal victimization in eleven industrialized countries: Key findings from the 1996 International Crime Victims Survey.* The Hague: Dutch Ministry of Justice.

McAdams, J. (1998). Racial disparity and the death penalty. *Law and Contemporary Problems* 61 (4): 153–70.

McAnamy, P. (1992). Asset forfeiture as drug control strategy. Paper presented at the annual meetings of the American Society of Criminology, New Orleans, LA, November.

McCaghy, C., T. Capron, and J. Jamieson. (2000). *Deviant behavior,* 5th ed. Boston: Allyn & Bacon.

McCleary, R., B. Nienstedt, and J. Erven. (1982). Uniform crime reports as organizational outcomes: Three time series quasi-experiments. *Social Problems* 29: 361–72.

McCombs, M., and D. Shaw. (1972). The agenda setting function of the mass media. *Public Opinion Quarterly* 36:176–87.

McElhaney, J. W. (1998). The jury consultant bazaar. *ABA Journal* 84:78–9.

McEwen, T., and F. Leahy. (1994). *Less than lethal force technologies in law enforcement and correctional agencies.* Alexandria, VA: Institute for Law and Justice.

McGarrell, E. (1993). Institutional theory and the stability of a conflict model of the incarceration rate. *Justice Quarterly* 10 (1): 7–28.

McGinnis, K. (2000). Make 'em break rocks. In J. May, ed., *Building violence: How America's rush to incarcerate creates more violence.* Thousand Oaks, CA: Sage.

McLaughlin, C. (2000). Prisoner rehabilitation: Feeling better but getting worse. In J. May, ed., *Building violence: How America's rush to incarcerate creates more violence.* Thousand Oaks, CA: Sage.

McQuail, D. (1994). *Mass communication theory,* 3rd ed. London: Sage.

McShane, M., and F. Williams. (1992). Radical victimology: A critique of victim in traditional victimology. *Crime and Delinquency* 38 (2): 258–71.

Meddis, S. In twin cities, a tale of two standards. *USA Today* (July 26, 1993): 6A.

Meeker, J. (1984). Criminal appeals over the last 100 years: Are the odds of winning increasing? *Criminology* 22:551–71.

Meier, R., and J. Short. (1985). Crime as hazard: Perceptions of risk and seriousness. *Criminology* 23:389–99.

Mendes, S. (2004). Certainty, severity , and their relative deterrent effects: Questioning the implications of the role of risk in criminal deterrence policy. *Policy Studies Journal* 32 (1): 59–74.

Merlo, A., and P. Benekos. (2000). *What's wrong with the criminal justice system: Ideology, politics and the media.* Cincinnati, OH: Anderson.

Merriam-Webster's Collegiate Dictionary (2007). Entry for "drug." Online: http://m-w.com/dictionary/drug.

Merriam-Webster's Collegiate Dictionary (2007). Entry for "system." Online: http://mw1.merriam-webster.com/dictionary/system.

Merton, R. (1938a). *Science, technology and society in seventeenth century England.* Bruges, Belgium: Saint Catherine Press.

Merton, R. (1938b). *Social structure and anomie.* Indianapolis, IN: Bobbs-Merrill.

Messner, S., and K. Tardiff. (1986). Economic inequality and levels of homicide: An analysis of urban neighborhoods. *Criminology* 24:297–316.

Michalowski, R., and R. Kramer (2006). *State-corporate crime: Wrongdoing at the intersection of business and government.* Camden, NJ: Rutgers.

Miethe, T. (1982). Public consensus on crime seriousness: Normative structure or methodological artifact? *Criminology* 20:515–26.

Miethe, T. D. (1995). Fear and withdrawal from urban life. *Annals of the American Academy of Political and Social Science* 539:14–27.

Milbank, D., and J. Blum. (2005). Document says oil chiefs met with Cheney task force. *Washington Post*, November 16. Online: http://www.washingtonpost.com/wp-dyn/content/article/2005/11/15/AR2005111501842.html.

Mill, J. S. (1859). *On liberty.* Tokyo: Kenkyusha.

Miller, D. (2003). *Principles of social justice.* Boston, MA: Harvard University Press.

Miller, J. (1994). *African American males in the criminal justice system.* Alexandria, VA: National Center on Institutions and Alternatives.

Miller, J. (1997). African American males in the criminal justice system. *Phi Delta Kappan* (June): 22–30.

Miller, J. (1998). *Search and destroy: African-American males in the criminal justice system.* New York: Cambridge University Press.

Miller, J., and B. Holman. (1992). *Hobbling a generation: African American males in the Washington, DC criminal justice system.* Washington, DC: National Center on Institutions and Alternatives.

Miller, M. (1995). The road to Panama City. *Newsweek* 126 (18): 84.

Miller, R. (1997). Symposium on coercion: An interdisciplinary examination of coercion, exploitation, and the Law: III. Coerced confinement and treatment: The continuum of coercion: constitutional and clinical considerations in the treatment of mentally disordered persons. *Denver Law Review* 74:1169–1214.

Miller, S. (2000). Arrest policies for domestic violence and their implications for battered women. In R. Muraskin, ed., *It's a crime: Women and criminal justice,* 2nd ed. Upper Saddle River, NJ: Prentice Hall.

Miller, T., M. Cohen, and B. Wiersma. (1997). *Victim costs and consequences: A new look.* Washington, DC: U.S. Department of Justice, Office of Justice Programs, National Institute of Justice.

Milovanovich, Z. (2000). Prosecutorial discretion: A comparative perspective. In G. Mays and P. Gregware, eds., *Courts and justice: A reader,* 2nd ed. Prospect Heights, IL: Waveland Press.

Minow, M. (2000). Stripped down like a runner or enriched by experience? Bias and impartiality of judges and jurors. In G. Mays and P. Gregware, eds., *Courts and justice: A reader,* 2nd ed. Prospect Heights, IL: Waveland Press.

Mintz, M. (1992). Why the media cover up corporate crime: A reporter looks back in anger. *Trial* 28: 72–7.

Mocan, H., and R. Gittings. (2003). Getting off death row: Commuted sentences and the deterrent effect of capital punishment. *Journal of Law and Economics* 46 (2): 453–78.

Mokhiber, R., and R. Weissman. (1999). *Corporate predators: The hunt for mega-profits and the attack on democracy.* Monroe, ME: Common Courage Press.

The Mollen Commission. (1994). *Police brutality and excessive force in the New York City Police Department.* New York: The Mollen Commission.

Moore, W. (1995). Targeting Harlem, not Hollywood. *National Journal,* February 11:388.

Morgan, M., and N. Signorielli, eds. (1990). *Cultivation analysis: New directions in media effects research.* Newbury Park, CA: Sage.

Morgan-Sharp, E. (1999). The administration of justice based on gender and race. In R. Muraskin and A. Roberts, eds., *Visions for change: Crime and justice in the 21st century,* 2nd ed. Upper Saddle River, NJ: Prentice Hall.

Morris, E. (1988). *The thin blue line* [film]. New York: Miramax Films.

Move On. (2002). Online: www.moveon.org.

Muraskin, R. (2006). *It's a crime: Women and justice,* 4th ed. Upper Saddle River, NJ: Prentice Hall.

Muraskin, R., and S. Domash. (2006). *Crime and the media: Headlines vs. reality.* Upper Saddle River, NJ: Prentice Hall.

Murray, C. (1984). *Losing ground—American social policy, 1950–1980.* New York: Basic Books.

Murray, C., and R. Herrnstein. (1994). *The bell curve: Intelligence and class structure in American life.* New York: The Free Press.

Myers, S. (1987). Introduction. Special issue on race and crime. *Review of Black Political Economy* 16:5–15.

Nacos, B. (2002). *Mass-mediated terrorism: The central role of the media in terrorism and counter-terrorism.* Lanham, MD: Bowman & Littlefield.

Nadelmann, E. (1991). The case for legalization. In J. Inciardi, ed., *The drug legalization debate: Studies in crime, law, and justice.* Newbury Park, CA: Sage.

Nadelmann, E. (1998). Experimenting with drugs. *Foreign Affairs* 1:111–26.

Nagin, D., and G. Pogarsky. (2001). Integrating celerity, impulsivity, and extralegal sanction threats into a model of general deterrence: Theory and evidence. *Criminology* 39 (4): 865–91.

Nakell, B., and K. Hardy. (1987). *The arbitrariness of the death penalty.* Philadelphia: Temple University Press.

Nardulli, P., J. Eisenstein, and R. Flemming. (1988). *The tenor of justice: Criminal courts and the guilty plea process.* Urbana: University of Illinois Press.

National Association for the Advancement of Colored People (NAACP). (1993). Online: www.naacp.org.

National Association for the Advancement of Colored People (NAACP), Legal Defense Fund. (2006). Online: www.naacpldf.org.

National Association of Criminal Defense Lawyers. (1996). *Racism in the criminal justice system.* Washington, DC: National Association of Criminal Defense Lawyers.

National Association of State Budget Officers. (1996). *Capital budgeting in the states.* Washington DC: National Association of State Budget Officers.

National Center on Addiction and Substance Abuse. (1998). *Behind bars: Substance abuse and America's prison population.* New York: National Center on Addiction and Substance Abuse.

National Center on Institutions and Alternatives. (1999). What every American should know about the criminal justice system. Online: www.ncianet.org/ncia/facts.html.

National Institute of Justice. (1997). *A study of homicide in eight U.S cities: An NIJ intramural research project.* Washington, DC: National Institute of Justice, US Department of Justice.

National Institutes of Health. (1997). *SAMHSA's National Clearinghouse for Alcohol and Drug Information: A Service of the Substance Abuse and Mental Health Services Administration.* Bethesda, MD: NIH.

National Institute on Drug Abuse. (1998). *25 years of discovery to advance the health of the public.* Bethesda, MD: National Institute on Drug Abuse.

National Institute on Money in State Politics. Online: www.followthemoney.org.

Nazario, S. Odds grim for black men in California. *Washington Post* (December 12, 1993): A–9.

Nelson, L., and B. Foster. (2001). *Death watch.* Upper Saddle River, NJ: Prentice Hall.

Nettler, G. (1984). *Explaining crime,* 3rd ed. New York: McGraw-Hill.

Neubauer, D. (2007). *America's courts and the criminal justice system,* 9th ed. Beverly Hills, CA: Wadsworth.

Newman, G. (1990). Popular culture and criminal justice: A preliminary analysis. *Journal of Criminal Justice* 18:261–74.

The New York Times. (2006). Lethal cruelty. April 26. Online: http://select.nytimes.com/gst/abstract.html?res=F40E15F7395B0C758EDDAD0894DE404482.

Nisbet, M. (2001). Media coverage after the attack: Reason and deliberative democracy put to the test. Online www.csicop.org/genx/terrorattack/.

Nobling, T., C. Spohn, and M. DeLone. (1998). A tale of two cities: Unemployment and sentencing severity. *Justice Quarterly* 15:459–85.

Nolan, B., C. Bradley, D. Cole, G. Stone, H. Koh, K. Sullivan, L. Tribe, M. Lederman, P. Heymann, R. Epstein, R. Dworkin, W. Dellinger, W. Sessions, and W. Van Alstyne. (2006). On NSA Spying: A Letter to Congress. *New York Review of Books* 53 (2).

Norris, P., M. Korn, and M. Just. (2003). *Framing terrorism: The news media, the government, and the public.* London: Routledge.

North Carolina Department of Correction. (2000). Online: www.doc.state.nc.us/.

Nuro, D., T. Kinlock, and T. Hanlen. (1998). The drugs-crime connection. In J. Inciardi and K. McElrath, eds., *The American drug scene: An anthology,* 2nd ed. Los Angeles: Roxbury.

Nutt, D., and C. Blakemore. (2007). Results reported by BBC. Scientists want new drug rankings. *BBC,* March 23. Online: http://news.bbc.co.uk/1/hi/health/6474053.stm.

O'Brien, D. M. (1993). *Storm center.* New York: Norton.

O'Connell, M., and A. Whelan. (1996). Taking wrongs seriously: Public perceptions of crime seriousness. *British Journal of Criminology* 36:299–318.

Office of National Drug Control Policy. (ONDCP). (2006). Online: http://www.whitehousedrugpolicy.gov/.

Oliver, W. (2003). *The law & order presidency.* Upper Saddle River, NJ: Prentice Hall.

Omi, M. (1987). We shall overturn: Race and the contemporary American right. Dissertation, University of California at Santa Cruz.

Omi, M., and H. Winant. (1986). *Racial formation in the United States.* New York: Routledge and Kegan Paul.

Orcutt, J., and J. Turner. (1993). Shocking numbers and graphic accounts: Quantified images of drug problems in the print media. *Social Problems* 6:217–32.

Packer, H. (1968). *The limits of the criminal sanction.* Palo Alto, CA: Stanford University Press.

Page, J. (2000). Violence and incarceration: A personal observation. In J. May, ed., *Building violence: How America's rush to incarcerate creates more violence.* Thousand Oaks, CA: Sage.

Palermo, G., M. White, and L. Wasserman. (1998). Plea bargaining: Injustice for all? *International Journal of Offender Therapy and Comparative Criminology* 42 (2): 111–23.

Parenti, M. (1993). *Inventing reality: The politics of the news media.* New York: St. Martin's Press.

Parton, D., M. Hansel, and J. Stratton. (1991). Measuring crime seriousness: Lessons from the National Survey of Crime Severity. *British Journal of Criminology* 31:72–85.

Pate, T., and L. Fridell. (1994). *Police use of force: Official reports, citizen complaints, and legal consequences, 1991–1992.* Ann Arbor, MI: Interuniversity Consortium for Political and Social Research.

Paulsen, D. (2000). Murder in black and white: The newspaper coverage of homicide in Houston, 1986–1994. Ph.D. dissertation, Sam Houston State University.

Pearson, D. (2000). Minority health. In R. Lauer and J. Lauer, eds., *Troubled times: Readings in social problems.* Los Angeles: Roxbury.

Peffley, M., and J. Hurwitz. (1997). Racial stereotypes and whites' political views of blacks in the context of welfare and crime. *American Journal of Political Science* 41 (1): 30–60.

Peoples, E. (2000). *Basic criminal procedures.* Upper Saddle River, NJ: Prentice Hall.

Perlmutter, D. (2001). Before rushing to judge cops for their actions. *Law Enforcement News* 27 (557): 11.

Petersilia, J. (1983). *Racial disparities in the criminal justice system.* Santa Monica, CA: Rand Corporation.

Petersilia, J. (1985). Racial disparities in the criminal justice system: A summary. *Crime and Delinquency* 31:15–34.

Petersilia, J. (1998). Probation in the United States. *Perspectives* 37:30–49.

Petersilia, J., and S. Turner. (1986). *Prison versus probation in California: Implications for crime and offender recidivism.* Santa Monica, CA: Rand Corporation.

Pew Research Center for the People and the Press. (2006). State of the American News Media, 2007: Mainstream Media Go Niche. Online: http://pewresearch.org/pubs/428/state-of-the-american-news-media-2007-mainstream-media-go-niche.

Phillips, K. (1991). *The politics of rich and poor.* New York: Random House.

Phillips, K. (2003). How wealth defines power. *The American Prospect Summer:* A8–A10.

Phipps, A. (1986). Radical criminology and criminal victimization: Proposals for the development of theory and intervention.

In R. Matthews and J. Young, eds., *Confronting crime*. Beverly Hills, CA: Sage.

Pizzi, W. (2000). *Trials without truth*. New York: New York University Press.

Platt, L. (1999). Armageddon—Live at 6! In R. Hiebert, ed., *Impact of mass media: Current issues*, 4th ed. New York: Longman.

Podgor, E., and J. Israel. (1997). *White collar crime*. St. Paul, MN: West.

Pogarsky, G., K. KiDeuk, and R. Paternoster. (2005). Perceptual change in the national youth survey: Lessons for deterrence theory and offender decision-making. *Justice Quarterly* 22 (1): 1–29.

Pojman, L. (1998). *The death penalty: For and against*. New York: Rowman and Littlefield.

The Police Foundation. (1981). *The Newark foot patrol experiment*. Washington DC: The Police Foundation.

Pontell, H., K. Calavita, and R. Tillman. (1994). *Fraud in the savings and loan industry: White collar crime and government response*. Washington, DC: National Institute of Justice.

Pope, H., and D. Yurgelun-Todd. (1996). The residual cognitive effects of heavy marijuana use in college students. *Journal of the American Medical Association* 275:7.

Poporino, F. (1986). Managing violent individuals in correctional settings. *Journal of Interpersonal Violence* 1:213–37.

Potok, M. (2007). Active hate groups in 2006. Online: http://www.splcenter.org/intel/map/hate.jsp.

Potter, G., and V. Kappeler. (1998). *Constructing crime: Perspectives on making news and social problems*. Prospect Heights, IL: Waveland Press.

Pound, R. (1912). *The scope and purpose of sociological jurisprudence*. Cambridge, MA: Harvard Law Review Association.

Pratt, C. Police discretion. *Law and Order* (March 1992): 99–100.

Pratt, T. (1998). Race and sentencing: A meta-analysis of conflicting empirical research results. *Journal of Criminal Justice* 26 (6): 513–23.

Preble, E., and J. Casey, Jr. (1969). Taking care of business: The heroin user's life in the streets. *International Journal of Addictions* 4:1–24.

Prejean, H. (1993). *Dead man walking*. New York: Random House.

Project for Excellence in Journalism. (2001). The look of local news. Online: http//www.journalism.org/resources/research/reports/localTV/2001/look.asp.

Project for Excellence in Journalism. (2005). The state of the news media. Online: http://www.stateofthemedia.org/2005/narrative_localtv_intro.asp?cat+1$media=6.

Quan, S. (2000). A profile of the working poor. In R. Lauer and J. Lauer, eds., *Troubled times: Readings in social problems*. Los Angeles: Roxbury.

Quinney, R. (1970). *The social reality of crime*. New Brunswick, NJ: Transaction Publishers.

Quinney, R. (2000). *The Social Reality of Crime*. Edison, NJ: Transaction.

Radelet, M. (1989). Executions of whites for crimes against blacks: Exceptions to the rule? *Sociological Quarterly* 30 (4): 529–544.

Radelet, M., and R. Akers. (1996). Deterrence and the death penalty: The views of the experts. Online: http://sun.soci.niu.edu/~critcrim/dp/dppapers/mike.deterence.

Radelet, M., H. Bedau, and C. Putnam. (1992). *In spite of innocence: The ordeal of 400 Americans wrongly convicted of crimes punishable by death*. Boston: Northeastern University Press.

Raeder, M. (1993). Gender and sentencing: Single moms, battered women, and other sex-based anomalies in the gender-free world of the federal sentencing guidelines. *Pepperdine Law Review* 20:948.

Raine, A. (1993). *The psychopathology of crime*. New York: Academic Press.

Randell, D. (1995). The portrayal of business malfeasance in the elite and general media. In G. Geis, R. Meier, and L. Salinger, eds., *White-collar crime: Classic and contemporary views*. New York: The Free Press.

Ransby, B. (1999). The black poor and the politics of expendability. In L. Kushnick and J. Jennings, eds., *A new introduction to poverty: The role of race, power, and politics*. New York: New York University Press.

Rasmussen, D., and B. Benson. (1994). *The economic anatomy of a drug war*. Lanham, MD: Rowman and Littlefield.

Rauma, D. (1991). The context of normative consensus: An expansion of the Rossi/Berk model, with an application to crime seriousness. *Social Science Research* 20:1–28.

Rawls, J. (2003). *Justice as fairness: Restatement*, 2nd rev. ed. Boston: Belknap Press.

Reed, I. (1991). Tuning out network bias. *The New York Times* (April 9) A11.

Reed, I. (1993). It's racist. *American Journalism Review* 15 (7): 22–23.

Reeves, J., and R. Campbell. (1994). *Cracked coverage: Television news, the anti-cocaine crusade, and the Reagan legacy*. Durham, NC: Duke University Press.

Reiman, J. (1998). *The rich get richer and the poor get prison: Ideology, class, and criminal justice*, 5th ed. Boston: Allyn & Bacon.

Reiman, J. (2004). The rich get richer and the poor get prison, 7th ed. Boston: Allyn & Bacon.

Reiman, J. (2006). *The rich get richer and the poor get prison*, 8th ed. Boston: Allyn & Bacon.

Reiman, J., and P. Leighton. (2003). Getting tough on corporate crime? Enron and a year of corporate financial scandals. Online: www.stopviolence.com.

Reinarman, C. (1994). Unanticipated consequences of criminilization: Hypotheses on how drug laws exacerbate drug problems. *Perspectives on Social Problems* 6:217–32.

Reinarman, C. (1995). Crack attack: America's latest drug scare, 1986–1992. In J. Best, ed., *Images of issues: Typifying contemporary social problems*. New York: Aldine de Gruyter.

Reinarman, C., and H. Levine. (1989a). The crack attack: Politics and media in America's latest drug scare. In J. Best, ed., *Images of issues: Typifying contemporary social problems*. New York: Aldine de Gruyter.

Reinarman, C., and H. Levine. (1989b). Crack in context: Politics and media in the making of a drug scene. *Contemporary Drug Problems* 16:116–29.

Rendell, S., and T. Broughel. (2003). *Extra!* May/June. FAIR. Online: www.fair.org.

Rengert, G., and J. Wasilchick. (1985). *Suburban burglary: A time and place for everything*. Springfield, IL: Charles C Thomas.

Reppetto, R. (1974). *Residential crime*. Cambridge, MA: Ballinger.

Reuter, P. (1998). Hawks ascendant: The punitive trend of American drug policy. In J. Inciardi and K. McElrath, eds., *The American drug scene: An anthology*, 2nd ed. Los Angeles: Roxbury.

Ridgeway, G. (2006). Assessing the effect of race bias in post-traffic stop outcomes using propensity scores. *Journal of Quantitative Criminology* 22 (1): 1–29.

Ritzer, G. (2000). *The McDonaldization of society*. Thousand Oaks, CA: Sage.

Roberts, D. (1993). Crime, race and reproduction. *Tulane Law Review* 1945:1.

Roberts, J. (1992). Public opinion, crime, and criminal justice. In M. Tonry, ed., *Crime and justice: A review of research* (Vol. 16). Chicago: University of Chicago Press.

Roberts, J., and A. Doob. (1990). News media influences on public views of sentencing. *Law and Human Behavior* 14:451–68.

Roberts, J., and D. Edwards. (1992). Contextual affects in judgements of crime, criminals, and the purpose of sentencing. *Journal of Applied Social Psychology* 19:902–17.

Roberts, J., and L. Stalans. (2000). *Public opinion, crime, and criminal justice*. Boulder, CO: Westview Press.

Robinson, M. B. (1997). Environmental characteristics associated with residential burglaries of student apartment complexes. *Environment and Behavior* 29 (5): 657–75.

Robinson, M. (1998a). Tobacco: The greatest crime in world history? *The Critical Criminologist* 8 (3): 20–2.

Robinson, M. (1998b). Accessible targets, but not advisable ones: The role of accessibility in student apartment burglary. *Journal of Security Administration* 21 (1): 28–43.

Robinson, M. (1999). The historical development of CPTED: 25 years of responses to C. Ray Jeffery's work. *Advances in Criminological Theory* 8:427–62.

Robinson, M. (1999). Lifestyles, routine activities, and residential burglary victimization. *Journal of Crime and Justice.* 22 (1): 27–56.

Robinson, M. (2000). The construction and reinforcement of myths of race and crime. *Journal of Contemporary Criminal Justice* 16 (2): 133–56.

Robinson, M. (2002). The case for a "new victimology": Implications for policing. In L. Moriarty, ed., *Police and victims.* Upper Saddle River, NJ: Prentice Hall.

Robinson, M. (2004). *Why crime? An integrated systems theory of antisocial behavior.* Upper Saddle River, NJ: Prentice Hall.

Robinson, M. (2006). McDonaldization of American police, courts, and corrections. In G. Ritzer, ed. *The McDonaldization Reader,* 2nd ed. Thousand Oaks, CA: Pine Forge Press.

Robinson, M. (2007). The politics of terror. Online: http://www.justiceblind.com/politicsofterror.html.

Robinson, M. (2008). *Death nation: The experts explain American capital punishment.* Upper Saddle River, NJ: Prentice Hall.

Robinson, M., and R. Scherlen (2007). *Lies, damned lies, and drug war statistics: A critical analysis of claims made by the Office of National Drug Control Policy.* Albany, NY: SUNY Press.

Robinson, M., and B. Zaitzow. (1999a). Criminologists: Are we what we study? A national study of crime experts. *The Criminologist* 24 (2): 1, 4, 17–9.

Robinson, M., and B. Zaitzow. (1999b). Like the pot calling the kettle black: Criminologists who engage in criminal, deviant, and unethical behavior. Paper presented to the American Society of Criminology (November).

Rold, W. (2000). Legislating barriers to effective solutions: An indelicate tool for a complex problem. In J. May, ed., *Building violence: How America's rush to incarcerate creates more violence.* Thousand Oaks, CA: Sage.

Rome, D. (1998). Stereotyping by the media: Murderers, rapists, and drug addicts. In C. Mann and M. Zatz, eds., *Images of color, images of crime.* Los Angeles: Roxbury.

Rosch, J. (1985). Crime as an issue in American politics. In E. Fairchild and V. Webb, eds.,

The politics of crime and criminal justice. Beverly Hills, CA: Sage.

Rosoff, S., H. Pontell, and R. Tillman. (2004). *Profit without honor: White-collar crime and the looting of America,* 3rd ed. Upper Saddle River, NJ: Prentice Hall.

Rosoff, S., H. Pontell, and R. Tillman. (2006). *Profit without honor: White-collar crime and the looting of America,* 4th ed. Upper Saddle River, NJ: Prentice Hall.

Ross, D. (1999). Assessing the patterns of citizen resistance during arrests. *FBI Law Enforcement Bulletin* 68 (6): 5–11.

Rothman, D. (1971). *The discovery of the asylum.* Boston: Little, Brown.

Rouse, J., and B. Johnson. (1991). Hidden paradigms of morality in debates about drugs: Historical and policy shifts in British and American drug policies. In J. Inciardi, ed., *The drug legalization debate: Studies in crime, law, and justice.* Newbury Park, CA: Sage.

Ruprecht, C. (1997). Are verdicts, too, like sausages? Lifting the cloak of jury secrecy. *University of Pennsylvania Law Review* 146 (1): 217–68.

Rusche, G., and O. Kirchheimer. (1939). *Punishment and social structure.* New York: Columbia University Press.

Rush, G. E. (2000). *The dictionary of criminal justice,* 4th ed. Boston: Dushkin/McGraw-Hill.

Russell, K. (1998). *The color of crime.* New York: New York University Press.

Rutenberg, J., and B. Carter. (2001). Draping newscasts with the flag. *The New York Times,* September 20: C8.

Sabato, L. (1993). *Feeding frenzy.* New York: The Free Press.

Sacco, V. (2005). *When crime waves.* Thousand Oaks, CA: Sage.

Sacco, V., and L. Kennedy. (1996). *The criminal event,* 3rd ed. London: International Thompson Publishers.

Salant, J. (1999). Tobacco giant Philip Morris tops list of political contributors. Online: www.nandonet.com.

Samaha, J. (2007). *Criminal law,* 9th ed. Beverly Hills, CA: Wadsworth.

Sampson, R. (1987). Urban black violence: The effect of male joblessness and family disruption. *American Journal of Sociology* 93:348–82.

Sampson R., and J. Laub. (1997). A life-course theory of cumulative disadvantage and the stability of delinquency. In T. Thornberry, ed., *Developmental theories of crime and delinquency.* New Brunswick, NJ: Transaction.

Sandor, R. (1995). Legalizing/decriminalizing drug use. In R. Coombs and D. Ziedonis, eds., *Handbook on drug abuse prevention: A contemporary strategy to prevent the abuse of alcohol and other drugs.* Boston: Allyn & Bacon.

Sandys, M., and E. McGarrell. (1995). Attitudes toward capital punishment: Preferences for the penalty or mere acceptance? *Journal of Research in Crime and Delinquency* 32:191–213.

Sarat, A., and N. Vidmar. (1976). Public opinion, the death penalty, and the Eighth Amendment: Testing the Marshall hypothesis. *Wisconsin Law Review* 17:171–206.

Sasson, T. (1995). *Crime talk: How citizens construct a social problem.* New York: Aldine de Gruyter.

Scarr, H. (1973). *Patterns of burglary.* Washington, DC: National Institute of Law Enforcement and Criminal Justice.

Schafer, J., D. Carter, A. Katz-Bannister, and W. Wells. (2006). Decision making in traffic stop encounters: A multivariate analysis of police behavior. *Police Quarterly* 9 (2): 184–209.

Schatzman, M. (1975). Cocaine and the drug problem. *Journal of Psychedelic Drugs* 7 (1): 7–17.

Scheidegger, K. (2004). Smoke and mirrors on race and the death penalty. *Engage* 4 (2): 42–5.

Scheingold, S. A. (1984). *The politics of law and order: Street crime and public policy.* New York: Longman.

Schiraldi, V., P. Sussman, and L. Hyland. (1994). *Three strikes: The unintended victims.* San Francisco: Center on Juvenile and Criminal Justice.

Schlesinger, P., and H. Tumber. (1994). *Reporting crime: The media politics of criminal justice.* Oxford: Clarendon.

Schmalleger, F. (1999). *Criminal law today.* Upper Saddle River, NJ: Prentice Hall.

Schmalleger, F. (2001). *Criminal justice today,* 6th ed. Upper Saddle River, NJ: Prentice Hall.

Schmalleger, F. (2006). *Criminal justice today* 9th ed. Upper Saddle River, NJ: Prentice Hall.

Schneider, V., and J. Smykla. (1991). A summary analysis of executions in the United States, 1608–1987: The Espy file. In R. Bohm, ed., *The death penalty in America: Current research.* Cincinnati, OH: Anderson.

Schoenborn, C. A., and B. H. Cohen. (1986). Trends in smoking, alcohol consumption, and other health practices among U.S. adults, 1977 and 1983. Hyattsville, MD: National Center for Health Statistics, U.S. Department of Health and Human Services, No. 118: 1–16.

Sebba, L. (1984). Crime seriousness and criminal intent. *Crime and Delinquency* 30:227–44.

Seidman, D., and M. Couzens. (1974). Getting the crime rate down: Political pressure and crime reporting. *Law and Society Review* 8:457–93.

Sennott, C. (2000). The $150 billion "welfare" recipients: U.S. corporations. In R. Lauer and J. Lauer, eds., *Troubled times: Readings in social problems.* Los Angeles: Roxbury.

The Sentencing Project. (1997, 1998). Facts about prisons and prisoners. Washington, DC: The Sentencing Project.

The Sentencing Project. (2003). On-line: www.sentencingproject.org.

The Sentencing Project. (2007). Felony disenfranchisement. Online: http://www.sentencingproject.org/IssueAreaHome.aspx?IssueID=4.

Shapiro, B. (1997). Victims and vengeance: Why the victim's rights amendment is a bad idea. *The Nation* 264:11–9.

Shapiro, M. (1992). *Reading the postmodern polity: Political theory a textual practice.* Minneapolis, MN: University of Minnesota Press.

Shapiro, S. (1995). Collaring the crime, not the criminal: Reconsidering the concept of white-collar crime. *American Sociological Review* 55:346–65.

Shelden, R. (2001, 2007). *Controlling the dangerous classes.* Boston: Allyn & Bacon.

Shepherd, J. (2004). Murders of passion, execution delays, and the deterrence of capital punishment. *Journal of Legal Studies* 33 (2): 283–322.

Sherizen, S. (1978). Social creation of crime news: All the news that's fitted to print. In C. Winick, ed., *Deviance and the mass media*. Beverly Hills, CA: Sage.

Sherman, L., D. Gottfredson, D. MacKenzie, J. Eck, P. Reuter, and S. Bushway. (1997). *Preventing crime: What works, what doesn't, what's promising*. Washington, DC: U.S. Department of Justice, Office of Justice Programs, National Institute of Justice.

Sherrill, R. (1997). A year in corporate crime. *The Nation,* April 7.

Shipler, D. (2005). *The working poor: Invisible in America*. New York: Vintage.

Shover, N., and J. Wright. (2000). *Crimes of privilege: Readings in white-collar crime*. New York: Oxford University Press.

Shukovsky, P., T. Johnson, and D. Lathrop. (2007). The FBI's terrorism trade-off: Focus on national security after 9/11 means that the agency has turned its back on thousands of white-collar crimes. *Seattle PI,* April 11. Online: http://seattlepi.nwsource.com/national/311046_fbiterror11.html.

Sidel, R. (1996). *Keeping women and children last*. New York: Penguin.

Siegel, L. (1998). *Criminology,* 6th ed. Belmont, CA: Wadsworth.

Sigal, L. (1973). *Reporters and officials: The organization and politics of newsmaking*. London: D. C. Heath.

Signorielli, N. (1990). Television's mean and dangerous world: A continuation of the cultural indicators perspective. In M. Morgan and N. Signorielli, eds., *Cultivation analysis: New directions in media effects research*. Newbury Park, CA: Sage.

Sileo, C. (1993). Sentencing rules that shackle justice. *Insight* 11.

Simon, D. (1999). *Elite deviance*. Boston: Allyn & Bacon.

Simon, D. (2005). *Elite Deviance* 8th ed. Boston: Allyn & Bacon.

Simon, D. (2007). *Elite deviance,* 9th ed. Boston: Allyn & Bacon.

Simon, D., and F. Hagan. (1999). *White-collar deviance*. Boston: Allyn & Bacon.

Simon, J. (1994). *Poor discipline: Parole and the social control of the underclass, 1890–1990*. Chicago: University of Chicago Press.

Simon, J. (2007). *Governing through crime: How the war on crime transformed American democracy and created a culture of fear*. New York: Oxford University Press.

Simpson, D., K. Knight, and C. Pevoto. (1996). *Research summary: Focus on drug treatment in criminal justice settings*. Fort Worth: Texas Christian University Institute of Behavioral Research.

Singh, V. (1991). The underclass in the United States: Some correlates of economic change. *Sociological Inquiry* 61:505–21.

Skogan, W. (1990). *Disorder and decline*. Berkeley: University of California Press.

Skogan, W. (1995). Crime and the racial fears of white Americans. *Annals of the American Academy of Political and Social Science* 539:59–71.

Skolnick, J. (1966). *Justice without trial: Law enforcement in a democratic society*. New York: Wiley.

Skolnick, J. (1967). Social control in the adversary system. *Journal of Conflict Resolution* 11:52–70.

Skolnick, J. (1994). Wild pitch. *American Prospect* 17:31–7.

Skolnick, J. (1997). Rethinking the drug problem. In L. Gaines and P. Kraska, eds., *Drugs, crime, and justice,* 3rd ed. Prospect Heights, IL: Waveland Press.

Skolnick, J. (2007). Racial profiling—Then and now. *Criminology & Public Policy, 6* (1): 65–70.

Smith, D. (1986). The plea bargaining controversy. *Journal of Criminal Law and Criminology* 77:949.

Smith, P. (1990). *Felony defendants in large urban counties, 1990*. Washington, DC: Bureau of Justice Statistics.

Smith, P. (1993). Private prisons: Profits of crime. *Covert Action Quarterly* 4:1–6.

Smith, R. (1995). *Racism in the post-civil rights era: Now you see it, now you don't*. Albany: State University of New York Press.

Smith, W., D. Tomaskovic-Devey, M. Zingraff, H. Mason, P. Warren, and C. Wright. (2003). The North Carolina Highway Traffic Study. Online: http://www.chass.ncsu.edu/justice/reports/hwy_traffic_study_03.htm.

Smolej, M., and J. Kivivuori. (2006). The relation between crime news and fear of violence. *Journal of Scandanavian Studies in Criminology and Crime Prevention* 7 (2): 211–27.

Snell, T. (1997). Capital punishment 1996. *Bureau of Justice Statistics Bulletin* (December). Washington, DC: U.S. Department of Justice.

Son, I., M. Davis, and D. Rome. (1998). Race and its effect on police officers' perceptions of misconduct. *Journal of Criminal Justice* 26 (1): 21–8.

Sourcebook of Criminal Justice Statistics. (2003). Online: www.albany.edu/sourcebook.

Sourcebook of Criminal Justice Statistics. (2006). Characteristics and distribution of persons arrested. Online: http://www.albany.edu/sourcebook/toc_4.html.

Sourcebook of Criminal Justice Statistics. (2006). Persons under correctional supervision. Online: http://albany.edu/sourcebook/toc_6.html.

Sourcebook of Criminal Justice Statistics. (2007). Judicial processing of defendants. Online: http://albany.edu/sourcebook/toc_5.html.

Spelman, W. (2000). The limited importance of prison expansion. In A. Blumstein and J. Wallman, eds., *The crime drop in America.* New York: Cambridge University Press.

Spire, R. (1990). Breaking up the old boy network. *Trial* 26 (2): 57–8.

Spitzer, S. (1975). Toward a Marxian theory of deviance. *Social Problems* 22:638–51.

Spohn, C., and D. Halleran. (2002). The effect of imprisonment on recidivism rates of felony offenders: A focus on drug offenders. *Criminology* 40 (2): 329–57.

Spohn, C., and M. DeLone. (2000). When does race matter? An examination of the conditions under which race affects sentence severity. *Sociology of Crime, Law, and Deviance* 2:3–37.

Spohn, C., and D. Hollerman. (2000). The imprisonment penalty paid by young, unemployed, black and Hispanic male offenders. *Criminology* 38 (1): 281–306.

St. John, C., and T. Heald-Moore. (1996). Racial prejudice and fear of criminal victimization by strangers in public settings. *Sociological Inquiry* 66 (3): 267–84.

Steel, B. S., and M. Steger. (1988). Crime: Due process liberalism versus law and order conservatism. In R. Tantalovich and B. W. Daynes, eds., *Social regulatory policy.* Boulder, CO: Westview Press.

Steele, W. Jr., and E. Thornburg. (1991). Jury instructions: A persistent failure to communicate. *Judicature* 74:249–54.

Steele, W. Jr., and E. Thornburg. (2000). Jury instructions: A persistent failure to communicate. In G. Mays and P. Gregware, *Courts and justice: A reader,* 2nd ed. Prospect Heights, IL: Waveland Press.

Steffensmeir, D., J. Ulmer, and J. Kramer. (1998). The interaction of race, gender, and age in criminal sentencing: The cost of being young, black, and male. *Criminology* 36:763–98.

Steiker, C., and J. Steiker. (1998). Judicial developments in capital punishment law. In J. Acker and C. Lanier, eds., *America's experiment with capital punishment: Reflections on the past, present, and future of the ultimate penal sanction.* Durham, NC: Carolina Academic Press.

Stephen, J. (1883). *Liberty, equality, fraternity.* New York, H. Holt.

Sterling, J. (1983). Retained counsel versus the public defender: The impact of type of counsel on charge bargaining. In W. McDonald, ed., *The defense counsel.* Beverly Hills, CA: Sage.

Stevens, J., and H. Garcia. (1980). *Communicating history.* Newbury Park, CA.: Sage.

Stevenson, N. (1995). *Understanding media culture: Social theory and mass communication.* London: Sage.

Stewart, E. (2007). Either they don't know or they don't care: Black males and negative police experiences. *Criminology & Public Policy*, 6 (1): 123–30.

Streisand, B. (1994). Can he get a fair trial? *U.S. News & World Report*, October 3: 61–3.

Strinati, D. (1995). *An introduction to theories of popular culture*. London: Routledge.

Stuckey, G., C. Robertson, and H. Wallace. (2001). *Procedures in the justice system*, 6th ed. Upper Saddle River, NJ: Prentice Hall.

Sullivan, D. (2006). *The handbook of restorative justice: A global perspective*. New York: Routledge.

Surette, R. (1992). *Media, crime, and criminal justice: Images and realities*. Pacific Grove: Brooks/Cole.

Surette, R. (1998). *Media, crime, and criminal justice: Images and realities*, 2nd ed. Belmont, CA: Wadsworth.

Sutherland, E. (1977a). Is "white-collar crime" crime? In G. Geis and R. Meier, eds., *White-collar crime: Offenses in business, politics, and the professions*. New York: The Free Press.

Sutherland, E. (1977b). White-collar criminality. In G. Geis and R. Meier, eds., *White-collar crime: Offenses in business, politics, and the professions*. New York: The Free Press.

Swezey, R. (1973). Estimating drug crime relationships. *International Journal of the Addictions* 8:701–21.

Sykes, G. (1958). *The society of captives: A study of a maximum-security prison*. Princeton, NJ: Princeton University Press.

Tashkin et al. (2007). Results reported by *Washington Post*. Study finds no cancer-marijuana connection. *Washington Post*, May 26. Online: http://www.washingtonpost.com/wp-dyn/content/article/2006/05/25/AR2006052501729_pf.html.

Tillman, R. (1987). The size of the "criminal population": The prevalence and incidence of adult arrest. *Criminology* 25:561–79.

Tillman, R., and H. Pontell. (1992). Is justice "collar-blind"? Punishing Medicaid provider fraud. *Criminology* 30:547–73.

Tinklenberg, J. R. (1973). Alcohol and violence. In P. G. Bourne, ed., *Alcoholism: Progress in research and treatment*. New York: Academic Press.

Tomaskovic-Devey, D., C. Wright, R. Czaja, and K. Miller. (2006). Self-reports of police speeding stops by race: Results from the North Carolina Reverse Record Check Survey. *Journal of Quantitative Criminology*, 22 (4): 279–97.

Tonry, M. (1992). Mandatory penalties. In M. Tonry, ed., *Crime and justice: A review of research* (p. 16). Chicago: University of Chicago Press.

Tonry, M. (1995). *Malign neglect: Race, crime and punishment in America*. Oxford: Oxford University Press.

Torrey, E., J. Steiber, J. Ezekiel, S. Wolfe, J. Sharftein, J. Noble, and L. Flynn. (1992). *Criminalizing the seriously mental ill: The abuse of jails as mental hospitals*. Washington, DC: National Alliance for the Mentally Ill and Public Citizens Health Research Group.

Treaster, J. (1990). Is the fight on drugs eroding civil rights? *The New York Times* (May 6) A1, 9.

Trebach, A. (1997). *The great drug war*. New York: Macmillan.

Tuchman, G. (1978). *Making news: A study in the social construction of reality*. New York: The Free Press.

Tunnell, K. (1992). Film at eleven: Recent developments in the commodification of crime. *Sociological Spectrum* 12: 293–313.

Tuohy, L. (1995). CCLU suit lays bare a public defense system in crisis. *Hartford Courant* (January 8) A1.

Tyndall, A. (2005). Results reported in *Just News*. Online: http://www.richmonddiocese.org/ojp/jn2003-09.pdf.

UCR Handbook. (1999). Online: www.fbi.gov/ucr.htm.

Unah, I., and J. Boger. (2001). Race and the death penalty in North Carolina. On-line: www.deathpenaltyinfo.org/article.php?scid=19&did=246.

U.S. Census Bureau. (2001, 2006). Income, poverty, and health insurance coverage in the United States. Online: http://www.census.gov/prod/2006pubs/p60-231.pdf.

U.S. Department of Education. (1999). *Early warning, timely response: A guide to safe schools.* Washington, DC: U.S. Department of Education.

U.S. Department of Justice. (1996). *National data collection on police use of force.* Washington, DC: U.S. Government Printing Office.

U.S. Department of Justice. (1998). Online: www. usdoj.gov.

U.S. Department of Justice. (1998). Sourcebook of criminal justice statistics. Washington, DC: U.S. Government Printing Office.

U.S. News & World Report. (2000). The rich get richer: What happens to American society when the gap in wealth and income grows larger? *U.S. News & World Report,* February 21.

Unnever, J., and L. Hembroff. (1988). The prediction of racial/ethnic sentencing disparities: An expectation states approach. *Journal of Research in Crime and Delinquency* 25:53–82.

Uphoff, R. (2000). The criminal defense lawyer: Zealous advocate, double agent, or beleaguered dealer? In G. Mays and P. Gregware, *Courts and justice: A reader,* 2nd ed. Prospect Heights, IL: Waveland Press.

Utt, R. (2005). The bridge to nowhere: A national embarrassment. Online: http://www. heritage.org/Research/Budget/wm889.cfm.

Van den Haag, E. (1982). In defense of the death penalty: A practical and moral analysis. In H. Bedau, ed., *The death penalty in America,* 3rd ed. New York: Oxford University Press.

Van den Hagg, E. (1997). The death penalty once more. In H. Bedau, ed., *The death penalty in America: Current controversies.* New York: Oxford University Press.

Vandiver, M. (1998). The impact of the death penalty on the families of homicide victims and of condemned prisoners. In J. Acker, R. Bohm, and C. Lanier, eds., *America's experiment with capital punishment: Reflections on the past, present, and future of the ultimate penal sanction.* Durham, NC: Carolina Academic Press.

Van Horn, C., D. Baumer, and W. Gormley, Jr. (1992). *Politics and public policy.* Washington, DC: CQ Press.

van Kesteren, J., Mayhew, P., and P. Nieuwbeerta. (2001). Criminal victimisation in seventeen industrialized countries: Key findings from the 2000 International Crime Victims Survey. Online: www.minjust.nl.

Varinsky, H. (1993). Trial consulting: The art and science of selling a case to a jury. *Washington State Bar News* 47:47–50.

Victor, J. (2006). Why the terrorism scare is a moral panic. *The Humanist* (July 1). Online: http://www.encyclopedia.com/doc/1G1-148674633.html.

Vila, B. (1997). Motivating and marketing nurturant crime control strategies: Reply to comments. *Politics and the Life Sciences* 16:48–55.

Virkunnen, M. (1974). Alcohol as a factor precipitating aggression and conflict behavior leading to homicide. *British Journal of the Addictions* 69:149–54.

Vold, G. (1958). *Theoretical criminology.* New York: Oxford University Press.

Vold, G., T. Bernard, and J. Snipes. (2002). *Theoretical Criminology,* 6th ed. New York: Oxford University Press.

Von Drehle, D. (1988). Bottom line: Life in prison one sixth as expensive. *Miami Herald* (July 10): 12A.

Walker, S. (1998). *Sense and nonsense about crime and drugs: A policy guide,* 4th ed. Belmont, CA: Wadsworth.

Walker, S. (2005). *Sense and nonsense about crime and drugs,* 6th ed. Beverly Hills, CA: Wadsworth.

Walker, S., C. Spohn, and M. DeLone. (1996). *The color of justice: Race, ethnicity, and crime in America,* Belmont, CA: Wadsworth.

Walker, S., C. Spohn, and M. DeLone. (2000). *The color of justice: Race, ethnicity and crime in America,* 2nd ed. Belmont, CA: Wadsworth.

Walker, S., C. Spohn, and M. DeLone. (2006). *The color of justice: Race, ethnicity, and crime in America,* 4th ed. Beverly Hills, CA: Wadsworth.

Waller, I., and N. Okihiro. (1978). *Burglary: The victim and the public.* Toronto: Centre of Criminology, University of Toronto.

Walsh, D. (1980). *Break-ins: Burglary from private houses.* London: Constable.

Warr, M. (1991). What is the perceived seriousness of crime? *Criminology* 27:795–821.

Warren, P., D. Tomaskovic-Devey, W. Smith, M. Zingraff, and M. Mason. (2006). Driving while black: Bias processes and racial disparity in police stops. *Criminology* 44 (3): 709–38.

Weaver, D., and G. Wilhoit. (1986). *The American journalist: A portrait of U.S. news people and their work.* Bloomington: Indiana University Press.

Webb, G., and M. Brown. (1998). United States drug laws and institutionalized discrimination. In E. Jensen and J. Gerber, eds., *The new war on drugs: Symbolic politics and criminal justice policy.* Cincinnati, OH: Anderson.

Weigl, A. (2006). North Carolina first to monitor consciousness of inmate during lethal injection. *The News & Observer,* April 21. Online: http://www.constitutioncenter.org/education/TeachingwithCurrentEvents/ConstitutionNewswire/16062.shtml.

Weil, A. (1998). Why people take drugs. In J. Inciardi and K. McElrath, eds., *The American drug scene: An anthology,* 2nd ed. Los Angeles: Roxbury.

Weinstein, C. (2000). Even dogs confined to cages for long periods of time go berserk. In J. May, ed., *Building violence: How America's rush to incarcerate creates more violence.* Thousand Oaks, CA: Sage.

Weisburd, D., E. Chayet, and E. Waring. (1990). White-collar crime and criminal careers: Some preliminary findings. *Crime and Delinquency* 36:342–55.

Weisburd, D., and K. Schlegel. (1992). Returning to the mainstream: Reflections on past and future white-collar crime study. In K. Schlegel and D. Weisburd, eds., *White-collar crime reconsidered.* Boston: Northeastern University Press.

Weisman, A. (2000). Mental illness behind bars. In J. May, ed., *Building violence: How America's rush to incarcerate creates more violence.* Thousand Oaks, CA: Sage.

Weitzer, R. (1996). Racial discrimination in the criminal justice system: Findings and problems in the literature. *Journal of Criminal Justice,* 24:313.

Welch, M. (1999). *Punishment in America: Social control and the ironies of imprisonment.* Thousand Oaks, CA: Sage.

Welch, M., M. Fenwick, and M. Roberts. (1998). State managers, intellectuals, and the media: A content analysis of ideology in experts' quotes in feature newspaper articles on crime. *Justice Quarterly* 15 (2): 219–41.

Wells, G., A. Memon, and S. Penrod. (2006). Eyewitness evidence: Improving its probative value. *Pscyological Science in the Public Interest* 7 (2): 45–75.

Welsh, B., and D. Farrington. (2005). *Preventing crime: What works for children, offenders, victims and places.* New York: Springer.

Welsh, W., and P. Harris. (1999). *Criminal justice policy and planning.* Cincinnati, OH: Anderson.

Welsh, W., and P. Harris. (2004). *Criminal justice policy and planning,* 2nd ed. Cincinnati, OH: LexisNexis.

Westmarland, L. (2005). Police ethics and integrity: Breaking the blue code of silence. *Policing and Society* 15 (2): 145–65.

Whitehead, T. (1997). Urban low income African American men, HIV/AIDS, and gender identity. *Medical Anthropologist Quarterly* 11 (4): 411–47.

Whitehead, T. (2000). The "epidemic" and "cultural legends" of black male incarceration: The socialization of African American children to a life of incarceration. In J. May, ed., *Building violence: How America's rush to incarcerate creates more violence.* Thousand Oaks, CA: Sage.

White House (2007). Office of Management and Budget. Defense Department. Online: http://www.whitehouse.gov/omb/budget/fy2007/defense.html.

Wice, P. (1985). *Chaos in the courthouse: The inner workings of the urban criminal courts.* New York: Praeger.

Wikipedia.com. Entry for "expert." Online: http://en.wikipedia.org/wiki/Expert.

Wilbanks, W. (1987). *The myth of a racist criminal justice system.* Monterey, CA: Brooks/Cole.

Williams, C. (1991). The federal death penalty for drug-related killings. *Criminal Law Bulletin* 27 (5): 387–415.

Williams, E. J., and M. Robinson. (2004). Ideology criminal justice: Suggestions for a pedagogical model. *Journal of Criminal Justice Education* 15 (2): 373–92.

Williams, J. (2000). The politics of jailing. In J. May, ed., *Building violence: How America's rush to incarcerate creates more violence.* Thousand Oaks, CA: Sage.

Wilson, C. (2006). Indiana inmate executed amid federal court drama. Law.com, January 30. Online: http://www.law.com/jsp/ article.jsp?id=1138356402268.

Wilson, E. (1995). *Effects of corporate downsizing on survivors: An empirical assessment.* University of North Carolina at Charlotte.

Wilson, J. (1975). *Thinking about crime.* New York: Basic Books.

Wilson, J. (1998). Foreword: Never too early. In F. Loeber and D. Farrington, eds., *Serious and violent juvenile offenders.* Thousand Oaks, CA: Sage.

Wilson, W. J. (1987). *The truly disadvantaged: The inner city, the underclass, and public policy.* Chicago: University of Chicago Press.

Winchester, S., and H. Jackson. (1982). *Residential burglary: The limits of prevention. Home Office Research Study No. 74.* London: Her Majesty's Stationery Office.

Wisotsky, S. (1991). Beyond the war on drugs. In J. Inciardi, ed., *The drug legalization debate: Studies in crime, law, and justice.* Thousand Oaks, CA: Sage.

Wolfgang, M., R. Figlio, and T. Sellin. (1972). *Delinquency in a birth cohort.* Chicago: University of Chicago Press.

Word, R. (2006). High court to consider appeal on last-minute challenges to injection executions. Law.com, April 25. Online: http://www.law.com/jsp/article.jsp?id=1145885163985.

Wright, R. (1993). A socially sensitive criminal justice system. In J. Murphy and D. Peck, eds., *Open institutions: The hope for democracy.* Westport, CT: Praeger.

Wright, R., and S. Decker. (1994). *Burglars on the job: Streetlife and residential break-ins.* Boston: Northeastern University Press.

Wrobleski, H. (2006). *Introduction to law enforcement and criminal justice,* 8th ed. Beverly Hills, CA: Wadsworth.

Wrobleski, H., and K. Hess. (2000). *An introduction: Law enforcement and criminal justice.* Belmont, CA: Wadsworth.

Young, R. (2002). Religious orientation, race and support for the death penalty. In J. Martinez, W. Richardson, and D. Hornsby, eds., *The Leviathan's choice: Capital punishment in the twenty-first century.* Lanham, MD: Rowman & Littlefield.

Yu, J., and A. Liska. (1993). The certainty of punishment: A reference group effect and its functional form. *Criminology* 31 (3): 447–64.

Zehr, H., and T. Toews. (2004). *Critical issues in restorative justice.* Sydney, Australia: Criminal Justice Press.

Zehr, H., and M. Umbreit. (1982). Victim offender reconciliation: An incarceration substitute. *Federal Probation* 46 (1): 3–68.

Zerbisias, A. (2003). Hawks turned media into parrots. Online: www.globalpolicy.org/security/ issues/iraq/media/2003/0612 censorship.htm.

Zimmer, L., and J. Morgan. (1997). *Marijuana myths, marijuana facts: A review of the scientific evidence.* New York: Lindesmith Center.

Zimmerman, P. (2004). State executions, deterrence and the incidence of murder. *Journal of Applied Economics* 7 (1): 163–93.

Zimring, F. (2003). *The contradictions of American capital punishment.* New York: Oxford University Press.

Zimring, F. (2006). *The great American crime decline.* New York: Oxford University Press.

Zimring, F., and G. Hawkins. (1986). *Capital punishment and the American agenda.* New York: Cambridge University Press.

Zimring, F., and G. Hawkins. (1997). *Crime is not the problem: Lethal violence in America.* New York: Oxford University Press.

Zinn, H. (2003). *A people's history of the United States.* New York: HarperCollins.

Zuckerman, M. (1994). The limits of the TV lens. *U.S. News & World Report* (July 25): 64.

INDEX

Abortion, 111, 112–13
Abramoff, Jack, 156
Absconding, defined, 211
Academy of Criminal Justice
    Sciences, 340
Acquittal, 63, 211
Acts, defined, 87
Actus reus, defined, 87
ADAM (Arrestee Drug Abuse
    Monitoring), 374
Adelphia Communications, 119
Adjudicators, defined, 208
Administrative law, defined, 61
Administrators, defined, 208
Admissibility of evidence,
    202, 206
Adversarial, defined, 11
AEI (American Enterprise
    Institute), 154
Affirmative defense, defined, 226
Afghanistan, 95, 147, 152, 154–55
African Americans
    arrest rate and, 180, 187–89, 424
    belief in criminality of, 113, 132,
        422–23
    court clients and, 204
    in courtroom workgroups,
        204, 238
    criminal justice network and, 34
    death penalty and, 311, 314, 315,
        316, 344, 345
    drug crimes and, 103, 265, 266,
        365, 389, 390
    drug use and, 185, 266, 388
    health insurance and, 419
    historical notion of black
        inferiority, 431
    income of, 425
    juries and, 347
    in law enforcement, 168
    as lawmakers, 66, 67, 188
    police corruption and, 193
    police discretion and, 181
    police profiling and, 182, 183–84
    police use of force and, 191, 194
    poverty rate and, 179, 180
    preventive detention and,
        211, 441

prison population and, 282, 298,
    299, 300
public defenders and, 222
recidivism and, 257
sentencing and, 260–61, 265, 266
stop rates and, 187
street crimes and, 103, 421, 423
three-strikes laws and, 240
U.S. Constitution and, 60
victimization and, 423
voting behavior and, 71
Age
    of court clients, 204
    death penalty and, 316
    fear of crime and, 144
    police profiling and, 182, 184
    recidivism and, 258
    of state legislators, 67
    street crimes and, 275
    support for capital punishment
        and, 326
    of U.S. Congress members,
        66–67
    voting behavior and, 71
Aggravated assault, defined, 90
Aggravated murders
    death penalty and, 322, 346
    defined, 315
Aggravating factors
    defined, 237
    in sentencing, 237, 238, 343,
        347, 357
AIDS, 401, 403, 427
Alaska, 317
Alcohol, Tobacco, Firearms, and
    Explosives, U.S. Bureau
    of, 166
Alcohol use
    as gateway to illicit drugs,
        381, 400
    harms associated with, 373, 383,
        384, 388, 399
    psychopharmacological
        violence effect and, 384
    trends in, 374, 378
Alibis, defined, 87, 226
Alito, Samuel A., Jr., 217
Al-Qaeda, 38–39, 131, 158

Altria, 105
American Bar Association, 206,
    207, 221, 340
American Civil Liberties
    Union, 80
American Correctional
    Association, 290
American Enterprise Institute
    (AEI), 154
American Medical Association
    (AMA), 144, 320
American Psychological
    Association (APA), 143
American Society of
    Anesthesiologists, 320
American Society of Criminology,
    114–16, 340
Analgesics, 372
Andrade, Leandro, 264
Anecdotal evidence, of
    deterrence, 341
Angelman, Alexa, 104
Anti-Drug Abuse Act of 1986, 388
Anti-Drug Abuse Act of 1988, 388
Antiopium movement, 385
Antipoverty programs, 428
Anti-terrorism and Effective
    Death Penalty Act of
    1996, 77–78, 322
AOL/Time Warner, 119, 126
APA (American Psychological
    Association), 143
AP (Associated Press), 124, 125
Appeals
    antiterrorism laws and, 78
    criminal justice process and, 12
    death penalty and, 310,
        312–14, 347
    defined, 12
    limiting of, 46
    public defenders and, 220
Appellate courts, 201, 202
Arbitrariness, of death penalty
    application, 343–46,
    357, 448
Arkansas, 310
Arraignment, 10–11
Arreola, Jose, 262

Arrestee Drug Abuse Monitoring
    (ADAM), 374
Arrests
    arrest rates, 180, 187–89, 424
    courtroom workgroups and, 209
    criminal justice process and, 8,
        9, 175
    criminal justice resources and, 22
    defined, 9, 186
    discretion and, 180
    for drug crimes, 185, 364, 365,
        368, 370, 390
    gender and, 433, 435, 436
    location of police on streets, 179
    media portrayal of crime
        and, 149
    police corruption and, 193
    police discretion and, 181
    police profiling and, 183, 184
    searched incident to lawful
        arrests, 170
    street crimes compared to
        corporate crime, 103–4
    Uniform Crime Reports
        and, 422
Arson, defined, 90
Arthur Andersen, 102, 119, 137
Ashcroft, John, 216
Assembly line metaphor, 18, 45,
    46, 133, 218
Asset forfeitures
    defined, 364
    war on drugs and, 47, 186, 364,
        366, 368–69, 392
Assigned counsel programs, 23,
    207, 208, 219
Associated Press (AP), 124, 125
Atkins v. Virginia (2002), 342
Attempts, defined, 87
Australia, 110, 111
The Aviation and Transportation
    Security Act, 78

Bagdikian, Ben, 126–27
Bail
    alternatives to, 212, 213
    courts' function and, 202
    criminal justice goals and, 201
    defined, 10, 210
    Eighth Amendment and, 58, 211
    going rates and, 48
    as injustice, 210–14, 447
    recommendations on, 457
    types of, 210
Bailly, Larry, 319
Bail Reform Act of 1984, 211
Barbiturates, 384
Batson v. Kentucky (1986), 225
Beard, Charles, 59
Beccaria, Cesare, 251
Bechtel, 96
Belgium, 110, 111

Bennett, Bill, 113
Bentham, Jeremy, 337–38
Berg, Nick, 142
Berger v. United States (1935), 206
Bertelsmann, 126
Best-bet hypothesis, 341
Beyond a reasonable doubt,
    defined, 11
Bias
    bail and, 211
    in corrections, 297–300, 445, 446
    in courts, 201, 202, 211, 219,
        223, 228–34, 412, 440–41, 445,
        446, 447
    criminal defendants and, 222
    in criminal justice network, 16,
        31, 33, 415, 419–33, 445, 446
    in criminal law, 65, 66, 164, 178,
        223, 344, 424, 445, 446
    innocent bias, 164, 178–86, 344,
        440, 441, 447, 449
    in interest groups, 74
    in law enforcement, 164,
        178–86, 440, 445, 446, 447
    in media portrayal of crime,
        130, 445, 446
    in plea bargaining, 219
    prosecutors and, 207
    in sentencing, 260–67, 412,
        441, 447
    in trials, 223
    in U.S. Constitution, 59, 60
    voir dire and, 224–25
Bible
    capital punishment and, 326,
        331, 332, 334–36
    retribution and, 247, 331, 332
Bieghler, Marvin, 319–20
Bill of Rights, 58, 63, 148
Bill of Rights Defense
    Committee, 80
Binder, Johnny, 230
Bin Laden, Usama, 37, 39
Bispectral index (BIS)
    monitor, 319
BJS. See Bureau of Justice
    Statistics (BJS)
Blackmun, Harry, 329–30
Blacks. See African Americans
Black's Law Dictionary, 186
Bloodworth, Kirk, 351
Blue code of silence, 196
Bohm, Robert, 311, 312, 315, 317,
    322, 330–31, 335, 339,
    346, 348, 351
Bolton, Terrell, 193
Booking, defined, 9
Boot camps, 243, 250, 259
Border control, war on drugs
    and, 363
Boston University Medical
    Center, 378, 380

Bowling for Columbine
    (documentary), 145
Boykin v. Alabama (1969), 220
Brady v. United States (1969), 220
Breyer, Stephen Gerald, 214, 215,
    216, 217
Bright, Steven, 219
Bristol-Myers Squibb, 119
British Broadcasting
    Corporation, 213
Brown, Nicole, 57
Brown, Willie, Jr., 319
Brownsberger, William, 261
Brutalization effect, 339-40, 357
Buchanan, Pat, 428
Bunyard, John, 263
Bureaucratization, 45
Bureau of Justice Assistance, 172
Bureau of Justice Statistics (BJS)
    adult correctional populations,
        245–46, 273, 278
    African Americans and, 298
    collateral damage on inmates
        and, 293
    drug abuse and, 370
    drug crimes and, 265
    face-to-face contact with police
        and, 182
    federal police officers and, 165
    female incarceration rate
        and, 436
    local police officers and, 169
    mental illness and, 280
    National Incident Based
        Reporting System and, 93
    police profiling and, 183, 184
    police use of force and, 191
    public versus private attorneys
        and, 223
    recidivism and, 257
    survey of inmates, 374
    victimization by race, 423
    victimizations and, 106–7
Burger Supreme Court
    (1969–1986), 19
Burglary, defined, 90
Bush, George H. W.
    corporations and, 275
    crime control and, 21, 42, 431
    death penalty and, 342
    Horton and, 451
    war on drugs and, 47, 362,
        386, 390
Bush, George W.
    alleged drug use of, 370
    corporate crime and, 121, 155
    crime control and, 21, 43–44
    death penalty and, 342–43
    domestic spying program and,
        17, 80
    enemy combatants and, 214–15,
        217, 292

Homeland Security Advisory System, 140
Iraq war and, 95, 154, 156
oil industry and, 76
terrorism and, 37, 38, 39, 78, 143
war on drugs and, 47, 365, 390
Bush, Jeb, 319
Buying, receiving, or possessing stolen property, defined, 91

Cable News Network (CNN), 104, 137
Caffeine use, 374
Calculability
criminal justice network and, 47, 445
defined, 45
McDonaldization and, 45
California, 239–40, 241, 262, 291, 310, 316–17, 352
Callins v. James (1994), 329–30
Camp X-Ray, 213–14, 216, 217
Canada, 110, 111, 253, 273
Cantu, Ruben, 348–49
Capitalism, 426
Capital Jury Project, 224, 346–47
Capital punishment. See also Death penalty; Executions
Bible and, 326, 331, 332, 334–36
calculability and, 47
defined, 307
deterrence and, 43, 315, 329, 331, 332, 338–41, 448
expert opinion on, 353–60
history of, 308–15
justifications for, 332–41
politics and, 44
public opinion and, 310, 326–32, 338, 341, 346, 351–52
Texas and, 36, 43
U.S. Supreme Court and, 36, 309, 310–11, 314–15, 319–20, 321, 329, 337, 342, 347, 440
wrongful convictions and, 228
Career criminals, 8, 279, 281
Carjacking, defined, 55
Carter, Nathaniel, 230
Case law
defined, 57, 61
precedents and, 55
Caucasians
arrest rate and, 188
court clients and, 204
death penalty and, 315, 316, 344–45, 412
drug use and, 185, 388–89, 393–94
income of, 425
juries and, 347
as lawmakers, 66, 67

police profiling and, 182, 183, 184
police use of force and, 191
poverty rate and, 179
prison population and, 282, 298, 299, 300
public defenders and, 222
sentencing and, 260, 261
support for capital punishment and, 326
three-strikes laws and, 240
victimization and, 423
voting behavior and, 71
Caveat emptor, 105
Center for Constitutional Rights, 217–18
Center for Environmental Health, 104
Center for Media and Public Affairs (CMPA), 125, 143, 147
Center for Public Integrity, 73
Center for Responsive Politics, 72, 73, 75, 76
Centers for Disease Control and Prevention, 401, 403, 437–38
Central Intelligence Agency (CIA), 79, 213
Cepeda, Michael, 263
Certainty of punishment, 251, 267, 276
Chain gangs, 250, 283, 290
The Challenge of Crime in a Free Society, 13
Challenges for cause, defined, 224
Charge bargaining, defined, 218
Cheney, Richard B., 38–39, 76
Chicken Little phenomenon defined, 143
fear and, 143–46
Children of incarcerated mothers, 437
Children's Defense Fund, 428
Child sex offenders, 36
China, 352
Chivalry or paternalism hypothesis, 433
Christopher Commission, 193
CIA (Central Intelligence Agency), 79, 213
Circles, 254
Circuit courts, defined, 201
Citigroup, 119, 121
Citizen involvement, 7, 8
Citizens Against Government Waste, 96–97
Citizenship and Immigration Services, Bureau of, 166
Civil law
criminal law distinguished from, 53, 63
defined, 63

victimizations and, 179
Civil liberties
erosion of, 21, 44, 80, 152, 157, 367
racial discrimination and, 439–42
USA PATRIOT Act and, 79
war on drugs and, 367
war on terror and, 17, 19
Civil liberties safe zones, 79
Civil Rights Act of 1964, 439
Civil rights movement
achievements of, 439
characterized as crime, 41, 433
racism and, 429–30
Clark, Joseph, 320
Class discrimination
criminal justice network and, 33, 419, 421
death penalty and, 343, 344, 356
due process model and, 18
jail population and, 280
jury service and, 225
justice and, 28
label of crime and, 31
market economy and, 432
police profiling and, 48
in sentencing, 260, 266–67
war on crime and, 413
war on drugs and, 400
Clear, Todd, 272, 275
Clearing a case by arrest, defined, 8
Clinton, Bill
alleged drug use of, 370
crime control and, 21, 42, 146
crime rates and, 174
executions and, 310
health insurance and, 419
incarceration rate and, 32
war on drugs and, 47, 390
Clinton, Hillary, 419
Closing arguments, 226, 226–27
CMPA (Center for Media and Public Affairs), 125, 143, 147
Coca-Cola, 118–19
Cocaine
crack cocaine, 385, 386–90, 406, 440
dangerous substances added to, 393
harms associated with, 373, 383, 384, 399
importation of, 397
myths associated with, 402
use of, 375, 377, 406, 407, 408, 409
Codify, defined, 53
Coercion, defined, 220
Cohan, Ethan, 196–97
Cohen, Jeff, 158
Cold crimes, defined, 8, 175
Cole, Ervin, 263

Coleman, Tom, 193
Collateral damage, defined, 293
Collective conscience, defined, 70
Collective incapacitation, 249
Colleges of crime, 295
Colombia, 394
Columbia Law School, 348
Columbine High School, 136
Commerce, U.S. Department of, 117
Commercialized vice, defined, 92
Common Cause, 75
Common law
    corporate crime and, 100
    defined, 61
    as type of law, 61, 63
Community
    intrusive law enforcement and, 186
    prosecutors and, 206
    treatment programs, 280
Community corrections, defined, 271
Community defender organization, defined, 208
Community Epidemiology Work Group (CEWG), 386, 387
Community policing
    crime prevention and, 171–75
    defined, 171
    recommendations on, 456
    zero-tolerance policing contrasted with, 194
Community service, 243, 254
Comprehensive Drug Abuse Prevention and Control Act of 1970, 372
Conaway, Charles, 418
Conditional release
    as bail alternative, 212, 213
    defined, 213
Conferencing, 254
Confessions
    false confessions, 233, 350
    Miranda warning and, 20
Confidentiality, 177
Conflicts of interest, 67
Conflict view of the law, 65–66
Connecticut, 283
Consensus view of the law, defined, 64
Conspiracy, defined, 87
Constitutional law, 57, 58–60
Constitutional protections
    Constitutional law and, 58–60
    criminal law and, 64
    defense attorneys and, 207
    due process and, 3, 58
    due process model and, 18, 21
    media portrayal of crime and, 133, 151
    plea bargaining and, 218, 220

police corruption and, 192, 194
    prosecutors and, 206
    role of police and, 169, 180
    unwarranted government interference and, 24
    war on drugs and, 367, 390, 391–92
Consumer countries, defined, 394
Consumer Product Safety Commission, 104–5
Contextual discrimination, 420, 421, 447
Contracting attorney programs, 23, 207, 208, 219
Control. See also Crime control; Crime control model; Population control; Social control
    criminal justice network and, 49–50, 445
    defined, 45
    McDonaldization and, 45
Controlled Substances Act (CSA), 372–73
Convict School of Criminology, 290, 301–3
Corporate crime
    crime information and, 117–18
    crime rates and, 86
    elite deviance and, 94
    harms associated with, 65, 76, 99–100, 102–3, 120, 129, 137, 412
    media coverage of, 127, 129, 137
    Model Penal Code and, 100–101
    prosecution of, 103, 104, 105, 111
    ratio of police to criminals, 8
    scandals and, 118–21, 137, 155
    sentencing and, 267
    street crimes compared to, 76, 103–4, 120, 137
Corporate violence, defined, 94
Corporate welfare, 96
Corporations
    media owned by, 125, 126–27
    taxation of, 275, 418, 428–29
Corrections. See also Incarceration; Jails; Prisons
    adult correctional populations, 245–46, 271–72, 448
    bias in, 297–300, 445, 446
    calculability and, 47
    control and, 49
    corruption and, 196
    criminal justice process and, 12–13
    criminal justice resources and, 21, 22, 24, 25, 46, 219, 445
    criminal law and, 66
    efficiency and, 46
    employees of, 6, 22, 23, 32

law enforcement and, 165
    media portrayal of crime and, 133, 134
    organization of, 271
    predictability and, 49
    problems with, 441
    recommendations on, 458–59
    responsibilities of, 5, 6
    risk classification in, 49
    war on drugs and, 390–91
Corrections Corporation of America, 32
Corrective justice
    defined, 18
    emphasis on, 19
    lack of achievement of, 179
Corruption
    bribery and, 196
    in criminal justice network, 195–98
    defined, 192
    drug crimes and, 185–86, 192, 193, 196
    law enforcement and, 192–95
    minorities affected by, 440
    police and, 180, 185–86, 192–98, 440
    war on drugs and, 196, 392, 397
Counsel, right to, 58
Counterfeiting, defined, 91
Courthouse regulars
    criminal justice resources and, 456
    defined, 207
    indigent clients and, 208
Courtroom workgroup
    bail and, 212
    characteristics of, 48, 204–5, 448, 456
    defense attorneys and, 205, 207–8, 210
    defined, 205
    effects on justice, 205, 223
    ethics and, 5
    judges and, 205, 208–9
    power in, 202, 206, 412, 448
    prosecutors and, 205–6
Courts. See also Federal courts; State courts; U.S. Supreme Court
    bias in, 201, 202, 211, 219, 223, 228–34, 412, 440–41, 445, 446, 447
    calculability and, 47
    characteristics of clients, 204
    convictions by gender, 434, 436
    courtroom workgroup and, 204–9
    crimes defined by, 55
    criminal justice resources and, 21, 22, 24, 46, 219, 445, 456
    criminal law and, 66
    drug crimes and, 185, 203, 448

efficiency and, 46
employees of, 6, 22–23
function of, 202
law enforcement and, 165, 169
organization of, 201–2
power imbalance in, 209–10, 412
predictability and, 48–49
preventive procedures and,
    210–21
public versus private attorneys,
    221–23
recommendations on, 456–58
responsibilities of, 4–5, 6
television in, 133
trial as exceptional case and,
    223–27
types of crimes handled by,
    203–4
war on drugs and, 369,
    390–91 Court TV, 133
Credit Suisse First Boston
        Corporation, 119, 121
Crime. See also Media portrayal
    of crime; Reducing
    crime; Victims of crime;
    War on crime
  causes of, 42
  comparison of harms associated
    with crimes and noncrimes,
    99–100, 102–6
  conceptions of, 94–97
  criminal justice process and,
    7–8
  defined, 7, 17, 86
  drug use linked with, 366, 367,
    368, 384, 385, 391
  label of, 31, 53–54, 57, 62, 65–66,
    98, 99, 102, 105, 127, 413
  legal definition of, 86, 87–89, 92,
    105–6, 445, 452–53
  natural definition of, 86
  politics defining, 36, 107, 114
  seriousness of, 64–65, 86, 89–94,
    105, 107, 188, 223, 238, 260, 412,
    415, 417
  social reality of, 36, 86
  sources of information on,
    106–18, 422
  types of, 89–100, 102–6
Crime analysis, defined, 173
Crime control
  defined, 3
  due process and, 64, 80
  industry and, 32
  juries and, 346
  reducing crime and, 14
Crime control model
  bail and, 212
  basis of, 296
  criminal justice resources and,
    22–23, 24
  defined, 18

due process model compared
    to, 18, 21, 218
  media portrayal of crime and,
    133–34, 149, 150, 151, 446
  politics and, 19, 42, 43, 44, 149
  shift toward, 3–4, 19, 21, 417, 445
  terrorism and, 77
  war on crime and, 413
Crime prevention
  community policing and,
    171–75
  criminal justice resources
    and, 25
  defined, 14
  politics and, 39, 42
  punishment and, 255
  recommendations on, 460
  role of police and, 168
  studies of, 258–59
Crime rates
  crime control model and, 18
  criminal justice resources
    and, 24
  incarceration rate and, 274, 275,
    276, 295
  media portrayal of crime
    and, 149
  police's effect on, 171, 174
  politics and, 41, 44
  property crimes and, 108, 109,
    110, 174, 274, 275
  public opinion and, 113–14,
    139, 145
  public perception of, 130
  three-strikes laws and, 240, 265
  Uniform Crime Reports, 90, 107
  validity of, 107
  violent crimes and, 32, 47, 86,
    108, 109, 174, 275
Crimes associated with a drug-
        using lifestyle, 366
Crimes by any other name,
        defined, 94
Crimes known to the police
  defined, 106
  media portrayal of crime
    and, 135
  percentage of, 169
  property crimes and, 107, 108
  Uniform Crime Reports
    and, 422
  violent crimes and, 107, 108
Crimes of privilege, defined, 94
Crimes of the state, defined, 94
Crime tariff, defined, 391
Crime trends
  defined, 107
  factors affecting, 111
  media portrayal of crime and,
    138–39
  street crimes and, 111–14
Criminalblackman, 422

Criminal class, media portrayal of
        crime, 137
Criminal conviction, defined, 63
Criminal homicide, defined, 90
Criminal justice goals
  achievement of, 25, 448
  alternative goals, 30, 31–33, 279,
    445, 450
  criminal justice network and, 6
  doing justice, 14–15, 19, 31, 44,
    114, 148, 179, 198, 412, 420,
    445–49
  government statement of, 13
  performance assessment
    and, 450
  planned change and, 40
  population control and, 30, 31,
    33, 445
  reducing crime, 14, 19, 31, 44,
    114, 164, 180, 198, 412, 445–49
  serving limited interests and,
    30, 31, 33, 60, 279, 445
  social justice and, 465
Criminal justice network
  bias in, 16, 31, 33, 415, 419–33,
    445, 446
  corruption in, 195–98
  criminal justice resources and,
    22–23, 114
  defined, 6
  efficiency and, 45–46, 172, 445
  functions achieved by, 33–34
  gender discrimination and, 16,
    419, 433–38
  ideology underlying, 31, 35–36,
    43, 44
  inner cities and, 24–25, 189, 412
  McDonaldization of, 45–50, 445
  media portrayal of crime
    and, 150
  minorities and, 16, 30, 34,
    419–33
  myth of leniency, 111
  politics and, 31, 35–36, 195, 417,
    442, 451
  protection of innocent citizens
    and, 24
  racial discrimination and, 33,
    300, 421, 429–33, 439–42
  reforms for, 302–3
  role of, 6
  typical crime processed
    through, 6, 7–13
Criminal justice process
  appeal and, 12
  arraignment and, 10–11
  arrest and, 8, 9, 175
  Bill of Rights and, 58, 63
  booking and, 9
  corrections and, 12–13
  due process and, 58
  fairness and, 5, 7, 15

Criminal justice process
(*continued*)
impartiality and, 5, 15
initial appearance and, 9–10
investigation and, 8–9
media portrayal of crime
and, 133
police and, 6, 7–8
politics and, 44
power and, 195
preliminary hearing/grand jury,
10, 205
release and, 13
sentencing and, 12
trial and, 11–12
typical process, 7–13
Criminal justice resources
distribution of, 21, 22–24, 46,
219, 221–22, 258, 445, 454, 458
expansion in, 114, 277
source of, 23–24
three-strikes laws and, 239–40
war on drugs and, 362, 363
Criminal justice system. *See also*
Criminal justice network
definition of system and, 4, 5–6
interdependent components
of, 4–5
Criminal law. *See also* Law
enforcement
bias in, 65, 66, 164, 178, 223, 300,
344, 424, 445, 446
civil law distinguished from,
53, 63
crime as violation of, 7
defined, 61
failure to protect Americans,
74–76
legal definition of crime and, 86,
87–89, 105–6, 445
power and, 66, 98
purpose of, 64–66
recommendations on, 452–53
types of, 61, 63
Criminal procedure, rules of, 58,
66, 205
Criminal sanctions. *See also*
Intermediate sanctions;
Punishment
criminal law and, 414
defined, 242
Criminal subcultures, 366
Crop eradication
defined, 364
war on drugs and, 363–64
Cruel and unusual punishment
capital punishment as, 342
Eighth Amendment and, 58,
308, 309, 311
lethal injection and, 317, 319–21
Marshall hypothesis and, 328,
329–31
Cruz, Rolando, 351

Culpability
defined, 89
media portrayal of crime
and, 137
victimization and, 98–99, 178,
179, 454
Cultural perspectives, 426–27
Curfew violations and loitering,
defined, 92
Curtis, Dennis, 26–28
Customs and Border Protection,
Bureau of, 166

Damiens, Robert-François, 321–22
Dark figure of crime
defined, 8, 106
National Crime Victimization
Survey and, 108
Darwin, Charles, 87
Davis, Robert, 192
DAWN (Drug Abuse Warning
Network), 374, 375, 377
Day reporting centers,
defined, 243
DEA (Drug Enforcement
Agency), 367, 381
Death penalty. *See also* Capital
punishment; Executions
antiterrorism laws and, 77–78
costs of, 352
defense attorneys and, 208, 351
as deterrence, 250, 315, 316,
322, 343
facts on, 315–26
as incapacitation, 249
jury instructions and, 227
media portrayal of crime
and, 143
minorities and, 207, 311, 316,
344, 412, 429, 441, 448
offenses punishable by death,
322, 323–26, 340
politics and, 36, 43, 313–14, 338,
342–43, 351
problems with administration
of death, 341–52
racial discrimination and,
343–46, 355–56
recommendations on, 459
Rehnquist Supreme Court
and, 19
trends in application of, 308–9
voir dire and, 224
wrongful convictions and,
312–14, 329, 347–52, 356
Death Penalty Information
Center, 321, 343,
347–48, 351
Death-qualified juries, 346–47
Death row inmates
demographics of, 344–45
population trends, 310, 315, 316,
317, 318

wrongful convictions and,
347–52
Decertification, defined, 394
Decision making
criminal justice system and, 5
of juries, 346
police discretion and, 180
police profiling and, 182
Declaration of Independence,
16, 221
Decriminalization of drugs
defined, 397–98
drug abuse levels and, 400,
401–2
harm reduction and, 403
medical problem of drug abuse
and, 401
as policy alternative, 87, 394
Decriminalization of victimless
crimes, 279, 453
Deeb, Muneer, 349
Defense, U.S. Department of, 374
Defense and Homeland Security
Appropriations Acts,
96–97
Defense attorneys. *See also*
Private attorneys; Public
defenders
bail and, 211
closing arguments and, 226–27
courtroom workgroups and,
205, 207–8, 210
criminal justice resources and,
221–22
death penalty cases and, 208, 351
defined, 207
media portrayal of crime
and, 134
peremptory challenges and, 224
power of, 209–10
predictability and, 48
presentation of case, 226
Defenses, valid defenses, 87–88
Democratic Party
crime control model and, 42, 43
due process model and, 19
money in federal elections and,
72, 73
money in state elections
and, 74
oil and gas money and, 76
tobacco money and, 75
Denmark, 110, 111
Depressants, 371, 372
Deprivation of goods and
services, 292
Deregulation, defined, 104
Destutt de Tracy, Antoine, 35
Determinate sentences,
defined, 237
Deterrence
capital punishment and, 43, 315,
329, 331, 332, 338–41, 448

death penalty and, 250, 315, 316, 322, 343
defined, 250, 338
expert opinion on, 354–55, 359
imprisonment and, 295
as justification for punishment, 250–52, 447
legalization of drugs and, 398
motivation of criminals and, 251, 252, 256, 338–39
punishment and, 47, 237
recommendations on, 458
sentence certainty and, 48
war on drugs and, 391
Devlin, Patrick, 247
Diallo, Amadou, 191
Difference principle, 462
Differential association theory, 149
Differential opportunity, defined, 428
Differential reinforcement theory, 149
Directed verdict, defined, 226
Discretion
death penalty and, 345–46
defined, 7, 180
of police, 176, 180–81, 346, 440, 447
of prosecutors, 207, 209, 238, 261, 343, 346, 440–41, 448
stops and, 187
use of force and, 190
Discretionary releases, 296
Discrimination. See also Class discrimination; Gender discrimination; Racial discrimination
contextual discrimination, 420, 421, 447
death penalty and, 343–46
defined, 343
degrees of, 421
due process model and, 18
individual discrimination, 421
institutional discrimination, 385, 420, 421, 432
recommendations on, 450
systematic discrimination, 420, 421, 430
Disorderly conduct, defined, 92
Disparities
in criminal justice network, 429
death penalty and, 343–45, 440
defined, 297, 343
innocent bias and, 344, 440, 441, 449
war on drugs and, 369, 385, 388, 389–90, 393–94, 397, 400
Displacement model, 395–96
District courts, defined, 201
Dixon, Vallerie Ann Roberson, 319
DNA exoneration cases, 231

DNA tests, 348, 349, 351
Doing justice
courtroom workgroups and, 205
as criminal justice goal, 14–15, 19, 31, 44, 114, 148, 179, 198, 412, 420, 445–49
defined, 14
Domestic violence, 437–38
Dope fiend mythology, 368
Double jeopardy, 58, 63, 201
Dragnet approach, 25
Draper v. United States (1959), 186
Driving under the influence, defined, 92
Drug abuse
decriminalization and, 400, 401–2
drug use distinguished from, 370–71
as medical problem, 401
nicotine use and, 378–80
outcomes of, 371
war on drugs and, 398
Drug abuse violations, defined, 92
Drug Abuse Warning Network (DAWN), 374, 375, 377
Drug courts, 259, 401
Drug crimes. See also War on drugs
African Americans and, 103, 265, 266, 365, 389, 390
arrests and, 185, 364, 365, 368, 370, 390
courts and, 185, 203, 448
incarceration rate and, 273, 365, 449
innocent bias and, 184–86
law enforcement and, 165, 365
location of police on streets and, 179
media portrayal of crime and, 139
plea bargaining and, 219
police profiling and, 184
preventive detention and, 213
prison population and, 278, 279, 281, 298, 300
probation and, 242
rearrest and, 213
recidivism and, 257
sentencing and, 261, 265, 266
three-strikes laws and, 265
Drug-defined crimes, 366
Drug Enforcement Administration, 79, 166, 362
Drug Enforcement Agency (DEA), 367, 381
Drug Policy Alliance, 196
Drug prevention education
decriminalization and, 398, 400
legalization and, 399
war on drugs and, 364, 365
Drug-related crimes, defined, 366

Drugs. See also War on drugs
availability of, 375, 377, 378, 398
classification system for, 373
definition of, 369–71
examples of, 372
harms associated with, 378–84
legal status of, 372, 384–90, 391
types of, 371–73
Drug treatment
availability of, 303, 365, 378
cost effectiveness of, 401
funding of, 273
legalization and, 399
reducing drug use and, 259
reducing recidivism and, 286
war on drugs and, 364, 365
Drug use
crime linked with, 366, 367, 368, 384, 385, 391
deaths attributed to, 375, 377, 378, 383, 392–93, 404
definition of drug and, 369–71
drug abuse distinguished from, 370–71
drug scares and, 385–86
emergency room mentions of, 375, 377, 383, 392
extent of, 373–78
harm reduction and, 402, 403
harms associated with, 368, 373, 378–84, 401–2
health and social costs of, 363
myths about, 368
plea bargaining and, 46
poverty and the poor, 31
punishment for, 44
rate of, 47
trends in, 375, 376, 377, 404, 405, 406–9
war on drugs and, 362, 363, 398
Drunkenness, defined, 92
Dual court system, defined, 201
Dualistic fallacy, 127
Dubner, Stephen, 112–13
Due process
capital punishment and, 342
common law and, 61
Constitutional protections and, 3, 58
crime control and, 64, 80
defense attorneys and, 207
defined, 3, 17
efficiency and, 46
juries and, 346
legal technicalities and, 206
Due Process Clause, 58
Due process model
crime control model compared to, 18, 21, 218
criminal justice resources and, 22, 24
defined, 18

Due process model (*continued*)
  media portrayal of crime and,
    133, 134, 149, 150, 151
  recommendations for, 450
  terrorism and, 77
  wrongful convictions and, 19, 347
Dukakis, Michael, 42, 342, 451
Duress, as excuse, 88

Early release programs, 42
Easley, Mike, 321
Economic compulsive
    homicides, 366
Ecstasy, 373, 375
Educational level
  court clients and, 204
  jail population and, 280
  plea bargaining and, 219
  poverty and the poor, 428
  prison population and, 281, 298
  recidivism and, 258
  support for capital punishment
    and, 327
  voting behavior and, 71
Educational programs, 34, 277,
    294, 303, 459
Efficiency
  crime control model and, 18,
    42, 45
  criminal justice network and,
    45–46, 172, 445
  defined, 45
  McDonaldization and, 45
Eighth Amendment
  bail and, 58, 211
  cruel and unusual punishment
    and, 58, 308, 309, 311
  USA PATRIOT Act and, 79
Eisenhower Commission, 13
Electronic monitoring, 243, 259
Elite deviance
  conceptions of crime and, 94–97
  crime information and, 109,
    117–18, 453
  defined, 94
  harms associated with, 99, 102,
    105, 117, 146, 165, 203, 412, 421,
    445, 446
  lack of focus on, 99, 121, 412,
    424–25
  law enforcement and, 165
  media portrayal of crime and,
    127, 446
  sentencing and, 267
  in state and federal courts,
    203, 204
  war on drugs and, 390
Embezzlement, defined, 91
Employees, of criminal justice
    network, 6, 22–23, 32
Employment programs, 25, 277, 303
Enforcing laws, defined, 168

England, 110, 111, 173–74, 253, 273
Enron, 102, 119, 121, 137, 155, 418
Entrapment, as procedural
    defense, 88
Environmental racism, 417
Equal opportunity, illusion of, 431
Equal opportunity principle, 462
Equal Protection Clause, 58, 342
Escalation, defined, 248
Estonia, 110
Ethics
  police and, 176–77
  responsibilities and, 5
Ethnicity. *See also* Minorities
  police profiling and, 48
  voting behavior and, 71
European Union, 110
Evidence
  admissibility of, 202, 206
  exclusionary rule and, 17,
    170–71, 206
  preponderance of, 63
  prosecutors and, 205–6
Evidentiary requirements, 17, 63,
    170–71
Evil woman hypothesis, 435
Ewing v. California (2003), 241
Excessive bail or fines, 58, 211
Exclusionary rule
  defined, 169, 170
  evidence and, 17, 170–71, 206
  law enforcement and, 170–71
  Rehnquist Supreme Court
    and, 19
  wrongful convictions and, 71
Excuses
  defined, 88
  as valid defenses, 88
Executions
  brutalization effect and, 339
  geographical distribution of, 343
  lessening cruelty of, 308, 317
  lethal injection and, 317, 319–21
  methods of, 317–22, 327–28
  moratorium on, 358
  by state, 316, 317
  trends in, 308, 309
  wrongful executions and, 312
Executive clemency, 347
Exigent circumstances, defined, 170
Ex-offender assistance, 254
Expert, defined, 353
Expert opinion, on capital
    punishment, 353–60
Extra Sensory Political
    Participation (ESP), 71
Eyewitness testimony, wrongful
    convictions and, 228,
    229, 231–32, 348, 351

Factually guilty, 19
Fagan, Jeffrey, 312–14

Failures to act, defined, 87
Fair Housing Act of 1968, 439
Fairness
  Constitutional protections
    and, 58
  criminal justice process and, 5,
    7, 15
  death penalty and, 311, 343
  due process model and, 18, 19
  justice and, 15–16, 17, 461, 463
  Justitia and, 26, 28
  prosecutors and, 206
  punishment and, 248
  in sentencing, 260
Fairness and Accuracy in
    Reporting (FAIR), 154
False confessions, 233, 350
Falsification of police reports, 192
Families
  of condemned prisoners,
    336–37, 357
  effects of imprisonment on, 295
  of murder victims, 337, 354
Family skills training, 303
Fastow, Andrew, 121
Faust, Frederic, 333
FBI. *See* Federal Bureau of
    Investigation (FBI)
Feagin, Joe, 59, 60
Fear
  corrections and, 46
  criminal justice resources and, 24
  legal definition of crime
    and, 105
  media portrayal of crime and,
    43, 114, 132, 139, 142, 143–46,
    148, 302, 446
  politics and, 14, 37, 43, 146, 151
  serious crime and, 89
  support for capital punishment
    and, 327
  terrorism and, 43, 113, 141,
    142, 145
Fedderson, David, 229
Federal Bureau of Investigation
    (FBI)
  civil rights movement and, 41
  corporate crime and, 121
  employees of, 165
  law enforcement and, 166
  preventive detention and, 213
  spending on war on drugs, 362
  terrorism and, 165
  Uniform Crime Reports and,
    89, 91, 106
  USA PATRIOT Act and, 79–80
  white-collar crime and, 117
Federal Bureau of Prisons, 165, 166
Federal courts. *See also* U.S.
    Supreme Court
  defense attorneys and, 208
  jurisdiction of, 201

punishment statistics, 244
rearrest and, 213
types of crimes handled by,
203, 223
Federal Defender
Organization, 208
Federal government
crime information collected
by, 106
criminal justice resources and,
23, 24, 34
death penalty offenses, 322,
324–26
general recommendations,
450–52
Homeland Security Advisory
System and, 140
inner cities and, 34
law enforcement agencies of,
165, 166–67
legal definition of crime and,
105–6
sentencing guidelines, 238
spending on war on drugs,
363, 364
Federal Trade Commission, 104
Ferguson, Malcolm, 191
Field training officers (FTOs),
defined, 182
Fifth Amendment
double jeopardy and, 12,
58, 201
USA PATRIOT Act and, 79
Filtering, 7, 9
Fines, 259
Finland, 110
First Amendment, 79
Fixed sentences, defined, 237
Fleischer, Ari, 38
Florida
death penalty and, 36, 343, 352
executions and, 319
incarceration in, 260
myths concerning prisons,
283–86
sentencing and, 436
silly statutes and, 54
Food and Drug Administration
(FDA), 104–5, 392–93
Force, use of
code of conduct and, 176
continuum of, 189, 190
law enforcement and, 189–92
limits on, 189
police corruption and, 194, 198
police discretion and, 180,
181, 440
police profiling and, 183
stops and, 187
Forcible rape, defined, 90
Forgery and counterfeiting,
defined, 91

Formal social control, 172, 173
Fourteenth Amendment, 58, 311
Fourth Amendment
exclusionary rule and, 170
unreasonable searches and
seizures and, 58
USA PATRIOT Act and, 79
France, 110, 111, 273
Franklin, Benjamin, 60, 80
Fraud
defined, 91
preventive detention and, 213
sentencing and, 266
Freedom
due process model and, 18, 21
ideals of, 16
media portrayal of crime and,
150–51
French Revolution, 322
FTOs (field training officers), 182
Fuller, Kenneth, 263
Fully secured bail, defined, 210
Furman, William Henry, 310–11
Furman v. Georgia (1972), 309,
310–11, 313, 316, 318,
329–31

Gain time, elimination of, 46
Gambling, defined, 92
Gandhi, Mahatma, 333
Gans, Herbert, 33, 65, 413–14,
415, 419
Garcetti, Gil, 198
Garcia, Michael, 240
Garza, David, 349
Gates, Robert, 213–14
Gateway drug hypothesis,
381, 400
Gattis, Dan, 37
Geidel, Paul, 241
Gender
arrests and, 433, 435, 436
capital punishment and,
308, 315
court clients and, 204
in courtroom workgroups, 204
death penalty and, 316
fear of crime and, 144
incarceration and, 435, 436–37
in law enforcement, 168
police profiling and, 182,
183, 184
police use of force and, 190
prison population and, 298,
299–300
recidivism and, 257
of state legislators, 67
support for capital punishment
and, 326
of U.S. Congress members, 66
victimization and, 433, 434
voting behavior and, 71

Gender discrimination
criminal justice network and,
16, 419, 433–38
death penalty and, 343, 344
due process model and, 18
justice and, 28
police discretion and, 181
police profiling and, 48
in sentencing, 434
General Accounting Office, 185,
196, 345
General deterrence, 250, 338
General Electric (GE), 126
General incapacitation, 249
General jurisdiction, defined, 201
General Social Survey (GSS), 431
Geneva Conventions, 215, 217
Geographical disparity, capital
punishment and, 343, 357
Georgia, 311, 315
Germany, 273
"Get tough" environment
capital punishment and, 342
Constitutional protections
and, 169
media portrayal of crime
and, 150
minorities and, 441–42
overzealousness and, 234, 275
parole and, 13
police and, 440
politics and, 36, 39, 42, 43–44,
111, 276, 278, 342–43
prosecutors and, 206–7
war on drugs and, 389
Ghetto poor, defined, 413
Gideon v. Wainwright (1963),
208, 222
Gilmore, Gary, 309
Gingrich, Newt, 428
Ginsburg, Ruth Bader, 214, 215,
216, 217
Global Crossing, 119
Going rates
defined, 48, 211
plea bargaining and, 218–19
Goldman, Ronald, 57
Goldman Sachs, 119
Goldwater, Barry, 41
Good faith exception, defined, 170
Goods and services, deprivation
of, 292
Gore, Al, 43, 342–43
Gottlieb, Gerald, 309
Governmental deviance,
defined, 94
Graham, Gary, 350, 351
Grand jury, criminal justice
process and, 10, 205
Grant, Ulysses S., 60
Gray, James, 239, 266, 367
Greenspan, Alan, 417

Gregg v. Georgia (1976), 309, 311, 330, 337
Griffin, Larry, 349
Group A offenses, 92, 93–94, 106
Group B offenses, 92, 94, 106
GSS (General Social Survey), 431
Guantánamo Bay, Cuba, 213, 216, 217
Guilty pleas
  bail and, 212
  plea bargaining and, 219–20
Gun control, 143

Habeas corpus petitions, 78, 215, 216, 217
Halliburton, 96
Hallucinogens, 371, 372, 375
Hamdan, Salim Ahmed, 217
Hamdan v. Rumsfeld (2006), 217
Hamdi, Yaser, 214–15
Hamdi et al v. Rumsfeld et al (2003), 214–15
Hamilton, Alexander, 60
Hancock, John, 60
Harm reduction, 402, 403, 452
Harris, Donald, 320
Harris, Robert Alton, 310
Hart, H. L. A., 237, 247*Harvard Law Review*, 207
Hate groups, 145
Hawaii, 317
Health insurance, 419
Henry, Patrick, 60
Herndon, Clarice, 230
Heroin, 373, 375, 376, 383, 384, 393, 399
Herrera v. Collins (1993), 347
Heterosexual relationships, deprivation of, 291
Hewitt, Brian, 196, 197
Hicks, James, 229
Higher level courts, 202
Hill, Clarence, 319, 320
Hispanics
  court clients and, 204
  death penalty and, 316, 344, 345
  drug crimes and, 365, 390
  drug use and, 185
  health insurance and, 419
  income of, 425
  in law enforcement, 168
  as lawmakers, 66, 67
  police corruption and, 193
  police discretion and, 181
  police profiling and, 182, 183, 184
  police use of force and, 191
  preventive detention and, 211
  prison population and, 282, 298, 299, 300
  public defenders and, 222
  sentencing and, 260, 261, 266

stop rates and, 187
  victimization and, 423
  voting behavior and, 71
HIV, 401, 403
Hobbes, Thomas, 64, 65
Holmes, Oliver Wendell, 247
Homeland Security, U.S. Department of
  Homeland Security Advisory System, 140–41
  law enforcement and, 165, 166–67
  USA PATRIOT Act and, 79
Homeland Security Advisory System, 140–41
Homelessness, 137, 156, 395
Horizontal bargaining, defined, 218
Horton, Marvin, 349
Horton, Willie, 42, 138, 431–32, 451
Hot spots of crime, defined, 174
House arrest, defined, 243
House counsel for police, defined, 206
Housing programs, 34
Houston, Sam, 60
Huffington, Arriana, 418
Human rights, 463, 464
Human rights violations
  in prisons, 290–91
  war on drugs and, 401
Human Rights Watch, 291
Hung jury, defined, 227
Hurst, Gerald, 350
Hussein, Saddam, 37–38, 39, 152, 156, 157, 158
Hypnotics, 372

IACP (International Association of Chiefs of Police), 89, 175, 176–77, 190, 455
ICVS (International Crime Victims Survey), 109–10
Idaho, 310
Ideology
  criminal justice network and, 31, 35–36, 43, 44
  defined, 35
  media portrayal of crime and, 138, 150
  policy development and, 41–43
  Political Action Committees and, 72
  politics and, 35, 37
  terrorism and, 37, 39
  war on drugs and, 367
  war on terror and, 153
ImClone, 119–20
Imitation
  defined, 148
  peer culture and, 148–49
Immaturity, as excuse, 88

Immigration and Customs Enforcement, 166–67
Immigration and Nationality Act of 1965, 439
Immigration and Naturalization Service, 79
Immigration offenses, 278, 440
Impartiality
  criminal justice process and, 5, 15
  justice and, 15–16, 17
  Justitia and, 26
  police duties and, 176
  punishment and, 248
  voir dire and, 224–25
Impartial jury, 58
Imprisonment. *See also* Incarceration; Life imprisonment without the possibility of parole (LWOP)
  boom in, 273, 274
  pain of imprisonment, 283, 294–96
  political imprisonment, 290
  rate of, 272–73, 298
Incapacitation
  capital punishment and, 329, 331, 332, 341
  expert opinion on, 355, 359
  as justification for punishment, 248–49, 447
Incarceration. *See also* Imprisonment
  costs of, 243, 249, 277
  defined, 243
  destructive nature of, 12
  as deterrence, 250
  drug crimes and, 273, 365, 449
  gender and, 435, 436–37
  likelihood of, 255, 256, 257, 423
  rate of, 32, 42, 44, 46, 47, 111, 245, 271–77, 282, 295–96, 302, 448
  statistics on, 244
  trends in, 278
  war on crime and, 414, 415
Inciardi, James, 366, 385, 397, 400
Incident-driven policing, defined, 171
Income
  defined, 425
  stigmatization and, 293–94
  voting behavior and, 71
Income inequality, 417–18, 427, 451, 462
Indeterminate sentences, 48, 238
Indiana, 326
Indictment, defined, 10, 205
Indigents
  court-appointed counsel for, 23, 207–8, 457

criminal justice resources
    and, 219
defined, 204
plea bargaining and, 220
quality of legal service for, 210
as typical defendants, 208
Individual discrimination, 421
Industry, crime control and, 32
Inevitable discovery, defined, 170
Infant mortality rates, 432
Informal social control,
    defined, 172
Information, defined, 10, 205
Inhalants, 371–72
Initial appearance
criminal justice process and,
    9–10
defined, 10, 210
Inner cities
criminal justice network and,
    24–25, 189, 412
intrusive law enforcement
    and, 186
location of police in, 179,
    412, 447
police corruption and, 194
police profiling and, 184
programs for, 25, 34
residential segregation and,
    426, 430
victimization and, 423
Inner ring of the media
corporate ownership of media
    and, 126
coverage of terrorism and, 153
crime information and, 124–25,
    127, 149, 446
defined, 124
peer culture and, 157
Innocence, presumption of, 192,
    211–12, 223, 226
Innocent bias
defined, 178
disparities and, 344, 440, 441, 449
drug crimes and, 184–86
focus on certain types of crimes,
    178–79
in law enforcement, 164,
    178–86, 447
location of police on streets,
    179–80
police discretion and, 180–81
police profiling and, 181–84
Innovation, defined, 427–28
Insanity, as excuse, 88
Inspections, law enforcement, 165
Institute on Money in State
    Politics, 73–74
Institutional corrections,
    defined, 271
Institutional discrimination, 385,
    420, 432

Institutional racism, 430–32
Integrity, police and, 177
Intentional acts
culpability and, 99
defined, 89
harms associated with, 100
Interdiction efforts
defined, 364
war on drugs and, 363–64
Interest groups. See also Serving
    limited interests; Special
    interests
defined, 74
Intermediate sanctions
defined, 243, 271
recommendations on, 458–59
statistics on, 244–45
types of, 243
Internal Revenue Service
    (IRS), 167
International Association of
    Chiefs of Police (IACP),
    89, 175, 176–77, 190, 455
International Crime Victims
    Survey (ICVS), 109–10
Internet, as news source, 129
Investigation
criminal justice process and, 8–9
law enforcement and, 165, 169
police profiling and, 182
Involuntary intoxication, as
    excuse, 88
Iowa, 317
Iran, 352
Iraq
death penalty and, 352
defense budget and, 95–96
media coverage of war on
    terror and, 137, 147, 152, 153,
    154–58
rebuilding effort in, 121
Iraq Study Group Report, 95
IRS (Internal Revenue
    Service), 167
Irwin, John, 301

Jackson, Andrew, 60
Jackson, Jesse, 422, 423
Jails
bail and, 211–12
characteristics of population,
    280, 282
crimes committed within
    and, 249
defined, 12–13, 243, 271
drug crimes and, 185, 365
Japan, 110
Jefferson, Thomas, 60, 247
Jeffery, C. Ray, 257, 267–69, 333,
    334, 337
Jessica's Law, 36–37
John Paul II (pope), 335

Johnson, Cladius, 262–63
Johnson, Lyndon, 41
Johnson, Paul, 142
Johnson, S., 334–36
Johnson & Johnson, 120
Jones, Leo, 349–50
Jones, Willie, 233
Jordan, 352
Journalism. See Media portrayal
    of crime
J.P. Morgan Chase, 120, 121
Judge Judy, 63
Judges
bail and, 211, 212, 213
common law and, 61
courtroom workgroups and,
    205, 208–9
defined, 208
discretion in sentencing and,
    238, 311, 436–37, 456
jury instructions and, 227
mandatory sentencing and,
    238–39
power of, 209
predictability and, 48
sentencing guidelines and,
    49, 238
Judicial Watch, 76
Jumping bail, defined, 211
Juries
death penalty and, 346–47, 448
discretion in sentencing and, 311
prosecutors and, 206
recommendations on, 457–58
voir dire and, 224–25
Jurisdiction
of courts, 201
defined, 164, 201
of police agencies, 164
salience of race and ethnic
    minority groups in, 420
Jury consultants, 224, 225, 458
Jury deliberations, 227
Jury instructions, 227, 458
Just desserts, 27, 133, 247, 333, 415
Justice
adversarial nature of, 11, 18, 46,
    133, 218
conceptions of, 14–15
conflicting views of, 16–17
courtroom workgroups and,
    205, 223
due process versus crime
    control, 18–19, 21
imbalance of power in court
    and, 209–10
"Justitia" and, 4, 16, 26–28
meaning of, 15–19, 21, 24–25
as outcome, 18, 19
pretrial procedures and,
    210–21, 441, 447
as process, 18, 19

Justice (*continued*)
  scales of, 15, 26–27
  social justice groups, 460–67
Justice, U.S. Department of
  crime prevention and, 258
  law enforcement and, 166, 167
  probation and, 242
  street crimes and, 102
  USA PATRIOT Act and, 79, 80
  use of force and, 189–90, 192
Justice as outcome
  death penalty and, 352
  defined, 18
  juries and, 346
  justice as process compared
    to, 19
  plea bargaining and, 221
  prosecutors and, 206
  retribution and, 248
  wrongful convictions and, 228
Justice as process
  death penalty and, 352
  defined, 18
  juries and, 346
  justice as outcome compared
    to, 19
  plea bargaining and, 221
  prosecutors and, 206
  wrongful convictions and, 228
Justice Policy Institute, 239, 240
Justifications, defined, 88
"Justitia"
  conception of justice and, 16,
    26–28
  meaning of, 4
Just Say No program, 401, 406,
    407, 408, 409
Juvenile justice system, 9, 201
Juvenile offenders
  crime prevention, 259
  death penalty and, 342

Kansas City Patrol Study, 174
Kant, Immanuel, 247
Kendall, George, 308
Kennedy, Anthony M., 214, 215,
    216, 217
Kerner Commission, 186
Kerry, John, 44
King, Martin Luther, Jr., 41,
    439, 466
King, Rodney, 113, 138
Klaas, Polly, 113
Kmart, 120, 418
Knowing acts
  defined, 89
  harms associated with, 100
Kozlowski, Dennis, 418
Krajicek, David, 125, 130, 132–33,
    134, 135, 137–38, 142,
    144, 147, 149, 151
Kyzer, Dudley Wayne, 241

Labeling theory, 294
Laissez faire, 105
Lambert, Bobby, 350
Lamphear, Bruce, 105
Larceny-theft, defined, 90
Latvia, 110
Law. *See also* Civil law; Common
    law; Criminal law;
    Natural law; Positive law
  crimes created by, 53–54
  defined, 53
  demographics of lawmakers,
    66–70, 411
  media portrayal of crime
    and, 138
  origin of, 55–56
  silly statutes, 54–55
  supremacy of, 61
  types of, 52–53, 56–57, 61, 63
Law and Society Association, 340
Law enforcement. *See also* Police
  behavior of police and, 175–78
  bias in, 164, 178–86, 440, 445,
    446, 447
  community policing and, 171–75
  corruption and, 192–95
  criminal justice resources and,
    24, 219
  drug crimes and, 165, 365
  employees of, 6, 22, 164, 165
  federal government and, 165,
    166–67
  image of, 163–64
  innocent bias, 164, 178–86, 447
  local governments and, 22,
    164, 165
  organization of policing, 164–68
  roles and responsibilities of
    police officers, 168–69, 171
  state government and, 167–68
  stop rates and arrest rates,
    186–89
  use of force and, 189–92
Law Enforcement Code of
    Conduct, 175, 176–77,
    186, 455
Lawmakers, demographics of,
    66–70
Lawmaking process
  demographics of lawmakers
    and, 66–70
  special interests and, 72–74
  voting behavior and, 70–71
Lay, Kenneth, 121, 418
Lazarus, Edward, 20
Leadership Conference
    Education Fund, 439
Leadership Conference on Civil
    Rights, 439
Legal definition of crime
  criminal law and, 86, 87–89,
    105–6, 445

  defined, 86
  degree of harm and, 452–53
  limitations on, 92
Legalization of drugs
  defined, 397
  increased recreational drug use
    and, 398
  as policy alternative, 87, 394
  reducing crime and, 384
  regulation and, 398–99
  social management and, 400
Legal technicalities, 12, 19, 205, 206
Leighton, Paul, 121
Levitt, Steven, 112–13
Liebman, James S., 312–14
Life expectancy, 432
Life imprisonment without the
    possibility of parole
    (LWOP)
  costs of, 352
  deterrence and, 339
  expert opinion and, 354, 355,
    358, 359, 360
  incapacitation and, 341, 355, 359
  Marshall hypothesis and, 331
  public opinion and, 326
  recommendations on, 459
Lifton, Robert, 327
Lindsell-Roberts, Sheryl, 54–55
Liquor law violations, defined, 92
Lithuania, 110
Lobbying
  criminal law and, 53, 75
  money in political system and,
    72–74
Local governments
  crime information and, 106
  criminal justice resources and,
    23–24
  law enforcement and, 22,
    164, 165
Locke, John, 64
Lockyer v. Andrade (2003), 241
Loewen, James, 16
Loitering, defined, 92
Loss of autonomy, 289–90
Loss of security, 290–91
Loss of voting rights, 293
Louima, Abner, 191–92
Louisiana, 55, 283
Louis XV (king of France), 321
Lower courts, 202
LSD, 373
Lunsford, Jessica, 36
LWOP. *See* Life imprisonment
    without the possibility
    of parole (LWOP)
Lynchings, as capital punishment,
    307, 308

Mack, David, 196, 197
Madison, James, 60

Magna Carta, 333
Maine, 317
Mala in se crimes
    defined, 53
    natural law and, 56
Mala prohibita crimes, 53–54
Malvo, Lee Boyd, 131, 132
Mandatory releases, 296
Mandatory sentences
    death penalty and, 308, 311
    defined, 48
    drug crimes and, 265, 369,
        391, 441
    gender and, 436–37
    as minimum sanction, 238
    minorities and, 441, 447
    predictability and, 48–49
    prosecutorial control and, 209
    truth-in-sentencing laws
        and, 241
Manifest Destiny, 16
Manipulative model, defined, 146
Manning, David, 320
Mapp v. Ohio (1961), 17, 170
Marijuana
    antimarijuana movement, 385
    classification of, 373
    decriminalization of, 401, 403
    dope fiend mythology and, 368
    drug offenses and, 185, 365
    harms associated with, 378, 379,
        381–83, 384, 399
    importation of, 397
    use of, 368, 374–75, 376, 406,
        407, 408
    war on, 369
Market model, 146
Marr, Melanie, 215
Marshall, Thurgood, 223, 328,
    329–31
Marshall hypothesis, 328, 329–31
Maryland, 310
Massachusetts, 317
Mathews, Rich, 192
Mathews, Steven, 264
McCleskey v. Kemp (1987),
    314–15, 440
McDonaldization
    of criminal justice network,
        45–50, 445
    defined, 45
MCI, 96, 105, 120, 121
McMillan, Walter, 351
Media
    corporate ownership of, 125,
        126–27, 137, 145, 147, 157, 446
    defined, 124
    drug scares and, 386–90
    as for-profit entities, 139, 147,
        446, 447
    inner ring of, 124–25, 126, 127,
        149, 153, 157, 446

middle ring of, 124, 126, 154
minorities and, 427
news-related information and,
    123–24
organization of, 124
outer ring of, 124, 126, 154
poverty and the poor, 427
public exposure to, 129–30
recommendations on, 453–54
role of, 128–29
Media portrayal of crime
    bias in, 130, 445, 446
    class discrimination and, 31
    corporate ownership of media
        and, 127, 157
    crime entertainment narratives
        and, 148
    crime information and, 106,
        125, 129
    crime trends and, 138–39
    fear and, 43, 114, 132, 139, 142,
        143–46, 148, 302, 446
    focus of, 134–38
    inaccuracy and, 132–33,
        146–51, 157
    lack of criminal justice
        education and, 149, 157,
        447, 453
    lack of critical coverage and,
        139, 141–43, 153, 155, 156
    legal definition of crime
        and, 106
    minor problems transformed
        into major problems, 125, 128
    organization factors and,
        147–48, 157
    peer culture and, 148–49,
        157, 447
    politics and, 125, 126, 128,
        132–33, 138, 148, 149–51, 447
    repetitive coverage of crimes,
        128–29, 132
    terrorist attacks of September
        11, 2001 compared to, 152
    unplanned change and, 39
    violent crimes and, 113, 135,
        136, 138–39, 203, 412
    war on drugs and, 367–68
    Washington, D.C. snipers and,
        130, 131–32
Mempa v. Rhay (1967), 208
Mens rea, defined, 87
Mental illness, 280, 347, 357,
    382, 395
Mental retardation, death penalty,
    342, 347
Merrill Lynch, 120, 121
Methadone maintenance
    programs, 401, 403
Mexico, 394
Michigan, 317
Micke, William, Jr., 311

Middle ring of the media
    corporate ownership of media
        and, 126
    coverage of terrorism and, 154
    defined, 124
Military Commissions Act of
    2006, 80, 217–18
Military death penalty
        system, 344
Mill, John Stuart, 247, 255
Miller, David, 461, 463–65
Miller, Jerome, 24–25
Miller, Kimberly Jane, 319
Miller, R., 188, 189
Miller, Tommy, 319
Minimum-maximum sentences,
        defined, 238
Minnesota, 317
Minorities
    aggressive police patrols
        and, 186
    arrest rate and, 189
    bias in courts and, 201, 202, 211,
        219, 223, 412, 447
    bias in sentencing and, 260, 261,
        265, 266, 447
    court clients and, 204
    in courtroom workgroups,
        204, 456
    criminal justice network and,
        16, 30, 34, 419–33
    death penalty and, 207, 311, 316,
        344, 412, 429, 441, 448
    drug scares and, 385
    jury service and, 225
    in law enforcement, 168
    overpoliced and underpro-
        tected, 174
    police corruption and, 192, 194
    police profiling and, 184
    police use of force and, 190–91
    population control and, 31
    prison population and, 282,
        299–300
    stop rates and, 187
    three-strikes laws and,
        261, 262
    war on drugs and, 362, 390,
        393–94, 412
Miranda v. Arizona (1966), 9, 20
Miranda warning, 9, 19, 20
Mississippi, 283
Missouri, 322, 343
Mistrial, defined, 227
Mitchell, Greg, 327
Mitigating factors
    defined, 237
    in sentencing, 237, 238, 343,
        347, 357
    three-strikes laws and, 239
Mobbs Declaration, 214
Mock, Ronald, 350

Model Penal Code
  corporate crime and, 100–101
  death penalty and, 311
Mollen Commission, 192
Mongolia, 352
Monitoring the Future Survey
    (MTF), 374, 375, 376,
    377, 405, 408
Monroe, James, 60
Moore, Michael, 145
Morales, Manuel, 263–64
Moral panics
  defined, 141
  drug use and, 386
  imitation and, 149
  media coverage of terrorism
    and, 145, 146
  media portrayal of crime
    and, 446
  three-strikes laws and, 239
Moratorium
  on death penalty, 308–9
  defined, 308
  on executions, 358
Moreno, Juan, 349
Moss, Quintin, 349
Motivation of criminals
  deterrence and, 251, 252, 256,
    338–39
  effectiveness of punishment
    and, 255–57
  false assumptions concerning,
    296, 302
  mitigating factors and, 237
  potential gains and, 116
Motor vehicle registration, 224
Motor vehicle theft, defined, 90
Muhammad, John Allen,
    131, 132

NAACP, 194
Nader, Ralph, 117
Narcotics, Bureau of, 368
Narcotics/opiates, 371, 372
National Academy of Sciences,
    401, 403
National Advisory Commission
    on Civil Disorders, 186
National Association of State
    Budget Officers, 277
National Center on Addiction and
    Substance Abuse, 366
National Center on Institutions
    and Alternatives, 24–25
National Coalition to Abolish the
    Death Penalty
    (NCADP), 342
National Conference of Catholic
    Bishops, 335
National Conference of State
    Legislatures, 67
National Crime Survey, 129

National Crime Victimization
    Survey (NCVS)
  crime information and, 108–11,
    422, 423
  crime trends and, 111, 112, 139
  defined, 108
  gender and, 438
  Uniform Crime Reports
    compared to, 424
National Criminal Justice
    Commission
  community policing and, 174
  courts' function and, 202
  criminal justice goals and, 13–14
  decision making in criminal
    justice, 5
  families and, 295
  female incarceration rates
    and, 436
  incarceration and, 272
  jury system and, 225
  media portrayal of crime
    and, 144
  police corruption and, 193
  police discretion and, 180
  politics and, 37
  prison conditions and, 290
  prison legislation and, 283
  replacement model and, 396
  right to attorney and, 221–22
  sentencing and, 42
  zero-tolerance policing and, 194
National defense spending, 94–96
National Household Survey on
    Drug Use and Health
    (NHSDA), 407
National Incident Based
    Reporting System
    (NIBRS), 92–94, 106, 117
National Institute on Drug Abuse
    (NIDA), 374, 386, 387,
    388, 401
National Institute on Justice
    (NIJ), 374
National Institutes of Health
    (NIH), 382
National Institutes of Mental
    Health (NIMH), 143–44
National League of Cities, 79
Nationally known attorneys,
    defined, 207
National Pretrial Reporting
    Program, 212
National Rifle Association, 239
National Science Foundation, 346
National Security Agency, 17, 80
National Security Letters, 80
National Survey on Drug Use and
    Health (NSDUH), 185,
    373, 374, 375, 376
National White Collar Crime
    Center, 117

Natural definition of crime,
    defined, 86
Natural law
  defined, 56
  as type of law, 56–57
  violation of, 86
NCADP (National Coalition to
    Abolish the Death
    Penalty), 342
NCVS. See National Crime
    Victimization Survey
    (NCVS)
Nebraska, 310
Necessity, as justification, 88
Needle exchange programs,
    401, 403
Neely, Todd, 230
Negligent acts
  defined, 89
  harms associated with, 100, 102
Negotiators, defined, 208
Nelson v. Campbell (2004), 320
Netherlands, 110, 401–2, 403
Neurotransmitters, 370
News Corporation, 126
Newspapers
  coverage of terrorism and, 153
  media portrayal of crime and,
    129, 130, 135, 138, 139, 144
New York, 310, 317
NHSDA (National Household
    Survey on Drug Use and
    Health), 407
NIBRS (National Incident Based
    Reporting System),
    92–94, 106, 117
Nicotine use
  addiction and, 388
  as gateway to illicit drugs,
    381, 400
  harms associated with, 373, 378,
    379–82, 383, 384, 388, 399, 407
  trends in, 374, 378
NIDA (National Institute on
    Drug Abuse), 374, 386,
    387, 388, 401
NIH (National Institutes of
    Health), 382
NIJ (National Institute on
    Justice), 374
NIMH (National Institutes of
    Mental Health), 143–44
Nixon, Richard, 42, 366–67, 390
No-bid contracts, 96
Nolo contendere (no contest), 10
North Carolina
  corrections and, 283, 287–89
  death penalty and, 319, 321, 345,
    348, 352
  salaries of lawmakers, 67
  silly statutes, 54, 61–62
North Dakota, 317

Northern Ireland, 110
NSDUH (National Survey on
    Drug Use and Health),
    185, 373, 374, 375,
    376 *Nulla poena sine
    crimine*, 210
Nurturant strategies, 252

Objectivity, rule of procedure
    and, 205
Obstacle course metaphor, 18
Occupational crime, defined, 94
Occupational Safety and Health
    Administration, 104
O'Connor, Sandra Day, 214, 215,
    216, 241
O'Dell, Joseph, 349
Offenses against the family and
    children, defined, 92
Office of National Drug Control
    Policy (ONDCP)
    budget of war on drugs, 364
    creation of, 388
    cultivation of illicit drugs
        and, 394
    distortion of statistical
        information, 362, 404–9, 449
    drug use trends and, 375,
        376, 377
    gateway hypothesis and, 400
    goals of war on drugs, 363
    harms associated with war on
        drugs, 403
    marijuana use and, 368
Ohio, 320
Oil and gas companies, political
    contributions of, 76
Oklahoma, 343
Oklahoma City bombing, 77
Olbermann, Keith, 140
ONDCP. *See* Office of National
    Drug Control Policy
    (ONDCP)
Opening statements, defined, 225
Operation Iraqi Liberation, 76
Operation Sunrise, 194
Opiates, 369, 383, 384, 385
Oregon, 310
Organizational model, 146
Original jurisdiction, 201
Outer ring of the media
    corporate ownership of media
        and, 126
    coverage of terrorism and, 154
    defined, 124
Overcharging practices, 184
Overpoliced and underprotected,
    defined, 174

Packer, Herbert, 17–18, 21, 237,
    279, 391
Padilla, Jose, 215–16, 292

Pain relievers, 375
Pains of imprisonment, 283,
    294–96
Pakistan, 352
Panel attorneys, defined, 208
Parks, Bernard, 193, 197
Parnell, Kenneth, 262
Parole. *See also* Life imprisonment
    without the possibility of
    parole (LWOP)
    characteristics of parolees, 299
    crime prevention and, 259
    defined, 13, 241, 271
    elimination of, 46, 241, 441
    harassment of parolees, 297
    mandatory releases and, 296
    recidivism and, 258, 297
    recommendations on, 459
Part I Index Offenses, 90, 91,
    106, 178
Part II Offenses, 91–93, 106
Paternalism hypothesis, 433
Patrol
    arrests and, 180
    inner cities and, 179
    law enforcement and, 165,
        169, 174
    minorities and, 186
PCP, 384
Pearl Harbor attacks, 152
Peel, Robert, 173–74
Peer culture, of journalism,
    148–49, 157, 447
Pennsylvania, 322
People of color. *See* Minorities
The People's Court, 63
Percentage bail, defined, 210
Peremptory challenges
    defined, 224
    jury service and, 224–25, 457
Perez, Rafael, 197
Personality, police subculture and,
    194, 195
Pew Research Center for the
    People and the Press,
    129, 130
Physical dependence, drug abuse
    and, 371
Plain touch doctrine,
    defined, 170
Plain view doctrine, defined, 170
Planned change
    defined, 39
    unplanned change compared
        to, 39–41
Plea bargaining
    convictions achieved
        through, 203
    crime control model and, 18, 23
    criminal justice goals and, 201
    defined, 10–11, 218
    efficiency and, 45–46

going rates and, 48
    as injustice, 218–21, 447
    media portrayal of crime
        and, 133
    overzealousness of prosecutors
        and, 233
    police corruption and, 193
    public defenders and, 222, 223
    recommendations on, 457
    trials and, 11, 218, 219, 221, 223
    types of, 218
Pluralist view of the law,
    defined, 66
PNAC (Project for a New
    American Century), 154
Poland, 110
Police. *See also* Law enforcement
    asset forfeiture and, 47, 186,
        364, 366, 368–69, 392
    behavior of, 175–78
    bias in, 440, 445, 446, 447
    calculability and, 47
    cases sent to courts, 209
    community policing and,
        171–75
    corruption and, 180, 185–86,
        192–98, 440
    crimes known to, 106, 107, 108,
        135, 169, 422
    as criminal justice employees, 6
    criminal justice resources and,
        21, 22, 24, 46, 219, 445, 454
    criminal law and, 66
    discretion and, 176, 180–81, 346,
        440, 447
    displacement model and,
        395–96
    educational requirements of,
        175, 177, 178, 455
    efficiency and, 46
    harassment by, 187
    harassment of parolees, 297
    image of, 163–64
    innocent bias and, 178–86
    investigation and, 8–9
    manipulation of crime data
        by, 107
    media portrayal of crime and,
        134, 138, 168
    militarization of, 185, 191,
        194, 368
    organization of policing, 164–68
    overzealousness of, 230, 233–34
    plea bargaining and, 221
    predictability and, 48
    professional model of, 172,
        177, 180
    prosecutors and, 206
    recommendations on, 454–56
    reducing crime and, 14, 164,
        172, 174, 175
    replacement model and, 395, 396

Police (*continued*)
  responsibilities of, 4, 5, 6,
    168–71, 176
  salaries of, 177–78, 455
  subterfuge model and, 394–95
  war on drugs and, 368, 390–91,
    394–97, 401
Police corruption, 180, 185–86,
    192–98, 440
Police Executive Research
    Forum, 455
Police interrogation, *Miranda*
    warning and, 20
Police profiling
  defined, 48, 182
  innocent bias and, 181–84
  racial discrimination and, 48,
    182, 184, 261
  recommendations on, 455–56
  selective prosecution and, 88
  typical criminal and, 187, 447
  war on drugs and, 392
Police subculture, 194–95
Policy development. *See also*
    Death penalty; War on
    crime; War on drugs;
    War on terror
  alternatives to current practice,
    449–60
  criminal justice academics
    and, 149
  media as source of information
    on, 125, 137–38, 139
  planned versus unplanned
    change, 39–41
  politics and, 35, 36, 41–43, 149,
    276–77
  reality construction and, 389
  treatment-based programs
    and, 253
Political Action Committees
    (PACs)
  defined, 72
  political donations and, 72–73,
    75, 412, 445
  top committees in federal
    politics, 73
Politics
  concentrated criminal
    victimizations and, 418
  criminal justice network and,
    31, 35–36, 195, 417, 442, 451
  criminal justice resources and, 24
  death penalty and, 36, 43,
    313–14, 338, 342–43, 351
  defined, 34
  executive clemency, 347
  fear and, 14, 37, 43, 146, 151
  function of, 34–35
  ideology and, 35, 37
  incarceration and, 278, 279, 296
  law enforcement and, 169

McDonaldization and, 50
  media portrayal of crime and,
    125, 126, 128, 132–33, 138, 148,
    149–51, 447
  money in, 72–74
  policy development and, 35, 36,
    41–43, 149, 276–77
  political imprisonment, 290
  rehabilitation and, 39, 42,
    252–53
  seriousness of crimes and, 107
  terrorism and, 31, 37–39, 146, 153
  unemployment rate and, 32
  unplanned change and, 39
  war on drugs and, 368, 369
Politics of fear, defined, 151
Polk, James, 60
Popular culture, 124
Popular rule, 59–60
Population control
  criminal justice goals and, 30,
    31, 33, 445
  defined, 31
  incarceration and, 415
  serving limited interests and,
    32–33
Portugal, 110
Positive law
  common law and, 61
  defined, 57
  as type of law, 57, 61
Poverty and the poor
  arrest rate and, 180, 187, 189
  bias in courts and, 201, 202, 210,
    211, 219, 223, 412, 447
  conception of crime and,
    132, 223
  conflict view of the law and,
    65–66
  court-appointed counsel for, 23
  criminal justice network and,
    16, 30, 419, 449
  criminal justice process and, 7
  cultural perspective of, 426–27
  defined, 425
  increase in, 417–19
  inner cities and, 179
  interest groups and, 74
  jury selection and, 225
  media portrayal of crime
    and, 133
  police corruption and, 192, 194
  population control and, 31
  prison population and, 281, 298
  recommendations on, 451
  structural perspective of,
    426, 427
  three-strikes laws and, 262
  as undeserving underclass, 33,
    413–14, 415
  U.S. Constitution and, 59
  violence and, 418

voting behavior and, 71
  war on crime and, 281, 412–19,
    424–25
  war on drugs and, 362, 390,
    397, 412
Poverty wage, defined, 425–26
Powell, Colin, 38, 153
Power
  conflict view of the law and,
    65–66
  corporate crime and, 102
  corruption and, 196
  in court, 209–10, 412
  in courtroom workgroup, 202,
    206, 412, 448
  criminal justice network and,
    195, 417
  criminal law and, 66, 98
  defined, 35
  media portrayal of crime and,
    125, 150
  pluralist view of the law and, 66
  politics and, 35
  of prosecutors, 206, 209, 226,
    233, 265, 412
  sentencing and, 260, 266
  sentencing guidelines and, 49
  social reality of crime and, 36
Precedents
  courts and, 55, 201
  defined, 201
Predictability
  criminal justice network and,
    47–49, 445
  defined, 45
  McDonaldization and, 45
  positive law and, 57
Prediction problem, 249
Preliminary hearings
  courts' function and, 202
  criminal justice process and,
    10, 205
Preliminary investigation,
    defined, 9
Preponderance of evidence,
    defined, 63
Prescription drugs, nonmedical
    use of, 375, 383
Preserving the peace, defined, 168
President's Commission on Law
    Enforcement and
    Administration of
    Justice, 13
President's Task Force on Victims
    of Crime, 17
Presumption of innocence
  bail and, 211–12
  for criminal defendants, 226
  defined, 223
  police corruption and, 192
Pretrial phase, defined, 210
Pretrial procedures

bail as injustice and, 210–14
justice and, 210–21, 441, 447
plea bargaining as injustice and, 218–21
war on terror and, 213–18
Preventing crime. *See also* Crime prevention
defined, 168
Prevention. *See also* Crime prevention; Drug prevention education
defined, 364
Preventive detention
African Americans and, 211, 441
defined, 10, 211
likelihood of conviction and, 212
recommendations on, 456–57
types of crimes and, 213
war on terror and, 213–18
Primary goods, 462–63
Prior record
racial discrimination and, 421, 429
sentencing and, 238, 260, 261
Prison Fellowship International, 254
Prisonization, 292
Prisons
characteristics of prisoners, 277–82, 298
as colleges of crime, 295
costs of, 277
crimes committed within, 249
crime trends and, 111
defined, 13, 243, 271
deprivation of goods and services, 292
deprivation of heterosexual relationships, 291
drug crimes and, 185
loss of autonomy and, 289–90
loss of dignity and, 293
loss of liberty and, 283, 286
loss of security and, 290–91
loss of voting rights, 293
media portrayal of crime and, 134
myths concerning, 282–86
overcrowding of, 42, 46, 243, 369
pain of imprisonment, 283, 294–96
recommendations on, 459
sample day of, 287–89
stigmatization and, 293–94
super-maximum prisons, 49–50, 291
Private attorneys
death penalty and, 344
defined, 207
public defenders compared to, 221–23, 227, 344
Private property rights, 59

Probable cause
arrest and, 186
defined, 9, 186, 271
Fourth Amendment and, 58
police profiling and, 184
race and, 48
Probation
bias in, 261
crime prevention and, 259
criminal justice resources and, 258
defined, 12, 242
as deterrence, 250
as incapacitation, 249
reasons for using, 243
recidivism and, 243, 258, 378
recommendations on, 459
statistics on, 244
typical rules of, 242
Problem-oriented policing, 46, 171, 172, 456. *See also* Community policing
Procedural criminal law
defined, 63
rules and, 66
Procedural defenses
defined, 88
as valid defenses, 8
Procedural justice
defined, 18
lack of emphasis on, 19
Producer countries, defined, 394
Profit without honor, defined, 94
Program development, planned change and, 40
Program on International Policy, University of Maryland, 158
Project for a New American Century (PNAC), 154
Property crimes
arrest rate and, 188
buying, receiving, or possessing stolen property, 91
crime rates and, 108, 109, 110, 174, 274, 275
crimes known to the police and, 107, 108
defined, 106
media portrayal of crime and, 135, 136, 147
preventive detention and, 213
prison population and, 273, 278, 281, 298
rearrest and, 213
recidivism and, 257
state courts and, 203
three-strikes laws and, 262
Prosecutors
closing arguments and, 226–27
courtroom workgroups and, 205–6

criminal justice resources and, 219, 222
defined, 205
discretion of, 207, 209, 238, 261, 343, 346, 440–41, 448
media portrayal of crime and, 134
overzealousness of, 230, 233–34
peremptory challenges and, 224
power of, 206, 209, 226, 233, 265, 412
predictability and, 48
presentation of case, 225–26
sentencing guidelines and, 49
Prostitution and commercialized vice, defined, 92
Providing services
community policing and, 172
defined, 168
role of police and, 168–69, 171, 180
Psychological dependence, drug abuse, 371
Psychopharmacological homicides, 366
Psychotherapeutic drugs, nonmedical use of, 375
Public assistance programs, crime linked to, 41
Public defenders
criminal justice resources and, 219, 221
death penalty and, 344
indigent clients and, 23, 204, 208, 210
media portrayal of crime and, 133
plea bargaining and, 222, 223
private attorneys compared to, 221–23, 227, 344
salaries of, 219–20, 223
work environment of, 220, 223
Public defender systems, defined, 207
Public hysteria, 367
Public opinion
of accuracy of news sources, 130
capital punishment and, 310, 326–32, 338, 341, 346, 351–52
crime rates and, 113–14, 139, 145
decriminalization and, 400
of drug treatment, 273
Iraq war and, 158
media portrayal of crime and, 129, 130, 137, 138, 145–46, 150
punitive sentencing alternatives and, 25
rehabilitation and, 253, 281, 447
three-strikes laws and, 240
war on drugs and, 386, 388, 399
white-collar crime and, 118

Public order offenses
    federal courts and, 203
    law enforcement and, 165
    plea bargaining and, 46, 219
    prison population and,
        273, 278
Punishment. *See also* Capital
        punishment; Cruel and
        unusual punishment;
        Sentencing
    continuum of, 242
    defined, 237
    deterrence and, 47, 237
    effectiveness of, 255–59,
        267–69
    facts on, 244–46
    failure of, 267–69
    justice and, 16
    Justitia and, 27
    media portrayal of crime
        and, 133
    methods of, 241–46
    reasons for, 246–53, 447–48
    stability of, 272
    utilitarianism and, 255
Punitive attitude, 24
Pyrrhic defeat theory, defined, 31

Quinney, Richard, 36, 86
Qwest, 120

Race
    of capital juries, 347
    crime as code word for, 42
    criminality and, 422–25
    imprisonment rates by, 298
    income and, 425
    victimization and, 423
    of victims of crime, 345, 346,
        347, 412, 441, 448
    voting behavior and, 71
Racial discrimination
    capital punishment and, 309,
        316, 327, 329, 440
    criminal justice network and,
        33, 300, 421, 429–33, 439–42
    death penalty and, 343–46,
        355–56
    drug crimes and, 185, 369
    due process model and, 18
    justice and, 28
    police discretion and, 180, 181
    police profiling and, 48, 182,
        184, 261
    in sentencing, 260–61
    stealth racism, 184
    U.S. Constitution and, 60
    in war on drugs, 385, 393–94,
        400, 430
Racial relations
    intrusive law enforcement
        and, 186

support for capital punishment
        and, 327
    war on drugs and, 367
Radio, 129, 144
Rampart Area Corruption
        Incident, 193, 196–98
Rand Corporation, 265, 344, 401
Rasul et al v. Bush et al (2003),
        216–17
Rawls, John, 461–63, 464, 465
Reagan, Nancy, 401, 406, 407, 408
Reagan, Ronald
    corporations and, 275
    crime control and, 21, 42, 431
    war on drugs and, 47, 362, 368,
        386, 388, 390
    welfare programs and, 428
The Real War on Crime, 13, 37
Reasonable doubt, defined, 226
Rebuttal witnesses, defined, 226
Recidivism
    defined, 249
    drug offenders and, 378
    drug treatment programs
        and, 286
    effectiveness of punishment
        and, 257, 265
    parole and, 258, 297
    probation and, 243, 258, 378
Reckless acts
    defined, 89
    harms associated with, 100, 102
Recreational programs, 294
Reducing crime
    community policing and,
        172, 174
    as criminal justice goal, 14, 19,
        31, 44, 114, 164, 180, 198, 412,
        445–49
    defined, 14
    effectiveness of punishment
        and, 257, 267–69
    incarceration rate and, 274, 275,
        276, 295–96
    police and, 14, 164, 172, 174, 175
    recommendations on, 450,
        451–52
    war on drugs and, 363, 400, 404
Regulatory agencies,
        victimizations and, 179
Rehabilitation
    crime prevention and, 259
    defined, 252
    as justification for punishment,
        252–53, 447–48
    politics and, 39, 42, 252–53
    public opinion and, 253, 281, 447
Rehnquist, William, 20, 214,
        215, 216
Rehnquist Supreme Court
        (1986–2005), 19
Reich, Robert, 428

Reiman, Jeffrey, 31, 33, 34, 60, 64,
        65, 102–4, 121, 132, 222,
        366, 412, 418, 424, 465
Reintegrative shaming, 293
Release
    conditional release, 212, 213
    defined, 13
    discretionary releases, 296
    early release programs, 42
    mandatory releases, 296
Release into third-party custody,
        212, 213
Release on own recognizance
        (ROR), 10, 212, 213
Reliability
    due process model and, 18
    of self-report studies, 116
Religion, support for capital
        punishment, 326
Renewal, defined, 253
Replacement model, 395, 396
Representative of the court,
        defined, 206
Republican Party
    crime control model and, 19,
        42, 43
    crime rates and, 41
    money in federal elections and,
        72, 73
    money in state elections and, 74
    oil and gas money and, 76
    support for capital punishment
        and, 326
    tobacco money and, 75
Residential programs, 259
Residential segregation, 426,
        430, 440
Resnick, Judith, 26–28
Restitution
    defined, 253
    life imprisonment without the
        possibility of parole, 341, 459
    restorative justice and, 254
    support for capital punishment
        and, 326
Restorative justice
    defined, 253
    as justification for punishment,
        253, 255
    principles of, 254, 448
Retreatism, defined, 427
Retribution
    defined, 247, 333
    expert opinion on, 353–54, 359
    as justification for punishment,
        15, 237, 247–48, 447
    support for capital punishment
        and, 328, 329, 331, 332, 333–34,
        336–38
    vengeance contrasted with, 248
Rhode Island, 317
Rice, Condoleezza, 38, 76

Richardson, James, 234
Richardson, Nicole, 238
Riddle, Debbie, 37
Ridge, Tom, 140
Right of *habeas corpus,* 215
Risk classification, in
        corrections, 49
Rite Aid, 120
Ritzer, George, 45
Robbery, defined, 90
Roberts, John, 21, 217
Roberts Supreme Court
        (2005–), 21
Robinson, Matthew B., 114–16,
        140, 181, 257, 293, 308,
        346, 360, 413
Roe v. Wade (1973), 111
Roper v. Simons (2005), 342
ROR (release on own
        recognizance), 10,
        212, 213
Rousseau, Jean-Jacques, 64
Rules of procedure, 58, 205
Rumsfeld, Donald, 38, 215
Rumsfeld v. Padilla et al (2003),
        215–16
Running away, defined, 92
Russia, 110
Ryland, Kendall, 350

Safety
    control and, 50
    crime control model and, 21
    incarceration rate and, 47,
        282, 295
    media portrayal of crime
        and, 133
    social safety net approach, 25
    support for capital punishment
        and, 337
    war on drugs and, 400
Salinas, Ramon, 349
SAMHSA (Substance Abuse and
        Mental Health Services
        Administration), 185,
        374, 406
Santabella v. New York (1971),
        220, 221
Sarbanes–Oxley Act, 121
Saudi Arabia, 352
Scalia, Antonin, 214, 215, 216, 217
Scared Straight programs, 259
School violence, 124, 136, 146
Scientific management, 45
Scotland, 110
Searched incident to lawful
        arrests, defined, 170
Searches with consent, defined, 170
Secondary crimes, 366
Secondary investigation, defined, 9
Security/protection, law
        enforcement, 165

Sedatives, 375
Selective incapacitation, 249
Selective prosecution, as
        procedural defense, 88
Self-defense, as justification, 88
Self-incrimination, 58, 61
Self-report studies
    crime information and, 114,
        116, 422
    defined, 114
Sensenbrenner, James, 79
Sentences, defined, 237
Sentencing. *See also* Mandatory
        sentences
    bias in, 260–67, 412, 441, 447
    courts' function and, 202
    criminal justice process and, 12
    defined, 12
    deterrence and, 47–48
    gender and, 434, 436–37
    going rates and, 48
    judges' discretion in, 238, 311,
        436–37, 456
    plea bargaining and, 219, 220
    politics and, 42
    predictability and, 48–49
    public opinion on, 25
    recommendations on, 456
    state legislatures and, 253
    types of sentences, 237–41
Sentencing guidelines, defined,
        49, 238
The Sentencing Project, 257, 293,
        298, 364, 365, 388
Serious crime
    defined, 89
    lawmakers defining, 188
    as type of crime, 89–94, 223,
        412, 415, 445
Serious reversible error, death
        penalty and, 312–14, 448
Serving limited interests
    conflict view of the law and, 65
    criminal justice goals and, 30,
        31, 33, 60, 279, 445
    defined, 31
    population control and, 32–33
    war on drugs and, 361
Sessions, William, 170–71
Sex offenses, defined, 92
Sexual assault, 437, 438
Sherman, L., 258–59, 274
Shock probation, 259
Simple assaults, defined, 91
Simpson, O. J., 57, 133, 211, 221, 225
Singapore, 352
Sixth Amendment
    right to counsel and, 222
    right to trial and, 11–12, 58
    USA PATRIOT Act and, 79
Skillern, Bernadine, 350
Skilling, Jeffrey, 121

Slavery, 59, 60
Smith, Anna Nicole, 156
Smith, Robert, 426, 430–33
Social class. *See* Class
        discrimination; Poverty
        and the poor; Wealth
        and the wealthy
Social contract, defined, 64
Social control
    law enforcement and, 172
    retribution and, 333
Social control theories,
        defined, 150
Social disorganization, 277
Social isolation
    police subculture and, 194
    poverty and the poor and, 417,
        418, 426, 430
Social justice, 460–67
Social learning theories,
        defined, 148
Social order
    crime and, 65
    retribution and, 333
Social programs, 25, 34, 94, 277,
        365, 393, 428
Social reality of crime, defined,
        36, 86
Social safety net approach, 25
Soft money
    defined, 75
    political contributions and, 75,
        76, 445
Sourcebook of Criminal Justice
        Statistics, 192, 433
Souter, David, 214, 215, 216, 217
South Africa, 110
Spain, 110
Special deterrence, 250, 338
Special interests
    conflict view of the law and, 65
    criminal law and, 53, 411
    lawmaking process and, 72–74
    pluralist view of the law and, 66
Specific deterrence, 250, 338
Specific or limited jurisdiction,
        defined, 201
Speeding laws
    police discretion and, 181
    police profiling and, 182–83
Spence, David, 349
Stare decisis, defined, 201
State courts
    defense attorneys and, 207–8
    intermediate sanctions and,
        244–45
    jurisdiction of, 201
    organization of, 201–2
    punishment statistics, 244–45
    rearrest and, 212–13
    sentence length and, 244, 245
    types of crimes handled by, 203

State governments
  crime control and, 14
  crime information and, 106
  criminal justice resources and,
    23–24
  death penalty offenses, 322,
    323–24
State legislatures
  crimes defined by, 55
  demographics of, 67
  money in state elections and,
    73–74
  salaries of legislators, 67, 68–70
  sentencing and, 253
  statutory law and, 57
State supreme courts, 202
Status quo
  criminal justice network and,
    33, 34
  media portrayal of crime
    and, 150
Statutory law, defined, 57
Stayner, Steven, 262
Stealth racism, defined, 184
Stephen, James, 247
Stereotypes
  media portrayal of crime
    and, 127
  police discretion and, 180, 447
  of typical criminal, 187
Stevens, John Paul, 214, 215,
    216, 217
Stewart, Martha, 120
Stigmatization, 293–94, 416–17, 448
Stimulants, 371, 372, 375, 383, 384
Stops
  defined, 186
  discretion and, 180
  stop rates, 187
Strain theory, defined, 427–28
Street crimes
  corporate crime compared to,
    76, 103–4, 120, 137
  crime peak for, 112–13
  crime rates and, 49, 111, 113, 275
  crime trends and, 111–14
  criminal justice network and,
    86, 99
  defined, 87
  deterrence and, 251
  distribution of, 107
  harms associated with, 99, 100,
    102, 104, 114, 137, 178
  ideology and, 39
  label of crime and, 66
  law enforcement and, 165, 171
  media portrayal of crime and,
    127, 132, 135, 137, 412
  police focus on, 178
  property crime and, 109
  ratio of police to criminals, 8
  serving limited interests and, 31

social disorganization and, 277
sources of information on, 106
three-strikes laws and, 265
as type of crime, 89–94
typical offenders, 103
Streeter, Jeffrey, 231–32
Street-level drug enforcement
  defined, 364
  war on drugs and, 363–64
Stress, police subculture and, 195
Strickland v. Washington (1984),
    220, 351
Structural perspectives,
    defined, 426
Subcultures
  criminal subcultures, 366
  police subculture, 194–95
Subordination, 430
Substance Abuse and Mental
    Health Services
    Administration
    (SAMHSA), 185,
    374, 406
Substantive criminal law
  defined, 61
  defining crimes and, 66
Subterfuge model, 394–95, 396
Super due process, 348
Super-maximum prisons
  control and, 49–50
  defined, 49
  inmate contact and, 291
Survey of Health Related
    Behavior Among
    Military Personnel, 374
Survey of Inmates in State
    Correctional
    Facilities, 374
Survival of the fittest, 87
Sutherland, George, 206
Sweden, 110
Switzerland, 110
Sykes, Gresham, 283
Symbolic crusading, 36
System, defined, 4, 5–6
Systematic discrimination, 420,
    421, 430
Systemic homicides, 366

Taxation, 418
Taylor, Zachary, 60
Technical violations, 297
Technology
  corrections and, 49
  police and, 46, 185
Television
  in courts, 133
  coverage of terrorism and,
    153, 155
  media portrayal of crime and,
    129, 130, 133, 135, 138–39, 144
Temperance movement, 385

Tennessee, 308
Tennessee v. Garner (1985), 191
Terrorism. See also War on terror
  antiterrorism laws, 53, 77–80
  fear and, 43, 113, 141, 142, 145
  Homeland Security Advisory
    System and, 140–41
  law enforcement and, 165, 167
  media coverage of, 125, 131,
    135, 136, 141–43, 144, 146
  moral panic and, 141
  politics and, 31, 37–39, 146, 153
Terrorist attacks of September 11,
    2001
  history of terrorism and, 77
  law enforcement and, 165
  media coverage of, 142–43, 145,
    147, 152–58
  public concern over
    terrorism, 113
  Washington, D.C. snipers
    and, 131
Terry stop, defined, 186
Terry v. Ohio (1968), 186
Testilying, defined, 192
Tetrahydrocannabinol (THC),
    378, 381, 382, 383
Texas, death penalty and, 36, 43,
    316, 317, 343, 352
THC (tetrahydrocannabinol),
    378, 381, 382, 383
Therapeutic community resident
    programs, 259
Thomas, Clarence, 214, 215,
    216, 217
Three-strikes laws
  bias in, 261–62, 447
  defined, 49, 239
  facts about, 239–40
  individuals sentenced under,
    262–65
  recommendations on, 458
Times Mirror Center for the
    People and the
    Press, 145
Tobacco, 373. See also
    Nicotine use
Tobacco industry
  advertising of, 378–80, 381
  negligent actions of, 388
Tobacco legislation, influence of
    money on, 75–76
Tolerance, drug abuse and, 371
Torts, 57
Totality of circumstances,
    defined, 186
Tranquilizers, 375
Transporter countries, defined, 394
Treasury, U.S. Department of, 167
Treatment, defined, 364
Trial counsel for police,
    defined, 206

Trials
bail and, 210–11
bifurcated trials, 311
crime control model and, 18, 23
and criminal justice network
goals, 201
criminal justice process and,
11–12
defined, 11
efficiency and, 46
as exceptional case, 223–27
media portrayal of crime
and, 133
plea bargaining and, 11, 218,
219, 221, 223
police corruption and,
192, 193
right to fair trial, 208, 221
right to trial by jury, 58, 61
stages in criminal trial, 224–27
truth and, 206
Trop v. Dulles (1958), 309
Trusted criminals, defined, 94
Truth-in-sentencing laws, 47, 241
Tyco, 120, 137, 418
Tyler, John, 60
Typical criminals, defined, 187
Typical police officer, defined, 168

UCMJ (Uniform Code of Military
Justice), 217
UCR. *See* Uniform Crime
Reports (UCR)
Underclass. *See also* Poverty and
the poor
defined, 413
drug use and, 385
jail population and, 280
law and order movement
and, 33
as undeserving, 33, 413–14, 415
war on crime and, 415
Underemployment, defined, 425
Unemployment rate
cultural perspectives and,
426–27
curbing drug use and, 386
incarceration and, 415, 416
prison inmates not counted
in, 32
race and, 425
Uniform Code of Military Justice
(UCMJ), 217
Uniform Crime Reports (UCR)
crime information and, 64, 89,
106–8, 109, 111, 139, 422, 423
defined, 106
limitations of, 106–7
National Crime Victimization
Survey compared to, 424
Part I Index Offenses,
90–91, 106

Unplanned change
defined, 39
planned change compared to,
39–41
Unreasonable searches and
seizures
Fourth Amendment and, 58, 170
Rehnquist Supreme Court
and, 19
Unsecured bail
as bail alternative, 212
defined, 210
Upholding rights, defined, 168
USA PATRIOT Act of 2001, 53,
78–79
U.S. Congress
antiterrorism laws and, 77–80
crimes defined by, 55
death penalty and, 310
demographics of, 66–67
deregulation and, 104
drug crimes and, 388, 389
income inequality and, 418
Iraq War Study Group Report
and, 95
power of, 35
statutory law and, 57
war on terror and, 214
wasteful spending and, 96–97
U.S. Constitution. *See also*
Constitutional
protections
Constitutional law and, 57,
58–60
criminal justice decision
making governed by, 180
criminal justice goals and, 14
purpose of, 59–60
use of force and, 190
U.S. Customs and Border
Protection, 165
U.S. Immigration and Customs
Enforcement, 165
U.S. Marshals Service, 166
U.S. population, demographics of,
66, 67, 71
U.S. Secret Service, 167
U.S. Sentencing Commission,
365, 388
U.S. Supreme Court
abortion and, 111
attorney competence and,
220, 351
bail and, 211
capital punishment and, 36, 309,
310–11, 314–15, 319–20, 321,
329, 337, 342, 347, 440
as court of last resort, 201
enemy combatant status and,
214–15
evidentiary requirements
and, 17

mandatory death sentences
and, 308, 311
Miranda warning and, 9
peremptory challenges and, 225
plea bargaining and, 220
police use of force and, 191
purpose of, 58–59
right to counsel and, 208, 222
right to trial and, 11, 221
sentencing guidelines and, 238
stops and, 186
three-strikes laws and, 241
war on drugs and, 367, 392
war on terror and, 214–18
U.S. Surgeon General, 438
U.S. v. Booker (2005), 238
U.S. v. Cortez (1981), 186
U.S. v. Dickerson (2000), 19, 20
U.S. v. Salerno (1987), 211
Utah, 309
Utilitarianism, 255

Vagrancy, defined, 92
Validity, of self-report studies, 116
Vandalism, defined, 91
Van den Haag, Ernest, 338,
339, 340
Vengeance
assumptions of, 415
defined, 247, 332
retribution contrasted with, 248
support for capital punishment
and, 332–33, 337
Vermont, 317
Vertical bargaining, defined, 218
Viacom, 126
Victim assistance, 254
Victim impact statements, 357
Victimization. *See also* National
Crime Victimization
Survey (NCVS)
conceptions of, 97–99, 105
defined, 97
police focus on types of crimes
and, 178–79, 454–55
portrayal of victims, 114
poverty and the poor and,
418, 423
of prisoners, 290–91
race and, 423
reporting of, 107
risk for, 110–11, 143, 144, 452
typology of, 97–98
Victimless crimes
decriminalization of, 279, 453
defined, 47
Victim-offender mediation,
254, 303
Victims of crime
plea bargaining and, 220–21
police providing services for,
169, 171

Victims of crime (*continued*)
  prosecutors getting justice
    for, 205
  race of, 345, 346, 347, 412,
    441, 448
  restorative justice and, 254
  retribution and, 333
  social justice and, 466
Victims' rights initiatives, 17
Vietnam, 352
Vigilantism, 64
Violence
  corporate violence, 94
  domestic violence, 437–38
  media and, 124, 135, 136, 137,
    143–44, 147
  poverty and the poor and, 418
  in prisons, 290–91
  recommendations on, 450–51
  school violence, 124, 136, 146
  war on drugs and, 391
Violent crimes
  arrest rate and, 188
  corporate crime and, 117
  crime rates and, 32, 47, 86, 108,
    109, 174, 275
  crime trends and, 112
  defined, 106
  drug use and, 384, 385
  incarceration and, 243, 296
  media portrayal of crime and,
    113, 135, 136, 138–39, 203, 412
  politics and, 43
  preventive detention and, 213
  prison population and, 273–74,
    278–79
  public opinion and, 113
  punishment and, 253
  rearrest and, 213
  recidivism and, 257, 258
  reporting of, 107
  state courts and, 203
  three-strikes laws and, 239, 262
  victimization and, 99, 423
  war on drugs and, 390
Virginia, 343
Virginia Polytechnic Institute
    and University, 136
Visual reality
  defined, 148
  Iraq war and, 155
Vocational training, 259, 294, 302,
    303, 459
Voir dire, 224–25, 447, 458
Voter registration, 224
Voting behavior
  corporate ownership of media
    and, 127
  jury pools and, 224
  lawmaking process and, 70–71
Voting rights, 59, 60, 439
Voting Rights Act of 1965, 439

Wackenhut, 32
Waksal, Sam, 120–21
Wales, 110, 111
Walt Disney, 126
Walters, John, 404
Ward, Miriam, 349
War on crime
  benefits of, 32
  costs of, 277
  defined, 191
  effects of, 276, 298, 300
  expansion of, 21
  functions served by, 416–17
  lack of success, 31, 37
  poverty and the poor and, 281,
    412–19, 424–25
War on drugs
  alternatives to, 87, 394–403
  asset forfeitures and, 47, 186,
    364, 366, 368–69, 392
  benefits of, 32
  corruption and, 196, 392, 397
  costs of, 365, 393, 399
  criminal justice interventions
    and, 47
  data on, 364, 365
  defined, 362
  effectiveness of, 376–78, 402–3,
    404, 449
  elements of, 363–66
  environmental damage and, 394
  expansion of, 21, 44
  federal sentencing and, 266
  goals of, 363
  harms caused by, 390–94, 402,
    403, 449
  history of, 366–69
  honesty and dishonesty in, 362
  hypocrisy of, 384, 399–400
  innocent bias and, 184–86
  mandatory sentencing and, 238
  media's role in, 386–90
  prison population and, 278
  success of, 397
  war on crime and, 415
War on Poverty, 276
War on terror
  civil liberties and, 17, 19
  crime control and, 21
  enemies abroad and, 25
  media coverage of, 137, 147,
    152–58
  preventive detention and,
    213–18
  U.S. Supreme Court and,
    214–18
Warrants, defined, 186
Warren Supreme Court
    (1953–1969), 19
Washington, D.C., 317
Washington, D.C. snipers, 130,
    131–32

Washington, George, 60
Watson, Dale, 167
WCTU (Women's Christian
    Temperance Union), 385
Wealth and the wealthy. *See also*
    Elite deviance
  bias in sentencing and, 266
  corporate crime and, 103
  criminal justice process and, 7
  death penalty and, 344
  defense attorneys and, 226, 227
  defined, 425
  drug use and, 384
  imbalance of power in court
    and, 210, 412
  income inequality and, 427, 462
  increase in, 275, 279, 417–19
  interest groups and, 74
  jury selection and, 225
  of lawmakers, 67
  media portrayal of crime and,
    125, 133, 137
  support for capital punishment
    and, 326
  U.S. Constitution and, 59, 60
  voting behavior and, 71
Weapons offenses, prison
    population, 278
Webb, Johnny E., 350
Weems v. United States (1910), 309
Weld, William, 286
Welfare programs, 428
Welfare reform laws, 34, 428
Welfare-to-work programs, 34
West, Valerie, 312–14
West Virginia, 317
White-collar crimes
  crime information and, 117–18
  elite deviance and, 94
  harms associated with, 65, 102,
    137, 412
  law enforcement and, 165,
    167–68
  media portrayal of crime
    and, 137
  National Incident Based
    Reporting System and, 92
  preventive detention and, 213
  prison population and, 278
  private attorneys and, 223
  prosecution of, 103, 104, 105,
    111, 165, 167
  ratio of police to criminals, 8
  sentencing and, 267
  typical offenders, 103
Whites. *See* Caucasians
Williams, Jerry, 264
Willingham, Cameron, 350
Willis, Ernest, 350
Wilson, William Julius, 413
Wisconsin, 317
Withdrawal, drug abuse, 371

Without defense or justification, defined, 87
Women's Christian Temperance Union (WCTU), 385
Woodson v. North Carolina (1976), 308, 311
WorldCom, 102, 120, 121, 137, 155, 418
World Trade Center, 77
World War II, 309, 310
Writ of *habeas corpus*, 214, 215, 230

Wrongful convictions
bias in courts and, 202, 228–34
death penalty and, 312–14, 329, 347–52, 356
due process model and, 19, 347
exclusionary rule and, 71
eyewitness testimony and, 228, 229, 231–32, 348, 351
life imprisonment without possibility of parole and, 341
overzealousness and, 230, 233–34
police corruption and, 193

Xerox, 120

Yemen, 352
Young, Francis, 381

Zaitzow, Barbara H., 114–16, 181
Zero-tolerance policing
defined, 46, 194
war on drugs and, 395–96
Zimring, Franklin, 111, 327
Zinn, Howard, 16